ELI
EL

ELISABETH ELLIOT

OMNIBUS

THROUGH GATES OF SPLENDOUR

SHADOW OF THE ALMIGHTY

NO GRAVEN IMAGE

OM
publishing

This Elisabeth Elliot omnibus edition first published 1997 by
OM Publishing

03 02 01 00 99 98 97   7 6 5 4 3 2 1

OM Publishing is an imprint of Paternoster Publishing,
P.O. Box 300, Carlisle, Cumbria CA3 0QS, U.K.

British Library Cataloguing in Publication Data

A catalogue record for this book is available from the British Library

ISBN 1-85078-265-2

Printed in the UK by Mackays of Chatham PLC, Kent

ELISABETH ELLIOT

THROUGH GATES OF SPLENDOUR

OM
publishing

> *'Give of thy sons to bear the message glorious,*
> *Give of thy wealth to speed them on their way.*
> *Pour out thy soul for them in prayer victorious,*
> *And all thou spendest Jesus will repay.'*

The parents of the five men have, in a very literal sense, fulfilled the words of this hymn. This book is dedicated to them.

CONTENTS

ACKNOWLEDGEMENTS

MANY PEOPLE, scattered from the jungles of Ecuador to the skyscrapers of New York, have helped in the writing of this story. The four other widows, Barbara Youderian, Marj Saint, Marilou McCully, and Olive Fleming, when they suddenly found themselves with doubled responsibility, took time to gather their husbands' diaries, letters, and other writings, and were willing to share them. Abe C. Van Der Puy, of the missionary radio station HCJB in Quito, Ecuador, spent many months assembling material for *The Reader's Digest* article, prepared by Clarence W. Hall, which appeared in the issue of August, 1956. I have freely drawn on this material in the expanded version of the story. Jozefa Stuart, of the Magnum research staff, made a special trip to Ecuador for the publishers to collect extensive additional data which I needed in writing the book. Many of the facts on the Auca Indians came from Rachel Saint, sister of the missionary pilot, who learned them from an escaped member of the tribe. Nate Saint's brother Sam played a unique role as adviser and official representative for the five of us widows. Decisions which would have been beyond our ability to make, Sam made, consulting with us by overseas telephone, personal conference, and mail. The hours and the miles of travel he devoted on our behalf cannot be counted. The editors of

9

Harper & Brothers, my original publishers, were unstinting in giving of themselves to make this book what it ought to be. Their counsel and encouragement have been invaluable. To all of these people I am deeply grateful. With Barbara, Marj, Marilou, and Olive, I thank God for allowing us to share so intimately in the lives recorded in these pages. And to Him who made them what they were, we repeat the words which our husbands sang a few days before they died:

> *'We rest on Thee, our Shield and our Defender,*
> *Thine is the battle, Thine shall be the praise*
> *When passing through the gates of pearly splendour*
> *Victors, we rest with Thee through endless days.'*

ELISABETH ELLIOT

Quito, Ecuador
February, 1957

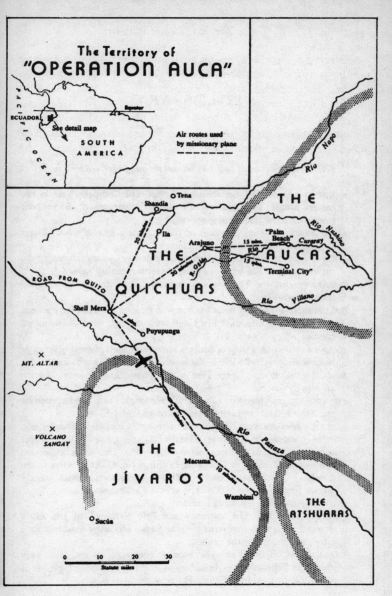

GLOSSARY

(All a's are pronounced half-way between the a in father and the a in cat)

ARAJUNO a-ra-*hoo*-no. An abandoned Shell Oil Company base in the eastern jungle. The station where the McCullys worked; also the base from which the rescue party set out.

ATSHUARA at-*shwa*-ra. A group of Jivaro Indians among whom Roger Youderian established an outstation.

AUCA *ow* (rhymes with cow)-ka. A group of savage Indians inhabiting the eastern jungle. The word is a Quichua term meaning 'savage'.

CURARAY coo-ra-*rye*. The river on which the five missionaries established their 'beach-head'.

DAYUMA dye-*u*-ma. An Auca woman who escaped from her tribe several years ago. She furnished Jim Elliot with the data used on the initial contact.

JIVARO *he*-va-ro. A group of Indians known for their ancient practice of head-shrinking, who live in the south-eastern jungles of Ecuador.

MACUMA ma-*coo*-ma. Home base of the Youderians. A jungle station among the Jivaros.

PUYUPUNGU pu-yu-pungu (all four u's are long). Outstation opened by the Elliots; later the home of the Flemings.

QUICHUA *keech*-wa. Any of a number of groups of Indians in Ecuador who were conquered by the Incas. Also the language spoken by these people now (it was forced on them by the conquerors). This is the Ecuadorian spelling of Kechua, or Quechua. In this book, Quichua refers to the Lowland Quichuas—those who live in the eastern forests, among whom Jim Elliot, Ed McCully, and Pete Fleming worked.

QUITO *key*-toe. The capital of Ecuador.

SHANDIA *shan*-dya. The station where Pete Fleming and Jim Elliot worked when they first went into the forest. McCullys lived here for a time, and later only the Elliots.

SHELL MERA shell-*meh*-ra. The base of operations of the Missionary Aviation Fellowship in Ecuador, at the edge of the jungle. It is accessible by road from Quito. Home of the Saint family.

— I —

'I Dare Not Stay Home'

THE *SANTA JUANA* IS UNDER WAY. White stars breaking through a high mist. Half moon. The deep burn of phosphorus running in the wake. Long, easy rolling and the push of steady wind.'

It was hot in the little cabin of the freighter. Jim Elliot, who was later to become my husband, was writing in the old cloth-covered ledger he used for a diary. It was a night in February, 1952. Pete Fleming, Jim's fellow missionary, sat at a second desk. Jim continued:

All the thrill of boyhood dreams came on me just now outside, watching the sky die in the sea on every side. I wanted to sail when I was in grammar school, and well remember memorising the names of the sails from the Merriam-Webster's ponderous dictionary in the library. Now I am actually at sea—as a passenger, of course, but at sea nevertheless—and bound for Ecuador. Strange—or is it?—that childish hopes should be answered in the will of God for this *now*?

We left our moorings at the Outer Harbour Dock, San Pedro, California at 2.06 today. Mom and Dad stood together watching at the pier side. As we slipped away Psalm 60:12 came to mind, and I called back, "Through our God we shall do valiantly." They wept some. I do not understand how God has made me. Joy, sheer joy, and thanksgiving fill and encompass me. I can scarcely keep from turning to Pete and saying, "Brother, this is great!" or "We never had it so good." God has done and is doing all I ever desired, much more than I ever asked. Praise, praise to the God of Heaven, and to His Son Jesus. Because He hath said, "I will never leave thee nor forsake thee," I may boldly say, "I will not fear...."

Jim Elliot laid down his pen. He was a young man of twenty-five, tall and broad-chested, with thick brown hair and blue-grey eyes. He was bound for Ecuador — the answer to years of prayer for God's guidance concerning his life-work. Some had thought it strange that a young man with his opportunities for success should choose to spend his life in the jungles among primitive people. Jim's answer, found in his diary, had been written a year before:

> My going to Ecuador is God's counsel, as is my leaving Betty, and my refusal to be counselled by all who insist I should stay and stir up the believers in the U.S. And how do I know it is His counsel? "Yea, my heart instructeth me in the night seasons." Oh, how good! For I have known my heart is speaking to me for God!... No visions, no voices, but the counsel of a heart which desires God.

Jim's mood of the moment was felt by Pete. Pete was shorter than Jim, with a high forehead and dark wavy hair. The two had learned to understand and appreciate each other long before, and their going to Ecuador together was, to them, one of the 'extras' that God threw in. Pete, too, had met with raised eyebrows and polite questions when he had made it known that he was going to Ecuador. An M.A. in literature, Pete was expected to become a college professor or Bible teacher. But to throw away his life among ignorant savages — it was thought absurd.

Only a year or two before, the problems of Ecuador, on the north-west bulge of South America, had seemed remote. The two young men had talked with several missionaries who had been there, who described the enormous problems of transportation, education, and development of resources. Missionary work had done much to help the country bridge the cultural span of a millennium between primitive jungles and modern cities. But progress was pitifully slow. Evangelicals had been working among the head-shrinking Jivaros for twenty-five years, among the Quichuas of the high Andes, and among the red-painted Colorados of the western forest. The Cayapas of the north-western river region had also been reached with the Gospel, and advances were soon to be made into the Cofan tribe of the Colombian border.

But there remained a group of tribes that had consistently repelled every advance made by the white man: the Aucas. They are an isolated, unconquered, semi-nomadic remnant of age-old jungle Indians. Over the years, information about the Aucas has seeped out of the jungle: through adventurers, through owners of haciendas, through captured Aucas, through missionaries who have spoken with captured Aucas or Aucas who have had to flee from killings within the tribe. Whatever Jim and Pete had been able to learn about them was eagerly recorded, so that by now the very name thrilled their young blood. Would they some day be permitted to have a part in winning the Aucas for Christ?

They were aware that the first missionary to have entered Auca territory—a Jesuit priest, Pedro Suarez—had been murdered by spears in an isolated station near the confluence of the Napo and Curaray. That was in 1667. His murderers were Indians who might have been the ancestors of some present-day Aucas. For about two hundred years after this the Indians had been left in peace by the white man. Then the coming of rubber-hunters wrote a dark page in the history of this jungle area. For some fifty years—from about 1875 to 1925—these men roamed the jungles, plundering and burning the Indian homes, raping, torturing, and enslaving the people. It was a time when the concept of 'lesser breeds without the law' was almost universally accepted. For the Auca to have no love for the white man was understandable. Could Christian love wipe out the memories of past treachery and brutality? This was a challenge to Jim and Pete as they hoped to bring the message of

God's love and salvation to these primitive people. It was a challenge and leading for which they had both been prepared since childhood.

God *had* led Jim — since boyhood, when, in his home in Portland, Oregon, he learned that the Book of all books is the Bible, and that to follow its teaching is not necessarily to live a cloistered, dull life. Now as he sat in his cabin on shipboard his mind went back to his family house on a hillside facing snow-covered Mt. Hood. Jim's father, a red-haired, iron-jawed Scotsman, would gather his four children each morning after breakfast and read to them out of the Bible, trying always to show them that this Book was to be lived, and that the life it depicted was a happy and rewarding one. The children would squirm in their seats in the little breakfast nook, but some of the truths sank in, and Jim, third of the Elliot sons, soon received Jesus Christ as Saviour and Lord.

When he entered high school, Jim, following the example of the Apostle Paul, was 'not ashamed of the gospel of Christ.' A Bible always rested on top of his stack of textbooks when he entered the classroom. Academically his early interest was in architectural drawing. His talent in this was exceptional, and his drawings were kept by the teacher to be used as examples to future classes. Before finishing Benson Polytechnic School, however, he began orienting his life towards the mission field.

While at Wheaton College in Illinois, Jim limited his extracurricular activities, fearing that he might become occupied in non-essentials and miss the essentials of life. He refused requests that he run for several offices on the campus. He did, however, go out for wrestling, explaining his choice in a letter to his mother:

I wrestle solely for the strength and co-ordination of muscle tone that the body receives while working out, with the ultimate end that of presenting a more useful body as a living sacrifice. This God knows, and even though He chose to allow it to be strained, the motive was for His glory and the faith He honours. Simplicity of heart and freedom from anxiety He expects of us, and gives grace to have both.

During his sophomore year in college Jim came to the conclusion that God wanted him in a Latin-American country, preaching the Gospel to those who had never heard it. This decision was immediately followed by action; he began the informal study of Spanish. He chose Greek as his major, preparatory to translating the Bible into some unwritten language. His professors remember the vigour, if not always the accuracy, with which he translated some of the ancient classics—Xenophon, Thucydides, patristic literature. It was a thrill to him to read for the first time in Greek the old stories of the New Testament, so familiar in English.

'Today I read the story of the Cross in John 19 for the first time in the original,' he wrote to his parents. 'The simplicity and pathos made me almost weep; something which has never occurred in my English reading. Surely it is a wonderful story of love.'

In November, 1947, Jim wrote a letter to his parents which showed where his ambition lay:

The Lord has given me a hunger for righteousness and piety that can alone be of Himself. Such hungering He alone can satisfy, yet Satan would delude and cast up all sorts of other baubles, social life, a name renowned, a position of importance, scholastic attainment. What are these but the objects of the "desire of the Gentiles" whose cravings are warped and perverted? Surely they can mean nothing to the soul who has seen the beauty of Jesus Christ. . . . No doubt you will hear of my receiving preliminary honours at school. They carry the same brand and will lie not long hence in the basement in a battered trunk beside the special gold "B" pin, with the "ruby" in it for which I studied four years at Benson. All is vanity below the sun and a "striving after wind". Life is not here, but hid above with Christ in God, and therein I rejoice and sing as I think on such exaltation.

Jim and my brother, Dave Howard, were both members of the class of 1949 at Wheaton, but although I was also at Wheaton, I had not met Jim until Christmas, 1947, when Dave brought him home with us for the holidays. I smiled later when I learned Jim had written his parents about 'a tall, lean girl, far from beautiful, but with a queer person-ality-drive that interests me'.

His junior year at college completed, Jim wrote to his parents:

> Seems impossible that I am so near my senior year at this place, and truthfully, it hasn't the glow about it that I rather expected. There is no such thing as attainment in this life; as soon as one arrives at a long-coveted position he only jacks up his desire another notch or so and looks for higher achievement—a process which is ultimately suspended by the intervention of death. Life is truly likened to a rising vapour, coiling, evan-escent, shifting. May the Lord teach us what it means to live in terms of the end, like Paul who said, "Neither count I my life dear unto myself, that I might finish my course with joy...."

During that summer, after preaching to a group of Indians on a reservation, Jim wrote:

> Glad to get the opportunity to preach the Gospel of the matchless grace of our God to stoical, pagan Indians. I only hope that He will let me preach to those who have never heard that name Jesus. What else is worth while in this life? I have heard of nothing better. "Lord, send me!"

In his diary of the summer he wrote:

> "He makes His ministers a flame of fire." Am I ignitible? God deliver me from the dread asbestos of "other things". Saturate me with the oil of the Spirit that I may be a flame. But flame is transient, often short-lived. Canst thou bear this, my soul—short life? In me there dwells the Spirit of the Great Short-Lived, whose zeal for God's house consumed Him. "Make me Thy Fuel, Flame of God."

18

The man who wrote these words was no recluse. He was an American college senior, school-champion wrestler, consistent honour student, president of the Student Foreign Missions Fellowship, amateur poet, and class representative on the Student Council. Jim was warmly admired by fellow students. He was known as 'one of the most surprising characters' on campus. Able to recite such poems as 'The Face on the Bar-room Floor' and Robert Service's 'The Cremation of Sam McGee', he was at the same time recognised as a man of spiritual stature above his classmates. George Macdonald said, 'It is the heart that is not yet sure of its God that is afraid to laugh in His presence.' Jim spoke of 'joking with God'. 'Every now and again,' he said, 'I ask for something—a little thing, perhaps, and something answers. Maybe it's only me, but something answers, and makes the request sound so funny that I laugh at myself and feel that He is smiling with me. I've noticed it several times lately, we two making fun of my 'other self' who does so hate to be laughed at!'

Sure that he belonged to God by faith in His Son Jesus Christ, Jim was equally sure that the God who had redeemed him would also guide him. 'I am as sure of His direction as I am of His salvation,' he used to say. During his senior year a large convention was held at the University of Illinois for students who were interested in foreign missionary work. Jim attended and asked God to show him what He wanted him to do.

At the end of the convention he wrote:

The Lord has done what I wanted Him to do this week. I wanted, primarily, peace about going into pioneer Indian work. And as I analyse my feelings now, I feel quite at ease about saying that tribal work in South American jungles is the general direction of my missionary purpose. One more thing: I am quite confident that God wants me to begin jungle work single. Those are good-sized issues to get settled finally in a week, but just now I am happy about them.

Towards the end of the summer of 1950 Jim's 'general direction' became specific. He met a former missionary from Ecuador who told him of the needs in that field, and mentioned the great challenge of the dread Aucas. This was the climax to several years of seeking direction from God. Jim devoted ten days largely to prayer to make sure that this was indeed what God intended for him. He was given new assurance, and wrote to his parents of his intention to go to Ecuador. Understandably, they, with others who knew Jim well, wondered if perhaps his ministry might not be more effective in the United States, where so many know so little of the Bible's real message. He replied:

I dare not stay home while Quichuas perish. What if the well-filled church in the homeland needs stirring? They have the Scriptures, Moses, and the prophets, and a whole lot more. Their condemnation is written on their bank-books and in the dust on their Bible-covers.

This feeling is reflected in his diary account of Gospel meetings that he and his college pal Ed McCully conducted in southern Illinois:

Sterile days. Have had thirty-two nights of "Youth Rallies" in Sparta, with fifty or sixty out in the public-school gymnasium. There is little interest, and very few young people are reached in this way, I'm beginning to see. This problem of meeting a culture with truth from God is the most difficult kind of thing. One comes as a renovator, a conditioner of society, and society is in no mood to be conditioned. The fixedness of the human mind is the "wall of Jericho" to Gospel preaching. *God* must shake, or there will be no shaking.

There has been a sense of discouragement and doubt come over me through this. . . . There is a strong pull to the philosophy that "chaos created this lump of clay in his own image" —and to let fall the whole gamut of theological arguments. Again, I'm held by the resurrection of Jesus Christ. Were it not that I believed that Jesus was seen of men and proved Himself to be supernatural in out-witting death, I would throw the whole system back to the troubled skies and take a raft down the Mississippi today. But the fact is founding, settling, establishing. It holds as nothing else, and gives the sense that there *are* answers, not yet discovered, for which I must wait.

It was typical of Jim that, once sure of God's leading, he did not turn aside easily. The 'leading' was to Ecuador, so every thought and action was bent in that direction. Jim practised what he preached when he wrote in his diary: 'Wherever you are, *be all there*. Live to the hilt every situation you believe to be the will of God.'

Jim had been praying for some time that God would give him a comrade with whom to go to the mission-field, a single man ready to enter tribal work with him. For a while he thought that it might be Ed McCully, but when Ed married in June, 1951, Jim began to pray for another. In August he saw an old friend, Pete Fleming, who had just obtained his master's degree and was at that time seeking God's direction for his life-work. Jim later wrote to him:

> I would certainly be glad if God persuaded you to go with me, but if the Harvest-Chief does not move you, I hope you remain at home. To me, Ecuador is an avenue of obedience to the simple word of Christ. There is room for me there, and I am free to go. Of this I am sure. He *will* lead you too, and not let you miss your signs. The sound of "gentle stillness" after the thunder and wind have passed will be the ultimate word from God. Tarry long for it. Remember the words of Amy Carmichael: "The vows of God are on me. I may not stay to play with shadows or pluck earthly flowers, till I my work have done and rendered up account."

Jim's hopes were to be fulfilled when he and Pete set sail from San Pedro in 1952.

Their paths had crossed when groups of young people interested in studying the Bible had got together from Seattle and Portland for conferences and mountain-climbing expeditions.

Pete had once gone east to join Jim Elliot in a series of speaking engagements at religious conferences and other meetings. Six weeks of travelling together brought them into a deeper comradeship than they had known before. Driving back across the country to the north-west, Jim wrote:

> Pete is a most engaging travelling partner, interested in all the things that I notice—geology, botany, history, and the sky and all the good things God has scattered through the west in such extravagant variation.

Pete, who was born in Seattle, Washington, in 1928, early learned to appreciate the Bible and to hold it as his supreme rule of life and conduct. Those who knew him in his late teens and early twenties were impressed by his intelligent grasp of Scripture, and by the breadth of his spiritual knowledge. Converted at the age of thirteen after hearing the testimony of a blind evangelist, Pete, like Enoch, 'walked with God' in a way that set him apart in the eyes of fellow high-school students. He earned his letters in basket-ball and golf, and the members of the letter club asked him to be their chaplain. In his valedictory speech at graduation he said: 'Where shall we look? Where shall we go? I believe that we have a right to go back to the Bible for our anchorage. Here we have a recognised foundation . . . let us build upon it.'

This conviction stood Pete in good stead when, in the fall of 1946, he entered the University of Washington as a philosophy major. He was a man with a critical mind, and the study of philosophy challenged him to re-examine his whole view of life and of the world around him. For a while he almost foundered on the shoals of conflicting thought, but at last the God to whom he had long since 'committed the keeping of his soul' brought him back to the harbour of truth, His eternal Word.

Pete worked part time, studied hard, and was president

of the University Christian Fellowship. He was a man who drove himself, yet in his busy schedule he took time for prayer and study of the Bible. In 1951 he received a master's degree, his thesis being on Melville's *The Confidence Man*.

In the meantime, having seen and corresponded with Jim, he reached a decision about his life-work. He surprised his friends by announcing that he believed God was calling him to Ecuador.

'I think a "call" to the mission-field is no different from any other means of guidance,' he once wrote to his fiancée, Olive Ainslie. 'A call is nothing more nor less than obedience to the will of God, as God presses it home to the soul by whatever means He chooses.'

He had known Olive since childhood; the two of them had attended the same worship group on Sundays. When he responded to God's call to Ecuador, however, he went with the intention of serving Him without the responsibilities of home life—at least for the first year or so.

On September 6, 1951, he wrote to Dr Wilfred Tidmarsh, an English missionary with twelve years' service in the Ecuadorian jungle, who had addressed many Christian groups in the States:

> Since your visit I have been very much in prayer about going to Ecuador. In fact, I have never prayed so much before the Lord about anything. Jim and I have exchanged several letters in which I told him of the increased desire to go forth, and of the Scriptures which God seemingly had brought to mind to confirm it. My thinking, both in and outside of the Scriptures, was directed towards the stringency of Christ's words to His disciples, when he sent them forth: "I send you forth as sheep among wolves...." "He that loveth father or mother more than Me is not worthy of Me...." "He that taketh not up his cross, and followeth after Me is not worthy of Me...." "He that findeth his life shall lose it: and he that loseth his life for My sake shall find it." It has seemed that the severe requirements of a difficult field like Ecuador are matched on a spiritual level by the severe requirements placed on real disciples. Ecuador, as it seems, is a God-given opportunity to

place God's principles and promises to the extreme test.

This door seems to be opening at a time when I was looking to the Lord regarding the future, and thus is the Lord's answer to my prayers.

On the verge of his sailing from the States, Pete said to one of his college friends:

Remember the last few verses of 1 Corinthians 3: "For *all things* are yours... and ye are Christ's; and Christ is God's." Throughout all our personality we are God's, and since God has made our whole selves, there is great joy in realising who is our Creator. This realisation is to permeate every area and level of life. In appreciation of beauty, mountains, music, poetry, knowledge, people, science—even in the tang of an apple— God is there, to reflect the joy of His presence in the believer who will realise God's purposes in *all things*.

— 2 —

Destination: Shandia

AFTER EIGHTEEN DAYS AT SEA Jim Elliot and
Pete Fleming arrived in Guayaquil, Ecuador.
'About half-way up the Guayas River,' wrote Pete,
'I finally comprehended that this, *this* was Ecuador. I felt a
tingling sensation for the first time. Jim and I sang quietly,
'Faith of our Fathers', as the boat pulled into the harbour:

> *'Faith of our Fathers, holy faith,*
> *We will be true to thee till death.'*

Leaving the ship, the two young men made their way
through the stacks of baggage out into the hot sunlight on
the Malacon, the parkway beside the Guayas River. The
tide was coming in, and out in the centre of the current
great masses of water hyacinths rode swiftly up-river. A
gleaming white fruit-ship stood at anchor, and beside it
crowded the barges and long, slim dugout canoes of banana
vendors. A ferry was disgorging its sweating, shouting
multitudes, with their straw suitcases, cloth bundles,
chickens, and baskets. Jim and Pete stopped to watch the
faces until the crowd dissipated in all directions; then they
turned and crossed the street. Portals over the sidewalk
shaded them from the tropical sun, and they gazed at the
store windows with their astonishingly heterogeneous dis-

25

plays; sweaters and typewriters, frying-pans and automobile tyres, fake shrunken heads from the Jivaro Indians, and Camay soap. In one side street, cocoa beans were spread out like a nubbly red-brown carpet to dry in the sun. Businessmen, dressed in crisp white suits and Panama hats, were coming out of the buildings for their two-hour lunch break. Cadillacs and donkeys, nudging each other for the right of way, epitomised this land of contrasts.

With a growing population of over three hundred thousand, Guayaquil is the country's largest and most modern city, with wide streets and imposing office buildings. The streets are crowded, as owners, managers, and clerks from the various importing and exporting firms bustle about their business. Guayaquil is the banana capital of the world, and also from here, since World War II, more than three million bags of coffee, some seventy million pounds of cocoa, and more than three hundred million pounds of rice have annually been loaded for the export market. An air of prosperity prevails, production is constantly rising, and this port city serves as the country's trade barometer.

Pete and Jim spent their first night in a third-class hotel. Heat, mosquitoes, the occasional bray of a burro, and the Latin rhythm of a dance band nearby made the night a memorable one. The next day they took a plane to Quito, travelling up over the western cordillera of the Andes, crossing a 13,000-foot pass, and landing in the capital of Ecuador. Quito is 9,300 feet above sea level, and to the west rises the volcanic mountain Pichincha.

Here was a new opportunity to 'live to the hilt'. This old-world city, with its adobe houses, high mud walls, cobblestone streets, ornate churches, with its red geraniums and eucalyptus trees, was to be their home for the next six months. For before they could get to the Oriente—the eastern jungle area of Ecuador, goal of their tireless preparation and planning—there remained this last requirement, the learning of Spanish, the national language of Ecuador.

They signed up for Spanish lessons with a *señorita* who

expected nothing short of perfection, and they also engaged a room in the home of an Ecuadorian doctor who had five children. Here was an unparalleled opportunity for practice. They were forced to speak Spanish, and the children were quite uninhibited in pointing out the mistakes and peculiarities of their guests.

'Señor Jaime,' said little Moquetin, a bright-eyed imp of six, 'Why is it that your face is always red?' Jim countered, 'Why is it that *your* face is always brown?' 'Because it is much prettier that way,' was the unexpected reply.

'Language is a tyranny of frustration,' Pete once said. But learn it they must. During those months of study Pete wrote in his diary:

> I am longing now to reach the Aucas if God gives me the honour of proclaiming the Name among them.... I would gladly give my life for that tribe if only to see an assembly of those proud, clever, smart people gathering around a table to honour the Son—gladly, gladly, gladly! What more could be given to a life?
>
> These almost six months have been crammed full of goodness, and God has given us special privileges by way of having no set responsibilities, of giving us the money and the freedom to live with a national family, and undoubtedly we have learned things that will stand us in good stead all our missionary lives. And it has been a terrific boon; praying together and seeing God give us faith, getting more and more from the Spanish Bible, gradually finding Spanish easier and getting useful phrases fixed in my mind so I didn't have to think out every one. It has all been good and we have learned things: how to cope with situations and how to keep our mouths shut on some subjects, how to get along with the nationals, what their perspective on missionaries is.... God is going to give us Spanish by one means or another, and Quichua as well.

Finally the day came when Jim and Pete were to leave Quito. They saw their gear thrown up on top of a fat, ungainly vehicle that served as a bus. An American truck bed had been surmounted by an amazing superstructure that protruded on both sides, accommodating perhaps thirty or more passengers inside, and as many as dared cling on the outside. Squeezing themselves and their cameras, hallmark of the missionary as well as of the tourist, in among the other riders, they each found a seat—a board perhaps ten inches wide, with as much room again for the legs, between it and the next seat. They were fortunate indeed to be in a bus with an aisle, for in some vehicles passengers cheerfully clamber over the backs of the seats to their places. And they were able to sit up straight and still see out of the low windows. To have one's knees close to one's chin is not the most comfortable position, but then, they could take turns sitting by the aisle to stretch their legs.

'*Vamos!*' called the driver. Jim and Pete rejoiced that the bus was going to start on schedule. But no such luck this time—for this is the land of *mañana*. Everywhere there are unexplained delays, and perhaps the most trying thing of all to an outsider is the fact that no one seems to be the least interested in giving an explanation. No questions are asked. Silence. In this case, the delay lasted only ten minutes or so; and, without warning, the driver gunned his motor and the bus lurched to a start.

Leaving the city, the bus climbed up over the paramo, where a cold drizzle added to the bleakness of great stretches of brown grass. An occasional Indian galloped by on horseback, red wool poncho flying in the strong wind. A woman dressed in a heavy wool skirt and embroidered blouse passed at a dog trot, the usual gait of the Indian of the high Andes. Her baby, dressed exactly as she was, complete with fedora, joggled in a cloth on her back. The mother's hands moved nimbly, spinning wool on a spindle.

At 12,000 feet the men could see the small grass huts of the highland Quichuas. They eke out a living herding cattle and sheep, growing potatoes and certain grains. This scene was soon replaced by the arid territory surrounding Ambato, the city of the earthquake of 1949, and the 'gateway to the Oriente'. Here the bus stopped, and was immediately besieged by women with their trays of fried pork, meat pies, glasses of fruit drink, or slices of pineapple piled into an enamel basin. Each called her wares in a peculiar sing-song.

The trip was resumed once more, with the bus climbing up between lofty, snow-clad peaks, then tipping forward to swoop down in dizzy, hairpin turns into the vast gorge cut by the Pastaza River through the eastern cordillera of the Andes, past the cone-shaped Tangurahua, an extinct volcano. With startling suddenness the desert of the western slope and the high mountain pass were replaced by lush greenness on the breath-taking eastern descent. Purple orchids nodded out over the road as the bus swayed and jerked along the narrow shelf of road, a precipice on the right, a steep wall of rock shouldering up on the left. Towards late afternoon the bus rounded another curve, and the Pastaza spread itself out before them, flowing in broad ribbons over black beaches. This was the western extreme of the mighty Amazon basin, which terminates 3,000 miles to the east, as the river empties into the Atlantic Ocean. Another little town or two, and Shell Mera was reached. A former base of the Shell Oil Company for prospecting operations in the area, it is now an unpretentious huddle of dilapidated wooden buildings: houses, an hotel, and stores on one side of the road, and an army base and a mission-sponsored Bible school on the other.

The Ecuador base of the Missionary Aviation Fellowship was at the southern end of town. Here Jim and Pete met Dr Tidmarsh, the missionary with whom they had corresponded before coming to Ecuador. And with him they were soon flying north from Shell Mera, over the green sea of jungle, following the Ansüc River towards the Atun Yaku, headwaters of the Napo.

They were headed for Shandia, the Quichua mission station which Dr Tidmarsh had had to abandon because of his wife's health. They planned to re-open the station, Dr Tidmarsh staying till they could get established. Shandia did not at this time have an airstrip, so the three flew to another station nearby. Here they landed and set out on foot through the jungle. It was late in the afternoon when they started, and knowing that it was normally a three-hour hike, they raced against the sudden tropical twilight. Slipping on grassy roots, stumbling and struggling through deep mud at times, they pressed eagerly on to the place that would be their home for months to come. They were full of anticipation for what lay ahead, but at the same time they drank in the beauties of the great Amazon rain-forest through which they passed.

It was virgin jungle. Trees with great buttress-shaped roots grew to tremendous heights, often with no branches except at the top. Under these umbrellas an incredible variety of flora thrives. It was often impossible for Jim and Pete to distinguish the leaves which belong properly to the trees, for the huge tangle of lianas, air plants, and fungus that sponge a living from them. Orchids everywhere lent their soft colours to the living green. Fungus grew in vivid colours and bizarre shapes—vermilion, shaped like the ruffle on a lady's dress; turquoise, shaped like a shell, half hidden under a rotten log.

Just as the moon rose over the forest, the three men burst into the clearing that was Shandia. Pete wrote:

Indians immediately gathered around, and I remembered a couple of faces from Tidmarsh's pictures, and felt a kind of pride in remembering. My first thought was, "Yes, I can love these people." The ink-coloured designs on the women's faces interested me and the pitiful drape of the faded blue skirts. Lots of children were about, smiling shyly. Babies sucked on big, tremulous breasts, and the young, eager faces of boys looked up at us. Heard Tidmarsh's first conversation in Quichua; wondered how I would ever learn it.

At the same time Jim wrote:

We have arrived at the destination decided on in 1950. My joy is full. Oh how blind it would have been to reject the leading of these days. How it has changed the course of life for me and added such a host of joys!

At the far end of the clearing stood the small thatched house in which Dr Tidmarsh had lived. It was walled with split bamboo, floored with boards, and set on posts to ensure circulation of air and to give protection from both the damp ground and the invasion of insects.

Pete wrote in his diary:

At my first glance the house looked spacious and comfortable, and I thought how easily Olive and I could live in such a set-up, feeling joy in the knowledge and anticipation. Afterwards we got cleaned up a bit, washed our muddy feet in the ice-cold Napo, took a look around, and settled down to a meal of rice soup, plantain, manioc, and rice, with coffee. Now by the light of the kerosene lamp I am writing on the dining room table . . . tired but full of thankfulness to the Father, who leads on. In reality, this is not an end but a beginning.

— 3 —

'All Things to All Men'

IN SHANDIA, JIM AND PETE became full-fledged missionaries for the first time. They had come to reach the Quichuas with the Word of God, a task for which they were prepared but could accomplish only if they gained the Quichuas' confidence and love. So by living among them, sharing in their lives and thus laying the foundations of mutual trust they hoped to open the minds and hearts of the Indians to the Christian message. And Jim and Pete knew that whatever knowledge they gained from their experiences among the Quichuas would prepare them for work among other tribes further removed from today's civilisation.

The two young missionaries learned quickly that the Quichuas hunt a little, farm a little, and work occasionally for a neighbouring hacienda owner. They are subject to a variety of diseases and debilitating intestinal parasites. They are caught between two cultures — the disappearing one of their forebears and the rising white man's world of today. They are a gentle people, unlike their neighbours to the south, the head-hunting Jivaros, and to the north-east the feared Aucas. Every facet of the lives, health, language, education, birth, and death of the Indians was of immediate interest to Jim and Pete.

Night after night they sat in their little hut, listening to the jungle tuning up its nocturnal orchestra, and recording their experiences in diaries and letters. Moths and flies swarmed against the lantern, dropping to the paper and clogging pen-points. Great beetles zoomed at their faces, which glistened with sweat from the heat of the lamp. Every evening they were surrounded by a circle of dark, laughing faces — schoolboys who came in to watch whatever the missionaries might be doing.

'Don't white people ever get tired of paper?' said one to Dr Tidmarsh in Quichua. 'These two, all they do is look at paper and write on paper. My father says white men smell like paper. He gets mad at me for smelling like paper when I come home from school.'

Pete Fleming smiled as Dr Tidmarsh translated. How was a man to concentrate for five minutes? But then — he loved these Quichua boys. This is what he had bargained for — this is why he had renounced the solitude and silence for study which had been his pleasure before.

I was by this time in the western jungle of Ecuador, and Jim kept in touch with me as frequently as jungle mail service would permit. Soon after he reached Shandia he wrote:

Days begin at 6 am with the swooshing of the gas stove on which Dr Tidmarsh heats his shaving-water. The box we use for a wash-stand sits on the corner of the front porch, and the drain is over the wall, where you aim the basin at a ditch which runs right around the house. Breakfast, usually consisting of a bowl or two of banana soup or ground corn, a fresh banana and a cup of coffee, has so far been interrupted at 7.15 each morning to make radio contact with the other mission stations of the region. At meal-time we speak only Spanish. Breakfast is followed by a reading of Daniel in Spanish, and morning prayer.

So far my mornings have been consumed in watching the doctor do medical work, studying, or making some gadget to bring things to a little better state for comfort, and interspersed with visits to the airstrip to see if the men are working. Today, as a herd of wild pigs up-river sent most of them scurrying to the hunt, there were only a dozen or so working. They had arrived at that part of the strip which was planted in patches of plantain [a tropical fruit, "cooking cousin" of the banana] and they were loath to cut them down. I helped them push over the trees to get them started. It's like destroying food to them, and it hurt me a little, too, but there are other plantains and no other airstrips.

Our room is exceedingly pleasant; a huge window looks out on a beautiful view. Door is monk's cloth curtain, between our room and the living-room. Two throw rugs and the two aluminium chairs make the place look very civilized and the Indian, Venancio, sweeps it daily to clean out the mud and dead cockroaches.

Old Venancio, a typical Quichua, was Dr Tidmarsh's right-hand man. He dressed as the white man does, in ordinary pants and shirt, his parents having years ago left the old costume of the Quichuas, the *kushma*. Travel on jungle trails, sometimes in knee-deep mud, makes shoes an absurdity for him, though a few others wear them on special occasions as a sign of prestige. A safety-pin adorns a conspicuous spot on the front of his unironed shirt, handy for removing chonta palm thorns from his feet. As he travels the trails, he carries a well-worn machete, which he swings aimlessly at trees. If he comes to a steep or slippery bank, he can cut steps for his toes as he ascends. If a vine hangs in his way, one swipe removes it. His wife Susanna trudges behind him, carrying her baby in a cloth on her side, and a great basket containing cooking-pot, chickens, blanket, and plantains. This basket is strapped with a jungle 'rope', a strip of bark or a long, fibrous leaf, which is passed around the basket and up over Susanna's forehead. She, too, carries her machete, with which to dig and peel the manioc which is their main diet, trim her fingernails, or discourage the weeds around their front door. The machete is their most valued implement — indeed, often the only implement. It makes an excellent hoe, shovel, axe, knife, scissors, or what have you. Jim and Pete soon learned that it is indispensable in the jungle, and wondered how they had ever done without one in the States.

Venancio spends much of his time making small baskets for storing eggs, trumpet-shaped traps and nets for scooping fish, woven sieves, and monkey-skin drums. His wife does all of the heavy work, such as clearing the land of trees and other jungle growth, planting, carrying water and firewood, washing of clothes on the rocks by the river, hauling of heads of plantains, which may weigh up to one hundred pounds each.

Venancio's bed is made of a few slabs of split bamboo laid across a few poles. For chairs he has chunks of wood, five or six inches in height, on which he squats by the fire. A soup plate and spoon make up his eating utensils, and he uses half-gourds for drinking, along with the clay bowls. The staple food of Venancio and his fellow tribesmen is a drink known as chicha. This is made from manioc, a starchy tuber dug daily by the womenfolk, peeled with deft whacks of the machete, and steamed in a clay pot. When it is cooked, the women pound the manioc with a wooden pestle to the consistency of mashed potato, but coarser and heavier. Taking mouthfuls of this, they chew it and spit it into a tray, thus beginning the fermentation which continues as the mass is put back into the great clay urns. It is left for a day or two, or even a week if strong chicha is desired. The Quichuas literally live on this stuff for most of their lives, supplementing it when they can with wild meat or fish, perhaps a little jungle fruit, and eggs.

Day by day in their observation of the Indians as individuals and in a group, Jim and Pete learned to fit themselves into this new fabric of living. One night as the two men, with their senior worker Dr Tidmarsh, sat with the school-boys in their little bamboo house, running steps were heard outside.

'Doctor! Doctor! *Tiangichu*? Are you there?'

'*Ikui. Ikui.* Come in.'

'My sister-in-law is dying!'

This, in Quichua, may mean anything from a headache to a snake-bite. If one is in excellent health, he is 'living'. Otherwise, he is 'dying'.

'What is the matter with your sister-in-law?'

'She is causing a child to be born. Will you come?'

Unless there is some complication, the missionary is not usually called to attend a delivery, but Dr Tidmarsh knew that in this case the woman had lost five babies. He was a doctor of philosophy, not a medical doctor, although he had studied homoeopathy. So he collected the simple equipment he had for such emergencies, and with Pete, started down the river. Venancio, serving as guide, plunged ahead in the darkness, while they swung their flashlights to try to augment the little circle of light they threw on the muddy trail. The Talac River, a shallow stream perhaps fifty feet wide, had to be crossed two or three times, and finally the house was reached, a rectangular building constructed of split bamboo and palm-leaf roof, woven beautifully and evenly. As they entered the narrow doorway, stepping over a low sill designed to discourage pigs and chickens, they could see several fires glowing dimly through the smoke that always filled the house and incidentally acts as a preservative for the roof leaf, coating it with tars that resist insects. In one corner sat a man, weaving a string fishing net. Another sawed away on a home-made violin.

Pete wrote later in his diary:

The woman was lying on a bamboo board, partly shielded from public view by two loosely hung blankets, and was attended by the "midwife". Gradually all became dark, the smouldering fires died to embers, and the families went to their boards for the night, the little children with their parents, older boys together in one corner, girls in another. They gave Tidmarsh and me a bed and we lay down as there was no sign of the baby's arrival, labour pains still seven minutes apart. As the bamboo had none of the usually-associated attributes of flexibility which it has in the minds of many,

36

and as our shoes and pants were still wet from walking in the river, we soon chilled, and later rose and sat on small log seats around a smoky fire which refused to stay alight. In company of two mangy skeleton-ribbed dogs we sat listening to the whine of the crickets, the strange goose-like honking of the tree-toads, the occasional waking cry of a child, the creaking of the bamboo as someone rolled over, and the periodic moans of the woman which rose shrilly to a short scream.

Gradually as the pains increased and intensified the girl rose to her knees and reached for the vine-rope which hung from the ceiling above, intertwining her hands in the rope and lifting her body when the pains came. For me, those small brown hands held high over the head, and the arms, lined with taut tendons, communicated something of the simplicity and yet binding custom of their means of giving birth. After she had passed the water, the pains waned and finally the baby began to descend. The midwife gave a word, everybody woke up and moved sleepily to the corner and stood peering over the curtains. Privacy is a word and concept unknown. They prepared a drink for the mother by scraping the claw of a sloth and mixing the powder with water. I think this is supposed to hasten the arrival of the baby.

Venancio, our cook, then stepped inside, grasped the girl by the shoulders and began shaking her violently, which he continued to do until the baby arrived, dropping half on to the banana leaves, half on the earthen floor, a tiny frail thing attached to an intestine-like cord, motionless in the flickering kerosene light. It burped a couple of times, sputtered and cried, then adopted normal breathing. Tidmarsh stepped in to tie off the cord, and the midwife cut it with a sharp edge of a bamboo stick. The midwife then picked up the baby, took a mouthful of water from an iron pot, and spat it out over the baby, thus washing it. Then wrapping it in an old dirty cloth and tying it with a woman's embroidered belt, she handed it to a small naked child, who tottered across the floor with it. A woman took it, laid it on a bamboo plank, where it was apparently forgotten. Meanwhile the mother continued in her martyr-like position, wincing and writhing under the continuing contractions. Tidmarsh committed the baby to the Lord in prayer.

Slowly the men became more familiar with the language. They were never without their little black notebooks and pencils. Since the language was not a written one, they had only to write down what they heard, try to find out by one means or another what it meant, and then memorise.

Jim wrote home:

> I find the language fascinating. The freshness of discovering a language from the speaker's mouth, without the aid of a textbook, is most stimulating. And an especially interesting feature to me now is the onomatopoeic value of certain words. For example, I heard it said of a free-swinging broken wrist, "It goes whi-*lang*, whi-*lang*." The word has no dictionary meaning, so far as we can discover. Or a lamp flickering goes "li-*ping*, li-*ping*, tiung, tiung, and dies." The word "tukluk, tukluk" describes rapid swallowing or gulping. And there are myriads more.

As Pete and Jim's knowledge of the language grew, so grew the Indians' confidence in them, and they began to invite the missionaries to greater participation in their life and customs. 'You speak Quichua better than we do,' said Wakcha, a proud young Indian who always wore a pith helmet, a sign of great prestige among his people. 'You hear us too well. We are talking away saying to ourselves, "They do not hear," and then you answer us!'

Dr Tidmarsh eventually left the forest to return to his family in the mountains, but before he went he gave Jim and Pete a few simple instructions about caring for the sick. On their own, they would have to give what medical aid they could with the help of medical books and prayer. Sick calls had to be answered. One night in January a distraught father came to them on behalf of his baby who was ill.

'Will you not stick it with medicine?' he pleaded. It had not taken the Indians long to learn the healing power of antibiotics for their frequent tropical infections, and they soon began to feel that unless they were injected, the missionary had really done nothing at all. It was useless for the missionary to try to explain that if a man had a bad case of worms, penicillin would not cure him. 'Drinking-medicine' was not nearly so effective, in the Indian mind, as 'sticking-medicine'. This time, however, that baby's case seemed to be pneumonia, so Jim gave penicillin. The parents were satisfied that he had done what he could—but the baby did not show immediate signs of recovery. They fell back, then, on the greatest power they knew, the witch-doctor. Jim asked if he might stay to watch the ceremony. He recalled later:

A bed was pointed out to me. I was told they were going to drink *ayak waska* and that I was to stay on the cane bed and not turn on my flashlight.

All lamps were extingushed by 8.30 and the three Indians who were to drink the herb, *ayak waska*, could be heard speaking across the room occasionally. I feigned sleep and drowsed, but woke when one of the watchers sleeping on the floor beside me was roused to be alert to listen as the drinking passed and the "swoon speech" expected. I heard the quick, steady, swish beat of what sounded like a bunch of dry leaves being shaken, and from somewhere, I cannot say if it was from the same source, the rather melodious whistle of the three-tone pattern so usual among them. This was interspersed with a spitting, retching sound, and the curious pop of the smoke blowing on the patient's head, as I had seen done earlier. (I had offered another injection of penicillin and been refused at supper-time. The witch-doctor insisted that we wait till morning.) The swishing and blowing and whistling were joined by an occasional heavy snore and I dropped off to sleep.

At eleven I was awakened by an Indian playing a violin. We chatted. I checked the baby at midnight and was told that the witching had not amounted to much, as the drinkers had not taken enough to do much talking. Fever seemed a little higher, breathing and general conditions not changed. Around one I fell asleep again. The mother and an old woman were awake, making applications of leaves and tobacco. Lamps and kerosene lanterns made things somewhat less eerie than earlier.

I slept until the death wail awakened me at three. No struggle; just quit breathing. Made our third small coffin this morning.

These happenings gave insight into the life of these people. Superstition and fear bound them tightly. Would the New Testament answer the longing of the Quichua for freedom from fear, peace of heart, deliverance from evil spirits? The missionaries prayed and discussed these problems, but still they felt themselves foreigners — felt that they would always be foreigners. The Indian himself must be the answer — he must learn the Scriptures, be taught, and in turn teach his own people. To this end Pete and Jim re-opened the missionary school at Shandia that Dr Tidmarsh had been forced to close. Here in a one-room schoolhouse the youngsters of the community were taught to read and write so that ultimately they could read the Scriptures for themselves.

But there were others, Indians who had as yet never had one chance to hear the story which these boys listened to daily. Would God send Jim and Pete to take the message to the Aucas?

'The thought scares me at times,' wrote Pete, 'but I am ready. We have believed God for miracles, and this may include the Aucas. It has got to be by miracles in response to faith. No lesser expedient is a short-cut. O God, guide!'

– 4 –

Infinite Adaptability

EVER SINCE THEIR COLLEGE DAYS Jim Elliot and
Ed McCully had wondered if some day they might
work together on the mission-field. When Ed, his
wife Marilou and their tow-headed toddler Stevie arrived in
Quito in December, 1952, it seemed that their hopes would
be realised. The McCullys planned to stay in Quito for their
required Spanish study and then join Jim and Pete in
Shandia. In June, 1953, Ed left his family in Quito and
made a quick trip to his future home in the jungle. He wrote
to his folks in the States of the scenes he had witnessed:

> I have just returned to Quito, after spending twelve days in the
> jungles with Jim Elliot and Pete Fleming among the lowland
> Quichua Indians. If the Lord permits, we hope to be located
> there in a few months. During these twelve days, after viewing
> the Indian boys in school and the endless line of people seeking
> medical aid, after visiting Indian homes, after hearing the
> weird chant of witch-calling, and the hopeless cry of the death
> mourners, I praise God for bringing us to this land to work
> with these people. I pray that we might be faithful to our
> calling and that God will use us to bring many of these Indians
> to Himself.
>
> I stood by the bed of an eighteen-year-old Indian boy in the
> eastern jungle. I watched him vomit blood and in a few
> minutes I watched him die. In that hour, as I stood looking at

his lifeless form lying on bamboo sticks on the dirt floor of the hut, I was to realise more fully what Paul meant in 1 Thessalonians 4, "Ye sorrow not, even as others which have no hope." I will not soon forget the screaming-chanting wail of these heathen folk as they beat their breasts and mourned for two days and nights. It was a pathetic picture of "no hope". Tonight I pray a peculiar prayer... that God will spare the lives of these Indians until He enables us to bring to them the message of hope, of eternal life, of salvation in their own language.

Eldest son of a Milwaukee bakery executive, Ed McCully grew up in the Midwest, in a home which knew something of sacrifice for the work of the Lord. Ed's father was active in preaching, travelling thoughout the United States, speaking of Christ to his business associates at every opportunity, and to Christian groups in many places. When Ed entered Wheaton College in the fall of 1945, it was not with the idea of becoming a foreign missionary. He chose business and economics as his major.

Six feet two inches tall, weighing one hundred and ninety pounds, he soon distinguished himself as star end on Wheaton's championship football team. His surprising speed for so big a man made him a track star as well. His track coach, the national champion miler, Gil Dodds, tells of an incident in Ed's senior year. Ten 440-yard men were in training for a special meet in Boston; from the ten, five would be picked to go. Ed wanted to go to Boston. So, in spite of the fact that he was a 100 — 220-yard man and had never run a 440 in his life, he asked if he could try out with the others. It was typical of Ed that he made the relay team by one-tenth of a second. 'He was always coming through with the impossible when the chips were down,' was Dodds' concluding comment.

Ed was at his best on the platform. His simple, direct approach to his audience enabled him, with no formal training whatever in public speaking, to win the 1949 championship in the National Hearst Oratorical Contest in

San Francisco, a competition in which over ten thousand students had competed. His essay on Alexander Hamilton was nearly memorised by his classmates, who insisted on his reciting it at every class gathering. When he came to the climax,

> *And like a silver clarion rung,*
> *The accents of that unknown tongue,*

the class would rise simultaneously and shout with Ed, '*Excelsior!*'

Such was the spirit which Ed, senior class president, had generated. Of his election my brother Dave wrote: 'Ed was elected (or shouted in) without a contrary vote. I frankly doubt if anyone even entertained the idea of proposing anyone else for the position. It was a foregone and unanimously accepted conclusion.'

The following year Ed McCully, having turned his thinking towards the bar, entered the law school at Marquette University. At the beginning of his second year there he took a job as hotel clerk at night, intending to spend the time studying. But God, who ordains men of His own choosing and moves in them to the accomplishment of His eternal purposes, had other plans. Ed told his Wheaton classmate Jim about it in a letter dated September 22, 1950:

Since taking this job things have happened. I've been spending my free time studying the Word. Each night the Lord semed to get hold of me a little more. Night before last I was reading in Nehemiah. I finished the book, and read it through again. Here was a man who left everything as far as position was concerned to go do a job nobody else could handle. And because he went the whole remnant back in Jerusalem got right with the Lord. Obstacles and hindrances fell away and a great work was done. Jim, I couldn't get away from it. The Lord was dealing with me. On the way home yesterday morning I took a long walk and came to a decision which I know is of the Lord. In all honesty before the Lord I say that no one or nothing beyond Himself and the Word has any bearing upon what I've decided to do. I have one desire now—to live a life of reckless abandon for the Lord, putting all my energy and strength into it. Maybe He'll send me someplace where the name of Jesus Christ is unknown. Jim, I'm taking the Lord at His word, and I'm trusting Him to prove His Word. It's kind of like putting all your eggs in one basket, but we've already put our trust in Him for salvation, so why not do it as far as our life is concerned? If there's nothing to this business of eternal life we might as well lose everthing in one crack and throw our present life away with our life hereafter. But if there *is* something to it, then everything else the Lord says must hold true likewise. Pray for me, Jim.

Man, to think the Lord got hold of me just one day before I was to register for school! I've got my money put away and was all set to go. Today was registration day so I went over to school to let them know why I wouldn't be back. I really prayed like the apostle asked the Ephesians to pray, that I might "open my mouth boldly". I talked to all the fellows that I knew well. Then I went in to see a professor I thought a lot about. I told him what I planned to do, and before I left he had tears in his eyes. I went in to see another professor and talked to him. All I got was a cold farewell and good luck wish.

Well, that's it. Two days ago I was a law student. Today I'm an untitled nobody. Thanks, Jim, for the intercession on my behalf. Don't let up. And brother, I'm really praying for you too as you're making preparation to leave. I only wish I were going with you.

Ed's period of boot-training came when he went with Jim Elliot to Chester, Illinois, in the winter of 1951. Besides the tent meetings and children's classes which they held in an attempt to preach the Gospel in that town, Ed frequently preached on a weekly radio broadcast which he and Jim shared. As the Apostle Paul wrote, 'I am debtor both to the Greeks, and to the Barbarians; both to the wise, and to the unwise. So, as much as in me is, I am ready to preach the gospel to you that are at Rome also. For I am not ashamed of the gospel of Christ: for it is the power of God unto salvation to every one that believeth...' So Ed believed and so he preached.

On May 16, 1951, he used civic law as an illustration in one of these radio messages. Ed's sermon explains better than most theological statements the belief shared by all five of the men who were ultimately to combine forces in Operation Auca.

Ed said:

> "The fate of the criminal, is to fulfil the condemnation by being punished—for some this means serving a term of years, for others it means imprisonment for life, for others it means death. God's condemnation upon all sinners is death. "The wages of sin is death..." One sentence, and one punishment for those who do not believe.
>
> But, you say, God is a God of love. He will not punish anyone eternally. It is true that He is God of love. And His condemnation does not in any way alter the fact. God is not willing that you or I experience the punishment we justly deserve. Therefore He offers us and escape, if we choose to accept it. At the price of His only begotten Son, God provided pardon.
>
> This is the simple, plain, and clear Word of God from His book, the Bible. "He that believeth on My Son," says God, "is not condemned, but he that believeth not is condemned already, because he has not believed on my only begotten Son.

As in the days when the Lord Himself walked on the earth, the results were not startling. A few wrote to the radio station for further information. A handful of people professed conversion as a result of the meetings held in school auditoriums and tents. But Ed knew that he had been obedient to God in the work of those months. Just prior to going to Chester, Ed had accepted an invitation to speak at a young people's banquet in Pontiac, Michigan. God had more in mind than Ed had imagined. It was there that he met Marilou Hobolth, a pretty dark-haired pianist in the church where he was to speak. During the months in Chester, Ed sent more letters, no doubt, to Marilou than he had posted to others in several years. Early in the correspondence he wrote:

> I'm praying definitely for two things: first, that the Lord will give us wisdom in our relationship—even in the business of letter-writing. Second, that as long as we've got anything to do with each other, that each of us will be an influence upon the other for closer fellowship with the Lord. I don't mean that we'll be *preaching* to each other—but just that our attraction for each other will be a means of attracting us more to the Lord. I know that's the way you feel too.

Their friendship ripened fast and in April Ed and Marilou became engaged. A few days later Ed wrote her:

> When you pray, ask the Lord definitely to show us where He wants us to spend our lives, and that we'll be willing to spend them there, even anxious to.

Ed's love for the girl he was going to marry was whole-hearted:

> When anybody speaks to me, it takes everything I've got to stay with them in conversation. It's the craziest sensation! I'm beginning to believe everything the poets and song-writers have to say about love!

On May 29, 1951, he was writing:

> One month from today you will have lost all your freedom and will be subject to my iron rule, my unflinching law, and my cruel command. You have exactly thirty-one days to reconsider. Do you think you'll really be able to put up with me for the rest of your life? It won't be easy. There'll be plenty of times you'll wonder why on earth you married me. Have you reconsidered? Now let me tell you that I love you with all of my heart.

Marilou did not reconsider. They were married in June in her home church, the First Baptist of Pontiac, Michigan.

Ed's decision to become a foreign missionary led him to enrol at the School of Missionary Medicine in Los Angeles, where he spent a year of intensive study in tropical diseases and their treatment, obstetrics, dentistry, learning the fundamentals in order not only to be of help to the Indians, but also to keep himself and family in shape.

On December 10, 1952, with eight-month-old Stevie, Ed and Marilou sailed for Ecuador, the country where God had indicated He wanted them to spend their lives.

In the jungle Jim and Pete had been looking forward to the day when the McCullys would join them. They were building a house for them, along with other mission buildings. In the meantime, the McCullys were living in a stucco house in Quito with an Ecuadorian family, learning Spanish. It was not an easy life and they found themselves subject to discouragement and a sense of uselessness. 'We ask in prayer that we might have aptness and accuracy in the studies, and grace to carry us over the 'hump' so we will be able not only to converse but also speak the Word of Life,' Ed wrote to friends who had promised to pray for them. He and Marilou were eagerly looking forward to having their own home down in the jungle, and to getting into the work which they longed to do. One day Ed was called to the short-wave radio.

'I didn't read that transmission too well — did you say *all* of the buildings?' he asked. 'Over.'

'All of the buildings at Shandia have been destroyed by flood. *All* of the buildings at Shandia have been destroyed by flood. Jim and Pete would like you to come down as quickly as possible. Over.'

'Okay. Okay. Tell them I'll be right down.'

Ed McCully handed the microphone back to the short-wave operator. The message had been relayed to him from Shell Mera. Jim and Pete had sent a runner to Dos Rios, a mission station six hours' walk from Shandia. The missionaries there had informed Shell Mera by radio of the flood.

Ed was dazed. He walked over to the window and stood looking out across the valley of Quito, towards Antisana, the mighty snow-cap between him and the little mission station he had visited only a few weeks before.

The mission station at Shandia had been wiped out. In one day of thunderous rising water, followed by a nightmare that lasted through the long hours of darkness, the rampaging river destroyed everything. Five hundred hand-planed boards—each representing one full day's work for one man—stacked up for a new house, a new clinic, and a new school kitchen had disappeared in the night. Most of their personal belongings were saved, but Jim and Pete's invaluable Quichua vocabulary manuscript was strewn all over the ground and tracked in mud. Three hundred and thirty feet were sliced off the end of the airstrip. It was a poignant reminder to the men of the temporal quality of their present 'city'.

Just as they had instinctively sought Ed's help, so now he turned to Marilou. 'Babe, the whole station at Shandia has been destroyed by flood!'

Marilou was incredulous. Ed told her of the disaster and of Jim and Pete's having asked him to go down to the forest. She agreed immediately that this was the right course of action.

'But—what about you and Stevie?' he asked.

'Oh, we'll be fine,' Marilou replied. 'We'll just stay right here, and you let us know by radio whatever you plan to do. I'm sure it'll work out okay.'

As usual, Ed was cheered by her spirit, and began making preparations for the trip. 'Elliot,' he had said one day to Jim, 'I've married an efficient wife. She plans—and she makes me plan. And we get it done!'

She got him ready in record time, and soon thereafter he was seated on a canvas chair in the tent which Jim and Pete had pitched in Shandia. Discouragement gave way to planning and the young men quickly turned to rebuilding the mission station and getting things ready for the McCullys. As soon as possible Ed went to Quito to move his family down. An excerpt from Ed's diary tells of their first days in the rain forest:

> *September, 1953.* We are well settled by now. Life gets to be a routine of buying, selling, treating sick, fixing kerosene and gasoline appliances, trying to learn a language. It's a fight to try to get time for the latter. Also time for Bible study and prayer. It's hard to stay on top of it all, hard to keep rejoicing, hard to love these ungrateful Indians. It's hard to keep our primary purpose in view when we get so swamped with secondary things.

The life of a missionary calls for infinite adaptability— from winning a national oratorical contest to struggling with an unwritten language . . . from starring on the college football field to teaching a bunch of small Indians to play volley-ball . . . from prospects of a law career in a North American city to a life in the jungle of South America. Marilou, who had been director of music in a large church, slowly and carefully taught Indian children to sing two-line songs which she and Ed had written in the Quichua language. With all this, they were ready. They were fully prepared to be 'fools for Christ's sake.'

— 5 —

'Expendable for God'

AVIONETA UYARIMUN! The little plane is coming into hearing!'

These words, shouted by the Indians, announced to Jim, Ed, Pete, and other missionaries in the Oriente that the bright yellow Piper of the Missionary Aviation Fellowship was about to land on the station airstrip. The most welcome sound in the jungle was the approaching hum of its engine. The missionary would interrupt his business for the morning — treating a baby for impetigo, selling a bottle of worm medicine, teaching a Bible class, or sawing boards for a building. There would be a grand scramble to clear the strip, the missionary would pace it for a final check of the surface, and then, when dogs and children were at a safe distance, the plane would glide on to the grass. As the prop stopped spinning, the door would swing open, and a sunburned, sandy-haired man with a wide grin and frank blue eyes would hop out — Nate Saint, the man whose vision had changed missionary life in the jungle.

Nate would dig out the cargo listed for that station, checking aloud the list which his wife Marj had made out for him beforehand:

'Let's see — a sack of flour, fifteen gallons of diesel oil, meat, vegetables, two brooms, and the mail. Your penicillin is in the mail-sack. Guess that's it. How's it going, Ed?'

As the two men talked beside the plane, Indians would eagerly gather round. One would stand rubbing one leg down the back of the other continually, to keep off the flies. A baby would cry, or a dog would escape from the captivity of a child—nothing would distract the Indians from looking at the plane, no matter how many times they had seen it.

And then, without warning, a tiny alarm would sound —Nate's watch! A methodical man, he had figured out exactly how much time he could spend in that station and still make his deadline home before sundown, or, if he had another flight scheduled, he would know precisely when he must take off for that. After piling and lashing down the empty diesel oil-cans in the back of his plane for refilling at his headquarters in Shell Mera, and rechecking his list, he would jump in, fasten safety-belt and shoulder harness, wave good-bye, and take off. It was a bright spot in the week for the isolated missionary.

'Man, there's nobody like old Nate,' Ed would say to Marilou, as they walked back to the house.

Truly the coming of Nate Saint with the Piper had marked the beginning of a new way of life on the isolated mission stations of this jungle area. Heretofore the missionary and his family would be completely cut off from the outside world long months at a time—four, six, eight days of heartbreaking struggle on a dangerous jungle trail separated him from medical and other help. Then, one by one, airstrips were hacked from the jungle. Radio transmitters and receivers were installed, and the airplane, when it came, covered in five minutes the distance of a long hard day on the trail. Housing was vastly improved—from vermin-ridden bamboo and short-lived thatch to boards cut and planed by machinery brought in by air. Nate worked out a special frame underneath his plane for hauling sheets of aluminium. These provided a durable and easily-constructed roof. Electric light plants and fuel to run them, kerosene refrigerators, filing cabinets, stoves, power saws, and cement—all helped to make life in the jungle safer, healthier, and more efficient.

Nate and his wife Marj arrived in the Oriente in September, 1948. His first job there was to set up some kind of living quarters for himself and Marj in Shell Mera. A tent sufficed during the weeks he was building a small frame house, which soon became 'warehouse-dormitory-toolshed'. But the job of serving the missionaries was not allowed to wait until the Saints were comfortably settled. Nate had come down as a pilot of the Missionary Aviation Fellowship, an interdenominational organisation founded by two ex-Navy pilots whose aim it was to transport evangelical missionaries, their supplies, their sick, to and from remote outposts. Thus, by lightening the physical burden which the missionary carries because of the primitive nature of his surroundings, the MAF could give him more time and energy for his spiritual ministry.

Almost at once Nate started ferrying missionaries in his plane, transporting their cargo, making courtesy flights, and handling all the maintenance on the plane himself. Marj began entertaining all the missionaries and their visitors who came through Shell Mera. These were numerous and she was the only available hostess for miles around. She never knew whether supper should be cooked for two or twelve. 'And they eat like harvest hands!' she said. 'I cook what I think ordinary people would eat, and then double it.'

For the stringent requirements of their unique job, Nate and Marj were eminently suited. Nate's appreciation of Marj's role was once expressed in a letter: 'How glad I am to have you working at my side *always*. I have felt that I had sufficient 'snort' and drive for the sprints, but God knew I would need a flywheel to steady me for the long haul.'

Nate's first concern in flying was that it should be safe, efficient, and economical: 'Missionaries who used to travel the old trails made sure they weren't carrying anything that wasn't neccessary. Today, in the airplane, we, too, make sure we don't carry anything that isn't necessary. When our mission bought the plane, it had nice, soft seats in it. But we found that these seats weighed almost eight pounds each. So we decided to use harder seats that weighed only one pound, and take seven pounds of extra food and cargo.'

Every ounce counted in a plane of this type. When Nate found that the streamlined wheel-covers were collecting mud, he took them off. Characteristically, Nate turned this to spiritual illustration: 'When life's flight is over, and we unload our cargo at the other end, the fellow who got rid of unnecessary weight will have the most valuable cargo to present to the Lord.'

Nate had always regarded himself as 'expendable' for the cause of Christ. In a short sermon delivered over the missionary radio station HCJB—The Voice of the Andes in Quito—he shared his belief with others:

> During the last war we were taught to recognise that, in order to obtain our objective, *we had to be willing to be expendable*.... This very afternoon thousands of soldiers are known by their serial numbers as men who are expendable.... We know there is only one answer to our country's demand that we share in the price of freedom. Yet, when the Lord Jesus asks us to pay the price for world evangelisation, we often answer without a word. We cannot go. We say it costs too much.
>
> God Himself laid down the law when He built the universe. He knew when He made it what the price was going to be. God didn't hold back His only Son, but gave Him up to pay the price for our failure and sin.
>
> Missionaries constantly face expendability. Jesus said, "There is no man that hath left house, or brethren, or sisters, or mother, or wife, or children, or lands for my sake and the Gospel's but shall receive an hundredfold now in this time and in the world to come eternal life."

However, Nate's convictions about expendability did not lessen that sense of caution which is ingrained in the fibre of any first-rate flier. On the contrary, his brain teemed with ideas for improving the safety of his plane. 'I am trying to steer clear of gimmicking for the sake of gimmicking,' he wrote. 'Nevertheless, I can't help the gadgets that run through my head, but I do try to sort out stuff that might have some value.'

One of the devices of real value which he put into operation was an alternate fuel system. He often tried out his ideas on his older brother Sam, an airline pilot with long experience in the field of aeronautics.

Nate wrote to Sam:

> As I sit above the jungle listening for the symptoms of trouble that I never want to hear, I have in the back of my mind little things like the fuel line that fell off in my hand in Mexico a few years back. The flare had broken off one end of the tubing, but natural spring tension had kept it in place. I also think of the quick work of mud wasps when they decide to plug up a fuel vent. To be sure, I am impressed by the "long end" of statistics, but I am also impressed by the dire consequence to my passengers, not to mention my own bones, if I should come out on the short end somewhere over these tall trees.

While turning over in his mind methods of eliminating a breakdown in the fuel system, Nate was working one day at the hangar at Shell Mera when he noticed a truck en route to Ambato, high in the Andes. Trucks in that region were not common and this one had an additional attention-catcher. A small boy was clinging to the roof of the cab holding a five-gallon can of gas and a syphon, while an older boy sat on the front fender holding the lower end of the syphon, pointed in the direction of the carburettor under the partially opened hood. Whatever had caused the failure of the regular fuel system, here was a truck preparing for an ascent of 6,000 feet, most of the way in second or third gear with a great deal of shifting, while a boy metered gas to the engine through a rubber hose!

Nate's lively imagination immediately transferred this method of feeding gas to his own need. He lifted the cowl of his plane, removed the temperature-gauge fitting from the intake manifold, and squirted in gasoline. Each squeeze on the gas-loaded tube produced a burst of power. Encouraged by his experimentation, he went into the kitchen and borrowed one of Marj's cooking-oil tins to use as an auxiliary three-gallon tank. To provide a streamlined fairing for the tank he sent an Indian boy for a piece of balsa wood, which the lad obtained by chopping down an eighty-foot balsa tree. The tank and fairing were then strapped to the struts under the left wing. Salvaged fittings, strainers, and a screw-type valve finished the rig. Nate mounted the valve on the fire wall and extended a control rod to the instrument panel. So far so good, but darkness forced him to wait until morning to test his home-made safety device.

He put in a sleepless night, thinking of various reasons why his idea was totally impracticable — but still there *was* that truck racing along in second gear without its normal fuel source. Then, too, from his long experience as a mechanic he knew that the complexity of a modern carburettor arises from the need to accelerate smoothly from slow speeds to higher speeds. And a dead engine in the air, he told himself, will windmill fast enough to stay out of those critical lower speeds.

The next morning, first tests proved that the alternate fuel system could work without a hitch on the ground. The moment had come to test it in the air. He described the experience:

Two thousand feet above the landing-strip I pulled the mixture control to idle-cut-off. It was quite a novel experience for a fellow who had listened so long, hoping never to hear it happen. But a turn of the new little T-handle on the instrument panel brought with it a wonderul feeling as the engine wound back up to smooth full-power. For the next twenty minutes the normal fuel source was shut off tight. Even though the carburettor was by-passed completely the engine never missed. It picked up from the windmilling condition without a cough.

I put the plane into every imaginable attitude at various power settings. It never faltered. "Feeling" for the best mixture setting with the emergency T-handle was no more difficult than "leaning" the engine with the regular mixture control. Same thing.

The whole rig, tank and all, weighs only four pounds. The only thing it has in common with the ship's fuel system is the engine. It takes care of all the common troubles such as clogged vents and broken lines. With the simplicity and low cost of a deal like this, why do we fly along with our only source of fuel supply in jeopardy at several points between tank and engine, and no alternative? We are all sold on dual *ignition:* why not an alternate fuel system for emergencies?

With government permission, every MAF plane now goes out to the jungle a safer machine because it is equipped with Nate's alternate fuel system.

Another ingenious invention of Nate's has astonished many in the aviation world. He developed a method of lowering a canvas bucket from an airplane in full flight into the hands of a person on the ground. This 'spiralling-line technique', as he called it, later made possible the first direct contact with the Aucus. A canvas bucket is let out behind the airplane on a line about 1,500 feet long. As the airplane goes into a tight turn, the bucket moves towards the centre of the circle—the drag of the cord across the circle overcoming the centrifugal force tending to throw the bucket outwards. As the bucket moves towards the centre it falls until it eventually hangs almost motionless at the bottom or vortex of an inverted cone. Not only could the person on the ground receive mail, medicine, and small parcels, but, more important, could send messages or other things back to the airplane as the bucket is pulled up again. Sometimes Nate substituted a telephone wire for the cord, with a field telephone in the bucket. In this way he could talk by telephone to a missionary on a sandbar or in a jungle clearing in areas where there was no landing-strip.

One of the essential safety measures was the maintenance at all times of short-wave contact with the plane. This was Marj's job. Whenever the plane was in the air, she stood by for regular checks of location, altitude, and fuel load. She checked on weather conditions in Shell Mera, and kept in touch with the missionary to whose station Nate was flying for a check from that end. Each missionary station was equipped with transmitter and receiver, and at seven o'clock every morning the missionaries called in to Shell Mera. If a medical emergency had arisen since the previous call, help could be obtained, and flights arranged for evacuating the patient. Routine supplies were ordered, and flights scheduled by means of this contact. It meant hours and hours of sitting by the radio, but Marj was as convinced that this was her share of missionary work as Nate was that flying was his. Thus on any morning a visitor to Shell Mera might have heard something like this:

'Shell Mera is standing by for Macuma, Macuma. Over.'

'Macuma standing by. We'd just like to know how many carriers to have at the airstrip when our cargo arrives. Over.'

'Good morning, Macuma. I think two will be enough. Over.'

'Okay, thanks. And how is the boy we sent out to the clinic? Over.'

'I'll phone the clinic and find out if he can come home on Thursday's flight. Incidentally, you'll be having a visitor on Thursday. A missionary just came in on the bus and would like to see a typical jungle station. Over.'

'Okay, Marj. We'll be glad to have him. Better send us a little more food than our usual order this week, though. Over.'

'Okay. Okay, Macuma. Shell Mera calling Shandia, Shandia. Do you have any traffic? Over.'

'Shandia standing by. No traffic, Marj. Over.'

And so the morning would pass, Marj taking orders for food, supplies for the Indian schools, medicine for the dispensaries; standing by while one station talked with another, relaying messages from missionaries to the doctor, getting his answer by telephone and relaying it back to the missionary, and calling '56 Henry', Nate's plane, as he flew out over the jungle, carefully noting down his position every five minutes.

There were those back home who smiled at Nate's

constant concern for safety. 'After all,' they said, 'a mission-ary is supposed to trust the Lord!'

Nate wrote home:

Perhaps my reasoning *is* pagan, as I've been told. I do belive in miracles. They are nothing to God, surely. But the question is one of finding the pattern that the Lord has chosen us to conform to. I wouldn't be here if I weren't trusting the Lord. Chances are that those who shrug it off by saying, "The Lord will take care of you," are the same ones who would hardly expose themselves to the bacteriological risks of working in a downtown rescue mission. Forgive me if I feel a little strongly at this point. I'm concerned about safety, but I don't let it keep me from getting on with God's business. Every time I take off, I am ready to deliver up the life I owe to God. I feel we should be quick to take advantage of every possible improve-ment in carrying out the job before us.

Besides facilitating the work of the jungle missionaries, Nate had a direct influence on the Ecuadorians at his own doorstep. He never appeared to be hurried, and many a national came to him just to talk, recognising in him a love for God and a sympathetic heart which drew them. He improved steadily in the Spanish language, and was respected for this effort. Street meetings, Sunday School and literacy classes, personal chats — these things made Nate a missionary as well as a pilot.

Small contrivances to add to the convenience and pleasure of his family also took his attention. He built a concrete cistern to catch rain-water from the roof, and also built up a lower outer wall so that the children — Kathie born in 1949 and Stevie born in 1951 — could have a place to wade in the overflow from the larger tank. He put a bell-ringing timer on the washing-maching to save Marj steps while she was at the radio. Dampness is a major problem in Shell Mera, so Nate created a drying-room behind the kitchen by building the kerosene refrigerator flush with the kitchen wall and backing the heating unit into the little room. Here he also put the hot-water heater. Thus clothes and other equipment could be kept dry.

What had brought a man with this inventive, ingenious turn of mind, with these modern technical skills, into the primitive jungle of Ecuador? Like Ed, Pete, and Jim, Nate came from a family whose guiding principles of life were rooted deep in the teachings of the Scriptures. As a small boy, he understood the personal implications of the New Testament, and placed his faith in Christ as the only ground for his hope of salvation. In the Saint home in Philadelphia, where Nate was born in 1923, movies and dancing were not allowed, nor any form of gambling, from pitching pennies to playing poker. But it was no monastery. The children went fishing, trapping, sledding in winter-time, and were allowed such adventures as sleeping out-of-doors. Nate blueprinted and built model gliders, boats, and locomotives. His elder sister Rachel was 'like a little mother' to him, reading him missionary books about Africa, Japan, India, and South America. His imagination fastened eagerly on to these stories, and he once said, 'I don't expect ever to be a preacher, but some day I would like to talk to someone who has never heard about Jesus.'

His eldest brother Sam took him flying when Nate was seven — so small that he had to stand on the seat to see out of the cockpit of the old biplane. From that time on he was captured by wings and the wide sky.

At thirteen he suffered a severe case of osteomyelitis in his leg, and enforced inactivity gave him time to think. Could it be that God wanted him to be a missionary?

Later he recorded:

> Through high school everthing was evaluated in terms of flying machines and all emotions were tuned to imagined air adventure. All else became almost unbearably confining, in fact, any occupation that keeps me where I can't see the sky for a day is still one of my rougher tribulations.

The four walls of the classroom finally did become unbearable, and in his senior year Nate took a daytime job in a welding shop and went to night school, completing his high-school course in a few months. A job at a small airport, where he learned to fly small planes, took up the next six months. After this he worked in an airline overhaul shop and gained a mechanic's licence. The next step was to sign up for the Air Force pilot cadet programme. 'It looked as though the Eagle was about to lay the golden egg!' he said. 'Twenty-five thousand dollars' worth of pilot training!' By this time he had piloted a 40-horse-power light plane about eighty hours, but he had dreamed long of flying the big powerful planes of the military.

The night before he was to report for his first military flying instruction he became aware of pain around his old osteomyelitis scar. Yanking up his trouser leg, he knew the truth. It was inflamed. All his boyhood ambitions of the past years, wrapped up and focused on this shining opportunity to get into big-time flying, suddenly collapsed.

> I didn't say a word to my room-mate, but jumped into bed and turned out the light without a word. There I barred myself into the small, dark confines of my heart, which had now become a dungeon for solitary confinement. Except for the tossing, and choked, then sighing, respiration, no one would have known the thing that was almost overwhelming me. No fooling; I was hearbroken.

The shock of losing the opportunity of getting out of the flying 'put-puts' into real airplanes left Nate in a state of numbness, not caring much about anything. When he came out of the hospital the Air Force made him a maintenance crew chief. On this job he had time to burn and he used it for Bible-reading, which he had neglected. One year after he was grounded, he was sent to Detroit on detached service to study new and larger engines that were soon to be on the line, and there, at a New Year's Eve worship service, he felt

that the Lord was turning his heart to the mission-field.
He recalled later:

> What was going on in the service wasn't important. I wasn't
> hearing anything with my ears, anyhow. I pleaded helplessly
> with my Heavenly Father for the answer that stood between
> me and the peace that Jesus had said should be ours. Now,
> you've heard about people being spoken to by God. I don't
> know about the other fellow, but that night I saw things
> different...BING...like that. Just as though a different
> Kodachrome slide had been tossed on to the screen between
> my ears. As soon as I could, I stepped out of the building and
> started out...just to get away from people. It was snowing
> and there was already a deep virgin snow on the ground, and
> the moan of city traffic had been muffled as it is when deep
> snow is around. A joy, such as I had never known since the
> night I accepted Jesus' forgiveness for my sins, seemed to leave
> me almost weak with gratitude. It was the first time that I had
> ever really heard that verse: 'Follow me, and I will make you to
> become fishers of men.' The old life of chasing things that are
> of a temporal sort seemed absolutely insane.

It was at this juncture, when Nate thought that he would
have to say good-bye to planes and flying and buckle down
to a couple of years of college in preparation for the mission-
field, that he heard of the Missionary Aviation Fellowship.
He wrote to his mother: 'Methinks the aircraft industry has
suffered the loss of a "big operator", and the Lord has won
for Himself a "li'l operator".'

Shorly after V. E. Day he was shipped out to Salinas,
California, to work as crew chief with the Fourth Air Force.
There he met the two ex-Navy pilots who had founded
MAF. It sounded like the perfect, made-to-order spot for
Nate Saint. He got hold of an old, beaten up, 40-horse-
power airplane, fixed it up, and began flying in every spare
minute—practising, always practising.

While he was still in the Army he met Marj Farris, whom
he later described in a letter:

Among other blessings, the greatest. She has just finished her State exams and is now a practising registered nurse in California. She is a graduate of U. of California at Los Angeles, an ardent student of the Word, and has a challenging love for the lost. She is the most selfless person I have met in my life except my Mother. She is a meek girl of deep conviction, ready for service for the Lord of the Harvest....

When Nate was discharged from the Air Force he asked God specifically to show him his next move. Suddenly he found himself with his first assignment with MAF. Early in July, 1946, he was asked to go down to Mexico to repair a plane that had crashed there during a landing. 'When God took over my life a couple of years before,' Nate said, 'He had not defined my duties but somehow it seemed immediately clear that this was to be my first [missionary avaiation] assignment.' Less than two weeks after he accepted the job, he found himself near the Guatemalan border, in the town of Tuxtla Gutiérrez, with a knowledge of Spanish 'limited to my childhood acquaintance with the Lone Ranger'.

He knew he was something of a sight, with a duffel bag containing forty pounds of tools, plus all his worldly goods. He wondered, too, if he might have difficulty at the customs office — 'It's not exactly usual for tourists to carry seven-foot airplane propellers under their arms.'

'I tried to imagine the damaged plane. It wouldn't be too bad — a damaged landing gear, and probably a splintered prop. Little did I dream that I would find two completely demolished wings in a bushel basket.' The plane had crashed in the bush at the edge of a jungle airstrip. Pieces of wing-struts, landing gear, and the panels had been brought out to the Tuxtla airport for Nate to rebuild. With the help of a Mexican cabinet-maker to whom everything had to be explained by drawings, he set to work to put the pieces together again. He was impeded by the fact that the blueprint he had been given did not match the plane and that a factory-made wing-spar sent down as a replacement matched neither the blueprint nor the plane. When he had finally reassembled the parts, the problem arose of taking the wing-panels out to the airstrip in the bush where the wrecked plane lay. It was not feasible to crate them and send them on the trail, where narrow canyon walls had to be scaled; the crates would never make the turns. So the wings were built up like a model plane kit, piece by piece without any glue, then each piece labelled, the whole works disassembled, tied up in bundles, and flown out to the jungle airstrip. When Nate got to the wrecked plane, he found that some parts had been stolen and that mud wasps had lodged in the fuel tank and lines. For lack of rigging data, he had to prop the tail up on a stump and rig the new wings to match the old by eye, just as he used to rig model planes as a child. Thus he finished his first MAF assignment, the plane being flown out barely within the work-permit time limit.

Later Nate went to Los Angeles and spent ten happy days with his little nurse. As he bade her good-bye he said, 'Well, Marj, as far as I'm concerned, it's all settled but the hardware!'

The winter of 1947-48 found him enrolled at Wheaton College, and in January Marj took a nursing job in a nearby town, studying the Bible at the college in preparation for the missionary life they anticipated together. They started a Bible club for teenagers. Nate called the programme 'a sort of candy-box, loaded with Gospel dynamite'.

But their training practice period was shorter than they had expected. The need of a pilot in Ecuador was presented to them. They cut short their courses, pooled their funds, bought an engagement ring and a Model-A Ford, and set out one midnight for Long Island, New York, nearly 1,000 miles away. They stayed with his brother Sam, and were married. After a four-day honeymoon, they headed their old Ford west, all their worldly goods stacked up in the back seat. Meals were cans of food heated on the engine. Finally they reached California and Nate began final work on a plane that had been purchased by the MAF for its operation in

Ecuador. Marj took another nursing job.

On September 8 the plane was ready and Nate, with another MAF pilot, flew it to Ecuador, leaving Marj to follow later that month by commercial transportation.

The years at Shell Mera passed quickly. The house grew into a large chalet of dark wood, with spacious porches, wide eaves for protection against tropical rains, a running water system for kitchen and shower, connected with the rain-pipes from the aluminium roof and with tanks under the eaves. After they raised the roof and built in a second storey, there were ten bedrooms to accommodate the many guests who came through, and a radio room where Marj could work efficiently and where radio repairs for the missionaries could be made.

Another pilot, Johnny Keenan, arrived with a second airplane to help in the work, and Nate soon had a comfortable house well on the way for the Keenans, plus accommodations in the hangar for the two planes. He installed a hydro-electric plant down by the river behind his house to furnish electricity for the establishment.

They were now set up to operate with the greatest efficiency; jungle stations were all being supplied, and Nate and Marj began to ask God in what new way they might forward His work in the Ecuadorian jungle.

Nate, despite the unceasing load of responsibility that weighed on him, had never forgotten that the Auca Indians lived only some sixty air-miles from Shell Mera. Shortly after arriving in South America Nare had written home:

> Not long ago we talked with another missionary who is longing to reach a tribe of killers, the Aucas. Few white persons have contacted them in a friendly way and lived to tell about it. We expect the airplane to play an essential part in reaching these people with the Gospel.

Nate used his plane to make an occasional survey flight over Auca territory, but not much was located on any of the

flights—only a house or two which had been abandoned.
He was beginning to wonder where they were. Then one day
in July, 1954, the jungle grape-vine carried the news that
there had been another Auca killing and this time Nate
became personally involved. He wrote home his own account
of what happened:

Yesterday I landed at Villano, about 45 miles west of here.
Just after I got on the ground a runner came up and told me of
an Auca raid. Later two Quichua survivors arrived at the
airstrip. The woman was being carried on a bamboo stretcher
and had a serious-looking lance puncture under the armpit.
They told us that the lance broke off in the wound. Her
attacker was going to jab at her again but she grabbed the end
of the lance and hung on to save her life. She is about six or
seven months pregnant. The man arrived under his own power
although considerably crippled up with chest punctures, a
hole all the way through one thigh and a hole through his hand
where he had apparently tried to stop one of the deadly shafts.
We loaded the two patients on to the plane. Once in the air I
told Marj what had taken place so that when we arrived here in
Shell Mera she had cots set up and, with another woman
helping, the Indians got the best care that local facilities
would permit.

We can't talk directly to our patients but our hired couple
speak Quichua and converse easily with them. Last night our
hired man read the Bible to them in Spanish, interpreting into
Quichua as he went along. They had never heard of the Bible.
Apparently the truth had not yet found its mark because this
morning the man asked if I couldn't fly back out there in the
plane and kill at least one of the Aucas for him. Again the
hired man explained that we were not interested in taking life
but rather in saving it through the Lord Jesus Christ.

Greatly as this incident intensified Nate's sense of urgency
about reaching the Aucas, there were also other tribes whose
ignorance of the Gospel offered a spiritual challenge to
missionaries. In 1954 came an unusual opportunity for
Nate to help push deeper into the dark reaches of the jungle.
One of the key figures in this new page of missionary history
was Roger Youderian.

– 6 –

Missionary to the Head-shrinking Jivaros

AT MACUMA, a mission-station in the southern jungle served by the little yellow plane, lived Roger Youderian, his wife Barbara, and their two children, Bethy and Jerry. Macuma, run since 1945 by Frank Drown, is reminiscent of a busy farm in the United States. As the plane comes in, chickens scatter off the airstrip, while cows continue chewing their cud undisturbed. Buildings are made, not of split bamboo, but of sturdy wooden planks, and an atmosphere of stability and permanence pervades the compound. Macuma is located in Jivaro territory. The Jivaros, whose lives are punctuated by fierce inter-family feuds, are famous the world over for their custom of shrinking human heads. They live throughout 7,000 square miles in the southern part of the jungle, independent of the white man who has nominally ruled their country for four hundred years.

Roger, tall and thin, with a shock of black hair, had been born on January 21, 1924, on a ranch near Sumatra, Montana, the seventh child of a ranching family. From his mother he received a devoted and thorough Christian training. Roger had been an active youngster, and on the way to becoming a good pianist, when polio struck him at the age of nine. This crippled him so that he not only lost his musical touch, but for the rest of his life walked and ran like an old man.

In high school in Lewistown, Montana, he overcame the effects of polio sufficiently to play basket-ball. From high school, Roger went to Montana State College with three scholarships. He planned to become a teacher in agriculture. He was chosen the outstanding freshman of his year in 1942 and worked during the following summer drawing maps of farms around Lewistown that are still used by the Federal Land Bank. In October, 1943, Roger enlisted in the Army, eventually becoming a paratrooper. He was stationed in England, where he became assistant to Army Chaplain Paschal Fowlkes, who wrote to Roger's parents: 'Christian work in the Army is not greatly different from Christian work outside, in that the leader must learn to depend on a comparatively small number to carry the load and give inspiration to others. I thought you would be proud and happy to know that I count Roger one of those "strong pillars".' During this time in England, Roger's faith was deepened and strengthened and in December, 1944, we find him writing to his mother:

> The happiest day of my life was the day I accepted Jesus Christ as my Saviour for the remission of my sins, duly repented for, and with God's help I hope and pray for the faith and strength to glorify our Father through my daily living as a witness and follower of Christ. Searching the Scriptures is my greatest source of hope and inspiration, having yet to learn the full power of prayer. I used to say, "This is a great world." With this new faith, this feeling has increased a thousandfold, and I fairly ache within from happiness and rejoicing in sharing God's manifold blessing which He gives to this world with Infinite mercy and grace.

Roger survived the Rhine jump of 1944 and was decorated for action in the Battle of the Bulge. The idea of dedicating his life totally and completely to the Lord was taking root in Roger's mind and in August, 1945, he wrote from Berlin:

> I've a secret to tell you, Mother, in this more than anything in the world I want the action to precede the announcement.

Ever since I accepted Christ as my personal Saviour last fall and wanted to follow Him and do the will of the Lord, I've felt the call to either missionary, social, or ministerial work after my release from the service. Can't say now what the calling will be but I want to be a witness for Him and live following Him every second of my life.

Roger returned to Montana in January, 1946, and during that winter his conviction that he had been called to the mission-field was confirmed. He enrolled in the College of Liberal Arts at North-western Schools in Minneapolis, where he met Barbara Orton, a quiet, fair-haired girl who was also studying Christian Education with the mission-field in mind. She came from a Baptist family in Lansing, Michigan, and all her childhood she had heard of mission work, listened to missionaries speak at her church, and met them in her home. 'I believe that the Lord just spoke to me, while I was a child,' she says now, 'and made me feel that that was what I should do.' In September, 1950, Barbara and Roger enrolled in the missionary medicine course at North-western Schools. All winter they sat next to each other in a little classroom with nine other students, learning how to set bones, deliver a baby, give injections. They were engaged on Easter Day, 1951, and married in September. They were accepted as candidates by the Gospel Missionary Union, a non-denominational board, and left immediately for six months' probation work in Kansas City. Here they had Spanish classes, learned how to approach some of the practical problems of a mission station, took turns leading Sunday services, and worked with groups of children from the city slums.

In January, 1953, they set out with six-month-old Beth Elaine for Ecuador. After a period of Spanish study in Shell Mera, the Youderians went to Macuma. Frank and Marie Drown, senior missionaries at the Macuma station, had come to Ecuador eight years before from the farm country of Iowa. It was through letters written back to the States by

Marie that Roger became interested in working with the Jivaros.

Once settled on the station to which God had sent them, Roger and Barbara plunged into a study of the Jivaro language and were soon able to help in the development of a method of teaching the Jivaros to read and write their own language. Roger made little pen-and-ink drawings of famil- iar sights—a sloth hanging upside down on a branch, a blow-gun, a lizard lazing on a tree-trunk—and next to the drawing he printed the sound of the Jivaro words.

Although Roger had come to preach the Gospel, there is much a missionary must accomplish and learn before he can expect to make successful contact with a primitive tribe. And even after he has mastered the language, built himself a home, gained the confidence of the Indian, he still has to spend a large amount of time in what is best described as maintenance. The jungle grows with incredible speed and therefore has to be kept at bay by the constant use of the machete. The generators that are used for current at the bigger stations break down with irritating frequency, roofs leak in the hard tropical rain, and the only person who can cope with all this is the missionary himself. Roger's skill as a carpenter and his pleasure in this kind of work stood him in good stead when he first came to Macuma. Barbara wrote:

> Roj is in his glory in Macuma; they have two men sawing boards, two fellows are planing, two are grooving, two more sawing and planing 2 by 4's. Roj has his power-saw going and they have poured pillars to set the house on. Roj has planted 74 tomato plants from the seeds he got from the station in Costa Rica.

It was not to do construction work, however, that Roj had left his home. Soon he was driving himself to reach the Jivaro Indians with the Gospel. A fiercely independent people, the Jivaros combine war-like hostility and a boister- ous sense of humour. 'All they do is laugh and spit,' said one missionary in describing them. They seem to laugh with little provocation, and have a way of punctuating their conversation by spitting through the second and third finger with an explosive sound. Like the Quichua, the Jivaro never tires of pressing his face to the screen of the missionary's window, watching all that goes on inside. Roj became accustomed to this after a short time, though he found their *sotto voce* comments and sudden outbursts of smothered giggles upsetting at first.

Wearing shorts, a sweat shirt, cotton cap, and canvas leggings and sneakers, Roger spent much of his time visiting Jivaro houses. He followed the twisting and exhausting jungle trails, more often than not knee-deep in mud. He might pause sometimes, arrested by an indescribably sweet fragrance, sweeter than orange blossom, but because of the forest, he would be unable to locate the source. The most striking flowers are found high up in the tree-tops, nearly smothered by the ubiquitous green foliage. He would also have to be on his guard against the most dangerous of jungle fauna, the snakes. Protective colouring renders many varieties almost impossible to detect. The tiny viper may lie in the centre of the path, but the dappled pattern of its skin so blends with the pattern of the sunlight on fallen leaves that the traveller seldom sees it. The bushmaster carries enough poison in his sacs to kill one hundred men. The coral snake, whose poison attacks the central nervous system and causes death without previous symptoms in twenty-four to forty-eight hours, is one of the smaller species, and therefore more difficult to see. Suddenly, the forest path would end and Roger would step into a clearing, his eyes blinded by direct sunlight after the twilight zone of the jungle. Each Jivaro house stands in its own clearing. It is oblong-shaped, a narrow slit about five feet high at either end serving as window and door, and covered with a palm-thatched roof of pointed leaves whose fringe almost touches the ground.

Strict rules of etiquette govern the behaviour of the Jivaro host and the visitor who enters his clearing. A formal greeting, which may take ten or fifteen minutes, is proper.

It is a series of utterances which may go something like this:

'I have come.'

'You've come?'

'Yes, I've come to your house.'

'You have come well.'

Roj learned that no matter how many people are present, the newcomer goes through this dialogue with each one.

Bending his head to get his five feet eleven inches through the slit, he would enter the murky interior through which he could just barely see the dim figures of women moving about at the far end of the house, trailed by several little naked children. Hard-packed earth serves as a floor in these houses and small fires glow at intervals down the long thirty-foot interior, the smoke creating an acrid odour and adding to the lack of visibility. The Jivaro house is strictly divided between the men's section, the front part, known as the *tangamash*—somewhat the equivalent of the small-town front porch, a place where men can sit and gossip for hours on end—and the back part of the house, which is exclusively for the use of women. The women wear a long piece of cloth that hangs down straight to the knees, the two ends tied at one shoulder. The men are bare-chested, but wear a cloth tied around their waists. Like the Quichuas, the Jivaros have long, straight black hair. It hangs loosely around the women's faces, little attempt being made at any kind of coiffure. The men, as befitting their position as superior beings, go in for an elaborate hair-do. The waist-long hair is combed and then dressed in bright red, yellow, or blue tropical bird feathers.

Roger would be invited to sit down on a bench alongside the wall, and facing him, on a low stool, sat the head of the house. If the man were trying to impress his visitor with his position, he would go through an elaborate charade for the first five minutes before he permitted conversation to begin. One of his two or three wives would bring him a bowl of water, from which he took a mouthful but not to swallow. He spat it out over his hands and then washed his face with his wet hands. After that he combed his hair slowly and deliberately. The entire performance was carried through wordlessly and with dignity and deliberation. He would then be served his chicha, the bowl offered to his guest and conversation begun. Thus Roger spent many hours talking to the Jivaros in their houses, slowly acquiring their language, absorbing their way of life, and above all, telling them the story of Jesus.

Among the Jivaros, witchcraft and sorcery, hate and murder, take deep roots early in life. Children as they fall asleep at night are taught to repeat a list of names of those they must learn to hate. Writing of the tribe, Nate said:

> They aren't cruel, except that they are made that way by the religion of fear and evil spirits with which they hope somehow to cope with their sin problem. For instance, a witch visited the Macuma Indians a couple of months ago. He was from another section of the forests. For some reason or other he got mad and cursed a certain woman. Usually Jivaro difficulties are over women, who are soulless possessions of the man and are frequently stolen or traded in business deals. At any rate, the woman that had been cursed died within twenty-four hours. Her husband, brothers, and father then felt duty bound to avenge her blood because the witch was as guilty as if he had shot her outright. They went over to the other tribe and brutally killed the witch and another fellow. The thing is a couple of months old now, so life goes on as usual, but one of these days there will be another killing. It's routine in the Jivaria. There's no end to the killings. The miserable part is that to pay off these debts, as they call them, they don't necessarily have to kill the very murderer himself—any relative will do. Their consequent fear determines even the construction of their houses, which are very much like military fortresses. They often put traps in the trails for their suspected enemies. Not long ago one missionary in the Jivaria was out doing visitation work in the jungles. His bare-foot carrier was in front and as they approached a Jivaro clearing, he pulled up to a sudden, painful halt. A needle-sharp palm wood spike was sticking out of the top of his bloody foot.

These were the people with whom Roger had lived for over a year. He had learned their language on the Macuma station, and helped to make up primers for the literacy programme. At times the atmosphere of vengeance and murder affected Roger deeply, but with typical energy he kept driving ahead. Nate Saint once said of him: 'Roj is one of the few missionaries I know who display a real sense of urgency in the task of winning souls.'

Now this sense of urgency was prompting Roger to consider making a move. Knowing that Frank Drown could carry on the work of this established station alone, Roj began to pray for a wider sphere of service, as the Apostle Paul wrote: '[It is] my ambition to preach the Gospel, not where Christ has already been named, lest I build on another man's foundation.'

— 7 —

Breaking Jungle Barriers

AMONG THE TRIBES where Christ had not yet been named were the Atshuaras, first cousins of the Jivaros but their deadly enemies. Roger prayed often for an opening in this group and talked it over with Nate, who had shared his concern for some time. Frank and another missionary had tried to contact them five years before. On that occasion, Frank and his colleague had almost reached the house of the chief when they were met by a boy carrying a verbal message: 'If you do not turn around at once, you will be killed.' The reputation of the chief was such that there was no doubt about the accuracy of the message. The missionaries turned around.

Roger finally decided to move closer to the Atshuaras. On June 5, 1954, he left Macuma and travelled south-east two days on foot to a place called Wambimi, where the Shell Oil Company had abandoned an airstrip and a few dilapidated houses. He wrote:

This location is particularly important as a possible doorway [to the Atshuaras]. It was marvellous how the Lord worked for us in preparing this outstation. He enabled us to erect a new building 20 by 60 feet, with a permanent roof to augment the small houses already available on the spot. He protected us in those eleven days from snakes (I stepped on one), scorpions, tarantulas, injury, complications from nails, from roofs caving in while dismantling old buildings, etc.

The airstrip needed only a little grass-cutting, and was ready for Nate's plane to land. Nate recorded the subsequent events on magnetic tape:

We flew in Barb and the two children, and they set up housekeeping, started language study and literacy work among the local Jivaros as well as evangelism. While Roj was down there, as any missionary does, he carried on medical ministry. One of the sicknesses that plagues the Jivaro is leishmaniasis. It affects nasal cavity, nose and the back of the throat, the roof of the mouth. It's a hideous disease that is long drawn-out, eventually kills them and, of course, is very shameful—it disfigures the face terribly and the Indians dread it with a passionate dread. Several years ago missionary doctors ran down a cure, a drug called 'Repodral'. Roj had some with him and he scored a couple of notable cures among the local Jivaros. Despite the continual running feuds that go on between the Jivaros and Atshuaras, as well as within both groups, there is some liaison on the trail and word of the cures got across the line to the Atshuaras. One of the chiefs over there in the Atshuaras country was called Santiaku (a chief in this case, as in most jungle situations, is just a Number One man in a given small area; Jivaros and Atshuaras don't group up; they're scattered all over Timbuktu and the fellow that's the strongest or the most feared in a small area is a chief). The chief, Santiaku, had come down with this dread disease, and despite fear and happenings of the past, he finally showed up at Wambimi. And, of course, it was a milestone and a cause for great rejoicing because it was an answer to prayer. Roj did help him; the Repodral helped his nose condition and he showed up again later and invited Roj to go back to his house. Of course, this is what everybody had been waiting for, but in the case of the spider and the fly, Roj wasn't going to accept this offer carelessly. So he said to Santiaku, "Okay, I'll come to visit you at your house if you come and take me over there." And so, good enough, the escort did come and escorted Roj Youderian, Frank Drown, and another missionary into Atshuara country.

Somewhere along the way Frank coughed and the Atshuaras stopped right there; that was as far as they were going to go because they are deathly afraid of catching cold. Apparently it's a cold or grippe—what we call flu—that kills them off because they haven't much resistance to it, the disease never having touched their group while the generation was younger. It was with great difficulty that Frank convinced them he was just clearing his throat. Frank says that that night when they were camping along the trail somewhere he felt a tickle in his throat again and he just didn't know what in the world to do, so he feigned that he had business off in the bush and got away from them and cleared his throat, fearing, of course, that he might break up the whole expedition by coughing and being heard by the Atshuaras.

When they got to Santiaku's place it turned out to be a great big house, about three times the size of the long Jivaro houses. Roj says it was just about big enough to put a basket-ball floor inside. The Atshuaras speak a somewhat different dialect but understand Jivaro, their facial features are different, and the women have narrow hips, instead of wide hips like Jivaro women. When they got there, Frank started to give them the Gospel in Jivaro, telling them of the love of Christ and how he had died for us. It was a question of giving these Indians a story from scratch that they had never before heard any suggestion of. Frank talked until he was hoarse and exhausted. They had a little wind-up phonograph with them and they played Gospel recordings made in the Jivaro language and they would play these until Frank got his voice back and then the Atshuaras would say: "All right now, Panchu (an affectionate Spanish nickname for Frank), tell us more." And for three days, the Atshuaras went on like that—just sitting around, listening to the story of Christ, a most amazing opportunity and Santiaku showed real interest.

Because of the isolation of the Atshuaras and the tense situation with the neighbouring Jivaros, it seemed as though the key to getting in there and actually doing some good was air communication. Frank suggested right off the bat that they build themselves an airstrip. It seems to me that it was a really bold stroke of genius and I'm sure I wouldn't have had the faith to suggest it the very first time. The idea took hold—the Lord blessed the suggestion and brought it to fruition, because they started clearing an airstrip; the missionaries, while they were there, showed them where they could cut down the trees in line with their manioc patches, so that they would have some natural approaches to take advantage of the forest they had already cleared. Then the missionaries retired.

After several months, we thought it time to encourage the Atshuaras, so we flew down over there to see how they were coming along and found that they had cleared about 100 yards of the jungle floor for an airstrip. But 300 feet with trees standing all around it, trees that grow to 100, maybe 120 or 150 feet, is hardly an airstrip. So we dropped them a couple of pieces of cloth to encourage them, and then we went away again and a few more months went by.

The other day we went down and had a look again. And to our disappointment we found that the direction of the strip in the forest was such that it was lining right up with the great big house, and, of course, it's not ideal to have a house sitting right on one end of a strip in the approach. And the work didn't seem to have gone very far—looked like they needed help at this point. So we went back and had a short council of war and Roj said: "Well, it sounds to me like they need help and I think I should go." He had a little hand-crank radio, but he didn't have enough provisions. He really hadn't contemplated such a trip at all. Well, I guess he had a machete. But the need was there, the opportunity was there, and he could be there within two days' walk. He decided to try to get some Jivaro to help him carry the radio and guide him over the trail from Wambimi to the Atshuara country.

We left Roj at Wambimi on a Wednesday and on Thursday we listened on the radio for him. We thought it might just be that he would have set it up along the trail somewhere or maybe he was still in Wambimi. We didn't hear from him on Thursday, Friday, or Saturday. Monday we thought surely we'd hear from him—that he'd be with the Atshuaras and surely be on the air. We still didn't hear a word from him and there he was with no other missionary, but with those unconverted Jivaros who were known to be rascals. And, I guess many of them out there have killed—they're killers and some have survived killings—not the choicest group to have for company on a dangerous trail. At any rate, we decided on Monday when we didn't hear from him that we ought to go in and check on him and make sure he was all right. So we assembled provisions, notes to drop him, food, and medicine. And we took out the air-to-ground telephone. Frank and I went together in the airplane. We flew with the door off, of course, so we could operate the telephone if necessary. We got down there and when I first saw the strip my heart sank. In the first place, because I couldn't see right off the bat that anything at all had happened to it—and I knew that if Roj had got there, something would have happened to that strip, because Roj just doesn't have anything in hand very long before something happens to it—especially if it needs something to happen to it. Then I started looking around for a white shirt. We looked for several anxious minutes before we finally distinguished him down there on the airstrip. I'll tell you for sure, I hadn't realised how anxious I was about his safety until that moment when I looked for him and the thing was in the balance—either yes or no. Then I realised how concerned we had been about him on the trail, with just a Jivaro guide and a few provisions. There are snakes out there. But we saw him and our hearts were very rejoiced by seeing him.

We made a couple of low passes over the field. First we flew low over and throttled back the engine to quiet it down and I shouted down to Roj to ask him to get the Indians off the strip, that we had some stuff to drop to him. He heard us perfectly and cleared the Indians out of the way. We made about four runs, dropping the food and some axe-heads and cloth to the Indians as gifts for them. We needed to know what the situation was down there, so we pulled up and put out the telephone on a double-wire cable, using the spiralling-line technique. We reeled out about 1,500 feet of telephone cable and then started to circle. The telephone on that long line duplicated our circling, then slowly slid towards the centre and began to drop. Finally it hovered, drifting around in a slightly unruly way, its horizontal velocity perhaps six or eight miles an hour, while we above were circling at sixty miles an hour. With a little trial and error and compensating for the drift, we were able to finally get the phone down close to Roger. I heard Frank's voice saying: "Hello, Roj; hello, Roj," and I knew that we had contact with him down there.

Frank talked with Roj for about ten minutes there on the phone, getting data from him. And then he apparently had all the information he needed and we started to pull up to put tension on the line. Meanwhile, Roj had tied his mail-sack on to the cable—his outgoing mail and a note to his wife—and turned the phone loose. It went soaring up just about vertically, cleared all trees and we had it trailing behind us on the end of 1,500 feet of wire that we then had to reel in. We waved good-bye to Roj and shoved off to Wambimi.

When Nate landed again in Wambimi, Frank informed him that Roger had asked for a landing on the following Friday. 'It's impossible!' said Nate. 'The strip won't be ready. But then,' he added, 'I guess that's not my department. I'd better get in there as requested and then decide whether or not the strip is landable.'

Roger had also explained over the ground-to-air telephone that he needed medicine. The Atshuaras had contracted the flu from a group of soldiers who had passed through. This accounted for Roger's not having a radio. The Jivaro who had promised to carry it in had got wind of the sickness among the Atshuaras, and, knowing how deadly flu can be, refused to go near the place.

Nate continued on the tape recorder:

Friday came along and I was getting kind of keyed up about this business of inaugurating a new field. It isn't child's play; it isn't a Sunday School picnic, as they say; it is a very serious business, where you have to do your best possible calculating and double checking on everything and then trusting the Lord—go in and do your duty.

Friday morning woke up, as they say in Spanish, raining. By noontime we knew that it was out of the question for that day; the field would be wet anyway, and we can't add mud to other unavoidable hazards of such an operation, so we cancelled out for that day. We took it that it was God's indication that it was not the day to go and we left it pending for the next day. The next morning we made the preparations and Frank and I flew down to Wambimi after lunch. Frank got out and we unloaded the extra cans of gasoline and I took off alone with a very limited supply of gas. The airplane was completely stripped, with even the right seat taken out, so that it was as light as you could possibly get and have enough gasoline to be safe. I had a safe reserve—perhaps an hour and a half of gasoline aboard, and the round trip over to Santiaku's place and back would have been about forty minutes; so I had a hundred per cent reserve.

Taking off, Nate headed for a little river half-way between the Macuma River and the Pastaza, which was the only landmark for Santiaku's place. When he found it, figuring he must be south of the spot, he turned north, scanning the horizon near and far in search of the little island in the sea of green. Nothing. Suddenly, just below him, he saw a little house—of the square stockade style, but without a *chacra* [an agricultural clearing in the forest].

'That's strange,' thought Nate. 'Maybe it belongs to some Indian who's just killed somebody and is lying low here for a while. Probably his *chacra* is off somewhere else, to confuse the enemy.' Mystified, he kept on. Ah—there it was! He called in to Marj on the radio: '56 Henry—I'll be over Jimmy's place in two minutes. 56 Henry—I'll be over Jimmy's place in two minutes. Over.' Since Santiaku is a form of the Spanish name for James, they had nicknamed the spot for secrecy.

Nate's record continued:

Lo and behold, when I got over it two minutes later, there was no airstrip there! Looked just like his place, but no strip. That was a little disconcerting, because I didn't have a great deal of gas along, so I flew a little farther north and climbed on up, gaining altitude, trying to decide what I should do. I decided I'd better beat a track for Wambimi. Landed there around four-thirty. I hadn't been in a hurry before, because I wanted to get to Jimmy's place late in the afternoon when the air is cool and buoyant. It's steadier for this type of operation. Frank was a little surprised to see me back so soon. I described the house I'd seen and he recognised it as one they'd passed on the trail to Santiaku's. He passed me about five gallons of gas, and I took off, heading due east, picked up the little river and turned south.

Nate's blue eyes squinted through the plexiglass. Visibility that day was about a hundred miles, and 'you can almost imagine you see steamship smoke on the horizon', but in all that expanse there was not a sign of life.

He continued:

I went south. I went farther south. I was really beginning to make bets that I had never seen anything before, and goodness, I thought, there's no percentage in this! About that time I stumbled on to a house that was on a river bank, well stockaded, and the way that house was situated you just wouldn't see it unless you flew directly over it, that's all. Tucked down there in the forest, it was made differently from the other houses that I'd seen, Quichua or Jivaro. I didn't feel that I was exactly in a friendly neighbourhood. I decided that the Lord's hand must be in this somehow. (I was farther south than I had ever flown on survey).

Even though Nate by this time was greatly concerned about finding Roger, he looked this new house over carefully and made a mental note about its location,

because they would need to hear the Gospel, too, way out there in their isolated places. You feel convinced that it is the will of the Lord that we do everything possible, that each Indian have an opportunity to know of the grace of God, and to hear that Name that is above all other names.

So I went on. I felt buoyed up by the challenge of the very isolation of these people and the challenge to help other missionaries to get the Gospel to them, so the risk involved seemed to be offset and justified by the spiritual challenge of the situation.

Nate kept on flying till he figured the gas load was getting down. Then he switched on his transmitter: '56 Henry to Shell Mera. I've looked up and down the river. Can't find Jimmy's place. I'm turning around now, heading upstream, gaining altitude. Do you read, Shell Mera? Over.'

'Okay, okay,' came Marj's answer, and Nate started looking for smoke on the horizon, for surely he must be in Atshuara country, and if Roj had heard him he'd get a smudge going.

Presently he saw it—there, apparently to the south-west, was a column of smoke. But it seemed to be in the wrong direction. Was his compass off? Or was it that he was not as well oriented as he had thought he was? The situation seemed incongruous, but, Nate thought:

Once in a while you get in a situation like that, and the answer, when it comes, is a kind of surprise. So with that in mind, and with the fact also that where there's smoke there's fire, and where there's fire there are people, I decided to trust the Lord and head out across the stuff and see what in the world was producing that smoke. When I got there, I was well rewarded, but not in the way I'd expected.

Down a steep bank that had been cleared, in a little hidden river, set in the trees, there was a little flat place. And down in the flat place, sunken way down deep, was a big house, with rounded ends, and Indians all over the clearing.

Again Nate made a mental record for future use. After a quick look, with gas getting low,

I rolled out of the turn and started climbing and looked to the left, and, I'll be switched, there was a great big house, bigger than the one on the bank of the river, tucked down in there just off to one side. I just don't know how in the world it is that you can't see something until you're right on it. It's like hunting needles in a haystack.

Nate then started climbing, still circling.

I thought it just possible that if I got up really high, where I could look down into those little barrels of isolated pockets of mankind [he said], I just might see some more interesting things. I was all eyes and quite excited over these finds and thrilled to find myself completely thrust into the arms of the Almighty, because down there there's no question at all about that. If that old engine had quit up there, God alone could have saved me. I might just as well admit it frankly right here; I don't like to fly over stuff like that and I have to have a pretty good reason to be over it without a good position-check and a good river to identify my position by. But these are people for whom Christ died, and you have to find them before you can take the Gospel to them, so I was happy to have stumbled on them.

I had one last look around before turning over to Wambimi and on that inspection I noticed a little blemish, off to the east, and I thought I could afford to fly just a minute or two and see what it turned into. And so I did. And within two minutes I could distinguish a house and then a few seconds later I could see a clearing; some solid earth behind some trees, some tall trees that indicated that it was Jimmy's place, and there, completely hidden behind those tall trees, was the runway. I finally realised I'd had all this trouble finding the place because the late afternoon sun was hitting the low ridges at a different angle than I had been used to on previous trips over the area. Anyway, when I saw that clearing I got on the radio, but quick, and started down. That old airplane really let down in a hurry and when I looked over at the vertical speed indicator I was clocking about 1,500 feet a minute. I was spiralling down at a good clip, reporting in to Shell, getting confirmation of the position, circling over the clearing and having a look—a heart-saddening look—at the strip. It just wasn't what you would describe as an airstrip at all. My heart sank. I knew Roj needed to get out of there, because I know the way he works; he never spares himself. He'd been in there a couple of weeks almost and I knew he would be a wreck and needing badly to get clear of the place. So I was anxious to do my best, consistent with safety and our responsibility to MAF and the other folks that MAF serves.

While I circled back I shook my head and said to myself,

audibly: "No, that just is no good; it's just impossible."
Nevertheless, I figured I owed Roj a better look, so I came by
low a time or two, and one time I was about to cut the engine
and yell down to Roj and tell him: "I'm sorry; it's no soap."
But I went on by and took another look at it. He had it nicely
marked with bandage material. He had 50 yards on the lead
end towards the big house marked off, and then he had a line
with the word "WHEELS" on it. I knew I could touch down
from where the "WHEELS" sign was. Down at the far end he
had marked off 250 yards. Then I got to thinking that I can't
just say "no" on a hunch; but I can, too. Sometimes a hunch
saves a fellow's life, when a slide-rule says "yes" and a hunch
says "no". So I thought: "Well, the airplane is light; about
250 yards more or less of strip; maybe I should try one
approach." The air certainly was quite steady and I thought
that if I could get down there closer it might look different.
So, I prepared to buzz the field, let down steeply over the trees,
and down over the roof of Santiaku's house, going about 100
miles an hour. When I got down in there, there was one tree
sticking out along the edge of the strip, and I said to myself as
though someone could hear: "Roj, man, this thing does have
wings sticking out", and I pulled up and got to thinking the
problem over. The surface looked all right; I trusted Roj on
that; I know he's careful about making sure that there are no
soft spots; he's been through two other strip inaugurations
with me. That is to say, he's gone ahead to prepare and check
the ground, so I felt confident.

There wasn't much time left; I was well down in gas again;
so, "Here goes," I said to myself, "maybe I can get by that
tree." And then the thought came to me that I might not be
able to get *out* of there later. I figured that between the two of
us, with the Indians, we could fell enough trees in a couple of
days to get out of there. The radio was working on the
airplane; I could tell Marj where we were; I told Barb that Roj
was okay. "Okay," I called in quickly, "preparing to land at
Santiaku's place."

I reeled the antenna in, slowed the plane down, and put it in
the approach towards the trees. As I cleared the trees, I took it
into a very steep side-slip, pulled the flaps into full position,
and cleared Santiaku's house by about 15 to 20 feet. As I

measured the situation, I wasn't measuring just the tree sticking out but the whole thing, seeing everything at once. As a matter of fact, I didn't even see that tree; at least, I wasn't conscious of it. In a situation like that a pilot's subconscious drives him pretty much. It's a kind of automatic pilot that takes over because you haven't time to think out individual problems. They had been thought out while I was circling above, thinking through objectively and I'd decided that I could go in there safely and, as an old-timer said, from there on "the seat of your pants guides you".

I went on in there and I slipped that plane just as steep as she'd slip—a pretty solid 45 miles an hour; I straightened out just over the 50-yard rough stretch, plunked the wheels down just beyond the "WHEELS" sign and got stopped in a little over half of the 250 yards that was available.

I thanked God first of all for my being on the ground safe and sound. Naturally, the first thing you do in a situation like that is to get the trailing antenna out and transmit the news of the successful arrival without accident or incident to Marj and other loved ones and colleagues who are listening on their radios prayerfully. But this time I didn't. It never came to mind; there were too many things happening there too fast.

Roj came running up and said, "Have you got any medicine?" "Yes," I answered; "it's in here," and I tossed him the sack. I had it all bundled up ready to throw out of the plane. There wasn't any "Hello, I'm glad to see you" or "Dr. Livingstone, I presume" sort of stuff. Roj was haggard; he had a week's beard; a dirty tee-shirt, ripped full of holes; he was a really pitiful sight; emaciated. He was at the bundle, tooth and nail, taking that stuff out. Then he started shouting at the top of his lungs—voice almost breaking—to the Indians down the strip, barking orders. I've never seen Roj behave quite like that. I know that he can snap at people when things are tight, but in this case I didn't know quite what to make of the whole situation, so I grabbed him kind of firmly by the arm and said: "Slow down now, Roj; slow down; we've got time." He looked up out of those eyes and said, "We *haven't* got time; we *haven't* got time." So I didn't argue with him. He handed me two bottles of penicillin and said: "Here, shake these," so I did. He was barking orders at the Indians and I thought to myself, "My goodness, how on earth can these people think he's a friend when he talks to them like that?"

The first thing I knew, everyone and his brother were getting shots. It was soon evident that just everybody was sick with grippe. Some of them looked as though they were ready to die right there while we were working with the medicines. I did what I could to help Roj. Santiaku was sitting on a log, stoop-shouldered, looking sick, painted up "fit to kill", doing his best to look like a chief, but very, very sick. Roj told me while he was "shooting" that one of the chiefs had already died the week before. When he got there he had shot all the worst cases and they recovered and this was the next batch of light cases that were getting worse and worse and the people— well, you can imagine how they felt without any medical help.

We had two little bottles of penicillin. How precious those bottles were, standing between life and death. When Roj threw down the first bottle, I said: "Take it and try to see if there isn't another drop in it." Mothers would shove their little bare-bottomed babies towards Roj. He'd give them a swipe with a cotton swab of alcohol. It was just a tiny bottle that Roj might so easily upset because his hand was shaking like a leaf. He'd holler out at the Indians: "Now, don't move," and everybody just obeyed his orders. He was the chief in that outfit, at the moment, the real master of the situation. There was no question about it.

Roj peered into the faces of the Indians as they came along. The graver cases got the medicine. He looked across the clearing, and there coming out of the forest was Tysha, a close Atshuara friend. The Indians had tried to save his life by carrying him out to an army base, but the river was too great an obstacle for him in his weak condition. He arrived in time to get the last drop of penicillin from Roj's needle. 'Praise the Lord,' said Roj, 'it's unbelievable, but here he is, and this will probably save his life!'

Roj straightened up for the first time, looked at Nate, and smiled. The strain was off his shoulders. Nate looked at his watch—just a few minutes before their deadline for getting out of there. While Roj walked towards the plane, now at long last relaxed and at ease, Nate ran over and offered his hand to the bewildered chief. 'He didn't know what to do with it, but I just grabbed his and started talking English. They'd understand as much of that as of Spanish. "So long, glad to have known you fellows," I said, and headed for the plane.'

Roj was shaking his head, smiling. 'Well, God is certainly in this thing.'

Nate took off alone to satisfy himself that he could get out with the heavier load, and then came back in to pick up Roger. In the plane on the way to Wambimi, Roj told how the work on the strip had been hindered by sickness; how, because of the sickness, his Indian carrier had refused to bring the radio, and how he had worked on the strip himself for lack of anyone else to do it. At one point an Indian had shouted at hime: 'Watch out! There's a snake by your foot! Don't move!' Roj froze, and there, not two feet away from his foot, lay a bushmaster, coiled to strike. The Indian grabbed a stick. 'Nothing doing—that's too short!' yelled Roj. With the words 'God help me' on his lips, Roj slashed his machete at the snake's head, cutting it off cleanly.

Roj said:

You can't imagine how I prayed that you wouldn't make it on Friday, as we had originally planned. Then Saturday I prayed you *would* get here, and began to wonder if you'd make it. It got to be four o'clock, and no plane. I was getting pretty discouraged. Finally, there it was. We heard it coming, all right, but no—it was turning away! I just died a thousand deaths out on that field. I was really shot. After working all day in the rain on Friday, straining every muscle to get it done, and then straining our ears all day Saturday, well...then half an hour later, we heard you again. Again, instead of growing louder, the sound faded away. The Indians tore down to the *chacra*, and saw the plane disappearing. This was it. I decided to call it a day, and gathered the Indians together for a meeting and a little Gospel teaching. We had just started when the

Indians yelled that the plane was coming back. Some said,
"No, you're hearing it with your heart!" But soon we saw it.
Man, you can't imagine what it does to a guy to see this little
yellow job coming in over the trees!

These two men, imbued with the Christian pioneering
spirit of the first century, using the tools of the twentieth,
had pushed back the boundaries of their faith one more step.
Not only Roger and Nate, but also Jim, Pete, and Ed were
missionary pioneers—always looking to the regions beyond
immediate horizons. Just over the distant ridges were the
Aucas. 'One of these days we're going to spot those boys,'
Jim Elliot had said, 'and from then on they'll be marked
men!'

– 8 –

The Aucas

FOR A NUMBER OF YEARS,' Nate Saint once wrote, 'the Aucas have constituted a hazard to explorers, an embarrassment to the Republic of Ecuador, and a challenge to missionaries of the Gospel.'

Since his arrival in the Oriente, Nate had often flown over Auca territory, his trained eye trying to find houses or villages. It is no easy matter to find a people numbering perhaps five hundred to a thousand, in a dense jungle covering 12,000 square miles. No census, of course, has ever been made; the area is merely estimated by the Quichuas—an area undoubtedly far larger than the Aucas themselves would claim, as the Quichuas (quite understandably) give them a wide berth. This part of the jungle lies about 150 miles east of Quito. It is bordered by three rivers: on the west by the Arajuno, on the north by the Napo, on the south by the Villano. To the east it runs into the Peruvian border.

The history of the region goes back to the early days of the Spanish conquest of Ecuador. In 1541, Gonzalo Pizarro, brother of the famous Francisco Pizarro, who brought the Inca Empire to an end, crossed the Andes, explored their eastern slopes, and permitted one of his adventurous lieutenants to follow the Amazon to its mouth. In his astounding explorations he lost all but ninety-seven of his hundreds of soldiers. Some died of hardship but many were killed by hostile Indians. Some of these Indians were undoubtedly the ancestors of the Aucas. The conquistadors were followed in the seventeenth century by Jesuit missionaries, some of whom also were killed by hostile Indians. Little was done to settle or exploit the area from the seventeenth century to the middle of the nineteenth. Then the demand for rubber in the industrial parts of the world brought rubber-hunters to the Amazonian basin, at that time the source of the best rubber in the world. Unscrupulous, treacherous, cruel, the rubber-hunters wooed the Indians with presents only to raid their villages, plunder whatever of value they might find, carry off the able-bodied young men as slaves to work on haciendas, and murder the rest so that there would be no one left to drum up reprisals.

In 1874 a later Jesuit missionary made a trip down the Curaray intending to found a mission but instead spent his time — according to his own report — protecting the Indians from the rapacious rubber-hunters. Another record called the rubber-traders 'civilised savages against unbaptised savages'. Certainly from that time on, hatred spread throughout the Auca country, and a legacy of reprisal has been passed on from father to son. It was the behaviour of the white man that closed off this area to colonisation. There was a time when the country could have developed with the cooperation of the Aucas but that time is now past. In the early days of this century, haciendas were scattered throughout what is now a 'closed' country.

The Aucas' growing distrust of the white man is illustrated in a story told in the Oriente of a hacienda owner, a Señor Santoval, who lived in the Aucas' domain shortly after the turn of the century. Señor Santoval had two captured Auca families working for him and managed to carry on a lively rubber trade with the Aucas still in the jungle. They would leave rubber for him at the edge of his property and in exchange he would leave machetes, knives, and clothing for them. For about ten years this peaceful trading continued with no violence on either side. The captured Aucas were such superior workmen that Santoval asked them to approach their tribesmen with offers of work on the hacienda. Through his intermediaries, the patron offered them fair pay, good living conditions, clothing—anything they felt they wanted. The offer was refused out of hand and the answer came back that the Aucas wanted nothing whatever of the white man's world, that they were independent and wished to remain so. Santoval died in 1917 and his death was the signal for an Auca attack on the hacienda. Almost all his Indian workers were killed; those that survived, including some of the captured Aucas, moved permanently out of range of Auca attacks.

The Shell Oil Company, prospecting for oil in the Oriente from 1940 to 1949, had to contend not only with the usual hazards and inconveniences of the jungle but with attacks from Aucas on their workmen. In 1942 three of their employees were killed in the company's camp at Arajuno. The incident is described in a letter written by a Shell Oil Company executive:

> We regret to have to inform you that a most unfortunate incident occurred on Wednesday, January 7th last, in our camp at Arajuno. A group of hostile Indians attacked a gang of our labourers working near our camp and our foreman and two other Ecuadorian labourers were killed with spears. This attack caused some panic among our labourers which was aggravated when the following morning these Indians made another appearance and seemed to be surrounding the camp.... We fear it will become more difficult than before to engage an adequate number of labourers for our camp at Arajuno.

One year later the company lost eight employees. In an attempt to win the confidence of the tribe and ward off further killings, a visit was made to an Auca house. Gifts of machetes, shirts, magazines, and empty bottles were left for the inhabitants, who proved to be absent when the white men arrived. The Aucas responded with a present of a vine-woven basket which they left on the trail. This encouraged the oil-men, and one of them reported:

> It seems that our hope of friendship is going the right way. I think that this will become a reality in the near future, so long as our personnel always follow the indicated line of conduct which could be put down as "absolute respect of private property"... a stray bullet might, in my opinion, constitute something like a declaration of war, which could be fatal to our party.

An attempt at dropping gifts from an airplane was also made by the Shell Oil people, but, as Nate later observed, 'a two-thousand horse-power transport, roaring over the village at a low altitude, would seem sure to scare anyone, not to mention particularly a stone-age people with no knowledge whatsoever of science'. In spite of all these overtures, the hopes of the Shell Oil Company were not realised and no one made any further serious attempts to win the Aucas.

It was becoming increasingly important for these young missionaries to know every available fact about the Aucas. They read the reports of the Shell Oil Company and talked to anyone who had ever had any contact with the Aucas. An invaluable source of information was Señor Carlos Sevilla, who owns and operates a hacienda about ten minutes' flight from Shandia. Don Carlos had lived in Auca territory for twenty-six years, before he was driven out by repeated attacks. He is a tall, spare Ecuadorian in his middle sixties who has probably had more experience with Aucas than any other living man. His body still bears six scars inflicted by Aucas during his last encounter with them.

His first narrow escape came in 1914, when seven Indians and one Colombian who were working for him were killed on the hacienda 'El Capricho' on the Curaray. In 1919, while Sevilla was hunting for rubber, he left fifteen Indian families at a camp on the Tsupino River while he went upstream to get medicines. On his return he was met by an

Indian boy who was wounded in the arm, the sole survivor of an Auca attack on the camp. Hurriedly rounding up sixty Quichuas, Sevilla set off to find the Aucas responsible for the massacre at his camp. He found an Auca house, and one woman peacefully working in the manioc patch. She was captured, but as Sevilla's men surrounded the house, she broke away from her guards, and ran screaming into the bush. This sounded the alarm, and those who had been in the house were able to escape while the guards rushed to recapture the woman. As Don Carlos repeats this story, so many years later, there is still a note of bitter disappointment in his voice.

He has been able to observe Auca strategy closely. It seems that attacks are always by surprise, and that the Aucas invariably outnumber their opponents. One method of surprising travellers is to wait at the bend of a river until the current forces a canoe close to the shore, and while the polers are frantically trying to pull the canoe back into the mainstream, the spears are hurled, accompanied by wild yells to confuse the victims. The advantage is all with the Aucas. Sevilla's advice to any adventurer in savage territory is that he travel with at least two canoes, so that one canoe could fire to protect the other should an attack come.

In 1925 Don Carlos and his Indians were attacked twice within four months. Sevilla and his men were travelling by canoe upstream on the Nushino when, at a narrow bend in the river, they found themselves the target of dozens of Auca lances. The canoe capsized, five Indians were slain immediately, and Sevilla and one other escaped. Fighting his way through the hail of spears, he succeeded in killing two of the attackers with their own weapons, but emerged severely wounded himself. Eight days later he reached his hacienda on the Ansuc River, his body rotting with infection, his wounds worm-eaten.

An attack in 1934 finally drove him out of the territory, but it has not discouraged his making plans for a possible re-entry.

'I don't think it is too late,' says Sevilla. 'True, we've lost our best chances, but perhaps if we build a strong, lance-proof house fairly close to the Auca houses, make a large clearing around it, keep constant watch, and never use a gun, they would ultimately accept our friendship.'

But there are men in the Oriente, who roamed the region looking for rubber, gold, or oil in the days when this was 'open country', who say that never, never will the Aucas allow the white man to live peacefully in their land. It is too late. By the flickering light of kerosene lamps on the verandas of haciendas, these old-timers sit evening after evening recalling their experiences and conjecturing about the Aucas' real motives. Are they natural-born killers? Do they kill only to preserve their land from outsiders? Do they kill to rob? No one knows and there is no set pattern that shows any one single motive behind the killings.

It is known that a few killings have been followed by robbery. Articles which the Aucas considered useful, parti-cularly the machete, have been stolen. Other things, whose use they do not understand, they leave behind. In some cases all possessions of the victims have been left intact. Surprisingly, Quichuas are allowed summer fishing privi-leges in the heart of the Auca domain; undisturbed, they take their canoes down the Napo or the Curaray for weeks at a time. Then, for no apparent reason, the Aucas will attack. They may kill or wound a group of Quichua fishermen within Auca boundaries, or they move just beyond their frontiers and attack a Quichua family working in its *chacra*. One fact only seems firmly established: the white man is unwanted. When he sets foot within the area that the Aucas have marked off for themselves, he risks his life.

Killings, however, also occur within the tribe. Anger finds immediate expression in a killing. As it was with the Hatfields and McCoys of the Kentucky mountains, feuds flare up frequently, each death to be avenged by the surviving members of the family to form a chain-reaction of murder. Thus, the taking of life is not alien to the Aucas. From an early age on, young boys are trained in the accurate use of their nine-foot hardwood lances. Don Carlos tells of coming upon a deserted Auca hut, and finding there a life-sized human figure carved of balsa wood. The heart and facial features were clearly outlined with bright red achiote and the entire figure was torn with lance marks. This method, as modern as bayonet training for combat troops, had been used to develop the deadly marksmanship for which the Aucas are famous.

Don Carlos has working for him on his hacienda an Auca woman who escaped some years ago from a tribal killing. There had been a typical family feud, in which both her parents and brothers and sisters were killed by a neighbouring group. Dayuma, then in her mid-teens, had managed to escape by hiding out in the *chacra* until the invaders left. She then made her way to the nearest settlement of Quichuas, who took her to Don Carlos.

Like any refugee, Dayuma spent her first years among the Quichuas, adapting herself as quickly and totally as possible to their customs. One of her hardest adjustments was the food of her hosts. Aucas have no salt and it took her almost a year before she could enjoy seasoned food. Clothing was another major change. Aucas are entirely naked, except for vines that are tied tightly around wrists, ankles, and the waist. Now Dayuma wears the customary shapeless cotton dress of the Quichua woman. In an effort to hide her Auca ancestry she combs her hair down to cover her disfigured ear-lobes — ear-lobes once adorned with round balsa-wood plugs more than an inch in diameter. Watching her go about her work on the hacienda, feeding the animals, helping in the kitchen, there is little else to distinguish her from her Quichua fellow workers. The Aucas have the same straight black hair, the same tea-coloured skin, and about the same height — a few inches over five feet.

Dayuma has been able to give many facts of ethnological interest. Although the Aucas drink chicha, made just as the Quichuas make it, they drink it unfermented; consequently

Dayuma never saw drunkenness until she reached the outside world. Wife-beating was also unknown to her. Auca houses are long, oblong shaped, with mud-packed floors, and hammocks used as beds hanging from the roof. Living in each house may be anywhere from twenty to fifty members of a clan. The women work in the plantations of manioc and cotton. The men work on their lances, shaping the sharp points with stolen machetes. Every man in the household has his collection of nine or ten spears, which he takes with him on a foray for food or on a raiding expedition. Dayuma says that the Aucas can recognise a footprint — in much the same way that we would recognise a familiar face, they can identify the individual Indian who has passed by. She told Don Carlos that every step he had ever taken in Curaray country was known to her people. They also spent many hours spying on the Shell camp at Arajuno. At one time during the Shell occupancy, the people considered approaching the white man. They had talked seriously among themselves of the possibility of sending in two men as a scouting party and, if they were not killed, the rest of the group would follow. In actual fact, just the opposite happened; the Aucas attacked and killed three Shell employees.

Pets are common among Aucas; they snare parrots, monkeys, and the wild boar when they are still young and keep them in small huts surrounding the large main house. Like other people the world over, they have their legends and fairy stories. At one time, so goes the Auca legend, 'fire fell from heaven', spread out all over the world, and burned all the trees. The Aucas hid under the leaves of the sweet-potato plant until the fire was over and then came out and re-populated the earth. They fear evil spirits, as do all jungle people. They like their children and amuse them with tales. Dayuma tells one of the tales whose hero is a turtle:

One day a baby turtle met a powerful jaguar on the road.

'Ha!' said the jaguar. 'Your parents are far away and there is no one here to protect you.'

The little turtle in fear drew in his head.

'Put out your head,' the jaguar commanded.

And the turtle, hearing the mighty voice, put out his head. Then, looking into the jaguar's savage mouth, he said: 'What terrific teeth you have!'

The jaguar was flattered. He opened his mouth still wider to display all of his fine fierce teeth. So the little turtle, who was much quicker than he looked, jumped into the jaguar's mouth and bit his throat so hard that the jaguar forthwith died.

Then the little turtle left the jaguar and went to the neighbouring Aucas and told them that he had killed a jaguar and left it lying in the path. The Indians went to see, and there was the dead jaguar. Happily they snatched out the teeth and claws to make ornaments for themselves and went off, entirely forgetting to thank the little turtle. So the little turtle simply returned to the jungle and grew up to a big turtle!

Dayuma is constantly asked why the Aucas kill, and she can only answer that they are killers. 'Never, never trust them,' she repeats with emphasis; 'they may appear friendly and then they will turn around and kill.'

There are those, however, who have not and will not accept this verdict as final — those who cannot rest in peace while generations of Aucas remain beyond the frontiers of Christianity. Pete Fleming was one of those who could not be content while the Aucas remained in darkness. In his diary he wrote:

It is a grave and solemn problem; an unreachable people who murder and kill with extreme hatred. It comes to me strongly that God is leading me to do something about it, and a strong idea and impression comes into my mind that I ought to devote the majority of my time to collecting linguistic data on the tribe and making some intensive air surveys to look for Auca houses.... I know that this may be the most important decision of my life, but I have a quiet peace about it.

− 9 −

September, 1955

SEPTEMBER, 1955, was the month in which Operation Auca really started, the month in which the Lord began to weave five separate threads into a single glowing fabric for His own Glory. Five men with widely differing personalities had come to Ecuador from the eastern United States, the West Coast, and the Mid-Western States. Representing three different 'faith-missions', these men and their wives were one in their common belief in the Bible as the literal and supernatural and perfect word from God to man. Christ said 'Go ye'; their answer was 'Lord, send me.'

The missionaries who were about to join forces in Operation Auca had made several moves. After the flood it had been decided to rebuild Shandia, keep it as the main station of this area, and build outstations. The technique of maintaining a number of outstations is particularly important in the Oriente because the Indians in this part of the world, as already pointed out, do not congregate in large villages, but are scattered in small groups throughout large areas of the jungle.

It was agreed that an outstation should be established in Puyupungu. Jim and Ed and Pete had visited this little settlement of Quichuas on a survey trip down the Bobonaza River in August, 1953. There they had met Atanasio, the chief who had invited them to establish a school for his children. 'Because of God, will you not stay?' he had asked. 'We need you very much. I have—let's see—thirteen, fourteen, and another one, yes, *fifteen* children. No one has taught them. They want to learn to see paper. I have some orphans too in my house. Will you not come?'

Usually it is an uphill struggle to win the confidence of the people in a new area. Here, however, was not only an open door, but an outright invitation. The three men saw it as the answer to their prayer for enlarged borders. So plans were made. The McCullys moved to Shandia to begin their study of Quichua, and Pete, who was still single, was chosen to stay and help them learn the language and get established. Jim and I decided it was God's time for us to marry so that we could, together, open the station at Puyupungu.

Thus it was that Jim and I arrived there in November, 1953, with all our worldly goods in four canoes. After greeting us with much backslapping, handshaking, and laughter, the men carried the white man's incredible quantity of equipment up the high bank where Atanasio's two wives and throng of children waited expectantly.

The building of the house and airstrip did not take all of Jim's time. Together we began having meetings for the Indians, telling them in their own language the most wonderful story in the world, that of the Son of God who had come to earth and paid the price of man's sin with His own blood. The recognition of God's great love dawned slowly in the Indian mind. But one day we rejoiced as Atanasio said to Jim, 'I am very old. Perhaps too old to understand well. But it seems to me your words are true. I will die in your words.'

Meanwhile, the McCullys were making good progress learning the language in Shandia. Pete Fleming had built himself a little shack near their bamboo house, and took meals with them. He wrote in his diary:

It is surprising what joy and pleasure I had in building my

little two-room house. I really got a kick out of it, and though it took only four or five days, I could hardly wait to move in. It is *very* comfortable and it is *pure luxury* to have a place to myself, a bed, a desk, and chair where I will not be under observation. Best of all, it aids in leading a disciplined life, things are in a convenient place, and privacy for prayer is now possible. I have begun again to add to my file system on the New Testament, a thing I haven't done since I left the U.S. I am happy inside myself to be getting things done in an orderly way again. There is no question that it is the way I was meant to live, with regular bedtime, evenings free for study, and a full hour's devotional time in the morning.

As Pete watched the McCullys become oriented in the work, he began thinking more specifically about his own future. And about his fiancée, Olive Ainslie, a slim and beautiful girl, with dark eyebrows in striking contrast to lighter hair and blue eyes. They had become engaged in an exchange of letters while he was in the jungle. With typical candour this quiet, studious man wondered if there were any conflict between his coming marriage and his 'call' to the Aucas?

He wrote:

Last night Nate and I talked a long time about the Auca problem. Strangely enough, I do not feel my coming marriage will prohibit me from being eligible to help in efforts to reach them. I feel that if pushed to it, Olive would rather have me die after we had lived together than to indefinitely postpone our wedding on the possibility that something fatal might happen. Our life has become one, and I do not feel that God will separate us in our discernment of the will of God.

In June, 1954, Pete felt free to return to the United States to marry Olive. After Pete's departure Jim and I moved back to Shandia with Ed and Marilou McCully. Puyupungu having been established as an outstation, we arranged for future visitation and teaching sessions. Shandia, with a school, medical clinic, and small store, was considered our permanent base of operations.

We all agreed that Jim and I could take the responsibilities of the Shandia station, so Ed and Marilou began to consider a move to an area of their own—another place where the Gospel had not been carried. The McCullys knew of Arajuno, the abandoned Shell Oil Company base on the very edge of Auca territory. In survey flights over the area, Ed had estimated the Quichua Indian population to be somewhere around one hundred. Why not take advantage of the excellent airstrip which the company had built, and move in there for a while to preach to these Indians? The runway would need only a day's work at the most to clear it of grass, and the gravel base would be good as new. Arajuno, one of several Shell Company projects aimed at finding oil in the area, had been fabulously expensive. A small city had been hacked out of the forest; roads had been laid out; brick houses, with electricity and running water, had been built; a hotel and tennis-courts, bakery, and even a narrow-gauge railroad had been included in the project. Now, abandoned since 1949, the buildings had been claimed by the rot and ruin of the jungle. However, some useful materials might be salvaged. The idea of opening a station at Arajuno seemed a good one.

Ed began visiting Arajuno each week-end, flying over with Nate on Friday. Ed visited the Indians' homes and conducted meetings for them on Saturday and Sunday. The welcome he received encouraged him to build a simple house, using the foundations of one of the abandoned Shell Oil buildings and boards salvaged from round about. Finally when Ed decided to stay on full time at Arajuno, he moved Marilou and the two children to their 'new' quarters. Marilou soon had an attractive home fixed up—bright curtains at the screened windows, a 'sofa' made of a pile of salvaged bricks covered with a mattress and a sheet of plastic, pictures on the bamboo walls, and colourful Ecuadorian rugs on the cement slab floor. Nate Saint spent several nights rigging up a burglar-alarm system and an electric fence, for the

McCullys and their co-workers on other stations were fully aware of the dangers of living near the Aucas. The Arajuno River forms the western boundary of the Auca territory and the new mission station was on the Auca side of the river. It was the very site where the Shell Oil employees had been killed some years before. Such sporadic raids, with the Aucas darting from the jungle to kill swiftly and disappear again, had made the Aucas fearful and fascinating to their Quichua neighbours.

The Quichuas never allowed the McCullys to forget the possibility of a visit from the Aucas. The Quichuas refused to remain after four o'clock on that side of the Arajuno River. 'This is the Auca part,' they would say. Every so often rumours would spread around that Auca footprints had been found near the house, or that the grass was pressed down, indicating that Aucas had been lying there, spying on the foreigners.

The electric fence was set up a good thirty yards from the house, beyond accurate spear-throwing range, and Ed and Marilou always kept a pistol or gun handy. 'Even though we don't think they're around,' Ed said, 'it gives you a good feeling to know that the fence is buzzing. With our lights on in the house at night we'd make a good target!'

Thus it was that the Lord had placed Ed and Marilou in the strategic spot that was to become the base of Operation Auca.

Meanwhile, Pete had returned from the United States to Quito with his bride, Olive. They spent a year in the mountains while she learned Spanish and he translated Scriptures into Quichua, spoke at Indian gatherings, and refreshed his own knowledge of Spanish. In the fall of 1955, Pete and Olive came to the Oriente to begin Indian work together at Puyupungu, where they settled in the little thatched house which Jim and I had built. Pete began again to teach the Indians there, slowly and carefully, reviewing the things they had learned before, leading them into new truths.

Olive's initiation into jungle life included a spectacula display by the active volcano Sangay, visible from th living-room at Puyupungu.

Pete wrote:

> At night it looks like a huge bonfire out of which shoots flares
> in a long graceful arc landing a couple of thousand feet down
> the mountain-side. With the binoculars we could see indivi-
> dual balls of fire burst and spray out all over. It was a real show.
> Clouds of steam coming from the lava on the snow would
> momentarily blot out the pyrotechnic display, only to have it
> clear and start over again.

Their hearts were sometimes saddened by the drunken behaviour of many of the Indians at a fiesta. The results of such fiestas can be imagined — husbands beating their wives; pitiful naked children left to find their own place to sleep at night while parents stagger about until dead drunk. On one occasion a drunk mother rolled on her two-week-old baby, smothering it. An Indian will sometimes attempt to find his way home through the dark forest, usually ending up asleep on the muddy trail, waking hours later to find huge scavenger beetles digging under his legs in an attempt to bury him.

But there were signs, too, that the Gospel message was getting through to these sons of the jungle. Pete's journal records:

> Today the angels are rejoicing over Puyupungu, and so are we.
> How faithful God is. This morning a number of Indians
> decided for Christ. I felt led to speak on baptism since I had
> noted several misunderstandings while I listened to Indians
> talk. So after speaking from the story of Philip and the
> eunuch, I tried to explain simply and clearly the difference
> between faith and baptism. After an early fight with squalling
> babies the attention was excellent and I felt the Spirit moving
> in hearts, so asked for a show of hands after carefully explaining
> what a decision for Christ would involve. A number of hands
> showed — Tito, Benito, Pascual, and others. A number more

began to put up their hands when Alejo broke out from the back telling them that it would mean giving up drinking and living immorally. Some of the hands went down at that. I closed in prayer, inviting those who were really repentant to go into the back room of the school, where I could deal more carefully with them. Twelve came. We encouraged and exhorted them and arranged for a believers' meeting on Friday afternoon. Several others are very close. What joy! *This* is what we came here for.

At twenty-six years how good God has been and how full and blessed His ways. How continually I thank God for bringing me here, almost overcoming the impossible and pushing me out. I felt "thrust out" and how grateful I am for God's impelling.

In September, 1955, 'God's impelling' moved five pioneering missionary families to crystallise their plans of months and years into common action. Truly they were being 'thrust out' to carry the Word of God to the Aucas. The McCullys, in the station at Arajuno, provided the vanguard. Jim and I were in Shandia. The Flemings were in Puyupungu. Roger Youderian and his family had returned from their outstation at Wambimi and were again helping the Drowns at Macuma. Nate Saint with his little yellow plane and Marj at the radio remained at Shell Mera, their permanent base at the hub of these outlying jungle stations.

— 10 —

Operation Auca Begins

ON THE EVENING of the second day of October, 1955, Nate Saint fed some yellow tissue into his old typewriter and began:

This will be an attempt to note developments that have led to the recent decision to launch efforts towards contacting the Auca tribe. The notes, of course, will record only personal points of view of the situation and will not touch past efforts of other missionaries.

Last night Ed McCully, Jim Elliot, Johnny Keenan, and I were on the living-room floor on elbows and knees poring over a map of the eastern jungles of Ecuador. We had just decided that it was the Lord's time to try to contact the savage Auca tribe located somewhere east of Ed's Quichua Indian mission station at Arajuno.

Later, in the kitchen over a midnight cup of cocoa, we decided that our efforts should be carried forward as secretly as practicable so as to avoid arousing other non-missionary groups to competitive efforts. Their efforts would undoubtedly employ a heavily-armed invasion party going in overland. This we fear might set back for decades the missionary effort among these stone-age people.

This afternoon, in meditating on the situation, it seemed to me a shame that the secrecy required might deny our prayer-supporting colleagues at home the blessing of a fresh running account, reported at first-hand, of our efforts and of the Lord's good hand upon them. Therefore I have taken it upon myself to set down the *status quo* and hope to add to it as we progress in the days ahead.

A number of sporadic efforts have been made to change the status of these killers of the forests. Armed attacks and counter-attacks on the part of whites only thinned out the tribe and fanned the furor of hatred already present. Fear of firearms did not diminish the Aucas' desire for revenge even though it had to be carried out from ambush with hardwood lances.

The story of the exploration attempted by Rolf Blomberg, a Swedish explorer, and guided by a missionary in 1947, has been written in detail. The party was approaching the Aucas' location on balsa rafts when they were ambushed at a point where the current pushed the rafts close to the river bank. An Indian porter in the party opened fire immediately and then dived into the river, following the missionary who was swimming underwater. This experience makes us wary of combining our efforts with those who have no love or special regard for these people.

When Ed McCully moved his family to Arajuno he asked Nate for an aerial survey of the Auca territory, and together they looked up and down the Nushino River valley, where the Aucas were known to have been seven years before. They found nothing more than had Pete and Jim in their survey two years earlier—only the vast ocean of dark green tree-tops that stretches off into a smudgy horizon. The effect of an ocean is heightened by the choppy, wave-like hills that break up the terrain. The coffee-with-cream-coloured rivers snaking through the trees serve as a reminder that it is landscape, not seascape. Only the trained eye, however, would be able to spot human habitation in this wilderness—perhaps a ragged scarf of smoke rising above the green, of the infinitesimal spot which indicates an Indian *chacra*.

Nate's diary continues:

The actual search did not get under way until the morning of September 19, when I was letting down for Arajuno on the regular weekly vegetable-run. It was around 8.30 am, as I recall, and the atmosphere was unusually clear. Visibility was about seventy-five miles and all the little river valleys, which are usually camouflaged by the more common light-haze foliage combinations, were clearly discernible in the distance.

When I climbed out of the plane and greeted Ed, I asked him how he'd like to go looking for his 'neighbours'. He was all for it, so we set to work raiding Marilou's larder for canned goods and scrounged around for other special emergency equipment and took off about half an hour later.

We followed the Nushino east, but flying the north side this time. We were able to scan a six- or eight-mile swath. About fifty miles east of Ed's place, out over the middle of nowhere, we turned due north towards Coca on the Rio Napo. About five minutes later we spied some spots that looked as if they might have been planted manioc patches years ago. It's hard to be sure from a bird's point of view, even after you've been studying the woods for some time. We circled and then went on north until the Napo was getting close, without seeing anything more. The left turn towards home was inevitable. We didn't have gas enough to press on much farther and we had covered what we had outlined for this particular trip. However, it was hard to give up. It takes so long to get that far out, and it is so difficult to find such ideal weather. I'd been eyeing a blemish, barely discernible in the jungle, maybe five miles away. Ed couldn't make it out, but we decided to fly that way for just a couple of minutes, and if we didn't turn up something more concrete we'd beat it for home.

The blemish grew into a well-defined pockmark, and then into a good-sized clearing covered with well-cleaned manioc. *This was it.* We'd been cruising very slowly and our fuel consumption was getting low, but we could still hang around for fifteen minutes without cutting into the reserve. So we hung around. All told, we must have seen about fifteen clearing and a few houses. It was an exciting old time... a time we'd waited for.

We never did let down for a close look. In the first place, we had to watch fuel consumption; in the second, we didn't want anyone to get frightened on our first visit. We'd be back again with more thoughts on the best manner to approach these people.

On the way back Ed observed that he thought there must be other clearings closer to his place. He felt it would be a long hike for Aucas from this settlement to show up at his place or in its environs. I didn't think so. To me it seemed logical that they should all be way out there in the wilderness since there had been a raid at their old location on the Nushino. We decided to keep thinking about the whole thing and to compare notes later. We also decided to keep the 'find' in the family until we were sure it was okay to spill it.

The news was exciting to Marj and to Ruth and Johnny Keenan. As we reflected, it seemed providential that we had investigated that tiny spot that turned into the first Auca clearing we had ever laid eyes on.

A couple of weeks later (September 29) I was to take Jim Elliot and Pete Fleming over to Villano, where they were to spend several days preaching among a group of Quichuas who had never heard the Gospel. Our route was to be via Arajuno, so we decided that since we'd be flying over what was Auca territory, and since it would take two trips to move in the men and their equipment and two Indian guides—which would mean that I would cross the area four times—we would keep our eyes open and fly slightly different routes each time.

On the first trip over with Jim and the equipment we didn't see a sign of life. The return trip also yeilded nothing. Then Pete and the two guides and I started out. Having decided to go far enough east to see an area that hadn't been covered by the previous two crossings, we zigzagged slowly, favouring the more hospitable-looking jungle valleys.

About fifteen minutes from Arajuno we spotted some clearings. Pete and I spoke only in English, but there was no hiding our excitement. Our Indian guides spotted the clearings also. They were sharpies and immediately said 'Aucas'. It was their first time up in a plane, yet they knew just where they were and could name the rivers. We flew down a little river and spotted a half-dozen big houses with smaller ones around them. That was it. There they were as plain as the nose on your face *and only fifteen minutes from Ed's place at Arajuno by plane.*

As we approached Villano we talked over the problem of keeping the guides quiet. We decided that we would have to impress on them the danger to them personally if word of the location of the Aucas got around and if, as a result, there were attacks on the Aucas by the Quichuas or others, followed by Auca reprisal raids.

I landed from the inhabited end of the Villano strip, coming in fast so as to appear to have to use most of the strip. That took us away from the waiting crowd and gave Pete time to admonish the guides as per our agreement. They agreed to keep the secret . . . (probably as secret as a full-sized toy elephant under a Christmas tree).

Everyone who was in on our plan was again thrilled by the news. To some of us the most significant thing was not the information gained but the fact that after so much fruitless searching we had located the first group of Aucas and then in a couple of weeks had stumbled over the other group. It seemed to mean that now was the Lord's time to do somthing about them. Again we agreed to pray about the matter and compare notes further, after the whole episode had a chance to sink in.

Several days later, when Johnny Keenan was moving Jim and Pete and their guides from Villano back to Arajuno, he hit bad weather and finally had to come on back to Shell Mera to land and spend the night. That was the night that the map was on the living-room floor surrounded by four men who were now labouring under the conviction that the Lord was leading us to do something about the Aucas.

That night and into the wee hours of the morning we circumnavigated the problem a dozen different times. It is most fascinating to try to imagine how those people would respond to different approaches.

One of the problems that the missionaries grappled with that night was that of language. The need to convince the Aucas that here were friendly white men, could best be effected by communicating with them in their own language. This was of the essence. As the men talked over this problem, Jim Elliot came up with the answer. He remembered having seen Dayuma on Señor Carlos Sevilla's hacienda, which lay only four hours' walk from Shandia. He offered to go and talk to her to pick up phrases that could be useful in case contact were made.

A few days later, Jim trekked over. He found Dayuma cooperative, although he was very careful not to divulge to her the reason for his desire to be taught some simple Auca phrases. Among Quichuas gossip spreads as quickly as anywhere else. Fortunately, Dayuma—accustomed to the strange ways of strange people—assumed he was only casually interested in learning the language.

'*Biti miti punimupa,*' which means 'I like you; I want to be your friend,' Jim wrote carefully in his notebook. This was followed by '*Biti winki pungi amupa*'—'I want to approach you,' or, more colloquially, 'Let's get together.'

'How do you say, "What is your name?"' Jim asked in Quichua.

'*Awum irimi,*' Dayuma answered in Auca.

And so Jim built a practical vocabulary list.

Thus, one of the obstacles that lay in the path of the missionaries was partly overcome. A presentation of gifts seemed the obvious next step. Perhaps a carefully-planned, regular programme of gift-drops, made over a period of time, would show the Indians that the intentions of these white men were friendly, and the repetition would gradually convince them.

— 11 —

A Line from Plane to Ground

THE MEN DECIDED to begin the gift-drops to the savage Aucas at the earliest possible moment, employing the spiralling-line technique that Nate Saint had pioneered in Atshuara country. There, the accuracy of delivery had been of paramount importance. In the new venture, the technique would have the additional value of making it clear to the Aucas that the visitors in the plane had the power to give or retain the gift right up until the moment of delivery. From captive Aucas it had been learned that the Indians thought that the gifts from the Shell plane fell out of its 'stomach' as a result of its being wounded or scared by the lances they had thrown.

Nate typed out his continuing record of the start of Operation Auca:

> That night on the living-room floor it was decided that we would make our aerial visits regularly, leaving something different each week in order to work on their curiosity. We calculated that under the circumstances, sooner or later the hostile spirit would melt.
>
> The following day Johnny flew Jim and Ed back to Arajuno. At Shell Mera I began tests with the line to see what kind of simple, dependable mechanism we could use to release our gifts when they touched the ground. Johnny and I flew together on most of the tests and Marj and Ruth hooked on the test

weights and watched their release on the runway. We marked off a target on the runway and tried to hit it.

Finally we were ready for a dress rehearsal. The test went off fine, except that when we flew over the strip to drop the line, it fouled the strut and we had to tie a knife on a stick so that we could try to cut it loose. There was no danger except that it could have come loose by itself while we were not over the field. And that is just what happened. I saw the line drape itself in some tall trees just beyond the end of the runway. However, by the time we landed and got in there to hunt for it, it was too dark, so that it had to remain there till morning.

That night I was so keyed up I couldn't sleep much. On the other hand, I realised that the whole thing was in the Lord's hands. I had no way of knowing how long it would take the next morning to get the line out of the trees, but I told Marj that if I could be ready to take off by 9 am we would go through with it; if not, we'd cancel until the following day.

Next morning I rigged a 'fishing line' with a weight that I could toss over the lost line high in the trees. With that and a lot of trudging around through brush I finally got all the line and by 9 am we were ready for take-off.

October 6, 1955. The first gift was a small aluminium kettle with a lid. Inside we put about twenty brightly coloured buttons—obviously not for their non-existent clothes! But buttons do make good ornaments. Also we included a little sack with a few pounds of rock salt. We understand that they do not have any salt of their own. If only they could discover what the stuff was good for we felt sure we'd win friends. To these things we attached some fifteen brightly coloured ribbon streamers about a yard long. All was ready.

Out at Arajuno all was readiness and happy anticipation. I was very anxious lest by some fault of mine we might miss on this first attempt.

We loaded in our emergency equipment, rigged our special gear, made a 'dry-run' test of getting the rig overboard, and took off for points east. We could hardly believe that we were to have the privilege of making the initial effort. Fifteen minutes' flying brought us over the first clearings. It was Ed's first look at his 'neighbours', and he was plenty keyed up about it.

A Line from Plane to Ground

We decided to try to find the downstream edge of their domain so that if we had a forced landing we could travel downstream away from their territory. About fifteen minutes more of looking around assured us that we were over the house that interested us.

We were about 3,000 feet above the ground, and could not see anyone below; yet every indication showed that the house was occupied. The large house was thatched, with round ends, Jivaro style, and around it were several smaller squarish houses with thatched roofs, square on the ends. Well-beaten paths linked the smaller houses to the large central one. The main house was about forty yards from the edge of the stream and had a nice playa [sand-bar] in front of it, perhaps seventy-five yards long and twenty-five yards wide at the widest place. A path showed that they used the playa frequently. It would be our target.

We slowed the plane to fifty-five miles per hour and held the gifts over the side—the door having been removed at Arajuno—and hooked up the automatic-release mechanism. Slowly we lowered the gift packet until it was well clear of the plane. Then we allowed the airspeed to come up to sixty-five and began the heart-racking job of reeling out the line. I say heart-racking because if there is a bad knot anywhere in that bundle of cord, the whole effort is lost for that time. But all went well and we began circling at about sixty-five miles per hour.

Since our altimeter reads only the altitude above sea level, we had no way of knowing how high we were above ground. No sign of life below. We continued circling until the gift was drifting in a small, lazy circle below us, ribbons fluttering nicely. If no one was watching, it made it more important that we put the gift in an obvious place. The gift still seemed pretty high, so we started spiralling down, noting a considerable wind drift from the north, necessitating correction every time around in order to keep us over the target.

Finally the gift appeared to be pretty close to the trees below. Time for the attempt. The wind was making it difficult and the hills on either side of the stream were covered with tall trees. A couple of times it seemed that we snatched our charge upward just in the nick of time to keep it out of trees bordering the sand-bar. Once I believe the ribbons dragged across a tree and hung up momentarily. At any rate, that gave us our working elevation. We made about six attempts at this elevation, gradually drifting the prize against the wind until it was over the bar. Then we rolled the turn steeper and held our breath while it lowered towards the earth. It wouldn't be ideal for it to hit the water, and it was heading close... close... closer... plunk! It hit about two or three feet from the water, directly in line with the path to the house. They couldn't miss it, since they probably got their water for cooking right at that spot.

Now another problem. I thought I saw our gift move just a little as we began a slow climb, still circling. That raised the question as to whether it was released or dragging on the line. But finally we were sure the line was free... and there was our messenger of good will, love, and faith, 2,000 feet below on the sand-bar. In a sense we had delivered the first Gospel-message-by-sign-language to a people who were a quarter of a mile away vertically, fifty miles horizontally, and continents and wide seas away psychologically.

How much do these people know? What do they think of what little they have seen of the outside world? We know they used to watch airplanes of the Shell Oil Company land and take off at Arajuno, for the Shell workers saw the spots where they hid in the bush to watch these monstrous messengers of another world.

The trip back to Arajuno was short and happy. Back home again everybody who was in on the secret wanted to know if we had seen any Aucas. They were a little sceptical about anyone's finding our gift when we confessed we hadn't seen a soul. Nevertheless, a start had been made.

Friday, October 14, 1955. I haven't brought the narrative up to the moment, but rather than let the hottest stuff cool off while I catch up, I'm going to go ahead with what just happened today.

This morning the weather was good, so we took off around 8 am. On the way out we could see some early-morning fog still lingering in the river valleys to the east so we were in no great hurry. We landed at Arajuno and began to prepare for the 'drop', which was to be a new machete. We understand that these people have killed for machetes. That is, they have killed people working in the fields in order to steal their machetes or axes. It is easy to imagine the importance of such items among a stone-age people. We wrapped the blade in canvas so that no one would get cut and then tied on a number of coloured ribbon streamers. After rigging the automatic touch-release gadget, we climbed in the plane for a dress rehearsal. Going over all our plans and precautions again, it seemed that we were ready, so we had a word of prayer for the success of the trip and took off.

It is always a bit of a strain on me to reel out the line in the air. But I slowed the plane down and we carefully lowered our second 'messenger of good will' over the side. By the time the line was all out we were almost at our destination. We used a little less line this time than last.

Our plan was to check the sand-bar where we left the gift last week. There were some low clouds, but we found the house and the sand-bar. The gift was gone. The binoculars removed any doubt. Either they had 'accepted' it or a flood had taken it away. We saw no one, but it was evident that the site was well occupied. The plan was to fly upstream to the next house this time and leave the gift there. We figured that if we specialised on one house, the others might get jealous or become suspicious that the occupant of that house was in league with us, or was in some way a traitor to their cause. When we got to the target house, we found it directly under a cloud so we inferred that the Lord would have us go on to the next.

As we approached the house we had decided on, we spotted three or four canoes pulled up to the stream bank in front of the house. That was interesting because one report has it they don't have canoes...but there they were. That meant, too, that somebody must be around nearby.

As we started to circle about 2,500 feet above the house it became apparent that we were going to be inside the cloud about ten per cent of the time, but all other conditions seemed so favourable that we decided to go ahead. The high-riding machete was behaving nicely. Ed was glued to the binoculars. All of a sudden he let out a yell and all but crawled out the open door to get a better look. We were seeing our first Auca!

He was running around but not hiding. Pretty soon there were three of them out in front of their big leaf-covered house. Now we felt sure that they had received our gift of last week and that the idea had caught on in a hurry. If it was half the sport for them that it was for us, their excitement was understandable.

After about four circles we had compensated for the wind, etc., and started letting the gift down. I was no longer worried about their getting it because we felt sure they were already watching the dangling prize. We let on down. At first it looked as if it would hit the house, but it drifted towards the stream...Splash! Then, quicker than you could bat an eye, another splash; an Auca had dived after the treasure. Minutes later there must have been a half dozen or eight of the men on the bank examining the prize. Our hearts were grateful. We had not hoped to see this for perhaps months. Of course, we wonder what they were thinking.

Several things seemed evident: They got our first gift. They aren't afraid of us in this type of approach. They are as animated, in one way or another, about this thing as we are.

Back at Arajuno, Ed learned another interesting bit of news. His local Indians reported the tracks of Aucas who had apparently hidden in the brush near Ed's house to observe what was going on there. Although there was no way of verifying this conjecture, it was credible. A Quichua woman, Joaquina, who had been captured by the Aucas and later escaped, had once told Dr Tidmarsh that it was the Aucas' practice to sit on a certain hill overlooking the camp at Arajuno to observe what went on. It seemed that they had an intricate espionage system, which perhaps at this very moment was operating near the McCullys' house.

The men planned to make a wooden model of the plane — with ribbons dangling from it — to hang outside Ed's house in order to identify Ed with the operation.

Eight days after writing the previous report, Nate Saint typed a heading on a fresh sheet of tissue: Report on the third visit to the 'neighbours'. He continued:

We refer to the Aucas as "neighbours" and to their area as the 'neighbourhood' to avoid the use of the name on the radio, or in the hearing of those who aren't supposed to be interested.

We couldn't go out on 'visitation' on Thursday as we had planned because the Army called on us for a flight down the Curaray River in the interior looking for the body of a soldier who had drowned. We did not see any sign of the missing man but we did see a lot of Ecuador that lies beyond habitation. We understand that beyond the area we checked, out towards the Napo, some vestiges of civilisation reappear. However, we flew for forty-five minutes, following every curve in the river without seeing a single sign of human life . . . saw a little wild life: several tapir, some giant turtles, and an abundance of birds of paradise . . . beautiful things gliding over the woods below.

Next day, Ed and I got away from Arajuno at about eleven o'clock while Marilou kept all the Indians in school so they wouldn't ask too many difficult questions.

First we flew down the Curaray looking for possible camp sites or temporary landing-strip sites. (This was forty or fifty miles above the start of the area searched yesterday for the missing soldier.) We saw some interesting possibilites, but nothing ideal for an airstrip.

However, up on the horizon along the ridges we saw something that looked like smoke. It seemed to be about the place where the Aucas are, so we decided to have a look. Maybe the boys had a smudge going so we'd be sure to find them with our gift bag. The smoke turned out to be the remnants of a low cloud, but we found ourselves over the Auca neighbourhood at a lower altitude than we'd ever been before, and took the occasion to circle each of the four main houses and take some pictures. We saw Indians all over, some running down the stream-bed from the manioc patch towards home, others coming from other directions. They didn't seem at all afraid. We shouted Auca phrases until we were hoarse.

After we circled the house where we had received such open reception last week, and flew on towards the next house, the Indians apparently thought the show was scheduled there for this week, and all took off down the stream-bed to try to be in on it. At any rate, when we decided to repeat at the same house to reward their confidence, we came back over and found the place deserted except for what appeared to be two women. But soon the menfolk came charging back up the stream-bed. There must have been big excitement down there.

This week our gift was to be another aluminium pot containing a bunch of trinkets and beads, well ribboned. We also tied on a little ten-inch Indian basket (empty) in hopes they might put something in it and send it back up. But somehow or other, after we got the whole thing clear of the plane, the automatic release failed and we lost the kettle to the jungle below, perhaps 300 yards distant from a smaller manioc patch. It seems likely that they might find it, but not too probable since everyone was over at the big clearing waiting for the show to begin. We were already getting a little tired from all the photographing and shouting to them, but we felt we mustn't leave without giving them something, so we tied on a new machete from our emergency kit, left on the little basket, and lowered the whole works without any release mechanism.

One of the more tiring elements on this trip was the rough air. We were constanly bouncing around and had a snappy drift from the north-east, so that our machete drifted badly. Several times when it was lowering near them they would scramble helter-skelter in that direction. It is really great sport. We don't know whether or not they have any system for determining who gets the prize. But as long as the supply holds up they should all keep encouraged.

Finally after a couple of near misses, we set the packet within ten feet of the front door of their house. They had it immediately and took it out on the river bank. Here the wind fouled up the works because every time around I had to roll completely out of the turn to compensate for drift and thus stay over the house. And every time I'd roll out of the turn the pull on the line got really hard. They must have had the line for several minutes. We could not tell whether they were putting anything in the basket or not. They may have put in something too heavy to pick up, or they may have tied the line to something. At any rate we finally saw one fellow run diagonally into the river and stop abrupty and do something, suggesting that he was unsnagging the line. I felt the line loosen and we were free. We shouted at each other about the thrill of holding a line, the other end of which an Auca held.

Our next decision was to fly past them low enough so that they could see us. That meant pulling in the entire line, a tough job, but after ten minutes of hard work we had it all in. Then down we circled. As we got lower, the crowd, formerly eight or ten, thinned out until there were only two or three in sight. We tossed the ribbon from about 200 feet and a brown-skinned man had it like the spider takes a fly. We shouted. From the man's gestures and from the past experience in similar operations among other Indians, I feel sure that the man shouted back to us, flailing his arms. He was the only one in sight and when we circled around the other side of the house he ran in one side of the house and out the other.

I felt a keen disappointment as I thought how frightened they must have been when we swooped low. However, as we circled slowly higher and higher, they seemed to regain confidence and slowly reappeared. Finally everyone seemed to be present. How we hope that they regained their 'party' spirit and laughed off their fright.

Going away, we flew directly towards the Curaray, since we feel more and more that that will be the site of the first contact if the Lord is pleased to continue blessing our efforts.

— 12 —

The Savages Respond

FROM ALL APPEARANCES the Aucas understood the white man's attempt to introduce himself. They seemed to recognise the regularity of the flights, and in successive weeks appeared in large numbers, more eager than ever to receive the gifts. Had they any idea of reciprocating? What were their real reactions?

For the fourth flight Nate rigged up the plane with a battery-powered loudspeaker. As they approached the clearings, Jim called out the Auca words, 'I like you! I am your friend! I like you!' Then they dropped another machete, wrapped and decorated as usual. Jim's diary describes the reaction:

A group raced back into the trees behind the house and one lone man walked to the beach. He cupped his hands and seemed to shout, then flashed the new machete over his head. We dropped a small aluminium pot, with ribbons. It contained a yellow shirt and beads. The Aucas below us converged on it "like women at a bargain counter", as Nate put it, and one was soon flailing the shirt. As we approached the house, two canoes some distance below it going downstream turned and came back upstream hurriedly. At one time I noticed people come running up through the water on to the beach, and another time a single one with a white cloth.

We returned via the Curaray, looking for possible landing beaches. Hopes not good. Guide us, Lord God.

Back at Arajuno, the three pioneers had a council of war, deciding that the next full moon would witness the first attempt at a contact on the ground with these people who had won their hearts. Nate wrote that night:

> May God continue to put His good hand on the project and may we drop it when not fully assured of His direction. At present we feel unanimously that God is in it. May the praise be His, and may it be that some Auca, clothed in the right-eousness of Jesus Christ, will be with us as we lift our voices in praise before His throne. Amen.

On the next trip their reception was even more favourable. McCully manned the mike to call out, 'We like you! We like you! We have come to pay a visit.' The Aucas danced about eagerly, grabbing the machete the men had thrown, and stripped its canvas so that it shone in the sun. While circling low Ed leaned far out of the door and held out both hands. The Indians, about three of them, responded by reaching out their hands too.

Ed's observations on this trip were:

> No fear manifest today, even when the plane was down low. No running inside or away. Most stood under the banana trees, possibly because of the sun. The plane gets close but somehow one longs to get closer. No sign of malice or anger. No lances seen. If there were a ladder down from the plane to them it would seem a good and safe thing to go among them.

By this time each man on the team had had time to form a judgment. 'The team has a spectrum that ranges from impatience to conservatism,' wrote Nate. Pete, who constantly conferred with the other three, did not feel that the next full moon was the right time for the first attempt at contact. It was too soon to assume that a long-standing hatred of white men had been overcome. The language problem was a big one—and it lay within their power to gain more knowledge of it, by working with Dayuma, the escaped Auca woman from whom Jim had gathered his material. Ed's reaction was that the next move should not necessarily be an effort at contact, but rather the establishment of a usable airstrip down the Curaray, perhaps within five miles of the 'neighbourhood'. Meanwhile Jim was 'chewing the bit'. If a friendly contact were made, Jim and I were prepared to leave the work in Shandia for a time, and go in and live among the Aucas. Nate felt that the men should follow the already-established course of making regular contacts and that nothing should be done suddenly, but that each advance be allowed to 'soak in' before pressing another.

On November 12 Nate Saint returned to his self-imposed task of keeping the record of Operation Auca. He wrote:

This was the sixth week in succession that we have visited the "neighbours." It was a beautiful Saturday morning. There wasn't much cargo to go along, nor much fog in the river valleys, so I got out to Ed's place at about 8.30 am. He was waiting at the airstrip when I arrived.

We took off with the public-address system and reel aboard. Ed had a machete and a small aluminium pot and a large aluminium pot set up with ribbons. Again we flew down the Curaray at low altitude so as to familiarise ourselves with the sand-bars and various possible landing locations along the river. With familiarity, the sand-bars look increasingly useful for our purposes. When we got to the point where we were closest to the 'neighbours' we decided that rather than turn in to them, we would fly on down the big river to see if perhaps there might not be some ideal landing spot farther down. We found none. Then we decided that since we were down that far we'd go a little farther and turn back up the little branch river along which the Aucas live.

We flew perhaps eight to ten minutes up the small river before we stumbled on to a house...one that we hadn't seen before. It had the coarser-leaf type of roof which slanted all the way to the ground, a gable roof. The ends of the house were also of leaf and slanted perhaps ten to fifteen degrees out from the vertical. We saw no one by whom we could judge the size of the house. It appeared to be smaller than the others, but if in reality it is smaller, then the doors in the ends were such as to require one to stoop quite low to enter. Outside the house were two distinct plantings—two patches. The taller growth was darker green and covered perhaps an acre. It did not appear to be manioc, being taller and thicker in the foliage cover. But the interesting thing was that the plot was surrounded by a well-made fence comprised of upright posts perhaps six feet apart, interwoven with what could have been opened-up bamboo basket-weave style, so that apparently an animal larger than a cat might not be able to pass through the fence.

After circling three times to have a good look, we headed upstream to the next house, which was the one we had previously supposed to be the most easterly of this group. This house is also the one at which we did the first "line" drop of the little pailful of buttons. Here for the first time now on this trip we saw people, about six, I would guess. One went out on the sand-bar where we had left the kettle before and waited patiently. When we waved and yelled, he waved but not with the enthusiasm that is always displayed at the other place. We supposed that he was an older fellow. His body appeared to be smeared with something opaque such as clay. There were no clothes in evidence. We made a run and dropped him a machete, free-fall. It landed right on the sand-bar and was carried off with relatively little ceremony or enthusiasm. Nevertheless, there seemed to be no demonstration of hostility whatsoever; nor fear. We went on, after shouting with the public-address system that we were friends.

At the next house we ran across a few of the "neighbours" on the sand-bar. We flew quite low, shouting and waving to them without using the public-address system. Then we dropped them the little pot. It hit the playa near them and was enthusiastically received. They jumped around quite excitedly.

Also at this house (let's number them from the east, making this one No. 3) we noticed two items especially. First, at either side of the doorway were boards perhaps twenty-five inches wide and about five feet high, decorated with bold, bright red decorations. I suppose they are doors of some sort. The other item of note was that the owners had made a woven-leaf end for their house; heretofore it has been open where it faced on the river.

From there we went on to house No. 4, which is the one we've visited most often and at which we've been received with the most evident enthusiasm. There was a crowd on hand to welcome us. And to our surprise, out behind their house where there had been a stand of trees and undergrowth, there was now a clean clearing about seventy-five to ninety yards in diameter. Some of the stumps were still there, but aside from that it was as clean as a basket-ball court. From the reaction of the people below I would guess that they couldn't decide whether to expect the drop on their new clearing, or whether we would drop it down by the house as has been the custom.

Ed's diary picks up the account of his day's operation:

We went in low and threw an axe-head, wrapped in canvas. It lit just on the west side of the clearing in the bushes. They pounced on it immediately. Then we yelled, "We will give you a pot," and went up higher. Tied on the pot, and reeled it out. This was a definite leading of God, for we had almost decided to throw the pot free instead of bothering with the line. Nate made a perfect drop. I held the line and could feel their holding on to it. They cut the pot off—*and tied something on*! Nate spotted it and praised the Lord. When we got back to Arajuno we found that it was a *llaitu* or headband of woven feathers. A real answer to prayer; another sign to proceed, an encouragement that friendly relations are possible and that they will hear the Gospel!

On November 26 Nate Saint recorded later developments:

Last week, since Ed was not back from Quito in time for the usual run, Jim Elliot took it on with me. I picked him up in Shandia after doing some shuttling between Pano and Tena and Pano and Shandia. We stopped by Arajuno and picked up the "gear". There were two Indians near the plane and despite our caution they apparently managed to find out what was in the supply and said to Jim, "Why do you crazy fellows give all that good stuff to Aucas?" Jim ignored the question; but it meant quite surely that the secret was more or less out, even though they could not know any of the details.

We flew, as I recall, quite directly to the "neighbourhood" and started visiting around. At No. 4 house two men had climbed up on top of what we had previously thought of as a sun shelter—a high bamboo roof or platform perhaps six feet off the ground. We circled low several times and decided to go ahead with a previously-discussed plan aimed at getting them to cut down the trees at the far side of the clearing as a sort of approach or "go-around" which would permit us to fly low enough for them to see us so as to be able to recognise us later on the ground. The plan was to drop our gifts into the trees we wanted down.

First we dropped an axe-head. Unfortunately it landed at the foot of the trees in question. Next time around we tossed out four plastic combs with streamers of bandage material tied on them. Happily a couple of them at least got hung up in the trees.

Next we went to No. 3. Everyone was out in great style. One man had one of our gift shirts on. (The rest were in more typical uniform.) We circled and waved and then went on down to the old man's house. He was out with his two women. We didn't feel that he warranted too good a gift, so we tossed him a pair of "store-bought" trousers. After circling back to make sure he got them okay, we went on back to No. 3. We tossed the people there a machete with a pair of shorts attached.

From here we climbed on up over No. 4 to get ready to let down the kettle for the last act of the day.

I neglected to mention earlier that in rummaging in the emergency kit Ed had made up, we found a roll of tissue. We thought it might help to get those tall trees down if we were to drape the tissue along the tree-tops. Such a drop might seem to be utilising their curiosity to an unfair advantage but on the other hand they were amply repaid for any trouble that they went to. When we tossed the roll, however, it reeled off about six feet and then the wind tore off that length. This process was repeated until there was a curious white dotted line floating down into the trees.

The wind was rather strong today and I had trouble staying over the clearing as we let the kettle down. It required some six or eight attempts before the kettle landed in the little river at the edge of the clearing. They were at it in an instant. But in

that same instant I had to roll out of the turn upwind to keep
from getting too far from the clearing. That put quite a pull on
the line at the moment they were trying to work with it. In
about thirty seconds they let it go. It appeared to have a gift on
it . . . something small, perhaps, like the combs {received earlier
with the headband}.

As we left the area I called in and reported that we were on
our way back. Marj answered that the Drown baby was sick
and that I should make the best possible time so as to be able to
fly into Macuma if necessary. Therefore, I flew at seventy miles
per hour and somewhere along the line we lost the gift. About
half-way back I noticed that it was missing. It was a keen
disappointment.

In Jim's account of this day's operation, he said:

I saw a thing that thrilled me—it seemed an old man who
stood beside the house waved with both his arms as if to signal
us to come down! *Aucas*, waving to me to come! God send me
soon to the Aucas!

At the end of his record of the eighth visit, Nate wrote:

One of the problems we face now is getting another man to
bring our manpower up to strength. The Lord is abundantly
able!

Although five men would eventually make up 'Operation
Auca', only three—Nate, Jim, and Ed—were definitely
committed at this time. Pete, who had been as vitally
interested as these three, was, however, not clear whether
God's leading was for him to go or to stay.

It was now that Nate thought of Roger Youderian. They
had worked together opening up the Atshuara country,
building two other outstation airstrips, and Nate was sure
of Roger's capabilities. He saw him as a soldier of Christ, 'a
man capable of great effort, trained and disciplined.' He
wrote of him:

He knows the importance of unswerving conformity to the will of his Captain. Obedience is not a momentary option; it is a diecast decision made beforehand. He was a disciplined paratrooper. He gave Uncle Sam his best in that battle and now he is determined that the Lord Jesus Christ shall not get less than his best. Everything that made him a good soldier has been consecrated to Christ, his new Captain!

Ed and Jim hardly knew Roger; working with different Indians in another part of the Oriente, they had had little occasion for more than a passing acquaintance. But they trusted Nate's judgment implicitly.

As it happened, Roger was in Shell Mera at this time. He had come out from Macuma to help build a mission-sponsored hospital there. So one day, as Roger was nailing down sheets of aluminium on the roof, Nate came to him, told him of Operation Auca, and asked him to go along as the badly-needed fourth man. Nate did not want to leave his plane on the beach at night where it might be open to damage. Neither was he anxious to leave the two men alone overnight. Would Roj go?

Roger agreed immediately. But all unknown to the others, he was, at that time, passing through a deeply personal spiritual struggle, and he began to wonder if he should join the others in the physical venture when not with them completely in spirit.

Only he and Barbara were aware of the struggle he was going through. He questioned whether, after all, he was accomplishing anything whatever in the mission-field. He had broken the language barrier, to be sure, but why had there not been an immediate show of fruit for his labours?

A missionary plods through the first year or two, thinking that things will be different when he speaks the language. He is baffled to find, frequently, that they are not. He is stripped of all that may be called 'romance'. Life has fallen more or less into a pattern. Day follows day in unbroken succession; there are no crises, no mass conversions, sometimes not even one or two to whom he can point and say: 'There is a transformed life. If I had not come, he would never have known Christ.' There will be those among the Indians who say that they accept Christ, but what of the forsaking of heathen custom and turning from sin to a life of holiness? The missionary watches, and longs, and his heart sickens.

The forces of evil, unchallenged for so long, are now set in array against the missionary.

Roger Youderian was finding out the power of these forces. He wrote in his diary:

About ready to call it quits. Seems to me there is no future in the Jivaria for us, and the wisest thing for us to do will be to pull stakes. Will wait until I've had a chance to talk it over with Barb and see what she has to say. We might pass Christmas here, finish the hospital in Shell, and head home. The reason: Failure to measure up as a missionary and get next to the people. As far as my heart and aspirations are concerned, the issue is settled. It's a bit difficult to discern just what is the cause of my failure and the forces behind it. Since March, when we left Wambimi, there has been no message from the Lord to us. I just picked up my Bible to share with the same Lord who made me a new creature in England eleven years ago. There was no word of encouragement from Him. He had kept us safe wonderfully, and met our needs, but the issue is far greater than that. There is no ministry for me among the Jivaros or the Spanish, and I'm not going to try to fool myself. I wouldn't support a missionary such as I know myself to be, and I'm not going to ask anyone else to. Three years is long enough to learn a lesson and learn it well. Some people are slow to catch on. It will be tough on Barb and the children, but I've always been convinced that honesty and sincerity pay. The milk is spilled—I'm not going to cry over it. The cause of Christ in the Jivaria will not suffer for our having been there, but I must be honest and confess that it has not been *helped*. I don't think it will come as much of a surprise to many and will only be an "I told you so."

There is no spiritual pressure in the issue, and in fact very little of emotion or stress; perhaps none.

I realise that many along the way will say that we gave up too easy. Perhaps. But I believe that God's way is to face the issue and let our *yea* be *yea* and our *nay* be *nay*. I'm *amen* for the cause of Christ but believe that the part I ch—, no I cannot say the part I chose; I believe that the Lord chose the Jivaria for us but I just didn't measure up to it. You will say that when the Lord calls, He supplies. You can have my boots any time you want them. It isn't there. I'm not good at pretending.

I do not put any blame on personalities or circumstances involved; the failure is mine, and my failure to achieve the personal experience of Christ that could meet the needs here. It didn't pan out. It is not because of wife and family. Macuma station is ample for a home for them and all we need has been offered.

The issue is personal, and personal it shall remain. What is the answer? I do not know. And I'm discouraged about finding any satisfactory solution. Have been battling and thinking the issue for many months. There is no answer. It is a combination of situations and talents that has me buffaloed. This is the first time in my life that I have turned my back, but they say there is a first time for everything.

We are a happy family. He has kept us well and given us sound bodies and, we trust, sound minds. Whatever He has for us is fine but I'm afraid that anything along missionary lines has been scared out of me. If I couldn't make the grade here in Macuma I'm not foolish enough to expect a change of setting would change *me*. This is my personal "Waterloo" as a missionary.

It seems strange to try and sit back and view it in an impersonal way. Of this much I'm sure: it will draw me to read His word more, be more tolerant of others, and less venturesome in my activities.

Some will wonder why we don't seek a place in the Spanish or Quichua work. Frankly, I'm not interested. And, especially after this experience, I'm not begging for any more headaches. Only a fool makes the same mistake twice. One mess seems to me ought to be enough.

Here I sit at 11 am Wednesday listening to the services. I told them from the window that I would not come. First they sang "Wonderful Words of Life", and then "Oh Say but I'm Glad". I've found an English hymn-book to see if there might be some consolation in a hymn. There is none. It is beyond me. My, what a world of time I've wasted. The ruts are worn deep and it won't be easy to change habits and give up the lost ground or let it be gained by the Lord. But surely it will be worth the battle. My mind was made only to love Him; my body, also, which includes my tongue in all its activities. How slow some of us are to learn.

I will be led and taught of the Holy Spirit. God desires full development, use, and activity of our faculties. The Holy Spirit can and will guide me in direct proportion to the time and effort I will expend to know and do the will of God. I must read the Bible to know God's will. At every point I will obey and do.

A week spent in Shell Mera, prior to this period, when I reiterated many times a day "Thy will be done" helped much to fortify me for this struggle.

Roger had not yet emerged from his 'dark night of the soul' when Nate approached him. The days which followed found him in a desperate struggle to know the will of God. He had no doubt of his own desire—he would go if that were all that mattered. But to go without the smile of God—that would be impossible. 'If Thy presence go not with us, carry us not up hence.' Roger recognised something of what this decision might mean for him, and the hours spent on his knees with God witnessed agony of soul. But God, 'who causes us to triumph', brought him out of his slough of despond.

'He was cleansed through the Spirit for the task that lay ahead of him,' said Barbara afterwards, 'and went with a happy, expectant mind and his heart full of joy.'

On December 19 he wrote in his diary:

I will die to self. I will begin to ask God to put me in a service of constant circumstances where to live Christ I must die to self. I will be alive unto God. That I may learn to love Him with my heart, mind, soul, and body.

Just before he left Macuma to join the four in Arajuno, he wrote:

> *'There is a seeking of honest love*
> *Drawn from a soul storm-tossed,*
> *A seeking for the gain of Christ,*
> *To bless the blinded, the beaten, the lost.*
>
> *'Those who sought found Heavenly Love*
> *And were filled with joy divine,*
> *They walk today with Christ above*
> . . . . '

The last line eluded him and, as he put down his pencil, he said: 'Barb, I'll finish it when I get home.'

— 13 —

The Search for 'Palm Beach'

ALTHOUGH PLANS for meeting the Aucas on the ground occupied more and more time, the regular weekly visits to 'Terminal City', the name the men had given to the Auca village, were continued without a break. On December 3 Nate recorded the ninth visit:

We left Arajuno at about 8.45 with good weather. Before taking off, Ed and I shot some pictures that we hope will be suitable for enlargement up to almost life-size so that the 'neighbours' will recognise us when they first see us on the ground. We took close-ups of our faces, together with the combs and head-dress they had given us.

When we got over the first house, No. 4, we noted that a couple of pretty big trees were chopped down where we had tossed the gifts into the trees for that purpose. There are not many trees left now between the two clearings. If we can get them to cut down the rest, we will be able to make low passes.

Once this morning we swooped down so low that the two men who were up on the platform 'directing traffic' ducked down. When we swooped down again the two were content to view the proceedings from the ground. The platform-men had on shirts, period: shirts we had given them, of course. In these runs we dropped an axe-head, a plastic cup, and a cheap knife. We tried again to put these in the trees that still separate the two clearings. There were perhaps a half dozen other people around No. 4.

From there we went to No. 3. As we made a low pass we nearly fell out of the airplane, for there on the grass roof of the house was a model plane! We wondered if they made it after observing the model plane at Ed's place. In any case it indicates good will, and a craftsmanship hitherto unsuspected among such primitives.

We noticed another platform, larger and higher than the other and made of chonta. I'd guess it is fifteen feet off the ground. On top was a man complete with his uniform (shirt). He waved responsively as we waved to him. We made a couple of passes and tossed out a machete so that it fell just beyond the 'director'. We noted that the east wall of leaves was off the house, so that we could see inside... fire sites, etc. It was a very friendly-looking deal, but it's possible that they are going to put in a chonta wall to replace the leaves. Yes, I just checked the photo of No. 3 taken a while back, and it shows leaf-wall all the way around except at the river end which was open. It is easy to see how the availability of even so simple a tool as the machete can profoundly alter a culture.

Next we decided to have a close look at a fresh clearing that has been made on the ridge-crest just above No. 3. No-one was there. We discussed briefly the possible benefits of trying to lure them up and decided to try. First time around we tossed out an aluminium kettle. It was a poor shot and fell into the forest, fortunately on the slope facing the No. 3 house. It was then that we noticed that the undergrowth on the slope was in the process of being cleared out. That means that they will be tipping over the trees on that edge of the clearing which will enable us to fly within twenty feet of them in perfect safety. As a futher lure Ed decided we should toss out a cheap, plastic-handled knife. (All these gifts are generously trailed by ribbon and bandage material.) In view of the miss with the kettle I said to Ed as we approached, 'Let's put this one right on top of the house,' referring to the sketchy shelter that must serve as a sun-shade while they work on the new clearing project. And that's exactly where it landed... right on the roof.

"Let's go see how the old man liked his new pants," I suggested. "Okay"... so we went. He is about two minutes away from No. 3. He was waiting for us in pants and tee-shirt.

His two women were out, too. One "wore" a baby and the other nothing. The area around their house was nicely cleaned up, grass cut down to roots, etc. The old man evidenced the usual reserve and lack of enthusiasm. We dropped him a machete. One of the women had to go get it. His gestures are willing but slow. We flew by within 200 feet of them about three times, and headed back up-river to No. 3.

Back at No. 3 area we checked the hilltop clearing again. From a quarter-mile away I could see that someone was there. We were thrilled by this quick result since we had thought it might take weeks to coax them up. The figures proved to be two women, young; I would say about sixteen and twenty, maybe. They had got the knife and we passed within fifty feet of them taking pictures. We make about four passes and for the first time looked full into an Auca face. She was good-looking with hair cropped to bangs in front. The 'controller' of No. 3 was still on the platform. We waved good-bye to him and headed on towards No. 4.

Back a No. 4 the boys were all waiting for the last act, the 'bucket drop'. We climbed up to 3,000 feet and slowed down to forty-five miles per hour with power off. In this slow, power-off glide the kettle gets clear of the plane very nicely. It took only about three times around to set the kettle in the middle of the big clearing behind the house. They ran back and forth in a group, curiously to us. I was afraid that I was piling loose cord in after the kettle... however it seemed to have too much tension on it for that. Finally, after a minute and a half, they turned it loose and up it came with a gift... bright red and good-sized.

We flew back to Arajuno at fifty-five miles per hour so as not to lose the gift if we could help it. We had no trouble setting the gift down on the runway and then we dropped the cord. On the ground we ran to the spot. We found another feathered crown—a new one, freshly made, and attached to it a little hank of hand-spun cotton string. It was all attached to our drop-line with a square knot.

That night Ed noted in his diary: 'It is time we were getting closer to them on the ground.' To Jim he wrote:

I've been giving the trip some thought, and I feel this way: we should set a definite limit on the number of days we will wait on the Curaray for them, and if they don't show, we shoud be ready to go in to them. For myself, I am definitely ready to go in and feel that it would be reasonably safe . . . if we can ever use that term in our initial ground contact with these people! We should go in (1) wearing the head-dresses, (2) carrying small airplanes such as I have hanging here, (3) carrying gifts wrapped as we have been wrapping them, (4) shouting *'biti miti punimupa'* (I like you) or other phrases that we are making familiar from the plane. God being with us—and up to this point we have every confidence that He is—I think this would put us in. The whole project is moving faster than we had originally dared to hope, and while I'm not for getting ahead of God, I feel that we shouldn't lag.

On December 10 Nate's journal continues with an account of the next visit:

In spite of our evasive manoeuvre Ed's Indians tell him that they were down the Curaray last week and saw us go by. They say (what a sense of humour!) that they stripped off their clothes when they heard us coming and got sticks like lances so that we would think they were "neighbours". They probably thought that we would drop them gifts.

During the week, in talks with the members of the team it was decided that January 2 would be the tentative date for the entry attempt. We were thinking in terms of going down with Indians, setting up a house and then having the Indians retire while the team would wait for contact. Then with the plane we would try to get the "neighbours" to come over and pay a visit. We know how to say "come to my house" and also "Curaray" in their tongue. And I feel confident that by repeated circling right over the ridge from them we can use curiosity to bring them over to the big river.

Roughly, the strategy calls for the carrying of arms only by missionary personnel, and that out of sight. We presume that the first shot fired signals the failure of the entire project and the scuttling of any hope in the near future. Therefore utmost care will be taken and the guns will be used only to frighten the savages in case of need of self-defence.

There were two views or two possibilities under consideration: (1) Set up a little house at Palm Beach [the name agreed upon to designate the river beach chosen for landing the plane] and then retire until the "neighbours" would have had time to visit the site, and go back later; or, (2) Set up and attempt to make contact on that first trip. Since the events of this morning further affect this decision, I'll leave further discussion of it till later.

This morning we took off from "Centerville" [Arajuno] at about 9.15, armed with gift-wrapped machetes, axes and small knives and plastic items.

We also had three pairs of one-pound paper packages of paint pigment powder in three bright colours. These were for measuring playa sites that might serve for Palm Beach. Yesterday we ran tests here at Shell and found that when flying at sixty-five miles per hour we could drop little bags of flour at seven-second intervals and pretty consistently mark off from 190 to 210 yards. This measure was taken in view of the impossibility of satisfactorily estimating the length of sandbars where there is nothing that would serve as a basis for comparison.

We took a route down the Nushino, inasmuch as some of the Indians from Ed's station were down on the Curaray River fishing again this week. We gradually eased over to the south and picked up the Curaray in the area where we hoped to find a good site for Palm Beach. It wasn't long before we located a possibility. Most of the larger playas are on bends and therefore of no value without having approaches cut first. The river is so serpentine that there are few possibilities of a sand-bar along a straight stretch. We dragged [flew low over] the first. It seemed reasonable. The only drawback was that this beach would require take-offs with the prevailing wind . . . a serious difficulty. Nevertheless, after dragging it a time or two we "bombed" it with pigment and found that it had about 200 yards usable. Another difficulty was a big dead tree lying on the sand which forced the landing area very close to the river-bank foliage.

The next one we found was about a mile or less downstream. It looked better—better approaches, especially into the prevailing wind. The approach would be steep but possible. The playa is low to the water so that a flood would easily cover it, but it is pebbly and firm-looking. We "bombed" it and found a conservative 200 yards usable. I should not be surprised if a measure would show it to be more like 230 yards usable. Also it is such that an overshot landing would only put us into shallow water. We dragged it once, keeping good airspeed until more familiar with the pull-out area. In the pull-out the trees along the banks overhang enough that it is a little squeaky, but by tipping over two trees after we land, we can take care of that problem.

It began to look as if this would be our "Palm Beach". We decided to shoot a simulated landing on it. Down close to it I could see the surface well and I put the wheels down lightly twice as we accelerated again for the pull-up. The surface was smooth as a gravel runway and seemed hard. It is really ideal, except for vulnerability to flooding.

This finding brings into focus the possibility of landing the team right there with a prefabricated tree house and aluminium for a roof. It would mean that no Indians need to be in on the deal at all, and barring flood it would mean that I'd be able to fly them all out following a contact or whenever they should be ready to come.

The picture would be something like this: (1) On a Friday morning, Lord willing, free-fall supplies and equipment on to the Palm Beach site from very low (just off the runway) so as to be sure they would not be in the landing area. (2) We land with Jim and Roger, keeping the plane very light. (3) We land with Ed and aluminium. (4) We land with Pete and more supplies (if Pete should feel led to go).

On arrival, Jim and Roj would go to work tipping over the two or three medium-to-small trees in the approach. Then they would pick out a suitable tree for mounting the prefab tree house and start clearing around it. When the others are with them, all would go downstream to the first bend and tip over at least one of the two trees on opposite banks which make the pass rather narrow. (This is not an absolute must, but would be highly desirable.) During this part of the operation someone should always have a hand on a weapon inside a bag so that it could be fired on a moment's notice and thus upset the equilibrium of any possible lancer.

Next, back to the sand-bar, with two men widening the clearing at the foot of the tree while two work on getting the tree house up in place and the aluminium roof on. Once the house is all set, the men would rotate on the clearing, perhaps with one fellow still concentrating on getting food supplies, stove, water, etc., up on to the platform. One man, resting from the crew, could sit on the platform and cover the men on the ground, always keeping arms strictly out of sight. By evening, there ought to be a fair-sized clearing at the base of the tree, connected by clearing to the playa. The plane returns to Arajuno after checking radio set-up in the tree house, etc.

Next day the plane begins the invitation of the "neighbours" to the Palm Beach site, both by calling phrases as well as by coaxing, circling in that direction from where they are and then landing at Palm Beach and repeating every hour or so until we're sure they've caught on. Another detail will be the installation of a good-sized model plane on the site.

Maybe five days would be committed to the effort. If unsuccessful we would withdraw, either by air or by sending a crew of Indians down-river in canoes. Supplies in the tree house should be sufficient for two weeks to cover possible loss of the playa by flood or siege, the two rougher possibilities to be faced.

The practicability of a raft composed of air mattresses and bamboo should be reckoned with as a downstream exit to an Army base on the Curaray in case the Indians should refuse to go to the rescue.

Back to the narrative: We checked course and distance from the Palm Beach possibility to Terminal City—135 degrees and three minutes at ninety miles per hour. That makes about four and one-half miles from the beach on the Curaray to the Auca village.

While letting down we headed east to the old man's house. The old boy wasn't there but a young man was waving something like bark cloth and clearly offering it for trade. In the course of four passes we dropped (I think) a small knife, plastic cup, and possibly some article of clothing... not sure of the latter.

Next we moved up to the clearing on the hill above the airplane house, or No. 3. There were two women there. We dropped a small knife. The head man was down by the house on his platform directing traffic. He had on a red and black checkered shirt we dropped last week. We signalled and shouted to him indicating that we wanted him to come up to the hilltop. While we circled some more he disappeared from the platform and two younger boys took up his post. Next we made a low pass to drop an axe-head beyond the platform. We must have scared the younger fellows because one of them had a lance in his hand as we circled back. That was an unkind gesture and we swooped down low again to see if they would show any hostility. Someone must have given them the word because the lance had disappeared and all seemed well. Now we spotted the boss-man in the checkered shirt up on the hill. We couldn't afford to slight him so we made two passes and on the second dropped him a pair of pants which he caught in mid-air. (These fellows will be dressed like dudes before we get to see them on the ground.)

Next, up to No. 4 and the main act. The big shots, four of them, were clad in white tee-shirts. Youngsters and women were in the older uniform. The trees that we had tried to get them to cut down by tossing stuff into them, were now cut down. Also the walls (chonta) were off the house. (I failed to mention that they were also off No. 3) And beside the house they had built a new and higher platform like No. 3's.

We made a couple of low passes, calling to them, "I like you, I like you," etc. On the last low pass we tossed them a machete. While passing low we saw one of the four Big Wheels holding up a package, roundish and brown. We figured this was our trade item. We pulled up and climbed slowly. Ed was feeling pretty rough. It has been an unusually strenuous workout and Ed had had to attend to a sick baby across the river from his place earlier in the morning. He hadn't been feeling too sharp then. I was also feeling as though I'd been dragged through a keyhole, but it was worth it. At 3,000 feet I throttled all the way back, pulled flaps, and settled into the quiet of a forty-mile-per-hour glide while Ed got the gift overboard on the line. This week we gave them a couple of little bundles of string, a few smaller items, and four 6- by 9-inch portraits of the team-members, tinted and bearing the insignia of the operation, a drawing of the little yellow airplane. These were glue-mounted on Masonite board.

When this stuff got down over by the trees, they got it and quickly took it out to the centre of the clearing. They went into a 100 per cent huddle over the contents of the white cloth mail sack that carried the mentioned items, except for the fellow who was busy fastening on their gift to us. I saw the gift leave him, drifting lazily. I rolled out of the turn and added power. Within three or four secondes the package was swished skyward from them and the last man joined the huddle over the pictures. What wouldn't we have given to see those boys studying out our pictures and see their reactions!

We headed home at sixty-five miles per hour with the prize dangling at the end of the line. At Arajuno we set it down at the edge of the strip, cut the line, and landed. On the ground, I bashed my way through the brush at the edge of the strip while Ed lost his breakfast. This is the first time I've beat him to the prize. (His legs are at least a foot longer than mine.) When I got to the bark-cloth bag, it was moving. Since we had given them a chicken last week I figured it would be a bird, but as I started to peek in a hole the though of a snake crossed my mind. However, it was a nice parrot in a basket covered with bark. It was well tied and was complete with a partially-nibbled banana inside for the trip!

I had lunch with Ed and Marilou and talked of the possibilities opened to us by the finding of a beach we could land on. We praise God for this—another indication of His leading and care. We believe that in a short time we shall have the privilege of meeting these fellows with the story of the Grace of God.

— 14 —

An Auca on the Path

FRIDAY AM!' Nate tapped out this opening on a borrowed typewriter in Arajuno, and continued:

This morning in Shell Mera as I was dressing in the bedroom adjoining the office-radio room, I heard Marj checking a message just received from Marilou McCully, who was holding down Arajuno alone while Ed helped in a conference ministry at Puyupungu. Marilou said she had rather sound reason to believe that Aucas were in the neighbourhood.

Two things flashed through my mind: first, the opportunity to make contact with them, then the danger that a shot by one of the local Indians would ruin all the efforts made up till now—and the consequent closing of the door that seems to be opening to us.

While Marj got the message relayed to Ed down at Puyupungu, I was rolling the plane out of the hangar. Too much was at stake to hesitate. Also, the weather was threatening to sour to the north. The mission-house at Puyupungu is about five minutes from the airstrip. I got to the airstrip about one minute before Ed. We returned to Shell Mera immediately. Then while Johnny gassed the plane, Marj and Ruth got some cargo and vegetables ready, Ed loaded, and I got some equipment together for the special nature of the expedition. I found that the little blank pistol I had just bought in Quito felt very nice in my pocket. It must be because I feel that it would surely break up any attack, yet I can feel confident of not accidentally hurting anyone with it. It also shoots tear-gas cartridges, but as Ed notes, if there is an attack on and I get close enough to use tear-gas... well.

The weather held okay until we got over the Arajuno headwater valleys. There, low ceilings pushed us down into the valley and within five minutes of Arajuno the clouds were on the mesas that line the half-mile-wide valley. I kept a weather eye on the valley behind, got a final look at the clear area beyond the edge of the overcast and weighed the alternatives. In case of trouble, I could spiral up to 5,000 and head south-west into the clear area five minutes away. I yawed the plane to check the turn-and-bank indicator, without which this manoeuvre would be impossible. It was okay. Light rain—heavier in patches—made us circle a time or two to get a good look ahead. We slipped across the ridge and down the other valley. In about another minute (these are the long kind of minutes that seem to last about five minutes each) we had the strip under us. We kind of figured the Aucas might have wanted to take a look at the plane on the ground, and, not having found it at Arajuno, they might have headed for home. We then circled several times to let the "neighbours" know we'd come to welcome them. We landed around 8.30. As the bad weather moved south-west it became apparent that if we had delayed five or ten minutes we would have been too late.

Walking from the strip to the house we wondered if we were being watched. Ed went ahead with both hands full. If they are looking for large steaks on long bone, they passed it up this time. I had one hand in my pocket nonchalantly flipping the safety on and off on my blank pistol, all the while wondering how far things should go before allowing a shot to signal the end of the whole operation. Again we felt the need of God's guidance and intervention in a special way.

As we neared the house we heard a Christmas carol in Quichua. Ed explained that Marilou was rehearsing the local Indians for a Christmas programme. When we got in the house, Ed took over for a few minutes and gave the locals a pep talk on "How to win friends and influence people", also exhorting the Indians regarding our Christian obligations to reach the Aucas with the Gospel. It would seem that at this point the measure of missionary zeal among these new converts would depend pretty much on who saw whom first and under what circumstances.

The rehearsal for the Christmas programme proceeded rather anaemically a few minutes longer and was then dismissed. Ed politely asked the Indians to hit the road for home. But they hung around. Finally, Ed offered them candy if they'd go. They agreed. He gave the two leaders some special candy for extra bravery.

When we were finally alone, Ed ambled into the living-room like the friendly local patrolman and said to Marilou, "Now get a hold of yourself, lady. Everything's going to be okay. All we want are the facts." (The capacity of these guys to toss something like this into a serious situation is a great asset. It kind of double-clutches you into second gear when you've been pulling too hard in high.)

It seems that at 5.40 am, Fermin, the Indian who has been sleeping in the schoolhouse to help guard while Ed is away, went down the path towards the *chacra* to take care of the exigencies of nature. When about as far as the pole that holds the model plane aloft, he spotted a man at the end of the path . . . naked, with lance, and with hair tied up in a bun on the back of his head. As they saw each other the Auca ran into the forest. At 5.40 and ten seconds past, Fermin was calling at Marilou's window. Fortunately his gun (in the schoolroom) was not loaded and he needed powder and shot. Of course Marilou would not give him any. He was sure she had gone mad and proceeded to try to convince her with round advice on how to take care of Aucas. He was genuinely pale and excited. It looked like the real thing.

First Marilou took the empty gun from the poor fellow. Then, although she is seven months pregnant, Marilou took a machete for a gift and headed down the path calling "*biti miti punimupa*" . . . I like you . . . I like you. In between her calls she could hear Fermin calling after her in Quichua. . . . "You're crazy . . . you're crazy . . . they'll kill you first." When she was two-thirds the way to the spot where the savage had been seen, Fermin and Carmela, the Indian girl who lives with Marilou to help in the house, both came running and caught up just in time for them all three to see a fresh wet footprint on a dry board across a little ditch. The print was headed towards the house. Across the path they found grass recently stepped on, leading to the forest. Marilou then tossed the machete on the fresh path, called out some more, and returned to the house. Half an hour later when the local witch-doctor arrived for school, he accompanied Marilou to the spot. Finding no further indication of visitors, Marilou picked up the machete and they came back to the house. Carmela expressed a common feeling when she said she would have suspected that Fermin imagined seeing an Auca until she saw the footprint. When Marilou asked her if she was afraid she said she was only a little afraid, and that she was sure God would take care of them. Then Marilou heard Fermin call in to Carmela and ask if the Señora was scared. Carmela answered that as far as she could tell, she wasn't; to which Fermin answered that she would be when night came and he wasn't there to protect them. Marilou then asked him if he was going to stay that night. "I will stay," he said, "if I have a loaded gun. Without a gun we will all be killed."

We talked things over while Ed prepared a machete and a pot the way we do when we deliver them at the "neighbour-hood". At 10.30 (still raining lightly) we paraded down the airstrip decked out in the feather head-dresses they have given us on the line and calling in Auca phrases while waving the gifts over our heads. We must have looked like a couple of Don Quixotes in the role of Santa Claus delivering goodies to the trees.

At 2.30 pm we made another safari down to the far end of the airstrip making our most unusual offer. Then we decided that evening would be the most probable time to contact them here so we'd fly down to the "neighbourhood", count heads, and do tomorrow's drop today. We got ready and off, arriving over Palm Beach at 3.30. Spent about ten minutes there re-checking the beach. Dye and bandage material still on the sand, although nearby playas seem to have been under water at some time since last week's visit. We rolled the wheels of the plane on the beach about seventy-five yards and then poured on the coal. The approach is really difficult but the pull-out is good except for one narrow place, but that is a good way downstream. The whole site had a friendly look to us this time. We checked trees along the beach that might be suitable for the tree house and then took the three-minute trip over to the "neighbourhood".

We found our friends scattered, with no waiting traffic manager, making us think that maybe indeed we had got them on a seven-day week by the regularity of previous visits. We made a couple of low passes over the old man's house, taking movies in slow motion. One person showed up holding the same piece of material as last week. We dropped nothing. At the airplane house we found about four people around the house and platform and three up on the cleared hill. The fellow on the hilltop had on the red swimming trunks [an earlier gift]. We dropped him a small knife with appropriate ribbons and hurried on to the main house since by now we were convinced that men were clearly missing, making it probable that the visit at Arajuno was indeed real.

We made a couple of low passes taking movies and then pulled up and let out a pot on the line. The contents of the pot this week were: little packages of food wrapped in banana leaves, beef, chocolate, manioc, cookies, candy, and some beads. They received these gifts and helped themselves to about twenty to fifty yards of line and tied on a gift. It was larger and heavier than any so far. We made tracks for Arajuno with it. We let it down, cut the line, landed, and hit out through the brush trusting that any intelligent snake would know enough to get out of our way. (There's antivenin in the plane.) The gift was a large black bird, apparently their chicken, in a basket cage reinforced with netting and a piece of bark cloth. We still haven't decided what to do with the bird. Also in the cage there was a spinner's distaff loaded with cotton yarn, a well-received gift.

Evening and night in Arajuno...

— 15 —

Why Did the Men Go?

T HE TIME WAS RIPENING fast. The men and the other wives and I spent long hours discussing this project of which we had dreamed for so many months and years. Olive Fleming remembered what she had read in Pete's diary of his willingnes to give his life for the Aucas. I reminded Jim of what we both knew it might mean if he went. 'Well, if that's the way God wants it to be,' was his calm reply, 'I'm ready to die for the salvation of the Aucas.' While still a student in college Jim had written: 'He is no fool who gives what he cannot keep to gain what he cannot lose.'

Marilou McCully said: 'I hope no one feels any pressure is being put on Ed to go. This is a thing for each couple to face by themselves.'

Two gift flights remained before the actual ground operation was to begin. On December 23, when the Elliots and Flemings had gone to Arajuno to spend Christmas with the McCullys, Nate flew Jim over the Auca settlement. Seeing the same old man they had noticed before standing in a clearing, they swooped down past him at no more than fifty feet.

'Wow!' said Jim. 'That guy's scared stiff!'

Nate agreed. Later he wrote:

It's as though they had steeled themselves against doing anything that would express fear or hostility. Possibly afraid that they might scare away the chicken that lays the golden eggs. But their eyes don't lie—they're full of terror. Understandable, though. The expression is that of a six-year-old in the front row when the circus clown points a big gun right in his face. He's sure it's all in fun, but...oh, brother!

At the main house the "chief traffic director" was in full uniform—shirt and pants—everyone else more typically dressed, or undressed. Jim counted thirteen on hand. On our first swoop past, one of them held up what was apparently to be our gift. We dropped them a carrying net containing white cloth, a flashlight, a pair of pants, and other trinkets. What wouldn't we give to see them trying to make sense out of that flashlight!

Jim announced the take-off of their gift on the line, and I rolled out of the turn to hold it up. It is the heaviest yet. We cruised at sixty-five back to Arajuno, and let the bark-cloth bundle down hard. It hit in some bushes about twenty yards from Ed's house. Contents:

Cooked fish
Two or three little packets of peanuts
A couple of pieces of cooked manioc
A cooked plantain
Two squirrels, very apparently killed by the hard fall
One parrot, alive but a bit nervous
Two bananas in with the parrot
Two pieces of pottery, clay, busted to bits in the fall
A piece of cooked meat and a smoked monkey tail

This is by far the most all-out effort at a fair-trade arrangement on the part of the neighbours. We are all delighted. Jim and Ed sampled the meat, and we all ate some of the peanuts. Then, meaning no ill to the kind folks who mailed all those goodies to us, we sat down and ate the meal that Marilou had prepared.

Even though Pete had not yet made his final decision, he and Olive with three other couples who would be directly involved in the project were together on the 23rd for discussion. (Roger and Barbara Youderian still were on their station in the southern jungle.) The wives were particularly concerned to know exactly what provisions were to be made for safety. It was decided that arms would be carried, concealed, and that if the situation appeared to be getting delicate, they would be shown, simply to let the Aucas know that the white man held the upper hand. If this were not enough, shots would be fired with the intention only of scaring them.

Roger had drawn up a plan of operation. Jim was assigned to the task of prefabricating a house to put up in a tree. This would ensure safety at night, especially if a gasoline pressure lamp were kept burning to illumine the area at the foot of the tree. Ed was responsible for collecting items for trade with the Aucas. Roj would make up the first-aid kit, Nate saw to the communications and transportation, Jim took charge of arms and ammunition, and when later on Pete decided that he would go too, he was to be responsible for helping Nate on the flights to and from Arajuno, for flights over the Auca houses when he would shout over the loud-speaker, and for keeping supplies on the beach. Roj prepared a set of code signs to be drawn in the sand on the beach in case of emergency, and drew maps for each man with the code names he had made up for the strategic points.

The language material which Jim and I had gathered in previous weeks was organised and memorised by each member of the party. Marj's place was to be at the radio in Shell Mera, standing by at all times when the plane was flying, and keeping set schedules of contact with the men on the ground. It was decided that Barbara would stay in Arajuno, helping Marilou with the preparation of food which Nate was to fly daily to Palm Beach.

The appearance of the Auca at Arajuno, the fact that the Quichuas were guessing a little too shrewdly for comfort, the great encouragement in the drop flights — indeed, even the weather itself — seemed to be catapulting them towards their D-day with now-or-never exigency. Within a month the rainy season would start, flooding the rivers and making landings impossible. The ideal time for establishment of their beach-head in Auca territory would be early January during the full of the moon.

They set the date for Tuesday, January 3, 1956.

Christmas at Arajuno was made as much like Christmas at home as Marilou's genius could make it. She even had a little Christmas tree, made of bamboo and decorated with lights and tinsel. Ed and Jim, who already had 'reserved seats' for the trip to Palm Beach, were keyed up. Pete was still waiting on God in prayer before making his final decision to go.

The other wives and I talked together one night about the possibility of becoming widows. What would we do? God gave us peace of heart, and confidence that whatever might happen, His Word would hold. We knew that 'when He Putteth forth His sheep, He goeth before them'. God's leading was unmistakable up to this point. Each of us knew when we married our husbands that there would never be any question about who came first—God and His work held first place in each life. It was the condition of true discipleship; it became devastatingly meaningful now.

It was a time for soul-searching, a time for counting the possible cost. Was it the thrill of adventure that drew our husbands on? No. Their letters and journals make it abundantly clear that these men did not go out as some men go out to shoot a lion or climb a mountain. Their compulsion was from a different source. Each had made a personal transaction with God, recognising that he belonged to God, first of all by creation, and secondly by redemption through the death of His Son, Jesus Christ. This double claim on his life settled once and for all the question of allegiance. It was not a matter of striving to follow the example of a great Teacher. To conform to the perfect life of Jesus was impossible for a human being. To these men, Jesus Christ was God, and had actually taken upon Himself human form, in order that He might die, and, by His death, provide not only escape from the punishment which their sin merited, but also a *new kind of life,* eternal both in length and in quality. This meant simply that Christ was to be obeyed, and more than that, that He would provide the power to obey. The point of decision had been reached. God's command 'Go ye, and preach the gospel to every creature' was the categorical imperative. The question of personal safety was wholly irrelevant.

On Sunday afternoon, December 18, Nate Saint sat at his typewriter to tell the world why they were going — just in case. In speaking these words he spoke for all:

As we weigh the future and seek the will of God, does it seem right that we should hazard our lives for just a few savages? As we ask ourselves this question, we realise that it is not the call or the needy thousands, rather it is the simple intimation of the prophetic Word that there shall be some from every tribe in His presence in the last day and in our hearts we feel that it is pleasing Him that we should interest ourselves in making an opening into the Auca prison for Christ.

As we have a high old time this Christmas, may we who know Christ hear the cry of the damned as they hurtle headlong into the Christless night without ever a chance. May we be moved with compassion as our Lord was. May we shed tears of repentance for these we have failed to bring out of darkness. Beyond the smiling scenes of Bethlehem may we see the crushing agony of Golgotha. May God give us a new vision of His will concerning the lost and our responsibility.

Would that we could comprehend the lot of these stone-age people who live in mortal fear of ambush on the jungle trail...those to whom the bark of a gun means sudden, mysterious death...those who think all men in all the world are killers like themselves. If God would grant us the vision, the word sacrifice would disappear from our lips and thoughts; we would hate the things that seem now so dear to us; our lives would suddenly be too short, we would despise time-robbing distractions and charge the enemy with all our energies in the name of Christ. May God help us to judge ourselves by the eternities that separate the Aucas from a comprehension of Christmas and Him, who, though He was rich, yet for our sakes became poor so that we might, through His poverty, be made rich.

Lord, God, speak to my own heart and give me to know Thy Holy will and joy of walking in it. Amen.

— 16 —

'We Go Not Forth Alone'

NEW YEAR'S DAY, 1956, saw Ed and his family, and Pete and Olive Fleming, in Shandia with Jim and me, while Roger and Barbara Youderian stayed in the McCully house in Arajuno, to be on hand in case the 'neighbours' came calling. Nate was completing his preparations for the very serious task of transporting the missionaries and their equipment to the beach-head. Monday morning, January 2, was a clear day for flying. By this time Pete had decided to go, so Nate had planned to get Pete and Olive and the McCullys back to Arajuno from Shandia that day, and to shuttle Jim over on Tuesday. But on the morning radio contact he said: 'Think you better get ready to go to Arajuno today, Jim. We need time tonight for plans, and ought to take advantage of the good weather.'

Jim began throwing his things into an Indian carrying-net while the McCullys and Flemmings were flown over to Arajuno. Everything he could think of that might help or amuse the Aucas, should they pay the men a visit, Jim put into the bag: harmonica, snakebite kit, flashlight, View-Master with picture reels, yo-yo, and, above all, the precious notebook of Auca language material, with the carefully arranged morphology file. I helped Jim to get his things together, wondering all the while, 'Will this be the last time I'll help him pack? Will this be the last lunch he'll eat in Shandia?'

When the little plane returned, circling over the airstrip, preparing to land to pick up Jim, his baggage, and the last new pieces of the prefabricated tree house he had made, we went together out of the front door. Jim did not look back. At the strip he kissed me good-bye, and the plane was off.

That night in Arajuno the five men made a tentative schedule of timing for the next day's landings on Palm Beach in order to see whether the whole set-up on the beach could be ready by evening. No detail was omitted; lists of equipment for each flight were made, and copies distributed among members. After supper and schedule conference, the stuff was laid out. The place began to look like a full-scale beach-head as each man checked and completed his equipment lists.

When they turned in, sleep did not come easily for Nate, on whom rested the greatest burden of responsibility. He was spending the night at Arajuno in order to save time in the morning. His diary tells of that night:

I drowsed off quite soon, but was checking the luminous face of my watch dial at 12.30, again at 2.00, and from then on I was on horizontal listening-post guard duty. I prayed, tried repeating verses from memory, and even counting. My entire share in this business seemed to hinge on that first take-off and landing. Then, too, I had told the fellows that I would only take one in alone on the first trip. That meant a lonely vigil for someone. Roj was ruled out, because he spoke only Jivaro. Ed had already beat Jim by pulling straws, but Jim held out, claiming to be lighter. When I said a difference of fifteen pounds would be decisive, they dragged out the bathroom scales. Ed was only seven pounds heavier than Jim. "Why, you cotton picker!" said Jim. "You've lost weight."

Nate continued in his diary:

If I should misjudge, Ed and I would really be in a fix. If the plane were damaged it would mean vulnerability in a flood, possibly even dismantling it and making a strip on higher ground—all this in a forest inhabited by Aucas! We had faced it in the light of past tests and decided to go ahead. As I slept, or tried, it was still a rough decision. But there was no doubt in my mind that we should forge ahead. The stakes warranted it.

The last time I "punched in" was 4 am. From four until movement in the house woke me at 5.45, I slept.

The morning of January 3 dawned clear. Somehow Nate found time later to record the events of that day—the day of the first landings in Auca territory:

Roj and I got right out to the plane. We'd been losing fluid out of the right brake. With a ten-cc syringe and a No. 22 hypodermic needle we sucked brake fluid out of the left master cylinder and injected it into the right. No soap. Not enough. We'd lost too much when I fixed the brake fitting the night before.

The others were hauling boards and equipment and aluminium to the strip and arranging all in order of priority.

At the 7 am radio contact we asked Marj to ask Johnny to bring us brake fluid as quickly as possible. Also, Olive had had a rough night (sick) and planned to go back to Shell with Johnny. This delay gave us a peaceful breakfast and time for prayer together.

At the close of their prayers the five men sang one of their favourite hymns, 'We Rest on Thee', to the stirring tune of 'Finlandia'. Jim and Ed had sung this hymn since college days and knew the verses by heart. On the last verse their voices rang out with deep conviction.

> '*We rest on Thee, our Shield and our Defender,*
> *Thine is the battle, Thine shall be the praise*
> *When passing through the gates of pearly splendour*
> *Victors, we rest with Thee through endless days.*'

Nate's terse account continues:

It was a beautiful day. Chiggers kept us scratching, but spirits were all high. Johnny hove in sight at 7.40. We decided he should stand by till we'd see how the first landing turned out. Ed and I got airborne at about 8.02 am. Curiously enough we had started the tentative schedule on paper at 8 am—and when we got up over the first ridge we could see by the river fog over the Curaray that we never could have made it earlier. The fog got uncomfortably thicker under us but the holes allowed us to keep in touch with the river. The sun was shining and we figured it better to wait, if necessary, for the right holes rather than turn back and make a later attempt.

As we got within two minutes of the site, the fog thinned so that we could safely slip down under it and make an approach. We went in, simulating a real landing, checked the full length for sticks and other hazards and pulled up.

I had planned three runs before landing, but the thing was exactly as we had seen it several times before. As we came in the second time we slipped down between the trees in a steep side slip. It felt good as we made the last turn and came to the sand, so I set it down. The right wheel hit within six feet of the water and the left ten feet later. As the weight settled on the wheels I felt it was soft sand—too late to back out now. I hugged the stick back and waited. One softer spot and we'd have been on our nose—maybe our back. It never came.

We jumped out, rejoicing in the deliverance. The relief at being past that hurdle without damage damped my sensitivity to the glaring possibility that I might not be able to take off. It was great just to be there.

We ran up and down the sand hunting the best course for a take-off attempt and removing sticks that could puncture a tyre. Then Ed took the movie camera to the far end while I taxied back towards a take-off position.

About thirty yards from the end I felt the right wheel sink, and my heart sank with it. I cut the engine and Ed came on the double. He lifted the low wing and I hoisted the tail around. Then using the engine, and with Ed lifting the wing, we got out of the softer stuff and cut the engine. Again we searched for harder spots. Finally we pushed the airplane backwards into some bushes right at the edge of the beach. It meant losing thirty yards of the total 200 available—a critical loss in view of the generally soft consistency of the whole area. However, the plane had been lightened and we were now working only 1,000 feet above sea level, where we would get more lift out of the wing.

As I got back into the plane, Ed went again to the far end of the beach. It shook me a little to think what Ed might record with that movie camera. After a final check I let'er go. The sand really grabbed the wheels but the acceleration still seemed satisfactory, so I hung on and was airborne in about 130 yards (about forty or fifty before being over the water) at about thiry miles per hour. I held it down close to the water to gain speed and then pulled up steeply out of that hardwood canyon; circled back, saluted Ed, and beat a trail for Arajuno—not quite sure yet what I should do next. At least I knew now what I was in for.

At Arajuno everyone was glad to see the plane back, but my story dampened the festive spirit appreciably. We scrapped the scheduled list for flight No. 2 and took, instead, Jim and Roj and such basic equipment as was absolutely essential— like the walkie-talkie and a little more food. The men gave me more ballast aft. If anything went wrong—if we nosed over in landing—there would be four of us at least. Johnny continues to stand by now. He suggested softening the tyres to keep them up in the sand. It never occurred to me, but having taken them down to about twelve pounds each, I felt much better.

We took off three minutes behind schedule. The fog was almost gone. We circled once, checked safety harness and slipped down between the trees. The soft tyres stayed on top of the sand much better and the sun was drying things out.

The meeting of the three musketeers was jubilant. They set to work clearing débris from the playa while I got the plane into position for take-off just as I had done last time—same deal: cut over the water, and then up and out.

Trip No. 3 took in their radio and some tools and the first priority boards for the tree house. Running about ten minutes behind schedule, I believe.

The three fellows on the beach located a good tree, close to the open sand and slanted very slightly, in which they started to nail up the ladder and tree house. They hadn't figured on its being an iron wood tree, but that is what it proved to be—a

wood which lives up to its name. Next flights brought in
personal items, a larger radio, more food, and the last boards
and aluminium.

Later Nate recorded:

Now twenty-five minutes behind schedule because I was
spending time in unscheduled committee meetings on the
beach.

Working with safety-belts, plagued by myriads of sweat
bees and tiny gnats, the men managed to nail up the two
platforms on which they were to sleep, with an aluminium
roof overhead. With Nate's fifth flight completed, he headed
for Terminal City, where he called out to the Aucas over the
public-address system: 'Come tomorrow to the Curaray.'
Nate swung briefly back to Palm Beach and called to the
fellows that he had given the message to the Aucas. Then he
flew to Arajuno to sleep.

Next morning, Wednesday, January 4, Jim wrote me a
letter:

Just worked up a sweat on the hand crank of the radio. Nobody
is reading us but we read all the morning contacts clearly. We
had a good night with a coffee-and-sandwich break at 2 am.
Didn't set a watch last night, as we really feel cosy and secure
thirty-five feet off the ground in our little bunks. The beach is
good for landings, but too soft for take-offs. We have these
three alternatives: (1) wait for the sun to harden it up and sit
until a stiff breeze makes a take-off possible; (2) go make a
strip in Terminal City; (3) walk out. We saw puma [jungle
lion] tracks on the sand and heard them last night. It is a
beautiful jungle, open and full of palms. Much hotter than
Shandia. Sweated with just a net over me last night. Our hopes
are up, but no signs of the 'neighbours' yet. Perhaps today is
the day the Aucas will be reached. It was a fight getting this
hut up, but it is sure worth it to be up off the ground. We're
going down now. Pistols, gifts, novelties, and prayer in our
hearts. All for now...

Ed wrote to Marilou:

Dearest Baby:

It is 1.00 pm and we've just finished dinner and Nate is taking off to see if he can spot the boys. We are waiting for them to show up. Meals are fine and plentiful. I'll send some dirty clothes back with Nate this evening. Bugs are bad. Here's a list of things we need:

1. Two air mattresses — we are sending plastic ones back.
2. The pricker for gasoline pressure stove.
3. Three *shigras* [Indian carrying-nets] to hang up in our tree house to put stuff in.
4. 1 empty milk can to put candy in.
5. Alcohol for pressure stove.
6. My sun glasses.
7. Insect repellant.
8. More milk and lemonade.
9. Old scraps of meat for fish bait.

I love you very much. Give my love to the boys.

Ed

Thanks for everything

10. Sun helmet, if around.

On Wednesday morning Nate and Pete took off from Arajuno, flew over Terminal City, and noticed a definite 'thinning out of the crowd' there. This encouraged them to think 'the boys' were on their way to Palm Beach. Landing on the sandstrip at Palm Beach, they found Ed, Roj, and Jim pacing the beach holding out gifts and shouting welcome phrases to the trees. Nate set to work checking the radio and found the transmitter had not functioned because of a loose connection in the microphone. He was relieved to re-establish contact with Marj in Shell Mera. Roj and Nate built a beach house, then went swimming while Ed and Jim 'sacked out' in the tree house.

The afternoon drowsed by, and as the tropical sun began to slide down behind the great forest trees, Nate once more elbowed the little plane out of the river valley, and he and

Pete headed for Arajuno to spend another night. 'Thank God for the unusually evident blessing we have seen yesterday and today,' Nate wrote in his diary. 'Thank God for a good team, and forbid that any man should fail to praise HIM.'

Again on Thursday, January 5, Nate, with a driving sense of urgency, was writing of events as they happened. His account of the day's events, in that last week, was scrawled in pencil in a schoolboy's notebook (there was no typewriter on Palm Beach):

All's quiet at Palm Beach. However, we feel sure we are being watched. On the way in this morning Pete and I flew over Terminal City; two women and two children at Old Man's house. Airplane house is deserted. Probably women and children have gone up to big house. Big house showed five or six women, several children and possibly one old man.

While letting down for Palm Beach we checked about a mile of playas below camp site. Saw several tracks, probably of tapir and other smaller stuff. On way up to camp site we were down in river bed thinking to salute the fellows and pull up and around to land when, just one bend below camp, we sighted footprints. We pulled up and doubled back for another look. They were unmistakable. We buzzed on up past camp, saluted, pulled up and around checking the two playas above camp (no soap) and landed. News of the footprints livened up the party considerably.

Everyone had had a good night's sleep in the tree house. At 9 pm strong wind swayed trees and made such sounds that woke up the three men. But all three were soon asleep again. They had a lighted lantern up there to keep the target well lit. At 5 am they shone the flashlight down on the playa to check a gift machete left the night before. It was gone! For the next fifteen minutes the jungles rang with Auca phrases—perhaps with a Mid-Western accent. They then shone the light for a closer look. A big leaf had fallen on the knife so as to hide it. Tough!

As Pete and I pulled in here Jim was out in the river fishing almost in Auca uniform. Modesty seems a small consideration after seeing the dress of our "neighbours". If our dress is any criterion we're giving them everything. Pete's long-sleeved shirt, pants, and straw hat make him look like a beachcomber. Flies keep the rest of us pretty well clad in tee-shirts, pants, and tennis shoes. Jim sits in the smoke from the fire when not fishing or standing in the middle of the river 'preaching' out of his notebook of phrases.

Except for forty-seven billion flying insects of every sort, this place is a little paradise. With the help of smoke and repellant we are all enjoying the experience immensely. A little while ago Jim pulled in a fifteen-inch catfish. It is roasting over the fire now. Ed and Roj are up at the bend clearing a bad group of trees out of the approach. It's pretty close dropping down through there—will be much better now.

Pete is stirring. Getting interested in lunch. Just emptied a plastic bag of prepared raw vegetables into a pressure cooker already partly filled with meat chunks. He's gone up to the tree house now for salt.

The "armour" Roj made (breast and tummy plate) out of a gas drum worked very well for a stove. While getting steam up on the stew we tossed termite nests on the fire to chase the gnats like the Indians do. By the time the three musketeers got back the stew was done and everyone was ready to test it. It went down easily, flushed along by generous quantities of lukewarm lemonade.

Ever since Pete and I landed and reported the human footprints among the tapir and others, we were the objects of boisterous ridicule. However, curiosity brought on the acid test, and Jim and Roj started downstream, wading and running the beaches to check up at close range. We agreed that if they didn't show up in an hour, we'd look for them from the air. Fifty minutes later we saw them coming. I waded out to meet them and get the word—"Tapir," they called. Then at closer range—"Aucas—at least thirty of them." Characters! Sure enough, there were footprints—an adult, a youngster, perhaps twelve years old, and a little tot, but the prints were maybe a week old. The mud they were stamped in was cracked from drying. Sixty miles per hour or so, we had sure enough distinguished the prints from the many animal tracks.

Among other tracks there were alligator, puma, tapir, etc. we also saw some good-sized ducks. Someone said, 'Too bad they're out of season.' (We banned firing guns for fear of frightening the Indians.)

When someone noted with humour that although in Ecuador, we weren't speaking any Spanish the response was, "No one else around here does either."

We had all discovered the benefits of lolling in the shallow water nine-tenths submerged, and since I had just finished with the 2 pm contact, I shed my clothes and raced the gnats to the water, taking the sun helmet along. The fellows thought it a regal sight—nothing but a helmet and two bare feet sticking out of the water, so they dug out a couple of cameras. We enhanced some of the shots by adding *Time* magazine to the "hydraulic siesta".

Jim then started reading us a novel. We roared over even remotely funny suggestions and finally skipped to the end to see who married whom and set it aside in favour of some readings from *Time* magazine. One indulgent description really rolled us—"He looked like a tenement Tom starting his ninth life in the garbage can circuit."

At 3 pm I went aloft and circled up to 6,000 feet, where I could see the Auca clearing and Palm Beach at the same time. And then I glided down slowly, pausing now and then to circle tightly at full throttle so that anyone could hear me and judge the direction from the sound. As I approached to land I thought I saw fresh human tracks just two bends upstream from camp. They were among old tapir tracks—couldn't arouse any enthusiasm over it at camp. I was about fresh out of enthusiasm too—for everything.

By 4.30 everyone felt that the Aucas had not yet found our location. Yet everyone was determined to "sweat it out" till they should locate us and show themselves. One thing sure is that if *we* are fagged just waiting on the beach—the Aucas are really going to lose their zip by the time they locate us after tramping two or three days through the jungle. Pete and I were ready to take off for Arajuno at 4.45. The air was dead. We left all unnecessary weight behind. As we started slogging down through the soft sand on the take-off run we weren't doing at all well. At about the half-way point I cut the throttle and we stopped in about thirty yards. It looked like Pete might help guard the tree house for the night, but we ploughed back to take-off position for one more try. Roj talked us into shutting the engine off and pushing the plane by hand just as far back as we possibly could. The tail wheel was just a few feet from the water! Then Jim went down to the wind sock to give signals and with Ed and Roj pushing the wing-struts we started out. This time we made it okay and made a bee-line for Terminal City. We circled the main house twice, repeating the words "Curaray Apa" (River).

Engine skipped a beat over Terminal City (spark-plug trouble). A man was on the platform kneeling towards the direction of the camp site and pointing with both hands. This really gave us a boost. We hurried back and glided down over camp shouting the news. They signalled okay and we hit for home. At Arajuno we circled a couple of times, shouting a welcome to "anyone" who might be in the bush, then landed. After landing, Pete and I walked the airstrip with a gift machete—no soap.

We find we have a friendlier feeling for these fellows all the time. We must not let that lead us to carelessness. It is no small thing to try to bridge between twentieth century and the Stone Age. God help us to take care.

Everyone is in bed and asleep here now. So it is left to me to go down the path and shut off the diesel. My little blank revolver is a welcome companion on such a venture. But safety is of the Lord. May we see "them" soon. Nite.

— 17 —

Success on Friday

ABOUT ELEVEN O'CLOCK Friday morning, January 6, Nate and Pete sat in the small cooking shelter they had built on the sand. Ed was at the upper end of the beach, Roj in the centre, Jim at the lower end, continuing their verbal bombardments of the jungle. At 11.15 their hearts jumped when a clear masculine voice boomed out from across the river answering Ed's call. Immediately three Aucas stepped out into the open. They were a young man and two women—one about thirty years of age, the other a girl of about sixteen—naked except for strings tied about the waist, wrists, and thighs, and large wooden plugs in distended ear-lobes. the missionaries, temporarily struck dumb by the surprise appearance, finally managed to shout simultaneously, in Auca: *'Puinani . . .* Welcome!'

The Auca man replied with a verbal flood, pointing frequently to the girl. His language was unintelligible, but his gestures were plain. 'He's offering her for trade,' exclaimed Pete, 'or maybe as a gift.'

When it seemed that the Aucas wanted someone to come across, Jim peeled to his shorts and began wading over to them. The others cautioned him to go slow. Jim hesitated and the Aucas were slightly hesitant, but as Jim gradually approached, the girl edged towards the water and stepped off a log. The man and the other woman followed shortly. Jim seized their hands and led them across.

With broad smiles, many *'puinanis'* and much reference to their phrase-books, the five conveyed the idea that their visitors had 'come well' and need not be afraid. The Aucas' uneasiness fell from them, and they began jabbering happily to themselves and to the men, 'seemingly with little idea that we didn't understand them'.

Roj brought out some paring knives, which they accepted with cries of delight. Nate presented them with a machete and model airplane. The others, suddenly remembering the guns in the cook-shack and treehouse, went back to hide the weapons beneath their duffel. They dug out cameras and shot dozens of photos, while the women looked through a copy of *Time* magazine, and the man was being doused with insecticide to demonstrate civilisation's way of dealing with the swarming pests. The group spontaneously began referring to him as 'George'.

Presently the girl — the men called her 'Delilah' — drifted over towards the Piper, rubbing her body against the fabric, and imitating with her hands the plane's movement. She seemed 'dreamy', wrote Pete, 'while the man was natural and self-possessed, completely unafraid. They showed neither fear nor comprehension of the cameras.'

Pete continued:

Soon the fellow began to show interest in the plane and we guessed from his talk that he was willing to fly over the village to call his comrades. We put a shirt on him (it's cold up high), and he climbed into the plane with no sign of any emotion except eagerness to do his part. He acted out how he was going to call and repeated the words. Nate taxied down the strip and took off while 'George' shouted all the way. After circling and shouting briefly Nate landed again, thinking to give the fellow a rest before making the flight to his village. Nothing doing! He was ready to go right then.

Up they went again, this time to circle Terminal City. What must have been the thoughts of that primitive man as he peered down at the tree-tops and at the green sea below him, and suddenly recognised a familiar clearing, with familiar figures in it? 'George' chortled with delight, and leaned out to wave and yell at his fellow villagers. 'The woman at the Old Man's house,' wrote Nate '— her jaw dropped on seeing "George" . . . expression of delight on the face of the young man on the platform.'

Back on the sand strip, 'George' leaped out, clapping his hands. The five men immediately gave thanks to God, with heads up to try to show their visitors that they were addressing their Heavenly Father. As Ezekiel said, 'The Word was in my bones as a living fire,' and for these men the drive to deliver to the Aucas the message of redemption through the blood of Jesus was blocked only by the language barrier. If only they might suddenly leap over the barrier and convey to the Indians one hint of the love of God!

The missionaries demonstrated for their guests such modern marvels as rubber bands, balloons, and a yo-yo; served them lemonade and hamburgers with mustard, which they evidently enjoyed. Then they tried to get across the idea that an invitation to visit the Auca village would not be scorned. For this notion 'George' displayed no enthusiasm.

'Why is it he's so reluctant whenever we broach the subject?' one of the five demanded.

Another replied: 'Maybe he lacks the authority to invite us on his own.'

Nate wrote:

At 4.15 we decide to fly again. "George" decides to go along. We say 'no'. He puts his machete and envelope of valuables in the plane and looks at Pete as though he had already said it was okay and climbs in. On the way over we finally get Marj on the radio. Great rejoicing.

Back on Palm Beach we held a strategy meeting; talked of going over to Auca houses if a delegation of, say, six Aucas

arrive and seem happy to escort us. After that, every effort
would be bent towards building an airstrip in their valley. The
fellows tried to explain to "George" how an airstrip should be
cleared in his village.

At first he did not understand their word for trees. When
he finally got it, he corrected their pronunciation. They
stuck sticks in the sand to represent trees; then, with one of
the model planes, Nate showed 'George' how the airplane
would crash and tumble among the trees. With the model
lying on its back among the sticks in the sand, the fellows
all shook their heads and moaned in evident distress. The
scene was then re-enacted, only this time the fellows took
machetes and cut down all the trees (sticks) and smoothed
the sand carefully. The model airplane approached for a
smooth landing, accompanied by great rejoicing.

As the day wore on, 'Delilah' showed signs of impatience.
Once when Jim Elliot left the group to climb up to the tree
house, she leaped up and followed. When he then turned
and rejoined the others she seemed downcast.

Later, as Nate and Pete got ready to return to Arajuno,
'George' seemed to understand that he could not accompany
them. Before the airplane took off the fellows carefully
gathered all of the exposed film and everything that had
been written to fly it out for safe keeping. If something
unforeseen should happen, they did not want the record
lost.

When the Aucas indicated that they might spend the
night on the beach, the three musketeers hospitably offered
them the small shack they had been using for cooking,
motioning that it was theirs to occupy if they wished.
'Delilah', however, had other ideas. She wheeled and walked
off down the beach. 'George' called to her, but she kept
going. He followed her into the forest. The older woman
stayed by the fire 'talking a blue streak with Roj'. She stayed
on the beach most of the night. The next morning when Jim
come down to start the fire, he found her gone, but the

embers from her fire were still red.

The events of the next day, Saturday, January 7, were anticlimactic. The men waited hopefully, expecting the Aucas to arrive momentarily with an invitaton to their village. But no one came. Around noon Jim looked at his watch.

'Okay, boys,' he said. 'I give them five minutes. If they don't show up, I'm going over!' Wisdom prevented him from carrying out his threat, but he did go back into the forest on a rudimentary trail he had discovered behind the tree house, hoping to find some trace of them. He found the forest floor remarkably open, and abounding in animal trails, but no human footprints.

Nate and Pete then flew over Terminal City and were disheartened to find some signs of fear. On the first trip all of the women and children ran to hide. A few men in sight seemed relieved to hear Nate call 'Come, come, come!' He threw them a blanket and a pair of shorts to reassure them.

On the second flight 'George' appeared with a group of men. One old man pointed towards Palm Beach, and 'seemed friendly but not exuberant'. The third trip showed that fear had vanished. Nate reported: 'I got some good smiles from 'George' and another young man who, one can imagine, probably aspires to ride in the plane.'

Ed wrote a note to Marilou that afternoon:

Dearest Baby:

It's 4.30 and no sign of our visitors yet but we believe they'll arrive, if not tonight, then early tomorrow. Thanks for the clothes and food again. We are eating well. This has been a well-fed operation from start to end.

We feel now that we ought to press going over there and get the airstrip in as fast as possible—but we'll have to wait and see how God leads us, and them, too. Looks like Pete will be there to help you tomorrow morning. Give Stevie and Mikey my love and tell them I'll see them soon, and Carmela too. All for now. All of my love.

Ed.

Tossing on his bunk that night at Arajuno Nate wondered if everything possible had been done to interest the visitors and encourage them to return with their friends. Why had they been so casual? They seemed almost *bored* at times as he looked back on it. Jim's explanation had reassured him.

'That's Indian. If you landed him on the moon, he'd be satisfied in five minutes.'

As they climbed into the Piper on Sunday morning, Pete called: 'So long, girls. Pray. I believe today's the day.'

At Palm Beach the fellows enjoyed the ice-cream and warm blueberry muffins, fresh from the oven, Marilou had sent along. All then agreed on a visit to Terminal City. This time Nate went alone. Circling over Terminal City, he found only a handful of women and children. This sent his spirits soaring. Undoubtedly the men were at last on their way to the Curaray! And, sure enough, on the flight back he spotted a group of men 'en route' to Palm Beach. As he touched his wheels down he shouted to the four, 'This is it, guys! They're on the way!'

A contact with Marj in Shell Mera had been arranged for twelve-thirty. Breathlessly and still using their code words, Nate told of spotting 'a commission of ten' on the way from Terminal City, adding 'Looks like they'll be here for the early afternoon service. Pray for us. This *is* the day! Will contact you next at four-thirty.'

– 18 –

Silence

AT FOUR-THIRTY SHARP Marj Saint eagerly switched on the radio receiver in Shell Mera. This was the moment when the big news would come. Had the men been invited to follow the Aucas to their houses? What further developments would Nate be able to report?

She looked at her watch again. Yes, it was at least four-thirty. No sound from Palm Beach. She and Olive hunched close to the radio. The atmosphere was not giving any interference. Perhaps Nate's watch had run a little slow.

In Arajuno, Marilou and Barbara had their radio on, too. Silence. They waited a few minutes, then called Shell Mera.

'Arajuno calling Shell Mera. Arajuno standing by for Shell Mera. Any word from Palm Beach, Marj? Over.'

'Shell Mera standing by. No, no word as yet. We'll be standing by.'

Not a crackle broke the silence.

Were the men so preoccupied with entertaining their visitors that they had forgotten the planned contact? Five minutes . . . ten minutes . . . . No, it was inconceivable that all five would forget. It was the first time since Nate had started jungle flying in 1948 that he and Marj had been out of contact even for an hour.

But — perhaps their radio was not functioning. It happened occasionally. The women clung to each little hope, refusing to entertain the thought of anything really having gone wrong. Their suspense was the sharper because most of their missionary friends on the network were unaware that Operation Auca was in progress. In Arajuno, Barbara and little Beth Youderian had prinked up a bit, since it had been planned that Roj would come to Arajuno that night, while Pete took a turn sleeping in the tree house. Surely the little plane would come winging over the tree-tops before sundown. They walked up and down the airstrip, waiting . . .

Just after sundown Art Johnston, one of the doctors with Hospital Vozandes, affiliated with the missionary radio station HCJB in Quito, came into the radio room in Shell Mera. The radio was still on, but Marj sat with her head down on the desk.

'Is something the matter, Marj?'

She told him the situation briefly, but asked that he not divulge it yet. If nothing serious had actually happened, it would be disastrous to publicise what was taking place. There was little sleep that night for any of the wives.

By seven o'clock on the morning of Monday, January 9, 1956, Johnny Keenan, Nate's colleague in the MAF, was in the air flying towards the sandstrip which Nate had earlier pointed out to him. As he flew, Marj called me in Shandia: 'We haven't heard from the fellows since yesterday noon. Would you stand by at ten o'clock for Johnny's report?'

It was the first I knew that anything was amiss. A verse God had impressed on my mind when I first arrived in Ecuador came back suddenly and sharply: 'When thou passest through the waters, I will be with thee, and through the rivers, they shall not overflow thee. . . .' I went upstairs to continue teaching the Indian girls' literacy class, praying silently, 'Lord, let not the waters overflow.'

At about nine-thirty Johnny's report came through. Marj relayed it to me in Shandia:

'Johnny has found the plane on the beach. All the fabric is stripped off. There is no sign of the fellows.'

In Shell Mera, a pilot of the Summer Institute of Linguistics, Larry Montgomery (who is also a reserve officer in the USAF), lost no time in contacting Lieutenant General William K. Harrison, Commander-in-Chief of the Caribbean Command, which included the United States Air Rescue Service in Panama. Radio station HCJB was also informed and news flashed around the world: 'FIVE MEN MISSING IN AUCA TERRITORY.' By noon, all possible forces which might contribute to their rescue, including the prayers of thousands of people in all parts of the world, were set in motion.

Barbara and Marilou were flown from Arajuno to Shell Mera. They felt confident that there would be some survivors, and so left a note on the door of the house in Arajuno, stating where medicine and food could be found. What if one of them should stagger home wounded, or if all of them arrived back after a gruelling trip in the jungle? Marilou decided that she must return, to be there to help them. Late Monday afternoon she was flown home again, where she was to remain three more days. On Monday evening it was decided that a ground search party should be organised, on the assumption that one or more of the men still lived, and Frank Drown, Roger Youderian's colleague, a man with twelve years of jungle experience among the Jivaros, was unanimously elected to lead the party. Dr. Art Johnston offered to go along in his capacity as physician. Thirteen Ecuadorian soldiers promptly volunteered.

The news 'put me in a cold sweat,' said Frank, 'but I asked my wife Marie if she minded if I went.' 'Of course you must go,' was her reply, and Frank accepted without hesitation.

On Tuesday morning I was flown out of Shandia with Nate's sister Rachel, who had been with me while the men went on the Auca trip. Frank was brought out from Macuma, and many of the missionary men arrived in Shell Mera from Quito, some as volunteers to go on the ground party. Word was received via short wave that a helicopter was on its way from Panama, which lifted the spirits in Shell Mera. That night the pilot of an Ecuadorian airliner came to the house to tell the wives that he had flown over the scene at about six o'clock in the evening, and saw, a short distance upstream, a large fire, 'without any smoke', which would indicate perhaps a gasoline fire or a signal flare. Nate always carried signal flares in his emergency kit. This was a ray of hope for the five wives to sleep on that night.

On Wednesday Johnny Keenan took off again in MAF's second Piper Cruiser, a twin to Nate's plane, on his fourth flight over Palm Beach to see if there were any signs of life. Marj, who had hardly left the radio since Sunday afternoon, stood by for his reports. Barbara, Olive, and I were upstairs. Suddenly, Marj called: 'Betty! Barbara! Olive!'

I raced down the stairs. Marj was standing with her head against the radio, her eyes closed. After a while she spoke: 'They found one body.'

A quarter mile down-river from the little denuded plane Johnny had sighted a body, floating face-down in the water, dressed in khaki pants and white tee-shirt, the usual uniform of the men. Barbara felt it was not Roger; he had been wearing blue jeans.

Some of the land party went over to Arajuno to prepare the airstrip for the big planes which would be arriving soon from Panama. Late on Wednesday afternoon the roar of the planes was heard, and far on the western horizon where the volcano Sangay stands, a smoking pyramid, the great planes were silhouetted. As they drew near and circled the strip, the red, white, and blue of the United States Air Force became visible.

During the day the remaining volunteers who made up the ground party were transported to Arajuno where Indians, soldiers, and others of the missionaries were milling around the airstrip, waiting to start. In spite of the strain she was under, Marilou remained her efficient self; she had a meal ready for all the men before they headed down-river. There was some difficulty in securing Quichua carriers; they had long lived too close for comfort to the Aucas and did not want to get any closer. However, their loyalty to the men who had worked among them overcame their hesitancy, and about ten-thirty the party was ready to move off on foot, guns handy, eyes sharp.

Dee Short, a missionary from western Ecuador, who happened to be in Quito when news of the disaster arrived, had come to Arajuno. As the party left, Marilou turned to him and said with finality: 'There is no hope. All the men are dead.' Probably most of the ground party would have agreed with her but, nevertheless, every time they rounded a bend of the river they looked expectantly for one or more of the missing men.

Back in Shell Mera the radio crackled again. Marj answered: 'Shell Mera standing by.'

Johnny Keenan reported: 'Another body sighted, about 200 feet below Palm Beach.'

And once again, God, who had promised grace to help in time of need, was true to His word. None of us wives knew which two these bodies might prove to be but we did know 'in Whom we had believed'. His grace was sufficient.

At about four o'clock in the afternoon the ground party reached Oglan, an Indian settlement situated at the place where the Oglan River meets the Curaray. Here camp was set up for the night. Frank Drown organised the group, appointing one man to hire canoes, one in charge of cargo, one to plan seating in the canoes, one as mess chief, two for safety precautions. That night they slept on beds of banana leaves. Watches were kept all night.

Before the party set off on Thursday morning, the missionaries offered up prayer, committing themselves into the hands of God; and the Ecuadorian soldiers, of a different faith, prayed with them. The party moved cautiously down the Curaray; the river was at its lowest, making navigation difficult, and special care was exercised in rounding the many bends, for it was feared Aucas might be lying in wait.

At about ten o'clock Johnny Keenan again flew over the

ground party in the Piper, and Frank Drown was able to make contact with him by means of a two-way radio which the Air Rescue Service had supplied. Johnny told them of two canoes of Quichuas, proceeding up-river in the direction of the ground party; he feared that in their excitement some one of the men in the party might shoot at the first sight of an Indian on the river. Soon the two canoes of Quichuas appeared. They were a small group of Indians from McCully's station at Arajuno. On their own initiative they had boldly pressed into Auca territory ahead of anyone else, and had gone all the way to Palm Beach. The ground party was saddened when one of the Indians, a believer who had come to know Christ since Ed had gone to Arajuno, told them of having found Ed's body on the beach at the edge of the water. He had Ed's watch with him.

Now the missionaries knew who one of their fallen colleagues was, but a chance remained that at least three others had survived. They pressed on.

In the big house at Shell Mera, children played, babies were fed and bathed, the members of the Rescue Service came and went, Marj maintained contact on the short wave, meals were somehow cooked and served, visitors greeted and informed of the latest word, and prayer went up to God continually. The mechanics were making the final adjustment on the blades of the Army helicopter which had been dismantled and shipped from Panama in an Air Force cargo plane.

My diary recounts the events of Thursday afternoon, as the helicopter was dispatched to Palm Beach:

2.00. Johnny's Piper and helicopter headed for Arajuno. Also Navy R-4D, Captain McGee and Major Nurnberg in helicopter.

3.00. The aircraft are stacking up over the site of the incident now. I feel sick at my stomach.

3.20. "Blessed is she that believed...." The aircraft are circling the site.

3.30. "Yea, in the way of Thy judgment, O Lord, have we waited for Thee. The desire of our soul is to Thy name."

4.00. Still circling. "Hope thou in God, for I shall yet praise Him. . . ."

As the wives hoped and prayed and waited the procession of flying machines moved slowly down towards Palm Beach, the airplanes circling to keep pace with the slower helicopter skimming along at tree-top level and following the bends of the river. The airplanes chose different altitudes to avoid danger of collision as pilots circled with eyes on the jungle below. Johnny Keenan in the little yellow Piper was lowest. A few hundred feet above were the US Navy R-4D (the Navy version of the familiar DC-3), and, higher, the big amphibian of the Air Rescue Service. Close by, Colonel Izurieta in a plane of the Ecuadorian Air Force flew in wider circles ready to help should decisions be needed. The teamwork of the United States Army, Air Force, and Navy and of the government and military services of Ecuador was heartwarming to the wives.

Air Force Major Nurnberg, riding in the Army helicopter, landed briefly to talk with the ground party, still some distance up the river from Palm Beach. Ed McCully's name was mentioned guardedly on the radio. Those hearing guessed that somehow Ed's body had been identified. Was his one of the two bodies that had been seen from the air? Had three perhaps escaped into the jungle? Or been taken captive?

After a few moments the helicopter moved on. Finally, rounding a bend, it came at last to Palm Beach and landed. Nurnberg, carbine at the ready, jumped out and looked around. Anxious minutes went by. Back in the 'chopper' he radioed; 'No one here.' Hope flickered brighter in those who heard.

The helicopter was off again and started slowly down the river. Crossing to the other side it stopped, hovering, the force of its downwash disturbing the muddy surface of the water. Minutes later it moved on, only to stop again two hundred yards farther on. A third and a fourth time Nurnberg and McGee hung motionless ten feet above the water, rotor blades beating dangerously close to overhanging jungle trees. Hearts sank in the aircraft above as those watching guessed the meaning of those stops.

The aircraft returned to Arajuno. Once on the ground, Nurnberg, his face showing strain, confirmed suspicions. Speaking in low tones to the tight circle of military men, he explained that McCully's body, identified by the small party of Quichuas the day before, was now gone from the beach, no doubt washed away by the rain and higher water in the night. He leafed through his notebook for a moment. A few Indians stood silent in the tall grass near by, listening and watching. 'We found four in the river,' Nurnberg said, finally. 'I don't think identification will be possible from what I have here'— indicating his notebook. 'One of them may be McCully.'

He did not have to say what was in every mind. There might be one who got away, possibly wounded, still in the jungle.

How to inform the wives was the question uppermost in military minds. Should Marilou be told? She was right there at Arajuno, in the house.

'We'd better wait,' Nurnberg said. 'DeWitt is running this show. Let's get back to Shell and talk it over.' Captain DeWitt in the big Air Force amphibian was overheard, not wanting to risk a landing on the small strip at Arajuno. All returned to Shell and the military men gathered in the cabin of the amphibian. The wives would have to be told. But how?

Someone else had wisely decided to tell Marilou that four bodies had been found. Later in the afternoon Johnny flew her out to Shell to be with the four other wives.

In the end it was the wives who persuaded DeWitt and Nurnberg that there was no need to soften the blow. We wanted to know everything in detail. We gathered in Marj's bedroom away from the children. Major Nurnberg opened his notebook and in terse sentences described what he had found. It was immediately evident that identification could not be positive. One body was caught under the branches of a fallen tree; only a large foot with a grey sock appeared at the surface of the muddy water. In reading his notes of another, Nurnberg said: 'This one had a red belt of some woven material.' Four of us turned our eyes towards the fifth, Olive Fleming.

'That was Pete,' Olive said simply.

As the Major concluded, it was still not known whether Ed's body was one of those in the river. There was still the hope that one might have got away.

The military men, to whom the breaking of such news to loved ones was no new thing, left the bedroom silently. Their news had been met with serenity. No tears could rise from the depth of trust which supported the wives.

Barbara Youderian wrote in her diary:

Tonight the Captain told us of his finding four bodies in the river. One had tee-shirt and blue-jeans. Roj was the only one who wore them..:. God gave me this verse two days ago, Psalm 48.14, "For this God is our God for ever and ever; He will be our Guide even unto death." As I came face to face with the news of Roj's death, my heart was filled with praise. He was worthy of his home-going. Help me, Lord, to be both mummy and daddy. "To know wisdom and instruction...." Tonight Beth prayed for daddy in Heaven, and asked me if daddy would come down from Heaven to get a letter she wanted to write him. I said, "He can't come down. He's with Jesus." She said, "But Jesus can help him come down, and God will take his hand so he won't slip."

I wrote a letter to the mission family, trying to explain the peace I have. I want to be free of self-pity. It is a tool of Satan to rot away a life. I am sure that this is the perfect will of God. Many will say, "Why did Roj get mixed up in this, when his work was with Jivaros?" Because Roj came to do the will of Him that sent him. The Lord has closed our hearts to grief and hysteria, and filled in with His perfect peace.

That Thursday night the ground party pitched camp at 'El Capricho', the former hacienda where there had been some Auca killings. Throwing up some little leaf shacks, a guard was set up of two missionaries, two soldiers, and two Indians. The missionaries, when not on guard duty with the others, tried to decide the best course of action, knowing, through contact with the helicopter, that four of their colleagues were dead. It was a long night, and Frank Drown felt an old fear that had haunted him all his life of touching the body of a friend: 'Here I was, getting nearer and nearer to seeing the bodies of five fellows who were as dear to me as my own brothers.'

Starting out again at six in the morning of Friday, January 13, the party was on the last lap of its mission, with a date to meet the helicopter at Palm Beach at ten. The men had to hurry to get there and everyone was jittery from the strain of the trip and the thought of the job that lay ahead. At this point the course of the Curaray is a series of short, sharp bends and twists and offers an ideal ambush for an Auca attack.

At last the beach was reached. Quichuas were sent up first, as they were best able to spot evidence of recent Auca visits. There was none. The rest of the party followed. 'I remember,' says Frank Drown, 'that the first thing that struck me as we hit the beach was the smell from a pot of beans that had been overturned and were spread all over. I don't think that I'll ever forget that terrible, rotten smell.'

There was no sign as yet of the helicopter. The ground party set to work, everyone having been assigned different duties: the Ecuadorian soldiers spread out in a semi-circle in the jungle behind the beach to act as cover, two Indians set to digging a common grave under the tree house, others waded into the river looking for the men's possessions. Dee Short and Frank Drown crawled up into the tree house to try to find a clue to what had happened. Some of the men began to dismantle the plane, others looked for bodies. It was not until the helicopter arrived at twelve-fifteen and hovered over the bodies where they lay in the muddy waters of the Curaray, that the ground crew was able to find them. Frank Drown told of the scene:

> First Nurnberg pointed out one body downstream and Fuller jumped into the water and pulled the body across. Then Nurnberg shows us Nate Saint's body, and we got in a canoe and went downstream, and saw an arm coming out of the water, so I tried to attach a string to the arm and I just could not bring myself to do it. I'd reach out and try and then pull back, and have to try again until finally the man who was in the canoe with me did it. Now we were three canoes with three bodies attached to them, going upstream. We laid all four face down in a row on the beach. We never did get the fifth, which was Ed McCully's body. Then I got over my feeling of hating to touch the bodies, because a body is only a house and these fellows had left their house and, after the soul leaves, the body isn't much after all. The thing that is beautiful to us is the soul, not the body.

Identification of the four bodies was finally positive from wedding rings and watches, change purse, notebooks. Ed was not one of the four, so it was finally definite: all five were dead. In the providence of God the missing body was the one identified by the Quichuas the day before. Not only had they brought back his watch, but also they had taken off one of his shoes (a tremendous shoe — size thirteen and one-half) and thrown it up on the beach. The day before, Nurnberg had picked it up and brought it back to Shell Mera.

While the bodies were being drawn ashore a violent tropical storm was gathering. At that moment the helicopter came in low and fast. Cornell Capa, a photographer-correspondent on assignment for *Life* magazine, jumped out, camera in hand, and ran across the beach. Then the full fury of the storm struck and the missionaries felt as if the powers of darkness had been let loose.

Later Capa wrote an account of his landing and of subsequent events:

We floated above the jungle about two hundred feet over the tree-tops. The Naval Mission plane circling overhead did not let us out of their sight. Suddenly the sun disappeared and we headed into a tropical storm. The pilot looked grim and wasted not a minute landing on Palm Beach.

The atmosphere on the beach was fantastic. Everybody's hand was on the trigger, looking towards the jungle. I did not have to ask why. The rain was coming down in buckets; my handkerchief served no more to clean my water-soaked lenses. Suddenly I saw a struggling group of men carrying the last of the missionaries to his common grave. He was on an improvised stretcher, made out of the aluminium sheets that had covered the tree house where the men had lived.

It was a terrible sight. The light was eerie. The pall-bearers struggled against a muddy bank that led to the grave. I just made it in time to see the lifeless legs disappearing into the hole. Grim, weary missionaries looked for the last time at their friends, whom they could no more identify. One said: "It's better this way. I feel less miserable." They lingered for a moment, offering up a few words of prayer. At the end, Major Nurnberg, facing the jungle with carbine in hand, turned back towards the small knot of men about the grave and called: "Let's get out of here!"

The rain let up a bit, the helicopter was ready to leave and the time was near for decision. I could either go back with the pilot or stay with the ground party starting the overnight homeward trek. It was an easy decision. To leave now would be cheating. I gave my exposed film to the pilot. The struggle of the living to stay alive had just begun.

At last, we were off. The canoes were overloaded and at the slightest movement water poured through the side. This was to be no fun at all, I thought quietly to myself. Major Nurnberg was in front with his carbine and I could see from the back of his head that he had a mean look in his eyes. Nurnberg leaned back on Dee Short (a red-headed, *very* long-legged missionary, in a very small boat), who in turn leaned on me, and I leaned on the dismounted wheel of the ill-fated plane which we had salvaged. My back ached. Like a mother hen, I tried to protect my film pouches and to hide my cameras from the rain. It was futile.

Soon my range-finder clouded up. I had to guess the focus. A little later my view-finder fogged up as well. Now I only aimed the camera and prayed—like a missionary—that it was pointed in the right direction.

In and out of the canoe... marching with water squelching out of my boots. Anxious eyes everywhere. I unbuttoned my .45 holster. Fortunately, no sign of Aucas. This lasted for about two hours; then it was time to bed down for the night.

Major Nurnberg, Missionary Drown, and the Ecuadorian under-officer picked an open site for the camp. Their aim was to give us a chance to spot the Aucas before they had a chance to throw their spears. Guards were posted all around the perimeter and changed every two hours. We had a meal, cooked by one of the missionaries. Shelters were erected from the metal sheets we carried, and palm leaves formed the side walls and the floor. It was a temporary paradise.

Missionary Don Johnson, sitting in the darkness of the house, buried his face in his hands, and offered a prayer. He thanked the Lord for helping them to reach and bury their friends. Then, with great feeling, he evoked the modest and loved characters of the departed men. In the darkness of the night, with the firelight flickering on his face, and the sound of jungle birds and pumas' groans punctuating the air, this clearly spoken "conversation" with God was of great emotional impact. Don was not expressing sorrow for the departed so much as testifying to his faith in the Lord's will. When he finished only the crackling of the camp-fire filled the air.

But there was to be no sleep. All through the night we were in a wakeful readiness.

The rushing waters of the River Curaray were always in the background. There was the sound of an occasional tree falling to set off the trigger fingers of the nervous guards. And at intervals came the beams from their flashlights as the guards made their rounds. Slowly dawn came and our nervousness increased, for this was the hour, we had been told, when the Aucas liked to attack. Our Indian guides stirred, particularly when they heard the continuing sounds of a puma. The Aucas are well known for their clever imitation of the jungle animals, and the guides were sure that in the shadows of the early morning light our "neighbours" were everywhere. Major

Nurnberg crawled forward and with a sudden burst of fire silence the "puma".

Breakfast was oatmeal and coffee. Then we collected our gear and the march was on. Dried socks became wet again. Tired feet dragged. The searching eyes and ready fingers of Nurnberg and Drown brought up the rear. Sudden excitement: the "chopper" appeared overhead, always watched by its "Big Brother", the Navy's R-4D. Suddenly the Twentieth Century descended in the wilderness of the jungle. The helicopter had come for me.... As I took off I was sorry to leave my friends, but, no, not sorry to leave.

On Saturday morning Captain DeWitt of the Rescue Service asked us five widows if we would 'care to fly over Palm Beach to see your husbands' grave?'

We replied that if this were not asking too much, we would be grateful. The Navy R-4D took us out over the jungle, where the Curaray lay like a brown snake in the undulating green. Pressing our faces close to the windows as we knelt on the floor of the plane, we could see the slice of white sand where the Piper stood. Olive Fleming recalled the verses that God had impressed on her mind that morning:

"For we know that if our earthly house of this tabernacle were dissolved, we have a building of God, an house not made with hands, eternal in the heavens." *He who has prepared us for this very thing is God....* "Therefore we are always confident, knowing that, whilst we are at home in the body, we are absent from the Lord."

As the plane veered away, Marj Smith said: 'That is the most beautiful little cemetery in the world.'

— 19 —

'Yet Have We Not Forgotten Thee'

TWO DAYS LATER we widows—already we were adjusting ourselves to the use of the word—sat together at the kitchen table in Shell Mera. Dr. Art Johnston was describing the finding of the bodies. He had just returned with the weary, straggling ground party. When he hesitated, we urged him to give us all the facts.

It was evident that death had been caused by lance wounds. But how had ten Aucas managed to overwhelm five strong men who were armed with guns? Over and over we asked ouselves this question. The only possible answer was an ambush. Somehow, the Aucas must have succeeded in convincing the men of their peaceful intentions. Nate had assured Marj that they would never allow Aucas with spears in their hands to approach them. Perhaps the 'commission of ten' that Nate mentioned on the radio had been a decoy party. Certainly if this party had carried spears Nate would have reported this and the men would not have looked forward so eagerly to their arrival. This group may have walked peacefully on to the beach while a second party, carrying spears, moved up under cover of the jungle foliage to carry out a surprise attack. It seems likely that the missionaries and the unarmed Aucas had been mingling together, as they had on the previous Friday, with friendly words and gestures. And then, at a secret signal. . . .

There was evidence of a struggle on the beach — marks of Ed's leather heels in the sand; one bullet-hole through the windshield of the plane. However, no blood was found. If any Aucas had suffered, it was not apparent. Had the men tried to avoid shooting by backing into the river? A lance was found thrust into the sand in the river bottom near the body of Jim Elliot. The fact that all the bodies were in the water might indicate that they had tried desperately to show the Aucas that they would shoot only as a last resort.

The condition of the Piper showed real malice. Possibly some Auca had punctured the fabric of the plane with a spear, and, finding it vulnerable, had begun to peel it off. Others helped, and soon they had denuded it completely, tossing the strips into the water near by. But someone intended to put this man-carrying bird out of commission once and for all. Some of the framework was bent, and a part of the landing gear, made of tubular steel, was battered in as if by a very heavy object. The propeller and instrument panel, however, were intact. Perhaps to touch the 'soul' of the creature was taboo, but they had torn the stuffings from the seats, as if to disembowel the flying beast.

Why, after the overtures of friendship on Friday, had the Aucas turned with such sudden and destructive anger on their white visitors on Sunday? The answer can only be guessed. Among the most qualified to venture a guess is Frank Drown, whose work with the Jivaros has given him shrewd insight into Indian thinking. He says:

An Indian, when he first hears or sees something new, will accept it. Perhaps he accepts merely from normal curiosity, but he does accept. But after he has had time to think about the novelty he begins to feel threatened, and that is the time when he may attack. A group of Indians will sit back and discuss a new contrivance or a new way of doing things with some eagerness; but the witch-doctors, who are the real conservatives, can be counted on for rejection. They have a lot of authority and, when they work on their fellow tribesmen to reject an innovation, the people seldom go contrary to their advice. As in any culture, the younger men may be looking for a new way of life, but the older ones hang on to their traditions and maintain the *status quo*. Furthermore, most Indians are basically and understandably sceptical of anything the white man offers him. And don't forget that, after all, this was the first time within memory that the Aucas have had an encounter with the white man which was completely friendly. We can only hope they are pondering that fact right now.

In the kitchen we sat quietly as the reports were finished, fingering the watches and wedding rings that had been brought back, trying for the hundredth time to picture the scene. Which of the men watched the others fall? Which of them had time to think of his wife and children? Had one been covering the others in the tree house, and come down in an attempt to save them? Had they suffered long? The answers to these questions remained a mystery. This much we knew: 'Whosoever shall lose his life for my sake and the gospel's, the same shall save it.' There was no question as to the present state of our loved ones. They were 'with Christ'.

And, once more, ancient words from the Book of Books came to mind:

> All this has come upon us, yet have we not forgotten thee. . . . Our heart is not turned back, neither have our steps declined from Thy way, though Thou hast sore broken us in the place of dragons, and covered us with the shadow of death.

The quiet trust of the mothers helped the children to know that this was not a tragedy. This was what God had planned. 'I know my daddy is with Jesus, but I miss him, and I wish he would just come down and play with me once in a while,' said three-year-old Stevie McCully. Several weeks later, back in the States, Stevie's little brother, Matthew, was born. One day the baby was crying and Stevie was heard to say, 'Never you mind; when we get to Heaven

I'll show you which one is *our* daddy.' Was the price too great?

To the world at large this was a sad waste of five young lives. But God has His plan and purpose in all things. There were those whose lives were changed by what happened on Palm Beach. In Brazil, a group of Indians at a mission station deep in the Mato Grosso, upon hearing the news, dropped to their knees and cried out to God for forgiveness for their own lack of concern for fellow Indians who did not know of Jesus Christ. From Rome, an American official wrote to one of the widows: 'I knew your husband. He was to me the ideal of what a Christian should be.' An Air Force Major stationed in England, with many hours of jet flying, immediately began making plans to join the Missionary Aviation Fellowship. A missionary in Africa wrote: 'Our work will never be the same. We knew two of the men. Their lives have left their mark on ours.'

Off the coast of Italy, an American naval officer was involved in an accident at sea. As he floated alone on a raft, he recalled Jim Elliot's words (which he had read in a news report): 'When it comes time to die, make sure that all you have to do is die.' He prayed that he might be saved, knowing that he had more to do than die. He was not ready. God answered his prayer, and he was rescued. In Des Moines, Iowa, an eighteen-year-old boy prayed for a week in his room, then announced to his parents: 'I'm turning my life over completely to the Lord. I want to try to take the place of one of those five.'

Letters poured in to the five widows—from a college in Japan, 'We are praying for you'; from a group of Eskimo children in a Sunday School in Alaska; from a Chinese church in Houston; from a missionary on the Nile River who had picked up *Time* magazine and seen a photograph of her friend, Ed McCully.

Only eternity will measure the number of prayers which ascended for the widows, their children, and the work in which the five men had been engaged. The prayers of the widows themselves are for the Aucas. We look forward to the day when these savages will join us in Christian praise.

Plans were promptly formulated for continuing the work of the martyrs. The station at Arajuno was manned to be ready in case the Aucas should come out for friendly contact. Gift flights were resumed by Johnny Keenan, so that the Aucas would know, beyond any doubt, that the white man had nothing but the friendliest of motives. Revenge? The thought never crossed the mind of one of the wives or other missionaries.

Barbara Youderian returned to her work among the Jivaros, with the two little children, and I went back to Shandia with ten-month-old Valerie to carry on as much as I could of the work of the Quichua station. Another pilot, Hobey Lowrance, with his family and a new plane, were sent to the mission air base in Shell Mera, while Marj Saint took up a new post in Quito. After the birth of her third son in the United States, a few weeks after the death of her husband, Marilou McCully returned to Ecuador with her boys to work in Quito with Marj. For Olive Fleming, who had spent only two months in the jungle when her husband died, the problem regarding the future has been more difficult. But for her, as for all, one thing is certain: her life belongs to God, as had her husband's, and He will show the way.

In the months since the killing of the five men, Nate Saint's sister Rachel has continued with the study of the Auca language, working with the Auca woman, Dayuma. Many flights have been made over the houses of the Aucas. The first group of houses was found to have been burned, a common Auca practice after a killing, but not far away new houses were discovered, and gifts were dropped to the waiting Indians. When Johnny Keenan swoops over, 'George' appears, jumping and waving the little model plane given him by Nate Saint. 'Delilah' also seems to be there with him. Patches of bright yellow fabric from Nate's plane adorn the roofs of some of the houses.

Thousands of people in all parts of the world pray every day that 'the light of the knowledge of the glory of God' may be carried to the Aucas, a people almost totally unheard of before. How can this be done? God, who led the five, will lead others, in His time and way.

From among the Quichuas with whom Jim, Ed, and Pete worked, several have surrendered their lives to God for His use, to preach to their own people — or even to the Aucas, if He chooses. They have carried on the work begun by the missionaries, speaking to their relatives of Christ, reading the Scriptures that have been translated for them, travelling sometimes in canoes and over muddy trails to teach the Bible to others who do not know its message. A converted Indian, formerly a notorious drinker, came to me one day and said, 'Señora, I lie awake at night thinking of my people. "How will I reach them?" I say. "How will they hear of Jesus?" I cannot get to them all. But they *must know*. I pray to God, asking Him to show me what to do.' In the little prayer meetings the Indians never forget to ask God to bless their enemies: 'O God, You know how those Aucas killed our beloved Señor Eduardo, Señor Jaime, and Señor Pedro. O God, You know that it was only because they didn't know You. They didn't know what a great sin it was. They didn't understand why the white men had come. Send some more messengers, and give the Aucas, instead of fierce hearts, soft hearts. Stick their hearts, Lord, as with a lance. They stuck our friends, but You can stick them with Your Word, so that they will listen, and believe.'

For the wives and relatives of the five men, the mute longing of their hearts was echoed by words found in Jim Elliot's diary:

> I walked out to the hill just now. It is exalting, delicious, to stand embraced by the shadows of a friendly tree with the wind tugging at your coat-tail and the heavens hailing your heart, to gaze and glory and give oneself again to God — what more

could a man ask? Oh, the fullness, pleasure, sheer excitement of knowing God on earth! I care not if I never raise my voice again for Him, if only I may love Him, please Him. Mayhap in mercy He shall give me a host of children that I may lead them through the vast star fields to explore His delicacies whose finger-ends set them to burning. But if not, if only I may see Him, touch His garments, and smile into His eyes— ah then, not stars nor children shall matter, only Himself.

O Jesus, Master and Centre and End of all, how long before that Glory is Thine which has so long waited Thee? Now there is no thought of Thee among men; then there shall be thought for nothing else. Now other men are praised; then none shall care for any other's merits. Hasten, hasten, Glory of Heaven, take Thy crown, subdue Thy Kingdom, enthral Thy creatures.

ELISABETH
ELLIOT

SHADOW OF
THE ALMIGHTY

OM
publishing

To Valerie

I think the writings of your father, whom you do not
remember, will one day help you to know him in a way
which my descriptions of him can never do. And I pray that as you
know him, you will learn to love the One he loved, and to follow
Him as faithfully.

CONTENTS

Part Four   Ecuador, 1952–1956

ACKNOWLEDGEMENTS

O NE AFTERNOON about two months before Jim's death I was reading some of his letters and diaries. I turned to him and said, 'I'm glad I have these. I'm going to need them when I write your biography.' He made a remark about the absurdity of some of my ideas, and went on reading his *Time* magazine.

Shortly after his death I began putting together the writings which he left behind. Marilou McCully, Olive Fleming, Barbara Youderian, and Marj Saint have been my friends in the truest sense, and my strong supporters in this task from its very beginning. When they asked me to interrupt the writing of the biography in order to write *Through Gates of Splendour*, I flew to New York, and it was there that Melvin Arnold of Harper & Brothers read the first draft of this book. His encouragement then and his continued editorial advice have been a very great help.

For their help in supplying material on Jim's background and early years, and for their generously allowing me to use all of the letters Jim wrote to them, I am very grateful to Jim's family: his father and mother, the Fred Elliots of Portland; his brothers Bob, also of Portland, and Bert of Yurimaguas, Peru; and his sister Jane Hawthorne of Wheaton, Illinois. I would like to thank also Jim's friends Werner

Durtschi and Wayne McCroskey of Portland for their recollections of Jim's school days; Dick Fisher of Astoria, Oregon, for his vivid descriptions of Jim's early years, and for the use of a letter which Jim wrote to him; Olive Fleming for a letter Jim wrote to her husband Pete; Evelyn Corkum of Seattle for her testimony of Jim's influence on her life during her high school days; Ron Harris for his account of Jim's visit to his home in Mexico; Eleanor Vandevort of the Sudan and Bill Cathers of Ecuador for letters Jim wrote to them; and my brother Dave Howard of Costa Rica for his memories of college days. Sam Saint of New Jersey was kind enough to read the manuscript and give me some valuable suggestions. Mardelle Senseney and Ruth Keenan of Shell Mera, Ecuador, assisted greatly by checking the many Scripture references.

I should like to thank the Dohnavur Fellowship for their permission to quote from the work of Amy Carmichael.

Special thanks are due to Bill and Irene Cathers for assuming virtually all responsibility here on the jungle station so that I could be free to write.

ELISABETH ELLIOT

Shandia, Ecuador
April, 1958

PREFACE

*It is only when we obey God's laws that we can be quite sure that we
really know Him. The man who claims to know God but does not
obey His laws is not only a liar, he lives in self-delusion. In practice,
the more a man learns to obey God's laws, the more truly and fully
does he express his love for Him. Obedience is the test of whether we
really live "in God" or not. The life of a man who professes to be
living in God must bear the stamp of Christ.*[1]

THESE WORDS, written about AD 90 in the first
epistle of John, embody the radicals of Jim Elliot's
life. Obedience leads to knowledge. Obedience is
the expression of love to God. Obedience means that we live
in God. And if we live in Him, our lives bear the stamp of
Christ.

Some who pick up this book may make no claim to know
God. Others may make the claim but be victims of the
self-delusion that John observes. Yet others may know Him,
and obey Him, but wonder sometimes at the value of this
knowledge and this obedience. I think that this book will
have something to say to all three. If those in the first
category *want* to know God, they may perhaps learn how.
Those in the second group may find that they are missing a
great deal by not backing their claims with action. And those

in the third category may be encouraged to pursue their course.

Jim's aim was to know God. His course, obedience—the only course that could lead to the fulfilment of his aim. His end was what some would call an extraordinary death, although in facing death he had quietly pointed out that many have died because of obedience to God.

He and the other men with whom he died were hailed as heroes, 'martyrs'. I do not approve. Nor would they have approved.

Is the distinction between living for Christ and dying for Him, after all, so great? Is not the second the logical conclusion of the first? Furthermore, to live for God *is* to die, 'daily', as the apostle Paul put it. It is to lose everything that we may gain Christ. It is in thus laying down our lives that we find them.

The relationship between man and God is a very practical one. It finds its sphere of operation in the common life. Let us not forget that any relationship whatever between God and man rests today on the fact that *God* lived the life of a common man—was born in a stable, sweated in a carpenter shop, preached from a little fishing-boat, sat down tired beside a well and conversed with a courtesan, ate and drank and walked with ordinary men, and submitted to an ignoble death—in order that we could recognise Him. Nobody called Him a hero or a martyr. He was simply doing what His Father told Him to do, and doing it with *delight*.

Those who want to know Him must walk the same path with Him. *These* are the 'martyrs' in the Scriptural sense of the word, which means simply 'witnesses'. In life, as well as in death, we are called to be 'witnesses'—to 'bear the stamp of Christ'.

I believe that Jim Elliot was one of these. His letters and journals are the tangible ground for my belief. They are not mine to withhold. They are a part of the human story, the story of a man in his relation to the Almighty. They are facts.

'I write like I talk—without thinking much beforehand —and sometimes spiel stuff that were better left in the ink bottle,' Jim wrote to me in 1948. 'I think it was Browning who, having been queried on something he wrote in early life, said, "When I wrote that, two people knew what it meant, God and I. Now only God knows." So with anything perplexing, throw it out, discounted as an abortion sprung from a mind that is at times over-productive to its own hurt.'

Once in 1952 I mentioned to Jim that I had sent an excerpt from one of his letters to a friend. He replied:

> I'm not too excited about your sending my letters to others. I don't like to write a page knowing that perhaps a not-as-sympathetic reader as yourself may scan it. This is a confession that I am not trying to impress you with my letters. I barely reread them, pay little attention to grammar and punctuation, and know that my handwriting has suffered. I guess I will have to trust you to be choosy in sending representations of me to folks whose impression-factors should be delicately censored.

In the task of selection I have not 'delicately censored' anything at all which I felt would contribute to the faithful portrayal of the whole man as I knew him. The reader will notice the repetition of certain ideas throughout his writings. He will also wonder if perhaps in certain chapters I have included only those portions of his writings which indicate the growth of his soul, to the exclusion of those which would show a more 'human' side of his personality. Of both of these—the repetition, the long passages dealing with soul-exercise—I would say this: I have taken pains to let my choices represent the tone of Jim's writings as a whole, so that the number of excerpts on a given subject, or during a given period, are in direct proportion to the total content of the letters and diaries. There were periods when his writing was occupied almost exclusively with the metaphysical. There were others when it dealt with the mundane.

When Jim was twenty years old he prayed, 'Lord, make my way prosperous, not that I achieve high station, but that my life may be an exhibit to the value of knowing God.' His life was that to me, who shared it more intimately than any other. Was it extraordinary? I offer these pages so that the reader may decide for himself. If his answer is yes — if he finds herein the 'stamp of Christ', and decides that this is extraordinary — what shall we say of the state of Christendom?

Notes

1. 1 John 2:3–6, JBP.

PROLOGUE

WHEN JIM was a college student in 1949 he wrote these words:

He is no fool who gives what he cannot keep to gain what he cannot lose.

Seven years later, on a hot Sunday afternoon, far from the dormitory room where those lines were written, he and four other young men were finishing a dinner of baked beans and carrot-sticks. They sat together on a strip of white sand on the Curaray River, deep in Ecuador's rain forest, waiting for the arrival of a group of men whom they loved, but had never met — savage Stone Age killers, known to all the world now as Aucas.

Two days before, the hope of years had been partially fulfilled. Three of these Indians had met them on the beach where they now sat. The first friendly contact, long anticipated and carefully prepared for, had been completely successful. The young man and his two women companions stepped off the jungle green on the other side of the river and, after slight hesitation, accepted the hand of Jim Elliot, who led them across the river to the other white men. At first the naked tribespeople were distrustful and with reason. They had known of white men who flew in great birds similar to that which now stood beside them on the sand, who had proved that they could not be trusted. But somehow they had sensed, throughout the long weeks when these five men had attempted to show them their friendship, that there was no 'catch' here.

The white men had at first dropped gifts to the Aucas, similar to those they had received in other years—machetes, cooking-pots, ribbons, cloth. These things were most welcome, and the Indians began to wait for the sound of that yellow *ayamu* which appeared with regularity (though whether a people who cannot count beyond three would recognise the seven-day rhythm is questionable). When the sound of the motor was heard, they would run from their manioc patches, from inside the great, oval-shaped, leaf-thatched houses, or from downriver where they had been fishing in their dugout canoes. There they were again—those strange, white-faced men, waving and shouting, then lowering a bucket on a rope, from which the Indians could grab all manner of delights. And what was that? Suddenly a voice boomed through the air—in their own language! The man was speaking to them.

'Come! We are your friends. We like you. We are your friends.'

Could it be that they did not intend to take away the Indians' land, to destroy their crops, to kill their people, as others had done? There were some who began to believe. An idea came to them. Why not encourage these men? Would it not be worth while to find out what their true intentions were? Might there not be greater gains for the Indians if they played along with the strangers?

The following week they returned the airborne gift. A beautiful feather crown, carefully woven, with a palm-splinter facing, was placed in the basket which was slowly circling at their feet. Later an extraordinarily enterprising Auca made a little model plane, as much like the Piper Family Cruiser as he could make it, and set it up on the roof of his house. Had he been secretly spying on the house in Arajuno, which was the base of operations, where a model plane had been hung on a pole for just such an inspection? Or was it entirely his own idea to construct a model?

When the plane circled over one day, the Aucas heard one

of the men call, 'We are on the Curaray. Come. Come and see us.' This was too much for some of them. Still torn by doubts and long-held fears of these white men, they hesitated two days—possibly spying out the situation from the thick growth of jungle into which they know how to vanish as effectively as the dappled ocelot of their forest. But on the third day their curiosity—or who can say what motives—overcame their fears, and, answering the calls of the five men who strode up and down the beach, three young Indians made their appearance.

Who were these white men? Brothers of the monkey that swung in the vines, with their hairy faces and arms? Brothers of the armadillo who wears what must be an uncomfortable covering and never walks naked? Sons, perhaps, of the Sun-Maker, since they came from the skies? Yet they laughed, they spoke words which the Indians could understand, they offered gifts of food. Food, was it? It must be—it tasted good, though totally different from anything they knew (hamburgers, bread, lemonade, mustard; these could hardly be compared to the dry, heavy manioc root, tapir meat, and peanuts which formed part of their diet).

And that wonderful water! One of the men poured some into an Indian's hand (they called him 'George' among themselves), and when he rubbed it on his body the flies as if by magic stopped their biting.

The white men were constantly making strange marks with a black-tipped stick on a smooth white leaf. Then they would look hard at those marks, and speak the words the Indians had spoken. But to one another they made weird sounds—not words, surely? Yes, they must be words—they seemed to understand one another, to be talking. But it was not 'hearable'. And why did they not answer the Indians when they spoke to them?

The young girl discovered that the surface of the great *ayamu* was smooth. It was like—but it was not like anything she knew. How would she describe it to the others when she got home? Like a plantain leaf? But then, that is not broad and resistant. She rubbed her body against it ecstatically.

And just how did that creature fly? 'George' had to know. He peered into its crop, then into its belly. Those wings wouldn't flap. How did it work? Gesticulating and jabbering, he convinced the pilot that he was not afraid, that he wanted to fly. Up, up over the trees with a frightening roar they rose. How strange the world looked to his near-sighted eyes—for the forest Indian knows nothing of wide spaces, distant horizons. He knows only the brown mud at his feet, the height of a tree, the short reach of a river as far as the next curve. Perhaps he has climbed a tree and looked out over the greenness in search of the smoke which tells him of a house, but he has seen nothing like this which spread out beneath 'George' now.

Suddenly his eyes focused on a change in the scene below— people, tiny people, were running about. They looked the same size as the white men looked before, when they flew over his head. Yes, they must be *his* people. The plane circled lower. Ah, yes—there was his brother, his father, his old grandmother. He shouted wildly and they watched with astonishment. Now the plane circled up higher again. He was so overcome with glee that he shouted all the way back to the beach, where the white sand suddenly spread out huge and bright and rose to meet the plane. With a teeth-chattering grinding they bounced along the ground, and the trees finally stood still. There were the two women again. How describe to them what he had seen?

Late in the afternoon the young girl decided it was time to leave these strange people, who seemed to have no desire for her. She ran down the sand strip. 'George' called after her, but no, she was resolute. At last, as she disappeared into the forest, he followed. Later the older woman joined them, and they raced over the steep hills and through the mud to their village, breathless to tell of their experiences. But there were old matted heads of black hair back in the shadows which silently shook as they heard the tale. Between those cylinders of balsa stuck in their ear-lobes, dark plans were taking shape.

Back at the beach on the Curaray, the five men waited eagerly the next day for the return of their friends. Pacing the beach as before, they shouted the few phrases they had learned of the Auca language, phrases elicited from an escaped member of the tribe who lived on an hacienda near one of the mission stations. But their calls were answered only by the stillness of the virgin jungle on both sides of the winding river. Once a tree fell, alerting them all to tense expectancy. Nothing happened. Finally Jim Elliot looked at his watch.

'Okay, boys—I give them five minutes. If they don't show up, I'm going over!'

Wisdom prevented his carrying out this threat, but the long afternoon brought no reward for their vigil.

The 'neighbours' were apparently in conference—should they return and invite the white men to their village? Who should go? They could not know with what eagerness and longing they were awaited.

Sunday morning dawned clear. Again God had answered prayer. The river had not risen to obliterate the little landing-strip, and the skies were good for flying. Nate, the pilot, took off. After circling the Indian village, he spotted about ten Aucas making their way along the beach in the direction of the four foreigners.

'This is it, guys!' he shouted as the Piper bounced on to the beach. 'They're on their way!'

Nate's wife was informed by radio of the expected contact and was asked to stand by again at 4.30 pm.

Lunch over, the men busied themselves fixing up a miniature 'jungle' and model house in the sand, with the intention of demonstrating to the savages how to build an airstrip, should they be interested enough to want the white men to come and live among them. Then the five missionaries sang together, as they had so often done, spontaneously and joyously:

> *'We rest on Thee, our Shield and our Defender,*
> *We go not forth alone against the foe.*
> *Strong in Thy Strength, safe in Thy keeping tender,*
> *We rest on Thee, and in Thy name we go.*
>
> *'Yea, in Thy name, O Captain of Salvation,*
> *In Thy blest name, all other names above,*
> *Jesus our Righteousness, our sure Foundation,*
> *Our Prince of Glory, and our King of Love.*
>
> *'We go in faith, our own great weakness feeling,*
> *And needing more each day Thy grace to know,*
> *Yet from our hearts a song of triumph pealing,*
> *We rest on Thee, and in Thy name we go.*
>
> *'We rest on Thee, our Shield and our Defender,*
> *Thine is the battle, Thine shall be the praise*
> *When passing through the gates of pearly splendour,*
> *Victors, we rest with Thee through endless days.'*[1]

Committing themselves and all their carefully laid plans to Him who had so unmistakably brought them thus far, they waited for the Aucas.

Before four-thirty that afternoon the quiet waters of the Curaray flowed over the bodies of the five comrades, slain by the men they had come to win for Christ, whose banner they had borne. The world called it a nightmare of tragedy. The world did not recognise the truth of the second clause in Jim Elliot's credo: 'He is no fool who gives what he cannot keep to gain what he cannot lose.'

Note

1. Hymn by Edith G. Cherry in *Golden Bells Hymnal* 547.

PART ONE

Portland, Oregon,

1927 — 1945

— I —

Strong Roots

Those that be planted in the house of the Lord shall flourish in the courts of our God. [1]

TOWARDS THE MIDDLE of the nineteenth century the hardwood bush country of Ontario between Lake Huron and Lake Erie was still semi-frontier. Among the many who were attracted there by the promise of good cheap land were the Elliots, from a clan of the southern border of Scotland. They settled a hundred miles west of Toronto, near Molesworth, a tiny country village comprising two general stores, a schoolhouse, lodge hall, two blacksmith shops, and two churches. Of these last, the Elliots naturally chose the Presbyterian kirk. The choice was an auspicious one, for it was here that they encountered the MacAllisters, a family from the north of Scotland. Sunday after Sunday the eight Elliot children associated with the eleven MacAllister children. These friendships eventually led to four Elliot-MacAllister marriages, which in turn produced thirty-six double cousins.

One of the four couples, John and Margaret Elliot, owned a small frame house on a hill, surrounded by orchards and grazing land. John was a hard-working stock-trader, respected for his square dealing, eager that his eight children should

22

learn the value of honest labour. Opportunity for this was not lacking. There was stock to feed in the barns during the long winter from September to May, a large wood-house to keep filled behind the kitchen, crops to plant and hoe, reap and store, maple sap to collect and boil down, and of course cows to milk and chickens to feed. Often added to these were household chores, for the children's mother was subject to frequent violents attacks of asthma, and these finally necessitated the oldest son Fred's being taken out of school to help at home. Denied the remainder of his formal education, he became an avid reader, and learned many practical skills while helping his father with carpentry and the care of machinery.

When he reached teen-age, Fred went with his younger brother Will to work in the harvest-fields of Saskatchewan, and from there to British Columbia. Fred had been converted at the age of thirteen when he was taught that the Lord's return was imminent, but it was in British Columbia, under the teaching of Harry Ironside, that he recognised that life was worth living only if given over completely to God. He decided to surrender his life, and later began travelling with Mr Ironside as he went about preaching in rural communities of the north-west.

At about the same time that John and Margaret Elliot were married in Ontario, the call 'Go West!' lured a young man from Berne, Switzerland, where his father was civil engineer of that city. Emil Luginbuhl's money got him as far as Colorado, where he went to work in a smelter until he saved enough to take a homestead in the State of Washington. One day word came that a ribbon-maker's daughter, who had sung in the choir with him back home in Switzerland, had reached America. He lost no time in writing to her, and as soon as he could persuade her to come west, Emil Luginbuhl and Emma Maurer were married on a Methodist preacher's

23

homestead two miles from what is now Roosevelt, Washington.

In the midst of the vast grassland of eastern Washington, Emil created a beautiful oasis by irrigation, producing in time apples, pears, plums, peaches, cherries, apricots, grapes, and strawberries, as well as vegetables and flowers. There was such an abundance that he was able to supply not only his own family but also the neighbouring dryland farmers, who came in wagons and helped themselves to boxes-full of produce.

The acreage that was not planted in gardens or grain-fields was grazing land for sheep—wide, rolling hills stretching away as far as the foothills of Mt Adams, over which hung a blue-purple haze in the evening. The two Luginbuhl children, Jim and Clara, had only an hour a day for play. The chores of the barn and corrals for Jim, the baking of bread, housework, and occasional sheep-herding for Clara filled the remainder of the day.

It was to this ranch, with its large frame house set among tall poplar trees, that Mr Ironside, the travelling preacher, came one day with his young friend, Fred Elliot. Clara Luginbuhl was eighteen, and very much in love, she thought, with her uncle's foreman at that time. But three years later, while she was a student in chiropractic college in Portland, Oregon, she attended meetings in a little Baptist church where Fred—who had been encouraged by Mr Ironside to speak in public—was preaching, taking with her each night a different boy-friend. Fred noticed the pretty, blue-eyed girl on Monday night, and assumed her escort was the Elect. On Tuesday, however, he brightened to note a different one at her side. Seeing a third on Wednesday, he decided there was hope for him, and asked if he could see her home on Thursday. After that they saw each other daily. At Easter Fred sent her a lily, and a correspondence began which lasted two years, at the end of which time they were married, following Clara's graduation in 1918.

They made their home in Seattle for four years, where Clara practised chiropractic and Fred worked as an evangelist in the Puget Sound area. Their first child, Robert, was born there in 1921. The next year they moved to Portland, Oregon, to a small house which Clara's father had purchased years before as a summer home. Here three more children were born, Herbert in 1924, Jim in 1927, and Jane in 1932.

Clara had her professional office off the living-room of her home so that she could keep her fingers on the family pulse, for she considered the children her first responsibility. The idea of hiring baby-sitters never occurred to her. What the family could not do together, they simply did not do. The Elliot children went to worship meetings and Sunday School from the time they were six weeks old. 'I don't think it hurts any child to sit quiet through an adult meeting,' Clara declared; 'it's good for his nerves.' And as for any foolishness about 'forcing religion down their throats', the parents had not the slightest worry. They wanted the best for their children ('except money, which can become a curse,' they said) and gave it to them—spiritual as well as physical care, and all the other good things they could offer. If the child failed to appreciate the need for spiritual guidance, he probably failed, too, to see the need of physical rest when bedtime came around, but the parents guided him just the same, to God as well as to bed.

Fred Elliot read the Scriptures daily to his children, seeking to show them the glory of Christ above all else, striving always to avoid legalisms or a list of 'don'ts'. 'I prayed *with* them as well as for them,' he says. And each of the children at an early age heard the call of Jesus and set his face to follow.

Jim was only about six when he said to his mother one night as they returned home from a meeting. 'Now, mama, the Lord Jesus can come whenever He wants. He could take our whole family, because I'm saved now, and Janie is too young to know about Him yet.'

25

He began telling his small friends what he believed about salvation, 'preaching' to them from the lawn swing.

The Elliot home was always wide open to friends, including missionaries from many parts of the world. The impression this made on the four children was deep, teaching them the grace of hospitality as well as giving them priceless opportunities to know many kinds of people. 'The children loved to have company, even though it meant giving up their beds,' said Jim's mother, 'and because they met new acquaintances so often at home they were cheerful and free and uninhibited in public.'

Obedience and honesty were stressed above all else in the discipline of the children, while mischief was sometimes winked at and sometimes reproved with a brief scolding. The parents made an issue of nothing unless they intended to carry it through, believing that empty threats were dishonest and ruinous to a child's sense of justice. Fred Elliot administered the more serious punishments, occasionally postponing a spanking in order to give it in private. When the children reached the age of fourteen, they were told that from then on they were responsible to the Lord for their actions, since they had accepted Him as Saviour and Lord of their lives. 'And don't ever think you'll get by with something because we don't know about it,' their mother told them. 'God knows, and has His own way of punishing.'

They learned to appreciate the outdoors, tobogganing on Mt Hood in winter, picnicking on the rugged Oregon coast in summer or visiting the old Luginbuhl homestead in Washington, where they raced on the grass-covered hills, tumbled in the haymow, and were occasionally permitted to help care for the sheep and feed the new lambs. Their parents took them to stock shows, taught them to raise fruits, vegetables, and animals, and shared in their good times. Each child had his own hobbies, Jim's being the building of model sailing-ships and airplanes, collecting stamps and reading. His love for beauty was demonstrated in unexpected ways. His mother recalls how one afternoon, coming home tired from a shopping trip, she found a huge bouquet of autumn leaves which Jim had arranged for her on the dining-room table. He took a keen interest in the home and garden, in the colour of the breakfast-nook curtains or the rug in the living-room, as well as in the holly trees and roses outside. In grammar school the teacher was so pleased with his early efforts to draw that she lined the room with his pictures.

His interest in art was not, however, what his schoolmate Dick Fisher remembers. His most vivid recollection:

> I was a playground monitor, which meant that I locked the bicycles in the rack after everyone had arrived. I always had to wait for Jim. I can remember him tearing down 80th Street every day as the bell would sound, sliding on the gravel in front of the Gable Funeral Home as he rounded the fenced section of the pathway through the Seventh Day Adventist Church yard, and finally wide open across the school yard, until, in a big cloud of dust, he would brake to a stop at the rack, jump off the bike, mutter something about being late and thanks, and disappear into the school building. For one whole year that was my complete acquaintance with this picture of speed, fury, and recklessness.

Note

1. Psalm 92:13.

– 2 –

Orator and Garbage Collector

Whatsoever thy hand findeth to do, do it with thy might.[1]

JIM CHOSE architectural drawing as his major when he entered Benson Polytechnic High School in 1941. The *Tech Pep*, his high school newspaper, was sprinkled with his editorials, as well as with news items describing his performance as star in several school plays. Said a teacher who directed one of these, 'I have never had so talented an amateur. After the play, other teachers urged me to encourage Jim to enter the professional theatre.'

He had a reputation, too, as the 'oratorical king' of Benson. On the occasion of President Roosevelt's death, toward the end of Jim's high school days, he was given a few hours' notice to prepare a speech for a special assembly called for that afternoon. His coach commented, 'He gave the finest speech I've ever heard from a schoolboy—in fact, one of the finest speeches I've ever heard.'

Jim's grammar school pal, Dick Fisher, went on to Benson also. He continues with his impressions of Jim:

I was tall and skinny. Jim was a little shorter but had a real "build", brown hair and rugged good looks—the girls always looked at him twice. The thing I admired above all was his keen mind. He comprehended things and understood instructions

28

very fast, while I was always about a mile back. He would try to explain things to me in real simple terms....

When we got out of plumbing class, our next was drawing, which was about five city blocks away. To navigate through the middle of school, in crowded corridors, all in the five minutes between bells, was no simple feat. I can still see Jim bowling and pushing his way, his chin out, a picture of forward motion on the loose.

He usually carried a small Bible on top of his textbooks, and an audience of one or two was all he required to open it and start talking. He always said grace before he ate his lunch, and never missed an opportunity to talk to me about Jesus Christ, about whether I believed in Heaven, Hell, the Hereafter, et cetera. When he would have to prepare a talk for a meeting, he would get me alone, deliver his speech and ask for my criticism. At first I would laugh so hard he would get mad, but as time went on he developed the Hellfire-and-Brimstone, fist-pounding type of delivery (very effective in keeping the audience awake).

As wartime gas rationing began to have its effect on mass transportation, and as the weather got better, Jim and I started hitchhiking home from school. This not only saved us a nickel a day, but it gave us more time to talk and ponder the great things of the world. One night, Jim told me about his intention to become president of our country—an idea he earnestly worked on for a while.

One afternoon Jim took me home to meet his family. I especially noticed on that first visit the number of chores Jim had to do, and his methodical system of doing them. He had chickens, rabbits and goats to feed, the furnace to stoke, and the yard to keep up, with an errand or two to run. In no time at all, a portion of these jobs was allotted to me, and Jim's leadership ability advanced.

Jim and Dutch (Werner Durtschi) went out for football, and, after a lot of talking, they got me to join them. Jim played guard. I always thought he was about the funniest thing I ever saw in a football uniform. He reminded me of a big knock-kneed moose, out of water. His only bid for fame on the team was in getting more mud on his face than anyone else.

Jim was hot to get Dutch and me on a camping expedition, so after a few visits to the hock shops down on the waterfront to get some good buys in equipment, we started hitchhiking one Friday afternoon after school. You can see us, Dutch, Jim and I, all with pack sacks and rifle barrels with tin cans over them to keep out the rain—a tough looking bunch for any motorist. We always had a prayer meeting before we left on a camping trip, and I often thought if we had a guardian angel, he was kept on his toes and didn't get much sleep either.

No one would pick up the three of us, so while two of us hid in the brush, one did the "thumbing". Once when a car stopped, the three of us ran over to it, and the driver said, "How many are there, anyway?" and we said that there were only three and that we were very small—we managed to squeeze in along with the four already in the car.

Next day as we moved along the edge of a golf course we heard a duck quacking. We started across the fairway. Jim was in the lead, and when he saw the duck he pumped a shell into the breech, and then his rifle jammed. Dutch fired from behind me, his shell passing over the duck's back. I got off the next shot, and hit the duck on the fly, landing him in the lake about fifteen feet from shore. Jim took a stick and was trying to fish him out when he heard a yell from behind and turned to see a woman waving her arms frantically, yelling something about a pet duck. We felt panicky, but Jim was determined to get our prize, and finally succeeded, getting pretty wet in the operation. The woman was pretty close before we got moving, and was quite upset, yelling "murderers" and crying, so we didn't waste much time crossing the course and heading for a high ridge. We felt a little cruel, but we figured any duck that could fly was wild, and therefore fair game for us, although we regretted the lady's sorrow and asked the Lord to comfort her.

On another week-end we went to Louterelle Falls on the Columbia River. We climbed to the top, held hands, and peered over the edge. When it was Jim's turn he said, "It's the most terrific thing I've ever seen—just like looking from a cloud." We took the path in behind the falls to the rear edge of the pool at the foot of the cliff, and Jim assumed one of his Man of Destiny poses and peered up through the falling mist and meditated. He said if all this was the handiwork of God, what would eternity hold?

Another time, while attempting to get over a barbed-wire fence to examine a buzzard I'd shot, I accidentally pulled the trigger on my rifle. The shot went through Jim's hair. This had quite a sobering effect on us for a while.

Jim's older brother Bert had a lucrative garbage-collecting business in which Jim and Dick Fisher joined him on Saturdays. Bert drove the truck, while the two younger boys rode on top of the load, trying to swat sea-gulls out of the air with discarded fluorescent tubes, or picking through their collection of the morning. In this way they accumulated enough bricks to build themselves an outdoor barbecue, enough bottles to trade in for a goodly number of pies at the supermarket, and assorted useful objects which included several stoves, a bed, chairs, a bear rug complete with head, and even a set of autopsy tools, which inspired Jim to take taxidermy lessons. One of his first stuffed trophies was a sea-gull captured on the garbage route.

When the two entered the supermarket to trade in their armloads of bottles, the line at the cashier's booth simply melted away. In cold weather Jim dressed in a helmet-type hat with wool earmuffs dangling at the sides, sheepskin jacket with wool collar, coveralls, and an ancient pair of shoes worn down at the heels — all of this redolent of their cargo on the truck.

'We generally went in there twice a day on Saturdays,' says Fisher. 'Those poor girls hated to see us coming.'

Fisher continues:

We got interested later on in the slavery question in Africa. While I thought the use of force to break slavery chains was the answer, Jim was more interested in a missionary approach. However, I was quick to point out the dangers of cannibal soup

31

(an old-fashioned recipe consisting of one part missionary to a hundred parts of water); Jim's rebuttal to this was his faith in the Lord who, he said, had delivered many more men in their time than guns had ever done.

Somebody gave Jim a book of poetry, and he began to memorise passages from well-known works. Whenever I was in town I'd go to see him in the evening. He'd be sitting at his desk, and when I'd walk in the door, he'd start in on "Quoth the Raven, Nevermore". I'd sit there, wide-mouthed and awed, while he went through the whole thing with gestures and fanfare.

Jim was extremely wary of women, fearing that they only intended to lure a man from his goals. "Domesticated males aren't much use for adventure," he warned me. Whenever a young lady got a bit too friendly at a social function and I appeared to be taking the hook, I'd hear a voice in my ear saying, "Beware, Fisher, beware."

After I left Portland, and I was working in the Pentagon in Washington, Jim suggested that we correspond in poetry. His object was to make for better diction and sentence structure. I couldn't write nearly as good poetry as Jim, nor did I have his vocabulary, but I learned from him what I could. Then I determined to teach him something instead of always being on the receiving end. I got a book on the Chinook Indian language and sent Jim a copy. We started writing to each other in Chinook. This got our letters by the censor.

While they were in Portland, Dutch, Fisher, and Jim took many trips together and occasionally were away for weeks at a time without their parents knowing their whereabouts. On one occasion of which Dutch tells they hopped the gondola car of a freight train, which later stopped in a tunnel, and for a short time the boys wondered whether they would be asphyxiated. On another attempt to get a free ride Jim threw his fishing-pole into the freight car, reached for the handle to swing himself up, and was flung to the ground by the speed of the train. He had to continue the journey minus the fishing-pole.

Jim could not always be persuaded to join in these escapades, however, especially if the trip was to be over a weekend, because he was conscientious about his responsibilities at the Gospel Hall. When his father and Bert were away on an evangelistic trip in Arizona, Jim felt that he should be at home to help, as well as be present in the Sunday meetings. During this trip his father wrote to him frequently—letters which so impressed Jim that he read them to Fisher, remarking on his father's knowledge of the Scriptures and adding, 'The effectual, fervent prayer of a righteous man availeth much.'[2]

Fisher relates this incident:

One Friday night as Jim and I hitchhiked home together after school we had a little trouble getting a ride. Since it was raining we stood in the doorway of a store and ran out whenever a car came. There were "stop" signs on the corner, and every car stopped. After a couple of false alarms and a little embarrassment on our part, an elderly gentleman drove up. As he looked to the left to check approaching traffic before proceeding across the highway, Jim opened the door and we were in and had the door closed before he could figure out what had happened. Jim said, with a big grin, "How far you going?" The driver stuttered, "Sixtieth". "That's good enough for us," said Jim and we rode with him to Sixtieth Street, where he stopped and let us out. "Thanks for the ride," said Jim, but the driver looked as if he were the one who had been taken for a ride. Jim and I were almost hysterical with laughter, but we didn't try that trick again.

High school escapades did not divert Jim's attention from his goal of serving God. The third member of the Benson threesome, Werner Durtschi, recalls:

One day near Jim's last year in high school I saw him running around the outdoor track, training. I asked him what he was doing that for. He said, "Bodily exercise is profitable for a little."[3] He was building his body for the rigours of missionary life.

Another high school classmate, Wayne McCroskey, tells of an occasion when there was to be a big school dance.

Jim and I were eating lunch in the cafeteria when the student body officers came through selling tickets. I shook in my boots when I saw that none other than the student-body president himself was taking our table. He was a six-foot-three athlete, all-city baseball and basketball star, popular in the school. When he asked me to buy a ticket to the dance I stammered out some alibi about being too busy. Next he tackled Jim and was told "no sale". He knew Jim pretty well and, recognizing Jim's influence among the students, knew too that losing this sale would make others more bold to refuse, so he turned the heat on. He wound up his argument with, "Jim, you're in this student body as much as I am, and ought to support it." I won't forget the answer:

"Yes," Jim said, "I'm in the student body, but not the way you are. I'm a Christian and the Bible says that I'm *in* the world but not *of* it. That's why I'm not going to the dance."

The student-body president began to wilt, and tried to stop Jim's little sermon by saying, "Yeah, Jim, I understand... that's fine, fella.... OK, sorry I mentioned it... you bet...." He forgot his ticket-selling and slunk out of the cafeteria.

Jim and I were members of the public-speaking club, whose constitution stated that failure to complete an assignment would be penalised by expulsion from the club. The club president assigned us a political speech during the Roosevelt-Dewey campaign, but when Jim was called on, he replied that he had no speech. The president looked worried, because Jim was the backbone of the club.

"Jim," he said, "you know the rules. If you don't give a speech I'll have no choice but to expel you. Now come on up here. You don't need any preparation. Give us an ex-temp on your favourite candidate."

Jim looked right back at him and said, "I have no favourite candidate and I have no speech," and, rising out of his seat, "but I'll be happy to take three minutes to tell you why, if you wish."

The light suddenly dawned on the president's face. Jim had told him of his position as he understood the Bible—that a follower of Jesus could not participate in war or politics. With a face flushed with embarrassment, he said, "That won't be necessary, Jim. I believe we all understand your reasons, and I waive the rules. You are excused."

Although I shared Jim's views, it had never occurred to me to risk my club membership for so seemingly small an issue. Jim's attitude was Esther's: "If I perish, I perish."[4]

World War II was in progress during Jim's high school days, and although Jim was never forced, by a draft call, to take a public stand as a conscientious objector, his convictions on the question were settled. He believed that the Church of Christ, in contrast to the community of Israel in Old Testament times, has abandoned national and political ties. In the words of the writer of Hebrews: 'But we are citizens of Heaven.' 'Our outlook goes beyond this world to the hopeful expectation of the Saviour who will come from Heaven, the Lord, Jesus Christ.'[5] The principle of non-resistance which Jesus demonstrated once and for all on the Cross was one which Jim felt must be obeyed, in public life as well as in personal.

The war question, however, was one which he discussed at length with class-mates and teachers, and his views naturally enough diminished his popularity. So did his inviting a young Chinese, Mun Hope, to the school assembly. This young preacher gave a straight Gospel sermon on sin and judgment before the entire faculty and student body. These two factors, in Fisher's judgment, cut down Jim's chances (considered high) of becoming class president. However, he was given the position of vice-president of his class for his senior year.

Notes

1. I Ecclesiastes 9:10.
2. James 5:16.
3. I Timothy 4:8, ASV.
4. Esther 4:16.
5. Philippians 3:20, JBP.

PART TWO

Wheaton, Illinois,

1945–1949

— 3 —

Degree of A.U.G.

We should remember that while knowledge may make a man look big, it is only love that can make him grow to his full stature. For whatever a man may know, he still has a lot to learn, but if he loves God, he is opening his whole life to the Spirit of God.[1]

MANY A FRESHMAN entering college has no clear idea of what he is there for. Vaguely, it is to 'get an education', but many have done this without going to college, and many have gone to college without getting educated. The idea of an education presents itself to the freshman in a bewilderingly vast variety of forms—the orientation programme, with its lectures, examinations, and faculty receptions; the confusion of registration day, with its lines of frantic students trying to sign up for the course they have chosen before the loud-speaker crackles to announce that Section B of History 115 has closed; catalogues, listing professors who are only names to him so far, and courses elective and requisite; the booths representing organizations; athletic fees, chem-lab fees, dining-hall tickets, room keys— all these things are somehow included in that broad term 'education', and the student whose value scale places social acceptance and reputation high may be sucked into a whirl of extracurricular activity from which he finds it difficult to extricate himself.

38

When Jim Elliot entered Wheaton College in Illinois in the fall of 1945, his goal was clear. First of all, he had committed himself entirely to God and recognised the discipline that this commitment would involve. 'No man that warreth entangleth himself with the affairs of this life, that he may please Him who hath chosen him to be a soldier.'[2] This automatically eliminated many problems, and many 'good' things, in order to give place to those which furthered his purpose. Other students, however, lacking a defined primary aim, often pursued too many of the secondary ones presented to them.

It was this singleness of purpose which his fellow students noticed especially. If some thought he had a 'one-track mind' because he talked so freely about Christ, there were others who, for the same reason, regarded him as especially 'spiritual' and wanted him to be 'prayer chairman' of the freshman class. Neither opinion moved him. A frequent prayer of his was, 'O God, my heart is fixed.'[3]

One student recalls how Jim would stand in the tearing wind on the railroad station platform, head thrown back, fists jammed into his pockets, feet apart, as he waited for the 'Roarin' Elgin' (Aurora and Elgin)—a 'face-to-the-wind' personality.

Another remembers waiting in the dining-hall line reading her New Testament, when she heard a hearty voice behind her: 'Put up your sword, Van!' and turned to see Jim's friendly grin. In the dining-hall he would greet the girls behind the steam tables, the cashier, the bus-boys, as he shoved his tray along. He chose his food carefully: fresh fruits and vegetables, preferably raw; few starches, few desserts. He ate too rapidly, but in moderate quantity, in accord with the rules for wrestling training, as well as with his own ideas about preserving a rugged body for missionary work in the future.

Jim was sure that God had led him to Wheaton. He had

not come simply because father had sent him. Nobody was 'putting him through'. In fact, he did not know where the money would come from. God honoured this faith, however, and funds were supplied, through a friend, through a scholarship, and through part-time employment, so that in November he was able to write:

> This schooling experience is one wherein I can perpetually celebrate that all has been supplied by His ever-tender loving-kindness. To Him be all the glory and thanks.

The only record we have of his freshman and sophomore years is in his letters to his family which, aside from very brief notes on what he was doing, were heavily sprinkled with thoughts on eternity, and occasionally a bit of advice to a brother or sister, of which the following is a sample, written to his sister Jane early that fall:

> Begin each day with private reading of the Word and prayer. Bunyan has well said, "Sin will keep you from this Book, or this Book will keep you from sin." From the very first, as you begin high school, give out gospel tracts to those you meet. Make a bold start—it's easier that way, rather than trying to begin half-way through. Memorise Scripture on the street car. Buy up the time! It's costly because it's so fleeting. These are terse remarks, and trite, but I wish someone had said them to me about Labour Day, 1941. 'Do your best to present yourself to God as one approved, a workman who has no need to be ashamed, rightly handling the Word of Truth.'[4]

Jim set his alarm every night to waken him in time for prayer and study of the Bible. He wrote:

> None of it gets to be "old" stuff, for it is Christ in print, the Living Word: We wouldn't think of rising in the morning without a face-wash, but we often neglect that purgative cleansing of the Word of the Lord. It wakes us up to our responsibility.

A new appreciation of his home and parents was one of the fruits of that first year of college. In May he wrote:

> This is the spring of my nineteenth year. Slowly I have come to realise that my arrival at this point is not of my own efforts, nor merely by the sure ticking of this winged racer called Time, but by the quiet, unfelt guidance of a faithful mother and a father-preacher who has not spent so much time rearing other people's children that he hasn't had time for his own.
>
> My calendar says "Mother's Day", with Father's not far off. And so the people will pause for a few hours to honour those for whom Children's Day comes 365 days a year, those who dare not interrupt their labour of love to seek that honour. The florist shops will bustle, there will be a flurry of carnations, and the following Thursday it will all be forgotten until another May rolls around. I, too, pause, though not with flowers, for such are fast-fading sentiments for the immutable devotion of true parental care. I am grateful to you and to our mutual Father, who has loved us all with a love unknowable.

He wrote at the close of his freshman year:

> It has been a profitable year, drawing closer to my Saviour and discovering gems in His Word. How wonderful to know that Christianity is more than a padded pew or a dim cathedral, but that it is a real, living, daily experience which goes on from grace to grace. And its goal—sometimes seemingly distant, but bright and unfading, lit up and glowing with the beauties of the Sun of Righteousness.

Jim hitchhiked home that summer, and told his brother of the experience in a letter:

> Monday night I was walking a hard stretch of pavement at Cedar Rapids, Iowa, when a new Studebaker pick-up lived up to its name. "Where you goin'?" I queried. "California," retorted a tough marine sergeant. That word had a good effect, kinda warming and cheery, and I thought of God's word to Moses,

"My presence shall go with thee, and I will give thee rest."[5] Amen, said my spirit. We slept three hours Tuesday morning in the truck, pushing on through Nebraska and taking a good hunk out of Wyoming by midnight. At Caspar, Wyoming, the marine's ex-father-in-law owns a tavern. I slept in my clothes on a smelly couch in the back room. Two eggs and black coffee for breakfast. Mid-afternoon, at the junction of Routes 30N and 30S, a coal-truck found me and took me to Cokeville. The Lord is consistently good. Surely with Him there is no "shadow of turning".[6] An ancient Buick stopped, whose driver was a sailor with a throat like the one described in Romans 3, an "open sepulchre". He had a cracked head—that is, his auto did—and we were forced to stop frequently for gas, water, and oil. I was driving while the sailor slept, and within three miles of Boise there suddenly came a grinding crack from up front. I woke the sepulchre-throated gob. "What," said I, "is that noise?" "———," said he, "if I know." We slept till 6 am when a wrecker towed us into Boise. The sailor stuck with his car; I stuck with Highway 30. Got to Portland at 12.20. Total 20 rides, 70 hours, $1.32 in my pocket, and I beat the slow train! Haven't we a wonderful Lord? He says, "Command ye me concerning the work of my hands,"[7] and as we begin to mumble something about getting a ride, bang! there it is. "Before they call, I will answer."[8] I didn't wait over 15 minutes for any ride. That was a faith-strengthening experience.

Jim spent the summer at home, returning to Wheaton in September. In one of the first letters to the family he wrote:

The acquisition of academic knowledge (the "pride of life")[9] is a wearing process and I wonder now if it is all worth while. The shiny paint laid on by curiosity's hand has worn off. What thing better can a man know than the love of Christ, which passes knowledge? Oh to be revelling in the knowledge of Him, rather than wallowing in the quagmire of inscrutable philosophy! My philosophy prof says I can't expect to learn much in his class—all he wants to do is to develop an inquiring mind in order to "make explicit and critically examine philosophical problems of the wider generality." Ho hum.

A few days later he wrote home:

> Another Sunday gone, taking with it its joys, privileges, and
> opportunities, leaving a little good stored in memory's house,
> and an almost imperceptible amount of growth which every day
> of walk down here gives to our maturing process in the family of
> God. "And they shall see His face."[10] In hope of that event we
> rest, are purified and comforted.

Jim had made it a practice to stay in on Saturday nights
('Saves my mind for the breaking of bread on Sunday
morning'), but a football game in the afternoon was not
excluded.

He wrote on October 5:

> Attended my first social event of the year, a football game. Seems
> strange to be in crowds, and even stranger to find myself worked
> up by so small a thing as a ball game. The shouting seems a
> useless process—far better to be shouting God's praises. I feel
> that being alone is far more conducive to fellowship with my
> Father who daily grows more precious as I slowly learn His
> ways. Looking on His face with the eye of faith, we are changed
> into the same image, from glory to what? Asceticism? Bless
> God, more glory! Show a little faith to Him, and He gives more
> faith.
>
> *October 26.* They've asked me to take over the position of
> business manager of the *Tower* next year. It would mean that I
> would get six grade points, free tuition for a year, and a $ 12,000
> responsibility—but it would also mean late hours, a
> reduced class schedule, and participation in a lot of formal foolishness
> which I find difficult to reconcile with my non-conformist
> attitudes.

His rejection of the offer brought protests from the family,
to which he replied on November 2:

> Your letter arrived too late to dissuade me from my decision

regarding the post on the *Tower* staff. Last week-end I was quite upset about the whole matter, but after a long session of prayer my mind became settled, and I found peace in believing that it was not the Lord's will that I take it. Yet I still cannot set down reasons for the decision, save this, that the Lord showed the psalmist the path of life, evidently by his simply lingering in His presence. Psalm 16:11. I waited on Him and somehow the answer came—I trust it was of the Spirit. "A man's heart deviseth his way," said Solomon, "but the Lord directeth his steps."[11] My heart has devised to serve Him. I must leave the next step to Him.

Perhaps in the preparation of a young soul who has thus committed himself to serve Him, the Lord finds it necessary sometimes to narrow that one's vision until it is clearly focused. Before Jim graduated from college, he learned to appreciate the wider vision which it opened to him, but in these first two years he was not quick to accept the college programme as an unmixed blessing. His father, whose education had of necessity been curtailed, was anxious that Jim should fully apprehend the privileges that were his, and wrote to Jim in praise of education. Jim's reply:

You speak of it as "rounding out one's manhood". It rounds it out, all right, but I'm afraid sometimes it's more in the style of 1 Corinthians 8:1, "knowledge puffs up". "Culture", philosophy, disputes, drama in its weaker forms, concerts and opera, politics—anything that can occupy the intellect seems to turn aside the hearts of many here on campus from a humble life in the steps of the Master, though we sing about this most delicately! No, education is dangerous, and, personally, I am beginning to question its value in a Christian life. I do not disparage *wisdom*—that comes from God, not from PhD's.

Excerpts from further letters to his parents:

December 6. I'm finding my study load heavy just now, and it's almost impossible to split the sheets before 11 pm. I would much appreciate your prayers here, for it's difficult to keep from becoming drowsy in 7.30 Greek class in the morning, much more to keep one's mind in sincere morning prayer and study before that time. This, though, is what Paul meant when speaking of the rigour which must be sustained if one is to be a good soldier of Jesus Christ, enduring hardness.

January 3, 1947. I have felt the impact of your prayers in these past weeks. I am certain now that nothing has had a more powerful influence on this life of mine than your prayers. I was thinking today, Dad, how you used to read Proverbs to us. I can't remember much of what you read in the breakfast nook, but find that the experience has left in my mind a profound respect and love for the old wise man's words. Thank God you took the time—the value of such is inestimable.

January 27. My prayers have been much for the high school group lately as I realise more and more the guidance I needed in those reckless, golden days of glory and of grieving, when every problem was so monstrous and every detail loaded full of meaning. I think the "problem boys" would be less of a problem if we only would think back a few years to the time when our most common grief was a broken window, and our highest glory an apple war. A year's patient, prayerful shepherding will bring most of that flock home with Little Bo Peep's lambs, "dragging [*sic*] their tails behind them". It takes a while for revelry to turn to reverence, and much repetition of truth to eventually turn young zeal into habitual channels for good. Take care that well-doing does not become a weariness. It is "after ye have done the will of God" that you have most need of patience.[12]

Jim had gone out for wrestling during his freshman year, believing that participation in some sport contributed to his training as a soldier of Jesus Christ. As the apostle Paul wrote, 'But I pommel my body and subdue it, lest after preaching to others I myself should be disqualified."[13] Jim had no background in high school wrestling, but made the varsity squad his first year, and was known on the mat as tricky and daring. His ability to tie himself into knots led to the nickname 'India Rubber Man'. Often an opponent, sure that Jim's arm or leg would soon snap, was baffled to note the casual unconcern on his face.

Jim had written his mother:

> It's sure a good feeling not to be water-logged and flabby while one is studying. I think it definitely stimulates the entire body process, including thinking, to be physically alert. Like the horse in Job, one can rejoice in his strength.

Mother, however, was unconvinced, and continued writing to warm him of the dangers of the sport, so 'unnecessary', as sports often seem to mothers. It was during Jim's second season on the squad that he wrote:

> My first evil effect from this "ungodly" thing, as Granny [an elderly friend in Wheaton] calls it, showed up on Saturday. It is a puffing of the inner flanges of the ear, commonly called "cauliflower". Not considered very serious in wrestler's circles. Granny thought it was terrible for me to go off to the match singing hymns, and when I afterward told her that we always had prayer before a fight, it nearly shattered her faith.

He soon returned to the subject of education and of God's purposes:

> *February 8.* No, Dad, I have no chance at Darby's books, and if I had would have no time to read them. It is because of this that I begrudge myself an education, for at a time when my mind still functions quickly it is forced to work on subjects like René Descartes' rational epistemology or Laplace's nebular hypothesis, while I would so much more enjoy study on the things of God. Be that as it may, my Father knows best, and I'm confident that He has placed me here; my task is to labour quietly until the pillar-cloud removes and leads farther, working out God's purposes in God's time.

> *February 22.* Several of my housemates and I have begun prayer together here in our "den", and such times we do have! The first fruits of Glory itself. It's the sort of fest I'd call a

"consecrated bull session", where as soon as we hit a subject that has a need God can fill, we dive for our knees and tell Him about it. These are times I'll remember about college when all the philosophy has slipped out memory's back gate. God is still on His throne, we're still on His footstool, and there's only a knee's distance between!

My grades came through this week, and were, as expected, lower than last semester. However, I make no apologies, and admit I've let them drag a bit for study of the Bible, in which I seek the degree A.U.G., "approved unto God".[14]

March 15. The Student Foreign Missions Fellowship is paying visits to all of the Inter-Varsity groups in this area. Yesterday was my first time. Don't know when I've had so much joy. Left about 3 pm in a team member's car; started the meeting about 7.45. Six of us went, one as song leader, the other five to speak about ten minutes each. One spoke on the need—giving statistics on population, death rates, low numbers—of male missionary applicants (18 women to one man), presenting the logical challenge of the distribution of God's servants. I spoke on the Holy Spirit in missions. Another took methods: radio, translation, medicine, teaching, business, movies, air transport, building, etc. A fellow from Africa took the practical side—being able to resist temptation and disease, knowing something about building and digging, etc. Finally there was a question period—questions were varied and stimulating. Coming home we stopped for a bite to eat, and ran into a confused waitress. Had a heart-rending time trying to speak the Words of Life to her, and as I think of all this country now, many just as confused, and more so, I realised that the 39th Street bus is as much a mission field as Africa ever was.

March 22. I lack the fervency, vitality, *life* in prayer which I long for. I know that many consider it fanaticism when they hear anything which does not conform to the conventional, sleep-inducing eulogies so often rising from Laodicean lips; but I know too that these same people can acquiescently tolerate sin in their lives and in the church without so much as tilting one hair of their eyebrows. Cold prayers, like cold suitors, are seldom effective in their aims.

March 29. Only two more days, and another month will have marched quickly by to take its place in the ranks of past months—and as it does, I would say "thank God for those 31 days". By God's grace I have been able to sing two songs honestly, as I never sang them before. One is that thoughtlessly sung chorus, "Every day with Jesus is sweeter than the day before". These past two weeks have been of such progressive joy that I can say nightly of my Saviour's goodness, "it's sweeter today than yesterday". And the other is that hymn "Sweet Hour of Prayer". Nightly we have gathered here and usually it runs past the hour before we again rise from our knees, feeling as if our faces should be veiled for the small glimpse of Glory the Lord has given us. This, to me, is *real* Christianity, when fellows pray and see miracles worked on campus the following day. Each day becomes a time of wrought wonders.

From the last letter of his sophomore year:

What a brutish master sin is, taking the joy from one's life, stealing money and health, giving promise of tomorrow's pleasures and finally leading one onto the rotten planking that overlies the mouth of the pit. It is with honest praise to God I can look up tonight and rejoice in His loving-kindness in delivering me from a life of useless frustration and the ultimate agonies of the gnawing, undying worms of remorse and regret.

It was sometime during these first two years at college that Jim became conscious of the direct, personal implications of the Lord Jesus' command to go and preach the gospel. He decided that the command was directed to him. There is no record of the exact time when this decision was made, but a small black loose-leaf notebook, his companion in college days, contains evidence of his concern for the millions who had not had the chance to hear what God had done to bring man to Himself. This notebook was found on the Curaray beach after Jim's death, its pages scattered along the sand, some washed clean of ink, others stained with mud and rain but still legible. Besides the names of hundreds of people for whom Jim prayed, the notes contained also a recipe for soap-making (doubtless jotted down in anticipation of pioneer life on some mission field); notes for his own sermons preached in English, Spanish, and Quichua; notes on the Auca language, and several pages of mission statistics written while in college, of which the following is an excerpt:

1,700 languages have not a word of the Bible translated.

90% of the people who volunteer for the mission field never get there. It takes more than a "Lord, I'm willing!"

64% of the world have never heard of Christ.

5,000 people die every hour.

The population of India equals that of North America, Africa, and South America combined. There is one missionary for every 71,000 people there.

There is one Christian worker for every 50,000 people in foreign lands, while there is one to every 500 in the United States.

In view of the unequivocal command of Christ, coupled with these staggering facts, Jim believed that if he stayed in the United States the burden of proof would lie with him to show that he was justified in so doing.

He began planning to go to the foreign mission field, wherever God might lead, and took the first practical step in that direction in the summer of 1947, when he hitchhiked to Mexico with a college friend, Ron Harris, whose parents were missionaries there. Of his early impressions he wrote to his parents on June 23:

Ron took me to the Panteon (cemetery) and we wandered around there reading tombstones and looking for bones. When a person has been buried long, and they need more space, they just dig in all over again and let the femurs fall where they may. Decomposition is rapid here. Soon the funeral procession of a brother who died yesterday arrived, and we went over to observe. The hole was a little short, but the hand-carved coffin fit OK on an angle. It was let down on ropes and another box marked "gunpowder" was thrown in on top. They told me it held the bones of the dead man's wife, just dug up from another section of the cemetery. Both were buried in the grave of their grandmother who died thirty-five years ago!

When the preaching was over everyone who knew the man picked up a handful of dirt and chucked it on the coffin, then stood back while the diggers finished off the job. Then came the flowers. Everyone brings some and they are stacked like cordwood all over—beautiful glads, daisies, calla lilies, and more I can't name. What a place!

Mexico has stolen my heart. We've been here a fortnight (as Ron's folks say; they are very English) and they have invited me to stay as long as I wish. Right now I almost wish it were for life.... The Lord has been good to me in bringing me here and giving this brief opportunity to see the field and hear the language a bit. Missionaries are very human folks, just doing what they are asked. Simply a bunch of nobodies trying to exalt Somebody.

Jim was with the Harrises for six weeks, beginning the study of Spanish, observing the principles on which they worked, receiving counsel from them, and making notes about everything he noticed, even to Spanish names for birds, flowers, and mountains.

Towards the end of his stay in Mexico he was asked to speak in a children's meeting. With exactly one month's Spanish tucked behind him, he decided to attempt it without an interpreter.

Ron Harris recalls:

The subject was Noah's ark and the rainbow of promise. About 150 kids were very quiet and attentive while he spoke for over half an hour. There was a blackboard behind him, and every time he needed a word he didn't know, he would draw on the board and get someone to tell him the word needed. His enthusiasm and willingness to use what he learned made him get ahead rapidly with Spanish in so short a time.

There was little doubt in Jim's mind, as he hitchhiked back towards Oregon, that it was Latin America to which God was calling him. He knew then that he could never be satisfied with the "usual". His face was set towards those who had never heard.

Notes

1. 1 Corinthians 8:1–3, JBP.
2. 2 Timothy 2:4.
3. Psalm 108:1.
4. 2 Timothy 2:15, RSV.
5. Exodus 33:14.
6. James 1:17.
7. Isaiah 45:11, para.
8. Isaiah 65:24.
9. 1 John 2:16.
10. Revelation 22:4.
11. Proverbs 16:9.
12. Hebrews 10:36.
13. 1 Corinthians 9:27, RSV.
14. 2 Timothy 2:15.

— 4 —

Straight for the Goal

I do not consider myself to have "arrived" spiritually . . . but I do concentrate on this: I leave the past behind and with hands outstretched to whatever lies ahead I go straight for the goal, my reward the honour of being called by God in Christ.[1]

WHEN JIM ARRIVED at Wheaton in 1945 he thought that perhaps his stay would be just two years. But by the fall of 1947, after a few weeks at home on his return from Mexico, funds were available for him to continue, and he accepted this as God's signal to return. His first letter home was dated September 15:

Dr Brooks asked me to speak for a few minutes to the freshmen on Saturday, and the Lord gave strength to exhort and encourage. The subject was "What I as a Junior Wish Someone had Told Me When I was a Freshman". I mentioned that beyond "believing" and "behaving" in the Christian life, there is also "being", and I brought in New Testament exhortations such as

> *"Be not ignorant."*
> *"Be not deceived."*
> *"Be sober."*
> *"Be vigilant."*
> *"Be mindful of the Word."*
> *"Be steadfast," etc.*

52

May the Lord give me power to live as His Word demands.

In accord with his thinking of the previous year, Jim decided on a Greek major. Besides wanting to get to the bottom of the original language of the New Testament in order to gain a thorough grasp of its meaning for his own instruction, he believed that a knowledge of Greek would greatly aid him in translating the Bible into a primitive tongue.

For the same reasons, I too had chosen Greek as my major, and our schedule of classes that year was almost identical— rather a rare coincidence in a college of fifteen hundred students with so wide a choice of courses. It dawned on me one day that the Jim Elliot who appeared in Thucydides class, in Herodotus, the Septuagint, ancient history, and in the seminars on poets and dramatists, must be the same Elliot my brother had been talking about for two years, a buddy of his on the wrestling squad, whom Dave thought I should meet.

Jim sat across the aisle from me in ancient history class. Yes, I thought, he looks like a wrestler all right. Just under six feet tall, he had the bull neck and barrel chest I would have expected. Grey-blue eyes looked blue with the sky-coloured sweater he wore most of the time, accompanied by grey flannel trousers and slightly shabby gabardine jacket. Socks and bow ties usually matched, and I noted that he fell into the no-rubbers-or-briefcase category, a minor point in his favour in my eyes.

We talked occasionally after classes, and one day in October Jim asked me for a date, which on the spur of the moment I accepted but later broke. This, I was informed by my friends, was a poor move. Didn't I know that Jim Elliot was a woman-hater? I had rejected a unique opportunity.

Jim had gained for himself this reputation because of his determination to eliminate the non-essentials from his schedule. Dating he regarded as one thing he might well do without. Furthermore, during those early months of his junior year God had spoken to him through the word of Matthew 19:12, 'There are eunuchs who have made themselves eunuchs for the sake of the kingdom of heaven. He who is able to receive this let him receive it.'[2] No ascetic, Jim enjoyed to the full all that he believed God had given him to enjoy, but he felt it wisest to exclude from the sphere of activity anything which had the power to distract him from the pursuit of the Will. The precepts of 1 Corinthians 7 were inescapable to him, and it was not without reason that the Trainer of Souls set these lessons before him at this particular time. Whether God were actually giving him what he called the 'gift of single life' (an expression that Jim took from 1 Corinthians 7:7):[3] 'each has his own special gift from God'— he did not yet know; neither did he try to rationalise himself out of that possibility. He believed Christ to be utterly sufficient for the entire fulfilment of the personality, and was ready to trust Him literally for this.

Jim wrote in his journal:

> To that soul which has tasted of Christ, the jaunty laugh, the tempting music of mingled voices, the haunting appeal of smiling eyes—all these lack flavour. And I would drink deeply of Him. Fill me, O Spirit of Christ, with all the fullness of God.

In studying the separation of the Levites in Deuteronomy 9 and 10, and of their having 'no inheritance', he wrote, 'Lord, if Thou wilt but allow me to take this set-apart place, by Thy grace, I shall covet no inheritance. NOTHING BUT CHRIST.'

When my brother Dave asked Jim to spend Christmas vacation at 'Birdsong', our home in Moorestown, New Jersey, Jim accepted with alacrity, thinking (he revealed later) that it would be a good opportunity to get acquainted with me—a reason which at the time he kept entirely to himself. No one could have guessed the struggle he had during those two weeks because of the lessons he had been learning with regard to the dangers of getting himself 'attached', while at the same time he recognised a growing interest in me. However, I suspected nothing during those weeks.

He wrote to his family on December 21 from my home:

What God's way is in bringing me here I cannot now say, nor perhaps ever can while the ticking of clocks assails the ear, but that He is leading and that His purpose shall not fail, I know without doubt.... Here I am in the midst of a fine family: a fellow Bob's age and his wife (Phil and Margaret); Betty, who is twenty-one today and a senior at Wheaton, is next followed by brother Dave. Below him are Ginny, a bobby-soxer of fifteen who closes her eyes like Jane when she grins, which she does much; and Tommy, thirteen; with Jimmy, seven, who combine to keep the rest of us in fine spirits and good humour. Again I find God's people very good and these particularly godly. I went to "church" this morning and find myself appallingly ignorant of the form we so vigorously condemn (yet at times unwittingly follow) in the assembly.[4] I cannot repeat the Apostles' Creed or sing the proper Presbyterian tunes to the Doxology. Pray for me. I need constancy of spirit and mind.

My family was enchanted with Jim. As staid Easterners of Philadelphia and New England stock, we found his sudden wide smile and strong handclasp, his complete ingenuousness, refreshing. He fixed everything that needed fixing around the ageing place that had been home for eight of us for a number of years. He wiped dishes for a little old lady who was then a kitchen helper for my mother. 'That young man,' said the lady, 'will go places. When he finds a fork that is not well washed, he washes it again himself, instead of asking me to.' In spite of her deafness the old lady was able to hear Jim's singing. He knew hundreds of hymns by heart, and was quite uninhibited about breaking forth at any moment in his hearty, unmodulated baritone.

He went sledding and ice skating with my teen-age brother and sister, and shovelled snow for my father. I don't recall his doing very much for me except keeping me awake talking, long after the rest of the family had retired. We discussed a broad range of topics—his views on the war question (when my mother had innocently asked if he had been in the service, he said 'No, *ma'am*' with such vehemence she was taken aback), New Testament principles of the conduct of the Church, women, poetry, and many other subjects on which his views were, I thought, out of the ordinary. I enjoyed these sessions partly because at that time I disagreed with him on so many things. At any rate, I decided Jim Elliot was a 'character', and I liked him.

When we got back to Wheaton, Jim found that I always did my Thucydides assignment at a certain table in the hall of East Blanchard. He started joining me there quite regularly. There were moments when I was a little suspicious that I was doing most of the work, but I was totally unaware of motives other than the purely utilitarian on his part. We found it an efficient way to get through pages of the Greek classic.

When, months later, he told me that his interest in me had begun before Christmas vacation, I was surprised. I learned that his personal feelings had been held in check by a principle of which he once wrote to his parents:

> No one warns young people to follow Adam's example. He waited till God saw his need. Then God made Adam sleep, prepared for his mate, and brought her to him. We need more of this "being asleep" in the will of God. Then we can receive what He brings us in His own time, if at all. Instead we are set as bloodhounds after a partner, considering everyone we see until our minds are so concerned with the sex problem that we can talk of nothing else when bull-session time comes around. It is true that a fellow cannot *ignore* women—but he can think of them as he ought—as sisters, not as sparring partners!

As is often the case, despite a heavier schedule than ever

before, Jim found that his time alone with his Bible was even more vitally necessary. He began spending an hour before breakfast in the Old Testament, a few minutes at noon in the Psalms, and evenings in the New Testament. On January 18, 1948, he began recording in a notebook what he was learning:

> What is written in these pages I suppose will some day be read by others than myself. For this reason I cannot hope to be absolutely honest in what is herein recorded, for the hypocrisy of this shamming heart will ever be putting on a front and dares not write what is actually found in its abysmal depths. Yet, I pray Lord, that you will make these notations to be as nearly true to fact as is possible, that I may know my own heart and be able to definitely pray regarding my gross, though often unrecognised, inconsistencies. I do this because I have been aware that my quiet time with God is not what it should be. These remarks are to be written from fresh, daily thoughts given from God, in meditation on His Word.
>
> Genesis 23—Abraham calls himself a stranger and sojourner in a land he believed God was going to give to him. This is the first time he shows any real inclination to make a home on earth, and how slight it is—only a field, some trees, and a cave in which he can bury his dead. Lord, show me that I must be a stranger, unconcerned and unconnected with affairs below, as Abraham "looked for a city".[5] It was when he owned his strangerhood that the sons of Heth called him a "prince of God" among them. Abraham made no attempt to be a prince of men, as had Lot, and they all recognised his character and inheritance (qualities of a prince) as being not of men but of God. Oh to be known as Israel, a prince with God; no longer as Jacob of the carnal mind!
>
> Help me, Lord, not to mourn and weep for those things, once precious, which you teach me are but dead (whether desires, pleasures, or whatever may be precious to my soul now), but give me a willingness to put them away out of my sight (verse 14). Burying-places are costly, but I would own a Machpelah where corpses (dead things in my life) can be put away.

Such commentaries on his daily reading filled many pages of notebooks, which he called 'museums of pressed flowers, picked with Him, where He is leading me to "feed among the lilies".'6

It was during this year that Jim discontinued his practice of making notes in his Bible, or underlining verses. He bought himself a new version, and, though it was thoroughly thumbed and dog-eared within a year, it was without any markings. This practice, he felt, helped to keep him seeking new truth and allowed the Spirit of God, rather than a red pencil, to emphasise the particular words that he needed.

Jim was not always successful, however, in gleaning something 'fresh' from the Word. One morning not long after he began recording, he wrote:

> Yesterday though I had plenty of time for study and read the chapter faithfully, and earnestly sought truth that would be fresh, I cannot say that I found any. Perhaps I sought too hard. Perhaps I strove with the Spirit and frightened the Heavenly Dove in my eagerness. Teach me, Lord, how to listen and not always to seek to squeeze truth out of Scriptures which Thou dost not yet choose to open. My study and prayer time is not yet what I would have it.

After reading, digesting, and recording, Jim set himself to praying. He had lists of people to pray for, a list for each day of the week, and if time alone in his room was limited, he prayed as he walked up to breakfast on campus, or as he stood in line at the dining-hall. An odd moment here and there in the day was given to prayer for those names, or to memorization of Bible verses which he carried, written on small cards, in his pocket. These cards were kept till they were ragged, and occasionally were the cause of his being called antisocial, for there were times when they or the prayer-list notebook took precedence over small talk.

The sessions in the Psalms were sometimes shared with another. He wrote:

Happy time in Psalm 119 and in prayer with Dave at noon today. Oh what love God has led me into for them—Bob, Bill, and now Dave. What times we shall have, now and in His presence beyond, where looms no shade of terror! "Fear dissolved in blood." But still He waits, well knowing the Spirit's cry, and the Bride's and creation's groan.

It was Marcus Aurelius who said, 'A man's thoughts dye his soul.' Constant dwelling in the words of the Lord dyed Jim's soul, and its colour was not hidden from fellow students. 'His life had an impact on me,' wrote his room-mate. 'I remember the time he spent in prayer, and I remember with conviction, for he was walking closer to his Lord than his room-mate.'

To those accustomed to the shibboleths of 'Fundamental-ism' Jim's ideas sometimes seemed startling. Often in dining-hall bull sessions someone would say, 'Where in the world did you get an idea like that, Elliot?' The answer is found in his notebook:

2 Timothy 2:9 says, "The word of God is not bound." Systematic theology—be careful how you tie down the Word to fit your set and final creeds, systems, dogmas, and organised theistic philo-sophies! The Word of God is not bound! It's free to say what it will to the individual, and no one can outline it into dispensations which cannot be broken. Don't get it down "cold", but let it live—fresh, warm, and vibrant—so that the world is not binding ponderous books about it, but rather is shackling you for having allowed it to have free course in your life. That's the apostolic pattern.... And those who are arguing about fore-knowledge, election, and such: read those verses 14–26, and then look how the apostle is willing to leave it a paradox. "God gives repentance", and "they recover themselves". Yes, yes, I'm naïve, and glad to be so in such a case.

Jim studied the Word for himself, and if what he under-stood it to mean was not in conformity with what is commonly understood, his standard did not shift. He wrote:

> The pattern of my behaviour is not set in the activities of those about me. Don't follow the example of those you left in the world, nor those you find in the Church. Rather, the law of God, found in His Word, shall be my standard, and as I see it, there are few examples of this sort of living anywhere.

About a month after the Christmas holiday interrupted his college studies he wrote in his journal:

> Genesis 28: God's promise to Abraham was that his seed should be as the dust of the earth and as the stars of heaven. Stars suggest those children of Abraham which are so by faith, a heavenly people with a heavenly purpose and with heavenly promises. "In Isaac shall thy seed be called."[7] Jacob—later Israel—gives his name to the earthly people whose promises, purposes, and character were earthly. The differences of these destinations mark peoples so entirely different that to argue similarities in law, warfare, or inheritance is to be careless in the reading of the Scripture.

Thus Jim's views on warfare and law, theology and philosophy, while regarded as iconoclastic by some, had their basis in his simple, literal interpretation of Scripture and application of it to daily life. Even his birthday greetings were not run-of-the mill, as this to his brother Bert illustrates:

> For you, brother, I pray that the Lord might crown this year with His goodness and in the coming one give you a hallowed dare-devil spirit in lifting the biting sword of Truth, consuming you with a passion that is called by the cultured citizen of Christendom "fanaticism", but known to God as that saintly madness that led His Son through bloody sweat and hot tears to agony on a rude Cross—and Glory!

To his fifteen-year-old sister Jane, Jim wrote:

Fix your eyes on the rising Morning Star. Don't be disappointed at anything or over-elated, either. Live every day as if the Son of Man were at the door, and gear your thinking to the fleeting moment. Just how can it be redeemed? Walk as if the next step would carry you across the threshold of Heaven. Pray. That saint who advances on his knees never retreats.

Jim was doing a great deal of praying in these days concerning the mission field. He wrote, quoting Paul:

"Some have not the knowledge of God—I speak this to your shame."[8] And they must hear. The Lord is bearing hard upon me the need of the unreached millions in Central Asia. Why does not the Church awake? What a high calling is offered any who will pray, "Send me."[9]

Our young men are going into the professional fields because they don't "feel called" to the mission field. We don't need a call; we need a kick in the pants. We must begin thinking in terms of "going out", and stop our weeping because "they won't come in". Who wants to step into an igloo? The tombs themselves are not colder than the churches. May God send us forth.

He was a member of the Student Foreign Missions Fellowship, and attended its prayer meetings in the early morning. He often worked late at night, making up packages for relief in Europe. But his vision of world need included those at his own doorstep as well, and Sunday afternoon found him travelling into Chicago to talk of Christ to those waiting for trains in the large railroad stations. He wrote:

No fruit yet. Why is it I'm so unproductive? I cannot recall leading more than one or two into the kingdom. Surely this is not the manifestation of the power of the Resurrection. I feel as Rachel, "Give me children, or else I die."[10]

Love for God, Jim believed, must be manifested in love, not only for those who do not know Him, but also for those who call themselves by His name. 'If anyone says, "I love God,"' wrote John in his First Epistle, "and hates his brother, he is a liar."[11] There was a small group of Christians in a near-by town, who met regularly on simple New Testament lines. Jim jointed them, with the hope of being of some help. His diary shows that he felt something of the same discouragement there that he felt in the railroad-station effort in Chicago:

"The rod of the man I shall choose shall bud."[12] If Thou has chosen me, Father, then I should be budding, blossoming, bearing fruit for Thee.

His desire does not seem to have been visibly fulfilled, but the exercise of soul that it cost Jim did something at least to preserve him from what, for the average college student, is often a life of unmitigated selfishness.

He sought the help of older Christians in learning to live for God, and there were occasions when he asked them to pray with him. Of one of these he wrote:

Had fellowship in prayer with brother Harper, and discussion of the things of God. A happy experience. God, I pray Thee, light these idle sticks of my life and may I burn up for Thee. Consume my life, my God, for it is Thine. I seek not a long life but a full one, like you, Lord Jesus.

Further excerpts from the notebook of that junior year show his relentless pursuit of God:

February 3. O God, save me from a life of barrenness, following a formal pattern of ethics, and give instead that vital contact of soul with Thy divine life that fruit may be produced, and Life—abundant living—may be known again as the final proof for Christ's message and work.

March 10. Saviour, I know Thou hast allowed me absolute

liberty, to serve Thee, or to go my own way. I would serve Thee forever, for I love my Master. I will not go out free. Mark my ear, Lord, that it might respond only to Thy voice.

April 16. O Lamb of God, what a Sacrifice Thou art! Whose blood could avail like Thine? Goat's blood could not cleanse, for animals are amoral. My own would not avail for I am immoral. Only Thou art perfectly moral, and only Thy blood could be of any effect.

It was on this day that Jim and several other students were travelling as a gospel team. As they crossed a railroad track, the car stalled, and was wrecked by an oncoming freight only a few seconds after they leaped to safety. Jim sent a clipping from the newspaper to his parents with the following comment:

> The details are fairly accurate, but newspapermen know nothing about the ministering spirits sent by the Ruler of the Universe to be ministers for them who are to be heirs of salvation. It sobered me considerably to think that the Lord kept me from harm in this. Certainly He has a work that He wants me in somewhere. Oh that I might "apprehend that for which also I am apprehended".[13]

So Jim escaped accidental death for at least the second time—the first having been the bullet through his hair—and he was led on, for a few more years, to a very different kind of death, which seemed strangely prophesied in his journal entry of the second day after the railroad accident:

> (Leviticus 17:10): He who consumes blood will ever have the face of God set against him. So with me. If I would save my life-blood, and forbear to pour it out as a sacrifice—thus opposing the example of my Lord—then must I know the flint of the face of God set against my purpose. Father, take my life, yea, my blood if Thou wilt, and consume it with Thine enveloping fire. I would not save it, for it is not mine to save.

Have it, Lord, have it all. Pour out my life as an oblation for the world. Blood is only of value as it flows before Thine altar.

The school year was nearly over when Jim stopped me in the hall one day between classes. He handed me a small black leather-bound book, which I took back to the dormitory and found to be a hymnal. In the flyleaf he had written, first in his distinctive, flowing hand, and then in small, clear printing, a few words, a Scripture verse in Greek, and the notation 'Hymn number 46'. Turning quickly to the number, I found these words:

> *"Have I an object, Lord, below*
> *Which would divide my heart with Thee?*
> *Which would divert its even flow*
> *In answer to Thy constancy?*
> *O teach me quickly to return,*
> *And cause my heart afresh to burn.*
>
> *Have I a hope, however dear,*
> *Which would defer Thy coming, Lord—*
> *Which would detain my spirit here*
> *Where naught can lasting joy afford?*
> *From it, my Saviour, set me free*
> *To look and long and wait for Thee.*
>
> *Be Thou the object bright and fair*
> *To fill and satisfy the heart,*
> *My hope to meet Thee in the air,*
> *And nevermore from Thee to part;*
> *That I may undistracted be*
> *To follow, serve, and wait for Thee."*

—G. W. FRAZER

It had only been in the last few weeks before he gave me this booklet that I had had any idea that Jim was interested in me. Had I, however, entertained any hopes, the choice was clear to both of us now. It had to be Christ—alone.

We took a walk one evening, discussing what seemed to us a strange path in which the Lord had led us. We had dated only once—a missionary meeting in Chicago a month before. We had spent much time in study and conversation together, but neither had acknowledged anything beyond a very worthwhile friendship. Now we faced the simple truth—we loved each other.

Hardly aware of our direction, we wandered into a gateway and found ourselves in a cemetery. Seated on a stone slab, Jim told me that he had committed me to God, much as Abraham had done his son, Isaac. This came almost as a shock—for it was exactly the figure which had been in my mind for several days as I had pondered our relationship. We agreed that God was directing. Our lives belonged wholly to Him, and should He choose to accept the 'sacrifice' and consume it, we determined not to lay a hand on it to retrieve it for ourselves. There was nothing more to be said.

We sat in silence. Suddenly we were aware that the moon, which had risen behind us, was casting the shadow of a great stone cross between us.

The date of that night is marked in Jim's hymn-book, beside the following lines:

> "If Thou shouldst call me to resign
> What most I prize, it ne'er was mine;
> I only yield Thee what is Thine:
> Thy will be done!"
> —CHARLOTTE ELLIOTT

After my graduation Jim spent the first few days of the summer alone in his aunt's home in Glen Ellyn, a small town near Wheaton. During this time Jim thought over the decision God had brought him to. There was no question in his mind as to the rightness of it, but something of the conflict of his soul is revealed in the following journal entry:

> *June 18.* Joshua 5 and 6. "Devoted things." Here is something for my soul as regards Betty. As far as we both are concerned she was "devoted"—not to destruction as was Jericho, but to God, as a burnt living sacrifice. Now I agreed to this with God, allowing that He should have her and me both, wholly His, devoted. But the subtle danger was in retaining hopes ("nice things", gold and silver) that He would give her to me eventually, that our decision to go separately for God would be ultimately revoked by Him and on such fare I survived. But this was just as if I had never really "devoted" her at all, for there was still a future claim on her. Now comes this word: "...keep yourselves from the devoted thing and become...troubled" (verse 18). Ah, how like again—hidden in the tent in secret were those secret longings for something I may not have, gloated over in lonely moments. But the Cross is final. There is no turning now, nor half-way stopping place. I must go on, asleep until God sees my need of Eve—if such need ever arises. Fix my heart wholly, Lord, to follow Thee, in no detail to touch what is not mine.

Notes

1. Philippians 3:12−14, JBP.
2. RSV.
3. RSV.
4. This is a term that will appear frequently in the pages to follow. It is used in the New Testament sense of a local group of believers. It is the central meaning of the Greek word *ekklesia*.
5. Hebrews 11:10.
6. Song 4:5.
7. Genesis 21:12.
8. 1 Corinthians 15:34.

9. Isaiah 6:8.
10. Genesis 30:1.
11. 1 John 4:20, RSV.
12. Numbers 17:5, ASV.
13. Philippians 3:12.

— 5 —

Flame of Fire

Then flew one of the seraphims unto me, having a live coal in his hand, which he had taken with the tongs from off the altar: and he laid it upon my mouth, and said, Lo, this hath touched thy lips; and thine iniquity is taken away, and thy sin purged.[1]

DIRECTION WAS GIVEN in answer to Jim's prayer for guidance for the summer, which he had recorded several months earlier:

Guidance for Israel in their wanderings was unquestionable (Numbers 9). There could be no doubt if God wished them to move. Shall my Father be less definite with me? I cannot believe so. Often I doubt, for I cannot see, but surely the Spirit will lead as definitely as the pillar of cloud. I must be as willing to remain as to go, for the presence of God determines the whereabouts of His people. "Where I am, there shall also My servant be."[2] Very well, Lord—what of this summer?

In July, 1948, Jim and three other Wheaton students, Dave Howard, Roger Lewis, and Verd Holsteen, travelled together as a gospel team, representing the Foreign Missions Fellowship. The itinerary took them through the Midwestern states, from Michigan to Montana, where they spoke in churches, Bible conferences, camps, and schools, presenting to young people the need of a life given wholly to the Lord. They emphasised the responsibility of the Church to the tribes who have never heard of Christ. Jim did not want this trip to be just another 'junket'.[3] He wrote:

> [He makes] His ministers a flame of fire. Am I ignitible? God deliver me from the dread asbestos of "other things". Saturate me with the oil of the Spirit, that I may be aflame. But flame is transient, often short-lived. Canst thou bear this, my soul— short life? In me there dwells the Spirit of the Great Short-Lived, whose zeal for God's house consumed Him. And He has promised baptism with the Spirit and with Fire. "Make me Thy fuel, Flame of God."[4]

That prayer was answered immediately and also ultimately. Dave writes:

> During those weeks the Lord did a work in our own hearts, and to this day I can hear Jim preaching with a passion which I have seldom seen in anyone else. Several years later, when I was representing missions among students, more than once I ran into young people in colleges or Bible schools around the country who had originally responded to God's claims as a result of Jim's preaching on the FMF trip, and who are now preparing for missionary service.

The following are excerpts from his journal of that trip:

> Father, let me be weak that I might loose my clutch on everything temporal. My life, my reputation, my possessions, Lord, let me loose the tension of the grasping hand. Even, Father, would I lose the love of *fondling*. How often I have released a grasp only to retain what I prized by "harmless" longing, the fondling touch. Rather, open my hand to receive the nail of Calvary, as Christ's was opened—that I, releasing all, might be released, unleashed from all that binds me now. He thought Heaven, yea, equality with God, not a thing to be clutched at.

So let me release my grasp.

Have had much struggle of soul lately—doubts as to the truth of God's care for the world, springing I think from so little evidence of His power in the gospel. Comforted mightily yesterday morning by realizing that the rest of faith is upon fact, and that especially in the Resurrection of Christ. If he be not raised from the dead, my faith is vain.

Father, make of me a crisis man. Bring those I contact to decision. Let me not be a milepost on a single road; make me a fork, that men must turn one way or another on facing Christ in me.

And a letter to his mother, dated August 16, 1948, typical in its occupation with Christ of so many which he wrote over the years, I quote in full:

Beloved Mother *et al*: This will likely be my last letter home before I get there, I hope. It seems hard to write of news on the road somehow. We have been held up all afternoon getting repairs on the brake, so that we are now late for a meeting in an Indian reservation up in Red Lake, Minnesota. I type while we travel because it is exceedingly difficult to find time to write while we are staying in homes. Dave is reading Hudson Taylor's *Life* while I am trying to get the gist of his reading while I write.

I simply cannot explain what God is doing for us in this trip. I now begin to see why the Lord led me on this fresh experience of nightly ministering... [to see] the secrets of His working "in me mightily",[5] as Paul puts it. More when I get home. How unworthy a servant I have been, how absolutely insufficient to be given the Word of Reconciliation. But God is so very wise, I dare not ask, "Why hast Thou made me thus?"[6] The boys have stopped reading and Roj has burst into his powerful baritone with "Beyond the Sunset", inspired by the blazing throes of the dying sun which sprawls bloody riot in the western sky. Beautiful. I think I have never so enjoyed a sunset as the one we saw last evening. We are quite far north here and saw the northern lights the other night. Yesterday we had four services and a radio broadcast this morning. What glory to be weary in the work of the Kingdom!

From the last few letters I discover that all mention your physical condition, Madre. I do hope I can be of some encouragement. What have we down here, "unclothed",[7] anyhow? Oh, that we might be clothed upon with the glory of the Son of God. We *shall* be changed! Doesn't that grip you? I wish it were possible to transmit the inner flow of peace and power, the comfort the thought of translation has become to me. Of the flesh and its false emotions I have quite had my fill. Of Jesus I cannot seem to get enough. Thank God, though, He does not thwart the soul's desire for Himself, but only whets the desire, intensifying, sublimating. Oh, Mother, in patience possess your soul. He is on the threshold, waiting for His lovers to rouse themselves to answer His knock. Maranatha! Hallelujah! Lift up your heads. Soon shall the cup of glory wash down earth's bitterest woes. The dawn of Heaven breaks. There is balm in Gilead.

We are nearing our destination again. Oh that the power of God would again give us assurance of His working in us mightily. I have trouble keeping the prophet's spirit subject to the prophet.[8] The spirit is liquid and easily flows and surges, sinking and boiling with the currents of circumstances. Bringing every thought into the obedience of Christ is no easy-chair job.

Tuesday morning—Glad to get the opportunity to preach the gospel of the matchless grace of our God to stoical pagan Indians. Oh what a privilege to be made a minister of the things of the "happy God". I only hope that He will let me preach to those who have never heard that name Jesus. What else is worth while in this life? I have heard of nothing better. "Lord, send me!"[9]

> "Let us our feebleness recline
> On that eternal love of Thine,
> And human thoughts forget:
> Childlike attend what Thou wilt say,
> Nor leave our sweet retreat."[10]

—Love, Jimmy.

71

The journal continues on August 23:

I write on board the train, having just finished *The Growth of a Soul*, the life of Hudson Taylor. The month's trip is over and I trust Eternity will reveal fruit for the effort. I have not known before such freedom in ministering. Surely prayer has been heard and answered. What a mystery of Grace that God should allow me to take up the Sword to battle, being such a child. And this childishness today's soul-twistings well demonstrate. Boarded at Billings about 5.30 am and slept fitfully till nine. Woke with the realization that I am in Satan's realm still. One woman near me seemed to encourage the red-eyed imp Desire, and oh, how base and hateful I think of myself now having prayed and read some of the Word. What *will* Hell be like, enraged by unslaked Lust and made seven times hotter with the vengeance of an outraged God? Oh to think of these men and women, these happy boys and girls going there. Father, save them, I pray; grace only makes me differ. When will the Spirit's power make me a witness of the things which I have seen and heard?

Slept through the Continental Divide and awoke to find streams running west instead of east. Now a friendly river is ruffled by playful winds. The beauty of the West cannot be written, so high is it, it can hardly be enjoyed in its fullness. The battling of trees for foothold among castle crags, the thunder wars in distant mountains, the casual meadows, and the great rock laminations twisted weirdly and left clutching at the heavens—who can know these but the one who knows the Forger of the Lion and Enfolder of the Lamb?

Was sensitively touched at reading of H. Taylor's love victory. I cannot understand man, even a godly man. Having been conquered by a power unseen and willingly owning the sway of the Absolute, thus "finding himself" and satiating the ultimate longings of his breast, he can ache with a perfect fury to be subjugated still further to the rule of a woman's love. Or perhaps it is his desire to possess, having been strangely dispossessed by owning Christ as Lord. And within I feel the very same. Oh that Christ were All and Enough for me. He is supposed to be, . . . but oh, to be swept away in a flood of consuming passion for Jesus, that all desire might be sublimated to Him.

Copied out a few lines from Maxwell's *Born Crucified* yesterday, which I must learn:

> "The Cross falls like a two-edged sword
> Of heavenly temper keen,
> And double were the wounds it made
> Where'er it glanced between.
> 'Twas death to sin, 'twas life
> To all who mourned for sin.
> It kindled and it silenced strife,
> Made war and peace within." [11]

Jim arrived home in Portland on the 24th, and was there only a few days before going to a Bible conference in California, and from there back to Wheaton. On August 28 he wrote this letter to his brother:

Dear brother Bert: Saturday is at its peak here at 7272. [12] The girls are arguing in the kitchen over where they will each bake their cookies so that they will not be in each other's way. This pastry feud arises from an undefined idea which has led to much food being served at "sings" at the Elliot house. I cannot say that I understand just why so much worry is expended over such menials, but the women say that eats are an absolute essential, so there is no use talking. How I wish we could enter into the Saviour's meaning when He spoke of meat which they knew not of. Notice, He was actually *refusing* food which they brought from the city because he had an opportunity to do His Father's will. But this, of course, if carried to any sort of conclusion would make us all very hungry for meat which perishes, and the discomfort would doubtless stumble some. I have come to believe a little in the apostolic principle of fasting, though I cannot say that I have entered into it with much fervour. But we must remember that "good eating" is as much taught against in the New Testament as is idolatry or physical violence. Ministry

73

of this sort would bring a man into disrepute and gain for him the term "fanatic" so we can shy away from preaching it, I suppose! Oh, what vacillating, half-way slovens, dolts, and boors we are when it comes to careful and practical application of the more delicate demands of our Christianity. I have found that fasting is a tool for use as a "pry" on the Great Inscrutable's heart; when He sees one earnest enough in his pursuit of holiness that he neglects his daily food for prayer, He must be amazed and cannot help but honour such simple sacrifice. Hmmm— long enough on this—and all from cookies in the kitchen, too.

I could not help but be disappointed somewhat to learn of your remaining in Arkansas for a time yet. However, the Lord is teaching me to say with the psalmist, "I delight to do Thy will,"[13] instead of the usual, "Well, I suppose it's the Lord's will so we'll just have to put up with it." Oh the delirium of consciously being in the will of the Master: what joy, brother! And this brings a knowledge of His presence and this affords rest. "My presence shall go with thee, and I will give thee rest."[14]

Last night was the crowning event of Patricia's girlhood dreams. And like dream-fulfilment it did indeed appear! Not even the finery of the wildest Poe's fantasies could have been more gratifying to the aesthetic sensibilities. Glows and sparkles, pastels and flowing mesh veils with hats as delicate as the wings of dragon-flies, candle-glimmer and shuddering organ-strains, smiles and laughter and a sweeping spirit of affability upon every handclasp. Amalek assumes some subtle attitudes. I would have no complaints were I not dreadfully jealous for the person in whose name all this is carried on. Power we lack; paint we have in abundance. Somehow, I have not learned the poor simple Galilean to take on such airs. Well, one benefit I found was that everyone was in a mood to talk, and this afforded some good opportunities for quiet ministration. I pray that the sweetness of the Spirit will purge out the pride I sense arising as I write these comments. Oh, for grace in the inward parts, holiness unto the Lord.

Colleen [Bert's fiancée] was imposing as a Roman matron. She has a great soul and I sense in her a rising above these paltry and beggarly things of the seen world. Deal cautiously with her, Bert, she is as a railroadman's watch—great gold, and somewhat cumbersome, but full of good works, honest and well-regulated. She is all woman, and will doubtless emit some yet unforeseen eccentricities as well as some deep-buried beauties. Eve's daughters are as flowers and none can ever say they are through unfolding. And what man can predict the consummate end of such a life when its ultimate centre is Sharon's Rose?

Your exercise for Peru intrigues me no end. It is this I wanted most to discuss with you as I have felt a shifting burden from Latin American interests to Oriental fields, more particularly India. I cannot say why, but only that the sad neglect of the North American assemblies weighs heavily upon me. We have, to date, TWO brethren from North America, in a country of 400,000,000! More than all the people in North and South America and Africa combined!

And then, too, I wanted to fellowship with you before the Throne and in "holy discourse", as Wesley used to put it. . . .

I am not at all sure of the movements of the next two weeks. Dad wants to go to the Oakland conference and I should be in Wheaton to register for the draft again by September 12. If you have any plans please let me know. Perhaps you could come to Wheaton for a brief visit. This shall be before the Lord.

Must get into the Book for a little defrosting. God make us

"*. . . lone like the Tishbite, like the Baptist, bold,*
Cast in a rare and apostolic mold".

In the clutches of the Cross,
Jim.

Notes

1. Isaiah 6:6,7.
2. John 12:26.
3. Hebrews 1:7, ASV.
4. Poem by Amy Carmichael, 'Make Me Thy Fuel'.
5. Colossians 1:29.

6. Romans 9:20.
7. 2 Corinthians 5:4.
8. 1 Corinthians 14:32.
9. Isaiah 6:8.
10. Hymn by Gambold, *Little Flock Hymnal*, 1856.
11. Quoted in *Born Crucified* by L. E. Maxwell (Chicago: Moody Press).
12. The street number of the Elliot house.
13. Psalm 40:8.
14. Exodus 33:14.

– 6 –

Behold Obscurity

I called upon the Lord...
He heard my voice...
He made darkness His covering...
He delivered me...
Yea, Thou dost light my lamp,
My God lightens darkness.[1]

BACK AT COLLEGE by the second week of September, 1948, Jim Elliot wrote to his parents describing registration and his room situation:

Arrived safely though three hours late, and was not able to register at all on Monday, so began with the Class of '50 on Tuesday morning. My courses are eight hours of Greek (Church Fathers, Xenophon, Advanced Grammar, which is a terrific course from Tenney with a $14 textbook), elementary Hebrew, and two hours of textual criticism.

My room is nice, though a little small. I have it a good deal to myself as my room-mate is nephew of the house-mother and studies and eats his meals downstairs. I lack sheets, however. Blankets are plentiful and towels I have in sufficiency. Pillows are extravagant. Send three sheets when it is convenient, they are lending me those I'm using now.

I'm certainly glad I was able to get home when I did. What I learned while there I don't think I can express, concerning the centrality of Christ in the home, in the assembly and in individual life. Oh, He is enough, satiating every cell. May we learn to give Him the deserved place, and allow Him to preside. . . .

Time is gone, with space (as in Eternity) so I must get to my first Hebrew lesson.—Lovingly to each, Jim.

A week later I stopped in Wheaton for a few days on my way to Canada, having graduated from college the previous spring. Jim and I had agreed not to correspond during the summer, but when we saw one another again in September, we knew that the three months of silence had been a good test. Our love for one another had grown, but as to God's purpose in it, there was no further sign. As Jim said, in the words of Isaiah, 'We wait for light, but behold obscurity; for brightness, but we walk in darkness.'[2]

One evening Jim allowed me to read his first journal, a notebook begun in January, 1948, and filled by September of that year. With it he handed me this note:

There are a few things I should say about all of this, I suppose. Please excuse the form. I was at no time that I can recall writing for an audience, particularly *your* probings, so you will find abundant misspellings, horrors of punctuation, and some of the thoughts are so poorly expressed that they will be meaningless. Remember, too, that I usually wrote with some portion of the Word fresh in my thoughts giving a background to the entries which a reader cannot fill in without searching every little reference, and this, I think, you will not have time to do. In spite of what I entered as a prologue [see page 57] regarding the possibility of others reading this, I find on glancing over it that I have been more honest in places than I intended. You will know me as no one else does in reading this. Most of it is heart-cry from a little child to a Father whom I have struggled to get to know. Other is purely academic and will do you no good at all. I might say that you were more in my thoughts than these pages suggest. It is not written as a diary of my experiences or feelings, but more as a "book of remembrance"[3] to enable me to ask definitely by forcing myself to put yearnings into words. This I have failed miserably to do, but I don't apologise now. All I have asked has not been given, and the Father's withholding has served only to intensify my desires. He knows that the "hungrier" one is, the more appreciative he becomes of food, and if I have gotten nothing else from this year's experience He has given me a hunger for Himself I never experienced before. He only promises water to the thirsty, satiation to the unsatisfied (I do not say *dis*satisfied), filling to those famished for righteousness. So He has, by His concealing of Himself, given me longings that can only be slaked when Psalm 17:15 is realised. Betty, we shall behold Him face to face, much as you and I have looked with longing on one another. And He will tell us of His love in those looks as we have never known it here. "Thine eyes shall see the king in his beauty: they shall behold the land that is very far off."[4]

> "There the Red Rose of Sharon
>   Unfolds its heartsome bloom,
> And fills the air of Heaven
>   With ravishing perfume:—
> Oh, to behold it blossom,
>   While by its fragrance fann'd,
> Where glory—glory dwelleth
>   In Immanuel's land!"[5]

He knows our love, and is touched from a sympathy within, and I feel He holds us from each other that He might draw us to Himself. Let us pray individually, "Draw me . . ." and it may be that then we will be allowed to say together, ". . . we will run after Thee."[6]

"*And I will wait upon the Lord, that hideth His face from the house of Jacob, and I will look for Him*" (Isaiah 8:17).

"*Our eyes are upon Thee*" (2 Chronicles 20:12).

Jim had told his parents very little about me, but wrote to them on September 26:

I have just come in from a long talk with Betty Howard. I don't know what I have written of her, nor what impressions I have given, but somehow she is deliciously satisfying company—and this, strangely enough, is not on account of a fine-featured face, a shapely form, nor even on account of rare conversational powers. Of the former two she possesses little of appeal. Of the latter, though she has decided gifts of expression, she does not at all strike one as startling. This is what amazes me, for objectively she has practically nothing that would centre my interests. We find, however, that our thought-patterns coincide in a myriad of minutiae as well as in a great many major issues. There is a thought-bond that I have known with few others, and a huge thirst for God that may surpass my own in many respects. Both of us sense the kindred interests in one another, but are a little awed to speak of it, fearing it may lead to relationships neither of us intended.

I can hear Ruby [Jim's sister-in-law] laughing, but the Lord led us both to feel last spring that we were to go through life unmarried—she from Isaiah 54, I from Matthew 19:12 and I Corinthians 7. She is not playing a game.... I have said "Begone" to this feeling often, and even now wish it did not obscure my thinking, but it persists, not as something cumbersome, a "weight", but more as soul-pressure, almost as a prayer-burden persists, only in my emotions more distinctly. She leaves Tuesday, for which I'm thankful, as I must think clearly if I'm to understand Hebrew and Greek.

The Lord knows how I surrendered this "love-life" business to Him long ago, and the assurance that He will eventually lead into His way is strong tonight. Beloved, if you ever prayed for Jim, redouble your earnestness. I seek His will alone. Enough for now. All questions will be answered as honestly as a hypocrite of my experience can answer them.

During those few days together, one verse in particular of a hymn whose nineteen verses Jim had memorised was especially meaningful to us:

> *"But flowers need night's cold darkness,*
> *The moonlight and the dew.*

> *So Christ, from one who loved it,*
> *His shining oft withdrew;*
> *And then for cause of absence*
> *My troubled soul I scann'd—*
> *But Glory shadeless shineth*
> *In Immanuel's land.*"[7]

Jim decided that we should begin a correspondence when I left for Canada. His first letter to me is dated October 2, 1948, and shows that his purpose before God remained the same:

It's hard to pull out of the nebulae that have collected in thinking about this letter, some clever point with which to impress you right off. So I won't attempt it, but proceed as though I had been writing in my present capacity for a good long time. Got your card Wednesday afternoon: clever, devastatingly so. I wish I had here a "feel-o-meter" to transcribe what has been going on inside for the last few days. I began with that word I think I spoke to you of when we were together in chapel that last morning: trembling.

And what should a tuffy like me be trembling about? Three things: you, me, and God. I tremble to think that forwardness in declaring my feeling to you is actually affecting your entire life. I have an idea that it will be almost impossible for you to discern the Lord's mind for you without struggling through a maze of thought and feeling about me. What if, in the real test, your feeling should overcome your faith? Whose then the responsibility? Not entirely yours. For this I fear—that I, stepping out of the path of the Lord for just a moment, should draw you with me and thus be accountable for the "loss" of two lives.

There is within a hunger after God, given of God, filled by God. I can be happy when I am conscious that He is doing what He wills to do within. What makes me tremble is that I might allow something else (you, for example) to take the place my God should have.... I tremble lest in any way I offend my

81

Eternal Lover. Whatever passes between you and me, let us take note of this: all shall be revoked at His command.... Above all else I will that He might find in me the travail of His soul and be satisfied. Reading in Nehemiah these days—are we willing to build with a trowel in one hand while the other grasps a sword?

Our letters were very infrequent. 'Did I not sense,' Jim wrote, 'the value of discipline, I would counsel you to give way to any urges to communicate. However, we best learn patience by practising it.'

Excerpts from the journal of this time show that the state of his soul was not constant:

September 28. "He *hath* led me, and brought me into darkness, and not into light."[8] Because I cannot see, nor even assuredly feel, His satisfaction with me, I cannot doubt the leading simply because of the dark. The leading is nonetheless real, the pathway has simply been into a place I didn't expect or ask for.

September 29. Woke this morning with thoughts from Acts 5, about holding back part of the price. Ananias and Sapphira were not slain for not giving, but for not giving everything they said they had given. Holy Ghost, forbid that I should lie against Thee, not against man, but God. How can I know my heart as regards Bets? I cannot. Thou dost, my Father. Reveal myself to me, that I may see what Thou dost see.

> *"My soul is night, my heart is steel,*
> *I cannot see, I cannot feel.*
> *For Light, for Life, I must appeal*
> *In simple faith to Jesus."*[9]

October 1. Flood of peace within this morning as I seek God's face. "He came and preached peace to you which were afar off."[10] Lord Jesus, I thank Thee that Thou didst banish the very principle of distance on that Cross. Thou wast forsaken, thrust away from God, that Thou shouldst bring me near. GRACE! All grace.

October 3. Heavy and sorrowful because of my coldness, insincerity, and fruitlessness. Oh, how needy, what emptiness I feel. I am not ready to see the King in His beauty. I should be ashamed to meet Him this night. The Saviour's words come tenderly: "Blessed are those who feel their spiritual need";[11] πτωχοί —"crouching, cringing" becomes μακάριοι—happy. How is this possible? Yea, God looks at the end!

A letter to his parents on October 8 mentions two other issues which were before him then: the possibility of being drafted, and his urgent desire to get to the mission field. Excerpts from this letter:

Fellow-heirs: Mom's birthday letter just arrived with the five dollars, and has proved already a source of comfort. Somehow I've had trouble resting in His love the last couple of days but find afresh the truth of Romans 15:13, "in believing" we find joy and peace. I've found it hard to do just that, doubting in darkness what God made lucidly clear in the light. But the soul is built for struggle and the Spirit given to comfort and sustain. What a wretched ingrate I am for all the blessings He has laid to me, signs that He is designing my life. Faith is to be the life-blood of the just, but my spirit's circulating system is a little sluggish, I fear.

This is my twenty-first birthday. I suppose I should borrow seraphic fire and wax poetic, but I don't feel quite up to it. The sweater Werner sent fits beautifully. I expect the package will arrive this afternoon. Thanks for it all in advance. And to Auntie for the five dollars, many thanksgivings. I know these gifts are backed by your prayers, for (as one brother applied it) "where your treasure is, there will your heart be also"![12] Thanks for Neil's address. I wait still for a snap of the family. The sheets are in use, you didn't need to bother with a pillow, as I don't use one.

I sent in my CO registration this week. Here is a matter in which I am concerned at my own unconcern. Somehow I can't even pray with fervour that the Lord would let me finish Wheaton. I don't care what they do with me. Yesterday I prayed that God would take me to Peru or Brazil before I pass another October 8. I know inside that the flesh would like more training

—and perhaps I'm fitted to train more—everybody seems to be planning on it around here. But those generations passing away at this moment! They must hear of the Saviour! How can we wait? O Lord of Harvest, do send forth labourers! Here am I, Lord. Behold me, send me. How deaf must be the deafness of the ear which has never heard the story; how blind the eye that has not looked on Christ for light; how pressed the soul that has no hope of glory; how hideous the fate of man who knoweth only night! God arouses us to care, to feel as He Himself does for their welfare.

The journal continues:

October 9. "Every hour I need Thee."[13] My love is faint, my warmth practically nil. Thoughts of His coming flicker and make me tremble. Oh, that I were not so empty-handed. Joy and peace can only come in believing, and that is all I can say to Him tonight. Lord, I believe. I don't love, I don't feel, I don't understand, I can only *believe*. Bring Thou faith to fruition, Great Harvest Lord. Produce in me, I pray. This came today while meditating:

> *What is this, Lord Jesus, that Thou shouldst make an end*
> *Of all that I possess, and give Thyself to me?*
> *So that there is nothing now to call my own*
> *Save Thee; Thyself alone my Treasure.*
> *Taking all, Thou givest full measure of Thyself*
> *With all things else eternal—*
> *Things unlike the mouldy pelf by earth possessed.*
> *But as to Life and godliness, all things are mine,*
> *And in God's garments dressed I am;*
> *With Thee, an heir to riches in the spheres divine.*
> *Strange, I say, that suffering loss,*
> *I have so gained everything in getting*
> *Me a friend who bore a Cross.*

October 10. Have been vividly aware of seeking the praise of men today. Tonight the Lord Himself speaks from Matthew 6.

Lord; make me to forget myself. I would not be of those who already have their reward in receiving recognition from men. My God, Thou who dost see ἐν κρύπτῳ [in secret]! What dost Thou see in me? Purge! Tear off the shell and smash it to bits. Honestly, Father, I do not *now* want to be seen. Hide me in the brighter light of the Son within. And teach me to pray in simplicity as the Lord Jesus illustrated, concerned with seven things:

> *God's name*
> *God's kingdom*
> *God's will*
> *my bread*
> *my debts*
> *my debtors*
> *deliverance from evil*

Singleness, simplicity, is required of me. One treasure, a single eye, and a sole Master.

With a deeper love for Christ, Jim experienced what many others have found—his eyes were opened to beauty hitherto unseen, as another has written:

> *"Heaven above is softer blue,*
> *Earth around is sweeter green,*
> *Something lives in every hue*
> *Christless eyes have never seen.*
>
> *Birds with gladder songs o'erflow,*
> *Flowers with deeper beauty shine,*
> *Since I know as now I know*
> *I am His, and He is mine."*[14]

Jim wrote to me in October:

I wish I could describe the colour. You may remember the great

85

oak, that sucks up sap from deep secret places and sends it to stiffen broad leaves unbelievably distant from the trunk. Chill nights have slowed its workings and the little sturdy green sentinels writhe in sackcloth now. Brilliant red sumac copses shout along the roads. The landscape has wholly gone surrealistic, unscathed greens boldly standing alongside fading orange, while yellow tries in vain to reconcile. And black starlings pepper bizarre, pungent sunsets which really need no condiment. I can't remember enjoying beauty in the fall as just now. Perhaps I am a little more aware than before.

Then in his next letter to his parents:

I was concerned after writing lest I should have been hasty in saying what I did as regards a soon removal to Peru. This morning the Lord came with thoughts of "hastening"—Proverbs 4:12, "When thou runnest, thou shalt not stumble," Isaiah 40:31, "They shall run, and not be weary," *et cetera*. Now, I know that this could never mean that I should rush out to the field. But it does mean that if I go in a hurry, there is nothing inherently wrong with hurrying if God is leading. The urgency impressed me mostly because of the language difficulties. If I ever intend to do any work among South American Indians, I might just as well determine to learn tribal languages as well as Spanish. One learns faster at 21 than he does at 25.

On the same day his journal contains this entry:

Father, if Thou wilt let me go to South America to labour with Thee and to die, I pray that Thou wilt let me go soon. Nevertheless, *not my will*.

By this time he had heard from his parents in answer to his letter about me. His father wrote:

Jim, I am jealous of any thing or person who could retard your progressive course to everlasting riches and a life completely devoted to that supreme and glorious Man at God's right hand.

Jim replied:

I wish I could describe the rest of soul I have just now. I believe in the God who pulls strings through circumstances. As regards Bets, I would have it no other way. God has made me as eager to go singly to the work as I ever was. It would be fine with me—and I say this as praising His over-abounding grace—if I never saw her again. Our fellowship has been wholesome and entirely beneficial. But as for talk of my getting married—I stand aghast at the suggestion! I have no clear leading as to what work I am to be doing, so that a wife simply cannot be decided upon. I fear for Dad in this regard. I know your heart, Padre—it beats often with my own, and God has made me willing for Christlike loneliness, thanks to your prayers. But cannot we leave all that with Him? We shall not be without signs when there are turns in the road.

And to me, his confidence in God was expressed in a letter dated October 24:

The confidence of Philippians 1:6 assuages all doubt for me. He cannot fail us. Oh, He may lead us oceans apart (and can we not trust Him for that, too?), but are we so childish (I do not say childlike) as to think that a God who could scheme a Jesus-plan would lead poor pilgrims into situations they could not bear? Dost thou believe that God doth answer prayer, my heart? Yea, I believe. Then will He not most assuredly answer that frequent cry of thine, "Lead me, Lord"? I am as confident of God's leading as I am of His salvation. May He not so often have to address us ὀλιγόπιστοι ["little-faiths"]!

The journal continues:

October 26. Prayed a strange prayer today. I covenanted with the Father that He would do either of two things: either glorify Himself to the utmost in me or slay me. By His grace I shall not have His second best. For He heard me, I believe, so that now I have nothing to look forward to but a life of sacrificial sonship (that's how my Saviour glorified Him) or heaven—soon. Perhaps tomorrow! What a prospect!

The month of October ended on a happier strain than it had begun, as a letter to me, dated the 31st, evidences:

It's a late Sunday afternoon, a grey, gloating October day of the sort that makes you downcast when you have not had any mail all week. It would make one that way if God had not previously foxed grey October and the mails and a whole lot more by providing what Nehemiah called "the joy of Jehovah",[15] which is also to be one's stronghold. I almost took offence at the post-mistress when she said all the mail was put out, and I had an empty box. However, this queer "joy" is a patent panacea for all such ills and I marvel at my light heart while looking at the date of your last handwriting.

He is giving me such good things I wonder that I could want more. Much impressed lately with the blessing of being called to battle on the Winner's side. Think of it, sister—you and I shall one day share with Him the promised triumph when He comes with blood-bathed garments and eye of flame, mocking at twentieth-century wiseacres. Exulting we shall follow and wonder then that we ever disbelieved. Does He seem slow? Let not the counsel and spirit of a clod whose life is vapour cause us to think anything but that a "little while"[16] is just that! Not only is He sure to come, but suddenly and soon!... As soon as we believe, He will do. "The hour is coming,"[17] He says, but there's the rub—mustard seed is rare stuff today.

Notes

1. Psalm 18.
2. Isaiah 59:9.
3. Malachi 3:16.
4. Isaiah 33:17.
5. From 'Rutherford's Hymn' by Anne R. Cousins, 1857.

6. Song 1:4.
7. From 'Rutherford's Hymn'.
8. Lamentations 3:2.
9. From the hymn 'I've Tried in Vain' by James Proctor, in *Victorious Life Hymns* (Philadelphia: The Sunday School Times Co.).
10. Ephesians 2:17.
11. Matthew 5:3, Goodspeed's translation.
12. Matthew 6:21.
13. From the hymn by Annie S. Hawks.
14. From the hymn by G. Wade Robinson.
15. Nehemiah 8:10, ASV.
16. John 16:16.
17. John 5:25.

— 7 —

Wine of Bewilderment

Now Christ is the visible expression of the invisible God. . . . He is both the First Principle and the Upholding Principle of the whole scheme of creation.[1]

DESPITE THE PRESSURE of studies, Jim found time at midday to spend in the Word. He wrote to his family on November 7:

Beloved Family: Sunday night again and high time I was getting something on paper to let you all know what great faithfulness the Father continues to manifest on my behalf. I can never remember being busier with details (all of them "things honest"[2]) yet with such a happy state of rest of soul. "They that wait upon the Lord shall renew their strength."[3] Of course I can't do all I would like by way of service for the glorious Servant who offers me the yoke-sharing next to Himself in this "field" He has purchased, but I do certainly rejoice at the abiding source of power found through the supply of the Spirit. Been much in the psalms lately at noontime—incidentally, I would exhort you each to begin taking a few moments out with your Lover at midday, according to the pattern of the woman of the Song, "Tell me, where thou makest thy flock to rest at noon; for why should I be as one veiled beside the flocks of my companions?"[4] Often at noon there is a tendency for the soul to be "veiled", clouded with world-lore, filmed over with temporali-

ties. Just a few moments spent before the Shepherd, listening to
the silence of His love and telling Him the state of your soul
even if it's not warm toward Him, just to keep short accounts by
simple confession—this has been a great blessing to me.

As for coming home at Christmas, you will not understand
why I feel a responsibility to be at the Student Mission Convention here at Illinois University. And I will not take time to say
why, except that I am trusting God to make that a powerful
force in His hands to the thrusting forth of labourers and also to
speak to me regarding a definite field. I have not been able to
shake a pervading concern for Moslem work, especially as it
relates to unreached India. But He knows, and I wait.

Amused and a little mad at myself when you mention reading
my description of Betty last spring, Mom. I hate to break the
news to you now, but you have reared a good hypocrite in your
youngest son. I was deliberately striving for effect in that letter,
which I thought I had happily achieved. I was trying to throw
all you hounds off the track completely. One of your late letters
confirms that I succeeded in this and held up a fair front in
August. When I wrote that letter no one but me had any inkling
that I had feeling for Betty. She had none herself until I told her
on May 31. Even Dave had to be tipped off and he was thunder-
struck. Don't ask me why I held back from telling anyone my
feelings. I was, frankly, scared, not knowing my own heart in
the matter—and I have said some strong things about boy-girl
relations, you know. In it all I have been transparent before the
Lord. I did not court Betty's affections, though I may have done
some "stage-setting" which impressed her. I dated her once in
early spring; all other contact was commonplace and academic.
This will probably inspire more questions. I will try to be more
honest from here on out. As to her being critical and bossy,
Mom, those are things she never dared be with me. That
information comes from crafty drawing out of Dave things he
never knew he revealed. Betty is the sledgehammer type of
personality when she knows you, though she may appear quiet
at first glance. She is blunt and dominating and this makes her
tend to domineer, but I can't explain her. You must get to know
her yourself. This may never be necessary, as my life and hers are
"committed". I must feel more definite evidence from God and

circumstances before I take any more steps that way. He has not led me to pray for this.

On November 16 Jim wrote:

Enjoyed your letter, Padre, but find you are very evasive as regards what I am really concerned with, i.e., going to the mission field next year. Next time you get inspiration please give a line or two on what you think of my possible leaving. And Mother, please let's not have any more of this talk about staying home, telling people of the "need". That would be *augmenting* the need. There are too many good preachers berating people night after night about a lost world who have never faced the challenge of sacrificial foreign service themselves. I feel as if I haven't got any excuse whatsoever to let a body such as you have given me get fat leaning on pulpits. There's work to be done, and skilled labourers are needed to complete the building of God. May He grant that I be one of them. What greater privilege than to be able to aid in presenting a glorious Church to such a worthy Redeemer?

From the journal:

November 18. "... all the days of his vain life he spendeth as a shadow."[5] I find now the literal truth of these words in my daily round. I watch sunrise silhouette the Tower from my window, and without any sense that day is gone, see grey November deepen into moon-mixture. How few, how short these hours my heart must beat, then on—into the real world where the unseen becomes important. O my soul—what shall it be for thee in that Day when thou standest before the God who breathed thee?

Jim had been made president of the Student Foreign Missions Fellowship (FMF) on campus, and this, with other extra-curricular activities, made for a heavy schedule, which he outlined in a letter to me:

November 20. "They made me a keeper of the vineyards, but mine own vineyard have I not kept."[6] So the Lover of the Song. How I experience this daily only one who knows responsibility can understand. You wonder what it's all about. Here are some typical examples: FMF team to Aurora College (three meetings, for planning and prayer); complete reorganizing of FMF literature, plans for advertising a new practical missions course under Prof. Winsor and Dr Martin; gospel team to Baptist Church in Chicago Sunday night; Student Council meeting Monday night, prayer group leaders and Relief Board meetings Tuesday; FMF Wednesday; Christian Council meeting Thursday, and trip to North Central College with Student Council; Friday—FMF executive prayer meeting, then the sending of 800 packages of books to alumni missionaries in a workshop that lasted till 11.30 pm, and they're not stamped yet! Well, I think you get the idea. A yoke is a good thing for a young man, according to Lamentations 3:27, good for his neck and will, but oppressive to a zealous spirit. Especially when I'm supposed to be an honour student, and there is not a single course of which I can say, "Well, I've got *that* one under control." And ringing in my ears is Coach Olson's last remark, "Why weren't you out to practice last night, Elliot?" This is, I know, a wonderful context in which to bear Spirit-fruit.

And to his parents he made this comment:

Not that I don't enjoy the work, or would complain under responsibility—but I fear my heart is wizened and chilled, while my head is widened and warmed! Likely the same struggles will be faced anywhere else, but I like to dream of a little less *activity* and a little more production beyond that sheepskin which will make of me a BA, whatever that means.

The same letter continues, speaking of the partisan spirit which was destroying unity among Christians:

I am more convinced than ever that God deals with individuals as they individually respond to his Word, *regardless* of their

93

Church association. So that I am beginning to think that the thing to be stressed is not the form of assembly worship, but eager searching and obedience to the Scriptures. Nothing else will make the man of God "throughly furnished",[7] fruitful in every good work.

Discouragement is a Satanic tool that seems to fit my disposition and the Enemy knows it. When I look at the work in the assembly, and realise that I've been there almost four years but have not seen a single soul led to Christ, my increasing tendency is to throw in the sponge and call it quits. Gospel meeting after gospel meeting, with no one strange coming out—and worse yet, none of the saints seem very deeply exercised about it. "How long, Lord, when wilt Thou come unto me?"[8] Why does He wait till the fourth watch to come to us instead of in the evening? Well, all my doubts and fears (hinges on which swing the gates of Hell) cannot prevail to take Him from His throne nor stop Him from the building of His Church.

The journal continues:

November 24. My spirit is all aruffle again at the vast, inexplicable complexities of humankind, and the careless, ineffective manner we fool "fundamentalists" use in answering the cry of hearts which cannot understand themselves. I don't know what the Ecclesiast meant when he said "God hath set the world in the heart of men,"[9] but it might be suggestive of my feelings now. The world, with its huge broil of minutiae, is within! Time with its tempest; space with its apparent infinitude, motion, change, that sense of "something far more deeply interfused"— with the psychological and physiological factors—all these, and more. Whatever can relate them and bring meaning to this all? Surely not our little church-goings and doctrine-learnings. It overwhelms me. I would despair indeed were it not for things like this: καὶ αὐτός ἐστιν προ πάντων καὶ τὰ παντα ἐν αὐτῷ συνέστηκεν [1] ("He is both the First Principle and the Upholding Principle of the whole scheme of creation.")[10]

November 25. What I will be doing one year from today is a complete mystery. Perhaps a sick bed or a coffin—glory! Either

94

of these would be fine, but the latter would be immortality, a swallowing up by Life. For this I am most anxious.

To me on November 27 Jim wrote of a talk he had with a fellow student on Thanksgiving afternoon:

He was ready to throw Christianity overboard and turn modernist, terrifically confused because of all he saw pawned off in the name of Christ. Well, I happened to run into this fellow last Tuesday, and, sensing a little of his trouble, made a date to talk with him yesterday. He thinks now that he and I are the only heretics around here, and is glad he has found such a liberal as I am who believes that a man does not have to come all at once into the family of God with a jolt and accompanying spinal exhilarations. Personally, I wasn't "saved" all at once, but took some years coming into my present settled convictions about the truth of God. So why should I demand that conversion be immediate in all others? Christ healed men differently. Some, *in absentia*—He spoke a word, and there was a lightning-fast reaction. Others He touched, spat upon, made clay, spoke to and questioned, then when they saw men "as trees walking" [11] He went through the whole process again. Let not him who accepts light in an instant despise him who gropes months in shadows. It took the Twelve three years to apprehend what was being shown them. The natural, so often illustrative of the spiritual, teaches that healing and growth, yea, even birth, are processes, and I think we altar-callers often perform abortions in our haste to see "results".

Well, let's see—that takes us up to 10 am Thanksgiving Day. A couple of hours in Hebrew, then a turkey dinner in the dining-hall. Noon devotions (if you haven't begun yet, I exhort you, get started), then some time in the patristics and over to Auntie's for a 4.30 turkey with Ron. Home again by 7.15 for a time of soul-tonic with Dave, Art Johnston, Bob Weeber, and Bob Sawyer. Ah, what times! I'll look back on those hours of mutual exhortation, heart-searching, and prayer as building blocks which have laid the foundation of my life. We miss this intimacy with our insistence on "let's have a crowd out"—while the few gathering expressly "in His name"—find of a surety that He is in the midst....

God has blessed me with a queer twist that makes me laugh at almost anything, though sometimes it gets way out of hand. This may not be valid, but what do you think of translating μακάριος as "happy"? If this will pass the lexicographers I suggest it for I Timothy 1:11, "the gospel of the happy God". Whenever I get downcast, the Lord feeds me pills of praise.

A letter to his parents written the following day, typical in its occupation with Christ and eternity of many he wrote, is worth quoting almost in full:

November gone, and still no real winter in these parts. Frosty in the mornings but days are usually bright. Were it only for the weather I would be encouraged beyond measure, but the work schedule keeps me snatching at every moment for what it's worth. I suppose time has always gone as fast as it does now and it is silly to say "how time flies!" since it has always been the nature of time to "fly" and we are carried along in its current at the same rate from cradle to coffin, and should not act surprised at its passing. Only one is increasingly conscious of the rate as he finds more to be done and discovers the enormous obstacles, within and without, which oppose their accomplishment. Life? "It is even a vapour that appeareth for a little time." [12] And this musing spurs me on: "For yet a little while and He that shall come will come and will not tarry. Behold, I come quickly and my reward is with me." [13] What a challenge! What shall be my reward in that day? How much will have to be consumed at the glance of His "flaming eye"? How little remains to His everlasting praise? Looking at my days—how short they are, how unproductive, how full of incidentals, how little real production for the Harvest-Master.

Spent this afternoon with Ron at ————'s. They were most hospitable and were eager to be remembered to you all, especially you, Mother. E. says she has never met another like you or one even comparable, and I think I should countersign that with a hearty amen! They have a nice home and belongings and two cute kiddies, but are so like the rest of us that it is again disheartening. We are so utterly ordinary, so commonplace, while we profess to know a Power the twentieth century does not reckon with. But we are "harmless", and therefore unharmed. We are spiritual pacifists, non-militants, conscientious objectors in this battle-to-the-death with principalities and powers in high places. Meekness must be had for contact with men, but brass, outspoken boldness is required to take part in the comradeship of the Cross. We are "sideliners"—coaching and criticizing the real wrestlers, while content to sit by and leave the enemies of God unchallenged. The world cannot hate us, we are too much like its own. Oh, that God would make us dangerous!

Thanksgiving spent at Auntie's with the annual turkey and trimmings and accompanying results. Not much done for God that day, I fear. But had one suggested that we throw out convention and fast or pray, all would wonder what he had been reading or where his aesthetic sense of sentiment was buried—so why suggest, one so seldom finds a kindred heart....

Hard to imagine you so crippled, Mom. Auntie thinks you should come here and she could get you to rest a little. Utopian ideal, of course, but a noble suggestion. A deep sense of remorse prevails when I think of how much you have sacrificed on my account with such scanty results. God will have to reward you. I cannot. "Thy Father which seeth in secret shall reward thee openly." [14]

No opportunity to get into the big Chicago conference where the brethren rally year by year to encourage themselves in the grand old tradition. I fear I'm getting a bit cynical about these smug, powerless "PB's". [15] When it is good, it is very, very good, but when it is smug, it is horrid. I have met several earnest kids here from various backgrounds, completely muddled because of the confusion of "Fundamentalism" with what the New Testament represents as Christian. Talk of Evolution! One would hardly recognise the species today if it were not clinging to the old names. I sense fires burning, within which may make of me a fanatic reactionary, but as another has prayed, "Lord, deliver us from our sad, sweet, stinking selves." Oh why stand we debating whether or not children under the "age of accountability" (whatever that may mean) are going to heaven when we are dead sure that multitudes round us are pouring hourly into hell?

You ask whether Betty will go to Portland if I asked. I mentioned it, but she hasn't said a word. I'm quite sure she won't be going to Jersey and the only way I can think of getting a definite response is to just flat invite her. She certainly will not invite herself and I don't feel up to sending her home without your making the first move. Naturally I should like you to meet her, but you won't get to know her in a week or two. My mind is free from concern in the matter. I'm not ashamed of her nor of you all, nor of my present esteem of you both. Do as you feel the Lord leads.

If Mrs Rossler can secure at a rate any of that light airmail paper we got a year ago, I would appreciate some.

". . . in His temple doth everyone say 'Glory'." [16] The Lord is a hard taskmaster, telling me to rejoice and sing a praise-psalm when things oppress. Naturally, I rebel and quote Proverbs 25:20, "As he that taketh away a garment in cold weather . . . so is he that singeth songs to an heavy heart." "Sympathise," I cry, and He peels off my overcoat of self-pity by saying, "Praise, child, and be warmed within!" Ever notice that? Whenever I want comfort He tells me to "count it all joy" [17], and then, queerly, I heed, and it all becomes sweet.

> *"If our love were but more simple,*
> *We should take Him at His word,*
> *And our lives would be all sunshine*
> *In the sweetness of our Lord."* [18]

Ah, how many Marahs have been sweetened by a simple, satisfying glance at the Tree and the love which underwent its worst conflict there. Yea, the Cross is the tree that sweetens the waters. "Love never faileth. . . . Many waters cannot quench love." [19]

Resting in *that* love, then, and praying that we may be found abiding therein at the last trumpet, I wait as a loving son and brother, Jim.

The journal continues on December 4:

What would it be with no Spirit to restrain? Thou hast done well, my God, in getting hold of me. I would set this world ablaze with passion didst Thou not possess me. And even now I tremble lest, succumbing to these things, I should openly sin and bring reproach to Thy great Name. Listen, soul: "In that day that I am afraid, I will confide in Thee. I will not fear; what can flesh do unto me?"[20] "Thou hast delivered my soul from death. Wilt Thou not keep my feet from falling?"[21]

December 5. Deep sense of uselessness this morning. Enjoyed prayer, not for the thrusting out of labourers so much as for their heart-preparation in learning to know Christ. What a ragged, shoddy thing Christianity has come to be, honouring men and means, places and crowds—O Lord, deliver me from the spirit of this faithless generation. How I should long to see the simplicity and powerful beauty of the New Testament fellowship reproduced, but no one seems to be similarly exercised here, so I must wait. O Christ, let me know *Thee*—let me catch glimpses of Thyself, seated and expectant in glory, let me rest there despite all wrong surging round me. Lead me in the right path, I pray.

His Word came clearly just after writing the above, "Take heed...be quiet...let not thy heart faint.... If ye will not believe, surely ye will not be established."[22]

On the same day, Jim wrote:

Dearest Family: Much cheered in receiving two letters this week from Dad and Bob, with your enclosed note, Mom. It's a real joy to know your prayer fellowship on my behalf. Be assured of my burden for you each.... And your exercise re: waiting upon the Lord for thrusting forth into His harvest, Bob—how anxious I am that we should be accounted worthy of such a calling.... Fret not to go ahead in surgery or fracture or tropical disease, Bob—as your life is in His hands so are the days of your life. Remember you are immortal until your work is done. But don't let the sands of time get into the eye of your vision to reach those who still sit in darkness. They simply *must hear*. Wives, houses, practices, education must learn to be disciplined by this rule: "Let the dead attend to the affairs of the already dead. Go thou and attend the affairs of the dying."[23]

Wondering if Mom is at seaside this week-end. Wish she could get somewhere where honest-to-goodness rest would be possible, about six months of it. Don't know what I would like to do more than come home and pitch in and help a little. Likely, though, what's needed there is not more help but a little more discipline to "come apart and rest awhile"[24] with the Seated Saviour just a little more every day. Such would lubricate the days much better than another voice-box and two more hands.

December 7 (from the journal). Lord makes Himself very near and tender tonight. Spirit of gratefulness and much peace combined with an unworthiness so utter I hardly dare speak of it. War with Japan began seven years ago today. Thankful for peace and confidence within.

December 8. "Thou hast made me to drink the wine of bewilderment."[25] Strangely excited with—just the forces of Life, I guess. Feel "poured out" over a great many interests with intense desire to do but so little power and time to accomplish. For example, wrestling: I would love to be on the mat right now, not to be seen so much as just to be struggling, putting out for all I'm worth. And here I kneel, at 2.45 pm, writing! Hebrew: I can think of nothing I'd like better than to be able to pick up a page of Hebrew Old Testament and read it at sight. Greek loses a lot of its challenge when one gets to know a little. Betty: had a letter from her just now. Long to be with her, or at least sit down and write to her. Thus the body, the mind, and the soul are all pretty much awake, and I don't feel at all like studying. Perhaps this is the "wine of bewilderment". O Father, let me not be dissipated on non-essentials. Bring the Word to me in power; sublimate these huge hungers to the obedience of Christ. Above all these things, I would have holiness. Teach me the path of faith.

A letter to me, dated December 9, says:

Snow greeted me as I stepped from the gym after wrestling practice tonight—fine and silty, falling ever-so-softly on a wizened, autumn-swept turf, and mantling cheerless sidewalks with myriad diamonds which jump and vanish as one walks along. I get hungry for the big, husky mountains at times like this when seasons change—out West where evergreens are free for the hacking, where footprints of other than these sleek squirrels pattern an unusual trail. I get a little nostalgic and read Robert Service:

> "They have cradled you in custom, they have primed you with their
>   preaching,
> They have soaked you in convention, through and through;
> They have put you in a showcase; you're a credit to their teaching—
> But don't you hear the Wild?—it's calling you.
>
> Let us probe the silent places, let us seek what luck betide us;
> Let us journey to a lonely land I know.
> There's a whisper on the night-wind, there's a star agleam to guide us,
> And the Wild is calling, calling . . . let us go." [26]

The stuff really goes to my head and gets to be a real snare sometimes. He writes one piece called "The Men That Don't Fit In" that suits my spirit pretty much.

Your letter came yesterday but not until waiting had spawned fears and even doubts, I must confess! I think Solomon remarks somewhere that "hope deferred maketh the heart sick" [27] and perhaps this has been what's given such an unconventional spiritgraph this week. Jubilant and garrulous for a time, eager to wrestle or bat the breeze in the training room, then "vacant and pensive" (Wordsworth's "Daffodils", I think) with a gnawing yen to read Hebrew but little will to stick out the grind of consistent study for any length of time. Joy and confidence, then tight-lipped bitterness at nearly anything. Have felt an honest lonesomeness for Mom and Dad and an urge to be unclasped by all responsibility around here. And yet, with the covers tight around my neck last night in the dark, I felt as close to the Saviour as I have ever been, holding quiet communion. I

think these are signs of the birth of that second kind of faith—
expressed by Spurgeon in the now familiar phrase, "Little faith
will bring the soul to heaven, but much faith will bring heaven
to the soul."

On December 11 Jim wrote to his family:

Only a week more of school and a term paper due at the end of
this week, so I suppose the prospect of rest over the holidays will
grow sweeter as the next six days pass. As yet I don't know what
I'll do for vacation. Dave has invited me home to Jersey and I
would like to go except that it involves more expense than I care
to lay out just now, and then too it's only for a week so it would
be kind of a rush trip. We must be back to Urbana by Monday
the twenty-seventh, for the Student Missionary Convention.
Auntie has asked me to spend the vacation with them, and this
seems most plausible, as I feel the need of rest more than
anything else just now. It's all in the hands of the Mighty
"Planner of Lives" so I am at rest.

We lost our first wrestling meet to Illinois Normal today.
Quite a blow, since it's the first time they've beaten us in
remembered history and we're supposed to have an experienced
team. I took my match by a decision of 14 points to 3, but
couldn't seem to pin the guy. Sure fun and keeps me fit.

A couple of your late letters mention the thought that I am
not happy. I can't understand what nuances my letters contain,
but I fear you have misinterpreted. It is true I feel as never before
the pressure of studies and responsibility around here. The
uncertainty of the next year adds its sobriety to my thinking,
but for all these things, I would have no cause to call upon the
Remover of Hindrances. Banish your fears; my soul is glad in
God, though I tend to aggrandise the difficulties and fail often
to give glory to the Great Solver thereof.

You are all worried that my faith in the simple New Testament
principles of gathering for worship is being shaken. I think my
chief interest lies in the New Testament, and I can offer no
harsher criticism. Fret not yourselves as to my sincerity in
sticking on at the assembly; it is because I am positive that

God's pattern is preached there, if not practised. Mind you, there is much better "preaching" in the independent groups here in Wheaton, and far better practice, but the preaching is often man's pattern. The great mistake is in preaching to our fellow-believers, "Come out from among them and be ye separate,"[28] with the suggestion that they should come out to us and be separate. It struck me forcibly that only Almighty God can make that exhortation—for only He is above and beyond all our petty walls of party separation. Our exhorting should conform to Hebrews 13:13, "Let us go forth unto Him." Preach this and we shall not divide but unite. Ours is not to say "come out where we are" but to take our position within the admitted bounds of human doing and say, "Let us go forth unto Him." As for Betty: if she were not capable of receiving as the Word of God New Testament truth as it is *on the page*, though such reception lead her to do the costly unconventional, she would have no attraction for me whatever. In fact, I am coming to think that it is this—her divergence from the run-of-the-mill stock—that appeals to me most.

On December 18, in another letter to the family, Jim wrote:

I was quite startled to read the new wedding [brother Bert's] date. It falls exactly at mid-semester time. Exams start January 21 and it is possible I could take mine early so as to get home by Tuesday or Wednesday. School does not begun until Thursday, February 3, and I could preregister so as not to miss anything. However, the old problem of expense seems to me most pertinent now. Especially as you say what you do about next semester's tuition. Let us pray much before coming to any exciting conclusions. I would sure like to be there, but an extra $100 right now would seem pretty costly....

"And the work of righteousness shall be peace, and the effect of righteousness quietness and assurance forever."[29] "In quietness and in confidence shall be your strength."[30] I think the devil has made it his business to monopolise on three elements: noise, hurry, crowds. If he can keep us hearing radios, gossip, conversation, or even sermons, he is happy. But he will not allow quietness. For he believes Isaiah where we do not. Satan is quite aware of the power of silence. The voice of God, though persistent, is soft.... I am finding your counsel to get enough sleep most practical, Mother. Not only to be fit for the day and able to relax, but for spiritual awareness and reception one must simply be rested if he is to be blessed. Let us resist the devil in this by avoiding noise as much as we can, purposefully seeking to spend time alone, *facing ourselves* in the World.... Satan is aware of where we find our strength. May he not rob us!

The journal continues on December 22:

Feel deep urge to be moving above this slough of mediocrity which seems to characterise my days. Father, if these strong currents be flesh-driven, staunch them and slay them. But if they can be sublimated, channelled, into courses which will do Thy service, then intensify them, mobilise them, give them direction. For I long (Thou knowest how earnestly) that the Bride of Thy dear Son be made perfect and entire in my day. Yea, Lord, if it cost me my bride in this life, let me have Thy grace and power to bring to the Lamb the reward of His sufferings. "If Thy dear Home be fuller, Lord, for that a little emptier my house on earth, what rich rewards that guerdon were!"[31]

He wrote to me on the same day:

I trust the Source of Sacred Gladness will find you ready soil to receive the abundance of His showers. Somewhere Amy Carmichael writes of little joys, like flowers springing by the path unnoticed except by those who are looking for them. So have I known it since last writing—little things, like a quietly sinking sun, a friendly dog, a ready smile. We sang a little song in kindergarten which I've never forgotten:

> "The world is so full of a number of things,
> I'm sure we should all be as happy as kings."[32]

Simple, but such a devastating rebuke to the complaining heart! I am impressed with the joy that is ours in Christ, so that heaven above and earth below become brighter and fairer, would we only exult in our possessions.

I have recalled several times this week last Christmas time. I thought of the sledding that night in Philadelphia—how we called each other "brother" and "sister" every time our paths crossed. And it doesn't take vacation to recall those late conversations in the kitchen and living-room at Birdsong. I mulled over those times all summer, and have had to turn on my mental heels many a time, quoting "vanity of vanities"[33] from the Preacher. Much as I like to reminisce, I find it saps one's powers of meditation and concentration. But memory keeps throwing little lapping waves on to the shore of immediate consciousness, and one must keep the Son before his eyes, remembering heart-fixation that makes men flint.

Finished my seminar term-paper for Dr Stone Friday afternoon, on the ecbatic use of ἵνα in the New Testament. Saturday went by as I painted signs for the conference display. Monday I wrote letters, did a little Greek for Patristics, went sledding and snow-balling with some of the Lombard kids. Yesterday I went to Chicago with Uncle Earl to get a new suit, as he and Auntie had decided I needed one for Christmas. Good thing they're here—I never realised I needed one! Last night a gang of us went to the Inter-Varsity Christian Fellowship office in Chicago to pack some things for the conference. Bed at 1.00 am, up at 9 this morning. Encouraged my pagan instincts (and my Auntie) by putting up their Christmas tree this morning. I must go back there now, as they're having a missionary from Trinidad for supper, and I want to quiz him about a thing or two.

And now men talk of Christ-mass—weird monstrosity and mixture of bright lights, reindeer, tissue paper and scraggly evergreens; jumbled mobs, bargain-baited, "striving after wind",[34] singing "Silent Night"—but what know they of Immanuel? How can they understand the God who once was wrapped in swaddling clothes? How long, Lord, ere they bow the knee?

This week comes your birthday. I think you're twenty-two,

but I don't feel that merits congratulations. Lots of folks make it past that. This can be said appropriately, however: of our God the psalmist said, "Thou crownest the year with Thy goodness (*this* year, particularly). Thy paths exude abundance."[35] For the next, I charge thee, Beloved, seek *His* counsel. The next will be a crisis year for us both and we must individually find His path. His Word is sure, "Thou shalt guide me with Thy counsel and afterward receive me to glory."[36] He is called the Wonderful Counsellor. I think the first modifies the second. And listen as He speaks: "I counsel thee to buy gold."[37] Consider not the cost; get His gold, and your riches will be eternal.

Notes

1. Colossians 1:15,17,JBP.
2. Phillipians 4:8, para.
3. Isaiah 40:31.
4. Song 1:7,ASV.
5. Ecclesiastes 6:12,ASV.
6. Song 1:6.
7. 2 Timothy 3:17.
8. Revelation 6:10, AV, and Psalm 101:2, ASV, (both para.).
9. Ecclesiastes 3:11.
10. Colossians 1:17, Greek text.
11. Mark 8:24.
12. James 4:14.
13. Hebrews 10:37 and Revelation 22:12.
14. Matthew 6:6.
15. 'Plymouth Brethren', the name given by denominationalists to certain groups of Christians who seek to imitate (as literally as possible) the New Testament pattern for the local church.
16. Psalm 29:9, ASV.
17. James 1:2.
18. From the hymn by F. W. Faber
19. 1 Corinthians 13:8,ASV and Song 8:7.
20. Psalm 56:3,4.
21. Psalm 56:13.

22. Isaiah 7:4,9, ASV.
23. Luke 9:60, para.
24. Mark 6:31, para.
25. Psalm 60:3, JND.
26. From 'The Call of the Wild' in *The Complete Poems of Robert Service* (New York: Dodd, Mead & Co., 1940). Used by permission of the publisher.
27. Proverbs 13:12.
28. 2 Corinthians 6:17.
29. Isaiah 32:17.
30. Isaiah 30:15.
31. From poem by Amy Carmichael.
32. 'Happy Thought' by Robert Louis Stevenson, from *A Child's Garden of Verses*.
33. Ecclesiastes 1:2.
34. Ecclesiastes 5:16, para.
35. Psalm 65:11, para.
36. Psalm 73:24.
37. Revelation 3:18, para.

– 8 –

Sheep—Destined for the Altar

But he made His own people to go forth like sheep, and guided them in the wilderness like a flock. And He led them on safely, so that they feared not.[1]

THE END OF THE YEAR 1948 found Jim attending the International Student Missionary Convention at the University of Illinois. A letter to his parents described his impressions:

Conference here is more than half over, and I have mingled feelings about it all. I had come half-way expectant for a time of deep heart-searching and -breaking, with a resultant turning of lives to the more real things—the unseen treasures. That has come to my own heart in a sense, for I have had keen certainty of the Lord's presence in prayer and meditation at noon times in a quiet little Episcopal church near the campus. But the spirit of desperation to do God's will has not gripped this group of 1,450 as a whole—yet. We lack the intensity of feeling deeply, that sense of inevitable *must* which Christ possessed, the zeal for God's house that consumed Him. As I look about here in this comfortable lounge in the Student Union Building, I see all sorts of people. Two Anglican padres from Toronto converse in one corner. A prim little Mennonite bishop walks by. A dark-visaged Latin reads the daily announcement sheet directly in front of me. A nervous-looking Britisher purrs rapid cockney phrases into the ears of a painted American co-ed at my left. Plain grey-haired missionary ladies look wistfully about. Some read Scriptures, others write or gabble happily on any number of subjects.

Think for a moment of the potential here: students from all over the country and other parts of the world, met here specifically to study missions. How long shall we sit analyzing, questioning, arguing, discussing, before God lays hold on us with power to thrust us out to the billion and a half who have not yet heard? But one can pray—and I ask this of you *all*. Lay hold with all your powers upon the Lord of the Harvest that He would make the effects of this convention resound in dark places for His Name's sake.

He wrote to me of the convention's significance for him personally:

The Lord has done what I wanted Him to do for me this week. I wanted primarily a peace about going into pioneer Indian work. As I analyze my feelings now, I am quite at ease about saying that tribal work in the South American jungle is the general direction of my missionary purpose. Also, I am confident that God wants me to begin jungle work single. Those are some good-sized issues to get settled finally in a week.

And on January 18 he continued:

My decision was based on seeing a man from central Brazilian jungles who has done a work comparable to the sort I feel exercised for. He told of the impossibility of marriage in his particular context. That was all—no voices, no Scripture, just the settled peace of decision which often comes to the exercised soul. I will *not* say God is leading me to a life of celibacy. *I only know what I need to know for now*, and that is that the Lord does not want me seeking a wife until I have His definite sign. And apparently there is no immediate reason to expect that sign.

Let me tell you a story. When I returned from Birdsong last January, I had fallen—or grown very much into attachment to the girl you know better than anyone else. Because of heart-searching I had had regarding God's use of those who have made themselves eunuchs for the kingdom's sake, I determined that none should know of my affinity for that girl, even though it was evident that we should be much together. I can remember confessing to the Lord what I called "my love for her", and striving daily to forget and swallow hard. In those days of decision to keep silence, it seemed as if I had sealed the course of my whole life, and I must confess, I felt as if I were somewhat of a martyr. There came to me then this song:[2]

> *Why should I droop in sorrow? Thou'rt ever by my side!*
> *Why, trembling, dread the morrow?*
> *What ill can e'er betide?*
> *If I my cross have taken, 'tis but to follow Thee;*
> *If scorned, despised, forsaken, naught severs me from*
> *   Thee.*[3]

And in my hymn-book, there is a blue line drawn, with the date as I have indicated.

Dearest Betty, I charge you in the name of our Unfailing Friend, do away with all waverings, bewilderment, and wonder. You have bargained for a *cross*. Overcome anything in the confidence of your union with Him, so that contemplating trial, enduring persecution or loneliness, you may know the blessings of the "joy set before".[4] "We are the sheep of His pasture. Enter into His gates with thanksgiving, and into His courts with praise."[5] And what are sheep doing going into the gate? What is their purpose inside those courts? To bleat melodies and enjoy the company of the flock? No. Those sheep were destined for the *altar*. Their pasture feeding had been for one purpose, to test them and fatten them for bloody sacrifice. Give Him thanks, then, that you have been counted worthy of His altars. Enter into the work with praise.

This letter roused in me the old fear that I might be the means to turn Jim aside from God's purpose for him, and I wrote again, asking if he was sure that we did right to continue our correspondence. He was sure.

God has led us together in writing, and I have no sign that His will is anything else than that we continue. If such a course leads ultimately to a more bitter renunciation than withdrawal just now should mean, the more bitter way is to be God's way. Remember Marah. "And the Lord showed him a tree, which, when he had cast into the waters, the waters were made sweet."[6] The *cloud* led Israel to Marah.

Notes

1. Psalm 78:52,53.
2. January 8, 1948.
3. From the hymn 'Lord Jesus, Friend Unfailing' by Samuel C. G. Kuster.
4. Hebrews 12:2, para.
5. Psalm 100:3.
6. Exodus 15:25.

− 9 −

Goaded by God

*My son, hear the instruction of thy father, and forsake not the law of
thy mother: For they shall be an ornament of grace unto thy head,
and chains about thy neck.* [1]

IN JANUARY Jim's proposed trip West to attend his
brother Bert's wedding began to materialise when his
professors consented to his taking the final examinations
early. Upon receipt of this news, Jim's parents sent him
money for the train fare, begging him to come. He replied:

If I do come, may I make one stringent request? That there be *no*
eating engagements planned prior to the wedding—either our
going out or anyone's coming in. I should like if possible to get
in a time of real quiet with you all and feel that since this may be
the last family get-together before Glory, we should make it
specially *family* with sufficient time for family prayer and Bible
study. If it's to be a week of social hubbub, I refuse to come
home. I can have that here on campus with bands and flowers.
Promise?

He went home, and, as he predicted, it was the last family
gathering for the Elliots. Jim spent much time with his
father, and wrote to me:

Betty, I blush to think of things I have said, as if I knew something about what Scripture teaches. I know nothing. My father's religion is of a sort which I have seen nowhere else. His theology is wholly undeveloped, but so real and practical a thing that it shatters every "system" of doctrine I have seen. He cannot define theism, but he knows God. We've had some happy times together, and I cannot estimate what enrichment a few months' working with him might do for me, practically and spiritually.

The journal adds this:

January 29. When I think of how far he has gone into the secret riches of the Father's purposes in Christ, I am shamed to silence. O Lord, let me learn tenderness and silence in my spirit, fruits of Thy knowledge. Burn, burden, break me.

> *O God that goadest me*
> *With hunger pricks for Thee within,*
> *By stealing from my heart its dearest stays,*
> *And staying me with tendrils of Thy love—*
> *A token of friendship from a dear one in Thee,*
> *A word of Holy Writ, a song,*
> *A thousand things of spider-thong*
> *Which lift my heart from seen things, sturdy, strong,*
> *And rest me, relaxed, hung from an unseen stay above—*
> *Wise-goading God, teach me to rest in love.*

Undoubtedly it was his father's counsel which prompted this journal entry:

January 31. One does not surrender a life in an instant. That which is lifelong can only be surrendered in a lifetime. Nor is surrender to the will of God (*per se*) adequate to fullness of power in Christ. Maturity is the accomplishment of years, and I can only surrender to the will of God as I know what that will is. Hence, the fullness of the Spirit is not instantaneous but progressive, as I attain fullness of the Word, which reveals the Will.

If men were filled with the Spirit they would not write books on that subject, but on the Person whom the Spirit has come to reveal. Occupation with *Christ* is God's object.

After a week in Portland, he said good-bye to Bert and his bride, who were soon to leave the United States for Peru, and travelled east on the streamliner. He wrote his parents:

Never have felt such difficulty in leaving home as yesterday. Always before I've been possessed of some sort of youthful bravado which gloried in being unaffected. Yesterday's leaving, somehow, forced me to concerted action to keep a stiff upper lip as this steel serpent wound eagerly through Sullivan's Gulch. The "City of Portland" is running true to form, two and a half hours late. Snow was beautiful as it caught the first slants of dawn this morning, appearing a glistening sea of coiled and choppy billows. In some places the little slat snow-fences protruded just an inch or so above the swirl, causing long series of streamlined drifts trailing from the wind. Just now the sky is ice-blue, thawing into an occasional blur of cloud. The hills are ribbed with crusted sheep trails and broken with scrub brush. Most of those on board, however, are unappreciative. Cards, westerns, comic books, cigarettes, and worn timetables occupy the attention of most.

Still exceedingly grateful to God for the opportunity to come home this past week. Can't say why He should allow it as far as my ministry is concerned, for I felt far more ministered unto than I should have been had the Spirit of the Great Well-Pleasing Servant been more in possession.

Arriving back at Wheaton, Jim began his final semester in college. The journal for that first day reads:

I note that my jotting of a year ago seeks a time when I shall forget all my failure. Psalm 107 has wrought much peace of heart in this regard. Just today I was thinking of how God loves in spite of all my sin and has promised to bring us to the "desired haven".[2] He will perform until the day. What matters then the resident Adam? What care for my bloating pride? What concern for attacking lust whose inner fifth-column betrays me to that enemy so often? Perfect love casts out fear, and this blessed rest—in knowing He loves through all these things—makes them seem too worthless even to be thought upon. I know them. God knows them. I confess them. He forgives them. Oh, that I might praise Him worthily!

February 23. Some time since I made any note, I see. Too busy to take time out . . . and then, too, I haven't been getting fresh things every day. "Too busy"—cursed words, those. Father, forgive me for being so academic and material in my outlook, so much feeding of the mind and outer man, so little genuine concern for spiritual things.

Wrestling was responsible for part of the 'busy-ness', and Jim tried to encourage his mother with his letter of February 26:

This is the Wheaton Invitational Wrestling Tourney, and I'm sitting in my room after having tucked away a steak after semi-finals this afternoon. Finals begin in an hour. I'm wrestling opponents ten pounds over my weight at 175, but have been fortunate in getting some easy material thus far. Pinned one man this morning and won on points this afternoon. Will hit the Chicago University 175-er tonight. We've got the meet in the bag with so many men running to the last bouts, but there'll be some rowdy times in the gym tonight. Take heart, Mom—only one more meet, and maybe I won't wrestle that one, unless I get hot suddenly and the coach decides to send me to the Cleveland Invitational in March, but there's little danger.

Two weeks later he wrote to his parents:

We came in second at Cleveland. I have not yet determined how much the Lord uses athletics to honour His name in the world, but I have wrestled my last collegiate match in faith that it was His will, and asked Him to establish the work of my hands.

And in the journal, this:

We won second place at the tournament in Cleveland, but what is that? Nothing abides. Behold, the Son of God comes! One flash of His burning eye will melt all our polished marble and burnished gold to nothing. One word from His righteous lips will speak destruction to the vast rebellion we call the human race. One peal of His vengeful laughter will rock the libraries of our wise and bring them crashing to a rubble-heap. The wise shall be taken in their own craftiness; mountains shall be brought low. What shall abide that Day? Lo, "He that doeth the will of God abideth forever."[3] Church of God, awake to your Bridegroom! Think not, America, to say in your heart, "We have upheld the common man; we have the godly for our heritage; we have respect to the religions." I say to you, God is able to raise up righteousness from your pavement stones. You have nothing but awful show before Him who comes. "O that Thou wouldst bow the heavens and come down."[4] Laodicea, when will you learn that fullness without Him is vacuum? Oh, the awful emptiness of a full life when Christ stands yet without.

Jim was responsible for getting speakers for the weekly meetings of the Foreign Missions Fellowship. He was not satisfied, however, with the emphasis that some of them had been placing on 'leadership' and training for the mission field. He wrote to me:

Everybody who comes to FMF these days tells us that we must be more educated than the past generation of missionaries. There is not a word in the New Testament about this "training for leadership". There all the training is for being a servant of everyone you meet. Training is to learn to follow, not to lead. But we must have "Christians who are leaders, you know". Jesus said, "He that is first shall be last."[5] "It is enough for the disciple that he be as his master."[6] That is the sort of training that we need, to be as He is, sharing His rejection even by well-meaning Fundamentalists.

His brother's leaving for Peru as a missionary caused Jim to rethink the cost of that choice, and he wrote to his mother, near the date of Bert's sailing:

> Burdened to pray for you as Bert and Colleen leave, Mom. I can never share in the terrific struggles which you must know in this testing of your mother love. I only know that no testing can overtake you but what God will faithfully provide a way of escape so that you can endure it and glorify Him. Remember— and I don't want to sound pedantic or impudent as if I knew all the costs—remember that we have bargained with Him who bore a cross, and in His ministry to those disciples His emphasis was upon sacrifice, not of worldly goods so much as of *family ties.* Let nothing turn us from the truth that God has determined that we become strong under fire, after the pattern of the Son. Nothing else will do. Our silken selves must know denial. Hear Amy Carmichael:

> *"O Prince of Glory, who dost bring*
> *Thy sons to glory through the Cross,*
> *Let us not shrink from suffering,*
> *Reproach or loss."*

Notes

1. Proverbs 1:8,9.
2. Psalm 107:30.
3. 1 John 2:17.
4. Psalm 144:5.
5. Mark 10:31, para.
6. Matthew 10:25.

— 10 —

The Renaissance

Let no one boast of men. Everything belongs to you! . . . For you belong to Christ, and Christ belongs to God![1]

SINCE HIGH SCHOOL days Jim had judged his own conduct, and probably the conduct of others, by what he later called his 'code of don'ts'. Late in his senior year in college he began to see that this was contrary to the teaching of the apostle Paul. Furthermore, it was cutting him off from a certain percentage of the student body whom he wanted to know.

Paul says,

One man believes that he may eat anything; another man, without this strong conviction, is a vegetarian. The meat-eater would not despise the vegetarian, nor should the vegetarian condemn the meat-eater—they should reflect that God has accepted them both. After all, who are you to criticise the servant of somebody else, especially when that Somebody Else is God? . . . We shall all be judged one day, not by each other's standards or even our own, but by the standard of Christ.[2]

With a new understanding of these principles, Jim discarded some of the old inhibitions which before he had regarded as prerequisite to holiness. The Scriptural teaching was not always properly applied, however, as he later recognised, but he entered into many activities with a new liberty. Among these were the rivalries between the classes of '49 and '50. On March 19 he wrote:

Wednesday, besides being the 49-er's Centennial Day, was also our annual Reverse Day, when the girls date the fellows and open the doors and generally behave like gentlemen. They were far more interesting than the men, with their long hoop-skirts, bustles, piles of lace, and hair done up. One of them asked me to the student-faculty basketball game. I went over to uncle's and got his spats, top hat, stiff collar with wings, black bow tie, and then picked up an old Prince Albert coat with tails, and a cane (fancy dandy's, with carved dog's head and built-in gun chamber), and duded it in rare style. Set off shouting "Hail 49!" with great gusto. I have never in my wildest dreams hoped to see Wheaton, from prexy to janitor, in such high spirits. The faculty put on a skit between halves of the game that laid us all out. Strangely, I have never sensed a more unified school in four years. I received a tie, along with about twenty other faithfuls, for sticking out a three weeks' beard-growing.

On March 26 Jim wrote:

Dear Mom, Dad, and family: Good to get two letters this week: yours Monday, Mom, and then the combined of yours and Dad's this morning. Thanks for the two dollars, as well, and the stamps. Haven't the faintest idea when I will have opportunity to get the stamps in order of classified, but I'll keep hoarding them anyhow.

Sylvia MacAllister just interrupted this letter by walking by our window on her way over to Jackson's place. Couldn't resist shouting to her for old times' sake. Auntie invited her for the week-end, but since they're invited out for the evening, I volunteered to take Sylvia to the Chapel Choir concert tonight. All the boys in the house have dates and we are coming here for cookies and ice-cream afterwards. Four of us worked up a little harmonica quartette for entertainment.

I bought a harmonica last week in Maxwell Street—saw a German double-reed job brand new at $1.50. That's less than half what I priced the same thing for in Cleveland, so I bought it right off.

Saw the buds begin to sprout for the first time today. It's grey and dripping out, but we've had two warm spring days this week and things are on the burst. Just ten more weeks of classes. Junior-Senior activities are showing dangerous rival sproutings as well. Both classes are determined that the other shall be chagrined. The Forty-Niners showed such spirit as Juniors last year and did such a bang-up job with this Centennial Day affair that the Class of '50 is rankling with jealousy. My room-mate is a junior. They had a big party last night, and I noticed he came in with a sheet of most derogatory and barbarous songs about the senior class. The house lights grow dim—a hush comes over the audience—and the curtain rises on Act I——

In a letter of a week or so later:

Wrestling banquet is tomorrow night. It will likely be a high time. I'm to quote "The Shooting of Dan McGrew" and "The Cremation of Sam McGee", besides singing some of the old songs with my southern date, "Tex" Carlson. She owns a ukelele, so we'll harmonise and dummy around till the boys feel entertained. They sure do put one to work if he shows the least tendency to combine audience ability and foolishness. The thing that bothers me most is that I enjoy it.

Paul exhorts: 'Take care lest this liberty of yours somehow become a stumbling-block to the weak.'[3] Jim's liberty to participate in class activity to the extent of growing a beard was an offence to at least one fellow student. A girl came to him one morning to say that she considered his beard a sign of vanity. 'It went down the drain the next morning,' he wrote to his parents.

The journal continues:

April 14. Fellowship with the gang is enticing fun, but I feel carried away tonight with soul-excitement. Nothing bad—just nothing good. Taken up with comp studies, Robert Service, the old songs that keep ringing in my ears. Strange place, this soul of mine. I think it is more *place* than *person*. It rings with whatever enters, be it high thoughts of the seated Christ or idle rhymes from any poet. The soul does not seem to mind what it is occupied with, but only cares that it be kept occupied. It is passive as to choice. I choose, my soul responds, with ringing laughter, emotion, or pure worship. It is a tool, not a craftsman, and must be controlled. It is as amoral as a bed, but beds can become places of illegitimate activity. Son of God, Purger of the inner parts, Discerner of my sittings down, my risings, wilt Thou hallow this soul of mine? The choice is mine, you say? Ah yes, the choice is mine.

From a letter of April 16:

Went to Lake Michigan sand dunes with a gang of seniors. Had a good time. Wish I didn't have to go to class at all, but could just fellowship with these Wheatonites. So few of them understand life lived to the hilt for and with the Lord Jesus. I wish now that I had understood how to deal with them. Seems like I've only caught on myself this spring.

He wrote on May 10:

This week-end a gang of seniors is going to Rockford and camp out on one of the girls' farms. We'll be leaving Sunday night, skipping classes on Monday, so it looks like we're in for a high time. Pray that I'll be a help, they've asked me to take devotions. Next week-end after is the "Sneak", leaving sometime Friday and returning Monday. They've asked me to take Communion Service there. I've never done anything like that, so pray for me.

I thought of you all yesterday with Bert and Colleen leaving. Bet you felt it hard, Mom and Dad, and the Lord knows why. It's hard to know how to pray in such instances, except that each find strength in the Lord's goodness, as Amy Carmichael puts it,

> *"For my beloved I will not fear,*
> *Love knows to do for him, for her,*

> As hitherto. Whom my heart cherishes
> Are dear to Thy heart too!"

Seems that the Lord Himself must do. I cannot, cannot even pray aright for you. But if He has called them, what right have we to even whisper to our sleep-, ease-loving souls, "Why this waste?"[4] And yet we must learn to pray in words for them. God grant us grace that we may learn travailing intercession first for their soul's edification and strength and then for those to whom they are to minister. Paul wrote to the Philippians that although they were not in bonds nor in open battle with the enemy, *their faith was*, and he exhorts that they should enter into the conflict of the gospel, since it was given them not only to believe, but also to suffer for Christ's sake. So let us learn to strive together with them.

The moon is almost full tonight. It could be seen nearly all day up in the "brooding blue".... Just think—about one month from today I'll be seeing you. Hope you will feel well enough to enjoy your stay here, Mom.

The end of May was the time for the 'Senior Sneak', when the class of '49 successfully evaded the class of '50 to go up to Wisconsin for a week-end retreat. A year earlier Jim would probably not have allowed himself to indulge in this sort of fun, but, as he wrote to me:

A disruption of my previously pious "code of don'ts" that used to motivate much of my action has occurred in the last three months. The Lord has freed me from many things—good, "consecrated" attitudes, priggish little laws whereby I used to govern my conduct. I experience new fellowship, new freedom, new enjoyment. But my pendulum swung too far. My liberty became licence in some things, and a stumbling-block to some people.

He wrote to his parents while on the 'Sneak' on May 22:

Sitting by Lake Michigan with a gang of '49-ers on this terrific Sunday afternoon. Best loaf I've ever experienced. All inhibitions released by this northern Wisconsin air and outdoors, things really have cut loose. You'll be hearing reports and seeing pictures later. The Juniors didn't get a clue as to our luggage or destination, so this was a Sneak with a vengeance.

Thought about you much last week but failed to get a letter off to you. Wondering how the farewell was, and the trip to LA. Ed McCully, our senior class prexy, won the national oratory contest in Frisco last week. He's from the assembly in Milwaukee and a good buddy of mine. He flew back here yesterday and we promptly chucked him in the lake for his success.

Trust Bert and Colleen will have the confidence and peace of sensing the Lord's nearness on the trip. Been exercised afresh about the unreached "of every tribe"[5] today. Wish there was more wide-awake interest in the regions where pioneer efforts are needed. But one must be sure of a call to such a work and I'm not sure yet just where the Lord is preparing me for. . . .

I passed comprehensive examinations without undue strain on my part, though I don't know how I rated as yet. Still have two term papers to do before next week, so will be a busy little beaver till then. . . . Seems like there have been entirely too many worthwhile activities for me to do some very insistent writing which I have been neglecting. Pray that I might not become so involved that I fail to apply myself to the Scriptures and apply all the Scriptures to myself.

To me, on May 26, Jim wrote:

The Sneak is over, with much indecision on my part as to what profit it brought. I had one terrific lot of fun, got to know some kids on a spiritual plane whom I had always hankered to know. Sorry I was so foolish as to believe I could have a good time without the regular emphasis on the Word in private. *Nothing* substitutes for that.

You would have enjoyed the Communion Service we had during that week-end. We had a huge glass flagon and an oversized loaf of bread. After a few opening remarks we began to pray and sing familiar hymns as different ones led. McCully broke the bread and gave thanks for the cup. It took a long time for the single cup and plate to get around to 180 people, so we sang as it was passed, "Spirit of God descend upon my heart", "When I survey the wondrous Cross", "Amazing Grace", "O Love that will not let me go", "Crown Him with many crowns", etc. Hardly a soul that wasn't moved to worship. Oh, why cannot the Spirit lead us more often thus? How long shall we trust in man's programming to accomplish the work of His Spirit in men's souls?

One of the lessons Jim felt that his 'renaissance' experience had taught him was expressed in a later letter to me:

One of my renaissance experiences was to get among kids who were on a different spiritual level than my own, and enjoy fellowship with them. I found a very subtle snare in so doing. I sought their fellowship in order that I might minister to them, "be a help", you know, to these "weaker" ones. What a rebuke came when I sensed my real motive—that *I* might minister. Love hacks right at this, for she refused to parade herself. I learned to recognise no "spiritual planes", but simply to *love*, purely, in every group. Trying to "be a help" even has a smell of good works in it, for it is not pure. Our motive is only *to be*—do nothing, know nothing, act nothing—just to be a sinful bit of flesh, born of a Father's love. Then you see, Beloved, there can be no defeat.

> "*If you can meet with triumph and disaster*
> *And treat those two impostors just the same.* . . ."[6]

So whether knowledge tends to swell me up, or the despair of the flesh would make me shrivel up, the love of Christ "holds me together".[7] Any little occasion that has meaning, if only I can love while it lasts. Keble reminds us of Christ, who with a great task before Him.

> "*Yet in meek duty to abide*
> *For many a year at Mary's side,*
> *Nor heed, though restless spirits ask,*

'What? Hath the Christ forgot His task?'''

Only a few weeks remained before graduation, and Jim was seeking the will of the Lord for the summer. His brother Bob had written him of plans for building a house for himself and his wife, and Jim looked forward to helping on that project.

I feel sure that three months' building would prepare me more for the mission field than another three months in the books. Most pressing is a sense of responsibility to the home which has made me all I am, and paid all the bills without a question. God knows best. He will not reveal His will by fires nor earthquakes but by that quiet dwelling in His presence which sons soon learn to interpret in their lives. Strange that we should be so slow to "tame". Brute flesh is rebellion incarnate within, and it takes some seasons of hammering and healing both, to bring it into subjection.

Let us earnestly have these decisions before God. I think we can all sense that this is a crisis year both for family and country. Let us not be found with the frenzied of earth, cast about with no foundation upon which to base their lives. We can boast with David in his prosperity, "I shall never be moved."[8] "My heart confided in the Lord and I was helped, therefore my heart exulteth."[9]

Notes

1. 1 Corinthians 3:21,23, JBP.
2. Romans 14:2–4,10, JBP.
3. 1 Corinthians 8:9, RSV.
4. Matthew 26:8, para.
5. Revelation 5:9, para.
6. From 'If', by Rudyard Kipling in *Rewards and Fairies* (Garden City: Doubleday & Co., 1910).
7. 2 Corinthians 5:14, para.
8. Psalm 30:6.
9. Psalm 28:7, JND.

PART THREE

Portland—Oklahoma—Wisconsin—Indiana—Illinois—Portland,

1949–1952

— 11 —

The Test of Free Time

When the time came for God to reveal His Son within me so that I might proclaim Him...I did not, as might have been expected, talk the matter over with any human being...I went away to Arabia...It was not till three years later that I went up to Jerusalem.[1]

AFTER GRADUATING with highest honours from Wheaton, Jim drove West with his parents, expecting to spend at least the next three months there. It had not been easy to leave the 'old gang' at college, especially since Jim was not yet sure of God's intentions for him in the coming year. When asked the usual question posed to seniors, 'What will you be doing?' he had no answer. But he knew where to find it. In his journal on July 8, 1949, he wrote:

Home at last. Mingled feelings of "not belonging" and of thanksgiving for all God's grace these past four years. God, preserve me from living a life which conforms to the general pattern. Oh to live above the world, "in public duty and in private thinking", as J. G. Holland puts it. How many Christians will find with the character in Service's poem,

"Came out with a fortune last fall,—
Yet somehow life's not what I thought it,
And somehow the gold isn't all"?[2]

To whom shall I go for counsel for a way of life? To whom for example? To Thee, Lord? Yea, I come to Thee.

The Lord's counsel this time was that Jim spend a year in Portland, helping where he could in the assembly, but most of all preparing his soul through concentrated study of the Bible. He started out by helping to paint the assembly hall, but used even these hours for spiritual profit, as will be seen by a letter written to Bill Cathers on July 12:

While high up on the hall tower with a paint brush on a swinging scaffold with Dad the other day, we got talking about methods of preparing young fellows for the Lord's work. We agreed that the artificial atmosphere of Bible school was unsatisfactory, then started discussing Paul's way of training those about him to teach others. By the time we reached for the ropes to lower the pulleys to an unpainted place, he was saying, "Well, Jim, you pray about it, and if it is the Lord's mind I'll go with you and Billy into Montana next summer." What say you, brother? Of course it will mean no wedding plans for you, until some time after graduation, since I feel it is God's order to relieve young married folks from the burden of active battle until they are settled. Check Deuteronomy 24:5 on this. Pray about it, and I will, too. We would support ourselves, hold tent meetings and open-air meetings, or wherever there is an ear for the Word, and if we find interest and can help souls we would stay as long as is necessary to get them established and formed into assemblies. We ought to know how to do this in our own language before we try it in another, don't you think?

Your word about serving the Lord as Paul and Barnabas did together was not a new idea to me. It has often been my secret wish, and I should not be surprised if it is one of those things that is in the mind of our Great Shepherd-God to stir us on by one another's faith. But we can wait His time in this, too.

I have experienced some little stirring in my soul since last I wrote. The study of Acts has been engaging much of my time, and I sense hunger to know His way, that is, His method of doing His work. Oh, how we need the Holy Spirit to give us a godly distaste for Laodicea! And nòt to go sour, but to maintain the gladness of heart that is to characterise that people whose God is the Lord.

> "Aye, *amid all men bear himself thereafter,*
> *Smit with a solemn and a sweet surprise,*
> *Dumb to their scorn, and turning on their laughter*
> *Only the dominance of earnest eyes.*"[3]

I charge you, by the concern we bear for one another's souls, and by the love of God, that you warn and exhort me with patience if you see in me those turnings back of heart which I do not perceive in the blindness of my flesh. Rest in the knowledge of His doing all for you, Billy. — Earnestly, Jim.

On July 19 he wrote to me:

These days seem strange ones of waiting, sorta marking time till all the red-tape gets time to pass, but I am sure I have not missed the Lord's mind. We have not yet begun building [a house for his brother] because of a little snarl with the city over property lines, getting a loan, and agreeing with each other on blueprint details. Meanwhile Dad and I are working around here, painting the house, fixing the car, cleaning up the meeting-hall, details that seem so unimportant, but somehow needful.

How easy it is to lag spiritually at such times! Though there is challenge among the saints to stir them up and Sundays are crowded with jail and street meetings, there is a very decided tendency to let the days slip through your fingers. The Lord challenged me from the eighty-fourth Psalm last Saturday night. A different translation of verse 5 is "Blessed are they whose strength is in Thee, in whose heart are the *highways*". For me it meant, is your heart really in this business of getting out into those byways or are you willing to settle down and lag while others wait help? Just now I don't happen to *be* in the highways — my experience is more like the sparrows' of verse 3, resting beneath the altar. But that need be no cause for my heart to lose its eagerness for the highways. Then, too, verse 7 is both a warning and a promise "strength to strength" — but each one shall appear before God. How then, my soul?

I have had to reconcile myself to staying in the US until I've proved myself in the work here. The brethren would have it no other way, so unless I go out with Dad to British Guiana [this had seemed a possibility for a short time] I will have to wait until the way is clear for the Regions Beyond. Still, it is not wasted time, as I'm sure you, if anyone, will understand, Bets.... Confident of the Lord's glad promise, "He will give *grace* and *glory*; no good thing will He withhold from them that walk uprightly."[4]

The journal continues on July 23:

Painted part of the hall today. Restless to do other things more directly related to the Lord's work. Longing for a companion who will be a David to me, and me his Jonathan. Lack spiritual stamina to keep fresh in all this eating and doing. Oh, there is time to read and seek God, but my desire slackens. Lord, uphold Thy lily-saint. Stay me, Jehovah, for Thine is a strong right arm, and mine so weak! Saturday night again, and weary from work, but seeking something from the Lord now. How shall I build with these weak and slack hands, Lord?

Tuesday, July 26. Confession of pride—suggested by David Brainerd's Diary yesterday—must become an hourly thing with me. How vile and base my thoughts have been lately. Not just unkind or unsympathetic, but rotten, lewd thinking that cannot be overcome simply by *willing* to be rid of them. How dare I minister to God's saints in such a condition? Lord, rebuke my flesh and deliver my heart from evil.

August 4. I must confess much leanness of soul today, oh Patient Shepherd. How often I have been angered at delay, short-spirited, anxious to criticise. I noticed tonight, too, that one does not live to himself in this regard, but that a little leavening of dissatisfied temper will spread through a group and change outlooks. Then too, Meek Saviour, I must bring a boisterous tongue, roguish lips to Thee for cleansing. Oh to be holy! Just to sense for a moment that I have somehow, however feebly, simulated some measure of Thy character, Lord Jesus. A word from Horatius Bonar spoke to me tonight: "Holiness is not austerity or gloom; these are as alien to it as levity and flippancy; it is the offspring of conscious, present PEACE."

August 21. I sense tonight that my desires to be great are likely to frustrate God's intents for good to be done through me. O Lord, let me pray again with earnest, honest heart: I will not to be *great*—only, God, grant to me Thy *goodness*.

In September, at the repeated invitation of Jim's mother, I visited Portland on my way home from Alberta, Canada, where I had spent the summer in rural missionary work. Jim met me at the station, and drove me out to Mt Tabor, where his home stood facing snow-capped Mt Hood. The house had been greatly enlarged since the Elliots had first moved into it in 1922, and now it sprawled comfortably over a steep hillside, surrounded by fruit trees and flowers of many varieties. The glassed-porch was filled with flowers and plants, set in pots of every description.

Inside, I met for the first time Jim's mother. Soft grey hair and a wide, loving smile contributed to the general impression of motherliness. Mr Elliot, stocky and of strong build, with grey hair betraying its former redness, greeted me next. Then 'Auntie Frostie', a little old lady for whom Mrs Elliot had cared for over twenty years, prim and tiny, with a slight British accent. Jim's sixteen-year-old sister Jane and older brother Bob, a chiropractor, were also there.

One day Jim took me to the beautiful Oregon coast, where we swam at the foot of a great headland of rock, and, later, sat by a driftwood fire, watching the sun die in the Pacific. On other days we hiked on Mt Hood, canoed in the Columbia River, drove to Multnomah Falls.

'Strange, but oh such happy days,' Jim wrote later. 'Were those not of Thee, my God? And wilt Thou deny fruition to such love as we have known? As Thou wilt. But how impossible it seems—to wait—yet, with God nothing shall be impossible.'

After we said good-bye at the Greyhound Bus station, Jim wrote in his journal:

September 13. She has been gone one hour. What thunders of feeling I have known in that short time. I could not read the neon lights as I turned away from the bus, and couldn't face the people as they passed me. Leaving her is terrible. Teasdale's poem comes back:

> *"I asked the heaven of stars*
> *What I could give my love—*
> *It answered me with silence,*
>   *Silence above.*

> *"I asked the darkened sea*
> *Down where the fishes go—*
> *It answered me with silence,*
>   *Silence below.*

> *"Oh, I could give her weeping,*
> *Or I could give her a song.*
> *But how can I give silence*
>   *My whole life long?"*[5]

Each time I see her, I have no answer. Only that I must wait. How long? For what? I know not. O God of my bitter moments, Father of Christ who wept, grant me guidance directly from Thee. May I ask it in Spirit-spawned faith? Please let us not part again in silence. How bitter is love unexpressed!

These words came as I wept between sunset and moonrise on the side hill beneath the firs:

> *"Wheels carried her into silence,*
> *Out of my reach.*
> *I feared, lest darkness closing round us*
> *Might gain our souls,*
> *And we lose sight*
> *Of real things.*

But nay, the Sun that ruled our days
Has lit the moon to rule our night.

October 7. Realised today that I am on a very stiff trial—it is the test of free time. The Lord took away all outward activity. No work, no money to spend, nothing to do. I fear lest I should waste such days. Spent this one in writing, reading, and a little prayer.

October 16. Very happy in the Lord tonight. Sense that I am being tested in the matter of learning to "abound".[6] Everything seems directed to my good. I am free now of all work obligations except what minor affairs living at home entails. My health is perfect. The state of the assembly is happy and there is evidence of prosperity in the fellowship, though the miraculous is little known among us. Still there are many burdens to be lifted if I choose the path of sacrifice here at home. Lord Jesus, Lord of the apostle who knew how to abound and how to be abased, grant to me faithfulness this week. Let me not retrograde.

October 18. Last night those great, sweeping desires for the glory of God seized on me, seasons when the thoughts pour ahead of the words in prayer and my attitude is as one heaving great gasps of want. Desire there is aplenty. Words are few at such times and faith, I must admit, is not really great.

October 24. I see the value of Christian biography tonight, as I have been reading Brainerd's Diary much today. It stirs me up much to pray and wonder at my nonchalance while I have not power from God. I have considered Hebrews 13:7 just now, regarding the remembrance of certain ones who spake the word of God, "consider the outcome of their life, and imitate their faith."[7] I recall now the challenge of Goforth's *Life* and *By My Spirit*, read in the summer of 1947, the encouragement of Hudson Taylor's *Spiritual Secret*, and *The Growth of a Soul*. There are incidents which instruct me now from the reading of J. G. Paton's biography, read last winter. And now this fresh Spirit-quickened history of Brainerd. O Lord, let me be granted grace to "imitate their faith".

October 27. "Enjoyed much sweetness" (as he puts it) in the reading of the last months of Brainerd's life. How consonant are his thoughts to my own regarding the "true and false religion of this late day". Saw, in reading him, the value of these notations, and was much encouraged to think of a life of godliness in the light of an early death.

October 28. One of the great blessings of heaven is the appreciation of heaven on earth. He is no fool who gives what he cannot keep to gain what he cannot lose.

October 29. On reading a letter to Bert from Wilfred Tidmarsh I responded to a simple urge to offer myself for the work there in Ecuador. This morning it struck me as quite a presumptuous action and I covenanted with the Lord quietly that I would not post the letter unless I had some definite word from Himself. It seems the situation he is in demands that he abandon the Indian work among the Quichuas, because of his wife's health.

Later: after reading in Ephesians 4, 5, and 6, the words "redeeming the time"[8] struck me. The marginal reading encouraged me even more, "buying up the opportunity". And when I turned to the Greek, ἐξαγοραζόμενοι τον καιρόν, I had certainty that I should mail the letter.

On October 31 Jim wrote to me:

Today I went out to the Christian School to place my application as a substitute teacher. Tonight I went to the local detention home for boys to tell a Poe mystery story at their Hallowe'en Party. Tomorrow eve I am to help in a newly beginning craft class for unsaved kids in one of the suburban assemblies. Wednesday afternoon, children's meetings at the hall; Friday morning, chapel service for the Goodwill Industries employees. Days I spend in the books. Tell your father I was deeply impressed with Brainerd's Diary which I finished last week. Other reading material is a book on Ephesians by Van Ryn; Orr's *View of God and the World;* *The Pilgrim Church* by Broadbent; *The Holy War* by Bunyan. I try to get in what I call "reprobate reading", a little every day, just to keep from dropping into the stereotyped and conventional. This is either *Thus Spake Zarathustra* by Nietzsche, something from Service or Poe, the *Rubáiyát* of Omar Khayyám, John Masefield. It takes strict and careful discipline to keep my heart in Bible study in the forenoon, and in prayer. The rest of the day is desecrated with these others, secular and sacred.

From the journal:

November 6. Sweet, sweet grace of God! It was a happy day, spent with saints and sinners. Street meetings tonight brought me into contact with a successful man who has an empty heart. How shall I praise God sufficiently for the inexplicable miracle of divine grace in my soul? And how explain it to others? I have committed this man's soul to God, and His Word, expecting to write one day in these pages of his turning to the Lord and finding great peace. You see these words, Lord, and are my Judge as to whether they are in faith.

Had thoughts of eternity lately. Eternity shall be at once a great eye-opener and a great mouth-shutter. It shall be the Rectifier of all injustice and how vast is injustice!), the Confirmer of martyrs' blood, the Explainer of years of labour swallowed up in meaningless ruin on earth. Lord, deliver me from sweet doctrinal nothings.

November 8. I had just discovered Paul's use of the word καρπός ["fruit"] in Galatians, Ephesians, and Philippians when Mom called me to vacuum the living-room. Finishing that I noticed the table decoration was meagre, so went out and cut a couple of holly sprigs. That reminded me of the shoots growing under the chestnut tree (from seeds dropped by birds in the tree) that had to be moved if they were to grow. Decided to put a hedge of them around Jane's wing of the house, so removed the azalea that was there to the rockery and put in a dozen holly roots out there. Heigh ho! So goes the Greek for this morning!

November 9. It's almost midnight. Don't feel like bed. Spent the evening in the *Reader's Digest* and Wordsworth and Coleridge. Not profitable for sanctifying, but good broadening. Stepped out just now to mail a letter. The moon seems ulcerous, oozing yellow through torn gauze of cloud. Slow-drying pavements, the gutters sopping rotten leaves, motionless cold whose intensity lies in its quiet qualities rather than its chill.

November 10. The gaining of Christ is both an inward reckoning of loss and an outward suffering of it. I have known myself to lose something for Him, yet cherish it in my thoughts. Paul says, "I not only reckon them scraps fit for the heap but I have actually undergone loss of them."[9]

November 11. I am spending this drizzly afternoon reading *The Pilgrim Church*, by Broadbent. Who can describe the waves of pity, excitement, self-searching, and holy desire that have gone through me as I lift my eyes from the page to stare upon the soaked side yard? I find myself constantly trying to bring these ancient arguments up to date, to apply anabaptism, separation from nominal reform, fasting, Quaker freedom, etc., to my own day. "But Thou, O Lord, how long?"[10]

I see clearly now that anything, whatever it is, if it be not on the principle of grace, it is not of God. Here shall be my plea in weakness; here shall be my boldness in prayer; here shall be my deliverance in temptation; at last, here shall be my translation. Not of grace? Then not of God. And here, O Lord Most High, shall be your glory and the honour of your Son. And the awakening for which I have asked—it shall come in your time, on this principle, by grace, through faith. Perfect my faith, then, Lord, that I may learn to trust only in divine grace, that Thy work of holiness might soon begin in Portland.

November 19. Stupefying weakness and dullness in the things of the Lord. Seemed to lack communion on the Holy Spirit for spiritual energy. Show me my failings and goings-backward, Lord, for who can understand his own faults? Depressed and sensible of uselessness tonight. Satisfied that Fritz (see entry for November 6) is in the Lord, a brother. Thanks be to God for His deliverance!

November 24. Lord, give me firmness without hardness, steadfastness without dogmatism, love without weakness.

November 25. I see that a year ago today I was questioning what I would be engaged in today. Of six possibilities then supposed, I am engaged in none. The first two are still the most real exercises of my heart. Still, even in meditating on these (Peru or India), fears seize me and my inadequacy and unpreparedness, my real lack of intensity regarding them, come to me so forcibly that I can hardly believe I am being led in either direction. Yet, I say, "Lead on, O King Eternal, I follow, *not* with fears."[11]

Enjoyed the truth of singing "psalms and hymns and spiritual songs"[12] this morning. Found my prayer list so unstimulating to real prayer that I laid it aside and took the Inter-Varsity Hymnal and sang aloud with much heart-warming such songs as seemed to fit my need. This is as decidedly a means of grace as anything given by God to His people, but how little we use it!

November 29. I think there is nothing so startling in all the graces of God as His quietness. When men have raged untruths in His NAME, when they have used the assumed authority of the Son of God to put to death His real children, when they have with calloused art twisted the Scriptures into fables and lies, when they have explained the order of His creation in unfounded theories while boasting the support of rational science, when they have virtually talked Him right out of His universe, when they, using powers He grants them, claim universal autonomy and independence, He, this great Silent God, says nothing. His tolerance and love for His creature is such that, having spoken in Christ, in conscience, in code of law, He waits for men to leave off their bawling and turn for a moment to listen to His still, small voice of Spirit. Now, after so long a time of restrained voice, bearing in Almighty meekness the blasphemies of His self-destroying creatures, now—how shall break upon the ears, consciousnesses, hearts, and minds of reprobate man the Voice of one so long silent? It shall thunder with the force of offended righteousness, strike with lightning bolts upon the seared consciences; roar as the long-crouched lion upon dallying prey; leap upon, batter, destroy, and utterly consume the vain reasonings of proud human kind; ring as the battle-shout of a strong, triumphant, victory-tasting warrior; strike terror and gravity to souls more forcefully than tortured screams in the dead of night. O God, what shall be the first tones of that voice again on earth? And what their effect? Wonder and fear, denizens of dust, for the Lord Himself shall descend from heaven with a battle-cry, with the voice of the archangel and the trumpet blast of God Himself, made more terrible, if that could be, by the long-suffering of His silence.

December 1. Much disturbed at noon today by a report that "people are talking" about my not being employed. I trust I have had more exercise than they all in this matter. Some think I ought to go to work for a year. God knows I am willing. Felt this charge came as a cutting criticism and sensed a strong desire to retaliate by justifying myself before them, telling them of my application for three jobs lately; of my prospect of going to British Guiana; of my Bible studies; of reading and work—small indeed—of keeping up the place here. But the word of the Lord Jesus came to me. "Ye are they which justify yourselves before men."[13] Not wanting to be found such, I knelt to pray and read the noon psalm for today. It was number 17. Verse 2 smote me: "Let my sentence come forth from Thy presence. . . . Thou hast tried me . . . my steps have held fast to Thy paths. . . . Deliver my soul from men who are Thy hand (v. 14, margin), from men of this world whose portion is in this life . . . they are satisfied with children, but I shall be satisfied when I awake with Thy form." So, Lord, I am in Thy hand, and say now in faith that Thou hast led, searched, exercised, and tried me. If there lacks now that which I should be doing and am not, hide it not from Thy servant who would follow Thee.

December 5. "Give attendance to reading."[14] Finished a short biography of Allan Smith, missionary to the Paraguayan and Amazonian river systems. Stirred for Tidmarsh's work among the Ecuadorian Quichuas again. Prayed to be sent out soon with definite steps of guidance for my path. Took some confidence from Psalm 18:36, "Thou has enlarged my steps under me and my feet have not slipped."

On December 17 Jim wrote me a letter which showed that his field of vision was at last being focused:

I have had detailed correspondence with two missionaries to whom I wrote; one, Wilfred Tidmarsh of Ecuador (whose wife was injured in a Missionary Aviation Fellowship plane crash when Nate Saint was pilot), who is having to leave an established forest work among Quichua Indians; the other Rowland Hill of

Bangalore, India. Both describe fields of tremendous interest to me and both are quite anxious regarding my leading from the Lord. From one standpoint the works are almost opposite, as the Ecuadorian work is among primitive unlettered tribespeople, while the Indian project is among high school and college-age upper-crust Hindus who are studying in English. Brother Hill wants to start a Bible school for some of them, and is looking for someone who would qualify as a teacher of Greek, etc., as well as work in the wide-open schools. How is one to decide when the heart is equally torn for both works, and one's capabilities fit either sphere?

This was a new test of faith, in view of the decision to go to South American Indians, which Jim had made a year earlier at the Student Missionary Convention. But he believed that the way would be obvious when the time came, provided he continued fulfilling the duties which stared him in the face. As George Macdonald wrote, 'Obedience is the opener of eyes.'

For December 19 the journal contains this note:

I must act in a holy manner, not for reward or appearance, but because of God's nature. The Law continually reminds me that commandments are to be kept, not for their own sake, but for God's sake. I will be righteous, then, because God's nature is such. His character determines my conduct. "This do...for I am Jehovah."[15]

Jim wrote to me on December 27:

I forgot to mention your birthday in my last. I can't remember if we ever discussed giving gifts or not, but somehow it seems such a cheap sort of thing to do—entirely too conformist a practice to have much place in our relationship! The practice at Christmas has gotten to be such a commercialised hoax that I will be sincerely glad when all good Christians abandon it. The excitement of the week-end left us all weary-eyed and untalkative at supper tonight. Seems to me we would have a better attitude toward the whole thing if someone would write a realistic poem on the "Night After Christmas", to counterbalance the magical effects of the imaginative "Night Before".

The journal entry for the same night reads:

"The thirst that from the soul doth rise doth ask a drink divine."[16] Felt deserted this morning and utterly unable to pray because of the crowded passages within. Too much excitement at the reunion last night. I was reminded of the "rubble"[17] instruction of last fall. Desire for the earthly was increased and enlarged, still I recognised that were it sated I would not be at rest. Left my Greek to turn to Ecclesiastes, which I read partway through. The kindred pessimism helps me some, but I cannot tell why. Passages that seemed to say what I feel stood out:

"All things are full of weariness, man cannot utter it: the eye is not satisfied with seeing, nor the ear filled with hearing."

"I said of laughter, it is mad; and of mirth, what doeth it?"

"So I hated life, because the work that is wrought under the sun was grievous to me; for all is vanity and a striving after wind."

"I have seen the travail which God hath given to the sons of men to be exercised therewith."

"Better is a handful with quietness than two handfuls with labour and striving after wind."

Let me read this page when I get to hungering after civilisation's excitements and excesses in some lonely place. Take counsel, then, my soul; the whole of life is vanity and you would be no happier in brighter atmospheres. Woe and loneliness may be miserable, but hollow happiness and many in a crowd are much more so. You may say justly of it all, sighingly, "When will it end?" Shelley's "Ozymandias" fits fairly:

> "*I met a traveller from an antique land*
> *Who said: Two vast and trunkless legs of stone*
> *Stand in the desert. Near them, on the sand,*
> *Half-sunk, a shattered visage lies, whose frown,*

And wrinkled lip, and sneer of cold command,
Tell that its sculptor well those passions read,
Which yet survive, stamped on these lifeless things.
The hand that mocked them, and the heart that fed:
And on the pedestal these words appear:
'My name is Ozymandias, King of Kings:
Look on my works, ye Mighty, and despair!'
Nothing beside remains. Round the decay
Of that colossal wreck, boundless and bare,
The lone and level sands stretch far away."

"One moment in annihilation's waste" (Omar Khayyám).

"O Lord, be not silent unto me, lest I become like those that go down into the pit." [18]

Evening—Much comforted later, though conscious of sin. Read Hebrews through aloud in English.

December 31. This is New Year's Eve. Light-hearted and empty all day. Moved to sober prayer again. O Lord, you see the places secret in me, you know all my wanderings and reserves. If you see anything in me that is holding back the clear revelation of your will about Ecuador, uncover it to me, I pray.

To me, he wrote:

Had a letter from India today which ended, "I would rejoice to think the New Year would find you here." Still I am waiting. I was challenged by that word of Abraham in reading Hebrews tonight. "He went forth, not knowing whither he went." [19]

"I know that the way of man is not in himself—it is not in man that walketh to direct his steps." [20]

With a prayer for 1950 for you that is both directed by the will of Christ and executed by His power,—Jim.

Notes

1. Galatians 1:15–18, JBP.
2. From 'The Spell of the Yukon' in *The Complete Poems of Robert Service* (New York: Dodd, Mead & Co. 1940), p. 3. Used by permission of the publisher.
3. From 'St Paul' by F. W. H. Myers, in *Collected Poems* (London: Macmillan & Co., 1921), p. 138.
4. Psalm 84:11.
5. 'Night Song at Amalfi' by Sara Teasdale, from *The Collected Poems of Sara Teasdale* (New York: The Macmillan Co., 1937), p. 97. Used by permission.
6. Philippians 4:12.
7. RSV.
8. Ephesians 5:16.
9. Philippians 3:8, para.
10. Psalm 6:3.
11. From the hymn 'Lead On, O King Eternal' by Ernest W. Shurtleff.
12. Colossians 3:16.
13. Luke 16:15.
14. 1 Timothy 4:13.
15. Allusion to the commandments in Leviticus, e.g. Leviticus 19:30.
16. From 'To Celia' by Ben Jonson.
17. Nehemiah 4:10, para.
18. Psalm 28:1, para.
19. Hebrews 11:8, ASV.
20. Jeremiah 10:23.

The Test of Service

Concentrate until my arrival on your reading and on your preaching and teaching. Never forget that you received the gift of proclaiming God's word....[1]

On January 3, 1950, Jim wrote to me:

THIS BEGINS a new file on the second half of the twentieth century according to the conventional reckoning. But what am *I* doing here? What is the significance of my being one of the elect upon whom the end of the ages is come? It gives me a sense of what I heard C. Stacey Woods call "destiny" to think I live in a day so near the Great Precipitation. The elders got to discussing prophecy in our prayer meeting last night and suddenly brother Gill looked me straight in the eye and said, "We are within forty years of the millennial reign of Jesus Christ, and that's a conservative estimate!" At supper tonight, Dad said, "Children born today will see the wind-up of the age." Do consider this, Bets, slowly, and for several minutes at a time. What is my relation, practically, to the end of the age? Oh, it is gripping to think that our eyes are to be so blessed as to see Him, "so coming in like manner"[2] as He went away. What means the enormity of faith in a returning Christ in such an hour? How poorly will appear anything but a consuming operative faith in the person of Christ when He comes. How lost, alas, a life lived in any other light!

Yes, I read with avid eagerness *Life's* editorial [on America's failure to produce great art because of the lack of a sense of sin] last week. Even went so far as to pay twenty cents for the fool magazine! It denotes the swing of the pendulum from fearful realism to a little softer, if less surely defined, way of thinking. Pessimism, the anodyne of all pantheism, is a bitter pill and does not well suit man, the laughing mammal.... The armchair American, untrained in brutality, will find palpable the honeyed lie of the False Prophet. Neo-Orthodoxy will be the rage; church union the patriotism, God the common topic of conversation, but not Paul's Orthodoxy, nor Christ's Church, nor my God. "The people imagine a vain thing!"[3]

A later letter comments on my reply to this paragraph:

I share your sentiments about the *Life* magazine editorial. I hope I hadn't a sneer in my tone. Despisers are not in the way of righteousness. Nietzsche would have his disciples learn great contempt; Christ would teach His great compassion, *tender* feeling, not *bitter* feeling. As Bunyan says, "Bowels becometh pilgrims." Maxwell quotes a quoter of Carlyle this month similarly: "Contempt is a dangerous element to sport in; a deadly one if we habitually live in it." I think we both need this. Criticism of things in general is so distant from Christlikeness, and I am sure the healthy attitude toward Mr Luce's recent word on belief is to rejoice.

The letter of January 3 continues:

The volcanic upthrusts we imagined as frozen explosions on Mt Hood are pure white, dazzling against late Wednesday's blue sky. A carload of us went up again yesterday and skied all day. I feel like the first day following wrestling work-out in the fall. I am no skier at all, usually ending up in a soft but chilly bank of snow. It's far more thrilling a sport than skating, on any surface, though I am no better on skis than on skates.

Snow came on here last Sunday night. We have about two inches now, but rain and warmth are predicted for tomorrow.

The full moon on the snow and the freighted evergreens, the scarlet spots in the holly, and the silence—dozens of passages from Service come to mind. Somehow it amuses me every time you quote him. I never knew anyone else who took him seriously, I guess. All literature profs I ever talked to sorta look wise and remark, "Well, his writing is not in the best taste." I have not had much peace to read during the holiday, but things have blown quiet now and I must get at my books again.

I got my acceptance letter from Camp Wycliffe[4] for this summer. Feel as though the Lord would have me take the time there, whether I go to India or South America. The British Guiana project is dragging, so I will likely spend my spring here. Pray for more openings for the Word, will you? Oh that God would cause His Word to "run and be glorified".[5] The Christian High School board verified a standing offer for me to take two weeks' meetings in their high school. I wish you'd enlist some prayer help on this score. The series is to begin January 15, half-hour morning sessions. I have never done any such thing, and feel quite insufficient for a crowd of active minds such as they will have. Pray that the Holy Spirit will do His work of lauding, lifting, and enlivening Christ before them.

The diary continues on January 4:

I have been musing lately on the extremely dangerous cumulative effects of earthly things. One may have good reason, for example, to want a wife, and he may have one legitimately. But with a wife comes Peter The Pumpkin Eater's proverbial dilemma— he must find a place to keep her. And most wives will not stay on such terms as Peter proposed. So a wife demands a house; a house in turn requires curtains, rugs, washing machines, *et cetera*. A house with these things must soon become a home, and children are the intended outcome. The needs multiply as they are met—a car demands a garage; a garage, land; land, a garden; a garden, tools; and tools need sharpening. Woe, woe, woe to the man who would live a disentangled life in my century. II Timothy 2:4 is impossible in the United States, if one insists on a wife. I learn from this that the wisest life is the simplest one, lived in the fulfilment of only the basic requirements of life—shelter, food, covering, and a bed. And even these can become productive of other needs if one does not heed. Be on guard, my soul, of complicating your environment so that you have neither time nor room for growth!

I must not think it strange if God takes in youth those whom I would have kept on earth till they were older. God is peopling Eternity, and I must not restrict Him to old men and women.

January 10. The announcement of Einstein's new theory of gravitation—which I fail to understand in any degree—caused no small stir in the news this week. All I see is the "integration process" at work again, the "One World" idea of Wilkie's. World Government, World Council of Churches, unification of ideals, and now, the explanation of all phenomena on the basis of a single formula—these are the signs of the End. Social, religious, political, and technical unification, men will find. But where will they find a Moral Integrator, a common denominator for Good and Evil? There is no unification of these, nor understanding of them apart from the consideration of the Christian God.

January 11. Most encouraging letter from Fritz today. Thank God for the faith to believe for him, that first night in November. He grows daily, it seems. How faithful my God!

January 15. Deserted all morning. Much time on my knees, but no fervency or any desire for prayer. No heed or hearkening in the study of the Word, either. What good are Greek, commentaries, insight, gift, and all the rest, if there is no heart for Christ? Oh, what slackness I feel in me now. Wasted half a day. Was to have spoken in chapel again at the Christian High School, but because of snow, school was closed. Good thing—I had nothing to say to the kids anyhow.

January 18. Spoke on fellowship with God at the nurses' and med-students' meeting. Felt that I wandered and joked overmuch. I must learn to be more sober, Lord, in such serious matters. How carelessly I handle the Holy Word, how dangerously off-handed. Help, Lord; let my ministry be Spirit-empowered, not put over by my personality. Feel I failed the

Lord in too much digging for sermon thoughts, and not enough time letting the Scripture speak to me.

Despite the near-despair which some of these journal entries reveal, Jim was being strengthened, in the long hours spent at the old roll-top desk in his bedroom, for later conflicts. On January 19, out of his own discouragement, he was able to write a letter which was of great encouragement to me. I was facing a decision which I feared considerably. His reply to my letter:

> I pray for you, that all your misgivings will be melted to thanksgivings. Remember that the shadow a thing casts often far exceeds the size of the thing itself (especially if the light be low on the horizon), and though some future fear may strut brave darkness as you approach, the thing itself will be but a speck when seen from beyond. Oh that He would restore us often with that "aspect from beyond", to see a thing as He sees it, to remember that He dealeth with us as with sons. Amy Carmichael's words come to me:
>
> > *"He hath never failed thee yet.*
> > *Never will His love forget.*
> > *O fret not thyself nor let*
> > *Thy heart be troubled,*
> > *Neither let it be afraid."*[6]

The journal presents evidence that God was offering him opportunity to give out some of what was being taken in.

January 20, 21. Four meetings with an Inter-Varsity Christian Fellowship gang at Jennings Lodge. Spoke on New Testament semantics and on what a Christian is called: Believer, Disciple, Brother, Saint, Christian—and the relations they entail. Felt the sustaining power of the Spirit, but oh, how I need Him!

January 23. Disheartened tonight because of my lack of discipline. How dare I be so careless and preach as I do? "To him that knoweth to do good (as I have been taught and taught others to be hard on ourselves) and doeth it not, to him it is sin."[7] Sinned by being intemperate in working all day on my stamps—while keeping up a rationalization that I would quit at any moment. Oh, what hypocrisy, what a heart of sin—and how it deceives! Father, forgive it, and let not those who put their trust in Thee—for tomorrow's high school chapel—be ashamed *on my account*. Deliver me from this strong conscience of sins. Let it not have dominion. Give the spirit of forgiveness, I pray.

Not only was his own soul's state the subject of much lamentation, but the state of his own generation as well.

January 24. Ah, tolerant generation, who pay the prophets and fondle them who are sent unto you—Woe. How much better had it been for you and for them if only they had found death at your hands! Cursed be your Judas-embrace. Damned be your friendliness. It speaks not well for you; it lays a shattering condemnation on your prophets.

Ah, generation that hears, but feels not, listens, but aches not, harks, but knows not pain nor the pleasurable healing-balm thereof. Tell me, does all fire extinguish save in Hell? Damned be this tepidity. Have we no fire to hate? Does no flame seize our prophets? Show me one burning heart. Let me see a single worldling afire with true passion, one Heavenling consumed with his God's eternal burnings. In them I would find excuse for you, my cheating, shamming, joyless generation. Well has your own poet said, you live and die "ox-like, limp, and leaden-eyed".[8]

February 4. Difficulty in getting anything at all from the Word. No fervency in prayer. Disturbance in the house, cold weather, and occasional headaches have made spiritual things less precious this whole week. I find I must drive myself to study, following the "ought" of conscience to gain anything at all from the Scripture, lacking any desire at times. It is important to learn respect and obedience to the "inner must" if godliness is to be a state of soul with me. I may no longer depend on pleasant impulses to bring me before the Lord. I must rather respond to principles I know to be right, whether I feel them to be enjoyable or not.

I do not understand why I have never seen in America what missionaries write of—that sense of swords being drawn, the smell of war with demon powers. Corresponding is the unity among Christians on the mission field, forced by the onslaught of a very real foe. Satan is not real—though we talk of belief in a "personal devil". As a result, our warfare takes on this sham-fight with shadows, a cold war of weary words. There is no shouting; rather, yawning. Laughter long ago stifled sobs in our assemblings together. Woe, woe, woe unto us. We have not submitted to sacrifice. We have not guessed the power of the calling to which God has called—its power to ruin and to revive, its strength to slay. Service's "Law of the Yukon" has some words peculiarly applicable to the life to which I think God calls:

"Send not your foolish and feeble; send me your strong and your sane—
Strong for the red rage of battle; sane, for I harry them sore;
Send me men girt for the combat, men who are grit to the core;
Swift as the panther in triumph, fierce as the bear in defeat,
Sired of a bulldog parent, steeled in the furnace heat.

And I wait for the men who will win me—and I will not be won in a day.
And I will not be won by weaklings, subtle, suave and mild,
But by men with the hearts of vikings, and the simple faith of a child;
Desperate, strong and resistless, unthrottled by fear or defeat,
Them will I gild with my treasure, them will I glut with my meat." [9]

February 20. Finished the chapel services at the Christian High School. Forbid, Lord, that any of those to whom I minister should be so foolish as to take my word as though it were Thine; or so daring as to set aside Thy Word as though it were mine.

Whether Jim knew of any results from that series of talks I do not know. But after his death I received a letter which demonstrates that prayer was answered. Evelyn Corkum, a student in the high school at that time, wrote:

> I was a sophomore, a little more conservative than the average. In all these years there are certain specific things Jim said which have stood out and become very basic factors in moulding my character and way of life.
>
> His entire series was based on Timothy. He explained that he chose that book because it was written to a young man. . . . It was through this series that I finally began to have a rather regular daily time with the Lord. Jim did not suggest that we start the morning out with five minutes of Bible skimming and hasty prayer. He challenged us to get up forty-five minutes early, ahead of the rest of the family, get to a place where we could be alone with the Lord, without interruptions if possible. At that time, the suggested forty-five minutes seemed to me a huge sacrifice, but it was like him not to try to *edge in* counsel in the hope of gaining the students' favour.
>
> One day he spoke frankly of boy-girl relations. . . . "Don't put yourself in a position to see how good your resistance is. When you feel temptation coming, *get out of there!*" . . . It was new to me to see a good-looking fellow so sold out for the Lord. His personality was magnetic and his spirituality did not in the least make him "creepish" or "fuddy-duddy".
>
> He dared us to give up ourselves to Christ. . . . I am sure I am not exaggerating when I say that Jim had the greatest influence on my life of any single individual outside of my parents. I do not regret having taken his advice seriously. I believe that because of it my life has been full and that I have known and am experiencing the Lord's leading.

Jim's journal continues:

February 11. I see tonight that in spiritual work, if nowhere else, the character of the worker decides the quality of the work. Shelley and Byron may be moral free-lancers and still write good poetry. Wagner may be lecherous as a man, and still produce fine music, but it cannot be so in any work for God. Paul could refer to his own character and manner of living for proof of what he was saying to the Thessalonians. Nine times over in the first epistle he says "You know", referring to the Thessalonians' first-hand observation of Paul's private as well as public life. Paul went to Salonica and lived a life that more than illustrated what he preached; it went beyond illustration to convincing proof. No wonder so much work in the Kingdom today is shoddy—look at the moral character of the worker.

February 13. Spoke tonight at the quarterly meeting of the Christian School Association. Touched on demon powers in the classroom ("We wrestle not against flesh and blood"[10]) and of the *institutionalization* of the child—the ability to develop good deportment without godly devotion; scholarship without spirituality; sincere, pure minds, without spiritual, powerful motives. Felt clumsy in expressing myself and not too sure all I said was of use. Oh for the lips of Samuel, from which the Lord let not a single word fall to the ground!

February 18. Teaching seventh and eighth grades all this week in the Christian School. The board want me to decide soon about what I'll be doing next fall, as they want me to teach for a year. O God, so many turns, so many ways, so many pits! Help me to do Thy will without consideration of any man. I can make no decision unless I hear Thee speak, Lord.

The same day Jim wrote a letter to his high school friend, Dick Fisher, who he felt was missing God's way for his life:

Have you sent in your Wheaton application yet? You are losing valuable time in your GI-bill money for school. I exhort you, Richard, to drop these lumbering trivialities pronto, pay your debts, and hit the road to college. If you can't get into Wheaton try something else. Further, I sense that you are in real need of some stalwart Christian companionship in both sexes, and feel that the conditional environment of a Christian college campus would supply your present lack. You can't fool yourself into thinking you can get along without more contact with the people of God than you have been having. I say this not without forethought, for I have felt often when with you that you and I should have been more together, or at least that you learn godliness along with some friend, as did Christian in *Pilgrim's Progress*. I know that it is not my place to tell you what you should do, but I feel this strongly for you, brother. It is dangerous to have companions among the devil's flock, and know little of travelling behind the Great Shepherd of the sheep of His fold. It is probable that you have before you a multitude of hopes and plans for work around Astoria, but I feel that you should take all that to the Lord and tell Him that you want more than a good business. In fact, this is so pressing and so important to your welfare that I even dare to say that the telephone company doesn't need you any more. It is evident after several years with them that you have gotten very little for all your pains. Certainly the work has been of little profit to you spiritually, your bank account is no larger, and I daresay that you are no happier personally than you were when you started with them. In short, you are getting nowhere.

It seems like this is sorta stern stuff to be coming from me, but I got keyed up about it today and thought I had better exhort you, because I can see the Great Day approaching fast, and perhaps it hadn't occurred to you that you have got to render up an account right away. I'd like to see you to talk it over, for I am afraid that I won't be around here this summer, and may miss a chance to spend much time with you. If it sounds like I'm sticking my nose into your business, remember that I say this with a regard to the eternal profit of your soul, and that the Lord has stirred me up to write of this.

Christ needs some young fellows to sell out to Him and recklessly toss their lives into His work. It seems to me like you ought to be one of them, Fisher. —Earnestly in the Lord Jesus, Jim.

A letter written on February 22 to his father, who was preaching in eastern Washington, reveals the seriousness of Jim's intent to see the New Testament church pattern set to work in modern practice. The letter shows, too, that his time was not entirely spent in the academic (teaching and studying) and the spiritual:

Beloved Dad: Your insistence upon short notes leaves me without excuse not to write, so here is one for you. Long pause here. I wrote the first sentence too hastily, I guess. Just as I clicked off the last who should come bursting in the door but that mad Dutchman Werner Durtschi, who had brought his mother and two sisters over for a lesson in knitting Argyle socks from Mom. So went the evening. It's late now, and I had to run in second gear all day today because of a late night last evening.

Much longer pause here. Thursday filled with work and study. No time for letter writing.... Got my first pay cheque from the Christian school today. They're paying ten dollars a day minus tax. Sizeable, and giving an increased responsibility in stewardship to me. Things are going a little more smoothly as I get to understand the kids more. Discipline remains a problem. Do you think that the fall set the human heart against all learning? Why must all be pushed and driven to that which can only do them good, even in the field of secular knowledge? I see that the heart rebels at all light, not only at the knowledge of God.

The meeting of two weeks ago at the Stark Street assembly was enjoyable, though not as well attended nor as warm as the previous one, I thought. The setting up of men on the platform discourages contributions from the floor. I have been under some exercise as to running our gospel meeting as the saints used to, not announcing a leader nor appointing a song leader, but waiting on the Lord for individual exercise in these matters. We saw the method work well at Forest Grove one night some years ago.

The chickens are producing five or six eggs a day. We noticed that the leaving off of the light at night does not affect their production, so we have abandoned the practice of keeping the light on. We got an oversized egg today that measured 2¾ inches long.

The Buick slipped out of reverse and low again, but Bob had it back with a few minutes' work. Same trouble we had in Bozeman, you'll remember. The Plymouth is grinding gears badly, so we use it very little, not knowing what might happen next.

Bryson cut down the two remaining trees on his lot, and I hauled them down to the chestnut this morning. Have not had time to buck them to lengths yet, but we need little wood just now. The bulbs are springing all over the place, but won't be blooming for another two or three weeks, I guess.

I must get some papers corrected and do some other correspondence, so will call this the end. I made this translation of 1 John 2:7,8 this morning. What do you think of it?—"Beloved, I am not writing a new commandment to you, but an old commandment which you have held from the start; the word which you have heard is the old commandment. Still, I am writing it as a new commandment because the darkness is passing along, and the true light is shining on." This last means, I think, that the command to love one another takes on fresh meaning as I step into new light, and the darkness dissipates. With the growth in my knowledge of the implications of the love that I am taught, I am determined to apply that love in an increasing number of situations.—Earnestly, your son Jim.

February 25. Spoke last evening to the junior class at Multnomah School of the Bible, on 2 Timothy 2:4 [says the journal]: the war with spirit-forces, disentanglement, and something of the call to service. What a mockery! I felt as though little or nothing was accomplished.... The Lord has been distant most of this week, and I have found myself too weary and sinful to draw near to Him. Desire seemed to fail and my soul lies faint, lapping at its own stale dregs.

February 26. I was asked to give up the breaking of bread meeting for a "service" next Sunday morning. What folly! Ah, for the spirit of Rutherford,

> *"E'en Anwoth were not heaven,*
> *E'en preaching were not Christ."*

How can one explain without bringing offence? I offended in refusing, but oh, the Lord was real tonight out underneath the moon. A February night it is, pregnant with spring.

> *"Too many devious paths lead down the land*
> *And I shall need in that strange, vast unknown,*
> *Thy hand upon my hand."* [11]

March 6. Dave was here last week-end, and wants some answer regarding Inter-Varsity and Foreign Missions Fellowship work. I see several restrictions, the primary one being the compromises I would be called upon to live under in recommending mission boards, while knowing that the way of God is so far from organised methods that none with whom I would deal would be able to see the consistency of my own attitudes and the things I would have to recommend. Further, the leaping from place to place, here a night, there a day, has been shown to be ineffective, in the summer of 1948, lacking the substantial quality of settled local building.

My exercise seems to be undergoing crucial fires just now. I sensed afresh last eve the truth of Paul's word, "How shall they preach except they be sent?" [12] O God, here I am. Send me, oh send me afield.

But further preparation was still needed. Instead of being sent "afield" Jim was sent to a small town in southern Oregon to preach in a series of meetings. At the beginning of the two and a half weeks there, he wrote:

The fulfilment of Psalm 65:5 is hoped, "By terrible things in righteousness wilt Thou answer us, O God of our salvation; who art the confidence of all the ends of the earth, and of them that are afar off upon the sea." I hardly dare believe for this, since my own soul is in such a state that I cannot find faith to lay hold on God prevailingly.

March 26. Spoke this morning on the Triumphal Entry.... Some freedom but much unnecessary shouting.

March 27. Spoke on Mark 14. Felt deserted, though much prayer had ascended for the meeting. Only two sinners out. Much humbled in heart afterward.

March 28. Spent this afternoon visiting with Phares about the country. Some stir, a certain "sound of going" [13] there seems to be up the valley, but no conviction generally among the people.

O God, soften sinners and save them to Thine eternal glory!

March 31. Spoke on Gethsemane.... Went into the meeting with a shaking at the horror of sin. Conviction sensed, but the souls of men were not shaken with the trembling as we had hoped. Came home questioning the Father's goodness and was rebuked with these answers:

(1) God is not frustrating our prayers. He has heard, and in wisdom withheld an unusual work. The wisdom of God seemed a good thing to ponder, though I could not understand it. God withholds blessing only in wisdom, never in spite or aloofness.

(2) James' word about asking came.

    (a) I had not been asking definitely enough—"Ye have not because ye ask not."[14]

    (b) I had not been asking purely enough. "Ye ask and receive not because ye ask amiss, that ye may consume it upon your lusts."[15] I still had my own concerns, my own name connected with the work, and had God granted it hitherto I would have consumed the answer in pride and selfishness.

A letter to his father dated April 13 indicates that the meetings were not without effect.

Beloved Padre: Just a brief note-report on the Lord's work down at Williams. I just now got in after an eight-hour bus ride since midnight. Am unpacked now.

The Lord gave me much freedom in the meetings and was Himself obviously working over the whole valley area. The town's chief drunkard and his wife came to the Lord one afternoon and both gave public confession of faith last night. One or two of the young folks came into assurance of salvation and are making a good beginning at the study of the Scriptures. Phares and I met with twenty-five young people, high school age and over, last night after the meeting before I went to the bus and had a serious time dealing with them about private study of the Scriptures, personal holiness, and down-to-business living for Christ. I think God wrought wonders—nothing emotional (except in me personally, where I felt much conviction for my inward corruption), but a sane and scriptural building process, done, I trust, in the Spirit.

Never has the meaning of the death and consequent exaltation of the Saviour been so clear to me, and I praise God for plainness of speech in ministering some of the doctrines of grace.

The journal continues:

April 16. Inter-Varsity conference over the week-end. Exercised re: I-V staff work. No leading concerning the foreign field. Back to the Greek this morning, after three weeks away from it for all practical study.

April 17. Turned down offer by the school board to complete the school year as seventh-eighth grade teacher. Found some difficulty in discerning the Lord's will, but believe He has guided. It is easy to be swayed by minor (or even major) points when one comes to make decisions if one cannot hark back to *principles* of guidance. I have learned three principles recently which make a fair beginning at a code:

(1) Remember always that God has taught you the importance of a building ministry. Staying for some time in one group, stressing certain things consistently, is the best way to accomplish lasting work for God.

(2) Do not put yourself in a position relative to any man or group which permits them to direct policies which you know must be decided upon through your own individual exercise before God. Never let any organization dictate the will of God. A move which so ensnares cannot be of God for me.

(3) Whenever the choice is between the doing of spiritual work, of whatever sort, and a secular job, again of whatever sort, the choice of me must be the former regardless of financial conditions.

April 19. Seeking a promise of God's acceptance of my trust in Him for guidance in the next month and a half. I got this encouragement from Isaiah 42:16, "I will bring the blind by a way that they know not, in paths that they know not will I lead them."[16] I fulfil the qualifications for once, Lord; most surely I am blind.

April 20. I asked earnestly for some token of guidance to be shown concerning my going to the Summer Institute of Linguistics.[17] Got none. It is clear to me tonight that I can do quite well without that guidance for now. God is going to give me a specific leading—not when I ask for it, but when I need it, and not until then.

May 18. Took up and finished a hasty browsing of the *Life* of William Farel, a Reformer of note. It was three hours before I returned to the Scriptures and prayer. I trust I learned a lesson, for it took special concentration and considerable difficulty to begin to feel the power of the Word. Anything, good as it may be, put before my study of the true and living Word becomes a snare, and I must assiduously avoid such, if the Word is to be my fresh meat every morning.

Last night I took a walk around the hill. Found myself again dedicating my clay, asking for God's presence to be sensed more continually. Analyzed afresh and repudiated my base desire to *do* something for God in the sight of men, rather than to *be* something, regardless of whether results were to be seen. The clouds scudding over the west hills seemed to speak to me: "What is your life? It is even a vapour."[18] I saw myself as a wisp of vapour being drawn upward from the vast ocean by the sun's great power and sent landward by the winds. The shedding of blessing upon earth must be as the rain, drawn up first by God, borne along by His Spirit, poured out by His own means and in His place, and running down to the sea again. "As water poured out."[19] So my weakness shall be God's opportunity to refresh earth. I would that it should be as He has shown.

And to me, Jim wrote:

Though these days may be quiet, as far as doing is concerned, they are jammed full of excitement in the inner man. I exult to know the God who maintains the path of the just as a shining light, brighter by the moment toward the Perfect Day.

Notes

1. 1 Timothy 4:13, 14, JBP.
2. Acts 1:11, para.
3. Psalm 2:1.
4. A study-camp in Norman, Oklahoma, conducted by the Summer Institute of Linguistics, Inc., in affiliation with the University of Oklahoma.
5. 2 Thessalonians 3:1, ASV.
6. This was a quotation from memory and is not in the exact words of the author.
7. James 4:17.
8. From the poem 'The Leaden-Eyed' by Vachel Lindsay.
9. From 'The Law of the Yukon' in *The Complete Poems of Robert Service* (New York: Dodd, Mead & Co., 1940), p. 12. Used by permission of the publisher.
10. Ephesians 6:12.
11. Source unknown.
12. Romans 10:15.
13. 1 Chronicles 14:15.
14. James 4:2.
15. James 4:3.
16. ASV.
17. The University of Oklahoma.
18. James 4:14.
19. Psalm 22:14, para.

— 13 —

Impelled by These Voices

Unto the upright there ariseth light in the darkness.[1]

JIM ELLIOT'S April prayer for guidance concerning attendance at the Summer Institute of Linguistics was answered in the affirmative, and June 2, 1950, found him in Wheaton again, *en route* to Oklahoma. This futher step taught him something else about guidance, which he recorded in his diary:

> Impressed with Ephesians 5, "understanding what the will of the Lord is", and Romans 12, "proving what is the will of God". Every moment I may be conscious and rejoice in the knowledge of God's will. Obedience to every command puts me on the track and keeps me there. Decisions of course must be made, but as in railroad, so in life—a block signal, a crisis, is lighted only where there is special need. I may not always be in sight of a "go" light, but sticking to the tracks will take me where the next one is. Understanding the will of the Lord is believing Him, that he will—in all situations where I have obeyed—make that way His own way, effectual for eternity.

At the University of Oklahoma, Jim, along with several hundred other prospective or returned missionaries, spent ten weeks learning how to study unwritten languages—how to write them down and analyze them. Phonetics, the study of sounds, he found not difficult, with his native ability to mimic others' accents and dialects. His analytical mind tackled with zest the problems of morphology (the study of the structure of words) and syntax (the structure of sentences). The course also gave opportunity for each student to practise in a simulated field situation. Informants from various language groups were brought in to the University, and the students worked with them individually, collecting and organizing language data just as they would do in an area where the langauage is not yet in writing. For this study Jim was allowed to use as his informant a former missionary to the Quichuas of the Ecuadorian jungle. This afforded an excellent opportunity for a start on the particular language which Jim was beginning to feel would be his task in the future. The missionary from Ecuado was the first to tell Jim of the Aucas. Jim's heart was immediately set on fire. A tribe untouched by civilization? A people who had repulsed every attempt of the white man to contact them? The pioneer spirit in him was kindled at the very thought. Some may say his was a romantic temperament. Very likely it was. But Ragland, the pioneer of South India (1815–1858), said:

> St Paul considered it as wages to work at Corinth without wages, and had a feeling (which in anyone else we should call romantic) about preaching Christ where he had not been named before. . . . Indeed, I am not clear that the feeling commonly called "romantic" is not, as much as any other natural feeling, sanctifiable and applicable to Christ's purposes.

Jim thought of the correspondence he had had with Dr Tidmarsh. He thought of the Quichua country, where large areas were as yet not reached with the gospel. And now the Aucas. This, to a man accustomed to expect God to 'pull strings through circumstances' as he said, did not appear to be mere coincidence.

Was it Ecuador, then, rather than India, to which he was to go? His leading in this case was as remarkable as it was clear. On July 4 Jim decided to set aside ten days for prayer for God's definite answer.

'Make my path sure, Lord,' he wrote in his journal. 'Establish my goings. Send me when and where You will, and manifest to all that You are my Guide.'

Four days later he added:

These are days of vision for me, days wherein are revealed to me those great "oughts" which must be if Christ is to have glory. Partly they are revealed in what I see around me by way of departure from the Word of God in practice. Partly they are known in the reading of the Scripture as I see the ideal and its beauty in days past. Oh, what manner of men we ought to be in light of what is now on us! Lord, Thou hast spoken once and again in my soul. What ought to be can be. And I believe. Vindicate Thy Name, Thy Word, Thy pattern by accomplishing these many "oughts" I see but afar off.

July 14. I asked for some word from God ten days ago, which would encourage me in going to Ecuador. It came this morning in an unexpected place. I was reading casually in Exodus 23 when verse 20 came out vividly. "Behold I send an angel before thee to keep thee by the way and to bring thee into the place which I have prepared. Take heed before him." Coming as it did, with such preceding feelings and such simple believing for some promise, I take this as leading from God that I should write Tidmarsh telling him that I will go to Ecuador in the will of God.

It was not in answer to his own prayers alone that Jim was thus led. Only a few days later he received a letter from Eleanor Vandevort, a college friend who was by then a missionary in Africa. She told of a peculiar compulsion to pray for Jim at the very time he had set aside for prayer. He wrote to her:

Dear Eleanor: I suppose it is very early morning in the Sudan, and that you rise to face the day with Christ, or that you still sleep with His Spirit brooding over you. In either case, two four-line prayers from Amy Carmichael are being prayed for you now. If the former,

> "My Lord, My Love, my heart's Eternal Light,
> Shine on thy lover through the hours of night,
> Shine on my thoughts, my very dreams be found
> About Thy business, on some holy ground."

And if the latter, then:

> "Walking the dawn-wind, Jesus, Heavenly Lover,
> In the still beauty of the waking morn,
> Unveil Thyself to me, and with the vision
> Shall come the strength for trials yet unborn."

... Your letter is dated July 12 and you say I had been much on your heart thereabouts. It was of God you were burdened, Van. For I had been having ten days of special prayer about going to Ecuador, between July 4 and 15. A recently abandoned station among the Quichuas had been offered to whomever will take it. Some here knew of the work and encouraged us to regard it as a door to be knocked on. If God opens the door, who can shut? And if He says, "Go", who will dare stay? So pray that my faith be strengthened against opposing powers.

Then, on July 25, he wrote to his parents of further confirmation of the decision:

The confidence given of the Lord that this is His will for me grows daily, and is confirmed on every side. Not by spectacular means always, but by very little things, something dropped casually in class regarding the Quichua language; a $20 bill in an envelope in the mail-box with an unsigned note, "Philippians 4: 19. God bless you. This is for Ecuador." A letter from Dr Tidmarsh yesterday. He was encouraged but not elated, grateful to God, but will not yet assume that God wants us right in Shandia, knowing our interest in the Quichuas generally.

If it is God's will, I am ready to go immediately, and would wait only the decision of the elders in Portland. Bob's wonderings about the draft board do not even cause me the slightest worry. After all, he who sets the open door before me promised "no man can shut".[2] It may seem naïve to take such a view, but after all, there is nothing I can do to "draft dodge', or pull strings. The Lord's promise to preserve the simple applies in my case, I think. He is God who regards kings and rulers as very small factors in the affairs that concern His work. And I think we can afford to share that attitude with Him. This is not to say they will not try to shut the door. It is simply to say that God will keep it open, regardless of who tries to shut it, and how hard they try.

How I praise God for you all. What a heritage falls to them whose surroundings from childhood have been illumined by the Book of God, whose winds have been freighted with the prayer and concern of others for their souls. Think for an instant of the little children digging yams today at the crack of a whip in Quichua-land, many of whom don't know their own fathers. Romanism dominates their souls and intoxicates their bodies. Oh that God would plant His Spirit in some of those families, as He has so graciously in ours, that they might know the blessing and recompense of living for God as we know it today. The missionaries say the spirit of the people is utterly broken, having been so long enslaved in such frightful excesses. They have no desire to alleviate their own needs, but drink themselves into their graves.

> *"Not that they starve, but starve so dreamlessly;*
> *Not that they sow but that they seldom reap;*
> *Not that they serve, but have no gods to serve;*
> *Not that they die, but that they die like sheep."*[3]

Men who live and never understand what they were created for may be said indeed to be "dead" as the Scriptures say. "Where there is no vision, the people perish."[4]

Jim's parents, along with others who knew him well, could not help questioning whether perhaps his ministry should be among young people in the United States. His gift for Bible teaching and preaching was an unusual one, as had been evidenced in college student work, radio preaching, and evangelistic meetings. They wrote to him, telling him their feeling, and mentioning as well their own sense of loss at seeing him leave home permanently.

He replied on August 8:

I do not wonder that you were saddened at the word of my going to South America. This is nothing else than what the Lord Jesus warned us of when he told the disciples that they must become so infatuated with the Kingdom and following Him that all other allegiances must become as though they were not. And He never excluded the family tie. In fact, those loves which we regard as closest, He told us must become as hate in comparison with our desires to uphold His cause. Grieve not, then, if your sons seem to desert you, but rejoice, rather, seeing the will of God done gladly. Remember how the psalmist described children? He said that they were as a heritage from the Lord, and that every man should be happy who had his quiver full of them. And what is a quiver full of but arrows? And what are arrows for but to shoot? So, with the strong arms of prayer, draw the bowstring back and let the arrows fly—all of them, straight at the Enemy's hosts.

> *"Give of thy sons to bear the message glorious,*
> *Give of thy wealth to speed them on their way,*
> *Pour out thy soul for them in prayer victorious,*
> *And all thou spendest Jesus will repay."* [5]

Does it sound harsh so to speak? Surely those who know the great passionate heart of Jehovah must deny their own loves to share in the expression of His. Consider the call from the Throne above, "Go ye," [6] and from round about, "Come over and help us," [7] and even the call from the damned souls below, "Send

Lazarus to my brothers, that they come not to this place."[8]
Impelled, then, by these voices, I dare not stay home while
Quichuas perish. So what if the well-fed Church in the homeland
needs stirring? They have the Scriptures, Moses, and the
Prophets, and a whole lot more. Their condemnation is written
on their bankbooks and in the dust on their Bible covers.
American believers have sold their lives to the service of
Mammom, and God has His rightful way of dealing with those
who succumb to the spirit of Laodicea.

The breadth of Jim's vision is suggested in this entry from
the journal:

August 9. God just now gave me faith to ask for another young
man to go, perhaps not this fall, but soon, to join the ranks in
the lowlands of eastern Ecuador. There we must learn: (1)
Spanish and Quichua, (2) each other, (3) the jungle and independence, and (4) God and God's way of approach to the
highland Quichua. From thence, by His great hand, we must
move to the Ecuadorian highlands with several young Indians
each, and begin work among the 800,000 highlanders. If God
tarries, the natives must be taught to spread southward with the
message of the reigning Christ, establishing New Testament
groups as they go. Thence the Word must go south into Peru
and Bolivia. The Quichuas must be reached for God! Enough for
policy. Now for prayer and practice.

Notes

1. Psalm 112:4.
2. Revelation 3:8.
3. From the poem 'The Leaden-Eyed' by Vachel Lindsay, in *Collected Poems* (New York: The Macmillan Co., 1925). Used by permission of the publisher.
4. Proverbs 29:18.
5. From the hymn 'O Zion, Haste' by Mary A. Thompson.
6. Matthew 28:19.
7. Acts 16:9.
8. Luke 16:27,28, para.

— 14 —

The Pattern Tested

I only say this, let the builder be careful how he builds! The Foundation is already laid, and no one can lay another, for it is Jesus Christ Himself.[1]

WHEN THE linguistic course was over, it seemed that the 'pillar of cloud'[2] was not lifting, and Jim decided to stay on in Norman, Oklahoma, for a month or two with Bill Cathers, helping in the small assembly in Oklahoma City, and in the Bible study group on the university campus. During this period he applied for a passport. Dr Tidmarsh had written from Ecuador to say he planned to take a furlough in the fall, and urged Jim and Bill to come as soon as possible.

Jim wrote to me on August 31:

We are trusting God to provide a place to live and eat here. We ran an ad as "handymen", in the *Norman Daily*, and we usually make enough money painting, repairing, or fixing up to keep us ahead financially. There is abundant opportunity to minister in the area: high school kids in Norman, needy country folk all around, welcome in the assembly, and when school starts, work on the university campus.

If it is God's mind we will leave for Ecuador as soon as we have passports and have seen home once more. There are some

168

supplies to be collected, but nothing like most married couples require. Special stuff you could be praying about includes a radio set, some dental supplies, and medical tools (which Dr Tidmarsh will show us how to use), and, lest I forget, passage money. We are working on a deal which would take us there on a banana boat as crew members.

The journal continues:

September 7. These are waiting-days for Bill and me. We had hoped by now to have secured passports and begun work on collecting supplies, but God has had other things in mind. We have worked when the opportunity came, waiting for word *re*: commendation from the assembly at home. Tomorrow J. M. returns and we must leave his apartment. But where should we go? Norman is a good place to work, but finding a place to live and cook is not easy.

Psalm 31:15 was a blessing: "My times are in Thy hands." And Psalm 139:16: "In Thy book they were all written, even the days that were ordained for me."[3] Ordained days, then, whether spent in waiting, working, or whatever. We have asked for guidance, been obedient where we understood what was to be done, and now wait word for the next step.

September 29. Word came from Ed McCully today *re*: his exercise before the Lord to quit school and begin looking for open doors for a sold-out life. How I praise God to hear! Even wept as I read of the Lord's dealings, for my desire for him, and the spiritual exercise of his gift has been much enlarged. Now I wonder if he may not be the man God would sent with us to Ecuador? I have prayed for one more for the work, and perhaps God will answer thus. Grateful if so, Lord, very grateful.

October 18. I leave, God willing, tomorrow for Wheaton, though I cannot now see why. Things are so needy here. The meetings in Oklahoma City require much, much more prayer than we are giving them; visitation must be done. There are several recent contacts on the university campus that should be followed up with personal contacts. There are calls for painting jobs yet undone. Yet I feel constrained to go to Milwaukee to seek Ed McCully, much the same as Barnabas went to Tarsus to seek Saul long ago.

Lord, I have trusted in Thee with all my heart, and now I confess that I have no understanding upon which I can lean. Grant that my way may be prepared before me, at Homecoming in Wheaton, in Milwaukee, and in Huntington, Indiana. Do the first work of knitting Ed and me, opening the believers' hearts to the truth of the Sanctuary. Waste not my hours of travel, Lord. Flood my pathway with light and give me grace to walk therein pleasing to Thee.

On the way up to Wisconsin Jim ran the car he was driving into the high shoulder of the road, turning it completely over. A friend of Jim's had bought the car only a few days before, and had not a penny of insurance on it. Jim wrote:

I felt sick, but it was plainly an accident, and I know that God had lessons in it. Good to know Psalm 121 in these days—"Thy keeper . . . neither slumbers nor sleeps."

The McCullys had almost hired a painter, so I took the job and have it well under way now. Ed is working as a night clerk in a downtown hotel and I go down every other night to study the Word with him, sleeping while he does the bookwork, and getting in about three and a half solid hours of Bible study. The interchange of thought is stimulating.

There is little indication of where I should go from here. The Lord has supplied every need abundantly, and I rejoice in knowing His presence in all my "goings out and comings in".[4]

In a letter of a few weeks later:

I certainly enjoy being with Ed, and could hope the Lord would send us afield together, but I do not think the decision should be made while I'm here. We influence each other too easily and our natural compatibility would override the Lord's leading if we're not careful.

A letter from Tidmarsh tell us he is going to England on

furlough this month, and since we feel it imperative to be introduced to Shandia under his counsel, we will probably wait until then and return with him next year.

At this point Jim received word from Bill Cathers that he planned to be married. Since Jim had expected to go to Ecuador with Bill, according to the New Testament pattern of working 'two and two',[5] this news was a jolt. He told his parents of it in a letter, adding this comment:

> Talk of marriage, rings, flowers, affairs, and (ugh!) housekeeping leaves me cold. I dread occasionally that my realism may keep me from really falling for anyone hard enough to feel like getting married. Rats. I am a bohemian loafer without enough sense of responsibility to keep my shoes shined.

His mother's reply was a defence of the institution, plus the gentle suggestion that Jim's attitude was perhaps one of sour grapes. Jim countered:

> If I am envious of dear Billy in his marriage, Mom, it is certainly the newest kind of envy I have ever heard of. When it comes to marriage (since your last letter contained so much on the subject) I am still faced with serious problems. It does not necessarily mean that a bachelor must be egotistical, unbalanced, talkative, and overbearing because he has not got a wife. He may be all of these things, as some I know are, but there are married people in the same category. Besides this, Paul, Timothy (we are led to believe), and others of the New Testament figures, to say nothing of other godly men in history and our Lord Jesus Himself, were not married men. If marriage is the only cure-all for unbalanced young men, these must have been unbalanced, and from their work, one could not fairly say it. So, whether to get married is still a problem, aggravated by the peculiar demands put on one who would follow the Pauline pattern in a tropical-forest situation. Bill is being led to marriage, and I exult that it is so, rejoicing with those who rejoice. To envy him

would be to covet his leading (and gift!), and covetousness in Scripture is denounced as idolatry.

By the 'peculiar demands of a tropical-forest situation' he explained himself thus:

It is difficult enough to get among people, learn their language and customs, get acclimated, and make all those emotional adjustments without adding the tremendous task of aligning to married experience. For the woman it is even more difficult and there have been cases where family responsibility so absorbed the wife that she never has become a missionary, simply lacking time to make the social adjustment because of the multiplicity of domestic details. W. E. Vine, whom I have been reading, shares this view, and believes that a man should go with another man until effective contact is made in the society. If, then, it becomes clear that one's testimony and effectiveness would be increased, one should marry.

From Milwaukee Jim went to a small town in Indiana in November where a group of young married couples was interested in studying the Bible. It was an opportunity for him to teach some of the truths which he had recently been examining anew.

Of the first Bible study he wrote:

I felt liberty to lay the cards on the table and flatfootedly blurted out something about the New Testament church pattern. Most of them were stunned, but came back eagerly for more. Have been visiting some of their homes since, and find a real stirring among half a dozen families, a hunger for the Word. Many are bound by traditional organization patterns and, although they feel something is wrong, are fearful of breaking the accepted modes of worship. Of course, I am already branded as a propagator of some new sect, but to this I exultantly reply in the words of the apostle on a similar charge, "But this I confess to thee, that after the way which they call a 'sect', so serve I the God of our fathers.''[6]

I charge you to pray for the saints here. God must do the work of centring their lives in Christ. None know the Scriptures well because of the devilish schemes of the clergy to keep them from thinking for themselves. Do pray for wisdom and grace for me that my witness might be effective for the glory of the Man at God's right hand.

Jim's convictions on the importance of conforming to the New Testament pattern in the structure of the local Church underwent severe fire in this effort.

He wrote home on December 6:

All are willing to admit that the assembly pattern of the New Testament is ideal, but none are willing to commit themselves, particularly the men. . . . Let those who claim New Testament conformity beware: we commit ourselves to a way of life which must be conditioned by the New Testament, and disciplined by *all* the principles therein. So pray for these men—they do not lack desire, but practical devotion, a setting to the task.

After a month's studies with the little group, Jim wrote to his parents:

Generally I feel quite useless. They are helped by my being here, but total ignorance of the Truth is the general status of church-goers hereabouts. I know that my time is limited, and unless someone else moves here to help them, there is little chance of their going on. Oh that God would shake up some of those married couples around Portland with their prim unconcern for souls and saints, dabbling with building lots, houses, jobs, babies, silverware—while souls starve for what they know! God shall not hold us guiltless, either. ''He shall suffer loss.''[7] What is needed here is a family to move in, take work, open the home, and teach Truth without reference to the schismatic heresy of ''Plymouth Brethren''. The urge comes on me at times to write in scathing terms articles for these piddling little magazines of "comfort and kind words for God's little flock". Baloney! When are we going to rise like men and face the world squarely? This drivelling nonsense which condones inactivity because of the apostasy of the day needs a little fire to show up the downright ungodliness it hides. We cuddle around the Lord's table as though it were the last coal of God's altar, and warm our hands, thinking that will appease the wrath of the indignant Christ when He charges us with the unmet, unchallenged, untaught generation of heathen now doing their Christmas shopping. It makes me boil when I think of the power we profess and the utter impotency of our action. Believers who know one-tenth as much as we do are doing one hundred times more for God, with His blessing and our criticism. Oh if I could write it, preach it, say it, paint it, anything at all, if only God's power would become known among us! ICHABOD.

I had forwarded to Jim a letter from a friend in a foreign country, which told something of conditions among Christians there. His answer reveals the importance he placed on the corporate conduct of the Church:

J's letter was interesting. Her attitude toward the Church of God is like the multitude of Fundamentalists—"anything will do". The pivot point hangs on whether or not God has revealed a universal pattern for the Church in the New Testament. If He has not, then anything will do so long as it works. But I am convinced that nothing so dear to the heart of Christ as is His Bride should be left without explicit instructions as to her corporate conduct. I am further convinced that the twentieth century has in no way simulated this pattern in its method of "churching" a community, so that almost nothng is really "working" to the glory and pleasure of God. Further, it matters not at all to me what men have done with the Church over there or in America, it is incumbent upon me, if God has a pattern for the Church, to find and establish that pattern, at all costs.

The clergy of Fundamentalism is a direct descendant of papism, and in spite of what J. says, has no basic principle in Scripture—where the priesthood of all believers is taught.

Further, J. says "the worship service is most satisfying to me as an individual!" What in all eternity has that got to do with it? Have her personal likes and dislikes any right to dictate method in the holy church of God? It is this attitude that has brought hopeless confusion into our present order, for "holy rolling", and snake-handling are most satisfying to some folks as individuals. "Let God be true and every man a liar." Is it His way? Then let my personal likes be filed in the waste-can. Let me follow by afforded grace. It is neither J's job nor mine to commend or condemn any system of gathering. It is the responsibility of both of us to search the Scriptural principles, find the all-important "Thus saith the Lord".

In spite of this strong conviction, there were times when Jim was tempted to wonder if there was any use in expecting to see those principles actually at work. He wrote in his journal:

I have had such conflict of mind lately with unsettlement because of sin, and discouragement in this situation that the very idea of there being "pattern principles" upon which to build for God seemed absurd. Who cares these days if things are done according to Pauline method? Get on with the gospel; we haven't time to bicker over how the work is to be established. It seems I hear this on all hands.

First came the encouragement of 1 Chronicles 28:9, "My son, know thou the God of thy father, and serve him with a perfect heart and with a willing mind; for Jehovah searcheth all hearts and understandeth all the imaginations of the thoughts. If thou seek Him He will be found of thee; but if thou forsake Him He will cast thee off forever. Take heed now; for the Lord hath chosen thee to build a house for the sanctuary; be strong and do it."[8]

Merciful God, but speak this to *me*, actually; make this apply with all its power, promise of good and warning of evil.

God never built anything among men without first delivering to them a pattern; e.g., Moses, Noah, David, Paul.

175

Jim's next experiment in following the Pattern was to be in Chester, a small town in southern Illinois. Ed came down from Milwaukee and they arrived on December 13. Jim's journal entry that night was:

> Feel that God is surely leading Ed and me there. Asking for (1) the establishment of an assembly, (2) radio, medical, and educational experience. Absurd to ask now for these things, as far as any outward possibility is concerned, but I think God is to be glorified in our asking the impossible of Him.
>
> *December 16.* Back at work in the post office in Huntington. Slow going with souls here, but there are encouraging signs. Men unsound in doctrine complicate the issues. Ah, for a place where Scriptures have not been twisted! Lord, send me to Ecuador!

The decision to go to Chester, like every other decision, was tested almost immediately; this time by invitations to return to Portland to help in the Bible studies and evangelistic work there. He replied:

> I firmly believe that God wants me to pioneer in Chester. I still maintain that there is too much collectivism of spiritual truth in Portland. There are sufficient numbers of believers to turn the whole city to God if they would once turn to Christ and confess their shameful neglect of His work. It is now time for a demonstration of God's power—and that is expensive in terms of sacrificial living, travailing prayer, and renouncing of private enjoyments....
>
> Pray for openings for us in Chester—in the gospel, in work, and ministry to "churched" believers. We do not want to build on another's foundation so are praying that souls will be saved there through our witness and that we can do a genuine New Testament work in seeing them drawn together.

As for 'renouncing private enjoyments' Jim practised his exhortation when Christmas time came and with it wistful hints from the family that a visit from him would be much appreciated, after his seven months' absence.

> Surely it would have been nice to be home, and I know it gives you joy to have me there; still, we must steel ourselves to sacrifice *joyfully*, exulting in the knowledge of the proven will of God, that sweet food the Lord Jesus tasted in speaking with the Samaritan. "It is my meat to do the will of Him that sent me."[9] Let us not say in our hearts that this is a heartless attitude; it may be realistic, and therefore harsh on our feelings, but it is always the *very best thing* that can possibly be, the doing of the will of God. There is no need to apologise for one's action, nor defend it if he is sure of God's will. And this is my confidence, that the Lord wanted me here for now.

Notes

1. 1 Corinthians 3:10,11, JBP.
2. Exodus 13:21, RSV.
3. Psalm 139:16, ASV.
4. Psalm 121:8, para.
5. Mark 6:7.
6. Acts 24:14.
7. 1 Corinthians 3:15.
8. ASV.
9. John 4:34, para.

— 15 —

Hemmed in to Nothing

I will say unto God my rock, 'Why hast Thou forgotten me?'...As with a sword in my bones, mine enemies reproach me: while they say daily unto me, 'Where is thy God?'[1]

JIM RESUMED HIS JOURNAL notes on January 6, 1951;

Chester, Illinois: Ed McCully and I returned here on Thursday, and were prospered on our way by the Sovereign; protected, provided for, and encouraged. We are seeking His face now with the prayer of Psalm 90:16,17, "Let Thy work appear unto Thy servants...establish the work of our hands." We want first of all to see His approach to this area, discover His method, and then see it established in our hands. Sense a high privilege as a Truth-bearer here, and want much grace to present the Word in power.

January 9. Last night Ed and I went to St Louis with Powley for a profitable visit with the aged Dr Morey and the young men of the St Louis assembly. Lord, the potential for work is tremendous, work among them, Spirit of God; deliver their souls from the conventional tediums, terms, and traditions. Raise up some men of God from the group.

January 10. For youth there is special wretchedness; for then the powers within conflict most bluntly with the powers without. Restraint is most galling, release most desired. To compensate for these, youth has special powers. "I have written unto you, young men, because ye are strong, and the word of God abideth in you; and ye have overcome the Wicked One."[2] Unusual strength is a premium for youth; acuteness and retentive powers are more real in youth; victory sweetest in youth. Lord, let me live to the hilt, exerting all its force, loosing all its fire. In Solomonic wisdom, I would *rejoice* in youth, yet *remember* my Creator.

January 15. There is that restlessness, that itching, urging discontent in me this morning. The milk of the Word curdles before me or seems to sour within. Hatefulness and rebellion against all restraint is not far from the surface; and it is good that I am not alone here. "Lead me not into temptation, but deliver me from evil."

January 16. Feel that I must write something tonight in praise of the God of delights. The day passed slowly with little affairs; two conferences for Hytool sales, contract signing for a radio programme, some poor script-writing, all with a sense of waiting on God for His time, His H-Hour. All day the sun dropped hints of spring, and at dusk, returning from the shop, I exulted in the distinct wall of purple—the Ozark foothills—close-guarded by the unblinking Venus. The night spread black and blossomed brilliantly with stars. I walked out to the hill just now. It is exalting, delicious. To stand embraced by the shadows of a friendly tree with the wind tugging at your coat-tails and the heavens hailing your heart—to gaze and glory and to give oneself again to God, what more could a man ask? Oh, the fullness, pleasure, sheer excitement of knowing God on earth. I care not if I ever raise my voice again for Him, if only I may love Him, please Him. Mayhap in mercy He shall give me a host of children that I may lead through the vast star fields, to explore His delicacies, whose finger-ends set them to burning. But if not, if only I may see Him, touch His garments, and smile into my Lover's eyes—ah, then, not stars, nor children shall matter—only Himself.

On January 17 Jim wrote to his parents:

Dearest Mom and Dad and all. Good to hear from you again and know that the grace of God abounds still among my dearest ones on earth. It is sweet, unspeakably sweet, to know the Father of Mercies, and to know He never forsakes, ever fortifies those whose confidence is in Him. Ed and I have been feeling more and more recently the need of Him. Here alone the fight is not so easy as when many surround to encourage. But He has been our encouragement, and it is in the Name of the Lord that we set up our banners here.

Friday morning we begin our radio programme. We signed the contract yesterday. Ed will be taking the fifteen minutes' programme on Friday and I will be preaching on the half-hour programme Sunday afternoon, each announcing for the other. Some earnest young men from St Louis will make up a male chorus. Never have I sensed such a great responsibility to do and say the right thing for God. We have entitled the programme 'the March of Truth', taking our theme from the Battle Hymn of the Republic, "His truth is marching on". Pray daily for this, as we are children here, needing more each day to know His grace to demonstrate that promise of Jesus' own lips. "He that believeth on me, the works that I do shall he do also, and greater works than these shall he do, because I go unto my Father. And whatsoever ye shall ask in my name, that will I do, that the Father may be glorified in the Son."[3] What a promise!

From the journal:

January 18. Seems like long waiting to get the work started in Chester. No sales or income thus far, just draining resources, and those will not last more than another week. I have had hopes of laying by some money for the field, but selling is not going to be able to do that, at our present rate.[4] Desired to share in the work of financing the radio here and other evangelical efforts otherwise, but God has hemmed me in to nothing, that I may have nothing, do nothing, want nothing, save Himself. Lord, Thou seest the impossibility of my hopes, and I expect deliverance from Thee in some days.

January 29. Sunday morning we had the service at the state prison, speaking to about 350 convicts up for everything from petty larceny to wholesale murder. A real thrill to declare the Word of forgiveness from Mark 2. "Who can forgive sins but God only?" That *means* something to outcasts of society who have to face both an unforgiving conscience and a bitter hard culture.

After dinner listened to Billy Graham, then went down "under the hill" (as they say of the river-front) to a small mission where a dirty-fisted little plumber proved the godliness of Saint Paul by saying something like this: "Ah tell yuh, they was thirty-five souls saved by the apostle between his dungeon and the chopping-block. They whacked off his head with a broadaxe and it bounced three times and rolled away. But everywhere it hit there busted out three fountains of water, and they tell me they are springing up with pure water to this very day!"

We figured we had plenty of "religion" for that day, so went off to "Zarit's" for coffee and contacting the high school kids.

We're having meetings every Thursday night in a town about twenty miles away. Also have an opportunity to conduct an assembly in the high school there. We are on the bill as a "programme for moral, religious, and uplifting purposes". By God's grace, we'll preach the Resurrection.

A later letter tells of the programme.

February 23. Today Ed and I had the assembly at the Sparta High School. It was a flop and we have been brooding all day. I can't figure it out. We prayed and trusted, but the message and music seemed to have little effect on the kids. It was a real privilege and I will be sorry if we find that we muffed it by some thoughtless neglect or lack of faith or some other thing. Tonight we went over to one of the town's dowagers and got her to grant us the use of a run-down store to begin Sunday School work in. It will give us something definite to stick to. It is not up in the part of town where most people live and shop, but down along the river, in the old dock town. We are thankful for this opening. Frankly, things have been very difficult to go on with here. There has been no real interest on the part of unsaved radio-listeners, a thing we had hoped for, and our efforts to get public places were blocked in a couple of ways, and so we feel frustrated. It is an easy thing to wonder, as we have done dozens of times, just why God sent us here. Six weeks so far, and no natives converted except that salesman who was from out of town. We feel God must be testing us, for He has certainly given us no evidence, beyond His provision of our needs, of any special sort that this move was His will. But what can one do? Doubt, after praying, waiting, and weighing as well as one can and still leaning on the Spirit to move? No. We cannot doubt, but search our hearts and pray more and believe more.... It would be easy to slip into the business world and just be a good guy with a lot of religion, rather than a producing son of God in enemy territory. Time's up. Look aloft and pray for me.

On February 24 Jim made this journal entry:

Ed and I have been in Chester six weeks. There has been no real work started here, and we have only this confidence: God sent us. It is Jehovah who has said, "I will work, and who can hinder it?"[5]

To me he wrote:

There is a certain despairing loneliness snooping about these days and I can almost hear the streets and buildings bristling with the note that haunted David, "Where is thy God?"[6] I don't mean to sound dismal, but there is bleakness about a place like this where no liberating truth is being sounded out. The synagogues[7] are full, but still hollow with unreality. Oh, if earth in its brighter shades be so drear, what must its denser ones be? Thank God for that sense of looking "for a city which hath foundations",[8] which prevails when one sees the basis of these. The business world is a crude one, almost animal in certain aspects, and powerfully affecting to a new-comer, as I regard myself. The very principle of making money by selling things at a profit is distasteful at times, but it seems to be my job for now. Made a couple of sales on Wednesday amounting to nearly $700 in turnover of funds, exhilarating but empty.

We went visiting in the slums last Monday night. Not easy, but comforting to be among those "blessed poor"[9]—with Jesus in a sense we are not when among the self-sufficient. We must go again soon. It makes one scornful of vanity and not much in love with life, especially this life of banks, bills, rates, and percentages.

When Jim and Ed returned from their selling jobs at night, it was to a cramped little apartment, where they took turns cooking their dinners: steaks once a week or so, accompanied by elaborate salads. After dinner, as they cleared up the dishes, the two men would often memorise poetry together. Ed had not been aware of this world of delight until their Chester days, when he 'discovered' Shelley's Ozymandias, first of all, and then Omar Khayyám, Coleridge, Poe, and others. They even copied poems and stuck them up on the wall with adhesive tape, to aid in memorisation.

Their mood was not always serious. One day as they stood waiting for a bus in Chester, Ed went into a nearby store, leaving Jim standing beside a little old lady on the street corner. Presently Ed barged out of the store, coat collar clutched up over his chin, hat pulled down over his eyes. He shoved up to Jim, snarled out of the side of his mouth, 'Meet ya tonight at the Blue Parrot at nine,' and vanished around the corner. The lady, darting a terrified glance at the criminal beside her, edged away.

The incident was only one of many which Ed and Jim staged, without rehearsal or discussion of any kind beforehand. They worked together; they were a true team.

The journal continues:

March 5. Started River Rat Sunday School yesterday. Seventeen out. Encouraged. I am learning the vanity of words. If God does not speak through me, as it is plain He does not through most preachers today, I had better leave off trying to preach. Have been praying the prayer of Psalm 51:15, "O Lord open Thou my lips", and trusting that promise made first to Jeremiah, "Behold I will make my words in thy mouth fire, and this people wood." [10] Mere declaration, no matter how eloquent or impelling, will never kindle the fire God's Word, spoken by God's man, will kindle. Lord, give me Thy Word for this people.

March 22. Felt assured again that the Lord is sending me to Ecuador, having no more place in the States since so many possess so much truth here. Checked on a passport again last week.

The following is from a letter to his parents, dated March 31:

Easter found all the folks of Chester out to church. We had a record crowd at "Club 66" as well, totalling 43 "river rats". They are utterly devoid of any knowledge of God and I suppose that work among them is the nearest thing I've ever done to moving into a pagan culture with the gospel. They had yesterday off from school, so we took two loads into the "Thunderbird" [11] and carted them off to the big ball park for a game. They insisted we repeat the process today, so we're stiff from throwing and running two days in succession. We'll see how effective our methods are tomorrow morning at 10 o'clock. We are praying that God will enter this gang and give us some lives for the glory of the Lord Jesus. They don't bother much about making moral distinctions, though we've noticed a decrease in swearing since we've been playing with them.

Sales dribble in, and I don't work too hard at it. Peole have read that note about our evangelistic efforts in *Letters* magazine, and are sending funds liberally. This we are not too happy about. In the first place we didn't volunteer the information to the magazine and didn't look for publicity. Then too we feel that the work is so very small and we so ineffective in it, that it does not deserve much financial support.

These months of working with Ed led Jim to hope that he was the answer to prayer for a single partner with whom to begin jungle work in Ecuador. This hope, too, was frustrated, as he wrote on April 28 to his parents:

> Ed's diamond arrived this morning. By the time you get this he will be officially engaged, for Marilou is coming on Monday for a week's visit. I cannot condition myself to think of marriage now, in spite of all the bells and rings, not to mention the abundance of marriageable women on the horizon. Things are too unsettled with me, and I do not feel it fair, either to the girl or to the work of the Lord, to tie myself up now with all that the relationship involves. I admit, it is not easy to see the wedding bells break up the old gang, and sit by immobile, but, though a wife would be lawful (even desirable at times) for me, it is not now expedient.
>
> We are in the middle of our two rallies in the Chester High gymnasium. We had about eighty out last night, not a third of what it should have been in view of the heavy advertising we've been doing. However, we feel that we are delivering our souls of the blood of the community. They know we are here, and that we are having meetings regarding the reality of the Lord Jesus. If they do not want to hear, then their blood is on their own heads.

Jim's preaching in meetings of this kind was usually simple, very direct, and serious. He was offended by men who began their sermons with a joke. As he gained in experience, he learned to eliminate a great deal of shouting which had characterised his earlier efforts. When he used notes, they were written on small slips of paper which fitted inside the pages of his Bible. He stood behind or beside the pulpit, body thrust forward, his gaze 'reaching out' to his audience. Whatever he said was linked closely with the actual words of Scripture, which he read or quoted from memory throughout the talk. He did not make a practice of asking members of the congregation to make any overt response to the message, feeling that if the Holy Spirit was at work in the mind and heart of the listener during the meeting, He would continue that work later.

On April 16 Jim wrote to me:

Your last letter was, like Paul's to the Corinthians, at once rebuking and comforting, and I am grateful for it. The *trial* of faith, a court-room drama constantly in session for believers, is more precious than gold, Peter says. It has been that here. Faith has been under fire, and I think because its Source is Christ, it has been strengthened and proved precious. Now problems have arisen and combined with some unsettled old ones sufficiently to dishearten me, but God is faithful and the prayers of His Son effectual when He prays that my faith fail not.

During their last month of working together in Chester, Jim and Ed held meetings in a tent in town. Crowds were small, but there were several who indicated a desire to follow Christ.

Jim wrote:

Why, oh why, are the forces of God so few and feeble while the Enemy counts multitudes on his side? Lord, how long will you hide yourself, concealing your power and letting men think low thoughts of you? Begin to move, Lord, for the sake of the *Name*! Move me, as well, and let me know the fullness of the Spirit.

June 14. Finished tent meetings in Chester, preaching from Acts 1:11, "This Jesus shall so come."[12] Impossible to register the good God has done in Chester. I can see several reasons for coming now that I did not see in January. Surely the Lord has led. Still nothing "big" or extraordinary in the work of the gospel, and this I judge to be only because I lacked intensity and perseverance in prayer. Lift me to heights of desire, Lord, and teach me to pray.

Looking over the last two years since graduation gives me a funny sense of uselessness. The way for me has certainly not been conventional or predictable in any way. But I have sought the will of God, and in this I rest. It is no use arguing what might have been if so and so had happened. We are only asked to do what we are told—small, strange, or simple as that may be—our orders are to obey, and in this my conscience is clear. I have walked in integrity, not purposing according to the flesh, that my path should be yea, yea, and nay, nay. But having purposed in Christ to do what is pleasing to Him, I find His approval (yea) and seal (amen) in the very smallest and unlikely things. Especially is this true of these months here in Chester. Who shall doubt, or say that our labour is in vain? "Thanks be to God, who *always leads us in triumph*."

Notes

1. Psalm 42:9, 10.
2. 1 John 2:14.
3. John 14:12, 13.
4. There is a marginal note here in a different-coloured ink: 'Little did I know! Saved nearly $500 by June!'
5. Isaiah 43:13, ASV.
6. Psalm 42:3.
7. Jim's poetic use of the New Testament term, applied here to churches.
8. Hebrews 11:10.
9. Matthew 5:3, para.
10. Jeremiah 5:14.
11. Jim and Ed's pet name for their rattletrap.
12. ASV.

— 16 —

Exactly Timed for Good

Moreover we know that to those who love God . . . everything that happens fits into a pattern for good.[1]

JIM TOOK PART in the weddings of his two friends, Ed McCully and Bill Cathers, and then headed West once more, arriving in Portland in July with a dollar and twenty cents in his pocket. He set to work immediately at odd jobs, and in August took a brief vacation with the family at Ocean Park, Washington. I was vacationing in New Hampshire when he wrote to me:

> The Tidmarsh family were here for ten days. Their visit served to fix my purpose regarding Ecuador. Things are working out, but slowly. My passport number is in progress for visa in Ecuador. The draft board has given an OK to leave the States. A cautious estimate for a sailing date is December 1, probably from Los Angeles. First, I'm coming East.
>
> Bill and I are scheduled for meetings in the New York-New Jersey area from September 21 to October 12!—some ministry, some missionary, but mostly to get acquainted with the believers. I have a few days open in a rugged schedule and would certainly like to see you if the Lord would have it. Will you be at Birdsong [my family home in Moorestown, New Jersey]?
>
> Ed and Marilou will be in the medical school of the Bible

Institute of Los Angeles this year, and we pray will follow us to Ecuador next year. Pray, will you, that God will strengthen Ed's conviction? I am asking still for a single fellow to accompany me to the school in Shandia, and a young brother from Seattle seems interested. You may remember Pete Fleming, the rather intellectual young blade from the University of Washington. We have had some keen times lately and he is definitely waiting the Lord's command.

On the same day Jim wrote to Pete:

Dear brother Pete: Thanks for your letter of last Thursday. Glad you enjoyed Tidmarsh. We missed you on Mt Adams—sorry I didn't get word to you about it sooner. It was a much more rugged climb than Hood. Choppier snow face, steeper, two miles longer, but some warmer, and done on a much clearer day. There is a false summit which we nicknamed "Frustration Point". You think the hike is all over at 7.00 am and then you round this ridge and see the real summit 1,500 feet above you and a mile beyond. However, it was great; indeed, the life we were made for—though we were all sick until we had a snooze on top.

Our family decided to take this week off, so we are at the beach just now. Won't be home until late Saturday, so I cannot make Seattle this week-end. Besides, I was drafted for two meetings and a special dinner date this Sunday. I intend to be at the Conference Labour Day week-end, and am in hopes the Lord will make your way clear to come. We have much still to discuss—which does not come easily or well out of a typewriter or the barrel of a pen.

I have no word for you *re*: Ecuador. I would certainly be glad if God persuaded you to go with me. But *He* must persuade you. How shall they preach except they be *sent*? If the Harvest-Chief does not move you, I hope you remain at home. There are too many walls to leap over not to be fully persuaded of God's will. All I can do is pray for a cleared path for you. The command is plain: you go into the whole world and announce the good news. It cannot be dispensationalised, typicalised, rationalised. It stands a clear command, possible of realisation because of the Commander's following promise. To me, Ecuador is simply an avenue of obedience to the simple word of Christ. There is room for me there, and I am free to go. This of course is true of a great many other places, but having said there is a need, and sensed my freedom, through several years of waiting in prayer for leading on this very point of "where?", I now feel peace in saying, "I go, sir, by grace."[2] My experience is by no means restrictive to your persuasion. You may require more or less of subjective evidence to find certainty. I have not the foggiest idea how or where God will lead you. Of this I am sure. He will lead you and not let you miss your signs. Rest in this—it is His business to lead, command, impel, send, call, or whatever you want to call it. It is your business to obey, follow, move, respond, or what have you. This will sound meaningless to you, unconvincing and "old stuff", and that is what it should sound, for it is only a man's counsel. The sound of "gentle stillness" after all the thunder and wind have passed will be the ultimate Word from God. Tarry long for it.

We are leaving for the East September 7, if the Lord directs as we now plan. Will be returning late in October, hoping for passage in late November from Los Angeles.

Seems craziness to speak of leaving alone that soon... and it must be either craziness or faith. But, remember the words of Amy Carmichael? "The vows of God are on me. I may not stay to play with shadows or pluck earthly flowers, till I my work have done and rendered up account."—Looking forward to Labour Day weekend, Jim.

En route to the east coast Jim wrote me a note from Chicago:

I am grateful to the Lord Jesus for allowing another meeting with you. There is much to speak of. Dave mentioned the South Pacific possibility, and I am praying.—Gladly, Jim.

At my home on September 20 he wrote in his journal:

Arrived at Birdsong. Nearer to her now than ever, yet more confident that God is leading me away from her, to Ecuador with Pete, and she to the South Seas! This is a strange pattern.

Between the date of this entry and Jim's next visit to Birdsong several events indicated that the door to the South Seas was closed to me. Had our experience of God's leading throughout the course of our relationship been other than what it had been, it would have appeared simple: become engaged, and go to Ecuador together. For a long time there had been no question in either of our minds as to whom we should marry should marriage be the will of God. Had He indicated that this was His will? For each of us, the answer was still No. Jim felt, however, that this was no reason to dismiss from our minds the possibility of God's leading me to South America. He asked me to consider this seriously before the Lord, fully realising that such a course would lead to criticism and misunderstanding. We knew our Guide, and had experienced His clear direction at every point thus far. We knew, too, that He leads 'in a way that they know not'.[3] Indeed, what need had we for a guide, were the path a familiar one?

So we set ourselves to pray, well knowing the difficulty of discerning God's will where our own wishes were so strong. Often the prayer written by Amy Carmichael of India was ours:

> *"And shall I pray Thee change Thy will, my Father,*
> *Until it be according unto mine?*
> *But no, Lord, no; that never shall be, rather*
> *I pray Thee, blend my human will with Thine.*
>
> *I pray Thee hush the hurrying, eager longing,*
> *I pray Thee, soothe the pangs of keen desire,*
> *See in my quiet places wishes thronging—*
> *Forbid them, Lord, purge, though it be with fire.*

And work in me to will and do Thy pleasure,
Let all within me, peaceful, reconciled,
Tarry content my Wellbeloved's leisure
At last, at last, even as a weanéd child."

Jim went back to New York City for more meetings, and a few days later wrote me this letter:

The will of God is sweet tonight, altogether "good and acceptable and perfect".[4] The considerate love of the Lord Jesus for us seems such a kind thing now. I know it has always been so, but somehow I didn't see how *wise* it was when it didn't seem kind. "With mercy and with judgment my web of time He wove, and aye, the dews of sorrow were lustred with His love...."[5] You know the rest. Remind me of this when I cannot regard His love as considerate some time.

Stayed overnight with a brother in Queens who raises chrysanthemums. He was telling me that they don't bloom until every other flower is gone or going with the frost. I suspected that the frost might be what brought them to bloom, but he said, "No, it's the longer nights". I really had never realised the point of Rutherford's

"But flow'rs need night's cool darkness,
The moonlight and the dew...."[6]

not just for rest, but for blossoming. Need I allegorise?
...Waiting on Him for whom it is no vain thing to wait,
Jim.

The answer given during the next four weeks of prayer, "cool darkness," and waiting, was that I should go to Ecuador. This decision led Jim to hope that God meant marriage for us eventually, but, believing that he should ask for no commitments whatsoever until he had lived in the jungle and evaluated first-hand the requirements of that life, he steadfastly kept his course, telling me nothing of his hope. His commitment was to God alone, for he believed, with Paul, that 'He is able to keep that which I have committed unto Him'.[7] No attempt was made to explain our position to others. To us, the reason was eminently adequate—this was God's way.

Driving West with Pete Fleming, who had flown to New York to share Jim's meetings, Jim wrote to me:

> If I went to the mission field singly of my own will, I should certainly halt. But God has directed, Betty. He knows I would rather go with you, were not His mandate the better good.

And, like everything else in his life, Jim accepted this gladly.

> I thank my God. Life has been made so rich, so full for me. Sea-like, but having no ebb. Nature, Body, Soul, Friendship, Family—all full for me, and then, what many have not—the *capacity to enjoy*. "And He said, 'Lacked ye anything?' And they said, 'Nothing.'"[8]
>
> The past is gone, and I am glad, both for its going and for the way it went. God has led in, through, and out, by the best route possible, we may believe. I am particularly conscious of the Christian's right to expect events to be *exactly timed for good*. "As for God, His way is perfect."[9]

Notes

1. Romans 8:28, JBP.
2. Matthew 21:30, para.
3. Isaiah 42:16, RSV.
4. Romans 12:2.
5. From 'Rutherford's Hymn'.
6. From 'Rutherford's Hymn'.
7. 2 Timothy 1:12.
8. Luke 22:35.
9. Psalm 18:30.

— 17 —

The Hand Is on the Plough

Anyone who puts his hand to the plough and then looks behind him is useless for the Kingdom of God.[1]

AFTER ARRIVING in Portland, Jim was busy buying supplies for Ecuador, speaking in the north-western area, and packing. But he kept up his private times of prayer and study, recording in the journal things he felt no liberty to speak of to others. On November 23 he wrote:

Just read again the story of Abraham. Convenient food just now—with this pressing sense of need, the want of warmth and woman, tenderness, relief, and children. The God who "prepared laughter"[2] for Sarah in her old age, whose promises made Abraham himself fall to the ground and laugh because they seemed so goodly and impossible—fitting thoughts for my present attitude because I feel now as though it may mean five years of single life, these next five resilient years, years when I will most want her, most need her, and best be able to satisfy her. These years, I see in the plan now, must be spent alone. Then, maybe after I'm thirty, getting paunchy, wrinkling and balding even—then the marriage bed! Mother said the other day "Who wants to wait until they're thirty to start raising a family?" Certainly not I. All I knew to say was, "You raise a family when God wants you to." And I believe. I feel sure that God is doing the best for us, and that in the face of what seems most unlikey. Perhaps I'm wrong in thinking I have years to wait—but a man can't feel "lustihood of his young powers"[3] swell and surge inside him and not be affected by restraining them. It may be that He hasn't planned to make us wait years, but it certainly looks like it from here. Of course I hope I'm wrong. But if I'm not, then El Shaddai, the God who saw and heard Hagar, considered Sarah's laugh, and disregarded Abraham's 100th year—this God is the One I believe to be guiding and governing me in these affairs. And in this, in prospect, I with Abraham can laugh.

November 28. The dozens of little arguments that flood me when I think of waiting to take Betty amount to considerable force if I let them work on me. But my refuge is not in answering them one by one and arguing them down—my refuge is in Jehovah, Whom I have asked to preserve me. For now, and always, "Jehovah is the portion of my inheritance and my cup; Thou maintainest my lot"[4] (Comforting in the extreme, that word "maintainest"—stronger than the prayer word "preserve".

Relegating all problems directly to the Lord, trusting implicitly in His guidance for past and future experience produces the remark: "I will bless Jehovah, who hath given me counsel."[5] My going to Ecuador is God's counsel, as is my leaving Betty, and my refusal to be counselled by all who insist I should stay and stir up the believers in the US. And how do I know it is His counsel? "Yea, my heart instructeth me in the night seasons."[6] Oh, how good—for I have know that "my heart" is instructing me for God. "My heart said *for Thee*, 'Seek ye my face.'"[7] No visions or voices, but the counsel of a heart which desires God.

And so I sense that I may share the Christ's words, "I have set Jehovah always before me; becuase he is at my right hand, I shall not be moved."[8] Not moved? With all the awful pressure of inward desire to move me to lust? Not moved. With all demonic hatred to move me to fear and doubt? Not moved. Wherefore? He is before me and at my right hand. THEREFORE MY HEART IS GLAD!

November 29. I am reading *The Return of the Native*. Poor Hardy. If only he could have once seen the hand of God. The tragic lines of Egdon Heath form patterns which resist any idea of the working of the Will. If he could once have experienced a well-timed incident that wrought the greatest possible good, perhaps he would not have written as he did. Each event is so meshed with unreasoning ill, and the reader gets to expect the blackest. Really he does in the negative what poor novelists do in the positive— accentuates improbabilities—only he does it to the detriment of his heroes; they, to the betterment of theirs. Neither is true to life. Granted, fate and tragedy, aimlessness and just-missing-by-a-hair are part of human experience, but they are not all, and I'm not sure that they are even a major part, even in the lives of men who know no Designer or design. For me, I have seen a keener force yet, the force of Ultimate Good working through apparent ill. Not that there is rosiness ever; there is genuine ill, struggle, dark-handed, unreasoning fate, mistakes, if-onlys, and all the Hardyisms you can muster. But in them I am beginning to discover a Plan greater than any could imagine. Witness three years of relationship with Betty!

December 1. In reading the Scriptures I find a great moral power. Therein I am made aware of two great forces for good in human experience: the *fear* of God and the *grace* of God. Without the fear of God I would not stop at doing evil; the fear of God restrains. Without the grace of God I would have no desire to approach positive goodness. The one is a deterrent from evil; the other is an encouragement to good. "Wherewithal shall a young man cleanse his way?"—not so much make up for what is past, but perfect what is future—"by taking heed thereto (from now on) according to Thy word."[9] "These things I am writing to you that you may not sin."[10] The Scriptures were written to this very intent: to be a means of grace in struggling against sin. Would that Christians read their Scriptures. We should have a holier band for it.

December 5. Terribly depressed after preaching tonight. Felt as though I had no preparation, no liberty, no power. Once I felt compelled to stop during the sermon and tell the people I didn't have a message from God, but then thought better of it, or rather thrust it from thought altogether. I never want to preach that way again. Lord God Almighty, let me speak Thy word as going forth out of Thy mouth. How sadly and how slowly I am learning that loud preaching and long preaching are not substitutes for inspired preaching. Oh, it's awful. To see a room full of people, waiting to hear a word from God, and to have no word. And then to try to make up for it by jumbling unripe, untested ideas with old, dry words, and to know that your heart isn't in it. El Shaddai! Deliver! Worst of all, the people can't even seem to tell the difference when I feel the Spirit and when I can't. Either I'm a frightful bluff, or the people are utterly undiscerning... maybe all of both.

December 6. Passion, bordering on frenzy, grips me at times; —not always, thank Heaven, but often enough to make my denial of her for the work's sake a very real, poignant thing. In this, just now, I feel more than ever the Lord Jesus' requirement, "Except a man forsake...." [11] Well, thank God for the privilege of giving up ought for His sake.

December 24. Just finished *For Whom the Bell Tolls*. A most intriguing work which raises some problems for a Christian. Realistic, psychologically penetrating, compactly detailed, it represents a literary landmark for me for its style alone. Would that I could be as aroused about experiencing *God* in life as these modern writer are aroused at just experiencing life. They make no comment, draw no conclusions, point no moral; simply state things as they are. Perhaps it is for this very lucidity that they hold such grip on me. Must we always comment on life? Can it not simply be lived in the reality of Christ's terms of contact with the Father, with joy and peace, fear and love full to the fingertips in their turn, without incessant drawing of lessons and making of rules? I do not know. Only I know that my own life is full. It is time to die, for I have had all that a young man can have, at least all this young man can have. If there were no further issue from my training, it would be well. The training has been good, and to the glory of God. I am ready to meet Jesus. Failure means nothing now, only that it taught me life. Success is meaningless, only that it gave me further experience in using the great gift of God, *Life*. And Life, I love thee. Not because thou art long. or because thou hast done great things for me, but simply because I have thee from God.

A letter to me, of December 28:

I'm glad your last letter was a long one. It was mailed the fourteenth, and was good to have something more to think on while waiting your next. I've been expecting one every day this week, but know you must have had a busy holiday. I couldn't go to sleep last night for some reason so I took to piecing together our meetings and conversation in order for September and October. I am thankful, deeply thankful for such happy memories. Well may we bless God for them, Betty. He was kind, *very* kind!

Monday. Perhaps your letter will come today. I woke this morning with my left eye badly swollen and sore. Certainly gives me a curious squint with one eye closed. You'd have trouble loving me if you went by looks today. I'm certainly glad that we have not based our relationship on good looks. "Favour is deceitful and beauty is vain." [12] Oh, Betty, we owe praise to God for teaching us the worth of inner adornment. There are so many painted and well-dressed butterflies around here. They distract the eye but do not touch the spirit, and it is good to know the God who looks within to the "hidden man of the heart" and to enjoy that part of a person with Him. True, there are some here with this meek and quiet spirit, but I have found in none of them the response and stimulation which I find in you—the understanding you have of me and the spoken witness of it. Others listen and assent; you seem to *hear*, "savvy", and contribute some return. It is as you said, "The marriage of true minds". You said that was from Shakespeare, I think.

January 1, 1952. This has been a good day, full of visiting and chatting, resting and remembering. No small sign was given me confirming my going to Ecuador via the *Santa Juana*. I have been asking God to seal my leaving, not knowing what to expect. Yesterday several cheques came in the mail, and I intended to cash them and send a cheque to Kelly, the travel agent, for my passage. But the bank was closed when I finally found a parking place and finished other pressing things yesterday afternoon. Today when I picked up some purchases from Tommy Dryden he gave me a cheque for fifty dollars. I made no special note of it until I got home and put it with the cheques I got in yesterday's mail. Then I discovered that they totalled $315, my exact fare to Guayaquil! All in twenty-four hours, from five separate sources. This is the first of these miracles I am encouraged to expect. Hallelujah! Praise to the King of Heavenly coffers. Cheques confined my leading to Milwaukee last fall, to Sparta this spring, home this summer, and home now, since all came from individuals whose contacts depended upon my being in those places. Wise God, my God. This is to encourage me for 1952.

Letters written during Jim's last two weeks in Portland were filled with the details of packing, farewell meetings, and other things. The following are samples:

Equipment is piling up all over my room, and I hope to get to packing today. Correspondence is stacked up here on my desk and invitations to speak piling up....

I'm in the midst of a series of injections. Typhus reacted strangely this week, centring in my eyes and making them itch and colour red. More shots Monday....

Spent some of the week organising about 1,500 slides given me by a brother here. Besides Bible-story pictures, there are also nature pictures, through butterflies and giraffes to snowflakes. A godsend for the Indians.

Mail came in the middle of my packing books. Tomorrow, that barrel. It's been staring me in the face for two weeks and I haven't had the heart to begin filling it. Now it's a must. The *Santa Juana* will be in Portland on the 18th, and we must have it on the docks when we leave here the 10th. Pete is putting his stuff aboard in Seattle and Mom and Dad will drive us south.

January 10. Last day in Portland. The past week has been very busy, full of visits and interruptions while packing. But God has been good and exceeding loving-kind toward me. The saints have given unhesitatingly at every turn and every need has been met, even beyond the need. It is as in the wilderness, "for the stuff they had was sufficient for all the work to make it, and too much." [13] Peter will arrive today and we will drive to Williams tomorrow. That will be the first step away. It is hard to say goodbye, but, as Pete wrote yesterday, "the hand is on the plough".[14] I have had difficulty keeping spiritual pace these last days, rushing through prayer and scanning the Word only. This is no way to have confidence in the soul. Still, God is gracious.

> *"We change, He changes not;*
> *Our Christ can never die.*
> *His love, not ours, the resting place,*
> *His truth, not mine, the tie."*[15]

January 15: Oakland, California. Your letter came a week ago today and I opened it with the end of the paint brush with which I was lettering my name and destination on my packing barrels. Later that evening, after a meeting and supper at Herb Butt's, I had a chance to read it over. Wednesday, more packing. Thursday, all the stuff had to be taken to the dock and billed for lading. I ended up with two steel barrels (the best way to pack anything), two foot lockers, two wooden crates, and a wardrobe trunk—seven pieces, 1,400 pounds. Pete had only 900 pounds, but I had most of the heavy stuff: slides, recorder, tubs, guns, pots, kettles, and dishes.

We're in the middle of visits and engagements again in Oakland, and I find no time at all for closet prayer. We haven't a room of our own and I miss the sense of "bowing my knees"[16] as Paul says. Privacy before the God who sees in secret is an integral part of true prayer, and one hates to be obvious in asking for privacy. God knows and hears, however. What will Shandia be with the curious eyes of Quichua boys!

January 25: Sunland, California. The tumult of these last days is ruinous to correspondence with you, but things are settled sufficiently today to write. We have our passports visaed, all but one crate on the docks, and are waiting for our tickets from Grace Lines.

Leaving the States is not too exciting yet. I feel very little emotion, and will probably undergo the whole gamut of good-byes without a tremor. Not that I don't feel sorry to leave the folks, but only that this part of the will of God is of little more significance than any given part of it up until now.... As for you, it may be that it will be worse when I am gone, but I can think of nothing to help. Only to say that the will of God is "good, acceptable, and perfect".[17] May it be for you acceptable.

January 26; Tujunga, California. Must write some acknowledgements and finish packing a box this morning. The afternoon we spend with Ed and Marilou. Tonight a big rally and they're expecting me to do something great in sermonising. "Let not them that trust in Thee be ashamed because of me."[18]

January 28, Monday. Perhaps you've noticed that our ideas merged about this matter of Ecuador only being one of many steps of obedience to the Will, and leaving the dock only one more, hardly any more thrilling than the initial realising, months ago, that the Will would have it so.

The *Juana* isn't in yet, and I doubt if we sail before Thursday.

January 30. What is one supposed to do with three extra days? Spent the morning reading family mail, getting in a little reading from Leviticus, writing a couple of business letters. When I came here last fall I brought a twisted little tree from the Grand Canyon, and today I got a chance to mount it so it will be usable for a centre-piece. Something like a ming tree, but without the rounded limbs and heavy leaves. There is a small, moss-like leaf on parts of it, dried green now, but which used to smell strongly of sage. The trees at the Canyon are fascinating in their ruggedness and this one seemed to be a perfect miniature of many I saw there. Aunt Mabel likes this kind of stuff.

When I expressed to him something of the sense of loss which I felt at missing out on these important events, Jim wrote:

Your "sense of loss" at our not being able to share things these past few months is not new to me. I *know* it, and often tell Him about it. And such thoughts as

"*If Thy dear home be fuller, Lord....*"

are a consolation. And then the realistic facing of non-accomplishment comes to me and crushes to silence all telling. For if, really, we have denied ourselves to and from each other for His sake, then should we not expect to see about us the profit of such denial? And this I look vainly for. It comes to this: I am a single man for the Kingdom's sake, its more rapid advance, its more potent realisation in my own life. But where is that advance and that realisation? I am willing that "my own life. But where is that advance and that realization? I am willing that "my house on earth be emptier", but not unless "His house be fuller". And I think it right that we hold God to His own bargain. I err, of course, in making the *visible* results of our separation the final test, and, I trust, rejoice in seeing beyond results which are obvious. But I reason thus that I should be more importunate in prayer, more "dogged" in devotion, and should not get, as you say, to a "weary acceptance of things as they are. . . . "

Besides this there is the somewhat philosophical realisation that actually, I have *lost* nothing. We may imagine what it would be like to share a given event and feel *loss* at having to experience it alone. But let us not forget— that loss is *imagined*, not real. I imagine peaks—enjoyment when I think of doing things together, but let not the hoping for it dull the doing of it alone. What is, is actual—what might be *simply is not*, and I must not therefore query God as though He robbed me—of things that are not. Further, the things that *are* belong to us, and they are good, God-given, and enriched. Let not our longing slay the appetite of our living!

Notes

1. Luke 9:62, JBP.
2. Genesis 21:6, ASV margin.
3. From 'The Hound of Heaven' by Francis Thompson.
4. Psalm 16:5, ASV.
5. Psalm 16:7, ASV.
6. Psalm 16:7, ASV.
7. Psalm 27:8, JND.
8. Psalm 16:8, ASV.

9. Psalm 119:9.
10. 1 John 2:1, para.
11. Luke 14:33, para.
12. Proverbs 31:30.
13. Exodus 36:7, ASV.
14. Luke 9:62, para.
15. From a hymn by H. Bonar.
16. Ephesians 3:14, para.
17. Romans 12:2.
18. Psalm 69:6, para.

PART FOUR

Ecuador

1952—1956

— 18 —

Under Way

'I promise you,' returned Jesus, 'nobody leaves home or brothers or sisters or mother or father or children or property for My sake or the Gospel's without getting back a hundred times over, now in this present life, homes and brothers and sisters, mothers and children and land—though not without persecution—and in the next world eternal life.'[1]

WHITE STARS BREAKING through a high mist. Half moon. The deep burn of phosphorus running in the wake. Long, easy rolling and the push of steady wind. The *Santa Juana* is under way.

Thus began Jim's journal for February 4, 1952.

We've just come from a walk on the upper deck after a meal served in the officers' dining-room. Black cod, mashed potatoes au gratin, fresh vegetable salad, good black coffee. The stateroom is quiet now as Pete begins a little typing. All the thrill of boyhood dreams came on me just now, outside watching the sky die in the sea on every side. I wanted to sail when I was in grammar school, and well remember memorising the names of the sails from Merriam-Webster's ponderous dictionary in the library. Now I am actually at sea—as a passenger, of course, but at sea nevertheless—and bound for Ecuador. Strange—or is it?—that childish hopes should be answered in the will of

206

God for this *now*.

We left our moorings at the Outer Harbour Dock, San Pedro, California, at 2.06 pm today. Mom and Dad stood together watching at the pier side. As we slipped away Psalm 60:12 came to mind, and I called back, "Through our God we shall do valiantly." They wept some. I do not understand how God has made me. I didn't even feel like weeping, and don't, even now. Joy, sheer joy, and thanksgiving fill and encompass me.

In his first letter to his parents written en route, Jim said:

I surely praised God for the valiant way you both took my going. It is true that I know very little about how you feel at seeing me leave. All I understand is that it must be very keen, deep, and closely linked with all that this life involves for you. I pray for you whenever you come to mind, asking the "help that is from God"[2] for you both. You are as well a constant source of praise for all that you have given of yourselves for my sake. The will of God is always a bigger thing than we bargain for, but we must believe that whatever it involves, it is good, acceptable, and perfect.

Weep not for me. We abound in everything here. This tramp steamer is the best set-up I've ever been in. We eat like horses— egg plant, zucchini, potatoes au gratin, fresh buttermilk, fresh-baked rye bread are some of the staples. For meats we have had ox heart, lamb curry, beef roast, stewed tripe, and, tonight, sirloin steak. It would be all right if I could ever get enough exercise to get hungry. We have complete liberty over the whole ship, and believe me, we take it. Poop to prow, that's us. Our fellow-passengers number seven: two married couples who sit all day and read novels and soak up sunshine, and three women. Of these latter, two are middle-aged married women who wear jeans and short suits, and the third is a semi-peroxided case who is always wishing we'd get shipwrecked. I'd judge she's about 37, but tries desperately not to let that be known. In all, what I would term a "hot sketch".

The crew is much better company, many of them being young men our age. We have met and spoken with several.

Everybody knows we are missionaries, and it makes it easy to talk of the things of God, though we haven't been satisfied with our contacts yet.

The sheer joy of being in the will of God and the knowledge of His direction heretofore is my general experience now. God has been in our going to now, and if life were to end at this point, I feel I could say with Simeon, "Now let Thy servant depart in peace."[3] Not that I feel in any way that my work has been done, but only that I am satisfied that God has been confirming His word to me. The evidence is before me of the veracity of the Lord, and with Jacob I can say, "It is enough."[4]

The clear weather and oncoming humidity tell us we are approaching the tropics. Further evidence is the wildlife that surrounds us out here. Today I saw a bird standing on what looked like a piece of wood, but after the man on the bridge pointed it out and gave me his glasses I discovered that it was a great sea-turtle. While I was looking at that a flurry of water startled me right near the ship. It looked much like the pattern made by a star-bomb on the fourth of July, sending spurts every which way from the centre. Just a school of flying fish, I am told. Yesterday we sighted some large lance-nosed marlin leaping toward port, and a whale spuming not far off. Who said the sea was monotonous?

The journal gives further cause for thanksgiving:

Our stateroom was to have had three in it, but we bless God that He has ordered it so that we are alone. It would be a little awkward with another. "Your Father knoweth."[5] Ah, we've proved that lately! When the Chrysler was being repaired, we needed a car for running around Los Angeles, and God gave us one. He knew we needed a near-by bed the night the ship failed to leave. Helen and John provided that. He knew we needed the extra time for equipment, and the *Juana's* delay from January 20 until February 4 gave us that time. We needed, too, the breaking of bread at Glendale yesterday morning; the presence of Jesus the Lord was real. Thanks, then, to you, Good Lord. I'm glad the Lord knows the way of the righteous. He knows the way that I take.

"Oh well it is forever, Oh well for evermore,
My nest built in no forest of all this death-doomed shore.
Then let the vain world vanish, as from the ship the strand,
For Glory, Glory dwelleth in Immanuel's Land."[6]

He wrote to me on February 9:

> We are in the Gulf of Tehauntepec tonight, fairly close to shore,
> passing the city of Salina Cruz. The wind is wild. I've never felt
> such blowing. Just returned from the flying bridge where I was
> able to do something I've wanted to do for a long time—literally
> lean on the wind. One can stand effortlessly at a fair degree of
> slant, feeling the air misshape the face or hearing it really
> whistle if you hold your mouth just right. The water is alive
> with spray and whitecaps, leaping under a full moon in a clear
> sky. We are right opposite the narrowest part of Mexico. . . .
>   This is the ideal way to travel. Accommodations are excellent
> and all the officers very friendly. The realism afforded by cargo
> freighting, the constant sight of cables, derrick booms and
> winches, the close contact with the crew—all make for fascinat-
> ing travel. This was our sixth day out, and time has passed
> surprisingly fast. Most of our day is devoted to reading Spanish,
> and speaking it with what crew members we are able to find
> willing to talk to gringos.

His next letter home was written from Champerico,
Guatemala, dated February 10:

> We are riding the hook here in the waters off Guatemala. There
> is no such thing as a harbour in this whole coast, so the loading
> problem takes on a little different aspect. We came to a halt
> opposite low-lying land, with only a steel-reinforced dock and a
> couple of red-faced buildings in sight. The stevedores came
> aboard bringing a large, tub-like barge to each side of the
> forward holds. They loaded into these, then took them to the
> dock to unload there. A slow process, but no one seems to be in
> the slightest hurry to speed it up. The captain and a couple of
> passengers are playing cards.

The journal, on the same day, adds this:

Strange that the other passengers get bored waiting around, and we hardly have enough time to get what we want done. Thank God for purpose in life. So many purposes come into existence when one works the will of God, that there is no excuse for laziness or wasted time. He is redeeming our lives, as well as our souls.

Another journal entry:

February 14. Rolling slightly in a strong breeze out of sight of land, but off Nicaragua. Tuesday afternoon we anchored off La Libertad, San Salvador, and went ashore with four other passengers. Hired a station wagon to take us all up to the capital. Eating tortillas in a restaurant we were approached by a pretty little harlot named Emilia. I will always wish I could have spoken clear Spanish. We tried to make plain our desire only to speak her language and she was willing for a while to walk and speak with us. She took us to the University Post Office, where we bought some cards. Then she became embarrassed somehow —curses on my Spanish—and bade us good-bye. My whole soul went out for her, so young, so sweet-faced, and yet so enmeshed in an evil net. How long, Lord, will the earth perpetrate its wrongs! Hurry the promise, Lord, that "the earth shall be full of the knowledge of the Lord".[7] She epitomises for me the wrong of earth and men. I could no more have slept with her than died at will. The whole idea violated all that I know and feel. But oh, I longed to speak about the Saviour of harlots, the Friend of genuine sinners. God help me in the language for just such cases as these. I am sure she thought us strange men, such as fit no pattern she has seen. But will she ever really know why we refused to have her go find her "amiga" for us?

From Buenaventura, Colombia, I received a letter from Jim:

The captain and steward invited Pete and me to go with them to net shrimp. The captain was high on martinis and went to sleep on the deck of the snub-nosed power launch, but the rest of us stayed sober enough to bring back about a hundred and fifty pounds of big, beautiful shrimp. Netting is great sport here, as you haul in about two hundred fifty pounds of everything imaginable at every lift—we found several squid, some hammerhead sharks, sharp-toothed corbina, sea cat, sting rays, big-headed blowfish, every possible shape and colour of jellyfish, besides dozens of other species no one could name. Came back slightly sun-kissed, but not before God gave real opportunity to witness to the captain (before he went under) and one of the engineers who was along. Praise God for the time. He always leads us in triumph and makes manifest the savour of His knowledge in every place.

February 24, 1952. Thursday, about 9 am, we dropped anchor off the ramshackle shore of the island of Puna. Our crew members were not allowed shore leave, by order of a bewhiskered and portly islander called "The Captain of the Port". By noon we were officially received, and Customs men all came aboard for their carton of Luckies. The islanders floated around our big hull in their little dugouts with banana stalks, beer, coconuts, and balsa-wood models of Grace Line ships like our *Juana*. By one o'clock the stevedores arrived with their bawling and bickering. Some of them brought leather goods—most of it pretty stuff of unborn calf—shoes, handbags, and what-nots. By 2.30 the beautiful little yacht *Santa Rosita* came alongside with the barges and called out for the passengers. We said our good-byes and had our stuff packed from the stateroom to the *Rosita*.

Glimpses of river life, and pleasant conversation with the Grace agent's wife and a friend of hers helped us forget the oppressive heat while we sailed the thirty miles from Puna. By six our eyes were checking the docks along the Guayaquil waterfront for a look at Tidmarsh. But no one was there to meet us. A stevedore escorted me pronto to an "evangelista" he knew of, and she recommended a German pension. I went back to the Customs dock to get Pete, and found they had passed all our hand baggage, twelve pieces, without even opening it. Praise

God. Off we went with it in a wheelbarrow to the pension.

It was a hot night and mosquitoes were treacherous. I heard the town clock every quarter of an hour from one till 3.45. I'm still scratching. Next morning we hit it off for the Grace office to ask about Tidmarsh. Learned that our baggage would not be up-river till afternoon, so walked over to the waterfront, and lo, along comes Tidmarsh. The office had not been informed of our arrival, so he had come a day late.

God gave us great deliverance at the Customs house. Our combined freight of 2,300 pounds was all passed without a cent of duty. "O Lord, Jehovah, Thou hast begun to show Thy servant Thy greatness and Thy strong hand, for what God is there in heaven or in earth than can do according to Thy works?" [8]

Notes

1. Mark 10:29,30, JBP.
2. Psalm 121:2, para.
3. Luke 2:29, para.
4. Genesis 45:28.
5. Matthew 6:8.
6. From 'Rutherford's Hymn'.
7. Isaiah 11:9.
8. Deuteronomy 3:24, ASV.

— 19 —

Dreams Are Tawdry

And God Almighty bless thee, and make thee fruitful ... that thou mayest inherit the land wherein thou art a stranger. [1]

The first journal entry in Quito—dated February 27, 1952, began:

CAUGHT THE Panagra flight out of Guayaquil yesterday afternoon about 1.30. Clear view of the coastal plain as we came north, but began hitting clouds as we moved toward the mountains. Scudded over the mountains suddenly, catching sight of high ridges not far below. Then, as the clouds cleared again, we saw the great quilt of the plateau, beautiful and quiet with terraced hillsides and occasional buildings. Quito was in sight immediately and our DC-3 bounced down onto the runway at about 2.45.

Jim and Pete were taken to the Tidmarsh home at first, until they should be able to secure rooms with an Ecuadorian family. The study of Spanish began immediately. Jim wrote to his parents on February 29:

There is a real problem connected with this moving into a new language. One sees at once the terrific need of speaking for the Lord, and speaking clearly, pointedly, so as to be well under-

213

stood, and then one feels the utter helplessness of the situation in being unable to speak even one word without an accent so that he is detected the moment he speaks. The tendency is to throw up one's hands and say "what is the use?" But the necessity of speaking for the Lord drives us to get this language perfectly. Pray that for us it will be the latter. We started classes yesterday. I have four a week.

The city is beautiful, old, and picturesque, lying between two high mountain ranges. To the west, the volcano Pichincha, active and with traces of smoke the last few days, rises green and gullied, cultivated most of the way to the top.

The market is quite interesting. There one sees an aristocratic Latin in a fur coat shopping beside a beggarman in rags. There is a wide selection of vegetables and a fair show of fruit, though one cannot afford to eat much of either raw. Rhubarb was on our menu yesterday, cauliflower, Swiss chard, carrots, celery—and all cooked. But I miss our raw "rabbit food", and apples. Bananas, in all their forms, I am getting on to. We have had banana-meal mush for breakfast, fried bananas, and raw ones so far. A great "head" of green ones is on the garage floor.

Another letter to his parents is dated March 9:

I have made contact with a young Ecuadorian up here studying English. We are together about an hour every day, exchanging English and Spanish expressions. Nice fellow, twenty-three, named Abdon. Pray that I might be able to help him in the Word while I am here. It becomes increasingly obvious that our job here is to train Ecuadorians. We will never be able to speak as they speak nor get next to their own people in the way they are next to them.

More and more we feel the burden of the Auca and Cofan off in the Oriente, but feel that our first experience, if not our permanent one, should be with the jungle Quichua. Do pray that we might find out His work for us and do it for the greater glory of His name.

The diary continues on March 11:

Felt a strange bitterness this evening, tending to sullenness and dissatisfaction with everyone. Coming outside and feeling my barrenness, the beautiful night lured me on a walk. The moon has powers to wash a man inside and I experienced it tonight, the laving of the spirit by chill air, old mud walls, the smell of eucalyptus, night birds, and moon-burnished clouds. It's a different world over the walls here and up beyond the hill.

March 14. My first night under mosquito netting. Came down from Quito with Dee Short and family, and slept here in their rented house in Santo Domingo de los Colorados. Saw my first Colorado in the plaza this morning. Leaving Quito on cobblestone you climb awhile in view of all three peaks of Pichincha—swallowed in cloud yesterday at least the top third. Suddenly you see the valleys dropping away below, sunk in mist. Watching, you can see the mist part and the utter green denseness break clear, shot here and there with whites: a dead tree, a flash of waterfall, or a show of smoke. Down, down, down, twisting into canyon heads, past the cascades and smoking *carboneros*, squeezing past upcoming trucks, down through the chill mist until it is not chill, but steamy. Above, shouldering mountains swim into cloud now, and still you go down. The total drop is something around 9,000 feet from the highest point en route. Took us six hours in the pick-up truck. Here in Santo Domingo—a fast-growing agricultural centre with Negroes, Indians, and mestizos in the population—there is no other missionary for a radius of one hundred kilometres.

March 17. Living with Shorts these days, trying to be of some help around as well as sizing up the work and keeping Spanish before me. Most of the time it amounts to plenty of little things—washing dishes, helping with the kids, playing the harmonica in the open-air meeting, helping drive the truck. Yesterday we had a good meeting in the room off the plaza; lots of interested men.

March 18–22. Spent these days in San Miguel de los Colorados with the two English girls, Doreen Clifford and Barbara Edwards. First real time in the forests, and first contacts with Indians. The road is almost impassable, with all manner of mud-holes. We went on horseback, arriving in four hours. In the afternoon the girls and Don Gustavo took me to the house of the two albinos. Found the mouth-harp of good use in making friends, accompanying Doreen on her autoharp. Discussed location of a school for the Indians.

March 27. Returned to Quito in a fruit-truck with Abdon on Monday. Enjoying Christ and counsel with the Father these days, though since I have taken to pure Spanish reading of the Scriptures I feel that I have forfeited some of the freshness I once enjoyed from the Word. But it must be, and I have the hope that soon I shall be getting things from the Spirit in still another language.

April 6. Lord's Day. More inner joy today than for several days. Enjoyed the breaking of bread, simply remembering Him. One sees clearly the necessity for it here, not to speak of its honour to God, but for one's soul, to keep one pressing after Christ, pursuing fresh realities, purifying old ones.

Betty should be in Ecuador a week from today, God willing. Strange that we are led so close together so soon, wonderfully strange! There will be talk, especially in the US, but I tend not to care a bit for it here. Let them talk—and God shall lead us on! Faith makes life so even, gives one such confidence in his movements, that the words of men are as wind.

Jim's urgent desire to learn Spanish found further expression in a letter to his parents, dated April 19:

We are quite concerned at the slow progress we are making in the language. But these are problems. We would like to go somewhere and live where we are not given the opportunity to speak English. Here it is too easy for us. The only contact we have with Ecuadorians is that which we make ourselves, and one hour a day with the Spanish teacher. Not sufficient for real progress.

Jim wanted to share as much as possible in the life of the people of Ecuador, and found that mountain-climbing, sight-seeing, even bull-fights, contributed to this end:

Watched our first *corrida de toros* today. This is Ecuadorian "Labour Day", and they had a six-bull fight. Betty and I went with a group of missionaries and nationals. It was wonderful! The picador action is especially thrilling, while the ballet grace of the cape-wielders is beautiful.

I don't know why I love bulls. Nothing has quite the fitness to act *bravo*, it seems to me, as a well-built bull. They do nicely with their front feet, striking straight, stiff from the shoulders. The head-feint just before the lunge is clever technique, and although they hardly have a chance to vindicate themselves, they do well for all the confusion they are put to. One feels it a little unjust that the matador has done it so many times before, while the bull is at it for the first time. It is not as spectacular as a good western rodeo, and, of course, somewhat bloodier, but the whole thing seems to fit the Latin mind...gold braid and blood...exultation at death...paper ribbons and "picks"... gracefulness and brutishness...a bull and a pair of ballet shoes. These people are extremists.

Despite the freedom and ease of living which Jim wrote of in outward things, there were struggles of soul. My presence in Quito, a thing for which Jim was glad, as it was the first time we had ever lived in proximity since college days, opened for him again the issue of engagement. He was not yet in jungle work, and could not know the conditions it might impose. Yet God had led us one step further since our last discussion of these issues — we were now in Ecuador, by His clear direction. Once again principles, rather than impulse, were his guide. He wrote in the journal:

You understand, Lord. It is not easy, but we've had it out lots of times. I stick by what I've told You. So long as I can do a work in reaching a primitive people *better* as a single man, I will stay single. And that brings me to the other things we've been digging around: *Aucas*. My God, who is sufficient for them?

May 2. Oh for a heart like David's. For all his obvious powers of leadership he never goes out to lead the people in battle without consultation with Jehovah. "Shall I go up?"[2] This lack of self-confidence marks him as God's man for guiding others. He allowed God to press His cause, and the kingdom was established in his hand. Good lessons for the basing of our thoughts about moving to the Aucas.

May 5. Gave myself for Auca work more definitely than ever asking for spiritual valour, good Spanish, plain and miraculous guidance, among other things.

Consolidated my thinking about Betty. Reading of David's sin against Uriah the Hittite, I got to thinking over Uriah's attitude. David, obviously thinking he could make Uriah think himself the father of Bathsheba's child, brought him home from war, made him drunk and all but forced him to his wife's bed. But Uriah stayed with the king's servants and his reason for so doing is: "The ark, and Israel, and Judah abide in booths; and my lord Joab, and the servants of my lord are encamped in the open field; shall I then go into my house to eat and drink and to lie with my wife? As thou livest, and as thy soul liveth, I will not do this thing!"[3] It was not *time* to return to his house—though he had the right to do so, and the encouragement. It was the *time* for battle, and Uriah was a warrior; there could be no mixing of home-goodness and the business of his life. So it came to me. Marriage is not for me now. It simply is not the *time*. (I do not say, and never did say, it is not the *thing* for me.) With tribes unreached which I now believe reachable only by unattached men, "I will not do this thing".

May 7. Near full moon found Betty and me in the open fields, under a sparse stand of eucalyptus after heavy rain. The sky was broken with clouds, and flashed stars, but the horizon was sufficiently clear to see Cayambe, Antisana, and Cotopaxi by moonlight. No night like it so far here in Ecuador. It was one of those "asked-for" times, with her, depending on the weather, which God openly controlled for us. He seems to do much "for us" these days. I have not lost one nameable thing by putting her and our whole affair in the simplest way possible into His hands. There has been no careful planning, no worrying over details in the matter. I have simply recognised love in me, declared it to her, and to Him, and as frankly as I could told

Him I wanted His way in it. There has been no leading thus far to engagement, but the symptoms of a beautiful courtship prevail—not, perhaps, a routine one, or a "normal" one, but a good one, nevertheless, and, withal, a deep sense that it is God-directed.

May 9. I am now aware that my reasons for not being engaged are hidden in the counsels of God's Spirit. I simply know it is not for now—that knowledge is inward, God-given, and to be obeyed at whatever cost. There are no explanations except that God leads, and He does not let a man know why He leads. Faith binds a man to what he knows inside, like my coming to Ecuador. The world could not shake the persuasion. "The just shall live by faith."[4] Faith—not alone in facts and a rational apologetic—but in the reality of the inward work of the anointing which he possesses through the gift of the Holy Spirit. I must maintain a surer belief in the Spirit of God. It is no mere tenet of faith that He indwells the believer. He does indwell, and there He accomplishes His work of informing the spirit of man.

Dr Tidmarsh began a brief course in homeopathy for the several new missionaries in the group. This Jim found very interesting, as his letter home on May 15 demonstrates:

Right in the middle of tropical disease this week. Finished leprosy this morning. Most interesting, and I confess that I can hardly wait to start medical work—pilling, pulling, and puncturing! Had a chance to adjust Pete's neck last night. He gets occipital headaches and a neck rub fixes him up, we find, so I'll not lose my technique! Of course, yesterday he had reason to be a little tense. As you know, there was a full moon on Friday, and the moon just after waning is the best time for climbing mountains around here. So—Tuesday, about 9 pm, we decided to climb Pichincha. After a few hours in the sack I heard the alarm ring at 2.30. I woke Abdon (my right-hand Ecuadorian buddy), who was sleeping on an air-mattress here in my room. We looked up at a misty sky with a breaking moon. Rob Gill, Bill, Pete, Abdon, and I walked out into the night with three meals and rainwear on our backs in packs. We hailed a taxi, picked up Betty, and rode as far as the taxi could go up the trail. As soon as we got away above Quito we lost all trace of mist and the moon broke clear over the inter-Andean plain, exposing three of our most beautiful snow caps off toward the Oriente. At dawn we were back in a valley that cut off all but 19,170-foot-high Cayambe, blowing with three sharp clouds, tinted rose and deep purple. Turning, we could see ourselves standing in moonlight, shining on our side of the ridge, while across the valley dawn-light cast an entirely different sheen on the long mountain grasses. Nearly wept with the beauty of it. Up, up, up, with cascading water on all sides, exotic mountain flowers, broad-backed, rolling hills running up to the jutting peaks. Treeless, of course, but with the sense of habitation still, because of flies, birds, butterflies, toads, and even some horses grazing. Our final altitude at reaching the mist-washed peak (snowless except for dashes a few feet across) was 15,500 feet, the highest I've ever been on foot. Because we could use "Keds" for climbing and needed no crampons for ice hiking, the trip was much easier than climbing the peaks around home, and it didn't make me nearly as stiff or tired, despite the altitude. In all, a beautiful trip, well worth the effort and time, if only for the sweetening and enlarging it accomplished in one's spirit. The Lord made mountains to climb, not just to look at, and up there one understands why—seeing the vista that most folks never see, with the sense of farness that most never feel.

The same letter goes on to speak of the thing that yet remained a problem:

One doesn't learn to speak a language in a couple of months. It will be plugging for a good while yet. Seems that I'll never get through "preparing" for the mission field. But I've been comforted this week thinking of our Lord's thirty silent years of readying Himself at home with His family and bending over a carpenter's bench. Were those days any less of a fragrance to God than His later work before the eyes of the people? I think not. A well-made piece of furniture and a healed blind man represented the same thing to the Father—a job well done; mission accomplished. So with us here. Nothing great, but what is that to Him with whom there is no great or small?

The journal continues:

May 27. Moved to Dr Hugo Cevallos' home today, a pure Spanish context at last. Thank God! Taking midday meal with Sr Arias and morning and evening here. Great provision from God to have this place. I want to make the best of it, Lord.

The situation is described in a letter to his parents:

As I write, Pete is out in the *sala* reading the paper. The five Cevallos kids are engaged in various diversions. Doña Bacha is at work in the kitchen. The doctor, a fairly conscientious, but terribly conventional medic, has gone off on a call. He cannot support himself in a regular practice. His schedule runs something like this: first thing in the morning he has a class or two in biology in one of the big secondary schools. Then he goes to his office to wait on calling patients. Home at noon for lunch and siesta. Then until 6.30 or later he is at the Sanidad (Public Health Service) clinic. Any hour of the night he is obliged to run on calls, and he can't afford financially to turn them down. To supplement his funds he has rented the biggest bedroom of the house to us two gringos; the rest of the family sleep in two rooms. Not so soft, but he is a happier man than dozens of much wealthier, less busy, successful businessmen I have met in the States. The most modern thing in the home is a telephone. He has a radio, but no car. His wife cooks on kerosene, without electric beater, refrigerator, or oven of any sort. And they are supremely happy. I haven't heard a cross word pass between them or any of the children since I moved in. Just who is civilised, anyhow? "A man's life does not consist in the abundance of things that he possesses."

In June Jim accepted an invitation to make a quick trip to the Oriente, the eastern jungle, which would include some survey flying in search of Auca houses.

He wrote to his sister Jane, then a student at Wheaton College:

Mission work by airplane is different from what you imagine. First, there is the thrill of it. What I've said about "missionary thrills" is true—you get over them. But that doesn't mean you don't *have* them at first! The sense of lift, just as the wheels leave the ground, the "gasp" of dropping in a wind current 5,000 feet up, the tilt of swinging on a wing-tip to take a look at a tiny group of houses hidden in the forest, the shiver of dropping below trees to get a good look and the back-throw of pulling out over the trees—these are terrific thrills that I've had these last two days. I may get over them, or I may get sick, as Pete did, but at least I've had them.

We've been here in Missionary Aviation Fellowship headquarters in Shell Mera making jungle surveys. We were interested to know about the Quichua population of the southern Oriente, and have discovered what we wanted to know. We also wanted to find out if there was any truth to the possible friendly contact southern Quichuas might have with Aucas, the one really savage tribe down here. There isn't. They have just killed five in the area. We were looking for Auca homes as well, but found nothing. Evidently they are hiding out or have moved east. More and more that tribe is brought before me as a possible field of labour for my life. They are utterly untouched, and so far they are inaccessible. It would take a miracle to open the way to them, and we are praying for that miracle. They may be only a few hundred in number, but they are a part of the whole creation, and we have orders for such.

Can't seem to get any news of the Portland gang. Mom wrote about A.'s death. Seems far away and hard to believe. One can't imagine death as a look on the face or the stiff position of a body, when he hasn't seen the person that way. You always bring up the living face in thinking about him. Another instance of what death really is—not just a coldness or a silence or a horror, but a removal, a separation. For those who are near it may be the former things, but for us who have not been closer than thousands of miles, it is always, "I can't imagine so and so without *her*." We don't think of her as she died, but in relation to what she left, and the idea of separation is constant with her death. Sad thing it was, and tragic. But it is very easy to mouth clear, flat platitudes about it and to draw old morals again for re-etching.

It is a warning to any of us who love. We should love hard, and not casually; fervently, playfully, and simply, never heavily or slowly. Slovenly loving makes for wearisome living. I think A. just got weary. If you ever love, Jane, love like a schoolgirl with giggles and sighs, and keep love alive by consciously keeping wonder and surprise at the core of it. For many "young-marrieds" get used to it after a year or two, because they think they have to. For me, I can't afford to with Betty. I've got to make it last and last. I have not found it hard, but I have found that love is not effortless. It needs control and direction.

I can't quite figure out how this got started, but there it is. Only know that I love you, Sis, and think of and pray for you often several times a day. We as a family have loved without saying so, just by enjoying and missing each other.

When Jim returned from the jungle he wrote to Eleanor Vandevort in Africa:

The Lord has brought Betty and me over some happy ground since last we had any contact with you. We are living right across the street from one another. Living in Ecuadorian homes is the only real way to learn Spanish, and we are enjoying it immensely. Oh Van, I couldn't have asked for more than God in deliberate grace has surprised me with! We didn't ask to be sent to the field together. We didn't ask to be sent to live in such close proximity. We hardly asked for each other. It seemed unreasonable to ask such things, six months ago. Dreams are tawdry when compared with the leading of God, and not worthy of the aura of wonder we usually surround them with. God only doeth wonders. He does nothing else. His hand can work nothing less. Praise to the Guiding God of Israel, and that Great Shepherd of the wayward sheep. When He directs a path, no way can seem bleak, no instance dull.

Betty and I are agreed that the Will of God for some time is to be undeclared to one another, though our feelings are clear, and I think known to you. So we go on, waiting and willing to do the Will of Him who sent us, and working away at the language, wondering sometimes at His ways.

We have found great joy in coming to the field as God's free folk. Answering to nobody but Himself, and with nobody's support or promise but His very own. It is a very inofficious way to work—without so much as a letterhead to make a man feel that he "belongs" to something. But it is most gratifying to look aloft to the God who keeps promises and is sufficient.

The days of Spanish study in Quito seemed golden. On July 11 Jim wrote in his journal:

I wonder sometimes if it is right to be so happy. Day follows day in an easy succession of wonders and joys—simple, good things like food well prepared, or play with children, or conversation with Pete, or supply of money for rent or board within hours of its being due. Grace upon grace in the outside sphere of living. But, simply because I am not really studying the English Bible, fresh truth for inner soul-refreshment is rare. I am supposed to speak at an English-language gathering again on Lord's Day, and find that I must go back to old truths, learned in the work-free days in Portland in 1949, to get solid material for peaching. I was reading my diary notes and noting the contrasting soul-soreness of those days with the freedom and joy of these. Those were certainly more productive from a point of view of getting things from the Word; these are more casual and less fruitful, but for reasons—Spanish *must* be gotten. I want God to speak as He did then, but I want Him to begin speaking Spanish, and I am not yet used to that, perhaps not ready for it. So I go on in these days, glad-hearted and simple in my thanks, lacking the profundity of material for depth of worship. But I have not left off seeking His depths and I believe He will take me back to those days of struggling and discovering in the Word.

How well I see now that He is wanting to do something in

me! So many missionaries, intent on doing something, forget that His main work is to make something of them, not just to do a work by their stiff and bungling fingers. Teach me, Lord Jesus, to live simply and love purely, like a child, and to know that You are unchanged in Your attitudes and actions toward me. Give me not to be hungering for the "strange, rare, and peculiar" when the common, ordinary, and regular—rightly taken—will suffice to feed and satisfy the soul. Bring struggle when I need it; take away ease at Your pleasure.

July 26. Oh, for a faith that sings! Thought of Jehoshaphat in II Chronicles 20. Threatened with defeat by a multitude that far outreached his powers of war he set his face toward Jehovah. He called a fast for the people, then publicly reminded God of His covenant with Abraham and Solomon: Stating the problem thus put God in a position of responsibility: "O our God, wilt Thou not judge them? for we have no might against this great company that cometh against us; neither know we what to do, but our eyes are upon Thee."[5]

Then, after an answer from a prophet, Jehoshaphat, himself humbled and believing, charges his people: "Believe in the Lord Your God!"[6] And then they broke out singing! Singing, in the face of such a problem! Lord God, give me a faith that will take sufficient quiver out of me so that I can sing! *Over the Aucas, Father, I want to sing.*

Jim's prayer for help in Spanish was obviously answered. Many Ecuadorians commented on Jim's excellent pronunciation, and looked suspicious when told that he'd been in Ecuador just five months. On July 27 Jim wrote to his parents:

Last Lord's Day morning and also today we went with Dr Tidmarsh to Sangolquí. Got my first crack at preaching in Spanish. Great joy in it, but not really fluent yet. Never felt more apostolic in my life than this morning, when I was actually "disputing in the marketplace"[7] with two or three interested questioners in the crowd of perhaps forty people. One feels all alone, but the joy of seeing people who do not know of the

225

evangel asking sensible questions about faith and works or our belief in the virgin is something I have not known before. Oh, to be able in their language! I look forward with great pleasure to this time of witnessing. It is true that we get a couple of hundred tracts torn up every week, and there are hecklers who throw an occasional jibe or orange peel, but in all we feel that we are making friends, and destroying the traditional prejudice. We believe God is supporting His Word and following it to the consciences of some. Pray for this work, won't you?

The next letter is dated August 9:

Next Wednesday or so Pete and I will be going down to Shell Mera to help in a boys' camp, and from there on in to Shandia. We've been trying to get a little studying done in Spanish for that, as we both have two messages to give to the boys each week. We spent two days at our *bodega* (learn this word—it means storeroom, but is just a little room where some of us keep our barrels and crates, etc.) going through all our things and sorting out what we want to take first to the jungle. We used those big black rubber bags to pack in, Dad. Filled four of them, and left some things, like our aluminium chairs and a buck-saw and an axe, unpacked. Every ounce of packing means extra weight in the little plane. This morning Pete and I have to go down to the market and get some things we were unable to bring with us—machetes, pots, some oil for the .22 and other such.

As Jim contemplated leaving Quito, after five of the happiest months of his life, he thought again of engagement, feeling it would be easier for us to part if God would give us His word of assent. But again the answer was clear, as Jim wrote in the journal on August 12, two days before he said good-bye to me:

Oh, for a heartiness in the will of God, "doing it from the heart".[8] I must confess that, though I am sure that engagement

226

is not for us this summer, the acceptance of that as the Will of the Father is no gladdening thing. It is not that my wants (1. for her, 2. for the work, perhaps among the Aucas) conflict. They are not contradictory, but they do not seem to mesh. They have come at the same time, so that instead of fitting into one another, as cogs would, they grind against one another, sometimes with awful concentration. It is too soon for me, not having seen the Oriente, to believe that God may not want me there entirely unattached. But all the while I'm mad for her, wanting to be with her night and day, the haunting hunger of body, the loneliness of mind—making book-study a farce at times, and making life itself seem useless without her.

Notes

1. Genesis 28:3,4.
2. 2 Samuel 5:19.
3. 2 Samuel 11:11, ASV.
4. Galatians 3:11.
5. 2 Chronicles 20:12.
6. 2 Chronicles 20:10.
7. Acts 17:17, para.
8. Ephesians 6:6, para.

— 20 —

The Realised Will

And he brought us out from thence that He might bring us in, to give us the land. . . . Know therefore that the Lord thy God, He is God, the faithful God, which keepeth covenant.[1]

ON AUGUST 17, 1952, Jim wrote to me from Shell Mera, where the boys' camp was held on Bible Institute property:

In the dark of Friday morning I walked across the street to your wall, and stalked the length of it while Pete checked the room for the last time. Almost called your name to your dark windows, thinking you might be awake. Then I dropped into silence, knowing I was leaving you and ending the happiest weeks of my life. We were first to reach the church, waiting twenty minutes for the HCJB[2] sound-truck to roll up to pile in our gear and crowd ourselves into the noise of eighteen kids. The bus didn't leave until six am and I shared a seat with a boy, Segundo, who was, thankfully, a little strange to the group and not too talkative. Drawing past the railroad station I felt the weepiness coming on, but stayed it—I don't know with what. But dawn—with its quiet rose glint on Mt Cotopaxi, making a black silhouette of Antisana and melting Cayambe against the cold grey of clouds to the north—teased the sadness out of me (still not the silence), but making me thankful for the work of the Master-hand and reminding me that

228

The Realized Will

"A Father's hand will never cause
His child a needless tear."[3]

Rising up into the paramo that runs to the slopes of Cotopaxi we came into fog and I slept fitfully until we reached Latacunga, where town activity roused me to watching things. We bought mandarins and bananas in Ambato and ate them all the way down here, killing a bottle of carbon water for lunch at Baños. Below Baños the trip was beautiful with a clear view of the Pastaza. Orchids are in season and flashed along the road cuts. I cut one yesterday while we were out on a hike, and brought it to the camp building, but you weren't here, so had to stick it in a tin cup with another bright red flower I found. The orchids thinned out as we moved out of the gorge and followed the Pastaza from its hurtling out into the semi-level where it begins to braid among the gravel beds.

The mountains are blue just now as it turns dusk and there is the far-off drumming of thunder. Husky clouds hide El Altar and Sangay, which were visible this morning. Sangay is like Cotopaxi in shape; I have never seen anything quite like Altar— it seems to be a whole range in itself with a half dozen peaks, at least, all snow-capped. They were beautiful last evening. They say you can see Sangay spewing fire at night, for with all its snow it is still active. A parrot is whining like a frightened dog perched on one of the store fronts across the street and field, a block away.

Now I must finish—the campers will be coming soon, and my group must walk the three blocks to the Institute to carry up the food tonight.

A week later Jim wrote to his parents of the results of the camp:

In all I believe it has been a profitable week. Certainly we have had God's help in the language. He blessed in our morning Bible studies evidently—we had two each week. Wednesday the Lord gave us a happy break. I had just finished a half-hour Bible study on the LORD, JESUS CHRIST, defining the words

229

from the Scripture and having the boys look up the references. Afterward four of my dear little kids went crying to their rooms. We prayed and talked with them, all of them shaking with that body-jolting sob of children, and all confessing faith in Jesus and sorrow for sin. A very simple thing, and very "sweetly moving", as Brainerd would say, and it has changed the whole face of the discipline problem.

We got up at six and had "café", their term for breakfast, which consisted of a cup of chocolate and two small bread rolls. After a brief break, we began with choruses and Scripture memorisation, then morning Bible studies, forty-five minutes of searching for passages to discover what the Bible itself says about us, the Lord Jesus, and so on. Usually a banana for mid-morning snack, or sugar-cane, or even "tostados", roasted corn kernels which, with salt, serve nicely in place of crackers. Then it was play, either teaching them American games or their own soccer, if not too wet outside. Lunch was followed by siesta and then more play or swim in a beautiful stream ten minutes' drive up the valley of the Pastaza.

Jim's journal says:

But the week was too short to train sons. One must live with them. Wanting sons these days, wanting to feed them, lift them, have them hound me, beg me in the name of a father. And for me, it looks like no sons are in sight. Still, as I read Job 12:10 again, "In His hand is the life of every living thing."[4] I recognised that all I am and have is the Almighty's. He could in one instant change the whole course of my life—with accident, tragedy, or any event unforeseen. Job is a lesson in acceptance, not of blind resignation, but of believing acceptance, that what God does is well done. So, Father, with happy commital I give you my life again this morning—not for anything special, simply to let you know that I regard it as yours. Do with it as it pleases you, only give me great grace to do for the glory of Christ Jesus whatever comes to me, "in sickness and in health."

On August 25 he wrote to me:

You won't know how glad I was to hear of the hardly believed-
for peace you describe. May the Spirit who gave, maintain.
More than once I have wondered at the way of God, a wonder
that shaded into resentment. And it is easier to know that He
who led, gave grace, lustring with love the sorrow once again.
He knows better that you do, Bett, why and how intensely and
how long I have desired you, and the struggle it has been to
commit you to Him alone to comfort when I wanted devilishly
hard to have you committed—insofar as engagement would
make this possible—to me. But now I know that His loving-
kindness, forever better than life, is better, too, than further
human loving, for I doubt that even engagement could have
wrought the impossible peace you speak of. Praise, then, praise
for peace.

When camp was over, Pete and Dr Tidmarsh went into
Shandia first, while Jim remained in Shell Mera to await a
second flight. He busied himself collecting things for a
garden in Shandia, as he wrote to me:

Saturday I went orchid-hunting down behind the house. Found
two more of those waxy "shoe orchids", white with brown-
spotted centre, growing on a fallen tree over the creek. They are
now in a small packsack with other orchid roots, roses, naranjilla,
coffee, hibiscus, geranium starts, and a poinsettia shoot. I hope
things grow like folk say they do in the jungle. I've got the
flower craze worse than I get it some springs in the yard at
Portland!

The afternoon has cleared so that the big pillars of cloud,
rising in a haze over the jungle, stand pure white against a blue
sky. Silhouettes of distant birds are sharp against them, going
east. And tomorrow, happily, and in the will of God, I follow.
Only too well I know again the inner weakness to return, to go
back to you, but I feel that I have set my hand, and to look back
now would be dishonour. He knows the inner part, and He
knows how much of me I really leave with you. And He knows
why I leave, and for how long.

The journal continues on September 3:

Shandia. As I write my praise mingles with the steady rush of the Atun Yaku, running like pure silver into the jungle under a full moon. Left Shell Mera at three this afternoon in a sky of scattered clouds. Landed at Pano around three-thirty and made the walk to beautiful Shandia in just two and a half hours. The moon rose as I stepped into the clearing with Eladio, the school-teacher and two carriers, prognostically telling me of the faithfulness of God. Surely life is full in His Will and brings promise of good things yet for us here. In spite of my wait since Friday, first for the teacher and then for the plane, the thought kept recurring as I came along the trail, "right on time, right on time—God's time". So with much joy we have arrived at last at the destination decided on in the Will when at Wycliffe in 1950, and my joy is full, full, full. Oh, how blind it would have been to reject the leading of those days! How it has changed the course of life for me and added such a host of joys. As I looked up over the notched horizon of hills, the grandeur of the jungle was on me, and gave me again the sense of rugged solidarity, the sense of living alone and feeling satisfied within.

The forest is not unlike the west jungle, bigger, and emptier, but not much different. The trees with concave bark, and the roots ribboning down to the ground—the straight hanging vines—the clear, warm creeks—all beautiful, simply beautiful.

He wrote to his parents on September 7:

I am seated at the table with the Coleman double-burner lantern. We had supper a couple of hours ago of boiled bananas and manioc-banana soup, topped off with a cup of "hierba luisa", a sweet green forest tea that is supposed to have powers to make a man return to the Oriente, once he has drunk it, though he cross the world. Food has been most interesting these first few days, and I have eaten things fixed by our cook boy that I never dreamt existed. Ate chonta palm heart yesterday when the men clearing the airstrip cut down a big palm. It is the tender leaves deep in the trunk, soft and white and with a taste not at all unlike our chestnut. Always there is fresh fruit, papaya, sweet bananas (called "sedas"); then, too, I had my first chonta palm, although I confess I did not relish them as did the doctor, with his jungle-perverted palate! Since we have few other fats here, I suppose I'll get accustomed to them. The pineapples are luscious and the avocado, of which I eat maybe one and a half daily, are huge. We are supplementing our vegetable-lack with those great bottles of vitamins that we have carried half-way across the world. We have also started a small garden, experimenting with chard, cabbage, spuds, and other vegetables. Yesterday the Indians discovered a herd of wild pigs and we had genuine boar soup today.

Shandia is beautiful. We are high on a sheer cliff right above a big green river called the Atun Yaku, the "big water", in Indian parlance. Right here the small warm Shandia River runs into the bigger and much colder upper Napo, which comes down from the great snow caps of Antisana and Cotopaxi. We take daily afternoon baths down the fifty-five mud steps, though it is not deep enough to swim in the Shandia, and too swift to swim in the Atun Yaku. Mornings we employ thirty-five to forty men in clearing the jungle for our airstrip, and while they work, we study their language here in the house.

We have a board floor and bamboo ceiling, and impermeable paper on top to hold out excessive bat-droppings. The roof is thatch. Long screened windows let us look, from our bedroom, right out to the river and the airstrip and ball-field, and from the dining-room table, out to the garden and the uncleared forest fifty feet away. Our bedroom is exceedingly pleasant—a huge window looks out on a beautiful view. Door is a monk's cloth curtain between our room and the living-room; we have two throw-rugs, and the two aluminium chairs make the place look very civilised. The Indian Venancio, or his son Luis, sweeps it daily to clean out the mud and dead cockroaches (none under an inch long). The insect life here is fantastic. Right now there are half a dozen interesting beetles and moths crowding around the gas lamp, and we have several butterflies pinned daintily to our walls. Last week, as I was wearing blisters on my hand with my first machete practice, a little furry thing fell by my foot—

yellow and round like a baby bird, which I took it to be. My curiosity was satisfied that it was not when I drew back, a thumb stinging as if with nettles. It was a huge caterpillar with hair two inches long that had fallen from the tree I was hacking.

In a later letter Jim described for his parents the duties which occupied their days:

Last Lord's Day it was a boy to be splinted for a broken wrist. Wednesday a man with a machete cut. Thursday and Friday a breech-baby case which Pete and the doctor attended. Saturday a man with a 104-degree fever who had walked miles to get here and was too badly off to receive an injection, but instead of taking our offer to stay until his fever subsided he slipped away with only two or three atabrine pills. Then a baby and mother for quinine injections. It sure makes for an interrupted life, and we find it very difficult to spend any consistent time in language study. We have the full responsibility now of keeping the men working in the forenoons, getting the school-teacher (who has turned out to be a lazy guy) to plane boards for blackboards and a bookcase for the school, buying eggs, plantains, and selling salt and matches—any of a hundred and one little things, to say nothing of swatting at the little mean biteflies that have been on us since the heat came. The airstrip should be done soon, though, and that will relieve us of a great deal of worrisome details and cut down expenses considerably. I never employed a man in my life and here I am with half a hundred to manage. Of course, I'm not alone. I would be crazy now if Pete didn't share all the efforts.

Slight interruption. When the plane came into Pano, they left vegetables for us. I just went out to get the celery, green onions, cucumbers, and tomatoes to wash in potassium permanganate, so we can eat them for dinner raw, as a salad. They don't know anything about these vegetables here, and were wondering what to do with them. Usually everything goes into the soup, of which we have two bowls a meal. We eat it with sticks of steamed manioc. There is no type of bread here, so manioc and plantain are our staple starches. I just bought some forest potatoes—great, long, root-like affairs that grow in the dark jungle by means of a long vine that climbs the trees to sunlight. We eat off the plastic ware, and I notice it does scratch some, all advertising aside.

In spite of the difficulties of language study where inter-ruptions were so frequent, Jim was gradually absorbing it, mostly by 'living it' with the Indians, swinging a machete, visiting in homes, with his pencil ever poised, slogging over the dim trails in company with these laughing, black-eyed brothers.

The Quichuas soon won his heart—indeed, they had done so years before he saw them. But now, living with them, he knew a greater love, just as Jesus, '*looking on* the multitudes',[5] was moved with compassion. They are short and stocky, with beautiful bronze-red skin, heavy black hair, and high cheek-bones. They live in one-roomed, palm-thatched houses, walled with bamboo or split palm, if they are walled at all. There are no villages, a factor which greatly increases the difficulty of reaching them. Their houses are located, one here, one there, along the banks of rivers, and are connected by trails which vary from seas of mud, reaching often to the knees, to putty-like mud which soils only as far as one's shoe-tops. After the first six months in the forest, the six pairs of tennis shoes which Jim had brought from the States were rotted.

But the mud did not bog down his spirits more than momentarily, as snatches from his journal will verify:

September 21. Using Luis as an interpreter makes language study too easy, so that I don't feel the strong necessity of knowing the idiom. But I know all the same that I must get it, get it good, and get it rapidly. By Thy grace, Lord, I'm going to.

Just finished a sing out of the Inter-Varsity Hymnal, *Believers' Hymnal*, and *Little Flock*. Great joy in going over "At Even E'er the Sun was Set", "The Lord's My Shepherd", "And is it so, I shall be like Thy Son?", "O God, we adore Thee".

September 24. Full, happy, useful days. How I thank God for Pete and our present relation. Great sense of unity in attitudes with him. We were not vainly sent "two and two".[6]

September 25. Had my first chicha in the Indian homes today, made of mashed chonta. Also my first cooked chonta fruit. The latter was rich, though woody; the former flat and watery. Returning I stopped at a chagra-hut where a man with fever was lying under mountains of flies wrapped in a blanket, with boils on knee and shin. Ate my first ants yesterday—toasted "ukui".

To me Jim wrote:

The last minute before I left Shell Mera the pilot said the load had to be cut twenty pounds, so the bulbs and rose roots are still there. Our garden, too, that showed such high hopes before, has been root-eaten before the things got up an inch. Only a few cucumber shoots remain. We are going to have to change our methods, starting things in some sort of planting box so that they get a solid root before we set them out to the mercy of the Oriente insects. The only things that do well are the things I pick up on the trail and bring home to plant in the little sand stairway that leads to the river—lovely patterned leaves, an orchid or two, a wild snap-dragon, and a furry bluebell. Such things make the great forest somehow gracious and often sweet-smelling. Found a strange, single-petalled calla lily on the way to Pano, and brought home a root.

To his parents Jim wrote:

Hope you remember to pray for the multitudes of Indians around here. They are such children—wanting attention, running to the priest for insect repellent which he gives free to those who attend mass, and coming here for free medicines, bragging him up to us so that we will do some favour and avoid being called stingy, or sending their boys there to school and letting them come here to sleep and eat with our schoolboys. I have seen none who really seems concerned about his soul, the Scripture, or the gospel, and this I think is accounted for by our lack of concerned prayer for them.

September 30. An important day for the work here. Radio contacts all morning covering the first flight to Shandia. Easily a hundred and fifty Indians gathered for the event—the boys running about, the women hooting, the men crowding into the stopped Piper. Praised God for success and rapidity in getting the strip done. He supplied us with funds in time, kept the men working in a good spirit, sustained us with joy in the doing of it. "This God is our God *forever*; He will be our Guide until death."[7]

A letter I received, dated October 1, told more of the beauties of Jim's new home:

Bird songs in the forest are enchanting—long, low, almost sly whistles, clucking and knocking, sweet canary-like tunes, or a high mellow hoot—for all the world like a wood-wind instrument. And we hear the birds at night, as well as during the day, although their songs and whistles are not so frequent, and are often obscured by the rattling hubbub of crickets and other singing insects. I often think I would like to get a recording of night sounds as I lie in bed, from the squeaking of the bats in the thatch to the constant pounding of the rapids below. It is really a roar—only not rhythmic, like the oceanside, but constant, full, and interminable (that is, if one stops to think how long he's been hearing it). But it passes from the mind most of the time, only recurring when you look at the river consciously, or lie in the dark and listen. The river rose about four feet during the night, and canoes that were tied up on dry beach yesterday afternoon were rocking on a full current this morning, and the blank stretch of white boulders between the island and the opposite mainland was a turbid rush of slate when I woke. One thing that startles me with a shifting breath of wind is the orange tree in blossom just outside the door.

Some of the trees are veritable wonders for size and majesty. One, that we can see on the other side of the airstrip from the house, has roots which run away from the trunk like walls, bracing the height like structural triangles. I have seen one of these *uchu putus* with holes five feet across in the roots, where the Indians have hacked out a piece of wood for their huge trays, which they use for mashing chonta fruit, or for a butcher's block.

To his parents on October 18 Jim wrote:

Made my first coffin this morning, from pieces of crates that the radio equipment came in. A gorgeous dawn broke over our little place in the forest with the news that our cook's wife had lost a breech baby during the night. Dr Tidmarsh attended but they resented his interference, and refused to wrap the lower body in warm cloths while the head was still engaged. Dr Tidmarsh feared that cold on the body would make the breathing process start while the head be without air. The Indian attending simply said no, lifted the mother by the arm pits and shook the baby out, the mother hanging on to a rope on the wall. It took twenty minutes after the feet for the head to appear, and of course it was strangled. But it's got to be done that way; they have done it so for years and the wizards—the "knowing ones", as they call their witches—say it must so continue. It left Doc helpless. The mother cleaned up the mess. I saw her dumping it all over the cliff this morning as I washed out on the porch. We made the coffin this morning; the father condescended to dig the grave. Life isn't very important here, and death even less. Nobody cried, for they don't regard as human a thing that has not breathed.

The day was hot, and we had about a dozen men working on the foundation of the clinic building and clearing the forest directly behind. This afternoon a sudden tropical thunder-shower came up and blew the ridge of the roof right off the school. It also took the clothes off the line, turned the calendars over on the wall, and made a general mess of our shelves and papers with its wind. It only lasted about ten minutes, but it can give a man a lot to think about in that time. Screened windows leave one without anything to close when a storm comes.

Here we keep well. We eat loads, drink tea or lemonade

mid-morning and mid-afternoon. One sweats terribly and needs the liquid. Bathe daily in the river, go to bed around nine-thirty and get up at five-thiry. A good schedule, not at all heavy, if at times confused by everything coming at once. I'm not losing any weight, Mother, so I suppose you can let your fears perish for me here. We find the daily walk with God as always, a simple thing of faith, patience, and love, superabounding in the sheer joy of living. Only, we need the language to get over the first great hurdle of missionary jungle life. Then the war really begins in earnest, and we are eager for it.

Jim's journal was an outlet for thoughts which he shared with no one else at the time, and when he received word by short-wave radio that I was leaving Quito for the western jungle to begin analysis of the Colorado language, he wrote:

It quieted me almost to bitterness, making me feel as though I were saying good-bye all over again. Mail service will be slower, contact less frequent, the possibility of seeing her more remote. The Father was told all about it again, how I wanted her, needed her here, and, I must confess, the comforts of faith, at least my poor faith, are not always completely satisfying. But I believe, for all it's being poor believing, and know that I will not lose for having believed. . . . O God, having made me thus, and led me thus, enable me to endure Thy making and Thy leading.

To me on October 27 he wrote:

This I know. That if next year is as full of sweet surprises and things to be wondered at as has been this last one (and I have no reason now to expect anything less; the situations are analogous in their impossibilities) it will be but stronger evdience of the good hand of God upon and over us, keeping His promises and cofirming all we have hoped in Him. Is it not, for all its sting, a wonderful way to live, Betty? To dream, and want and pray, almost savagely; then to commit and wait and see Him quietly pile all dreams aside and replace them with what we could not dream, the *realised* Will?

Dawn was another delight this morning. Broken clouds, scattered as from the bright breaking dawn itself, vanished in the blue zenith. None shaped even similarly, the whole was hued as one, lavender shading upward into a brown ridge and brightening into a rich cream below with such a uniformity that it seemed to give the sky perspective, as though one could really feel that east was "down" the sky and north "across". The river twisted out of the mist, one colour and one movement with it up-stream, sheened from grey to green as it came into the light below the cliff, then turned and melted back into the grey below. I feel like running and shouting and throwing myself at it all as though it were possible to deliver oneself as wholly physically to it, as one feels with it spiritually.

And now the moon makes the clearing, the river, and the trees all shine, but not like the sun this morning. A quietness, a gentleness is moonlight, so quiet and so gentle that sometimes I feel fear to stand in it out here alone. One feels the emptiness more at night, and I must confess I have come into the house gladly, on simply beautiful nights, not knowing quite why, but knowing that I could never run and sing and give myself to the tropic nights as I am tempted to do to the tropic day. The night, for all its variety of noise, does not converse like sunlight, nor invite like day.

Along with language-learning, medical work, constuction of new buildings, and other daily chores, Jim and Pete shared the responsibility of the four-grade school. He wrote about the schoolboys on November 5:

We are in the middle of introducing a game of volleyball to the Indians. They love to play, but have neither patience nor aptness to co-operate with each other in team sports. They are beginning to catch on, and we hope that ultimately we will be able to bring in more complicated games like softball and basketball. They play soccer quite well, but are always kicking the ball over the cliff, or booting it into the forest where it gets punctured on a thorn. So we have a rule that nobody kicks the volleyball. This rule is observed only occasionally, when we are in sight, or in our room in full view of the playfield. The boys, still only about a dozen, are great pals with us, but each one is a strong individual, wilful, and even spoiled to do what he wants, so there are constant petty arguments to solve among them. We have devotions with them in Spanish at the beginning of every school day, taking the story of Elisha while Dr Tidmarsh is away. At night we may do any of several things—show them movies when the electricity is on twice a week, or slides with a gas lantern, or gather them in the radio room to listen to music from the radio or victrola, or show them colour slides of ours in the little viewer. (They think our homes and families are fine, and wonder why we don't like them, that we should come down here!) Usually it is a game of checkers, or looking at *National Geographic* magazine over in the school by gas light. We have also gone on a fish-poisoning spree and caught hundreds of little fingerlings to fry. It was a great privilege to have the boys with us, and we feel that even though our twelve seem few, it is a victory to have each one here. We think too, that while we are getting started at it, it is better to work with a few. We can do more with them as individuals. One is standing by me now as I write, and he said, as I paused to think of the next sentence, *ñuka kilkasha*, "I will write." And while I wrote that sentence, the whole room filled with men who are discussing the artifacts of our culture here—bedspreads, pictures, meat-cleaver, harmonica. Each holds a fascination for them, and I only wish I could explain to them what they are all for.

A letter of November 16 describes the death of a baby which Jim and Pete had treated, after the witch-doctor had tried all his methods of healing:

We had lent kerosene to the family so that they could watch all night, but the whole house had gone to sleep and woke when our schoolboys arrived with their lantern. They found the baby dead then, and sent for us. The mother and grandmother had started the weird three-pitched descending wail of the bereaved —an awful thing to have to work beside. We tried artificial respiration as the body was still warm. Sweating and crying to

God for life to be given back, kneeling on a dirt floor beside a sunken-eyed baby, wondering if the throbbing felt at my finger-tips were his heart or mine, trying to shut out of mind the death-wails and incessant sobbing of the family, I worked for more than half an hour. When we finished and looked up into the gas-lit faces it only served to increase the wailing, as it dashed any final hopes. And then the wake began, the chanting of the parents mingling with the laughter of the play of the guests. All the guests are expected to play and drink all night from a half-gourd, to keep the bereaved amused. We only stayed till eleven pm, and played a few games of checkers. One interesting diversion was a ball of wadded kapok soaked in kerosene and lighted, tossed among the guests to keep them awake and shouting. We tossed it, too—and a couple of days later treated a boy who was burned with it.

It was on this occasion that Jim was introduced to the game of 'flip-the-bowl'. A bowl of chicha was placed on the floor, and one of the guests spread his legs, leaned over, seized the edge of the bowl with his teeth, and then flipped the bowl over his head. The milky liquid drenched him. A second Indian escaped without a drop touching him. After a third had spattered himself and also several kibitzers, Jim stepped forward. Whoops of laughter woke some who had dozed off in the corners of the house, and all gathered to watch the inexperienced white man. Imitating the Indian stance, Jim clamped his teeth on the lip of the bowl, flung it over his head in a perfect arc, emerging unscathed. *'Pacha!'* — the Quichua equivalent of 'Wow!' — was all that the Indians could say.

Jim's letter continues:

Now, I can hear the rumbles—"What kind of missionary work is that?" Such questions rumbled in me, too. But it is a true fact that this is their death ceremony, and one who did not enter into it would be regarded as impolite and unsympathetic as someone in the USA who didn't go to the funeral and look sober. It is their way of forgetting how sad and cruel and hopeless a thing death is. We build beautiful coffins and send flowers and light candles, and put on our dark suits. They play games and sit up all night and sip *wayusa*.

They came on Saturday morning to ask if they could bury the baby under our school house; they would have had to abandon their house if they had buried it there. I was just about to nail the lid on the coffin when the mother told me to wait, and came with a bit of banana and manioc, a broken mirror, and some water to put in the rough little box. They buried it with its head toward sunset, so as to rise feet first on Judgment Morning to face the sun. And an hour later it was all over, forgotten in the excitement of the plane's coming in.

That wholesome weariness is on me now. As I sit down I can feel my legs warm and tingling-tired in the muscles. After the meeting this morning we went with two Indians upriver to the place they call The Valley. Several families have summer homes up there, where game is more plentiful. We had heard of sickness there, and, since no missionary has ever visited the place, so far as we know, we decided to take a look. It was altogether worth the looking. The Atun Yaku narrows and runs glassy below forest-capped two-hundred-foot cliffs, breaking in spewing rapids over outcrops of native granite bedrock, winding back into the uninhabited and mist-shrouded foothills of the Andes. We took our own lunch: lemons and sugar for lemonade, a few peices of *buriju* (a jungle partridge we bought yesterday), a bit of chocolate and cheese and a hard-boiled egg apiece. We ate that at the first house we visited in The Valley; the Indians had gone elsewhere. Then every succeeding visit brought us favours in food—milky chicha (yes, we drink the chewed kind, and today even had some that was noticeably spiked), a tender bit of tapir shoulder (the best meat I've had while here), manioc, and steamed green bananas. Back home to bean soup after four river-crossings and a brief swim.

November 20. The work here is not going at a ripping pace. A couple of schoolboys have quit; the language suffers from the constant interruptions, correspondence lags, and visitation is not effective yet becasue we have only a smattering of Quichua. A visit from Arajune Indians yesterday made me long to travel in that area, and a visit last Lord's Day to Iluculin fanned the interest we had of a visit upriver to the gorge.

In a letter to me dated November 25:

You ask if I am speaking Quichua. No, I don't even understand it yet. The few words and phrases that I have memorised are a bare defence in any conversation. I can contribute nothing. But what can I do? This morning after devotions with the schoolboys I came in to study. Then it occurred to me that one of the men whom I had sent to cut bamboo for the clinic ought to be put on mowing the airstrip. By 9.10 or so, the grass is dry enough to cut, so I went out to break in a man on the lawn-mower. I hadn't been with him ten minutes when Pete shouted down the strip that someone had been bitten by a snake. The father took us upriver for twenty minutes; we found his twelve-year-old daughter lying quietly on a cane bed. The bite was already an hour or more old, and no blood had come out at all. I jammed a clean blade on to the scalpel and slit the fanged heel three times before the girl began to cry, "He's killing me", and I had to stop cutting because of public pressure. Pete read the snake-bite-kit instructions while I tried to work the suction syringe, but it made her scream, so I settled for pressure with one hand while keeping the slits open with wet cotton with the other. She bled slowly until about eleven-thirty, when there was nothing to do but give homeopathic *Crotalus horridus* and go home. We haven't heard how she is. But that cuts down a man's study time.

His next to me, of December 2, says:

I strongly sense the rightness of God's leading you and me as he has, Bett. I could not be doing now what I am doing and needing to do (such things as letting Indians invade the bedroom anytime we're here) if I were a family man. As it is, I feel we are making contacts and friends on such a level as is most advantageous for the future of our work here, playing and sharing with the Indians in a way I could not have time for if I were married. It is temporary. I, like you, don't feel a plastic table-cloth is for life, but in our present circumstances, there is nothing else, and we gain by having a table the Indians can touch with muddy hands. Newspapers line my three boxes of clothes, and I don't believe I would put up with boxes in a *home*, but would build some closeable shelf-and-drawer system. I was struck with the verse you wrote on the flyleaf of my gift copy of *Toward Jerusalem:* "Thy statutes have been my songs in the house of my pilgrimage."[8] That is what all houses are, and I feel it keenly about this one.

Thanksgiving passed with little more than a tremor of festivity. We had that can of salmon you sent for the evening meal, and a can of prunes for desert.

December 4. Somehow, this month especially with its rush of pressures, I have felt lost without you, Bett; felt like the world was going by in a whirl of wonder and I was dazedly letting it go by, in body participating, but somehow the "me" standing apart looking for something that didn't show in all the wonder, and aware that that something was you. It all goes over my head, it seems, and I go through the motions of keeping in the tide; however, if anyone were watching closely he would know, by the quiet sigh in a rowdy game of volleyball, the far-away glance upriver and over the tree-tops, from mid-current to the clouds away off to the west, and by the sudden creaking in our moonlit room as I roll to the other side of the narrow cot in an attempt to terminate a longing flight of imagination—he would know that I was not really all there where I seemed to be. Oh, what an ache wanting you can bring, when I know that the wanting itself is good, right, even God-granted, but realise that now it is wisely God-denied, and that He has not let me know all the wisdom of the denial. But I believe, and it is this that lets the living go on—the volley-ball, the swimming, and the sleeping, and keeps my arms moving and my lips making sounds while the most of me is with you.

Your picture has been a great help. It depicts you as I like to think of you—longly moulded, with clear, quiet eyes. It often speaks peace to a strong emotion in me, lending an antiquity to my thoughts, an old knowledge, a white-headed patience, as it brings back the dark oak chest of drawers in the dingy apartment in Chester where it stood, or the bird's-eye maple at home, the night stand at Cevallos' in Quito, the dozens of times, looking up sideways from a suitcase, it has surprised me. The picture makes it seem as if it has been forever with us, through every-thing—the way it is now, and seems to say: "Take it easy, Jim; we are not through the story yet, and you have no basis for believing it will turn out a tragedy." Still I do, Betty, I do fear sometimes, like a worrying mother, that something will happen to you and I will lose you, and then what would I do, where would I be when I wasn't where I seemed to be? Where would my imagination go when I went to sleep? There could be nothing else in life like this for me. Funny, but I never think of *my* having the accident and your losing me!

To his parents on December 18 Jim wrote:

Your day-dreaming about coming to South America is no joke. The rate on an Ecuadorian airline from Miami to Quito is something under a hundred dollars. So don't lose your day-dreams. "Nothing is too good to be: so believe, believe to see." [9] In my own experience I have found that the most extravagant dreams of boyhood have not surpassed the great experience of being in the Will of God, and I believe that nothing could be better. That is not to say that I do not want other things, and other ways of living, and other places to see, but in my right mind I know that my hopes and plans for myself could not be any better than He has arranged and fulfilled them. Thus may we all find it, and know the truth of the Word which says, "He will be our guide even until death." [10]

That same afternoon Jim wrote in his journal:

The house is full of workmen. Pete is selling in the bodega, the doctor is sharpening a plane. I just stepped here into the bedroom to think a moment, about what we're doing here, about progress, about hopes and prospects. O God, life is slow, for all the action it holds. The clinic work lags, not half a wall finished this whole morning. The widening of the airstrip mouth moves so slackly with such a few men, the language hardly seems more intelligible today than it did three months ago, at least in the lips of many Indians. Betty seems so far away.

What shall I say, Lord? That I am dissatisfied, not pleased with the way You have led me? Almost I would say it. Why cannot I shout orders to the workmen, urge on the projects, press ahead with the language, hasten marriage? The pattern of life thus in the Will seems to drag, to wait for the nothing that happens, to push quietly up like trees, and to eat slowly away, and the clouds like slugs ooze over the fixed sky. It would not be happier otherwise, I suppose, but it seems discouraging this hot afternoon.

Notes

1. Deuteronomy 6:23, 7:9.
2. The missionary radio station in Quito, known as 'The Voice of the Andes'.
3. Source unknown.
4. RSV.
5. Matthew 9:36, para.
6. Mark 6:7.
7. Psalm 48:14, para.
8. Psalm 119:54.
9. From the poem 'Not in Vain' by Amy Carmichael, in *Made in the Pans* (London: Oliphants, Ltd., 1918), p. 130.
10. Psalm 48:14.

— 21 —

Three Challenges to Faith

This is no accident—it happens to prove your faith, which is infinitely more valuable than gold, and gold, as you know, even though it is ultimately perishable, must be purified by fire.[1]

ON THE NIGHT OF January 29, 1953, I was sitting as usual at a little card table in a thatch-roofed house in the western jungle, working over my Colorado language notes. Suddenly the sound of horse's hoofs broke through the clicking, singing, rattling, and buzzing of the night noises. I took the lantern outside, and was greeted by a friend from a village about eight miles away. He handed me a telegram. Jim was waiting for me in Quito.

The next day I went by horseback to Santo Domingo de los Colorados, and the following day, after ten hours in a banana truck, climbing the nine thousand feet to reach the Inter-Andean plain, arrived in Quito.

Jim's next letter to his parents was written from the Tidmarsh house in Quito on February 1:

I left the doctor with Peter in Shandia on Thursday afternoon and came up with Gwen in their Dodge on Friday. I am enjoying the change, and the time with Ed McCully (who had just arrived in Ecuador) and Betty immensely. You will understand this better when I tell you that I gave Betty an engagement

ring last night in front of a fireplace. It was a thing settled for me
months ago, that I should become engaged, and only needed the
opportunity for us to be together and her to say yes. She did. I
wanted to give her the ring for her birthday, the twenty-first of
December, but, not wanting to leave Pete alone in Shandia since
Dr Tidmarsh was here in Quito, I had to wait forty days and
forty nights to pose the query. I think I have the Will of God in
this. It has certainly not been done in a hurry, and the rest He
has given in the matter since last fall has been a constant witness
to the certainty of it.

It was only a week later that the first test of this 'certainty'
came to Jim. We were informed that, according to X-rays, I
had an active case of tuberculosis. Knowing as well as Jim did
that he was called to the Indians of the jungle, I felt that this
news spelled the cancellation of our marriage plans, for, even
if I should recover, life in the jungle would not be recommended for me. Jim's attitude, however, was unchanged.

His journal records:

If I had any plans, they are not changed. I will marry her in
God's time, and it will be the very best for us, even if it means
waiting years. God has not led us this far to frustrate us or turn
us back, and He knows all about how to handle TB. I don't
know what this means. I only know that God is in the generation
of the righteous, and guides their steps aright. Beyond His
counsel and Will there is no going. I am there now, and want
nothing more.

'According to your faith be it unto you.'[2] Jim's was
rewarded—a week's further tests showed nothing whatever
wrong with my lung.

Returning to the forest this time, Jim was accompanied by
Ed McCully, who wanted a little preview of the life he looked
forward to. On March 2, Jim's journal continues:

Ed left yesterday after our first ten happy days in the forest
together. I am alone with Eladio now. Pete went out with

malaria on Wednesday, putting me in close fellowship again with Ed. It is better than ever to be with him, and I almost stand in awe sometimes to think that God has really brought us together. Hurry the rest of our preparation now, Lord, and get us in the language preaching with one another again. With all of this planning and building going on, I will certainly enjoy our dreamed-of itineration in the forests.

Monday a week ago Betty came to the radio and said "It was all a mistake." The TB fears are gone. I wonder if God healed her in those ten days or simply proved our faith by a mistake. Whatever, He has done well, and I bless Him for her health and for my own.

Henri Andi died last Friday afternoon. He began vomiting great mouthfuls of red blood last Monday. Got along OK until Friday, when he vomited again and became exceedingly restless, dangerously so for one so weak. He tossed and wailed and we watched his pulse drop from 104 to 38 and then to nothing. The first man I ever watched die. And so, one day, it will come to me, I kept thinking. I wonder if that little phrase I used to use in preaching is something of a prophecy?—"Are you willing to lie in some native hut to die of a disease American doctors never heard of?" I am still willing, Lord God. Whatever You say shall stand at the time of my end. But oh, I want to live to teach Thy Word. Lord, let me live till I have declared Thy works to this generation.

The widow and mother of the dead man just passed, wailing. There is a desertedness about death here that I never felt elsewhere. It is an end of everything. They broke his flashlight to pieces and threw it in the grave. The wife broke up a big clay family cooking-pot while the mother untied the bamboo walls and let them fall away for burning. And always there is the wailing; half the women hereabouts are too hoarse for speech. Two full nights they played and cried, and they are still at it, though the crowd that followed us with the coffin from the mother's house to his own has mostly dispersed.

Two excerpts from letters to his parents tell of building progress:

March 5. I have been alone since Monday, when the little yellow plane lifted Ed off the brow of the cliff over the river and left me standing in a knot of Indians. He had come down to discuss the new house-site. Since he left I have laid out the foundation, and today lined up the first two forms for concrete posts. Since we are short of planks we will probably make two or three at a time and let them set and then re-use the forms. Slow, but so is everything here.

March 15. I have eight pillars poured for the new house, and intend to set up forms and pour again tomorrow. Sure could use some help on this building deal, Dad, but I suppose it would be all over by the time you could get papers straight to come. Well, I need and appreciate the experience, so the time is not all being lost.

To me he wrote:

I cannot see beyond concrete and nails and planks these days. I keep hoping some miracle will happen, something will upset our plans, even our hopes for the work, like a carpenter coming to do the building, and freeing me now to travel. Anything that would get me doing something besides building houses for other peole. But yet I feel, Betts, that no one else can do it who is now on the field, and that God has put me here for it— personal likes and dislikes aside. It's strange, but I both hope for and dread some cataclysmic upset that would bring you and me together. I feel now that it would have to be that, with things so well-formulated and going along so nicely.

I can hear the chariots of Thor rolling far away into the east, and the sound of rain is refreshing. It was hot today and I could hardly force myself to pour concrete into two pillar forms I did not get finished yesterday. I used up all the water in the rain-barrel, so I hope I get enough to mix concrete again day after tomorrow. I poured and mixed alone today as all the workmen were out in the forest dragging in the girders for the sub-floor. It is hard work, and now I am ready for bed.

Jim had been in a Quichua environment for just over six months when he wrote:

It is a great joy to be having little meetings in Quichua now, although admittedly, my Quichua is plenty poor. This morning I took the parable in Luke 14 of the folk who rejected the invitation to the feast, and it was a delight to see comprehension on the faces of some. Oh, pray that God would give us souls for Christ from this jungle, and that we may rejoice together in that day for men and women of this tribe who have believed through our word and your prayers. For we know now, if we knew only in theory before, that "except the Lord build the house, they labour in vain that build it".[3] Nothing can change the heart of this people but the Spirit of the Life-Giver Himself, and it is to Him we cry in our mute helplessness in this language.

The diary continues:

April 12. Struggling desperately with Quichua, and feel we gained ground in a solid week's listening and studying and trying to speak at the conference in Dos Rios. There was no real stirring. Illustration of the truth is no substitute for a statement of the truth; a story will not suffice where a sermon fails. Again it is the exhortation and stern warning to believe without sufficient statement of what is to be believed. But the statement of the truth is regarded as "too deep", too difficult to express in Quichua, which is such a simplified language. Still, it is better to try to make them understand, in order that they may know what they are rejecting, than it is, by pressing the acceptance more than the understanding, to allow them to accept something they do not understand.

Was touched at the Mishahaullí River after the conference, as the believing Indians came to the river's edge to say goodbye. I was startled to find two of the girls, the cripple Serafina and Christina, taking my two hands and leading me before the rest of the group to the river, and saying, "In every prayer we make we will pray for you."

On April 19, Jim's letter to his parents told of more building problems:

The Indians tell us that the rainy season has set in. It has held us up every day this past week, with rains every morning, and clearing only a little in the afternoon. This enables us to hoist around and notch one of the seven girders we have set on our concrete posts for the new house. Three remain for next week before we can level off and set in joists, for which, because of the young moon, we must wait. The cutters refuse to cut trees in the new moon and we won't have much hope of joists for a couple of weeks—more if the rains keep up steadily. The river is running brimful these days.

To me he wrote:

We poured a little more than half of the concrete slab for the breezeway this morning—arduous and patience-claiming work when done with Indians who have never seen a slab poured and do not take well to mixing sand with a shovel.

We have been very much encouraged—through reading a book that deals with examples of apostolic missionary methods —to believe again for some sort of New Testament pattern to be worked out among forest Quichuas. How false and fleshly to reason that God will do a work here "because Pete, Ed, and Jim are trained, capable, young, and strong"! I have been much impressed lately of the *absolute* necessity of God *Himself* rousing the conscience. I do not know how, nor even where, to begin to make a man think seriously about sin and judgment, and must look to the work of the Holy Spirit for the beginning move toward any hint of such a working. And pray that it will be so here, Betts, that God would take this work in hand, and do it ON HIS OWN LINES. To see Christ honoured and testified to publicly by one of these young Indian fellows we now know as friends would be something like seeing a miracle before my very eyes. Indeed, it would be a miracle, but I have never realised this fact so clearly as now. God must do His work, or it will not be done, and we stand waiting for Him here.

From the journal:

April 27. Struggling to maintain real faith for the genuine conversion of adult Indians and for confession on the part of schoolboys. Concerned lest my faith not be of the believing sort, for there are fears connected with it—fears of failure in our work here. Reasoning, "what if we don't get converts; what then of New Testament principles of church order? What then of teaching the Bible study method and memorisation, translation seminars and Book Study retreats with young men?" O Christ, I want this speaking-to-a-mountain faith, this faith that is bold, publicly, for God.

In May Jim went out to Quito to attend the Inter-Mission Fellowship conference and to see me again. We spent a happy two weeks shopping for materials for the buildings in Shandia, and visiting friends, and finally went down to the station in the west jungle where I was working. Of his trip back to Quito on a banana truck Jim wrote to me:

Of all trips I have made, it was the most difficult, and, for its length, way and above the most expensive. We hadn't gotten much past town when the gas-pump was full of water. At kilometre 106 we had a flat that held us up in repair until three o'clock. From there to Chiriboga the thing averaged the aching pace of five miles an hour. We arrived at the chain at nine pm and the guard refused to let us pass. Finally after a miserable snooze in the cab I persuaded him to lower the chain at five am. The *chofer* then encouraged me to take another truck because he was not sure his could make Quito. So I went to get my bag and discovered that it had been stolen. In the long, slow grind up to Chiriboga the conductor had come into the cab because of rain. Evidently someone had hopped on the cargo bed and thrown off my bag with other baskets belonging to passengers, while we were all huddled thoughtlessly in the front. Keep your eyes open for a green tarp, a seventy-dollar camera, light-meter, harmonica, all my coloured slides, boots, nylon shirts and wool slacks. Tell all the señoritas in San Miguel that their letters will have to be re-written and posted by someone more reliable than I. . . . The Lord gave me a victory in the loss, reminding me to be thankful for the abundance of possessions I have had. God knows, and I believe He sent this that I might be weaned more and more from things material—even good, legitimate things —and have my affections set more firmly on Him whom to possess is to have everything. Who could ask for more?

The journal continues:

June 14. This may become known as the season of the big flood. It started a week ago nearly, and has rained for five days and nights. Day before yesterday we noticed several large slides on the cliff wall downriver, and in anticipation of a possible sudden rise we tied the motor-house base and the generator to a rope and knotted it to the orange tree in front of this house. This morning at breakfast the Napo was plainly heading for a rampage. We went down to the coffee grove below the new house to watch the slides eat away the trail and the forest on the east bend. It crested between ten am and noon. The motor platform and generator are now dangling on the rope over a sheer wall. The new house, once thirty yards from the cliff, is now a bare fifteen. The trail is completely gone. The river was frantic and huge—gnawing off great chunks of earth and stone and forest, and growling deep in its guts as it churned up the stones. A fearful thing to see, especially when one is so close to it. I am about fifteen yards from the brink myself now as I write, and although the crest has passed for the present, the island is still far from the shore. Skinned flotsam lies crashed against the trees down low, and tons more are rolling by, on the mud-gone-greenish water. The problem is: shall we go on building the new house, with the expensive fixtures, aluminium and all, with the chance of a sudden repetition of today's show? The Indians intimate that it hasn't been like this for thirty years, but who knows when it will come again? Only God, whose voice is upon many waters. And He will show us His will and power.

To me, on June 17, Jim wrote of their decision:

Ed and Marilou have decided to move everything—taking

down all we have done; moving the cement pillars and all one hundred yards back. It was a terrific struggle for them to decide. Moving will probably hold us up another two months in the work schedule, but the discouraging part is tearing down all our work. Still, I have heard the voice of the Lord and am glad to do here as He is directing.

July 12 brought this word of progress:

We have been slowed considerably by the rains. All the postholes are full of water and working the posts into line is almost impossible in such mud. But we only have two more rows to go, and should have the girders up by the end of this week, if we get even three or four good days. But I can't get heart for this rebuilding job, somehow. It is not satisfying to me—such as finishing the steps was the first time—and I fear the workmanship is second-rate because of it; posts out of line, and not perfectly vertical, etc. And to think we must start a teacher's house next!

His letter to me a few days later says:

Tried to get some work done on the house this morning, but was rained in, and with all the stir this afternoon I don't suppose I'll get anything more done, either. It all seems so secondary, darling; so unimportant in comparison with what I want to be doing. Houses, exams, and all this has nothing to do with our love, and that is what possesses me these days.

That same afternoon, Jim wrote this prayer in his diary:

Lord God and Father, I call upon Thee to enter all the avenues of my life today, and to share every detail of it with me, even as Thou hast called me to share with Thee Thy life, and all the wonders of it. As I am to share the destiny, glory, and future affairs of Thy Son, so would I now have Him share this small destiny of earth which is mine, the joys of it, and all its small matters, that we should be one, Thou and I, even as we are in Christ.

The very night of this committal of heart, God brought about the 'cataclysmic event' which Jim had both hoped for and dreaded. Rains which had been more or less continual for a week became torrential, and fell relentlessly for thirty-six hours. The following afternoon, as I stood by the radio in Dos Rios, the jungle station six hours' walk from Shandia where I had begun the study of Quichua, I heard Jim's voice from Shandia:

> The brink of the cliff is only five yards from the house now. The river is still eating away the base of the cliff, and if you hear nothing from us at two o'clock you'll know we have had to abandon the house.

Two o'clock brought silence. So did the next two days. Though I tried to get an Indian runner to go to Shandia to find out what had happened, all said that the rivers would be impassable, and they would not attempt the journey. Finally an Indian consented to go, and brought back this letter from Jim:

> *August 1, Saturday.* Shandia is no more. This is being written beside a fire outside with a dozen Indians looking on and telling me what to write. The first house went about 3.30 pm on Thursday, and we have spent the rest of the time moving our stuff away from the river, except for last night when we slept the whole night with about thirty Indians under one roof. Most of the stuff is here now, under temporary shelters, though the heavier items—barrels, motor, refrigerator, etc.—are at various points in the forest (we hope that they are out of the reach of the flood). Most of our stuff was saved, thanks to the invaluable help of all the Indians, though we have lost a little through thievery. We lost the boards we tore from the houses because the Indians were just too weary to pack them away from the river. The school went about midnight, and the school kitchen in early hours yesterday. Clinic and our Indian kitchen went late in the afternoon. Will you please send this telegram to Mr K. L.

Fleming, 1403 Tenth Avenue West, Seattle:

"FLOOD DESTROYED SHANDIA. SAVED STUFF. ALL WELL. INFORM PORTLAND. LOVE PETE."

We will try to get our tent up today and get housekeeping underway again soon. It was so thoughtful of you to send bread. We found some butter and honey and had chicken soup for supper—the first good meal in thirty-six hours—last night. Sorry I could not inform you sooner, but we were busy, carrying stuff the very moment your carrier arrived, and I had no idea where pen or paper were until last night. The new house is near the brink and we lost about one-eighth of the airstrip. I don't know if they will dare land or not. If they do, we need aerial wire for the radio. It was not well guarded by the Indians charged with taking care of it. Breakfast is on the fire and a beautiful dawn is breaking through the forest. We are both well and happy, and waiting on God to show us His Will for this station.

The waters have not quenched love. I do not know what this will mean for us. Housing here seems almost stupid now, and Ed and Marilou cannot come in for some time together. Still, in all the rain and mud and mess and sense of loss, I loved you strongly, and wished for some reason that you were here—I do not know why, for we could not have had a moment together. We have loads of invitations from Indians to stay in their homes, and our cookboy is doing well with what he can find in all the damp tangle of our possessions. We are doing very well, and should be getting settled, organised, stored, and dried out in the next few days. I see no hope for school here in October. We must use part of the foundation of Ed's house for smaller living quarters. The mush is cooked. All for now. Ever your own, Jim.

Upon receipt of this letter I left Dos Rios immediately with a group of Indians, to help in any way possible in Shandia. Arriving there the next day, Sunday, I was able to piece together more of the details in conversation with Indians who had been at the scene of the flood.

While I and others had been waiting at the radio on Thursday, hoping that Jim and Pete would manage to get their radio functioning again in another building, they were frantically throwing their possessions into kerosene-can boxes (which are the principal items of furniture in many a jungle home). These, in turn, were thrust into the arms of waiting Indians who had collected as they heard the thunder of the cliff's caving in. The loose stuff taken care of, they made a desperate effort to save some of the timbers of the house, which were of an imperishable wood, difficult to find in the forests. The entire inside of the house was dismantled, and Jim was just ripping the screens out of the kitchen windows when, with a wrench and a crack, the front porch dropped out of sight into the river. Jim decided it was time to get out.

The next thirty-six hours were spent in the kind of downpour that can be visualised only by one who knows tropical rainy-season rain. Ed and Marilou's steel barrels—eleven of them, which had been shipped into Shandia in advance of their coming—were rolled through trailless forest. (The trails had long since gone over the cliff along with the house.) An eight-cubic-foot refrigerator was dragged, with the aid of two boards acting as runners, through the mud and underbrush. Boxes of clothes, food, papers, valuable language materials, medical supplies—completely soaked through—and heavy tools, were hauled from place to place. It had hardly become dark when Jim—plunging through the jungle, trying to keep track of the things and the places where the Indians were dumping them—lost his shoes in the mud. There is a species of palm in this area which has, growing thickly up the length of its trunk, thorns two to four inches long. These lie scattered about in the forest, along with strong bamboo spikes which will pierce even shoe soles. The condition of Jim's feet, after twelve hours spent barefoot in this kind of terrain, in the dark, need not be described.

Each time that Jim and Pete felt that they had managed to get the equipment to spots where it would be beyond the reach of the disintegrating cliff, a cry of alarm would go up from someone stationed near the brink, and things would have to be moved again. In the morning the newest building which they had completed—the clinic—was in danger. In order to try to save the roof-leaf, which is scarce wherever Indians have been building houses, Jim tied a rope around the building, and, with the help of a number of Indians, pulled the clinic over. It lay on its side nearly on the edge of the cliff, and in order to release the rope Jim went around between the building and the cliff. Suddenly there was a roar, and all but the bit of earth on which he stood fell away behind him. The Indians, hidden from view by the thatched roof, shouted 'He dies!' But Jim yelled back 'I live! Pass me a machete *fast*.' They thrust one through the thatch and he chopped his way to safety before the rest of his foothold gave way.

Jim's next journal entry was August 15:

Two weeks have passed since I last wrote, and those two weeks have made me older. The day I wrote that prayer on the other page, the Atun Yaku wiped out Shandia. Week-end was a weary one, brightened only by Betty's coming here on Sunday. Then it was the job of collecting all the stuff, sorting it, drying it, storing it somewhere. Ed came on Tuesday, and we discussed the Will of God and talked, planned and discarded plans. Then, more sorting, saving, and throwing out. It rained that week-end and took some more off the cliff, leaving the newly-moved foundation useless, forcing us to alter our plans again. Tuesday we took off the girders of the foundation and in the night I got my first touch of malaria. Ed and Pete left Wednesday morning and I spent the day in chills, fever and utter weakness and quite a lot of pain. Managed to get the girders laid for the storage house half-way down the airstrip. That night I saw the luminous dial on my watch flash as I rolled over and read every hour from midnight to five. Dizziness and headache were constant, with total loss of appetite for everything but lemonade (which, in view of the gallons I have drunk to cool and fill and satisfy me these three days, I regard as a rich mercy from God; there is a teapot on the desk now about a third full).

Dr Tidmarsh left with Nate this afternoon. At supper the mental symptoms of malaria reached their pitch. With the cessation of any physical work (all I could do, anyhow, was sit and tell the men what to do) the mind works overtime. My thoughts were awful. I did not know I loved Betty. I could not sustain two sentences of prayer. I talked impatiently to the workmen. It was terrible. Slept from eight till midnight. Such a twisting serpentine mass of wretched and uncontrolled ideas I never thought the mind capable of, especially as I knelt in prayer. God forgive me. (Pardoned. Just took it in faith.)

Now it is cool and growing later than my recent early bedtimes. I may sleep tonight if I stay up a little longer. The wall studs, door, windows, and roof slats, with part of the aluminium, are on the storage house. By the great kindness of God I am feeling stronger and enjoying good food. Tonight it was raw carrots, tomatoes, lettuce, and cauliflower (a salad plate!) with a little home-made vinegar, vegetable soup and a snatch of chocolate cake from Shell Mera. God be praised. This is a good night in what used to be Shandia.

August 16. Not much better today. Had a meeting of some thirty Indians in the morning air (no buildings to have it in). Luis and Lucas preached. First time I ever heard an Indian preach the Resurrection the way it should be preached. Sickly and weak. Gave medical treatment to some folk, and folded laundry, in the kitchen. The tent was too hot to rest in this afternoon. Bathed leisurely and alone in the Talac river. First time I've felt I could walk that far in a while.

This came to me as I was sitting on the cliff after a light supper of manioc, raw carrots, and tea:

Because, O God, from Thee comes all, because from Thine own mouth has entered us the power to breathe, from Thee the sea of air in which we swim and the unknown nothingness that stays it over us with unseen bands; because Thou gavest us from heart of love so tender, mind so wise and hand so strong, Salvation; because Thou art Beginning, God, I worship Thee.

Because Thou art the end of every way, the goal of man; because to Thee shall come of every people respect and praise; their emissaries find Thy throne their destiny; because Ethiopia shall stretch out her hands to Thee, babes sing Thy praise; because Thine altar gives to sparrows shelter, sinners peace, and devils fury; because "to Thee shall all flesh come",[4] because Thou art Omega, praise.

Because Thou art surely set to justify that Son of Thine and wilt in time make known just who He is and soon will send Him back to show Himself; because the Name of Jesus has been laughingly nailed upon a cross and is even now on earth held very lightly and Thou wilt bring that Name to light; because, O God of Righteousness, Thou wilt do right by my Lord, Jesus Christ, I worship Thee.

Counsel with Pete, Ed, and Dr Tidmarsh led to a decision to make their first itinerary in the jungle, to spy out the southern area of the Quichua tribe in case God should be indicating, by the destruction of Shandia, that another location should be sought. I was asked to stay in the tent in Shandia while the men were away, in order to guard the stores of valuable equipment which were protected only by aluminium sheets set up on poles.

For three weeks the three men—Pete, Jim, Ed—travelled on foot and by canoe, visiting the Indians on the shores of the Bobonaza river, estimating the population and evaluating the possibilities for opening new stations.

Twenty-one days of scorching sun, of solid sheets of rain, and of sore muscles caused by the back-breaking position necessary in a dugout canoe gave the men a fair introduction to the itineration they had looked forward to. Jim and Ed soon got 'jungle rot', a softening and sloughing of the soles of the feet owing to prolonged wetness.

Despite what one finds in the adventure stories, the traveller on jungle rivers rarely sees anything exciting. Wildlife is extremely wary, and the knocking of the canoe poles and intermittent shouting of the *popero* (whose responsibility it is to choose the course) provides sufficient warning for any creature which might otherwise be visible from the river. The heavy growth of the jungle hangs out over the water, trailing lianas into its dark depths. Occasionally a fish flips on the surface and a flock of parrots flashes across the sky with strident screech. The odd *dumbiki*, or toucan, looking like a jet plane with its long beak and tail of equal length, flaps overheard, uttering its single-noted cry. However, for the most part the sameness of the river and its jungle borders is unbroken, and the one who sees a tapir or alligator is fortunate indeed.

Ten days of slow, arm-wrenching poling brought the canoes with their three 'gringos' back to Canelos, and from there they returned on foot to Shell Mera, confident that God had a purpose for the many Quichuas they had visited.

When Jim returned to Shandia he told me of the most promising spot that they had visited—the juncture of the Pastaza and Puyo rivers, where lived Atanasio, an Indian with fifteen children who had begged the men to come and live among them and establish a school. This plea, the first of its kind that the men had heard from Indians, was not to be lightly refused. Ordinarily the problems of winning friendship and establishing residence in a new location are great enough in themselves to require a long period of time. Here, these would be entirely obviated. The men agreed unanimously that they must accept Atanasio's invitation.

Ed felt that if they were to begin the study of Quichua then he and Marilou should not have the added responsibilities of opening a new work. So he decided to settle temporarily in Shandia, living in a simple split-bamboo house. The help of one of the unmarried men would be needed in the language as well as in the running of the station. Who, then, could enter Puyupungu? The answer seemed obvious to all three men.

'So,' said Jim to me as he told me of it, 'how soon will you marry me?'

Notes

1. 1 Peter 1:7, JBP.
2. Matthew 9:29.
3. Psalm 127:1.
4. Psalm 65:2.

— 22 —

Lo, This Is Our God

And it shall be said in that day, Lo, this is our God, we have waited for Him.[1]

ONE OF THE THINGS on which Jim and I had agreed years before was that a conventional wedding could never be for us. I, like most women, enjoyed attending them, but could not imagine myself in such a setting. Jim, on the other hand, held them in disdain, as a page from his journal of 1949 reveals:

Twentieth-century Christian weddings are the vainest, most meaningless forms. There is no vestige of reality. The witnesses dress for a show. The flesh is given all the place. The songs are absurd, if one paid any attention to the words, but no one does; they simply listen to *how* it is sung, not what it means. Candles are useless but expensive trifles. Ushers help no one, but appear very officious and the ceremony itself is the most meaningless hodge-podge of obsolete grammar and phraseology — sounds like a schoolboy's translation of something from Cicero. And the stupid form of asking who gives this bride in marriage. Who cares? Everyone knows it is her father or uncle or some such sweating pawn standing before the altar. Talk of Romanism! We Fundamentalists are a pack of mood-loving show-offs. I'm sure the minor prophets would have found subject for correction in this affair. I must read this to myself on my wedding day (if I have one!).

I do not think he remembered to read it. If he had, I am sure he would have smiled at his own vehemence, for he had matured in those four years. Maturity, however, had brought him no love for show. This is his comment on a newspaper account of a wedding which took place a few months before our own:

> For me, "heavy ivory satin... fitted bodice designed off-shoulder effect... embroidery, iridescent sequins... tiara of rhine-stones"... long aisles, tears and sniffling, waiters in white coats do not amount to a sublime event. It is no more than an expensive tedium with little remembrance value. There is something in me that resists the showy part of weddings with a passion I have against few other things in life, as I cannot abide a puny man who boasts of his achievements and cannot stand behind his words.

We decided on a civil ceremony on October 8, Jim's twenty-sixth birthday, and Jim wrote to his parents of our intention on October 3:

> Nobody can accuse us of rushing things just because we have decided to get married in less than three weeks—we have been in love for over five years and I think considered the Will of God in marriage as carefully as anyone could, except maybe Dad.... No one really understands our wanting only a civil wedding, but we are going ahead, believing that God is our leader and judge of our motives. Our wedding is not the first thing she and I have braved public opinion on. Few have really tried to understand our long waiting for engagement and my going to the jungle single. Few really thought we were the "perfect match" in the first place. To me the words and worries of the rest matter not at all. It has been a long lesson learning to live only before God, and letting Him teach the conscience and to fear nothing save missing His Will. But we are learning, and I would live no other way. I want always to say with the apostle, "God is my judge."[2]

It had been a 'long lesson' indeed—from the days of studying Thucydides together, through the months of silence, then correspondence; the days at Mt Hood and the Oregon coast; years of uncertainty about the mission field; subsequent guidance and assurance; then Ecuador; climbing Pichincha; noon meals at the Arias home; separation to the east and west jungles; Quito again, and engagement; separation again; the flood in July; the Bobonaza trip in August . . . and then October 8, 1953.

'They shall not be ashamed that wait for Me.'[3] We were married without fuss at the Registro Civil in Quito. It was a delightfully simple ten minutes—a dingy, high-ceilinged room in an antique colonial building; a suitably solemn official who read, in rapid monotone, several pages of Spanish, punctuated here and there by our 'si'. Dr and Mrs Tidmarsh, our official witnesses, were the only ones present beside the McCullys. We signed our names in an immense ledger, and were man and wife.

'Delight thyself also in the Lord, and He shall give thee the desire of thine heart.'[4] God had given us that desire, and perhaps in the sense in which Jim had interpreted it in a letter to me written in 1949:

> It does not say He will give you what you want. It does say He will give you *the want*. Delight in Christ brings desire for Christ. He gives the heart its desires—that is, He works in us the willing (Philippians 2:13). This is why He can say in John 15:7, "Ye shall ask what ye will . . . if ye abide." The branch takes its sap from the vine, the same surges the vine feels then become the surges of the branch. My will becomes His, and I can ask what I will, if I delight myself in Him. Only then can my desire be attained, when it is His desire.

After a honeymoon in Panama and Costa Rica we returned to Quito to pack equipment for the move into Puyupungu. Surrounded by boxes and barrels, Jim found a few minutes to write to his parents, the first letter following the wedding, dated October 28:

> Betty and I are extremely happy now, sharing all that we are and have. Just now we are staying in the *bodega*, a house that all of us rent to keep our things in, and half of our missionary staff is in Quito now, so we are having a fight getting things packed for going to Puyupungu. In Shandia we used only a very small part of the stuff I brought from the States, so that now, returning from the honeymoon and opening up the barrels and crates again is just like starting out with new wedding gifts. Together we really have a wonderful collection of stainless steel ware, pots and utensils. I am sitting beside a small drum which Betty is packing full of it now, really a lot of fun.
>
> We got back from Panama Sunday; each room in the hotel had its own balcony, and ours looked right out over the Pacific.

The employees of the hotel were mostly bilingual, and Jim and I had amused ourselves noticing how they seemed to know which language to speak to each patron. Jim decided that he would try to trip them up. Approaching the cigar counter one morning, he was greeted by a polite 'Good morning, sir.'

'Ay would laik wan rroll of teerty-fa-eeve meeleemeter feelm,' he said, in his nearly perfect imitation of a Latin speaking English.

'*Muy bien, señor,*' was the quick reply.

I of course was taken completely by surprise, but succeeded in maintaining my equilibrium till we were on the elevator. I realised that I was now the *wife* of this unpredictable man, and that I must identify with him.

The letter to Jim's parents continues:

> After a week there we took a plane to San José, Costa Rica, where we dropped in on Dave[5] and Phyl, right in the middle of Spanish classes. They had not even known we were married, let alone that we would be coming to see them.

We gaped and gawked at the store windows like a couple of palm-leaf savages, both in Panama and Costa Rica. They are both progressive countries.

With our things well packed in steel drums and boxes lined with waterproof paper, we left Quito at the end of October and flew to Shell Mera, where we spent the night with Nate and Marj Saint at the Missionary Aviation Fellowship headquarters. Next morning, Nate drove us to the last town on the road, Puyo by name, where Jim had arranged for canoes to meet us. Our gear was loaded in, and we started down the Puyo river toward our new home, Puyupungu.

In the late afternoon, as the sun slanted down behind our backs, a hoot was heard below us, and Atanasio, the head man from Puyupungu, hove into sight with several canoes full of friends. They hailed Jim heartily, and said,

'So you are a word-fulfiller!'

There was much back-slapping and laughter, and we proceeded on downriver together till we reached the mouth of the river, where it empties into the mighty Pastaza. High on the bank stood Atanasio's family—two wives, and a veritable battalion of children, peering shyly down through the trees. As the canoes scraped the sandy beach, all came running down the steep trail, and soon had our gear—a tiny iron stove, a steel trunk, folding bed, assorted boxes and drums, and a tent—carried up the cliff and deposited in a little thatched shack where we were to sleep that night. In short order we were supplied with wood, water, fresh eggs, papaya, smoked fish, and plantains. Our welcome was genuine.

We found that the thatched house, while it looked a haven for us that first evening, proved to be the same for the cockroaches. Moreover, neither Jim nor I could stand up straight under the low beams which supported the roof. Within two days Jim had the tent pitched—a sixteen-foot-square one which someone had given him at the last minute before he sailed from California. We did not imagine, when we pitched it, that this would be our home for five months.

Jim had just put up some poles for a tiny kitchen shack outside the tent, and was planning to lay an aluminium roof on it as well as to lay a bamboo floor in the tent, when he succumbed to a fever that we were not able to subdue with the usual malarial drugs. The short-wave radio set we had brought along had seemed rather a civilised luxury to us before this, but now became an essential as I tried to get into contact with a doctor to describe Jim's symptoms. The radio was powered by handcrank, which Jim was too weak to turn, so the difficulty of getting a willing Indian to turn it while I operated the transmitter was added to poor reception, and attempts to communicate were very frustrating experiences.

Jim lay in bed for three weeks, hardly able to lift his head, while the rain ran under the sides of the tent, making a slough of the mud floor, and poured into the wall-less kitchen.

Records in Jim's own words from the time of our marriage until his death are few and sketchy. There are several reasons for this, the first being an obvious one — that he no longer wrote letters to me. Then, other things which, for lack of any other means of expression he had formerly shared only with the journal, he was now able to share with me, thus 'delivering his soul'. Further reasons he wrote to his brother Bob:

Thanks, Bob, for your notes on the "Man" at God's right hand. I am sure my letters from the mission field have contained precious little of this sort of thing and I fear that it is representative of what goes on in my soul a good deal of the time. Some think the life of the jungles tranquil, and indeed if you ask an Ecuadorian why he likes the Oriente, he will tell you it is because of the quiet and easy life. I have not found it so. Occupation with affairs that I never had experience with before, and things arising any minute of the day or night have sapped my study programme of content, and I find myself wondering where passages are that once I had at my fingertips. It is a loss. I don't know how I will ever preach again in English. I have been using the Spanish Bible constantly for over a year, and most of the ministry I have done has been from what little there is of the Scripture in Quichua. It is a struggle even to get in a period of reading, to say nothing of meditation or study. Sometimes one is conscious of spiritual life only because he is still struggling to maintain it, not at all because he is purposefully living it. Pray for my soul. We need no funds here, really, nor more workers. What we need is spiritual power and vigour in the soul. Our enemy wields well his weapons, and his, no less than ours, are spiritual weapons, for the defence of those same strongholds which we are equipped to pull down.

Jim's journal was completely neglected until December 1, when he wrote:

It is not raining at the moment but the fresh-cut bamboo slats are chunked with fresh mud, and the other half of the tent, not yet floored, is slippery gum from an all-night rain on Sunday. We had to get this much of the floor in yesterday and they are supposed to be bringing more bamboo today so perhaps we will be fully floored this week. I am supposed to have had jaundice almost since the day we arrived, November 11, and am still a part-time bed-patient. Betty is out cooking in the kitchen shack while I sit at the card table, decked with an aster-flowered teacloth with a centre-piece of white candle and a graceful-leafed little forest flower set off beautifully in a tin can.

Married life is rich, as I have always known life to be, but richer in its complexity. We have known nothing but harmony. The marriage "adjustment" is something, which if it exists at all, I am going through effortlessly, unconsciously, even. Such is the love we know.

In December Jim and I walked from Puyupungu to Puyo, on our way to Shandia to spend Christmas with the McCullys. The trail was, even by jungle standards, a poor one, being little used by Indians, who had their own canoes for river travel. Densely overgrown in places where it was second-growth jungle, it was wide enough for only a single human

271

foot in most sections. We travelled, of course, in single file. A young Indian boy went with us as guide. He set the quick, steady pace used by Indians, unvarying even on hills or while crossing unstable log bridges. Jim fell in behind him, and I took my place last, according to Indian custom. Women carry the loads (in this, however, we deviated from local practice!), and herd the children along, while the men, carrying nothing but a muzzle-loaded gun or a blow-gun, walk ahead, to watch for game or snakes. As I followed Jim, I noticed again the extraordinary lightness of his movements as he moved along the trail—occasionally leaping over especially deep mud, swinging himself down a bank by a vine, or springing over a fallen tree. There were places where we had to bend double to get through; others, where the guide had to hack a way through a tangle of vines and airplants which had broken a branch with their weight. We waded across rivers, went uphill and down—for the Indian builds a trail, by preference, on the highest ground to provide some drainage. There is little opportunity for enjoying the scenery while on the trail, but when we stopped to eat our lunch Jim commented on the gigantic trees, the delicate moss, the faintly sweet, cool smell of the forest. After some nine hours' walking, we broke out into the sugar-cane country surrounding the frontier town of Puyo, where Marj Saint was waiting in the pick-up truck with four iced 'cokes' and some cake. She drove us to Shell Mera and we flew from there to Shandia.

Jim's next journal entry is dated January 20, 1954:

Spent a holiday in Shandia from December 19 to January 5 with much joy. First young-men's conference went off with not enough prayer nor study, but albeit the blessing of God. Baptised Eugenia Cerda and Carmela Shiwangu in the Talac river on Lord's Day, with great joy and confidence in God. Began work on the airstrip and house site here in Puyupungu, but have been discouraged by rain and slowed by personnel problems. Still, God helps and progress is visible. Not happy altogether with

Lucas as a schoolteacher, but am encouraged with the attention some show to the Word of God. Last night in a little meeting we have on Tuesday, Atanasio said, "I will die in your words." I don't know how much he understands, but he does hear some. Praying for a work of God among the school-children, who now number ten. I may start a literacy class for some young fellows when the house is underway and the airstrip finished.

February 5. Finished the roof of the house and outhouse today. Men wearying some, and dropping off work. Only the Lord is constant and sure. It must be by His grace we have accomplished all that we have this past month, both on airstrip and in the house.

Praying especially for Pablo and Atanasio these days. Oh that God would bring light to their minds and life to their souls. Began literacy class daily with Tito and Benito this week. Tito does well. Perhaps God will give him to me to father in the faith.

April 1. Pause late on a rainy afternoon. Gratefully settled in our home in Puyupungu for a week now. Been a long, but not unendurable five months in the tent. God has been faithful, though Satan has fought us to discouragement through long weeks of rain. Men came from Pano to help, or I would never had gotten the airstrip done by now. Plane landed on three hundred yards of it yesterday, but this end is still too wet for take-off.

April 15 (letter to his brother). You apologise for sending stationery with roses, Bob, thinking we might be all orchidified by now. Wrong. I'd give plenty to get a rose-bush going here. True we have plenty of the lovely big orchids right over the cliff here, and I have made a small hobby out of collecting as many different species as I can find. They bloom only in season, but are a fascinating study. The big kind we get in the States are a developed brand. The one type of big orchid here grows out of the dirt like any wild flower. The last couple of weeks we have been cutting the forest back to lengthen the approach to the airstrip and have found that great, mossgrown trees when cut have an abundance of tiny true airplant orchids. There is a lovely small white one, maybe two inches across, blooming now on a tree growing near the house that we brought in from the forest, but the bloom only lasts a couple of days, even if left on the plant. Another green one a little larger abounds down near the river level on the cliff and has to be gotten at with a canoe. A delicate spider-orchid with long petals from a tiny blossom is one I found on the cut trees.

I bring in the plants and stick them on my orchid garden—a tree by the house here. In all I think I have eight varieties, although some have never bloomed. The bougainvillaea shoots we brought from Shell Mera are doing well and we have a couple dozen pineapple plants stuck in to keep the forest away from the house a bit. This kind of thing keeps a man from going entirely Indian out here. Of course they think it's crazy for anyone to plant flowers, but accept our doing it as one of the crazy things we do and get away with. Vegetable seeds rot in the ground, we find, but I have several vines of a nice wild squash started. It's about six inches long and has a very hard shall, but tastes very like Danish squash. . . .

This is Holy Week and we find that the custom of having some religious festival is a convenient time for us to press home the gospel. We are having meetings every night here and Lucas and I are taking turns ministering on the Seven Words from the Cross, one each night. The Indians are most attentive and Atanasio told me the night before last, that even though he is old, his eyes are beginning to open and he is beginning to understand. He has a real desire to change his ways, but is a habitual drunkard and says he has lived like a burro and a savage till now. We pray earnestly for his conversion. His oldest daughter, who helps us by washing dishes, is not far from the kingdom, we feel. Pray that the family will wholeheartedly accept the kingship of Christ and that the work will spread to the other Indians who live one and two days away, too far for us to reach up until now.

Jim and I were looking forward eagerly to the arrival of his father, who was coming to help with the rebuilding of Shandia, and hoped and prayed that the airstrip would be usable before it was time to go out to meet him. On May 30 Jim wrote:

Both Dad and Pete are here with us now and their presence represents a great deal of answered prayer. Betty and I were able to fly out of Puyupungu on April 21. Met Dad with much thanksgiving at Puná six days later. One week took him and all the construction equipment he brought through Customs. We spent a week in Quito getting teeth fixed, attending the Inter-Mission Conference, and meeting people, coming down by truck to Shell Mera on May 14. Betty came here and I went to Shandia to choose a house site. O God, may it be the right one!

His next letter to Portland tells of progress begun on the new house in Shandia. It was the feeling of the men at that time that at least one of our stations should have a permanent-type house, while places like Puyupungu might serve as outstations. So they took advantage of the help of Jim's father to begin that project.

The boards are planing up fine, and although Dad was having trouble getting the big saw adjusted, I think the main work of preparing lumber ought to be over in a couple of weeks, barring breakdowns. Puyupungu is so nearly finished, and runs on so much smaller and simpler a scale than Shandia that it is a relief to come here after a stay up north. We are finishing the rail fence around the airstrip here now, so that the cows won't tear it to pieces at night, and there is furniture to make yet, but we are mostly finished with the physical plant at this outstation. We still eat from a card table and use folding chairs that I would like to replace with permanent things so we could use these for other outstations.

We said good-bye to Pete last week, as he leaves to go to the States to get married. Baptised six more Indian young people and had our first breaking of bread in Quichua on the previous Lord's Day.

The house site in Shandia is cleared now and we hope to get the cement a-pouring before long. Dad is a great help....

Now my wife is playing on her organ some nice Sunday evening music, and I will try to get this finished. I don't know if I will or not, as the longer she plays the more things seem to go wrong with the organ—there are a total of three keys sticking since she began to play. Another instance of things that are nice to have but difficult to maintain in the jungle, and therefore of doubtful value.

A little girl just came in from Atanasio's house to ask if there would be a meeting tonight. I told her there would be. Pray that we might see the hand of God working among this small group of Indians and that the Lord would protect us from the work of the enemy here.

Notes

1. Isaiah 25:9.
2. Romans 1:9, para.
3. Isaiah 49:23.
4. Psalm 37:4.
5. My brother.

— 23 —

The Pattern at Work

According unto the patterns which the Lord had shewed Moses, so he made the candlestick. [1]

AT THE END OF June we had a little 'commencement' programme for the schoolchildren and their parents in Puyupungu, and, with a promise to visit them whenever we could, we closed up the house and went to Shandia so that Jim could put full time on the building programme while his father was still in Ecuador. Jim and I lived in a tiny bamboo house which Pete had built for himself, and ate our meals with Ed and Marilou.

Jim's days were spent in heavy, exhausting construction, in clearing jungle, in hauling sand and rocks, in building concrete forms, and in supervising workmen. When I took a pitcher of lemonade in mid-afternoon I would find him standing by the little cement mixer, stripped to the waist, bronzed and glistening with sweat as he heaved buckets of sand and directed the Indians who were working with him. He would return to the McCully house, which was a twelve-minute walk through the forest, near sundown, and bathe in the cool river before supper. Evenings were spent in letter writing, language discussion, preparation for Bible teaching, or talking with the McCullys. Working with Ed in the forest was another of Jim's dreams come true—which of course is what he fully expected dreams to do. For Marilou and me it was pure pleasure to watch Jim and Ed. Their minds met, it seemed, at nearly every point, and they found that the old fellowship of Wheaton and Chester days had lost none of its joy; in fact, the sharing of work together on the mission field had immeasurably strengthened the bond.

On October 8 he wrote to his mother and brother in Peru:

This is our wedding anniversary. It has been the happiest and busiest year of my life. I hope that by next week we'll move into our third house since we were married—first the tent, then the thatch roof in Puyupungu, and now, boards, concrete, and aluminium! Where does one go from there?

Ed is in Arajuno over the week-end. He went in there and built a shack and was there with his family for a couple of weeks. It will be like Puyupungu now, a preaching point to which we can "ride circuit" and teach and preach while basing our operations here in Shandia. We started school on Thursday with eleven boys and with promise of more coming on Monday. Some older fellows are coming along, too, so we are going to give some special attention to the school ourselves and not leave the teaching up to the poor, young Christian schoolteacher whom we have asked to come this year.

December 12. Ed and I are sweating out a warm afternoon in this little shack that Ed built in a Shell Oil "ghost town", Arajuno. It's a weird place—great cement slabs, steel girders, well-drilling heads, pipes, bricks, tumble-down buildings all grass-grown, rotten, and rusty. Had about twenty-five out to meeting yesterday in this place, and fifty out to a meeting in an Indian house this morning. There is genuine interest in the gospel here. They are not so jaded as those at Shandia. It is surely a thrill (even when you're hoarse, as I am) to announce the gospel to people who've never heard it, and I think it helps one get to the main point, leaving out the sidelines and details. When one gets out in these places one feels as though the Word is being fulfilled literally: "This gospel shall be preached throughout the whole world."[2]

278

We spent Christmas of 1954 alone in Shandia, because the McCullys had gone to Quito for the birth of their second son, Mike. We had moved into the new house at the end of October, and were greatly enjoying fixing up the inside. Jim spent Christmas week building a room-divider between the living-room and kitchen. This consisted of cupboards and drawers, made of a beautiful almost-black wood which he had selected from the forest.

On January 16, 1955, his journal reveals a spirit of heaviness:

> Cast down on this Lord's Day morning. Just came up from the meeting with twenty-five Indians, mostly schoolboys and young women. Felt as though I preached powerlessly, without unction, and resultant effect was evident. Restlessness, interruptions, playing. Almost no adults come. Vicente's wife, Kuwa's, and Upuchu's; no adult men. My first thought is that they have tired of preaching, and they do not enjoy it. I may be preaching too hard; I think that I am worried too much of the week with the finishing of the house—right up till Saturday supper. Translated and preached from Titus, but felt little life or even continuity in what I said. House and furnishing must take second place now. Getting the Indians out to meetings and individual witness to them has got to be my foremost concern. Elias Cerda wants to be baptised, but he did not come out to meetings today. I must speak personally with Gervacio, Venancio Grifia, and Abelardo as well as to Elias before the young men's conference which begins the fourth of February.
>
> I am sorry I have neglected writing here. Many times fresh thoughts come, and I have failed to record them, so that now they are gone.

The Flemings and McCullys were able to come to Shandia in February to help with the conference. Some seventy to a hundred Indians attended the sessions. On the final Sunday four young men were baptised and told the spectators of the power of Christ in their lives. One had been a notorious drinker—his life was now transformed. This was a great encouragement to Jim, for the young men, especially—since they were the ones to carry the spiritual responsibility of the little church—were the principal concern to him. He taught them carefully and patiently; always with a view to teaching *them* to teach. A Bible class on Mondays was for the instruction of believers only, and went far beyond the evangelistic preaching they received on Sunday mornings With a small nucleus of baptised believers Jim began having a simple meeting for the breaking of bread, when Christ was exalted and worshipped. No one taught; the words of men were few. Hymns of adoration were sung, prayer was offered, and gradually the new believers began to understand the meaning of worship—offering to the Lord the love of their hearts, with simplicity and sincerity. Others began to observe this gathering from outside—some to scoff, some out of curiosity, some with a desire to understand. There was not much to watch. The room where we met was the schoolroom—bamboo walls and floors, thatched roof, backless benches. A small table stood in the centre of the circle with a loaf of bread and a cup of wine. The Indians gathered quietly, for once (with the dogs and babies outside), and sat barefooted and reverent around the symbols which spoke to them of the death of their Lord Jesus, whom they had so recently come to know and love. One by one, the young men would take part, suggesting a hymn, or praying, while all joined in lifting their hearts to Christ. Reminded of His death, they also thought of His coming again, and frequently ended the meeting singing '*kirikgunaga, kushiyanguichi—Cristo shamunmi!*' 'Be happy, believers—Christ is coming!'

At first Jim did most of the preaching, after Ed and Pete had left Shandia. This usually necessitated translating, first of all, the passage from which he meant to preach, for there were very few Scriptures in the lowland Quichua. All three men worked on this task continually, sharing their problems, and the results. The McCullys produced on their mimeograph in Arajuno an amazing variety of literary materials in a short time. Jim translated most of the Gospel of Luke—one of his last tasks—and also many isolated portions of Scripture, in the process of preparing his sermons.

Gradually, however, he felt that the responsibility of the preaching must go to the young Indians, and to that end he spent many hours with individuals, going over and over some portion of Scripture, helping them to study it for themselves, trying to lead them into a method of Bible study which they could follow when alone. Several young men exhibited a real gift in this, and it was not long before they were able to take charge of the entire Sunday morning gospel meeting—from leading the singing to preaching a sermon. It was something of a novelty for most of the Indians to see one of their own up front, and much patient teaching was required before they appreciated this. To them the gospel was for gringos, and for learned people only. An Indian preach? Absurd! But they came to see the fun.

Jim was able to show them that the Lord Jesus did not choose from among seminary graduates those whom He sent out to preach. They were common labourers in many cases, from the strata of society of their listeners. There was no dichotomy between clergy and laymen. Jim determined that in Shandia there would be none. The Bible was for all, and all could learn to read it if they would. He was planning to do all in his power to put it into their hands in their own tongue, and to teach them not only to read it, but to 'rightly handle' [3] it. If the Indians came to meetings only to hear a foreigner, they might as well not come. They must see that the written Word is the oracle of God—regardless of who is preaching it—or the missionary labours in vain.

In the United States there is usually respect for the Word of God—that is, outward respect, even where there is no thought of obedience to it. In the Ecuadorian jungle the

Indian has not reached that 'level of culture'—he has neither respect, manifested by apparent attention when it is being read, nor reverence, manifested in obedience to it. The women are the most difficult element in the meetings—they search their children's heads for lice, stand up in a body when anything passes outside, rush to the window if it promises to be interesting, thrust a foot up on the bench for the nearest person to examine for thorns, hustle in and out with children, and have discussions in a conversational tone of voice. The men will occasionally remonstrate with them from the back of the room, rise to rearrange the benches during the sermon, or stand up to talk with a passer-by through the window— but in general they pay much closer attention than the women. Pets are taken for granted, dogs going about through the rows, birds or monkeys perched atop the women's heads, puppies wrapped in carrying-cloths on backs. One is reminded of how the Lord Jesus was constantly trailed by a 'multitude'—the writers of the Gospels have left to our imagination all that meant to Him, but in spite of all, there were the few who came for more than loaves and fishes. These heard His word, and followed. And so it has been in Shandia. There have been the ones and twos, who, apparently seeing Him who is invisible, through all the distractions visible and audible, have believed, and have followed. These were the ones for whom Jim daily laid down his life. 'We ought to lay down our lives for the brethren.'[4]

His patience and wisdom in dealing with them was a source of wonder to me. The Indian reaction to a situation is as different from ours as his manner of sitting on the floor with a plate and spoon is different from our hugely complicated ritual of tables, chairs, cloths, napkins, assorted plates, and cutlery and flowers—to say nothing of the number of dishes served. If he makes a mistake, instead of registering embarrassment, frustration, regret, or fear, he usually laughs. This habit annoyed and baffled me. It must have been trying for Jim, too, though he had learned to love these people, and love has a way of showing what to do.

In February Jim and I went to Shell Mera, where he went to work helping on the construction of a hospital sponsored by the Quito missionary radio station HCJB, which was to serve all of the jungle stations. Two days after our arrival there, on February 27, our daughter was born. She had no sooner made her appearance than Jim stated simply, 'Her name is Valerie,' a decision he must have arrived at on the spur of the moment, for although we had discussed many names, Valerie included, we had agreed finally on no one of them.

Her birth took place in the home of the pilot and his wife who had done so much for us during our life together in the jungle. We stayed another week with Nate and Marj Saint, and found much to discuss with them, into the small hours, over cups of cocoa in their kitchen. On one occasion Jim held Valerie, looking into her face, and Nate, his own eyes shining with empathy (his own son was just two months old), said, 'Aren't they *terrific?*' Jim did not need to answer. It was evident that his daughter had captivated his heart. No rules of hospital asepsis or visiting hours for him. He picked her up within a few minutes of birth, and continued to do so whenever he pleased, be it her nap-time or whatever. He was not, however, one to change her diapers. Jim was a strong believer in a division of labour. There was man's work, and woman's work, and while the two met, they definitely did not overlap. This was something I had had to learn early in our Puyupungu days, for my months of jungle living had taught me to chop wood, nail up screens, or use a machete, while Jim in his bachelor days had had to see that the laundry was brought in when it rained and that a minimum standard of cleanliness was maintained in the kitchen. Jim made it clear that those days were gone forever. He was always ready, of course, to help me with my work if it became necessary, but I tried to see that it never did.

Jim's parents had come up from Peru, where they had been visiting his brother for several months, to be with us when Valerie arrived. Consequently, there are no letters to them until a month later, March 25, when Jim wrote:

> It's a frog-croaking Friday night in Shandia but we have put new mantles in the lamp and shined up the chimney and I feel full of noodles and desire to send a letter your way which I hope will beat you home. Spent the day painting a baby crib, and the kitchen side of the room-divider.
>
> We just learned of an Auca attack not far from Arajuno and even though the house is nearly ready to move into there, Ed is a little worried about going there with his family. The Aucas killed two children and their mother and were last seen heading up the Arajuno river in a stolen canoe. Pray for Ed as he wants to reach those Quichuas....

This was followed on April 16 by another letter to his parents:

> The last two weeks have been ones of reaping. I have never seen so many Indians openly receptive to the Word. In Dos Rios at the conference last week there were over twenty, in Pano about the same, and here in Shandia about a dozen. Now to the job of readying them for life in Christ. Praise for this break, and continue to pray for these who have made the break. Many of their families are upriver and the real test has not yet come.
>
> I am trying to get the water system done now. I am standing the barrels upright on a platform above the baby's room window. Have to borrow pipe-threading tools from the hospital gang in Shell Mera. They are using our cement mixer.... We are tearing down the old wood-shed and the Indians have built a chicken-house for those noisy roosters on the north-west corner of the lot; next we'll have to have another wood-shed and then a motor-shed for the light plant.
>
> Dinner is over now. Eugenia and Camilo have gone down Talac to see her folks. So Betty and I did the dishes and have just

sung a hymn—my current favourite, "I cannot tell why He whom angels worship should set His love upon the sons of men"[5] to the tune of Londonderry Air. She is going to feed Val now, and I hope to get a little literacy material for our believers to read. They will read if they can get their hands on something they can understand. Then I have a pile of unanswered letters to do, so hope you will excuse me if I cut this short. We have all things and abound, so please do not be telling such sad stories to the home folks that they will begin to pity us. We are the happy ones and are feeling great joy in these days working with God here in the jungles. We long for both establishment and outreach in the work. Looks like we are to do the establishing this year while McCullys do the outreach as we did at Puyupungu last year.

From the diary:

May 16, 1955. This has been a busy morning and one of those that doesn't leave one with a great deal of satisfaction after it's all done. Morning reading was in 2 Thessalonians 3: "If any man will not work neither let him eat." Yesterday I had told three girls to come to work. *Six* came to clean two measly manioc-patches. Then I went down to put Urpi and son to work planting pasture. They achieved a morning's success of perhaps thirty yards, ten feet wide. The men were waiting for tools and to be sent for roof-leaf. I sent them. More than twenty women brought plantains and chicha to sell me, for the schoolboys' meals, and I outraged them by buying enough for only two weeks, as I had sufficient for one week already. And one package of chicha from each one, leaving much unbought along with a basket of unnecessary sugar cane. Then my change ran out. Then the workmen on the teacher's house needed two-by-fours planed. I planed two-by-fours for the school building. After that, the girls who had been cleaning the manioc-patch arrived; they wanted me to buy *their* plantains. Domingo wanted ink powder for marking boards. A boy came to buy five sucres' worth of snails for Señora Rosa downriver. The workmen had cut a two-by-four too short and needed a hand. Venancio's leg needed massaging and he wanted to sell me beans, though I had

had to give *him* some yesterday, because he said that he had nothing to eat. Had to tell the men to start weaving the roof and not to stand around doing nothing. Then they all wanted to work the whole day instead of just till noon. Yuyu wanted money for thirty pounds of peanuts, and his mother wanted a sack Ed had not given back to her. Protaco wanted his work-money and the gun that Pete sent down from Quito to sell. Pete had been on the radio in the morning, and it was urgent that I write Tidmarsh. Believers' meeting this afternoon. My snake-bite patient at Limon Chikta is in bad shape. I was there Friday and yesterday and must go again tomorrow, an hour or more each way. Betty and the baby both have colds. I have just eaten a good lunch.

A letter to his home assembly in Portland is dated June 2:

We've been fighting sickness again. I have been making three trips a week downriver, an hour's walk, to care for an Indian who was bitten by a snake something like our western rattler. The Indians fear to lance and suck the bite, so the poison is generally absorbed into the blood stream, where it damages cells and rots tissue. This fellow is improving and I am sure will walk again,[6] but at present he has no skin on the front of his leg from the toes to the knee, and sinews are visible at several points. The danger, now that I have taken out all the rotted matter, is secondary infection. In connection with this we have been having a meeting each week down there and are making contact with Indians who up until now have regarded us as devils. Tomorrow I will go again with some believers. They are helping in the singing and testimony and we can only pray that God will bring light to these sightless and hopeless souls. There is not even a word for *hope* in this language. Betty and I were on our way down there two weeks ago on a Sunday afternoon when our girl who helps us in the house, and who was carrying Valerie, was bitten on the foot by another type of snake. I slit the foot with a jackknife, sucked it, stuck it in cold water and, when we got home, applied ice and injected ten cc's of antivenin serum. She bled at the gums and the foot swelled some, but had little pain. This is snake season here. Don't leave the house without your razor blade!

June 10. I'm in Puyupungu again for a few days. Came back to give the final exams for the little school, visit, and let the Indians know we are still interested. Elena, Atanasio's wife, died last Sunday of smallpox, and I have had a couple of good long chats with Atanasio since arriving. Smallpox has gone right through the Indians here. That's why Betty decided not to come and bring Valerie, because she hasn't been vaccinated. Can't remember if I have or not, but will know for sure in ten days!

I planted dahlias by the palms at our front door in Shandia, and they are blooming nicely. We also have a wide path out to the river so that we have a nice long view of the big bend of the river. I'm planting coffee, palms, and some pasture grass for future millennial herds to keep the forest down. It makes a beautiful homesite now.

Valerie is a giggler already, as sweet and dainty as babies can be. Betty has started giving her banana and papaya and she loves both. We are very busy and very happy—desiring only a fuller experience of the power of Christ.

Jim's sister was married in June, and he wrote to her then:

This is a one-pager to let you know that I am very glad for you both and praying for you these days.

I have been thinking lately that life in the will of God is better in each phase that we enter, so I can say honestly today, "This is the best year of my life." Only now I don't *shout* it as I once did, but I don't despise the shouting, either. I am praying this for you both: that there will not be a sense of climax and then a fading such as I have observed in some young married people. But, rather, that the full experience of life, as it was meant to be lived from the beginning for adults, might be an increasing thing. God deliver us from lolling back and saying, "I've had it." We haven't had everything—only all we could take for the time being.

My warmest congratulations, my very highest hopes and

earnest prayers are for you!—Brother Jim.

Another answer to a prayer of Jim's—perhaps it was an unspoken prayer, but one of those 'desires of the heart'[7] that the Lord sees and answers before we get around to asking for them—came in July, with the visit of Jim's brother Bert and his wife Colleen from Peru. He wrote on July 3:

> It is surely nice to be with Bert and Colleen again. We share a good many things now that we did not before, having lived in the jungle. Their work is quite different and makes conversation very interesting. We haven't been getting to bed at our usual early hour these nights! Bert spoke this morning at meeting while I interpreted, but many didn't need the translation, because he speaks a very understandable Spanish, and some answered his questions without the Quichua translation.

During July Jim proposed a visit to the McCullys so that Bert and Colleen could see the work in Arajuno. I baulked at the suggestion, and said that I would remain at Shandia to take care of things while the rest went. Jim would not hear of this. He reasoned with me, and tried several means to persuade me, without success. Months before, we had agreed—though of course the civil ceremony contained no vows of obedience—that the Scriptural principle must be followed: 'The willing subjection of the Church to Christ should be reproduced in the submission of wives to their husbands. But remember, this means that the husband must give his wife the same sort of love that Christ gave the Church....'[8] This was the only occasion when Jim found it necessary to use his prerogative. I went to Arajuno. Later it was evident to me that he was acting in accord with the principle—I was benefited by the trip. He had done rightly in insisting.

The work with the Quichuas was bearing fruit, and on July 17 Jim wrote to his parents:

Thursday some of the Indians who wanted to be baptised got the idea that we were to have a baptism after the school exams. Just where they got this idea I'll never know, but they were insistent that they had waited long enough, and it is hard to hinder such. So, even though I was alone, I called the believers together and we had a four-hour session Saturday afternoon examining eighteen of them. To my way of thinking, the older believers show a real interest and ability at discerning reality. They decided to hold back four of the young women who are silly and a little scared. There was a great victory in the case of Kupal Angu, a young fellow who left his wife in a huff more than a year ago, but now wants to be baptised. It was put squarely to him that he must fix it up with her, and although at first he did not want to at all, he finally said he would take her again. She was wanting to be baptised, too, so we called her in and settled the thing.

So with Venancio, the assistant schoolteacher, taking every alternate one, we baptised fourteen this morning in the Talac river, at the "Devil's Deep", as the unbelievers call it. They all gave good testimonies from the water, and we can only hope that the unbelievers will heed and soon follow in the way of obedience. Pray for Vicente, Dad; he is well again and working and we pray that God will speak to his soul. So far I have gotten nowhere in the things of God with the elder Venancio, who had the broken back.

That brings the number breaking bread to twenty-five at Shandia—a growth we would regard as phenomenal in any assembly at home but which appears to me to be normal where there is real application to evangelism by the believers and to sound teaching by the leaders. Remember—less than half of these are literate and must be fed and grow only on what they can hear and remember, so pray for them, won't you?

Jim's diary account of the baptism gives details not included in the letter:

My flesh often lacks the deep feeling that I should experience at such times and there was a certain dryness to the form this morning, but I cannot stay for feelings. So cold is my heart most of the time that I am almost always operating on the basis of pure commandments, forcing myself to do what I do not always feel, simply because I am a servant under orders. And there was enough of the physically distracting this morning to save me from walking in the clouds. A part of the cliff gave way and three girls sat down on the beach amid shrieks and laughter. The schoolboys threw stones into the water, Antonia's son fell headlong off the end of the airstrip onto the beach and set up a great wail just as his mother was being baptised. Venancio failed to get Carmela's face clear under, and a group of mockers came by and taunted the baptised ones about bathing with their clothes on. But God is my witness that I have fulfilled His word as I knew how.

In August Jim took the Shandia schoolboys on a hike with a group of Quichuas from the mountains, travelling on foot from Puyo to Papallacta, a journey of about five days. At one point a swift river had to be forded, and the mountain boys, having seen very little water of any kind in their lives, were terrified. Two of them were caught in the current, and it was only after he had lost his shirt with wallet and money in the pocket that Jim was able to rescue one of them, Ed McCully the other. Jim wrote to his parents:

> We were disappointed in the spiritual values of the trip, everyone being too tired to think after twenty miles or so of walking each day. However, I was glad to see the Indian boys get the enlarging experience of it—some had never ridden in a car, and none had climbed a mountain; they got their picture in a Quito newspaper and visited the government buildings.
>
> Valerie grows week by week. She is terrifically active, rolling about and bicycling and "rowing", as the Indians say—with her arms, lifting them first over her head and then whamming them down. She looks like Eisenhower at times with her wide grin and her fine, almost-invisible hair. She is getting over a cold and knocks herself out sneezing, as Dad always did. Nights

are some better—she has slept from five until five, but she usually wakes, cries a little, and goes back to sleep. Betty has started giving her plantain flour, which she makes herself, and the little squirt loves it.

On September 18 Jim's happiness in fixing up his home and garden were reflected in another letter to Portland:

I got some outside window casings on and varnished them and the barge boards on the house. Vicente and his son are clearing ground for a new school. I want to get at the upstairs flooring soon. I did some trimming on the coffee and avocado trees and have dahlias and white glads blooming in the front yard. Also got three rose bushes going and just planted three gardenias. The pineapples are ripening fast now and we eat papaya off the trees on the place, and have our own manioc. Planted corn beyond the clothes-lines and at the back of the house, so the site really looks nice. The pasture grass between here and the river is doing fine, so we thank God for the tropic growing-season. The rain has set in suddenly again and it is chilly at the moment.

Notes

1. Numbers 8:4.
2. Mark 14:9.
3. 2 Timothy 2:15, para.
4. 1 John 3:16.
5. Hymn by W. Y. Fullerton.
6. He died soon after of starvation, because of Indian taboos regarding food which a snake-bite victim may eat.
7. Psalm 37:4.
8. Ephesians 5:24,25, JBP.

— 24 —

Mission Accomplished

*I tell you truly that unless a grain of wheat falls into the earth
and dies, it remains a single grain of wheat; but if it dies, it brings
a good harvest. The man who loves his own life will lose it, and the
man who hates his life in this world will preserve it for eternal life.*[1]

ONE DAY IN SEPTEMBER, 1955, the McCullys
shared with us the most exciting news we could
have hoped for— Ed and Nate, the missionary pilot,
finally spotted some Auca houses not many minutes' flying
time from Arajuno. From that moment on Jim had, as the
Spanish say, 'one foot in the stirrup'. His prayer, his personal
committal, his hopes for Auca work years before, had not
been in vain. Perhaps God was going to give him a share in it
with Ed.

Ed and Nate had begun a regular programme of dropping
gifts to the houses, in hopes of winning friendship and later of
approaching the savages on the ground. They well knew the
failure of other attempts to reach these Indians. But they also
knew Him who said, 'All power is given unto *Me* . . . . Go ye
therefore.'[2]

The work in Shandia was being established. There was now
a nucleus of believers, some of whom could read and understand the Bible. There were a few Scriptures in their hands.

Literary programmes for the boys and girls had been conducted. Material needs had been met — a permanent home, the cement base for a new school building, an adequate airstrip. A foundation for the future development of an indigenous work had been laid. The prayer that had been in Jim's heart for years was prayed with renewed energy now — that those who still had never heard, who had never even had the chance to reject the gospel message, might hear. Many Quichuas had heard; many had rejected, but their blood was now upon their own hands. The blood of the Aucas, however, Jim saw on his own.

He began immediately an even more concerted effort to get the young men to take over responsibilities of leadership in the church. He wrote to his parents on October 23:

Had a great time teaching about patches on old clothes and sweet wine in old bottles this morning. In a culture where the basic drink in intoxicating, like chicha here, and wine in Italy, one gets the full force of such statements as the Lord Jesus' word about a man, who having drunk strong drink does not straightaway desire fresh-made brew. It is a never-failing source of amazement to me how the lofty teaching of our Lord — having been fitted to primitive situations — are frequently more readily understood by a jungle Indian than by a cultured person who is a product of twentieth-century civilisation.

I am working on two of the ex-schoolboys to get them to take the Bible lessons on Tuesdays and Fridays. Venancio has the Wednesday class and Hector (the schoolteacher) the Monday one, so that I have Thursday only — but of course I sit in on all of them. A school is only worth while so long as the truth of God is being taught in it daily, but we have seen in Venancio that the one who teaches profits 100% more than the boys who hear, so we are trying to expand the blessing by giving others a chance. We have begun Friday afternoon meetings at the mouth of the Talac again, and we had twenty in an Indian house day before yesterday.

There have been new Auca attacks recently at the mouth of

the Arajuno. Ed is alert and has an electric fence operating. Tuesday I want to go over and get some phrases in Auca from a captive Auca woman in Ila and I also intend to buy a pig there, for the schoolboys to raise.

October 29. Ed and I flew to Villano on Thursday to visit the Quichuas there for a couple of days. In the afternoon, while Ed and I were chatting downriver with the Indians, they came to tell us that a boy had drowned upriver right where we had bathed. We hurried back to find all the Indians sitting placidly at the beach, talking. They had searched the place for the body (none of it was over my head, and the boy who had drowned was a swimmer, about ten years old). They had found nothing. His mother took a canoe downriver to look for the body, wailing as she went. Two hours later we heard her scream and set off wailing anew. We went to the bathing hole just below where he disappeared and saw her paddling up with a stick, with the naked body in the bow of the canoe. It was too late for artificial respiration. The story is that he and his buddy were both going to bathe. He peeled his clothes off and dove in first, came up laughing, and then shouted, "What's got me by the legs?" At that he was dragged under. The Indians said it was a devil. To the rest of us it was pretty clear that a medium-sized boa, looking for food, had seen his feet, drowned him, and, finding him too big to swallow, had let him go.

That spoiled the afternoon for meeting, and their wake left them too tired to hear anymore, so we returned early Saturday morning. Pray for that group of Indians, for we would like to go there to preach the gospel often, but this may make a barrier in some of their minds.

We walked over to Ila last week and I bought two young pigs for the school to raise. A bunch of our boys are going to Tena today to vote, so our meeting will be smaller tomorrow. There has been a definite crystallising of lines between the Indians who are disposed to hear our message and those who are not. Pray that our testimony may be of God. Hope to go to Talac Pungu this afternoon to announce the good news there again. No real response from anyone there yet, though all seem friendly enough.

Since the Auca operation was kept secret from all but those directly involved at the time, Jim wrote nothing of it to his parents in the above letter. His journal account of the same trip gives also the sequel:

We flew together back to Arajuno, had a little talk about tactics and flew then with the battery-loudspeaker and the Auca phrases I had gotten from Dayuma, the escaped Auca girl in Ila. I repeated the phrases at the first circling of the houses at about two thousand feet: "Trade us a lance for a machete." "We are your friends." We saw perhaps eight Indians scurrying about the house, one crossed the river with something on his head and seemed to flash a new machete. I did not see him return even though it looked as though he only went to the manioc-patch. One rushed into the house and returned with a lance. I took this as evidence that one had gone to get food in exchange and another to get the lance I asked for. But when we dropped the machete on the string they tore off both the machete and the small basket we had tied on to receive some gift in exchange. One went about the house flailing the piece of canvas the machete was wrapped in. We hauled in the line (heavy work!), then dropped it again after several tries, thinking they might tie something on. It dropped into the water and they cut off a section of it, instead. It was old green line of other drops. We pulled it all the way in and set up the loudspeaker again this time, using the phrases "we like you: you will be given a pot". At this a group raced back into the trees behind the house and one lone man walked to the beach. He cupped his hands and seemed to shout. He flashed the new machete over his head. We dropped a small aluminium pot free with ribbons. It contained a yellow shirt and beads. The man on the beach pointed to the place of the fall. Those behind the house got it and one was soon flailing the yellow shirt. As we approached the drop houses two canoes, some distance below, going downstream turned and went upstream hurriedly. I noticed three people come running up through the water onto the beach at one time and a single man with a white cloth another time. Returned via the Curaray looking for possible landing beaches. Hopes not good. Decided to send for a Whittaker landing gear for the plane, and to plan a trip to make an airstrip whenever it arrives. Guide us, Lord God.

Jim carried the Auca phrases written on small cards in his pocket, whipping them out at odd moments to memorise them. At night he would take them to bed, for a last review before he went to sleep. Coming back from an Auca flight with Nate, Jim was so excited he could hardly eat—I am sure that if I had fed him hay he would not have given it a thought. I knew, then, that this was it. Those vows made to God years before, those declarations of willingness to go the whole way—here was the proving ground. I began to have vague, unsettling doubts. Was this truly the plan of God? Had Jim perhaps run ahead? Could God really mean for him to leave the work at Shandia so soon?

Vision is one thing, carrying it through is another. The tangible facts confronted us now. The men had seen the Aucas. They had known of them before, known of their killing apparently for sport, known of their disdain for the white man and all that he represented. But now they had seen them, shouted to them, watched the Aucas beckon and smile at them, and had received combs, feather crowns, and bracelets which Auca hands had made. And these people, these naked Aucas, were still total strangers to the message which the men held in their hands.

But there were other even more immediate facts for the men for face. For Jim, there was a school building just begun, some young Quichua men who needed nurturing in the Word of God, a house and garden which were only now getting into proper shape—to say nothing of a wife and nine-month-old baby who were dependent upon him.

Which way to go? As always, Jim acted on principle rather than on impulse. Had he acted on impulse, I do not know which way he would have chosen, for the impulse to go to the

Aucas immediately was certainly strong; his love for Shandia, for the Quichuas, and for his family was strong, too. But lessons learned in years of acquainting himself with God were applied. In 1948, after studying Numbers 32, where the sons of Reuben and Gad begged Moses to let them settle down in Jazer and Gilead, rather than go across the Jordan, he had written:

> The reason they wanted "this side of Jordan" was that they had seen it and saw it fitted their case. How like many today who never having seen the mission field and, having talents and training usable in this country, stoutly declare "bring me not over Jordan".[3] This is a land of cattle (and I have cattle) or this is a place where teachers are sorely needed, and ably used, and I think I could be a teacher. "Shall your brethren go forth to war and shall ye sit here?"[4] This very thing brought forty years' wandering and left 603,550 carcasses in the wilderness. "Cursed be he that doeth the work of the Lord negligently and withholdeth his sword from blood."[5] The only way to be guiltless is to leave your possessions and little ones and go across to war.

On June 10, 1950, Jim had written:

> Abraham was a slow learner. Commanded to leave his family he took Lot—probably as a kindly gesture, but disobedience all the same. This leaving of the family to God is common among the called, cp. James, John, and Zebedee. Any disobedience soon leads to doubt and dallying.

The question of relative population might also have been considered. Was it reasonable to leave a field of potential thousands of Quichuas in order to reach a tribe which in all probability did not number more than a few hundreds? Here again principles of Scripture gave the answer. Jim had written in 1951:

> The argument of numbers does not hold entirely, since if my

call were to go where a great number are needy, I would not have chosen South America at all, but India. The Scriptures indicate that God intends some from every tribe and tongue and people and nation to be there in the glory, sounding out the praises of the Redeemer. This is specific indication that the gospel must be gotten to tribes who are not yet included in the singing hosts. Hence my burden for cultural groups as yet untouched.

The principles were plain. Jim was prepared to act on them. I was doubtful of my own willingness to let him go, however, until I challenged him with the question that burned in me.

'Jim,' I began, 'are you sure *you* are supposed to go?'

'I am called,' was the simple reply. So, it was all right. Scriptural principles, God-directed circumstances, and Jim's own inward assurance were consonant. I could share in it, then; I could happily help him plan.

I went to Ila myself a few weeks later, and gathered more linguistic data which Jim and I worked over together, comparing my material with his, filing it carefully, studying the constructions. It was a thrill to be starting on a new language again. We talked of the possibility of our moving into the tribe together, as soon as a friendly contact had been established. In fact, as the plan then stood, the men would go down the Curaray river by canoe first, spying out the land and perhaps preparing an airstrip near the river. Jim said I might go along, a suggestion I jumped at eagerly.

For him, the decision meant further heart-searching of his own motives for coming to Ecuador in the first place. He wrote on November 6:

You wonder why people choose fields away from the States when young people at home are drifting because no one wants to take time to listen to their problems. I'll tell you why I left. Because those Stateside young people have every opportunity to study, hear, and understand the Word of God in their own language, and these Indians have no opportunity whatsoever. I have had to make a cross of two logs, and lie down on it, to show the Indians what it means to crucify a man. When there is that much ignorance over here and so much knowledge and opportunity over there, I have no question in my mind why God sent me here. Those whimpering Stateside young people will wake up on the Day of Judgment condemned to worse fates than these demon-fearing Indians, because, having a Bible, they were bored with it—while these never heard of such a thing as writing.

Meanwhile, life in Shandia continued. The old school building of bamboo and thatch looked as though the next wind would demolish it, so Jim was working full speed on a new structure of boards. On November 9 he wrote:

Spent the whole day planing boards, so I'm pretty tired. I'm afraid to leave the Indians alone on the machinery, but they do fine pouring cement. We got seven pillars poured this week and now can't get cement.... I'm thinking of starting Vicente on digging that ditch from the Churu Yaku to the cliff, to get our hydro-electric plant going.

Monday, Lord willing, we'll have another work day and get all the Indains together to drag the girders to the school site. We can get more work done by mixing up a good soup for them than by paying them five sucres.

Valerie has taken to pulling herself up to a standing position in her playpen and letting herself down again. You'd love her now. She's a regular giggling doll. She got sore gums again and it looks as if two more teeth may be coming in soon. She laughs an awful lot, looks like an Elliot. She surely does leave us without any leisure for ourselves except after supper, and we love it. What in the world does one do with triplets?

It has begun to rain a little and I guess we deserve it. Weather has been terribly hot and we've had some really dangerous wind storms. A tree right above the spring, loosened at the roots some time ago, fell over in a small wind today. It's a fight to keep the jungle off your head. We've got to get our land papers settled one of these days, so I must open up the border trails again.

Late afternoons and evenings were spent in concentrated Bible study with young Indians. Jim would get one or two at a time, and go over and over a few verses with them, asking them questions, answering theirs, helping them to dig the meaning for themselves. This, he felt, was the foundation of any indigenous Church. It must be founded on the Word: the members must feed themselves on the Word. He had translated a large part of the Gospel of Luke, and I had a few passages of it translated. He said to me one day, 'We've *got* to get that done before I go to the Aucas.' So we worked over it together, putting our translations together, checking them with Indian informants, and correcting them as best we could. We finished the rough draft before he went.

November 20. A lot of Indians went upriver this week-end, so the number in the meeting was down to forty. Venancio Tapui, the assistant schoolteacher, led the singing, and Gervacio preached. He spoke on "Weep not for me, but for yourselves."[6] Rather good, I thought, though they still need a little poise to look the audience in the eye. Tomorrow Hector will have the Bible class, Tuesday Mariano, Wednesday Venancio, Thursday I give a summary, and Friday Asencio teaches. I am trying to get them all doing something, and they respond. Abelardo will preach this Sunday, God willing. Friday morning Betty and I go to Pano, so Venancio it to take the Talac Pungu meeting.

We have about half of the pillars poured for the new school now. The boys do all right, once they get the swing of the thing. We have all the girders cut, but we will have to have a work day next week to drag them to the site. Betty delivered an Indian woman's baby yesterday while I baby-sat here and made up some reading primers for the girls' school. I have spent some time on the trails this week to get our land-title papers settled. Not a lot of Indians around to work now, as many have gone to the coast and they found a gold-washing spot here this week and have all been panning gold.

Finished the upstairs in the house, using several sizes of flooring from six to nine inches. I couldn't see going to all the work of ripping so much and I think I'll do the same with the school, as there is much less waste that way. We tongue-and-grooved it. I think I'll ship-lap the sides of the school.

I let Valerie go on her feet yesterday and she stood there grinning and teetering for about five seconds alone. Betty is weaning her now, and she is a little pestiferous at night again. Has three upper teeth, and is drinking—a little sloppily—from a cup.

The journal continues:

November 27. Nate and I made my second Auca flight. Flew down their river to the grass shack where there are fenced plantations but no people. Noted an increased amount of cutting down the forest and land-clearing since my last visit. They seem to know what to do with machetes and axes. On the way up we dropped a pair of pants at the first house, where we saw a woman wearing a grey slip that had been dropped on an earlier flight. The second house has a model airplane carved on the house ridge. There we dropped a machete, a pair of short pants, and I saw a thing that thrilled me: it seemed an old man, who stood beside his house, waved with both of his arms as if to signal us to come down. Aucas waving to me to come! At the next house they have made a large clearing and built a bamboo platform on which one, a white-shirted one, stands and waves. Nate dropped a roll of toilet paper and several streamered combs[7] into the trees at the edge of the clearing to try to give them the idea that we want those cut down, too. Dropped a machete there, too, with streamer, which they got. Dropped a pot and an axe-head on the string and they tied something with a red ribbon on, but we lost it trailing it on the way back. Nate was in a hurry as it was late afternoon and he stepped it up, so we lost it.

God, send me soon to the Aucas.

On the same day as the above diary entry, Jim's letter to his parents told only of progress in Shandia:

I am very grateful to say that the Indian fellows are going great guns on the foundation pillars with only one more pouring left before we start on the girders....

The Indians are doing well in taking school devotions, too, and Abelardo had the meeting this morning. He spoke with a little previous help on the epileptic demon boy, the Lord's impatience with the mob who would not believe, His encouragement of the man who believed but needed help in believing, and the disciples, who even though they were believers were impotent because they had not been fervent in prayer and had lost their power.

Every afternoon and some evenings I have young fellows here in the house, and we go over and over the portion and then I listen to them say it, in Quichua much better than mine and with the great advantage that they make real progress in study and delivery. My ministry consists almost entirely in this now, and I am leaving the public presentation of the Word up to them, apart from the Monday afternoon class for all the believers, which I take myself. God help them. They are so desirous of learning and need no pushing at all, but lots of help in understanding the Word.

Thanks loads for sending the seeds. Sorry to hear you had a cold snap before the apples were picked. Are there any good trees left?

Keep praying for the men, Dad, especially those four: Vicente, Venancio, Chaucha, and Capitan. I felt a particular burden for them this week and I believe they may not be far, sometimes. Also do not forget that as the believers establish themselves here we are thinking of outreach with the gospel. If God sends us elsewhere for a couple of months I think it would be a good thing for the young church.

The hibiscus are blazing in the front yard, until some Indian comes along and strips them off. I got some varnish for the house this week and some tar for the roof, so we may get some finishing done on this place before long.

Guess that is all for now. It is after six and the crickets and frogs have begun their dusk-to-dawn concert. We have made a deal with friends to trade a big refrigerator for a good milk cow.

Our pasture is booming now. Thanks for all your love and prayers and care for us. We are constantly encouraged by the hand of God in the work.

I do not know whether Jim had any premonition that God was going to take him up on all he had promised Him— going to answer literally his prayer of April 18, 1948: 'Father, take my life, yea, my blood if Thou wilt, and consume it with Thine enveloping fire. I would not save it for it is not mine to save. Have it, Lord, have it all. Pour out my life as an oblation for the world. Blood is only of value as it flows before Thine altar.'

One of the last of many Quichua hymns he wrote was one describing what happens when a man dies, using a simile from Ecclesiastes 11:3 which was simple and understandable to the Indian:

> *If a man dies, he falls like a tree.*
> *Wherever he falls, there he lies.*
> *If he is not a believer, he goes to the fire-lake.*
>
> *But on the other hand, a believer,*
> *If death overtakes him,*
> *Will not fall, rather will rise*
> *that very moment, to God's house.*

This has become one of the favourites in Shandia, and several have spoken of its peculiar significance for them now.

But the Enemy of Souls is not easily persuaded to relinquish his hold in any territory. Seeing that his authority in the Auca region was going to be challenged, he soon launched an attack on the challengers. Jim was beset with temptation such as had never before assailed him, and that master-weapon, discouragement, which to my knowlege had held no power over him since his arrival in Ecuador, met him at every turn. A gloom seemed to settle over his spirit in December, and it seemed that battles were being fought which I could not share. During this time he wrote a little song to the tune of Balm in Gilead, lovely, plaintive words which lose their poignancy in translation:

> *Sometimes I say to myself,*
> *I am a believer for nothing.*
> *But in the hour when I say, I'm quitting,*
> *Jesus says to me again*
>
> *'Believe me, little son.*
> *Please follow me.*
> *To my Father's house*
> *I wish to lead you, little son,*
> *To a beautiful country.'*

When the beach was discovered on which Nate felt sure a landing would be possible, the plans of going down the Curaray river by canoe were discarded, and also the necessity of a woman's going. I knew that Jim would be leaving without me, and we began to discuss the possibilities of his not returning.

'If God wants it that way, darling,' he said, 'I am ready to die for the salvation of the Aucas.'

Just before Christmas, the Flemings, who had recently moved into Puyupungu, held a fiesta for the Indians there, inviting Jim and Ed to come down to help in the Bible teaching. Jim wrote of this on December 22:

There were about a hundred Indians there from up the Puyo river. Ten or so of our schoolboys and a couple of their sisters went from here on foot (three days!). There was excellent attention, after we took the gin away from them the first night, and there was no more drunkenness either. Pete gave the drink back to the owner on Monday morning. The older men gave very good attention, better than I have ever seen among Indians, and I can only hope that God will give them help to understand their responsibility to choose Christ and make an open stand for Him. Several of the younger fellows have already stopped drinking. Pray for Atanasio and his brother Isaac. Luis Capitan started out from here but got drunk on his way through Puyo and never made it any farther.

Friday morning on the radio contact Ed and I were standing by for Marilou in Arajuno and she sounded scared. An Indian who was staying with her had gotten up early and almost ran head-on into a naked Auca standing with a lance in his hand not fifty yards away from Ed's house. So Ed and Nate flew out there in a hurry, but nothing more was to be seen of him. The Indian had wanted to kill him on sight, but Marilou took his gun away from him and went out shouting a phrase that means "I like you" and tried to give him a machete, but he was gone. One lone wet footprint on a board and some mashed grass where he took off into the jungle were all she saw of him. We would like to reach this tribe. They have never had friendly contact either with whites or Indians, but we know where they live and will make a definite effort to reach them soon. This needs two things. The first is secrecy. There are some who, if they got wind of our plan, could wreck the whole deal, so don't tell this to anyone till I write you to do so. The second thing is prayer. These people are killers and have no idea of getting along with outsiders. Our Indians are deathly afraid of them, as are the whites, and we will be called fools for our pains, but we believe that God has brought Ed to Arajuno for this contact and we want to do his will in taking the gospel to them. They have no word for God in their language, let alone a word for Jesus. There is a "tamed" Auca woman at Ila whom Betty and I have visited and we are working on their language at present. It is much more difficult than Quichua and will need more work at analyzing, so pray for us. You will be hearing more of this in a month or so as plans develop.

Don't bother sending anything with Ruth Jordan, Mom. She already has a big box of stuff which Betty got her mother to buy, including pants and things for me. We don't need a thing but the power of God and that cannot be sent by anyone except via the throne of God.

We spent Christmas with the Flemings and McCullys at Arajuno. Marilou had set up a little bamboo Christmas tree, complete with lights and tinsel. Most of our conversations were taken up with the Aucas, with plans for the first contact on the ground, to take place the following week, and with the study of language data which we had gathered. Nate had succeeded in recruiting a fourth man to go along with Ed, Nate, and Jim— Roger Youderian, missionary to the Jívaros of the southern jungle. Pete Fleming took part in all of the discussion, but had not yet decided to go.

Christmas over, we all returned to Shandia for a New Year's conference for the young Indian believers.

Jim's last letter to his parents was written December 28:

By the time this reaches you, Ed and Pete and I and another fellow will have attempted with Nate a contact with the Aucas. We have prayed for this and prepared for several months, keeping the whole thing secret (not even our nearby missionary friends know of it yet). Some time ago on survey flights Nate located two groups of their houses, and ever since that time we have made weekly friendship flights, dropping gifts and shouting phrases from a loudspeaker in their language, which we got from the woman in Ila. Nate has used his drop-cord system to land things right at their doorstep and we have received several gifts back from them, pets and food and things they make tied onto this cord. Our plan is to go downriver and land on a beach we have surveyed not far from their place, build a tree house which I have prefabricated with our power-saw here, then invite them over by calling to them from the plane. The contact is planned for Friday or Saturday, January 6 or 7. We may have to wait longer. I don't have to remind you that these are completely naked savages (I saw the first sign of clothes last week—a G-string), who have never had any contact with white men other than killing. They do not have firearms, but kill with long chonta-wood lances. They do not have fire except what they make from rubbing sticks together on moss. They use bark cloth for carrying their babies, sleep in hammocks, steal machetes and axes when they kill our Indians. They have no word for God in their language, only for devils and spirits. I know you will pray. Our orders are "the gospel to every creature".[8]—Your loving son and brother, Jim.

The conference ended on New Year's Day. The guests were to leave on the second, and Jim planned to depart for Arajuno, where the men would assemble for the Auca expedition, on the third of January. But on the morning of January 2 Nate called in by radio to say that since the weather was good, they should take advantage of it for flying, and shuttle Jim to Arajuno along with the others. So we were not to have another day together, as anticipated.

Jim began to pack his things. I helped collect everything we could think of that might amuse the Aucas, things that would hold their interest and give more time for the establishment of friendly relations, since the men realised that sustained conversation with the Aucas, by means of the few phrases they knew, would be impossible.

Finally Jim's list was checked off. Everything was ready. We had the radio contact with the plane, Jim slung the carrying net across his forehead, and started for the front door. As he put his hand on the brass handle I almost said aloud:

'Do you realise you may never open that door again?'

He swung it open, followed me out and slammed it, striding down the bamboo trail in his usual firm, determined gait. As we reached the strip, the plane was circling to land, and it was only a matter of a few minutes before Jim kissed me, hopped in beside the pilot, and disappeared over the river. On Wednesday, January 4, 1956, he wrote me a pencilled note from 'Palm Beach':

Betts darling: Just worked up a sweat on the handcrank of the radio. Nobody is reading us but we read all the morning contact clearly. We had a good night with a coffee-and-sandwich break at 2.00 am. Didn't set a watch last night, as we really feel cozy and secure, thirty-five feet off the ground in our three little bunks. The beach is good for landing but too soft for take-offs. We have three alternatives: (1) Wait till the sun hardens it up and sit until a stiff breeze makes it possible to take off, (2) go make a strip in "Terminal City" [the code name of the Auca settlement] and (3) walk out.

We saw puma tracks on the beach and heard them last night. It is a beautiful jungle, open and full of palms. Much hotter than Shandia. Sweat with just a mosquito net over me last night.

Our hopes are up but no signs of the "neighbours" yet. Perhaps today is the day the Aucas will be reached. It was a fight getting this hut up, but it is sure worth the effort to be off the ground.

We're going down now, pistols, gifts, novelties in our pockets, prayer in our hearts. —All for now. Your lover, Jim.

As far as I know, these were the last words Jim wrote. He had yet four days to live. All that we know of those four days is told elsewhere.[9] Suffice to say that on Friday the thrill of Jim's lifetime was given. He took an Auca by the hand. At last the twain met. Five American men, three naked savages.

Two days later, on Sunday, January 8, 1956, the men for whom Jim Elliot had prayed for six years killed him and his four companions.

Notes

1. John 12:24,25, JBP.
2. Matthew 28:18,19.
3. Numbers 32:5.
4. Numbers 32:6.
5. Jeremiah 48:10, para.
6. Luke 23:28.
7. White-cloth streamers were attached to the combs to help the Aucas find them in the forest.
8. Mark 16:15.
9. *Through Gates of Splendour*.

EPILOGUE

W. SOMERSET MAUGHAM, in *Of Human Bondage*, wrote, 'These old folk had done nothing, and when they died it would be just as if they had never been.' Jim's comment on this was, 'God deliver me!'

When he died, Jim left little of value, as the world regards values. He and I had agreed long before that we wanted no insurance. We would store our goods in heaven, share what the Lord gave us as long as we had it, and trust Him literally for the future, in accord with the principles Paul set forth to the Corinthians:

> It is a matter of share and share alike. At present your plenty should supply their need, and then at some future date their plenty may supply your need. In that way we share with each other, as the Scripture says,
>
> > "He that gathered much had nothing over,
> > And he that gathered little had no lack." [1]

When the children of Israel were given manna in the wilderness, they received enough for one day. They were not told to lay up for tomorrow.

So, of material things, there were few: a home in the jungle, a few well-worn clothes, books, and tools. The men who went to try to rescue the five brought back to me from Jim's body his wrist watch, and from the Curaray beach the blurred pages of his college prayer-notebook. There was no funeral, no tombstone for a memorial (news reports of 'five wooden crosses set up on the sand' were not true).

No legacy then? Was it 'just as if he had never been'? 'The world passeth away and the lust thereof, but he that doeth the will of God abideth forever.'[2] Jim left for me, in memory, and for us all, in these letters and diaries, the testimony of a man who sought nothing but the will of God, who prayed that his life would be 'an exhibit to the value of knowing God'.

The interest which accrues from this legacy is yet to be realised. It is hinted at in the lives of Quichua Indians who have determined to follow Christ, persuaded by Jim's example; in the lives of many who still write to tell me of a new desire to know God as Jim did.

When I was a student at Wheaton, I asked Jim to autograph my yearbook. Instead of the usual 'It's been nice knowing you', or some equally meaningless platitude, he wrote:

The dust of words would smother me. 2 Timothy 2:4.

The text cited says, 'No man that warreth entangleth himself with the affairs of this life, that he may please Him who hath chosen him to be a soldier.'

His death was the result of simple obedience to his Captain. Many thousands of men have died in obedience to their captains. The men at Gettysburg were among them. Abraham Lincoln's great words, spoken on that battlefield, apply as well to other soldiers whose obedience to commands is not the less to be imitated:

We cannot dedicate—we cannot consecrate—we cannot hallow—this ground. The brave men...who struggled here, have consecrated it, far above our poor power to add or detract.... It is rather for us to be here dedicated to the great task remaining before us—that...we take increased devotion to that cause for which they gave the last full measure of devotion.

Lincoln and those who were present at that ceremony viewed once again the ground whereon the men struggled—common green fields of Pennsylvania, but fraught with new significance. As I read again Jim's own words, put down in battered notebooks during the common routine of life, they become, for me, fraught with new meaning. To them I can add nothing.

He is no fool who gives what he cannot keep to gain what he cannot lose. (*1949*)

One treasure, a single eye, and a sole master. (*1948*)

God, I pray Thee, light these idle sticks of my life and may I burn for Thee. Consume my life, my God, for it is Thine. I seek not a long life, but a full one, like you, Lord Jesus. (*1948*)

Father, take my life, yea, my blood if Thou wilt, and consume it with Thine enveloping fire. I would not save it, for it is not mine to save. Have it Lord, have it all. Pour out my life as an oblation for the world. Blood is only of value as it flows before Thine altar. (*1948*)

Saturate me with the oil of the Spirit that I may be aflame. But flame is often short-lived. Canst thou bear this, my soul? Short life? In me there dwells the spirit of the Great Short-Lived, whose zeal for God's house consumed Him. "Make me Thy fuel, Flame of God." (*1948*)

Are we willing to build with a trowel in one hand, while the other grasps a sword? (*1948*)

Taking all, Thou givest full measure of Thyself,
With all things else eternal,
Things unlike the mouldy pelf by earth possessed.... (*1948*)

Father, if Thou wilt let me go to South America to labour

with Thee and to die, I pray that Thou wilt let me go soon. Nevertheless, not my will. (*1948*)

How few, how short these hours my heart must beat—then on, into the real world where the unseen becomes important. (*1948*)

Of the coffin: a swallowing up by Life. For this I am most anxious. (*1948*)

Ah, how many Marahs have been sweetened by a simple, satisfying glimpse of the Tree and the Love which underwent its worst conflict there. Yes, the Cross is the tree that sweetens the waters. "Love never faileth." (*1949*)

As your life is in His hands, so are the days of your life. But don't let the sands of time get into the eye of your vision to reach those who sit in darkness. *They simply must hear.* Wives, houses, practices, education, must learn to be disciplined by this rule: "let the dead attend to the affairs of the already dead, go thou and attend the affairs of the dying". (*1948*)

Overcome anything in the confidence of your union with Him, so that contemplating trial, enduring persecution or loneliness, you may know the blessedness of the "joy set before", for "We are the sheep of His pasture. Enter into His gates with thanksgiving and into His courts with praise." And what are sheep doing going into the gate? What is their purpose inside those courts? To bleat melodies and enjoy the company of the flock? No. Those sheep were headed for the *altar*. Their pasture feeding had been for one purpose: to test them and fatten them for bloody sacrifice. Give Him thanks, then, that you have been counted worthy of His altars. Enter into the work with praise. (*1949*)

To his mother when his brother Bert sailed for Peru:

Remember—and I don't mean to sound pedantic or impudent as if I knew all the costs—remember that we have bargained with Him who bore a Cross, and in His ministry to those disciples His emphasis was upon sacrifice, not of worldly goods so much as upon *family ties*. Let nothing turn us from the truth that God has determined that we become strong under fire, after the pattern of the Son. Nothing else will do.

> *"O Prince of Glory, who dost bring*
> *Thy sons to glory through the Cross,*
> *Let us not shrink from suffering*
> *Reproach or loss." (1949)*

I must not think it strange if God takes in youth those whom I would have kept on earth till they were older. God is peopling Eternity, and I must not restrict Him to old men and women. (*1950*)

Granted, fate and tragedy, aimlessness and just-missing-by-a-hair are part of human experience, but they are not all, and I'm not sure they are a major part, even in the lives of men who know no Designer or design. For me, I have seen a Keener Force yet, the force of Ultimate Good working through seeming ill. Not that there is rosiness, ever; there is genuine ill, struggle, dark-handed, unreasoning fate, mistakes, "if-onlys" and all the Hardyisms you can muster. But in them I am beginning to discover a Plan greater than any could imagine. (*1951*)

The principle of getting by spending is illustrated by the actions of God:

> *"He had yet one, a Beloved Son."*
> *"He giveth not the Spirit by measure."*
> *"He spared not His own Son."*
> *"He emptied Himself."*

Is heaven the poorer for this spending? Nay, both heaven and earth are enriched by it. Who dare not follow God's example? (*1951*)

Only I know that my own life is full. It is time to die, for I have had all that a young man can have, at least all that this young man can have. I am ready to meet Jesus. (*December, 1951*)

Gave myself for Auca work more definitely than ever, asking for spiritual valour, plain and miraculous guidance.... (*May, 1952*)

The will of God is always a bigger thing than we bargain for. (*1952*)

Give me a faith that will take sufficient quiver out of me so that I may sing. Over the Aucas, Father, I want to sing! (*July, 1952*)

I know that my hopes and plans for myself could not be any better than He has arranged and fulfilled them. Thus may we all find it, and know the truth of the Word which says, "He will be our Guide even until death."

Notes

1. 2 Corinthians 8:15, JBP.
2. 1 John 2:17.

Notes

EVERY EFFORT has been made to find the sources of
quotations in this book. The author will be grateful
for information regarding errors or omissions.

Jim's writings are full of allusions to Scripture which he
did not put in quotation marks. These are not included in
end-of-chapter *Notes*. I have also omitted any references to
quotations for which a reference is given in the main text,
even if the reference is only a partial one.

Owing to the fact that Jim usually quoted from memory,
there is sometimes a difference of a word or two between his
quotation and the original text. In other cases, he made his
own translation from a Hebrew or Greek text. Some references
which Jim put in quotation marks are allusions to Scripture
texts. In all three of these cases, I have listed the reference
with the word *para.* (paraphrase) following.

Abbreviations used in end-of-chapter Notes.

> JBP J. B. Phillips' translations of the New Testament
> ASV American Standard Version of the Bible
> RSV Revised Standard Version
> JND J. N. Darby's translation of the Bible

All other Biblical references are from the Authorized
Version.

ELISABETH ELLIOT

NO GRAVEN IMAGE

OM
publishing

FOREWORD
by J. I. Packer

When would-be writers ask me for advice on fulfilling their ambition, I warn them that there is more to it than Enid Blyton's formula, going broody over a typewriter, might suggest. I tell them there are three essentials: first, something to say, something you have seen and want to share; second, enough technique to enable it to find its own best shape on paper; third, a strong bottom on which you can sit for hours together handcrafting sentences, paragraphs, and chapters. Sometimes my advice stops folk in their tracks. How much real wisdom it contains others must judge; I only know that this is what has come home to me during twenty-five years of trying to write myself. I judge, however, from the vivid, economical, fastidious Anglo-Saxon which fills Elisabeth Elliot's shrewd and shapely books that she, at least, is a member of my club.

No Graven Image is a novel that grew out of personal missionary experience of which she has written elsewhere, notably in *These Strange Ashes*, *The Savage My Kinsman*, *The Liberty of Obedience* and a haunting article, "The Wake," in the March 1964 issue of *Eternity*. I suppose she turned from biography, autobiography, and essays to the novel form (i.e., an imagined story of people in relationship against a chosen background of scenes and events) because it was most apt for what she had to say. Certainly, the sense of significance for the reader which a good novelist evokes by rousing him to imaginative involvement in the story is more than nonfictional analysis can ever convey. (Thus, if you want to feel the force of Tolstoy's view of Christianity, you read, not *What I Believe*, but his novel, *Resurrection*.) *No Graven Image* shows its author to be a pretty good novelist, and anyone who can identify with her narrator's state of mind depicted in the opening chapters will find the story dynamite.

Christian novelists today have a hard furrow to plough. The secular world finds their vision of life unconvincing, and the Christian world lacks interest in their attempts to express that vision in their stories. Part of the trouble here is the prevalence of a different type of Christian fiction, stemming from the "edifying" tracts and children's stories of the last century, having the nature not of novels but of sermons. As musical comedies tend to embody what P. G. Wodehouse called the oldest plot in the world, boy meets girl—boy loses girl—boy gets girl, so this type of Christian fiction is usually built round a two-pronged plot formula, someone turns from God and finds trouble—someone in trouble turns to God and is blessed. Unhappily, these moral tales, though not novels, often claim this name, and so spread the idea that this is what "real" Christian novels are like. The result, both funny and sad, is that when folk fed on this diet read a genuine novel by a Christian novelist (Graham Greene, say, or Charles Williams, or George Target, or Flannery O'Connor, or Fyodor Dostoevski, or Aleksandr Solzhenitsyn) their appreciation, if any, is overshadowed by regret and puzzlement that the author did not so manipulate his characters as to produce a straightforward moral tale, clearly illustrating the gospel. No suspicion that the novel is a different thing from the moral tale enters their heads.

What, then, is the novelist's task? Karl Barth, who though no literary critic was a Christian, a reader, a thinker and very much a modern man, answered the question thus: "I expect him [the novelist] to show me man as he always is in the man of today, my contemporary... I expect the novel to give evidence on every page that its author not only knows this man (his character) properly and sees right through him, from the depths of his heart to his outward manners and mode of speaking, but also treats him honestly, i.e., loves him as he is and as he is not, without regret or contempt. Furthermore, it should tell me what its author finds special in this man—that and no more. In other words, it should have no plans for educating me, but should leave me to reflect (or not) on the basis of the portrait with which I am presented. Finally, its form should correspond to the portrait of the man whom it presents; its form should be necessary, strict and impressive to the extent that I do not forget the man I have been shown in his temporal and timeless aspects. I should be able to live with him, and indeed perhaps have to live with him, again and again" (quoted in E. Busch, *Karl Barth*, p.313). On this showing, Barth would have recognized *No Graven Image* as a true novel, just as he would have recognized its vision of God's sovereign freedom as a truth of biblical faith.

When the book first appeared in the USA, some took it as expressing disillusionment with evangelical missionary endeavor as such, and were offended. But this is clearly not its thrust, even though for the sake of the story some cultural aspects of that endeavor get guyed in a way which they might be thought to deserve. *No Graven Image* is not bitter or resentful (in fact, patient good-will suffuses it throughout). It is a simple story about knowing God, or (which is really the same thing) the growth of a soul, and the place where the action happens is in the narrator's mind. She starts as the victim of a well-meant, God-shrinking, success-oriented notion of the "work" (Christian work, missionary work, God's work, my work) which fills her with zany confidence but keeps her from realism about either herself or her God. By the end of the book she knows what the authors of Job and Ecclesiastes taught—that God's providence is inscrutable, that apparent tragedy, frustration and waste are the lot of God's servants no less than of other men (perhaps, indeed, more), that God exalts himself by putting us down, and that it is not for us to claim to see the meaning of all that happens. Learning this leaves her an outsider, no longer able to identify with the phony streak in what she embraced before; but in not identifying she finds herself free, God real, and life good. How powerfully the narrative builds to its climax, and how hauntingly it poses its questions about ends justifying means, results mocking motives, and the value of misguided sincerity, the reader will discover. I must stop, lest I spoil for you a story which will rivet your attention from the start, and at the end blow your mind.

I first read *No Graven Image* ten years ago, and it bowled me over; partly, no doubt, because its vision of God struck so many chords in my own experience. I thought it was a little classic; a miniature maybe, but a gem. Reading it again, this time without the surprise and excitement of unanticipated empathy, I find that I think just the same. I count myself honoured to be asked to commend it to a new generation of readers, and I do so with very great pleasure.

But do please remember—it's a novel; it is not anything else.

I will manifest my holiness among you in the sight of the nations.
And you shall know that I am the Lord.

And I shall be profaned through you in the sight of the nations;
And you shall know that I am the Lord.

And her prophets have daubed for them with whitewash, seeing
false visions and divining lies for them, saying, "Thus says the
Lord God," when the Lord has not spoken.

EZEKIEL 20:41, 42; 22:16, 28.

INSIDE THE railway car there was a vacuum of stillness which seemed to shut in the passengers, making us acutely conscious of the slightest sound or movement. For no good reason, I was listening, hardly drawing breath. It was not quite six o'clock in the morning. Everyone else was half-asleep and thoroughly chilled, for the sun had not yet risen, but they waited with far more patience than I for the train to begin its journey up into the western cordillera of the Andes and down to the coast. It had been scheduled to leave at half past five, and although I had been in Ecuador long enough to learn to expect delays, I was especially eager to begin the last leg of what had been a very long journey, a whole life's preparation for missionary work among mountain Indians.

The door opened, relieving the vacuum, and a timid voice spoke. "Little suitcases. Toys. One sucre."

A woman in a plaid shawl and long wool skirt came in, steering a basket in front of her between the closely set seats. She saw me as soon as I turned. A foreigner was always a likely customer.

"Only one sucre, señorita." She stopped by my seat, proffering the basket with a look of humility and hope.

[1]

One sucre. About five cents. I took one of the tiny valises from the basket. It was made of layers of newspaper, pasted together and covered with an imitation leather paper. There were a little handle and a strap with a gold-colored buckle to fasten it shut. The valise measured perhaps two inches across.

"Did you make it?" I asked.

"*Sí*, señorita. I made it myself."

"But what a lot of work! One sucre, did you say?"

"*Sí*, señorita, one sucre, no more. It is not very expensive, señorita. Look at how nicely it is made. It is very pretty. Just one sucre."

"Oh no, it is not very expensive," I agreed. "I don't see how you can make money on it at all."

"Well, I don't make much, señorita, but it is something. I have six children. I try to care for them. Sometimes my daughter helps me. She is twelve. She can paste the paper for me. Don't you want one, señorita?"

"Yes, I want one." I put the sucre into her hand and took the little suitcase. I would find some child to give it to. An Indian child, perhaps. The MacDonalds, who were to meet me at the end of the train trip, were older. Their children were grown.

It would be nice to be met this time by experienced missionaries, and to stay in their home. My arrival in Guayaquil, six months before, had been quite different. The thin line of shore that I could see when the ship dropped anchor was like a line drawn to mark off a section of my life. When I crossed it, everything would change. The days aboard ship had given me a taste of a world I had never known and would not know again, a world of luxuries such as Camembert cheese, deft waiters, soft music at dinner. Standing on deck during the last moments before

[2]

disembarking I felt a faint wind stir my hair and I turned to face it, closed my eyes, and tried to see the far-off shore with its palm trees and thatched huts, the brown children running on the sand where the wind came from. It would not be long. Unaccountably, I wished that it would be. The door opened behind me, giving forth the breath of the little world within—cooled air, smelling of perfumes, cigarette smoke, steaks, alcohol. I wanted to prolong, not just indefinitely but forever, those timeless days of the voyage, when I was no longer preparing to be a missionary nor had yet become one. The irresponsibility was intoxicating. Now I would have to cross the line.

I went below and put a few last things into my suitcase. My leather-bound Bible lay on the dresser and I reached toward it for reassurance. "Fear thou not, for I am with thee." The Bible had opened easily at that passage, for it was a favorite of mine and it was to me now the voice of God. I left the ship, and then there had been the trip upriver by launch and my first night in an Ecuadorian hotel, with its smell of plaster, mold, cheap soap and floor wax; the smothering heat, the short bed and unyielding pillow, the sounds of coughing and spitting in the hall, of dogs barking in the streets. A clock had boomed out the hour and the half hour, a mosquito sang his thin song close to my ear, and a trumpet in a nearby dance hall had hooted and shrilled. The place of God's choice for me, I had reflected, so little discomforts, little sacrifices, were to be welcomed.

"Toys, sir? Suitcases, señora? Toys for your children. Only one sucre." The poor woman was back, making another attempt to sell her trinkets. Small chance that anyone in the next car had bought one—it was second class, with long wooden benches facing the center on which huddled Indians in ponchos and women with great cloth bundles and baskets. The toy vendor's voice was drowned much of the time by the strident cries of white-aproned women on the platform who were selling plates of cooked food.

In front of me sat a man in a black hat and a dark red poncho, cradling a burlap-wrapped package on his lap; the smell of the damp wool of his poncho was mixed with the heavy sweet smell of brilliantine with which his wife had slicked her black braid. Across the aisle were two men in black suits and black ties, reading newspapers. Three children a little ahead of them had turned one of the seats around to make a cubicle of privacy. With their mother they made a small cosmos, squirming and twisting in the seats as they arranged themselves and their bundles, looking at last with satisfaction at one another. There was no one else in the train, so far as they were concerned. Yes, there was. One of them spied me. Three other faces turned toward me. *La gringa!* Look at the *gringuita!* There was that word again—the foreigner—but I was used to it now. I had heard it a hundred times in the streets of Guayaquil, and later in Ambato, where I studied Spanish. They turned back and looked solemnly at their mother as though their security had been jeopardized. The two who faced me shifted their eyes quickly toward me now and then, and I tried to meet their glances with a smile. I wouldn't hurt you. Really, I am not dangerous, even if I am a *gringa.* They pretended they hadn't seen.

"Eggs! Fresh-cooked eggs!" A woman stuck her head in the car, and behind her another pushed in and shrieked, "Eggs! Potatoes! Tender corn!"

A whistle screamed, the train suddenly hissed and jerked, the two vendors lurched against the doorway and

[4]

scrambled for the platform. Poor things! How much could they make in that business? I looked out the window and saw the woman pass with her little suitcases, the supply apparently undiminished.

"Now we are going!" cried the children.

"Shut up!" said the mother.

Another tremendous crash, a great grinding and clatter, and the train began to move.

I should have bought ten of those toy valises, I thought. At least ten. I could have done that for the poor woman. I twisted my neck to see if I could still see her. Yes. There she stood with her basket. I felt that she was looking at me, though we had moved too far away to be sure. She was still standing there as a curve in the track put us out of sight.

I was on my way. Not yet a bona fide missionary, not quite yet. But soon . . .

It was impossible to arrange my knees comfortably in the short space between the seats, for they had been built for Ecuadorians. I had never thought of myself as tall—I was of average height in my own country—until I rode in Ecuadorian buses where I could not stand up straight. A cold draft blew up from the floorboards of the squeaking, creaking train and I tried to twine my legs together to keep them warm. Once a position was found, the effort of changing it was too great, and my lower extremities were soon numb. I decided to ignore this, and turned my attention to the passing scenery.

The track wound through cobblestone streets lined with whitewashed adobe walls and stone-block buildings much like those of Ambato and other sierra towns. I would be glad to leave cities behind now, and reach at last the limitless freedom and purity of the high Andes.

[5]

When the train reached the outskirts of the city the dusty dirt roads, lined with mud walls which seemed to have grown out of them, depressed me, as the vast slum areas which circled the city of Guayaquil had depressed me. But somehow, Riobamba's poor did not seem quite so poor, nor its squalor quite so squalid as Guayaquil's. There were garbage heaps in doorways here, there were half-clad, filthy-faced children, some of them boys with shoulder-length hair (for, an Ecuadorian had told me, "If you cut their hair before they learn to talk, they'll never talk"), there were the same rows of windowless houses with tiny shops squeezed into the doorways and strange things floating in great copper basins of boiling oil set on charcoal braziers on the street, there were the blaring radios and, in even less prosperous districts, the empty stillness, as though a plague had carried off all the inhabitants. But as the train crept hesitantly toward the countryside, through the widening streets and more sparsely scattered hovels, I wondered whether I had become so accustomed to poverty that it no longer seemed deplorable to me, or whether it was perhaps the clearness of the mountain air with its blue sky and sunshine and absence of vultures that made Guayaquil's poverty seem, in retrospect, extreme.

For days I had waited in the port city for my baggage to be unloaded from the barges which lay at anchor in the Guayas River. I had nothing at all to do. The days melted into one another, a long, monotonous succession of almost unendurably hot mornings, afternoons and evenings. One day I had seen a man with no eyes and no feet who sat on the pavement with his back against a building, holding a hat to the passersby, his head lolling back on his neck. Two holes where his eyes had been were directed toward me. A girl of about eight lay in his lap, emaciated and limp, with

[6]

immense black eyes rimmed with shadows and shining with fever. She gazed up into my face without a sound. Her lips were dry, her mouth hung slightly open, and flies crawled around the edges of her hair. I stopped, stunned by the sight, and tried to think what to do. The Bible story of Peter and John and the lame man came to mind. The man had asked for money and been healed instead. If only I could give the man his sight, the child her health! I couldn't, so, like Peter and John, I said, "Such as I have give I thee," and dropping a few coins into the greasy hat turned away.

And what of the woman this morning, selling toy suitcases? I could still see her face, turned toward me as the train had taken me out of sight. I could, of course, have bought the whole lot of toys. Then, I argued with myself, where would she have been? Not very far ahead. And next week? What could I have done to be of any lasting use? Physical help for the man and child in Guayaquil, economic help for the woman in Riobamba (and for the dozens of beggars I had met in the intervening time)— always the same problem: what to do? Witness to them! came the answer. Missionary reports were always full of such cases, but the aim was supposed to be spiritual work. I found it hard to acknowledge that spiritual need was not somehow correlative to physical, and when confronted with especially pitiful individuals I struggled consciously with the mandate to tell them of Christ. Was it the voice of God, the voice of a dozen preachers I had heard, the voice of an enlightened conscience—or were these voices synonymous? In a dusty, high-ceilinged Sunday-school room with worn red carpets and a picture of the Good Shepherd at the front I had learned the Westminster Shorter Catechism: "The chief end of man is to glorify God and enjoy Him forever." Then, in a missionary service in another church years later I heard that the chief end of man is to stop as many as possible of the millions from perishing. "Witness to them! Speak to at least one soul a day—remember, they are headed for blackness of darkness"—and here the preacher shook his jowls—"FOREVER!" I was so appalled that I had not stopped to sort out the confusions the two ideas had brought to my mind. I had gone through life with a vague but constant consciousness of having left undone the most vital of things I ought to have done. Others did them, and told about them triumphantly: how they had spoken to a seatmate on a bus, a gasoline station operator, a hairdresser or a ticket agent. Whenever I determined to lay hold of such an opportunity it seemed to evaporate. But when I reached my destination things would be different.

A cinder blew into my eye and I turned from the train window to find my handkerchief.

"She is crying," I heard one of the three children say. I looked to find them all staring enthralled at the *gringa*. How long had they been watching me? I smiled, but again they pretended not to see. Their mother turned then and gazed directly at me, her curiosity undisguised. It was unsettling enough to have a foreigner on the train. It was unbearable that the foreigner should be crying. She saw, however, that I was not crying, and spoke in a whisper to the children, who stopped staring. Soon one of them, a charming five- or six-year-old with a frayed pink ribbon in her luxuriant black curls, came over to where I sat.

"Good morning, señorita," she began. "You are crying, aren't you?"

"Oh no! Something got in my eye. What is your name?"

"Felicita. And yours?"

"Margarita. Are you going to the coast?"

"Why is your hair red?" she asked, paying no attention to my question.

"Red? Do you think my hair is red?"

"Yes. Very red. Why is it red?"

My hair, I thought, was brown—perhaps it had a few reddish lights in it at times, but certainly no one had ever called it red. I had wished it were. Anything but this nondescript brown.

"Your hair is a beautiful black, Felicita. How lucky you are!"

"Why do you wear glasses?"

"Felicita!" Her mother had overheard the question. "Come here."

I smiled at the wide-eyed child. "Go quickly, but come back if your mother says you may."

She went back to her seat, on which she knelt, her chin resting on two small hands placed on the back of the seat. She continued to gaze earnestly at me, pondering the strangeness of this stranger. She *was* crying, and her hair *is* red, and she thinks mine is beautiful and why does she wear those glasses and that ugly coat? (I had on a trenchcoat, belted at the waist, bulky with a sweater underneath.) Why does the *gringa* keep smiling at me? She doesn't know me.

Yes, Felicita, I thought, I am an oddity to you. You would never understand what I am doing here.

There was only honest puzzlement in her face. In a child in Guayaquil I had seen, I thought, resentment. Was it I who had changed? Perhaps I had been overly sensitive to being an alien. There was a woman selling *empanadas*—a kind of turnover—on the sidewalk under an umbrella-covered stand. She had a child hung in a cloth from her shoulder, a long-legged thin boy of at least two who was pulling noisily on her pale breast. She fried the pastries on a tiny stove, turning them with a great perforated ladle, shouting *"Empanadas!"* as she lifted the flaky things from their immersion in the reeking oil and dropped them onto the pile in a washbasin. She took me in at a glance, swiftly comprehending all she wanted to know of me, from head to toe. She had her black hair fastened in a braid with a bit of brown wool entwined in it, and wore a faded cotton dress with the snaps open down the front, a stained apron of heavy duck, black scuffs on her short, wide feet and the look of knowing all on her hard face. The child's hair nearly covered his eyes as he peeked up sideways at me from the source of nourishment. "This is mine," he seemed to be saying to me, "and my mother is mine and we belong here in the center of the whole world, and who are you?"

A displaced person, I had felt—neither at home, nor yet in my appointed niche—but just as I was recalling the uneasiness of that moment I saw from the train a group of Indians trotting by on their way to market in the city, each with a lumpy shawl on his back stuffed with wares to sell. There, I thought to myself, goes my reason for being here. "Go ye into all the world, and preach the Gospel to every creature. . . ." You would never believe it, Felicita, but I belong here. I am under orders.

A low ceiling of mist still lay over the city, and the smoke from the little mud houses spread itself under the mist. Sunlight slanted through in places, exposing an unmade bed through an open doorway here, a cluttered counter in a shop there. Then the railroad track began to rise slightly. For a few seconds we were closed in cloud. Thus blinded I became aware of the sound of the train wheels on the track. They clattered and thumped, thumped and clattered. Suddenly we emerged into sunlight again. There, to the north of us, rose Chimborazo, glittering pure and proud in the morning sun, its tremendous shoulders smooth with snow, the deep ravines blue with shadow against them. The lower slopes, covered with brown grass, spread and spread and spread, out onto the misty *páramo*, patches of brown in varying shades showing where Indians had cultivated. The motion and the noise of the train faded again from my awareness and the city receded behind us. The maguey-lined roads we were passing, with eucalyptus groves and tile-roofed shacks, were blurred. I saw only the peak, that clear peak, radiant, towering, full of strength and peace. It drew me as it had never drawn me in the months when I saw it from Ambato. I felt magnetized, yet its cold brilliance and total inaccessibility cowed me at the same time that it drew me. The winding of the railroad track took me out of range again and once more I smelled the damp wool in front of me, the banana peels on the floor, the smoke of the engine.

"Here I am," I thought, with a muffled kind of excitement, wanting to savor every part. God knew the whole picture when He called me here, but I would have to find it out little by little. He knew the beginning and the ending and everything that fitted in between. For me, the beginning had been six years before. I was nineteen then, and had just finished my sophomore year in Bible college. A missionary from Africa was to speak and show slides at church. It was a very warm night, and a week night too, not a Sunday. Going to church would necessitate washing my hair and ironing a dress and it was too hot to do either, but the man was a friend of the family, my father was a pillar of the church and a great supporter of missions, and it was unthinkable for the Sparhawks not to attend, en masse, such a meeting.

He spoke on a verse from the Bible, "I the Lord have called thee." He emphasized the word "thee." I had heard a hundred missionaries speak, I had looked at thousands of slides, of which a large percentage showed natives of one color or another lined up with smiles on their faces before thatched church buildings. There was nothing distinctive about either the man or the message on that July evening, but there was something peculiarly personal—I could neither explain nor ignore it—about the way those words sounded to me then. "I the Lord have called *thee*."

Not that the idea of being a missionary was new to me. Not by any means. I had talked about the possibility since I was a small child. My aunt was a missionary in India and she sent me little brass bells and brought me a cobra-skin purse when she came home on furlough. She always stayed at our house for several months out of a year's furlough, and we had a picture of her in an elaborate brass frame— she was dressed in a sari and had a little brown baby in her arms—on the living-room table. I think my father, who almost worshipped her, secretly hoped that I would feel called to join her in the orphanage work. He was a construction engineer who tithed his income very carefully. He had wanted to be a missionary, he said, or at least go into what he called "full-time Christian work," but the Lord had showed him that He could use businessmen too, and He wanted my father to support missionaries rather than to be one. So he taught a Sunday-school class, belonged to a group of businessmen dedicated to winning their colleagues to Christ, and brought his children up in the fear of the Lord. One of my brothers had gone into the construction business on his own, and the other was in seminary preparing to be a minister. My father could not take issue with either choice, but he still hoped most fervidly that one of his children would go to the foreign field for the Lord. My little sister, four years younger than I, was the darling of the family, and although she talked about being a missionary nurse I felt that my parents were not really eager to see her leave her native shores.

Once, when I was about eleven, a visiting preacher had thundered about the unwillingness of Christians to "sell out" for God. We sang for the closing hymn "Is your all on the altar?" and he moved from the pulpit down to the altar rail and asked those of us who "really meant business" to come forward.

> You cannot have rest, and be perfectly blest,
> Until all on the altar is laid,

sang the congregation. I knew that I wanted to be blessed, I meant business with God, so whatever it was that needed to be laid on the altar I was determined to lay. I went forward.

There had been other times, too. In missionary meetings when volunteers were called for, I had never been sure enough to stand up, but usually an invitation was given for those who would be willing to go if the Lord should call. I stood up for that one. Now, it seemed to me, He had called. But the missionary from Africa did not ask anyone to stand or come forward. He did not even ask for a show of hands. For a moment I felt cheated, but then I was glad, for when I went home and knelt down alone in my room to pray I was confident that I had not been merely the victim of an emotional appeal, a public altar demonstration, but that I had indeed heard the call of the Lord, commissioning me to be His ambassador in some far-off place. India, perhaps, but that was not important to me just then. "Lord," I prayed, "I think You meant me tonight, and if I am not mistaken that it is You that have called, give me one more sign—tomorrow morning—to confirm it."

Next morning when I went to breakfast there was a copy of *Mary Slessor of Calabar* at my place. I found an inscription in the flyleaf: "To Margaret, with the prayer that this great missionary's life may inspire you, and that the Lord may lead you to the place of His choice. Love, Mother." How had she known? I had said nothing to her or anyone else. Clearly, this was the sign I had prayed for. I ate my toast and drank my coffee with a sense of wonder at the destiny that had been shown me. Only my sister was at the table—the others had eaten earlier—but I said nothing to her.

I went into the living room afterward and stood looking at the carved wood motto which hung over the mantel-piece: "Fear thou not, for I am with thee." This, too, was the voice of God. The motto had hung there for as long as I could remember—sometimes partly hidden by a vase of flowers or by Christmas cards or family pictures or mis-sionary curios which were later relegated to the attic—and I had looked at it without seeing it, but today it spoke to me, and the words "thou" and "thee" were in italics.

Now the train was passing through a desert area. Tall cactus, thick with dust, lined the railroad track. Sand was banked along the road which ran beside us and the wind blew it through the cracks of the windows and along the floor of the carriage. The sun was high now, shining on the dry landscape, and it seemed that it ought to be hot, but the cold wind kept wrapping around my legs. The snowcap was hidden from view by a hill now. A woman hurried alone up a stony path, her shawl pulled tightly across her mouth, her head pushing into the wind. No other human being was in sight.

I began to feel sleepy, and tried to lean my head against the window. The vibration was too much and my head dropped and snapped miserably, but I could not hold it erect. I slept a little and dreamed I was riding a subway on a snowy night, returning to Bible school with fellow students.

There was the sudden woof-woof of a whistle. The brakes screamed. Had we reached a station? I lifted my head. A flock of sheep was tumbling across the tracks, followed by a frantic woman waving a stick. Spread out on all sides was a valley, green and brown and gray, dotted with hundreds of grass-roofed huts, scored with earthen walls and maguey-plant fences, rows of dark-green, stiff-pointed clusters. The mountains swept up on both sides in vast, easy slopes as though some huge hand had smoothed them back from the floor of the valley, in which lay a great sheet of water, feathered with reeds and flecked with white birds. A field of tall wheat breathed in the wind, gently rising and sinking like a living thing in the sunlight. The sky was wide and brilliant blue, an immense canopy flung from the points of the mountains over this paradise beneath. The size of the valley made the speed of the train seem to diminish almost to a crawl. As we rounded the shore of the lake I could see Indians sitting astride their rush rafts in the water. They were gathering something in the reeds—perhaps it was the reeds themselves. No doubt that was it, I thought, for I had seen the mats they sold in the markets of Ambato, and had heard they were made from lake grass.

The little mud houses were everywhere. Nowhere in Ecuador had I seen so many. They seemed to peep suspiciously at me from under the shaggy, steeply-pitched roofs, like the child who had peeped at me so smugly from his mother's breast.

"Look on the fields, for they are white already unto harvest. . . . Pray ye therefore the Lord of the harvest, that He would send forth labourers into his harvest. . . ."

I had come. Here were the fields, teeming and ready.

"AND DID you find the train trip hard, dear?" Mrs. Mac-Donald passed me a cup of tea.

"Oh no," I said, "I was a little sleepy since I had to get up very early, but the scenery was so beautiful I didn't think much about the train itself."

"Not what you're used to in the United States, is it, though? I hear they've beautiful trains there." Mrs. Mac-Donald's t's and r's were still Scottish, though she said she had been away from her homeland for many years. She poured a cup of tea, moved an empty cup closer, and poured the tea from the first cup into the second. I watched with interest.

"And now you're wondering what it is I'm doing," she said, her pink cheeks lifting in a smile. "Oh, it's a funny custom. Ian likes his cup warmed first, so I pour him another one. That way he gets it really hot." She moved the sugar bowl toward me.

"Ian. Ian, dearie?" she called.

"I'm coming, Janet. Coming right away." He came into the room through a doorway covered by a flowered curtain. His feet scraped slightly as he moved. He paused a moment and looked steadily at us both—first at his wife, then at me. His hands trembled almost imperceptibly as he put them on the back of his chair and pulled it slowly out from the table. He smiled and sat down.

"Some of your oat cakes, dearie. I thought maybe Margaret would like them too. My mother used to make these," she said, lifting the china plate of little brown biscuits and passing it to me. "Ian likes them very much. But I can't get quite the right kind of oats here. I have to substitute."

"They never tasted better to me in Scotland," said Ian, picking one up almost tenderly. He lifted his face and closed his eyes. "Father," he said, "You've given us all things good, and we thank You from our hearts. Amen."

I had heard many prayers in my life, but few with which I so wholeheartedly joined. It was exactly what I wanted to say. The marvel of that broad valley with its lake and white birds and straw huts and mountain bastions; then the trip through the pass and up into further hills, across more desert and through fields of calla lilies, lovely in their classic simplicity, then the arrival at the Wairapamba railroad station, where I saw the kind face (like the Good Shepherd, I had thought at once) of Mr. MacDonald looking over the shoulders of some Indians who were waiting; now this room, with its sunlight coming through the geraniums on the windowsill, the taste of the hot tea and the crumbly cakes—for all of this, and for the honest warmth of the two people who had received me, I was more grateful than an elaborate prayer could have expressed. "All things good. We thank You."

It was as I had hoped. If God had called me to Ecuador there would be a sense of belonging, a confidence that things were as they should be. During those strange and uneasy first days in the country this confidence had been lacking, and I had wondered whether I had made a mistake.

The certainty of my call seemed to wane, perhaps at times because of the oppressive heat, perhaps because of the shock of finding myself an alien. My mind was soon at rest when such explanations could be found. When they could not, I was troubled. Why was it, for example, when I helped a group of missionaries in Guayaquil with the task of folding Gospel tracts, that their conversation seemed somehow staged? They spoke of people in terms of "souls," cities in terms of "need," and church meetings in terms of attendance. Not that I would at that time have found fault with this view. Far from it. The fault lay, I suspected, with myself in not being able wholeheartedly to share it. Had I not been called to cast in my lot with these servants of the Lord?

But here in the MacDonald home things were different. I found a peace and a simplicity, which acted like a balm to my spirit. The teacups were of bone china, and the spoons were thin sterling—they must be very old, I thought, probably an heirloom from Mrs. MacDonald's family. The furniture was crude and heavy, of Ecuadorian design. They lived neither in unrelieved ugliness nor in inappropriate luxury, it seemed to me, and I was reminded of home, where a few very beautiful things that had been given to us, such as an Oriental rug and a cloisonné vase, were mingled with practical and inexpensive things which my parents, who considered all their money the Lord's, had bought.

"You can't imagine how we've prayed for this," Mr. MacDonald said to me. "You know we thought we were going to work with the Indians. Thirty-one years ago we came to these mountains, selling Bibles in the little villages round about. We couldn't sell many—not many people could read, and they were afraid of us. They would see us coming. Foreigners. And they'd run. But God gave us some precious opportunities. There's an old brother who lives seven miles from here who bought one of those first Bibles. He couldn't read, but he'd always wanted a book. 'If I had a book, I could learn to read,' he had said. 'If only I had a book.' So when I came he said, 'That's what I want. I want that book.' His wife scolded him for wasting money. He didn't give her any heed. He went into the back room and I could hear him moving trunks and things. He must have kept his money in one of them. His wife was screaming at him, 'So you'll let the children starve, you won't buy me a good rooster, but you'll buy a book.' Well, he bought it, and he learned to read. I came back several years later and he was reading. He knows the book now, from cover to cover. And I think he knows the Author, too. So you see, Margaret lassie, the Lord knows what He's about." He passed the cakes to me again, and his cup to Mrs. MacDonald. She poured milk into it and then tea.

"But you were telling Margaret about our wanting to do Indian work, dearie. You do get off the track."

"Oh yes. We came here to live twenty-eight years ago. We had sold Bibles in the area for a few years—I think it was five years—and then we came here to live. We visited around with the people of the town and with the Indians in the hills. But the Indians only come to town on market day and they live far apart. We found we couldn't keep them here long enough to do any work with them, and we couldn't visit their homes often enough. We had the children, you know." He took a sip of tea.

"How many do you have?" I asked.

"We have three," Mrs. MacDonald answered, her eyes lighting. "Two lassies and a laddie."

"Isn't your son a missionary?" I asked.

"Oh yes—in Tanganyika. He's been there two years now and just last week we received a letter from him with the news that he's found a wife. She's an English girl—a nurse. They won't be married for another year or so—she's still studying the language. But we're so happy for him. You know, it doesn't seem right for a young man to be alone like that, away out there." She had risen from her chair with the teapot in her hands. She looked eagerly at me. "I'll show you the picture he sent of her. She looks like a dear girl. And here I am talking when your cup is empty. I'll just heat this up a wee bit." She went to the kerosene stove in the corner of the room, set the teapot on the side and poured water from the steaming kettle into it. Her husband watched her bent back from the other side of the room. She straightened up and stretched a wisp of white hair into the cluster of pins at the back of her head, looked at the clock, and then carried the teapot to the table again.

"Here, Margaret dear, let me fill your cup. You must be tired. No? Ah, you're young. And then we have the two girls—Joan is married to a doctor in Kansas and Mary's studying to be a teacher. Sometimes we wonder about Mary." She looked at the geraniums with her head angled slightly to one side. She lifted her cup and held it without drinking. "Ah, she's a dear girlie. She had a hard time being away from us at the first, and then later, somehow she didn't seem to want to come back home. She didn't write for five weeks once. We heard things from people in Scotland: Mary's running around, Mary's not going to church, Mary's a wee bit rebellious. We don't know. The Lord knows what she needs, and we just commit her to Him. He's the Shepherd of the sheep—He won't let His lambs go astray. That we know, don't we, Ian? But we've talked too much, and you must want a little nap, Margaret.

[21]

We haven't heard anything about you, dear, and we want to—tomorrow you'll tell us all about yourself—but not now. You're tired. Come. Let me show you your room. Ah, you don't know how good it is to have you with us. We prayed so long that the Lord would send someone who could work with our Indians." She put her hands on the edge of the table and pushed herself back and then up from the chair. "You'll love them. I know you'll love them. But you won't find it easy."

"No, I don't expect I will. Everyone tells me how hard they are to reach. But then nothing's too hard for the Lord." As soon as the words were out of my mouth I felt checked. Who was I to tell a veteran missionary such a thing? Mrs. MacDonald put her arm around my waist.

"Follow the Shepherd, Margaret. He knows the way. I will fear no evil, for Thou art with me. That's His promise —to be with us. Ian and I have known it here."

The room to which she showed me was very small and immaculately clean, with a chair, a dresser and a bed that had a crocheted spread on it.

"There now, dear, you just put your things here." She pulled back a curtain and showed me a closet. "And there in the dresser is drawer space. You'll need a wee nap, now. You just lie down there, and when supper is ready I'll call you."

She left me and I went to the window, which looked out on a small patio where there were a dovecote and a great many geraniums in brilliant bloom. I saw Mrs. MacDonald open the kitchen door. The doves burbled and cooed as she held up her hands to them.

"*Palomita, palomita!*" she called, as though they would understand her better in Spanish than in English, and obediently they flew to her, circled and picked up the crumbs she scattered.

On the dresser was a neat, fat pincushion, crocheted like the bedspread, and a crystal bud vase with a few corn-flowers. There was a plaster-of-Paris motto on the wall with the words "He careth for you" entwined with forget-me-nots and rosebuds.

I could have wished that the little room, in the quiet home, in the town of Wairapamba, were for me the end of the road. It might have been so, for the mission to which I belonged, Indians for Christ, Incorporated, had suggested that I settle there near the MacDonalds, at least until the arrival of the Gardners, a couple who were coming to work with me but had so far been delayed for medical reasons. But Wairapamba was not so centrally located for reaching the Quichuas as some of the smaller towns farther up in the mountains, and the mission, as well as the Mac-Donalds, was pleased to know that I was willing to start out alone in the attempt to gain a footing among the people whom I thought of as my own. Tomorrow the Mac-Donalds were to drive me in their jeep up to Indi Urcu, several hours away, and help me to move into the house they had procured for me.

I lay down on the bed and thought about all the way which the Lord had led me. There was a certain element of apprehension of the unknown as I contemplated my arrival in Indi Urcu, but the knowledge that the MacDonalds had prayed for someone to work with the Indians, when they had found that they themselves could not, was to me the final seal that the course I had chosen was God's course.

There had been some strained moments at home when my parents learned that not only was I not going to India with my aunt, but that I intended to apply to a small, newly organized mission instead of to an established one, and would probably end up in Ecuador. Ecuador! They were not even sure where it was, and they had never known anyone who had gone there. Africa, China, India— these were the known fields. Why Ecuador? I had finally succeeded in persuading them that it was God's will. The evidence was enough for me—a chance encounter with a missionary, a meeting in which the needs of Ecuador's Indians were presented, a series of circumstances which seemed to point toward my going there, and, most incontestable of all, an inner conviction that this was it. I did not try to prove it to others. I simply said that the Lord was leading me, and this was both understandable and believable to my family and friends. I had not thought much about how such a statement might appear to others until I happened to meet a young man in Guayaquil, a drug salesman from New Jersey named Bill who, when he learned that I was a missionary, said, "A missionary! God. What's your religion?"

The question took me off guard. I belonged to a small church called interdenominational where we thought of all religions as sadly mistaken. Ours, by contrast, was not called a religion at all. It was the Way. Believing this as I did, the only answer I could think of sounded lame.

"Well, I'm a Protestant. I'm hoping to work among Indians and translate the Bible for them."

"Going to work in the jungle, huh?"

"No—among mountain Indians. Quichuas."

"Mountain Indians! Jesus Christ. Do you think you'll like that?"

"Oh, I think so."

"Kinda tough for a girl. Some of those mountain Indians

[24]

can be pretty tough." He shook his head slowly and surveyed me as though assessing my capabilities for the job. "Well, I wish you luck. I suppose you've got the call, haven't you?"

"Yes," I said, wondering how I could change the subject, for it was not clear what "the call" might mean to Bill, and I cringed at the thought of trying to explain to him what it meant to me. "Do you like your work?"

"Oh yeah, it's a good job. Good pay, lots of travel, meet a lot of nice people. It's only a job, though—the work is all cut out, you put in your time, draw your salary. But take you—you've got something to do that's really worthwhile —if you can *get* anywhere with those Indians."

There was nothing to say to this. I smiled. It was true, I thought, that what I had to do was far more than a job, and there was no salary. My support had been partially pledged by individuals who wanted to have a part in missionary work. There was no guarantee, of course, that they would fulfill these pledges, and even if they did the amount would not cover my expenses. I was living on faith, which I had been taught was a very honorable position of dependence on the Lord, never to be confused with living on charity, which meant dependence on human beings. As for having my work cut out, as Bill had, there were moments when I wished that the term "missionary" were a little more clearly definable. If I had been a missionary teacher or doctor or nurse my goals would have seemed unequivocal. Just how I was to "get anywhere" with the Indians I was not sure.

"I knew a couple of missionaries in Colombia once," Bill went on. "I was up there before I came here. Couple of girls. Nice girls, they were, from New York. They invited me down to their apartment one night for dinner. I was glad—you know, a bachelor, living alone, eating out in restaurants a lot, traveling a lot—it had been a long time since I had a good old American home-cooked meal. So I was glad they asked me. I tried to think of something I could take to those girls. You know what I mean, some little thing. So I bought a bottle of Drambuie. There's just nothing like a little glass of Drambuie with your after-dinner coffee. I thought it was just the thing. So I arrived at their house and when they opened the door I could smell steaks broiling. I gave them this bottle—and you know what they did? *They threw me out.* They took one look at the bottle and they threw me out. Really. I couldn't believe it. Never even gave me the meal they'd cooked. Can you beat that?"

"Oh, I suppose some missionaries are like that. It *is* hard to believe, though. I hope we're not all alike."

There was a low murmur from the kitchen, where Mr. and Mrs. MacDonald were. They did not want to wake me, and I could hear her moving plates and pans and things very gently as she prepared supper. Now and then a white dove flashed across the square of sky that I could see as I lay on the bed. It was delicious not to sleep, but just to lie in the stillness and think.

"Thank God," I thought, "they are not all alike."

IT TOOK a long time to get ready for the trip to Indi Urcu
the next morning. Mrs. MacDonald packed a lunch of
sandwiches, oat cakes and several thermos bottles of tea.
She had to feed the doves and chickens and close all the
shutters in the house against robbery, for which mountain
Indians were famous. Mr. MacDonald went to the gas
station and filled two jeep cans with gasoline because there
would be none available farther up in the hills. It took me
no time to assemble my few things and then I offered to
help Mrs. MacDonald, but she said, "Oh, thank you, dear,
no dear, I'll just put these plants away from the window
and then we'll be ready." She scurried about, finding things
to do, glancing now and again at the clock, making sure the
doors were locked, and then she took off her apron, tucked
in a strand of hair, put on a coat and said, "Now. Is Ian
ready? Ian's all ready, I think. We can go now, dear. Do
you have a coat? Good girlie. It does get cold up in the
mountains." Her husband was just loading some boards
into the back of the jeep. They might be needed for
bridging an irrigation channel or a washed-out place in the
road, he explained.

The trip was long and very bumpy and dusty, but I did

not mind it at all. It was a comfortable feeling to be sitting between two veteran servants of the Lord, people who knew the country and the Indians, who were profoundly concerned with the work I had come to do, people I could trust. Other journeys in Ecuador had been alone: the endless trip by bus, ferry and train to Ambato when I could not speak Spanish and kept waking up all night long, fearful lest I should sleep through the stop where I was supposed to get off, or waken to find my purse gone; the bouncing ride from Ambato to Riobamba when I was squeezed against the window by an enormous man dressed in black with a gold-headed cane who kept smiling and leaning toward me, breathing garlic and asking in English, "What ees your name? Where are you going?"

For the first few miles out of Wairapamba the people whom we passed waved in recognition of the jeep and the MacDonalds. "Oh, now there goes a dear lady, Margaret. My, what a story! Her husband drowned himself and left her with five children and shortly after that twelve sheep that she was keeping for someone else were struck by lightning, and then her youngest child died of smallpox. She accepted a New Testament one day when we visited her and now she's just a radiant Christian, such a dear soul. Oh my, Margaret, if you could know her!" A man rode by on horseback and waved to us. He was a *simpatizante*, they said, very friendly and open to the Gospel. A priest in a brown robe and sandals raised his hand and nodded—the MacDonalds had had some long talks with him. "There are many true believers in the Church, I think, Margaret," Mr. MacDonald said. "Oh, I think we're going to be surprised to see who's there when we get to heaven. 'He that is not against us is for us,' Jesus said. He alone knows who they are. And then there are those we expect to see who won't be there—Not every one who says 'Lord, Lord' will enter the Kingdom of Heaven. Ah, it sobers me to think of it."

The rest of the journey was like the day before—great stretches of brown grass, patchwork of cultivated fields, maguey borders, Indians trotting in both directions, scarcely looking at the car, then turning their faces away to avoid the dust; sheep and cattle and horses, a few goats, even a pair of llamas looking over a broken mud wall near a thatched house. And on all sides the mountains rising toward the burning blue sky, with the snow-covered cone of Chimborazo always in view. We stopped beside a small stream to eat our lunch. The grass grew lushly green beside it, but before we got out of the car Mrs. MacDonald whispered to me to be careful walking in the grass. "You know the habits of the Indians, dear. One has to be careful." It was well that she had warned me, for although I had learned to watch my step near towns and villages, the freshness of the mountain air and the glorious cleanness of the wide landscape might have given me a false confidence. Mr. MacDonald spread a blanket for us and his wife unpacked the sandwiches and laid them in neat piles and then poured tea. It was quiet except for the far-off bleat of a sheep. Occasional cloud shadows floated over us but we were protected from the wind in the shallow ravine where the brook ran.

We drove on after lunch, the road becoming increasingly rutted and winding so that I marveled to find that the jeep kept going. No one seemed inclined to talk, and I sat with my thoughts. Here, now is the land of my adoption. I had heard missionaries use the term affectionately. "Yes, dear friends, my heart is in Africa, land of my adoption, and I long to return." Upon my arrival in Guayaquil I had tried to arrange the furniture of my mind to include the dim light bulbs in the hotel, the short sheets on the bed, the lukewarm water from the tap which I dared not drink without boiling, the towels that looked like dresser scarves. These things had not satisfied my idea of missionary hardship and I knew that I would have to wait until I got into my real work.

When I had walked the streets of the port city, my heart sick at the sight of the beggars with their streaming eyes and the precarious bamboo houses leaning against modern steel and concrete structures, I had felt almost offended that such poverty should exist. I had looked at the emaciated children in the slums and the empty faces along the waterfront and had thought of Jesus, weeping over a great city, for they were as sheep without a shepherd. What sacrifice would I not make, I had asked myself, to meet such need? Why is it that no one does anything about it *now?* As soon as I learn Spanish . . . But, of course, I was not called to those people. It was to the Indians of the highlands that I had been called, and now, as the village where I would live came into view around the shoulder of a hill, I wanted to give notice that help was on the way. A woman carrying an enormous clay water jar passed us, and I wondered if she might someday be a friend of mine who, when she saw me, would call out, *"Buenos días*, Señorita Margarita!" and be glad that I had come to the mountains. The street we entered first was cobblestone and perfectly empty, with rows of squat, whitewashed houses on both sides, windows shuttered and doors closed. A door opened, an arc of dirty water splashed into the street, and the door banged shut. Someday, perhaps, that door would open to let me in.

"This is Indi Urcu, Margaret," said Mr. MacDonald, "Hill of the Sun." The sun shone down on the dusty cobblestones, and little eddies of wind drew circles in the corners of the doorways. Each corner we passed revealed identical streets, empty and silent. Then a man driving an ancient donkey loaded with round metal water tanks went by, switching the beast with eucalyptus twigs. The flanks of the donkey were great sculptures of bone, swathed in mouse-colored skin so thin that it looked as though it might at any moment give way. The animal moved without modifying in the slightest his creaking pace, the switch falling regularly on his back, the two heavy cans scraping his sides. Someday, I hoped, the love of God would get through to that man, and he would learn to love his burro.

When we reached the plaza in the center of the little town the car was instantly stormed by energetic women with baskets.

"*Choclos! Choclos a un sucre! Queso!*" They bleated at us, thrusting their wares through the windows. Mr. MacDonald smiled and nudged his way gently through the little knot of people. Market was over for the day, so the rest of the plaza was nearly empty. A few people came to the doorways of small shops to watch the *gringos* pass, and an Indian woman who had just knelt on the steps of the Catholic church turned her head to gaze after us, still kneeling. Would she, too, perhaps someday know the liberty of the Gospel of Jesus Christ? Was she, like most of the Indians, Catholic in name only, and lacking in any personal relationship with Christ? How much of her native ignorance and superstition were bound up in the only form of worship she knew? I wanted to guide her far beyond forms and ceremonies to the living Savior.

Mr. MacDonald drove up another side street and stopped at a doorway where a woman with an apron and dangling earrings gave him the key to my house. We could see that she wanted him to come in, but with a gracious bowing and gesturing in the Latin way he explained that we could not take the time. The lady nodded to us and we drove away, up the hill to a street where grass grew between the cobblestones and each house had a tiny yard enclosed by white adobe walls.

"Here we are, Margaret dear. This one is your little house. Oh, and the geraniums I planted are blooming so nicely!" Mrs. MacDonald patted my hand. The house was low, with a rust-colored tile roof and small-paned windows with shutters.

"Oh, Ian dear, you must fix the latches on those shutters! I thought we'd shut them when we left last time!" said Mrs. MacDonald in dismay. The whitewash on the adobe walls was dusty and the door was unpainted. I liked these touches. They made it seem a quaint and rustic cottage. I will be happy here, I thought.

While Mr. MacDonald unlocked the door I turned to look at the view from the front gate. The main part of the town lay below us, and I could see over the roofs and far across the valley, where hundreds of thatched houses—Indian houses, I thought joyfully—studded the plain like haymows. I saw that the MacDonalds had chosen the location wisely, and my eye drew imaginary lines, like the spokes of a wheel, from the gateway to the little houses—that one with the smoke filtering through the roof, the one over there on that knoll, that tiny one I could barely see in the haze of the distance. Unreached, every one of them, but, God helping me, I would reach them.

"Come in, dear." Mrs. MacDonald beckoned me inside, and I surveyed my home, the first I could call my own. There were only a few things in it—a small table, a chair, a chamber pot in the bedroom and a set of rusty springs, besides the bigger pieces of my baggage and furniture which Mr. MacDonald had brought up a couple of days before. We unloaded the things from the jeep, including a box of food which Mrs. MacDonald had prepared for me, enough to last for several days. She went about from room to room, mentally placing me in each one, anxiously arranging the things she knew I had brought and questioning me about other things she was sure I would need. Eager to show her that I could manage, I went into the kitchen and made tea and we sat on boxes and foot lockers in the living room while we drank it.

"You'll be all right here now, won't you, dear?" she said. I thanked her for all they had done—finding the house, cleaning it, transporting my things, bringing me. They were to spend the night in a room at the landlady's house since there was no hotel and there were not beds enough in my house for three.

"We'll just pop round in the morning, then, dear, to see that you're all right," she said. "Oh my, how we thank God that you've come, Margaret! How we prayed, didn't we, Ian? And now you've come!" She gave my shoulders a squeeze, her husband tipped his hat to me, opened the door and gently helped her into the jeep. I watched them move slowly down the street, Mrs. MacDonald's handkerchief fluttering from the window.

THE HOUSE seemed very empty indeed, and I felt more alone than ever before. It was not loneliness, exactly. Nor was it the feeling of alienation I had known since I arrived in the country. It was, rather, the aloneness of responsibility that pressed on me like a weight. Ever since that hot night when I was nineteen I had known that the responsibility lay upon me—I was one of those to whom God had specifically said, "Go *ye*." And now the emptiness, the silence and the damp chill of the thick-walled little house assumed almost a physical presence which confronted me and said, "You. It is you, now, who must act. If you do nothing, nothing will be done."

I went to the window of the living room, where no curtains had yet been hung, and looked across the rooftops of the town to the valley filled with houses. This was the beginning in earnest, and I found in my heart, along with the burden of responsibility, a genuine gratitude to God for the privilege which I saw was mine. He had provided all I needed; He would lead me ("Fear thou not, for I am with thee"—the Scriptural words came as confirmation of my own thought); He was responsible, in the end, for the results.

I looked around the bleak little room. No point in trying to bring order out of chaos tonight. Tomorrow I would arrange things. I pulled some food out of Mrs. MacDonald's box and found enough utensils to fix myself some supper. I could hear the wind whipping around the corners of the house, but there was no other sound. The single light bulb which illuminated the supper table was almost as dim as candlelight. If my friends could see me now! "Oh yes—Margaret Sparhawk. She went to Ecuador, you know —lives all alone way up in the mountains someplace with the Indians. A million Indians, I think she said, up in the Andes." That's what they would say, of course, and I would make light of the hardships, tell them how beautiful it was, how I loved the work, how fascinating the Indians were, really, when you got to know them. . . . But I must write to my friends right away. Another prayer letter was long overdue. I had written my first one from Ambato, but had delayed the second, thinking it would be more interesting to wait until I reached my own station. That was what my friends were eager to hear about.

Rummaging in a file box I found the first circular letter —we had called them "prayer letters" at home, where my parents received every week a dozen or so mimeographed reports from missionaries scattered over the globe. My father would read excerpts aloud at family devotions and we would pray for the writers, mentioning the specific needs stated in the letters. It was virtually the only way missionaries had to keep from being forgotten in prayer and—though this was seldom referred to except obliquely —from being financially neglected. I accepted this method without question as one of God's ways of supplying my needs.

I read over the letter I had written from Ambato.

Dear praying friends:

When He putteth forth His sheep, He goeth before. The Lord has fulfilled His word to me, and at last I find myself in Ecuador, the country to which He called me three years ago. How thankful I am for the privilege of being an ambassador for Christ! And how grateful I am to you dear ones whose prayers and gifts made it possible for me to obey the Great Commission!

Here I am in Ambato, a beautiful city in the inter-Andean plane, about 7,000 feet above sea level. There are Spanish colonial buildings, burros and pushcarts and modern cars in the streets, palm trees in gardens and patios. I live with a very nice family, Señor Honorio Torres and his friendly, attractive wife, Señora Aïda. He speaks a little English, but she does not know a word, which is an advantage for me because I am forced to speak Spanish. She chatters away very amiably, apparently thinking that I can follow what she says even though I seldom can think how to answer her! The house is very clean and comfortable, and I have a nice little room overlooking the street. Just now as I write I can see a small boy with a huge flat basket of rolls on his head, a shawled woman carrying two live chickens by their legs, a policeman in a khaki uniform with a gleaming white belt who keeps issuing diffident little peeps on a tiny whistle. I wonder why he does this? It seems that if anyone were breaking the law the whistle would give him plenty of warning of the policeman's approach. Well, there are many things in a foreign country that one doesn't understand, but it is interesting to learn, and I have learned to say, "How do you say?" and "What is this?" and "Why?"

Every morning I have a Spanish lesson with a charming young señorita named Dolores who wears very high-heeled shoes, long fancy earrings and such well-cut clothes that I feel at times quite frumpy and timid in her presence. She lives in a huge colonial house with a carved front door and a patio in the center, where a fat Indian woman rubs clothes on a block of stone. I have my lesson in an upstairs room which is very dark since it has only one long narrow window. There are immense portraits of bearded gentlemen and solemn ladies—descendants, I suppose, of the *conquistadores* themselves—on the walls, and they are hung diagonally across the four corners of the room and slanted so that their gaze seems to rest on me as I sit at my lesson. My "desk" is a velvet-covered round table, and my teacher sits opposite me on a brocade throne.

"*Rápido, rápido, rápido!*" she shrills at me, snapping her fingers in rhythm with the words, and I struggle to conjugate a verb without faltering, "*Yo hago, tu haces, él hace.*" It is not easy to get them all straight, and I am having an especially difficult time learning the subjunctive, and trying to imitate the intonation pattern, which Señorita Dolores says is very important. My high school Spanish did not get me very far, I am afraid! So please pray for progress in the language study, so that I may soon move out to the Indian villages where I will begin the work to which God has specifically called me.

Pray, too, that I may be a faithful witness for Christ here in this home, and in the city. I am not sure whether the Torres family are true believers, though they are quite willing to discuss the Bible and my reasons for being here in Ecuador. I had a thrilling experience the other day, however, and I trust you will pray very especially for the Lord's blessing in this matter. I went on a picnic with the Torres family—by bus, over the hills to a lovely swimming place in a green valley—and there I got into conversation with a thin, dark-haired girl named Gladys who said that she had some reservations about the Catholic faith and many questions she wanted to ask me about my own. When I said I would love to come to her house (she lived not far from me in Ambato) and read the Bible with her she jumped at the chance. Consequently I have been visiting her almost every day since, and it seems clear that the Lord is working in her heart. I believe He led me to the encounter, and has been directing me in our talks together.

[37]

Pray that He will bring her to a definite decision. Perhaps He will give me this seal of approval on my coming, even before I reach the people of the mountains!

I have had correspondence with the MacDonalds, senior missionaries who work up in the mountains, and they have located a good spot for me to work in a Quichua area. I can hardly wait until my time here is up and I can reach at last that needy place. Pray that they may be able to find a suitable house for me when the time comes. Remember to pray, too, for the Gardners, that they may soon receive medical clearance and join me in the work.

Yours in Christ,
Margaret Sparhawk.

Five months had passed now, and it was time to write another letter. How to begin? "Dear praying friends" was a standard beginning, and had seemed all right in Ambato. Something had happened since then, something which seemed to call for a simpler form of address—was it a cooler, calmer view of things which I now took? I was not certain, and although "Dear friends" sounded a trifle distant I could think of no better beginning.

The time spent in Ambato has come to a close, and I want to thank each one of you for your prayers. The study of Spanish was very profitable and my teacher was pleased with my examinations. . . .

Here I am, at last, in Indi Urcu (the *i*'s are pronounced like *e*'s, the *u*'s are long), a little village much higher up in the Andes than Ambato was, in the center of a large Indian area. I am hoping to start the study of Quichua as soon as I can find an informant, and would ask you to pray that the Lord will guide me to the right one. As you know, my ultimate goal is the translation of the Bible into mountain Quichua.

Some of you, perhaps, are wondering about Gladys.

Here I paused, not knowing what to write about a thing which had caused me no end of anxiety and self-criticism. Things had worked beautifully in the beginning, I believed God had led me to her, she seemed as needy as any jungle savage, she was open to all I had to say. I had prayed, friends had prayed, but one week the maid said she was not at home and the next week she said she was sick. The following week she was at home, but told me she did not really want to read the Bible and was having difficulty finding time to study the English verb lists I had given her. In the end, she did not see me any more, and I wondered if after all I was never to qualify as a missionary. What could I tell those who had prayed?

She never came to any definite commitment of herself to Christ, so far as I know, although I believe that the Lord is able to bring fruit out of seed that has been planted. Keep on praying for her.

I paused again. Here, in Indi Urcu, things were bound to happen. Perhaps God was only testing my faith in the Gladys experience. After all, someone has to plant. Often another reaps.

Remember the words of Scripture, "When we believe not, yet He abideth faithful."

Yours for the salvation of Ecuador's Indians,

Margaret Sparhawk.

I rolled the paper out of the machine and started to read it over but realized that my feet were cold. The little house was drafty and the thick adobe walls held the cold. I got up and went to the bedroom to see if I could find my slippers in the jumble of boxes. A window was open and I discovered that the latch did not fit, so I wedged a piece of paper under it. Dust had blown over everything and felt gritty to my fingers as I opened the suitcases. Oh dear, I thought, where am I to hang all these things? There wasn't a closet in the house. But how petty! I scolded myself. Other missionaries had trekked over mountains, across deserts, through raging seas.

> They met the tyrant's brandished steel,
> The lion's gory mane,
> They bowed their necks the death to feel—
> Who follows in their train?

If I were to answer with my own name I had better stop worrying about cold feet, broken latches, dust and lack of closet space.

I DREAMED that I stood on a platform before a vast audience. There was a hush as I opened my mouth to speak. No sound came, and in that endless second of my dream I remembered other dreams in which I had been frightened and had tried to scream but had found myself incapable of uttering a sound. The agony of the effort had awakened me. Now, in my dream, I decided that the simplest way of escape from this expectant audience was to wake up. Yet I felt a sense of undeniable obligation to them. I had come to say something, and they were waiting to hear it. But I could not remember the words. I stood as motionless and breathless as one does when he is about to sneeze. Then I began to squeak and creak. My dismay gave way to relief. Quichua! I thought. Such sounds as I had never heard poured forth from my mouth, and suddenly I awoke. The sound went on, and my mind groped to identify it. A donkey. That must be what it was. I had never heard a donkey bray, but the squeaking and creaking were followed by a recognizable hee-haw, and then I heard the lash of a whip, the clanking of water cans and an angry shout. The donkey clopped down the road and I opened my eyes.

My own bedroom, in my own house. Indi Urcu. My mission station. I stretched my feet toward the corners of the bed, luxuriating for the first time in over six months in its comfort. It was my own, not the short, squarish Ecuadorian one I had used in Ambato. There was no one waiting breakfast for me. There would be no Spanish lesson today, no journey, no more half-unpacked living. I could settle and take possession of the whole house. I had a whole day before me. In fact, I thought, as I jumped out of bed, the whole town was mine now, and the Indians. A promising task, a life's work. Through the window I could see the valley shining in the sun, mist rising above the rooftops of the village, and the Indians trotting by on the road. Always trotting—one leading a donkey, one pulling a pig tied by a leg, women with great nets full of clay pots, men with straw mats in rolls on their backs, towering loads of fodder and corn and hay. They were all in a hurry, and I felt that I, too, must hurry to meet them. I dressed quickly and flung open the front door, prepared to shout a glad greeting to the world. My enthusiasm was tempered when none of the passing Indians lifted his head to glance in my direction. Their burdens were supported by a band slung across the forehead, and they kept their eyes on the road.

From many an ancient river, from many a palmy plain
They call us to deliver their land from error's chain.

From rivers and plains, perhaps, I thought, but not from the high Andes. Not this morning, anyway. Well, I reflected, it's gratifying to see the Indians so industrious, so bent on the business of the day. I, too, have business—the King's business—and they little know that it concerns them.

Breakfast was the first item, and I found enough food and utensils to make a hasty meal and then set about putting the house in order. Crates, barrels and trunks stood in every room, some of them unopened since that last day in the basement at home when my father had nailed down the lids. Friends and neighbors had come in to help pack, each one wanting a part in a missionary project which originated so close to home.

I sorted towels and sheets—a class of young married women at my church had supplied them, along with a beautiful bedspread, "because even though you're a missionary we want you to have some nice things"—and stacked them neatly in a foot locker in the back corner room which I planned to use as a sort of bath and storage room. The house had no bathroom indoors, but there was a faucet in the kitchen and an ancient flush toilet in a tiny shack at the back. I would buy myself an enamel basin and pitcher for indoor bathing. As I attempted to place some trunks and boxes parallel with the wall, I discovered that no corner of the whole house would have satisfied a carpenter's square. The walls of each room appeared to be approximately the same length, but my boxes sat askew in the corners, and my brain seemed likewise set askew. There were too many doors. Each room opened into two others and I found it hard to decide where I could place a dresser which I did not yet have. I pushed a trunk against the biggest piece of wall in the bedroom and hung a mirror over it. I had wondered, as I packed this mirror, if my having it might be indicative of an unseemly vanity in a missionary, but decided to bring it anyway, unable to visualize a five-year term on the field without so much as a critical glance at my own face.

I pulled things out of the trunks and thought—sometimes with amusement, sometimes with real affection and gratitude—of the people who had given them to me. A case of insect repellent and six embroidered dish towels from an old-maid schoolteacher who had taught me when I was in the third grade; a parka from a man who had once done some climbing in the Andes in Chile, and a pith helmet from a group of Girl Scouts who thought that Ecuador was all tropical jungle; tablecloths of all colors, odds and ends of dishes, camping equipment from Army surplus stores, old costume jewelry to trade with the Indians, Bible pictures and flannelgraph figures for teaching Bible stories "in places where you can't speak the language," as one eager Sunday-school pupil suggested; a braided rug made by a shut-in who collected scraps of wool and silk and nylon and tulle and cotton from her friends and worked slowly day after day twisting them into ovals of all sizes. "You'll want something pretty down there for your house. They won't have anything like this in South America, will they?" I had assured her that they wouldn't, and I spread the rug now on the floor of the front room on the right— this would be the living room. It made a bright mottled spot on the rough wood, and I decided that it was not so bad after all.

I went back into the bedroom, realizing that I was not carrying out my work in a very orderly fashion, and began to make the bed. Frances Rogers, wife of the director of my mission board, had written to tell me to bring a bed—if there was one thing a missionary needed after a long, hard day it was a good bed, and Ecuadorian beds were "impossible." I had been a trifle inclined to sneer at this kind of advice. I wanted to identify with the natives; I even wanted to suffer somewhat. But Frances was the wife of my boss, as it were, and I capitulated.

I took a look at the living room and decided it was hopeless to do anything there until I bought some furniture, so I began clearing the breakfast things from the dining room. A door led outside to the leanto kitchen at the back, and it was inconvenient to have to open the door, go outside, open another door and take the dishes into the kitchen, but it was out of the question to eat in the kitchen. There was no room for a table and it was without any windows whatever. If I closed the door it was like a dungeon; if I left it open it was too cold. There was nothing in the kitchen except a tile wood-burning stove with a rusted iron top, and a very low concrete sink with a single faucet. Everything was in need of an energetic scrubbing and sweeping and scouring, but at last it was acceptably clean and I felt I could properly introduce all my shiny new utensils and set about washing the dishes. I had a bright turquoise plastic dishpan, hot water from the stove and Ivory soap. Mrs. MacDonald had included the soap in her box of supplies, and although it was admittedly expensive I told myself that missionaries were justified in using it after I saw the alternative—dark brown blocks of waxy substance with bits of straw, paper or fluff embedded in them. It would be positively dangerous to use that for dishes. Maybe for laundry, but certainly not for dishes. You owe it to yourself, all the missionaries said, to keep healthy, and I agreed that they had a point; but then, had I a right deliberately to separate myself from the people I had come to serve? If they could use this soap all their lives, couldn't I? Was it legitimate to spend the Lord's money on expensive imports which could only widen the gap between us? Oh dear, I thought, why must life be complicated by such trivialities?

I plunged my hands into the hot, soapy water and began

rotating the dish cloth, a gift from my niece, a nine-year-old who saved her allowance so that she might help her missionary aunt, just as I had once done. The lonely mission station, the civilized soap; the dark kitchen and the shining pots and pans; the cold tile floor and the hot dishwater—these things jumbled themselves happily in my mind, a nice mixture of mortifications and gratifications.

It was very quiet in the kitchen. I could hear nothing from the street, for a high wall surrounded the back patio on three sides and the house was wedged between two other houses, part of a solid row of whitewashed walls which filled the block.

A patch of sunlight was sliding down the far wall of the kitchen. Indi Urcu, Hill of the Sun. A lovely name, and this morning it seemed to me a lofty, shining place.

> Great is Thy faithfulness, O God my Father,
> There is no shadow of turning with Thee. . . .
> All I have needed Thy hand hath provided—
> Great is Thy faithfulness, Lord, unto me.

I hummed the tune as I went from room to room, jotting down little tasks to be done, things to be bought. Such trivialities had at last become synonymous with missionary work, for I had arrived in "The will of God for my life." It had been a magic phrase, a thing sought after, prayed about and worried over since I had reached the age of accountability. I wanted to shout my achievement from the housetops, but the next best medium of announcement was the prayer letter, which I must mail right away. I took it out of the typewriter, read it over, decided it was quite a good letter, and imagined it being read aloud in missionary meetings ("Here's one from Margaret Sparhawk, our new missionary in Ecuador. She works with the Quichua Indians"—they will have trouble with the pronunciation of that name, I thought). I saw the letter tacked up on church bulletin boards and beside maps of the world, a colored pin marking the little country of Ecuador, a ribbon stretched to a photograph of myself at the side. Over the map a large caption read: "Unto the uttermost parts of the earth."

As I folded the letter and put it into an airmail envelope I thought of Mavis, who would mimeograph and mail out copies for me from Des Moines. She was a secretary who had worked at the Bible school I attended, and had offered to do this for me even though she worked all day and did the cooking and housework for her invalid mother. "The Lord wouldn't let me go to the mission field," she had said, "but He will let me do this much for you. I would count it a privilege to have this tiny share in your work." Bless her, I thought, God bless her! She's probably praying for me even now.

The MacDonalds popped in as they had said they would, their cheeks rosy and their eyes shining as they came up the walk to the front door. They had had a good night with my landlady; she had let them read a portion of Scripture to her before they retired and at breakfast they had given her a Gospel of John and elicited a promise to read it and to keep a watchful eye on the new missionary. They told me that they would drive up whenever they could for a visit, that I should keep my door and gate locked and not open the windows at night; be careful not to walk too fast or too far in this high altitude; wash my hands as soon as I came in after a trip to town or to Indian houses, and not eat any raw vegetables without scalding them first. All these instructions had been given me by other missionaries in Ambato and I listened politely, but a trifle less earnestly than I had the first time.

"Goodbye, Margaret dear girlie," Mrs. MacDonald said. "Remember we're upholding you *every morning*" (she rolled the r's beautifully) "before the Throne of Grace. The Lord will keep you. Write to us."

There were no Indians in the streets as I made my way toward the center of town. They must be already in the market place, I decided, doing whatever it is they come to do. It was a white man's town and I was sorry about that. I wished there were such a thing as an Indian village, with little houses in a circle, where I could live in their midst and be a daily testimony for Christ. But mountain Indians had no such villages. There might be a cluster of houses here and there, but it was not public as a town is public, and an outsider did not simply move in on them. I had read with envy of missionaries in Africa who lived in villages with the people, or in compounds near the villages into which the natives streamed by the hundreds seeking help of one kind or another. Someday I might have their advantageous position, but the first step was learning to know the town where the Indians did their trading.

It was very cold when the wind whipped down from the heights, but the sun shone fiercely when it was still and I was alternately too cold and too warm. The market place was bustling with Indians when I arrived, all of them impervious to the weather, with heavy ponchos and shawls. Nearly every individual, man, woman or child, wore a hat—great wide-brimmed white ones, dark fedoras, misshapen basins, shallow-crowned sombreros; some of them were set at a jaunty angle, tilted toward the forehead, others were crammed straight down to the ears. There were people wearing two or three hats, one on top of the other—perhaps they meant to sell some of them, or had bought a hat for a friend and found this the simplest method of carrying it home. Babies wore hats like their parents' or knitted caps. A few women had cloths folded in the shape of a hat, or cloths laid across the crowns of their hats. Some wore cloths over their hair with a hat sitting precariously on top. The throng of buyers and sellers was a dark, moving sea, bobbing with disks and bubbles.

I skirted the crowd, noticing that very few wore anything on their feet. How did they endure the icy dew of the mountains and the clammy cobblestones of the town?

My first stop was the post office, where I wanted to mail my prayer letter. Two of the women who sold stamps in little kiosks said they had no airmail stamps. A third found one with difficulty. "But, señorita, no one sends airmail letters from here," she explained. Mr. MacDonald had arranged for a post office box for me and I found that mail had been forwarded from Guayaquil and Ambato. There was also a notice of a package that could be retrieved from the window. This was not a simple matter, I discovered. First I must produce my *cédula de identidad*, then fill out a form which required a government stamp, and the stamp had to be purchased from another window. There was a line of people at this window, standing humbly waiting their turn. I could see no one behind the grill. I joined the queue and at that moment a well-dressed white man came up behind me, hesitated a moment, and then strode forward to where an Indian stood. The man snatched the Indian's hat from his head and flung it across the hallway, keeping his chin high and his eyes straight in front of him. The act nearly took my breath away and I watched aghast as the Indian stepped silently from the line and the man calmly moved into the empty place. Not a word was spoken, not an eyebrow lifted that I could see. No one, in fact, had apparently noticed. The Indian was a small man with a slope to his shoulders. He wore calf-length white trousers which flared out above his deeply creased insteps, and a ragged poncho of a nondescript dark hue. Bereft of his hat he looked frightened and ashamed, and he crammed it quickly on to his head again, went back to pick up his bundle, and then came and stood quietly behind me. I wanted desperately to speak to him but I knew it was impossible. Perhaps he spoke only Quichua, and if he knew Spanish I dared not use it before so many white people. What, indeed, would I have said? My heart was like a cold stone in my chest and I found that I was clenching my purse till my fingertips were white. I turned halfway around to give him at least a sympathetic glance but he was occupied with his bundle.

When I finally reached the window the man lifted his hands with a circular motion, palms upward, and said, "There are no more." What should I do? I asked. "Come back at five o'clock, señorita. There will be more stamps at five." He was so cheerful, so satisfied in the consciousness of doing his job well that one could scarcely be displeased with him. This was the way things were done in Ecuador, and the sooner I learned to accept it, the easier life would be. I turned away from the window and started toward the street. A woman swathed in black from head to toe laid a gnarled hand on my arm.

"Just a little token of love, please, señorita, for the love of God. Just a little charity for the love of God, I am poor . . ." I groped in my mind for the Bible's sanction as I fished in my purse for what she wanted. "Give to him that asketh thee." A coin in her hand shut off the petition. She murmured, "May God pay you," and walked away.

There was an overpowering stench of urine as I stepped

into the street from the post office. The walls of the building had a number of abutments which provided a modicum of privacy, and this encouraged the townsmen to make use of them. I began to walk toward the little food store I had seen as the MacDonalds drove me through the town toward my house.

Partly blocking the doorway of the store were two glass cases in which I saw rolls, some greenish-colored sugared balls, round white cheeses, and *empanadas*. I went inside. The woman who was reading a newspaper behind the counter pulled herself up and leaned over the worn board toward me.

"*Buenos días*, señorita. What little thing?"

"Various things," I said, studying my list, which I had written in Spanish lest I forget the words for the items I needed. Then I remembered I had not returned her greeting. How many more times would I make this blunder?

"*Buenos días*," I said sheepishly.

The shelves were packed with cans, bottles, packages, many of which bore familiar American labels, but the prices horrified me. Two and a half times as much as one would pay in the States. I eschewed the foreign imports except for a few things which seemed indispensable—a package of tea, a can of instant coffee, detergent and toilet paper. It gave me pleasure to buy the cheap national foods such as rice, flour, dried beans and peas, sugar, butter, cheese and bread. The woman went over to the doorway to measure out the sugar, which stood in a burlap sack with the top rolled part way down. Sacks of grains I did not recognize stood beside it as her display of goods, for the store lacked a show window, or, for that matter, windows of any kind. The open door provided all the light and display space it had.

Over the counter was a large sign which said:

> Goodbye remedies!
> With one of our healing bracelets it is no longer
> necessary to use medicines. These bracelets will
> cure any disease, pain, or sickness. s/100

The woman came back with a sheet of newspaper containing the coarse, yellow sugar. She laid it on the counter and skillfully began twisting the edges together to form a neat, tight package. She saw me reading the sign.

"They are very, very good, señorita. I have sold many of them, and they cure anything."

"Is that so?" I replied. "It is just a bracelet which one wears?"

"Yes. I will show it to you." She went into a back room and returned with a bracelet, a very ordinary-looking cheap plastic circle.

"You must wear it all the time," she said, "and you will find that your sicknesses disappear gradually. Why, my sister-in-law was dying with diseased kidneys. She bought one of these—she didn't have the money but I gave her credit—and she was absolutely cured in two weeks. Absolutely *cured*. I know many who have been cured."

I smiled and assured her that though I was not sick now the bracelet was indeed interesting.

"You are visiting here, señorita?" she inquired.

"No, I have come to live here."

"To *live* here?"

"Yes, if God wills."

"Ah, how good. You are an American?"

"Yes."

"And how is it that you come here?"

"I am a missionary."

"A missionary! Ah, how nice. But you are not alone?"

"Yes, I am alone."

"But—your family?"

"My parents live in the United States."

"Your parents are alive?"

"Yes."

"Both of them? Mother and father?"

"Oh yes. They are both alive, and my brothers and sisters live there, too."

"And they do not mind that you have come so far away?" She looked at me curiously, moving back to lean on the shelves behind her and folding her arms.

"No, they do not mind."

"But—you are alone . . . you are single?"

"Yes."

"Have you children?" The question startled me a little.

"Oh no, señora, I have no children."

"Ay, señorita. Not even one?"

"No, señora, not even one. You see—I am single."

A small smile played in her eyes as she looked intently into my face, then appraised my entire person.

"Ay, what a shame. How sad to be alone. But you are a missionary, no?"

"Yes. I am going to be a missionary to the Indians."

Her hands fluttered and dropped to her sides.

"To the *Indians?*"

"Yes, señora. I have much interest in the Indians."

"But señorita! The Indians have no souls! They are not souls. Do you think, señorita, that the Indians are like the rest of us?"

"I think they have souls. I want to teach them about God—about Jesus Christ."

"They will not learn, señorita. They will never understand you. It would be better—much better—to teach us. We need to learn. Indians do not need to learn. Only to work. They are like animals, isn't that true, señorita?"

"In my opinion, we all need to learn. But Indians can learn too. They are human beings like the rest of us. They are not just animals, señora. Christ died for them, too, did He not?"

"Perhaps. Who knows if it is so? But then what do they care if He died? They don't go to church. They don't listen to the priest—only to be baptized and married and buried do they go to the priest."

"I hope they will listen to me. I believe God has sent me. He can help me."

"Well, señorita, you are valiant! God doesn't make them listen to the priest, but perhaps He will make them listen to you! Well, may you have good luck. We are here at your service, señorita." She handed me the groceries one by one, for there were no paper bags to be had, and I put them into my basket.

"Until another day, señora, and thank you."

"At your orders, señorita. Until later!"

When I had succeeded in finding a seamstress and a shoe-maker, and had bought a broom and some straw mats, I went back to my house. Approaching it on the street, I decided it was an attractive little house with its white-washed walls and tiled roof, and it was, above everything, mine. When I went inside, it was not really warm, but there was shelter from the dry, cold wind outside, and there was privacy. I put my basket on the table and sat down to read the mail.

"We have put your prayer card with the pictures of you on our church bulletin board. We prayed for you by name last Wednesday night and the pastor mentioned you in his

Sunday-morning pastoral prayer," said a letter from the church secretary at home in Pennsylvania. The rest of her letter dealt with local church gossip and a visiting missionary whose ministry was "a blessing to us all. Ralph Stone went forward on the invitation to dedicate his life to foreign missionary service. Three others stood to say they would pray for the Lord's will for their lives."

The chair I was sitting in, for a foreigner who had known foam rubber and form-fitting construction, was far from comfortable. I shifted my weight, trying to make myself fit the shape of the chair, and tore open another letter. This one was from a college friend. "I can only try to imagine you there at your station, actually beginning on the missionary work you have looked forward to for so long. It must be thrilling. Remember when we were in the Africa prayer group and you thought you were going to Africa? Well, the Lord's ways are not our ways! Praise the Lord!" One from a former Sunday-school teacher: "We miss you here, Margaret, but we are thankful you have followed the Lord. Do let us know what your house is like. It is hard to picture you there, way up in the Andes, alone. May the Lord give you grace and wisdom and strength as you commence your work for Him."

There were some family letters, one of which enclosed a recent snapshot of my aunt, standing under a jacaranda tree in India with a group of eager children at her feet. There was a magazine containing reports of mission work among lepers in India, orphans in Korea, illiterate slum children in Rio de Janeiro. "The Heathen for Our Heritage," read the title of one article. It told of a meeting in Malaysia which Muslims had attended. "History was made that night as between 350 and 400 people turned out to hear the Gospel of Jesus Christ! Beloved, the seed is still growing for we receive reports of many people asking questions, coming to the services, and souls are being saved. God is giving us the heathen as our heritage! Pray for us!"

I marveled at the author's assurance of accomplishment, his candid claim to an extraordinary part in God's eternal program. Would I ever be qualified to make such claims? The activities of the day hardly seemed the antecedents of any history-making achievements. I gathered up the empty envelopes and realized I had no wastebasket. I put them in a pile in a corner and wrote "wastebasket" on my shopping list.

The day had come and gone, and the Indians were again passing my front gate, oblivious, returning to the hills of home, their grains and potatoes and fodder exchanged for kerosene, salt—what else did they buy there? Iron plow blades? Cheap cloth? Bread? They were still trotting, the children tagging behind, bearing like their elders burdens of varied sizes and shapes. I watched them go up the hill until their hats were mere specks against the shadowed fields, and longed to let them know in some way that they had a friend in the white man's village. I had had some vague understanding during my stay in Ambato of the distinction between the Indian and the white man, but it was not until today that I realized the magnitude of the gulf fixed between them. It dawned on me, moreover, that having chosen the Indians as my people I was now to be identified with the despised. The white people, who had always been polite—sometimes to the point of obsequiousness—would perhaps come to hate me. Would it be possible to befriend both classes without offending either? I wondered. "I the Lord have called thee." If this was true, might He not lead me in paths that He Himself had trod? The Scripture said of Him that He was "despised and rejected of men; a man of sorrows, and acquainted with grief." Would I shrink from such a calling? No, Lord, no—only give me an entrance with the Indians; let me accomplish what You have sent me to do.

For a long time the Indians streamed back up into the barren, gashed mountains where their homes were. They lived in the cold, scratching a hard living from hostile soil. I could hear the soft padding of their bare feet and the occasional clink of metal or creak of hemp, but few voices reached me. Was their silence hostile or fearful because they were in the white man's world, or were they just as silent within the mud walls of their homes? What pleasures did they know? Was there anything to laugh about in their lives?

I watched a young woman hurrying up the road, her hands nimbly spinning a skein of wool. A baby, wearing a soft felt fedora identical to his mother's, jounced on her back, one little brown foot patting her hip and one hand patting his own hip as he rode in the shawl sling. They seemed contented enough, but what of the baby's future? What kind of life had he to look forward to? And what did the mother know of lasting peace? I had something to tell her, and how gladly she would hear it when I had the chance!

IT WAS surprising how many days I managed to spend getting settled. It seemed that each day was full of little things that could not wait. I could not begin my work until my living routine was established and my house in order, and although I awoke each morning with the thought of going to visit Indian homes, each evening came before the thing was done. During the day I felt triumphant to see the time passing in useful ways, conscious that I was not sitting down and wasting time, but when evening came and I took stock of the day's accomplishments I felt guilty to see that no breach had yet been made in heathenism. Hudson Taylor had made an impact on China, Mary Slessor on Calabar, John Paton on the South Sea Islands, David Livingstone on darkest Africa. Just exactly how had they *begun?* It was strange to find the actual daily doing of missionary work so unspecific, so lacking in direction. "Margaret Sparhawk is working among mountain Quichuas." I could not get away from the image I knew I had projected at home, but here was the other side of the coin. "Working." What does she do? Missionaries wrote of "doing" visitation, of "reaching" people, of "witnessing." I did not need to read any more missionary books, prayer letters, or progress reports in magazines to learn the terminology. I needed to find out what was really basic in the operation, and I went back to the source, the Bible, and read avidly the Old Testament stories of men with a mission. Moses was sent to Pharaoh.

"But Moses said to God, 'Who am I that I should go to Pharaoh . . . ?' God said, 'But I will be with you; and this shall be the sign for you, that I have sent you: when you have brought forth the people out of Egypt, you shall serve God upon this mountain.'

"Then Moses said to God, 'If I come to the people of Israel and say to them, "The God of your fathers has sent me to you," and they ask me, "What is his name?" what shall I say to them?' God said to Moses, 'I AM WHO I AM.' And he said, 'Say this to the people of Israel, "I AM has sent me to you."' "

I read of Joshua. God said to him, "As I was with Moses, so I will be with thee."

And of Samuel, who grew, and "the Lord was with him, and did let none of his words fall to the ground."

There was a young sheepherder named David, ruddy and handsome, who had beautiful eyes. And the Lord said to Samuel, "Arise, anoint him: for this is he." And when Samuel anointed him, "the Spirit of the Lord came upon David from that day forward."

There was Matthew, in the New Testament, to whom Jesus said, "Follow me," and he rose and followed. There was Peter, to whom He said, "Feed my sheep"; Paul, whom He struck blind and later led into a life of unprecedented service; there was, finally, the old exile John, to whom God gave the vision of the Book of Revelation, in which He said "Fear not, I am the first and the last."

The God of these men was my God, and if my faith was worth anything at all, I must act on it. I must start out somehow, and the logical place was in the open-air market —why, it was, in fact, the very place where Jesus and Paul had ministered. There I might meet Indians in a casual way, where they expected to encounter white people and would not be on their guard against us. I had already bought the most essential pieces of furniture for my house in a carpenter's shop, but had learned afterward that cheaper furniture was sold on Thursdays in the market. I still needed a couple of chairs, and decided to combine this errand with the more serious objective of meeting individual Indians. In order to do this I rose early as they did. The wind had not yet begun to blow, and the air was cold and still as I left my gate and joined the trotting, spinning, burden-bearing file headed for the village. Great pale shawls of mist lay along the floor of the valley and the snowcaps floated above them, jagged, detached masses, faintly touched by the rising sun. My shoes tapped sharply on the cobblestones by contrast with the nearly noiseless movement of the Indians' feet. A burro tethered to a stake beside the road followed me with his sleepy eyes, slowly moving one ear forward as I passed, as though he recognized the difference between me and the rest of the traffic. Grass grew between the stones in the road and the dew made them of one color, silver-gray in the wetness. In a very short time the sun would dry the stones to desert dryness and the road would be powdery with dust along the edges.

I was not accustomed to the dogtrot, especially at this altitude, and most of the people passed me, wives following their husbands, children—small versions of their parents, for they were dressed exactly like them—scurrying at the rear.

The sun was just slanting between the houses as I reached the market place, an open square almost in the center of town. Along one side were flimsy stalls with white cotton awnings or umbrellas, some of them walled with sheets of cardboard or rusted iron roofing. Brilliantly embroidered blouses and cheap nylon shirts flapped on hangers from the tops of some of these stalls; others displayed plastic tableware, thin aluminum pots and pans, gaudy glassware and old bottles. There were stalls of gorgeous flowers—white calla lilies, dahlias, asters, geraniums, bachelor buttons, marigolds, sweet peas—and stalls selling meat and cheeses. Great garlands of entrails, tripe, kidneys, brains and testicles from sheep, pigs and cattle adorned the front of the meat stalls, and huge limp mounds of bloody beef and pork lay open on the counters, the flies walking unmolested over them. Beyond the stalls women sat on the ground in front of their open sacks of beans, peas, potatoes of every description, and rice. Nearly every woman had a baby, either peering over her shoulder from a carrying cloth, or lying across her lap.

A foreigner was not a common sight in this market, and the women called to me continually, "What little thing, little madam?" ("*Qué cosita, madamita?*" It was a form of address I objected to—somehow the word *madam* with this diminutive suffix sounded incongruous, especially since I was anything but "little." I hoped I would get used to the term—and after all, I realized, the diminutive was merely an affectionate ending—but it never failed to irritate me.) "What are you looking for, little madam? What may we offer?" I smiled and shook my head and kept walking, picking my way through the litter and trying not to get my shoes wet in the unidentified liquids which ran in the gutters. There was a smell of warm blood and fat from the meat stalls, fresh flowers with the dew still on them from the flower stalls, sour milk from the dairy stalls, high fish and fresh fish, frying tortillas and onions, garbage, wet wool and unwashed humanity—all of this mingled with the ever-present stench of urine from the walls of the buildings surrounding the market and from the cobblestones underfoot.

At the far side of the square I could see straw mats, brooms, baskets, and furniture stacked in crazy heaps. As I walked toward them an Indian with a red poncho and navy blue pants partially covered with burlap approached me.

"What little thing, *madamita?* What do you want, señorita?"

"I am looking for chairs, señor."

"Here! I have good chairs, *madamita*, which one do you like? Just go ahead and choose. This one, señorita? Or this?" Eagerly he snatched up one after another and planted them firmly in front of me. Another man ran up and beckoned to me.

"Come, señorita. I will show you good chairs. Come here, come this way, señorita. Come, *madamita!*"

"Just a moment!" I laughed. "I will look at these first." A woman shouted from down the line, "Come here, señorita! Here I have furniture of every kind. Whatever you want, señorita, everything. Anything at all."

The chairs were mostly of simple design, roughly finished but sturdy looking. I picked one up. It was much heavier than it looked.

"An excellent piece of furniture, señorita," the man said, looking up into my face with earnest hope. I thought of him as I had thought of the woman with the toy suitcases, working perhaps in a shop in the front part of his house, turning out the crude little chairs, and I wanted to help him. Then there was the other man, too, and the woman. I saw a problem created before me. Business matters in my own country had been easy enough, for my motives had been simple. Here, however, a project was at stake and I felt responsible to act in its interest. I must convince the Indians, in any way possible, of my good will, for it was not merely chairs that I wanted of them.

There were a few upholstered chairs in the market, constructed on the fat, ugly lines of the thirties, the sides forming quarter circles, the seats too low, covered with coarse cloth in appalling colors. To put one of those in my living room would be a high price to pay, even to promote my end. No, I would stick with the ordinary wooden ones. I walked along and looked at the others, all nearly the same, wondering how I was to choose the person I would please. I asked the prices.

"Sixty sucres, *madamita*," was the first answer, followed by a shout from the man farther on, "I'll give you one for fifty-five." The woman called to me, "Come, señorita. I am going to show you a good chair for forty-five sucres. Come here, señorita."

There seemed to be no other customers and I felt myself the object of everyone's undivided attention. Did they know that I wavered in the decision not because I was trying to decide which chair to buy but which salesman to gratify? I kept walking back and forth, not replying to their calls. I noticed that behind the mats which the woman was selling she had a pot of corn soup boiling on a little stove. A child of perhaps three or four, wearing only a raveled sweater, lay asleep on a pile of rags beside the stove. He held a piece of blackened banana skin in his hand, and his breath came in short rasps.

"Is this your child?" I asked the woman.

"Yes, señorita. *Buenos días.*"

"*Buenos días.*" I had forgotten again. "Is he sick?"

[63]

"Yes, señorita. He has fever."

"Where do you live?"

"Over that way."

"You could not leave him at home?"

"How could I leave him at home, señorita? There is no one to care for him. I have to come to the market."

"You come here every Thursday?"

"Yes, señorita. And I go to other towns for market on other days. That is how I live."

The decision was suddenly simple.

"How much did you say this chair is worth?"

"Forty-five sucres, *madamita*."

"I will give you forty." It was standard practice to bargain, but even as I did it I felt condemned. The woman needed far more than forty-five sucres, even if that were clear profit.

"No, señorita. Forty-five is the minimum. You can see that I am poor."

I gave her the money. Surprised, she looked at my face with gratitude—in fact, I thought, with something akin to love.

"Thank you, señorita. Shall I call a *cargador* to carry it for you?"

"Yes, please," I said, and she hailed an Indian who stood nearby with a rope over his shoulder. He wore a pressed-felt hat with a round crown and a warped narrow brim. It looked as stiff, as heavy, and as weather-resistant as asbestos, and it was a dirty, yellowish white, splotched here and there with darker stains. His hair was cut raggedly just under the level of the hat brim, a poor compromise, it seemed to me, between the white man's style and the Dutch-boy bob of Indians farther north. His face was broad and unlined with a few sparse whiskers on his chin which gave him a callow look that did not match the mixture of suspicion and question in his eyes. He wore loose, uncreased white trousers which reached almost to his ankles, and his poncho, which was blue-black, was folded so that the two outer edges rested on his shoulders. Underneath the poncho he had a homespun shirt of European cut, tightly buttoned at the cuffs and collar. I tried to decide if the poncho was what gave his torso such a top-heavy look, or whether perhaps Indians were normally shorter-legged than Americans.

"I carry this?" he said.

"Yes, please," I said, and he silently strung the rope around the chair and passed the leather portion of it across his forehead, bowing slightly as he hoisted the chair to his back. He followed me patiently as I went from stall to stall, my main purchase made, choosing a few small things to furnish my house—a feather duster, a little brass basin with handles, a moss-green, dull-glaze piece of pottery to put on my windowsill. He collected the things as I bought them, finding a place to carry each. Then we started home.

"Do you live near here?" I asked the Indian as we climbed the hill.

"Yes, señorita, over that way." He pointed with his chin toward the northwest. He did not look at me, for his face was bent downward with the strap across his forehead.

"Do you have a family?"

"Yes, señorita."

"Children?"

"Yes, señorita."

"How many?"

Silence. He plodded on slowly, giving no evidence that he had heard me.

"How many children do you have?" I asked again.

"How many will it be? Four? Four, señorita."

"Four alive?"

"Yes. And a baby too."

"Then you have five?"

"Yes, five, señorita."

"Did you have children who died?"

"Yes, señorita."

"How many?" Perhaps I was being too inquisitive. But what *did* one talk about to an Indian? How was I to befriend him?

"I don't know, señorita."

"You don't know?"

"No, I don't remember. They are born and they die. Or they grow a little, and, sickening, they die. That is how it is, señorita."

We walked on in silence for a while as I thought of this succinct statement of the man's life. That is how it is.

"What is your name?" I finally asked.

"Pedro."

"And your surname?"

He glanced at me through his eyebrows. If only I could get through to him. If only he knew how I longed to win him for Christ. He had probably had little experience of white foreigners, but his knowledge of other whites had made him suspicious. He regarded them as his enemies, people who were determined if not to destroy at least to exploit him. Since I was, furthermore, a woman, there was little hope that he would believe in my attempt at friendliness.

"Do you have land, Pedro?" I decided to forget the question about his surname for the time being.

"Yes, señorita."

[66]

"Do you grow things on your land?"

"Yes, señorita."

We had arrived at my gateway. I was reluctant to part with him without some hope of seeing him again.

"Does your wife ever come into town?"

"No, she takes care of the house."

I opened the gate and he put the things down in the front yard.

"There, señorita." I gave him three sucres.

"*Gracias,* señorita." He turned and went out. I watched his broad short back as he shuffled down the street.

Was this the contact I had set out this morning to make, or had Pedro and the others to whom I had spoken merely slipped through my fingers? I had pictured myself, Bible in hand, against a backdrop of high mountains, talking—*dealing* was the word used by evangelists—with an Indian. Sadly I thought that this was how my praying friends pictured me, too, and the picture was not a true one. Things were just not working out quite as expected. What would I not give—O God, what would I not give—to make the picture come true? But perhaps I am impatient, I thought, as I went into the kitchen to make some coffee. I had, after all, found a nice chair, and that was one of my objects. Not the most important, of course. God forbid that visible things should mean more to me than invisible, but on the other hand I should not overlook tangible answers to prayer. If God had guided me to the right furniture there was reason to hope that He had guided me to the right man, the man who might eventually become a believer and be willing to help me with the task of Bible translation. My hopes leaped ahead and I saw already Pedro's face, lit with joy, reading the Scriptures in Quichua. But it will take a long time, the MacDonalds had said. It is no easy thing to get next to the Indians. Perhaps I was taking too much for granted. Perhaps I had frightened Pedro by asking him so many questions. Well, the Lord could overrule that, too. I must tread softly. It was like putting salt on a bird's tail.

THERE WAS an unexpected sameness in the weeks that
followed. It was unexpected because I had pictured a nice
sequence of events which would visibly mark the progress
of the new work among the mountain Quichuas: Getting
acquainted, Visiting, Contact, Witnessing, Conversions,
Translation of the Bible. Oh, of course I had not expected
all this in a short time. It would be slow, but it would, once
it got started, be steady, and there would be things to
report. Instead of this, things seemed to have come to a
standstill as soon as I had met Pedro, and I found myself
getting up in the mornings, reading my Bible and praying,
eating breakfast and swallowing my vitamin pills, washing
dishes and dusting, thinking of excuses to visit as many
shops as possible in order to engage the shopkeepers in
conversation, going to the post office to get my mail,
strolling through the market in hope of making the acquaintance of more Indians, and wishing for something to
happen. If nothing happened, where was my *raison d'être?*
It was not that I was lonely or bored. Quite the contrary. I
loved the setting—the little house, the quiet street, the
bustling village, the gorgeous valley and mountains with
the big sky overhead. I loved watching the life of those

around me, trying to understand what they did and why they did it. But what right had I to enjoy myself if that was all I could do? The world was full of people who had no other aim in life. My very contentment became a rebuke to me. Here were these souls all around me, busy with occupations and preoccupations in which I had no part, and not one of them yet won.

When I was in college there was a red-haired girl with a beautiful voice who sang,

> Over the ocean, millions I see,
> Fettered in bondage, beckoning me.
> Crushed beneath sorrows, too heavy to bear—
> Gladly I answer, Lord, send me there.

The words always stirred me and I was puzzled to find fellow students unmoved by the song, or by the statistics presented to us of the numbers who die daily without Christ. Words like "apathy" and "complacency" ran through my mind and I wondered what such students would have to lay at the Master's feet. There was another song about "nothing but leaves" which came to mind then. Here I was now, over the ocean, surrounded by the beckoning millions, but their lives went on as usual. I saw in their faces sadness and the emptiness of despair at times; I saw poverty and suffering and injustice. At the same time I saw that the sun shone on their peaceful valley and the women spun with their skillful fingers and carried their plump, contented babies on their backs; the men drank firewater in the market place and laughed loudly and ate their potatoes and fried pork skins with gusto, and at evening everyone had a house to go to and the next day would be the same. Once I was on the point of approaching a woman whose face looked especially sorrowful. She was standing beside a display of shoes made out of rubber tires. Just then a man leaned out of a truck and shouted, *"Hola, bonita!"* and the woman laughed and shouted back at him and then turned and gaily swatted a child who ducked past her into the stall. How, exactly, was I supposed to interrupt their lives? If one has been summoned to loosen fetters where does one begin?

Daily I prayed that the Lord would lead me to the ones I should speak to and it seemed on several occasions that my prayer had been answered. I found a woman in one of the meat stalls who could read. She was not strictly an Indian, but belonged to the *cholo* class, of mixed blood, and had had several years of schooling. Since she was there every day I decided to buy my meat from her and concentrate some effort on winning her friendship. She was unusually friendly and interested and after two or three conversations she asked if I would give her a Bible. I hesitated to start out with a whole Bible and suggested that she read a portion such as one of the Gospels, and then we could discuss it and, if she wished, I would give her more. She gladly accepted the idea and each time I went to her stall I found her with the book. She was, in fact, so avid in her reading and so instantaneous in her agreement with all I said about the Gospel that I could not help suspecting that she was only seeking to satisfy a customer. How was one to know?

There was a little girl, too, who begged me for one of my pretty books and ran eagerly home to show it to her mother. She told me later that her mother had beaten her for bringing the foreigner's book into their house and had torn it out of her hand and thrown it away, but the child retrieved it secretly and was reading it. An Indian boy had come to market one day with a small pig to sell. Seeing me sitting on a bench he came over and began to ask questions about my books so I read to him and we talked of many things. But when I asked what he knew of God he was frightened and hurried off to sell his pig.

Pedro was often in the market place with his rope slung across his shoulder, and though he was naturally very reluctant to recognize me at first—my friendliness baffled him utterly—as time went on he summoned the courage to answer my greetings. I asked him again if his wife ever came to market and he said that she would perhaps be coming the following week. I tried to find out what day but he only shook his head and said that he didn't know. When she came she would come, he said, using an odd Spanish phrase which I took to be a literal translation from his own language. My faith that God had indeed directed me in the initial contact with this man was renewed, and I sent up a veritable storm of prayer that I might meet Pedro's wife and thereby gain the longed-for entrance into the Indian community. Perhaps she would be my "first-fruits"—for, in spite of the few earlier encouragements, I was still not at all certain that I had ever won a soul.

When I was a student in Bible school the principal had once electrified us by asking how many in the audience had never won a soul. "How many, now," he had said, knitting his brows and leaning toward us over the pulpit, "have *never won a soul?* I want you to stand." The palms of my hands went damp and I could feel the blood rising in my temples. So far as I knew, I had never brought a single person to a decision about Christ. I had tried—not many times, but several, diligently and sincerely, without any result. I stood up. Every head in the auditorium was supposed to be bowed and every eye but the principal's closed. Mine, however, opened for a moment, and I saw only two others standing. Nearly a thousand sat in their seats. I felt marked for life—and even, I thought with horror, for perhaps longer than that. Was I after all one of the damned? At the same moment I felt a loathing for those who ought to have stood and hadn't. Surely we could not be the only three. Yet perhaps we were. Perhaps it was true that of that crowd only three had been disqualified, unusable for God. Self-justification and despair alternated in my mind so that permission from the platform to sit down brought little relief.

Now God was giving me another chance. In answer to my prayer, "Lord, send me," He had sent me and I had every reason to believe that He would glorify Himself by bringing forth results. I went every day to the market during that next week, and at last I saw a woman following close behind Pedro, carrying a basket of vegetables. He eyed me surreptitiously from the side and made no move to recognize me, but I hurried over and greeted him. The woman kept her eyes on the ground until I asked Pedro if this was his wife.

"Yes, señorita."

"It is my pleasure," I said in Spanish, giving my name and hoping she spoke enough Spanish to understand my good will. She smiled diffidently, passed a hand quickly to the mass of gold beads around her neck, and shifted her feet.

"She does not speak Spanish," said Pedro. Good, I thought, for after all if I am to learn her language it is better that we have no recourse to another. Already I imagined myself seated in her hut, scribbling furiously as she talked to me in Quichua and cooked her corn and potatoes. This would be the real beginning of the transla-

[73]

tion work. O Lord, so let it be. Make this woman know that I want to befriend her. Open the door, Lord. Open the door.

"What is her name?" I asked Pedro.

He looked embarrassed. He glanced at his wife; she looked from him to me and back at him. I could not tell whether I had committed a *faux pas* or whether perhaps he could not remember her name. Then, as though with sudden resolution, he blurted out, "Rosa." The effort this revelation cost him made me feel like a thief. I had extorted something from him which he had not wished to give. I remembered that Mrs. MacDonald had told me that Indian women do not take the husband's surname. But I did not yet even know what Pedro's was.

"Rosa," I repeated. "Rosa and Pedro. What is your surname, Pedro?"

He looked sheepishly at his wife, who was watching me closely.

"My surname? My surname is Chimbu, señorita. I am Pedro Chimbu."

"And mine is Sparhawk," I said, smiling. "It is a kind of bird. Does Chimbu mean something?"

"It is my surname, señorita."

"Those are lovely vegetables, Rosa," I said. "Did you grow them?" Then I remembered she could not understand. Pedro giggled.

"Tell your wife that I think her vegetables are very nice," I said.

"*Bueno*, señorita," he said and was silent.

"Tell her what I said," I urged. He laughed nervously and made a move as if to go. Rosa followed and I said I hoped I would see them again. In my heart I resolved to see them. There was something winsome about Rosa's face and sad, humble eyes. If only I could show her that not all white people hated her. If only I could show her God's love. . . .

It took several encounters like this one, widely spaced since Rosa came to market only once a week or less, before I dared to ask the thing I really wanted. In between visits with them in the market I prayed very hard that God would speak to them and cause them to invite me to come to their home. Finally I felt that God was telling me I should broach the subject—after all, He had sent me to them, not them to me, and I should not be shy in the King's business.

I found them contemplating some stainless-steel spoons at a little stall. They talked together for some time and at last must have decided against the purchase and began to move away. I went up to them.

"*Buenos días, Rosa. Buenos días,* Pedro."

"*Buenos días,* señorita."

I gave the baby on Rosa's back an affectionate pat or two, asked about their health and that of their children, remarked on the lovely weather, which drew a blank look from each of them, and then asked, "Could I come, Pedro, to visit your house someday?"

He stared at me in wonder.

"To our house?" he said.

"Yes," I said, "I would like to visit your house."

He spoke in Quichua to Rosa. Her eyes shot a hard glance at me, then she said a few words to Pedro, who repeated as though to himself, "To visit our house."

"Shall I come?" I said.

"Come," said Pedro.

He went with me to the street where I lived, which commanded a view of the valley and mountains, and pointed out the road I was to take.

"When you come to a house, ask them where I live. Tell them Pedro Chimbu, son of Old Pedro. In each house, ask, and they will tell you. They will show you the road."

A LETTER from Woodrow Rogers announced the forthcoming annual conference of missionary organizations working in Ecuador, to be held in Guayaquil in three weeks. It would be well, he suggested, if I would prepare a brief report for my fellow missionaries on the effort that had been started in Indi Urcu. To establish an evangelical work among a million highland Quichuas was our object as a mission board, but to date only three couples were working in widely scattered stations, and now I, a woman, had come. This did not constitute a very significant breakthrough. The Indian work of other missions had been concentrated in jungle tribes heretofore, but the men of vision who had conceived Indians for Christ, Incorporated, saw the immense potential of a harvest among those poor, degraded descendants of the once-powerful Incas and their subjects. Earnest efforts to recruit young men and women for the task had yielded dishearteningly small results so far.

When I read the letter I knew that I must hasten my visit to the Chimbu house. Had anyone accused me of going to visit Pedro and Rosa the next morning as much because of my need of something to report as because of my concern for their immortal souls, I would have been indignant. I rose earlier than usual that day in order to have time to prepare myself in prayer for the task ahead of me. I saw it as a serious task, one on which I had staked my life, and I must not botch it now. The mission also existed for this, and I was their representative. Beyond all this, I was also an ambassador of Christ. He could not fail. It was not simply my own success and reputation that were at stake—it was clearly the success of the Gospel message itself, the reputation of God and all that He had promised in His Word. "For the Lord God will help me; therefore shall I not be confounded: therefore have I set my face like a flint, and I know that I shall not be ashamed." The words from Isaiah buoyed me.

The sun rose and I rose from my knees. After breakfast I put on my coat and picked up my Bible.

The road I lived on ran east and west, and I followed it west for about a half mile, past the last houses in the village and through some fields of corn and potatoes. Indians who hurried by on their way to market did not know that I was on my way to visit Indians. They kept their eyes on the crumbly earth of the road and passed me as though I might have been one of the magueys. You find me here on your road, I thought—a strange figure among your cornfields and potato plants—and you hurry by, resentful, I suppose, at the intrusion, anxious only to escape an encounter and be gone about your business. But when I meet you, I think, Here is one now. Can I catch him? as though I were a hunter. You do not know. You would laugh if someone said, "She has come only because of you."

Jesus once met a woman at a well. She too found it hard to believe that He needed something from her, and even more incredible that He had something to offer her.

I stopped for a moment to watch an ox pulling a wooden plow through the arid crusty soil. It was hard to imagine that any tender plant could push its way through such earth—pale, buff-colored stuff which cracked into great rocklike clods as the oxen strained with lowered necks and scraping hoofs. "And some fell on dry ground." Where would fall the seed I was about to sow? "Plow the ground, Lord," I prayed as I walked on. "Their hearts will be hard, but You can soften them."

Presently I came to the footpath which ran north from the road toward Pedro's house. It was a dry gully between the rows of magueys, climbing gradually at first and then more sharply, dropping suddenly into a great eroded gash in the hillside and ascending once again the steep slope of the other side. The land was so dry that the dust rose in little puffs with each footstep, and my shoes were full of it. I could feel the cold dry wind stiffening my nostrils and pinching my lips.

A woman passed me, her rigid braid, bound in red cloth, sticking out behind her head like the handle of a pitcher. Her dark blue shawl was caught in front with a long silver pin in the shape of a sword. She threw a dark glance at me and went on, barely pronouncing an *s* in response to my *Buenos días.*

Finally I reached a little mud house, huddled in the corner of a field of grain. It had a steeply pitched grass roof like untrimmed bangs over its one feature, an empty doorway. There was a skinny rooster clawing at the dirt in front of the door, and an old blue enamel washbasin with holes in it lay to one side. I called out a greeting and waited. No one appeared. I called again. Was anyone inside or were they all out in the field? I waited, and then went on, threading the edges of several more fields. In spite of the beauty of the valley and range upon range of mountains, I was conscious only of utter desolation—the sharp cold, the loneliness, the taste of dust, and the fear in my heart. There was no sound whatsoever for minutes at a time. Now and then I could hear the distant bleat of a sheep, and the wind came in choking gusts. I saw another hut, approached, called, and waited. There was a movement near the doorway in the shadows of the interior. I called again, *"Buenos días,"* and a head appeared. A boy with flashing black eyes scrutinized me for a moment, his lips tight, his chin thrust out.

"Can you tell me where Pedro Chimbu, son of Old Pedro, lives?"

"Buenos días," he said. He kept studying me for a moment, then pointed to the northwest. "Over there."

"Shall I just follow this path?"

"Yes. Then when you see another one which goes that way"—he pointed with his chin—"follow it."

"Thank you." I went on, conscious of his continued gaze as I walked up the trail. I could feel his question, What wrong has Pedro done, to be thus pursued by a white woman?

Finally after several more inquiries I reached Pedro's house. It was larger than the others and one section of the roof was tiled. Around it were fields of beans, peas, corn and potatoes, and there was a calf tied nearby and several chickens who squawked at my approach. I called a greeting and after a moment Rosa poked her head out the door. I had the feeling she had long since seen me coming but did not want to be caught watching, so had waited for my call. She came shyly toward me and I smiled, said good morning, and patted her left upper arm with my right hand as women in Ecuador do. Pedro had said she did not speak

Spanish, but I spoke to her slowly, hoping that Pedro had exaggerated.

"I have come, Rosa, to your house—to visit you. I have come to see you." I could hardly mistake the distrust in her face, but she said, "*Bueno*, señorita. Come," and led me indoors.

I had to stoop low to enter. It was as dark as pitch inside, and the smell of smoke, dried grains, dust and humanity was overpowering. There was a tiny fire of wisps of grass smoldering feebly on the floor. Around it several small animals were moving which I at first feared were rats, remembering the loathsome creatures in Guayaquil. At length I saw that they were guinea pigs. Back in the corner lay piles of sacks and sheepskins, wool ponchos, shawls and blankets. This collection I took to be the bed. There was no furniture in the house at all, but bulging grain sacks were placed about as though they were meant to be sat on, so I looked at Rosa for permission. She waved her hand toward one of them and I sat down, while she squatted back on her heels by the fire and began banging a woven rush fan up and down on the floor to encourage the embers. She set a small black pot on some stones over the little flame. Then I realized we were not alone in the room. Three or perhaps four children—I could not be sure because they were huddled so closely in the dim light—were solemnly surveying me from behind some sacks in another corner.

Rosa was making some kind of drink. She had to keep adding tufts of grass to feed the fire, but she added them very sparingly, inserting them delicately in just the right spots. She said nothing more to me, but spoke in Quichua to the children. The words sounded angry, but the children did not move or reply. She took the pot from the fire, lifting the hot handle with a twig, and set it on the ground. Tipping it quickly with her bare hands she filled two small painted enamel bowls and pointed to one of them.

"Drink, señorita," she said. It appeared to be some kind of gruel. There was so little flavor—not even any salt— that I could not identify it. Nevertheless the warm liquid was satisfying—for one thing, because I was hungry, it being close to noon, and for another, because it represented a welcome from a Quichua woman, the courtesy of an Indian home. I tried to say thank you. Rosa took my bowl and filled it again but offered it this time to the children in the corner. She filled her own empty bowl as well and gave it to them. Was this to be their lunch, I wondered?

When they had all finished drinking, I took out my pad and pencil and began asking the names of various objects, using the Spanish phrase for "What is this?" Rosa looked at me dumfounded. Did I not know a guinea pig or a spoon when I saw it? I repeated the question and she said a word. I wrote it down, using phonetic characters, and the children eased over toward me and peeked over my shoulder at the paper. One of them, a boy of perhaps eight, took the pencil from my hand and made a letter on the corner of the paper—he wanted me to know that he could write. I supposed he had been to school for a few days or weeks, though he looked too small and did not seem to speak any Spanish. At length the children began to answer my repeated question, and made a game out of pronouncing the words for me and laughing at my attempted imitations.

Then the boy who had written the letter said, "*Imatai?*" pointing to my watch. I hoped that he was asking the same question I had asked, "What is this?" in Quichua. I answered with the Spanish word for watch, and he grinned. He tried it again. Pointing to my shoe he said, "*Imatai?*"

and I again gave the Spanish word. He was elated. He had taught me something.

"What is your name?" I asked in Spanish. His black eyes danced, but he did not reply. I felt sure he understood. "Your name?" I said. "What are you called?"

"Romero."

I looked at the smaller boy, but before I had a chance to ask his name Romero said, "And this one—Jorge." Jorge in turn pointed to his sister, a lovely child who looked to be about nine, but was perhaps older than that. Indians do not seem to show their age.

"This one is Pava," he said in Quichua. I caught the name Pava, and assumed that the rest of the sentence meant "This one is." The word was *caiga*, I thought, so I wrote it down with the tentative translation.

"Pava?"

"*Arí!*" Jorge and Romero said the word in unison, then laughed delightedly. They must have given me the word for Yes. I was pleased with my score thus far.

Rosa went outdoors and the children began examining my coat, shoes, wristwatch, hair and skin. They had seen plenty of white people, but they had not been this close to one. They had learned from an early age to keep their distance from and pay to the white man the respect due a superior. But with the guilelessness of children they accepted my friendliness without suspicion. Life had not yet taught them much about treachery.

When their mother came back inside she placed some leaves on the ground where the guinea pigs could get them and made as if to sit down by the fire. Then she walked over to the bed in the corner and began fussing with the skins and clothing. I tried out my Quichua question on her.

[83]

"*Imatai?*" I said, pointing to the sheepskins. She mumbled the answer so that I did not hear. The children repeated it for me. Rosa was not enthralled by the game and was finding it difficult to entertain a visitor whose vocabulary was limited to a single interrogative. I tried a new tactic. I stood up and sat down, using the Spanish word for "I sit down." It was clear, from Rosa's expression, that she questioned my sanity. I laughed and tried it again. The children watched mystified and delighted, but offered no information. Rosa was at a loss. She said something to me which I did not understand. Several possibilities came to mind: "Are you crazy?" "What is the matter?" or "When are you leaving?" I thought it most likely that she was trying to tell me she did not understand. Well, enough of this, I decided, and resorted to drawing pictures in the ashes on the ground for the children. Still Rosa did not sit down but busied herself here and there doing nothing. Then she spoke sharply to one of the children and the child went outside, perhaps to get the cow, I thought, or fetch water. Their life must go on, and my intrusion was inhibiting the process. Rosa had done all she knew to make me welcome. Beyond that she was at a loss, and my presence confused her. I could not explain my mission and it would be a very long time before I would be able to. But this was a beginning. A visit to an Indian home, a bare beginning on the language—six or eight nouns and a question form; plus the word for "yes." Well, some other day. This was, at any rate, a contact.

I rose from the sack on which I sat, extended my hand to Rosa. "*Gracias*, Rosa," I said. "I will come again some other day." I think she understood the phrase "other day." She smiled.

"*Bueno*, señorita," she said.

[84]

I shook hands with each of the children. It occurred to me that Pedro had said he had five children. Here there were three, plus the baby. Perhaps Pedro could not count.

"Until another day," I said in Spanish.

"Until another day," they parroted.

The trail down the mountainside was like broken concrete layered thickly with dust. It had been a mistake to wear thin-soled shoes and nylon stockings, but then I did not own anything else. I would have to see about getting something more rugged. "Sensible" shoes carried all the stigma of the missionary spinster image which I loathed, but I could unhappily foresee my own progressive conformity to this image. Even that, however, could be endured for Christ's sake. "How beautiful upon the mountains are the feet of him that bringeth good tidings . . ." Absurdly this bit of Scripture popped into my mind, bringing a tiny wry comfort.

I stopped now and again to empty the dust and stones from my shoes, and to look at the enormous range of earth and sky spread before me. Never in my life had my eye held at once so much earth and so much sky. I am not very good at judging distances, but it seemed that at least sixty or seventy miles of valley lay before me, drawn up at the two sides like a huge blanket, stretched between invisible stakes where the peaks of the mountains made the horizon jagged. Far to the south the land faded into sky. The colors were muted, with no greens visible except close at hand. The fields were brown and purple and mauve and taupe and gray, spreading to the high country where nothing would grow, where there were only the black of rock, the gray of volcanic ash, and the gleaming white of snow. The lake lay like a silver ellipse far below, and the little village of Indi Urcu nestled, small and insignificant as a heap of pebbles. The sky was a luminous, burning blue, incredible in its clarity. Even the edges of the white clouds seemed sharply cut and superimposed on an infinity. The magueys outlined the fields faintly like strings of dark beads laid neatly and tautly in criss-cross. At odd corners of the square patches huts stood, a few with blurs of smoke escaping through the thatch. The afternoon sun threw a mantle of peace on the whole, and I wondered if I had ever seen such marvelous beauty. Indians passed me in ones and twos, each carrying his unsold wares or his purchases for the day. Their feet were bare—tough, strong-looking feet covered with the dust of the road, with the toes spread as human toes were meant to spread, not crushed and caricatured by the wearing of shoes. Would these feet someday be the bringers of good tidings? The words of Isaiah again . . .

I hurried on down the path. An Indian man was coming toward me, not evading my gaze. It was Pedro Chimbu.

"*Buenas tardes,* señorita," he said. His rope lay on his shoulder. Market would be over for the day, and he would find no more carrying work to do.

"*Buenas tardes,* Pedro."

He asked if I had been in his house and looked pleased when I told him I had.

"*Bueno, bueno,* señorita," he said, looking past me and then at me, as if waiting for my permission to go.

"Until another day, Pedro," I said. "I would like to come someday when you are home. Perhaps you would help me talk to your wife."

"*Bueno,* señorita, that would be a good thing. You come when I am at home."

"I want to learn your language, Pedro," I said, "so that I can translate God's word into it." I hoped this would arouse his interest.

[86]

"*Bueno*, señorita."

What did this reply mean? Was it all I was ever going to get from Pedro? If I did not understand him, he probably understood me even less. Of my declared intention, as of any declaration made by white people, he made nothing. He had never discovered any grounds for dealing with them. Whatever it was they wanted, he was bound to treat them respectfully. I tried again.

"Do you know God's word?"

"No . . . once I went to the church. The priest talked about God, but I did not hear well, I did not understand."

"God has given us a book, Pedro. Did you know that?"

"No, señorita."

"Would you like to hear it? Would you like to hear God's word?"

"*Bueno*, señorita." This time I decided that the reply indicated not a desire to know but a polite willingness to be told.

"Someday we will talk about it. Until another day, then, Pedro."

"Until another day, señorita."

He trotted on up the hill. Well, they aren't headhunters, I reflected with a slight trace of disappointment, for it was beginning to dawn on me that my position among these Indians was not really a very dramatic one. Where the need is not obvious, as it is (it seemed to me) among wild aborigines, sacrifice to meet the need loses some of its nobility. But then, they are certainly godless Indians. (The adjective was a sweeping condemnation, but I used it automatically, having been taught that all were godless whose personal commitment to Christ did not match mine.) They have no knowledge of God's word. What a privilege it will be to bring it to them! I thought exultantly.

It was said that they had a form of religion, but they needed what I had come to bring, needed it every whit as much as a demon worshiper. Godless heathens, pagan savages, degenerate serfs—they were all the same, and Christ had died for them. Any incipient misgivings I may have had about the effectiveness of my first visit were banished by these thoughts.

Rosa had wished me gone. No matter. Secretly I heaped coals of fire on her head. I was doing her an immeasurable favor, though she was as yet unaware of it. The day would come when she would thank me for what I had brought her. I could look for that day in faith. "My word . . . shall accomplish that whereto I have sent it."

I went on past my house and down to the post office. There was a missionary magazine in the mail and I quickly turned to the South America section. The item was there:

"Miss Margaret Sparhawk of IFC has now arrived at the new station among the mountain Quichuas of Ecuador, Indi Urcu. Pray for her as she begins her work among these neglected people. Pray for help in her study of the difficult tribal language."

I was satisfied. They had me in my slot and could start praying now for the things I knew were going to happen. The word "difficult" made me slightly uncomfortable. I had not used it in my own letters describing Quichua, for I had heard from a noted linguist that Quichua is one of the easiest languages in the world. Well, I thought, the responsibility does not rest with me. If faulty information inspires more earnest prayer, who can regret it?

IN THE three weeks before the Guayaquil conference I visited the Chimbu hut as often as I could, sometimes when Pedro was at home, sometimes when he was not. Rosa was always in or near the house, always working—cooking, spinning, carrying water, carding wool, husking corn—but she learned to accept my coming though she did not clearly understand that her language was incomprehensible to me, or that I wanted to learn to speak it. White people did not speak her language, she knew, but perhaps because she herself had never had to learn it she did not understand why I had to. Was it not perfectly "hearable"? She had certainly not come across a white person who wanted to speak Quichua in preference to Spanish. So my questions and antics, intended to elicit Quichua phrases, she took as a white person's whims, not to be fathomed or challenged. Pava, although she was very quiet and as busy as her mother, missed nothing, her great black eyes following every movement of mine while her hands went on scraping the steel combs over raw wool or beating the dirt out of the tangled piles with a rod. Jorge usually managed to disappear just before I came into the house, but Romero joined in with my work as though it were a game.

"Señorita!" he would call, popping out from under a sheepskin. "Who am I?"

"You are Romero!" I would answer, in Quichua, proud to remember the pronoun and verb form.

"You are Romero!" he would repeat roguishly.

"No, I am Margarita." This required two different forms.

"She says, 'I am Margarita, I am Margarita,' he would chant, mimicking exactly my faulty intonation, for it was no easy thing to forget the English way of answering a question and to reproduce accurately the Quichua intonation. When Romero imitated me, however, I caught the difference, so his mocking proved a great help.

He taught me to count up to ten, but when I thought I had it, he would deliberately confuse me by counting with me and skipping a number. He would point to his foot and give me the word for hand, or to his head and say, "hair." I wished ardently that I knew how to scold in Quichua.

I visited other homes as well, but I had not worked out any plan for covering the territory I called my own—it was far too vast. Any contemplation of a systematic coverage would have discouraged me. I merely set out in whatever direction my mood dictated, having asked God beforehand for guidance to the right places, trusting that circumstances, mood, weather, chance encounters on the road might indicate the ones to whom God wanted me to speak. Long ago, when the servant of Isaac sought a wife for his master's son, his prayer was that the woman of whom he should ask a drink might be the one whom the Lord had appointed. It seemed to me a fairly reliable method of guidance: let the one to whom I speak *be* the one.

Each home I visited seemed a duplicate of the last, and

the Indians themselves hardly differed in their response. They were overawed at the presence of a foreign woman and listened very politely but noncomittally to whatever I said, whether it had to do with the weather or their crops or salvation through Christ. They nodded in solemn agreement and said "*Sí*, señorita," and I knew that some missionaries would accept this as an indication of their hunger for God's truth. Sometimes things worked together happily and I would come upon a man or woman at just the right moment—when he was resting from his plowing or she from her water carrying—and they would be willing to listen for longer than usual. I would bring the conversation around to their need of a Savior and they would agree and then, at such times, I could readily believe that I had been led. More often it seemed that nothing had worked very well and I returned to my house disheartened, feeling that I had gained little either in friendship or in language data. These were the times, I decided, when I had not been led. My faith worked best when things worked as I had planned.

I was to blame, of course, I confessed privately. Two things were wrong—two, at least. I was uncertain as to exactly what I ought to be doing, and I was still lacking in spirituality. I looked forward to the missionary conference in Guayaquil, where I might once more be with English-speaking people and learn from older missionaries how to go about my work, and I hoped that the meetings would provide spiritual fortification.

My vagueness about the course my work should follow made me uncomfortable. I was always sure what needed to be done in my house. It was a pleasure to get up in the morning, cook breakfast, clean and straighten things, shop for food, collect mail, do errands and write letters. It was when those things were finished and I was at last free to do missionary work that I found I did not know just what missionary work was. But of course this is all a part of it, a physical framework for spiritual operations, I told myself. All that one does is to be done "to the glory of God." How familiar the idea was to me. Yet somehow one had to divide it into categories—one could not qualify either for financial support or for prayer support simply by washing dishes in another country. There had to be, besides this inspiring view of housework, a demonstration of deeds accomplished, worthier causes pursued.

I had heard of missionaries' having servants so that they might be "free to do the more vital things to which God had called them," and this sounded altogether justifiable. When I stopped to consider what vital things I would do if I had a maid the answer, surprisingly, was not ready, but I was confident that I would surely find something. There would be some program, some method or means or project I could adopt besides my present pursuit of the language. The real work would begin, I ventured to believe, when the language was conquered—but then, one read of so much that missionaries did without knowing the language at all! I would have to confer with Woodrow Rogers to find out just what the mission policy was. How stupid of me not to have inquired more carefully before I launched out alone! If I just knew the policy . . .

But then there was still my lack of spirituality, of which, God knew, I had plenty of evidence every day. Why, the very evening of the day I had first visited Rosa I had come home elated, praising God for progress, and as I turned the key in the lock a fingernail snapped. Damn it all! was my immediate response, followed by shock in thinking how shocked everyone would be to know that such a word was even a part of my vocabulary. Of course I had not said it aloud—the word was forbidden at home, was not so much as admitted to thought—but I had thought it, and I thought it again when, a minute later, as I was searching for a nail file to repair the damage, the bureau drawer stuck first on one side, then on the other, and suddenly jerked out and dropped to the floor with a bang.

"Missionaries are human beings, after all," was a phrase I had heard, and at that moment it struck me as being so patently ridiculous that I wondered if anyone had ever really uttered it. Human beings! Dear God, what else could I or anyone else have thought? Could we have imagined that they were superhuman, perhaps, or ex-human? People who had turned into something else, subject no longer to human passion and temptation, invulnerable to the ordinariness of living? My mind jumped back to the missionary homes I had visited since coming to Ecuador—the squalling babies, rickety ironing boards, endless discussions of hepatitis and maid problems and customs difficulties. But, I argued with myself, God wants more than this. He offers us something higher and richer, and by His grace I will appropriate what He offers, I *will* be spiritual-minded, even if I am a human being. Now and then my thoughts dwelt on a suitably spiritual level (it seemed easier when I was with the Indians than when I was at home) but I was not the missionary my friends hoped I was, of that I was certain, and I wanted desperately to qualify.

The MacDonalds took me to the Guayaquil conference in their jeep and as we bumped over the roads and ate oat cakes and tea in the grass we talked of the work and I told them about Pedro and Rosa and my hopes for them. They were amazed that I had gotten as far as I had with the Chimbus. "Why, that's wonderful! Why, what a story! It took us months to get into any Indian homes! Oh Margaret, the Lord is good, isn't He? The Lord sent you here!" said Mrs. MacDonald, "and He will fulfill His purposes, for the Indians, and for you, dear girlie."

When we reached the port city they took me to the home of Joe and Jenny Twombley, a couple sent out from home by the same mission as mine, who had recently written to invite me to stay with them during the week of conference. When Joe opened the door there was an odor of fried fish and vinegar, mingled with the steamy smell of clothes being ironed. We went along a dark hallway to the dining room, where a middle-aged woman stood hunched over an ironing board, her cotton housedress clinging to her perspiring back, her hair pasted in wisps to her forehead. The belt was missing from her dress though the loops which should have held it were there. She stopped ironing long enough to shake hands with me when Joe introduced us.

"Guess we're Ecuadorian now," she said, laughing. "We always shake hands!"

"Myrtle works in the Oriente—you know, the eastern jungle," said Joe, "with the Quichuas. You two'll have to get together and compare language notes. Have a powwow or whatever you call it. Here's Jenny—and our future halfback, George."

His wife came in from the kitchen with a very plump, beaming baby in her arms. The baby flourished a spoon with applesauce on it. Some of it got on his mother's hair.

"Oh, Georgie baby, be careful, honey. Come on out in the kitchen, Margaret, while I just finish up a few things, then we'll be ready to eat."

The kitchen was a tiny sort of cave—tinier and darker than mine—with a black sink in one corner and a gasoline pressure stove propped on a packing crate, on which stood the frying pan with the fish I had smelled and a pot of something boiling. Jenny began to bustle around, stirring things and getting out dishes, so I offered to feed George. I was greatly relieved to find that he had been fed. Jenny said there was nothing to do, really, so I went and stood by the open back door, where I saw a large rat sitting calmly in the middle of the narrow patio, nibbling a bit of garbage. He made no move when I appeared. There was a tree in one corner of the yard which threw its shade over most of it, but not a blade of grass redeemed the slick hard surface of mud. The only green besides the tree was the mold which colored the mud.

"I suppose you're used to these rats out here?" I asked.

"Oh yes—aren't they awful? Guayaquil's full of them, but you do get used to it all, I guess." Another one ran along the foundation of the house which backed up to the other side of the yard. Piercing Latin music came from a cheap radio behind one of the bamboo walls of the other house. The volume was turned up full and the music seemed ceaselessly to repeat the same five notes.

"About ready, Mommy?" Joe called to his wife.

"Yes, right away," Jenny answered. "If you'll just take George, Daddy—here, put him in his high chair. Go to Daddy, Georgie. Here's a cookie. Want a cookie, Georgie?"

When the meal was ready, we sat down at a heavy wooden table covered with a plastic tablecloth—the same one, I noted, that had been on the table when I was here before. It was hideous, really. On the first occasion I had viewed it and the heavy plastic dishes and steel flatware as good, practical missionary equipment—didn't I have the same sort of things in my baggage, all but the plastic tablecloth?—but now I couldn't help feeling that they had carried the denial of niceties just a bit far. This downright ugliness—the sticky rice piled in the bowl, the gray-green peas and greasy fish, the careless appearance of the women—was it necessary? Must soldiers of the cross look as though they had just survived a pitched battle? Was this what was required of us?

"Fold your handies, Georgie," said Jenny.

"Fold handies, George, we're going to thank Jesus," said Joe, bowing his head, watching to see whether the baby was prepared to pray. The baby put his two fat hands together and Joe asked the blessing and then began to serve the food.

A child began to cry.

"Oh—Sandy's awake. Will you get her, Joe?"

There appeared in the doorway a child of about three, wearing only underpants, her hair a tangled mat of straw, her face stained and contorted with crying. She kept crying. Jenny reached for her, but she stood on one foot and bawled. This set George to crying loudly too, and the parents tried in vain to quiet them.

"I guess it must be the heat. They've been doing this every day now. Maybe the water. Come to Mommy, Sandy." Sandy stopped crying for a moment, then caught sight of me and burst into fresh yells. Myrtle tried.

"Come to Auntie Myrtle, baby. Auntie Myrtle take baby bye-bye. Go bye-bye, Sandy?"

The two babies screamed, the three adults tried all their tricks. The music outside was as loud as ever, as unremitting. The heat inside was suffocating. Poor Joe and Jenny, I thought. They were kind to invite me, but they had their hands full. I might have done them a favor by refusing their invitation. Well, here I was, and I would try to make the best of it. It was the meetings I had come for, at any rate.

The conference was to begin the next morning, but the regular prayer meeting of the Ecuadorian church took place that evening and I went with the Twombleys.

The church was a square room with unpainted wooden benches and a green concrete floor. The walls were pale green and there was a text printed across the front, *La sangre de Jesucristo nos limpia de toda maldad.* (The blood of Jesus Christ cleanseth us from all sin.) An upright piano stood on one side, an elaborately carved wooden pulpit occupied the center, and at the left was a large piece of white cardboard with a picture of a thermometer painted on it, indicating the progress of a Sunday-school memorization contest. I had sat in countless similar rooms and squirmed on the benches as the congregation sang and the preacher preached—churches ranging from the plain community church in Pennsylvania to country school-houses where I had held services when I spent a year in rural home mission work. I thought now of the blue-and-gray carpet in the first Sunday school I attended, and the brand-new smell of the little low varnished chairs on which we Beginners sat, peeking through our fingers at the patent-leather shoes on the carpet next to our own, and then of marching round the rows of chairs singing, "Dropping, dropping, dropping, dropping, hear the pennies fall, every one for Jesus, He will take them all." I used to ponder just how He would do that. Did He really need them? I was told that He did, in order to get His work done. It made me feel sad to think of God waiting for our pennies. Mr. Lewis was the superintendent, and he always had an "object lesson" for the children. I remembered the glasses of colored water and the padlocks and different-sized spoons and posters and boxes and diagrams of hearts and crosses and crowns and clouds which he used for teaching us spiritual truths. I could not remember much about what those objects were supposed to illustrate. I watched and listened enthralled until he came to the part which began, "And now, boys and girls, this little box is like . . ." Then I would start studying his round steel-rimmed glasses and his tiny, neat mustache, and remember how he looked at his desk in the bank where he worked. My father had taken me in there one day and Mr. Lewis had admitted us behind the brass fence and then into a great, gleaming round door which led to a vault lined with little steel boxes, one of which belonged to my father. To have been permitted to pass that monstrous door seemed a very great thing to me, and I stood hushed in the sanctum, wondering why he had not told us about this round door instead of about cardboard boxes.

In the next Sunday school I attended, my teacher began each class by hissing, "All right now, girls, le's jes' have a word of prayer." I remembered nothing of what she taught us but could not forget the grammar she used. ("Oncet I read about a clock that all the works into it was made outen wood.") But she was, I understood, a "faithful soul," and I was therefore expected to listen to her Sunday after Sunday.

It was the missionaries who spoke on special occasions in these Sunday schools to whom I listened with close attention. They told us about teaching little black or red or yellow boys and girls about Jesus. They taught us to sing "Jesus Loves Me" in half a dozen languages. I responded to the appeals they made, and dreamed of sailing to some far-off land where people waited under palm trees, straining their eyes toward the horizon until I should arrive to tell them what they longed to hear.

It was now long past the hour announced for the beginning of the prayer meeting, but only a dozen people had gathered. An old man opposite me at the back was reading a small New Testament, holding the book close to his eyes and moving his lips slowly. Several women with their hair in braids were talking in low tones. A young couple and a few children made up the rest of the congregation.

Soon Woodrow and Frances Rogers arrived. I had met them only briefly before, but had been impressed with Frances' ability to look fresh and cheerful at all times in so hot and depressing a city as Guayaquil. She looked the same now. She was about thirty-five, plump and neat and self-assured. When she walked into the church her heels clicked lightly and her bracelets jingled.

"Margaret! How *are* you?" she said, coming over to where I sat waiting for the meeting to begin. "Oh, I'm *so* glad you got down to the conference. Well, how do you like it up there? How does this heat seem to you after being up there in those cold mountains? Woodrow! Here's Margaret Sparhawk! Excuse me a minute, Margaret—I have to go speak to these people." She sidled through to the aisle to greet some Ecuadorians, speaking not loudly, for we were in church, but not in a whisper either. Things seemed to be quite informal.

A few more minutes passed and a gray-haired missionary lady arrived whom Woodrow introduced to me as Miss Blake. She did not take time for more than the formalities of greeting me, and then went to the piano and began to leaf through some gaudily colored paperback chorus books before she began to play. The sustaining pedal on the piano was not functioning. She struck the keys briskly, as though they were the heads of naughty schoolboys which needed rapping, and the plink-plunk of the chords had a curious honky-tonk quality, even though I recognized the tune as one we had sung in English at a Bible conference, "The Whole Wide World for Jesus." She played with great earnestness, nodding her head up and down, as she looked first through her bifocals at the music, and then down at her hands.

A few more people straggled in and sat down diffidently as close to the back as possible. Then a door at the front opened and three men emerged—two short Ecuadorians dressed in black suits and black ties, and Woodrow Rogers, tall and bony and dressed in shirt sleeves and a bright bowtie. They went up the three steps onto the platform and the younger of the Ecuadorians stepped to the pulpit and began to speak in a very loud oratorical tone. There was a rustle of hymnbooks, Miss Blake thumped a brief introduction, and the congregation began to sing. This was followed by a prayer, led by the older of the two nationals. His voice rose and rose, then fell in little swoops till it reached the amen, in which several members of the audience joined him aloud. There was an audible sign, a soft scraping as feet were rearranged, another rustle of hymnals. There was a second hymn, a third, then the announcements and offering and finally the preaching, the same routine followed in every church service I had ever attended.

The speaker took a long time finding the place in his huge Bible. He cleared his throat, looked out over the sparsely scattered audience, pushed his glasses down on his nose in order to look over the rims, surveyed the audience once more, cleared his throat authoritatively, and turned his eyes down to read through the glasses. He read a few verses and then spoke, gesturing widely with both hands, slapping the Bible now and then, adjusting his glasses, pointing skyward and then at us, pausing to find his place in the Bible again, turning over a leaf of notes, emphasizing with great clarity every consonant in the name *Cristo*, pronouncing it as though it were an indictment on his listeners. There. He was finished. The Gospel had been preached. There followed a period of prayer which was open to the floor and all of the adults present took part, all of them alike intoning their phrases as the men on the platform had done, everyone joining in to put a period in the form of an amen to each prayer.

Woodrow was asked to pronounce the benediction and we opened our eyes. The meeting was over, and the people began to move around, speaking to one another, fussing with hymnbooks, collecting Bibles and purses. Most of them smiled and offered their hands to me as they passed. I said, *"Buenas noches"* and *"Mucho gusto"* and waited for Joe and Jenny, who were talking with the Rogerses. Myrtle and Miss Blake had their heads bent together over a large folder which looked like a Sunday-school lesson manual. Myrtle looked up.

"Hello, Margaret. Come and meet Miss Blake."

"Yes—we met just before the meeting."

Miss Blake put out her hand. "I didn't shake your hand, though. In Ecuador we always shake hands." She smiled at me, revealing yellowish but original teeth. Her handshake was very firm and brief. "We're glad to have you with us. Where is it you're working?"

"With the mountain Indians—not far from Waira-pamba, where the MacDonalds live."

"Well, that's a needy field. A *very* needy field. You'll

have to learn Quichua, you know. That's the first thing you'll have to do."

"Yes, I'm very much hoping to find an informant to help me."

"Miss Blake has been in Ecuador for thirty-seven years, haven't you, Miss Blake?" Myrtle said. "She worked with national pastors here in Guayaquil for some time, visiting homes and jails and handing out tracts and teaching Bible classes in some of the believers' homes. Now she's in Riobamba."

"Riobamba's a needy field, too," said Miss Blake. "I do the same sort of work up there, but there's a lot of opposition. A lot more than there is down here on the coast. This is a modern city, more open and tolerant. But we have some wonderful opportunities in Riobamba. Praise the Lord for that."

Joe and Jenny were ready to go, and I went with them, pondering what might be the true nature of the work of God.

CHAPTER

10

⚓

THE OPENING meeting of the conference was a devotional one in the morning. I stood with Jenny in the back of the church where we had attended prayer meeting, waiting for Joe to come and the meeting to begin. Missionaries of every size and shape, and of as many doctrinal persuasions as could be admitted among those who call themselves evangelical, poured through the door past us.

"Hazel! How are you? You cut your hair!"

"Hi, Harry pal. Whendya get down?"

"Stay here with Mother, Betsy; hold Mother's hand. Betsy! Stay here, I said. We'll sit down in just a minute."

"Well, praise the Lord, Mike, that's just what we've been hoping for. Wonderful. Just wonderful. Right in the main plaza? And they didn't bother you at all? Last time we tried to hold a meeting there we got rotten tomatoes. Say, I'd like to go back there and hold a campaign with you!"

"It's the most delicious stuff. I have the recipe if you want it."

". . . told her that was *not* what I meant but she went right ahead and *wrote* to the director . . ."

I would have known they were missionaries almost anywhere, except for a few who didn't quite fit the pattern. They were solid, serious, earnest types for the most part, the young men with a certain eager stretch to their necks, the older ones with a weariness around the eyes and a droop to the shoulders. The women were pale—make-up was worn timidly by a few—and most of their hair styles were several years out of date. They came in self-consciously, gently shoving their children before them, looking around for a place to sit near the back. Jenny introduced me to a few who stopped to speak to her.

"Margaret Sparhawk? Oh, you're the new one with the mountain Indians now, aren't you?"

"Oh yes—with IFC, aren't you? How do you like working with the Indians?"

"How is it up there—pretty rough, huh?"

My answers to these and other questions were not very articulate. Fortunately the people did not seem to expect answers.

I began to glance over some of the literature spread out on long tables on either side of the door. The titles revealed how other missionaries felt about their calling: "Latin America, Land of Opportunity for Christ," "What Is the Church's Responsibility to Lost Tribes?," "Is God Calling *You?*," "How to Know the Will of God for Your Life," "Ecuador in Her Hour of Crisis," "The Unfinished Task," "The Unreached Millions," "The Great Commission and You." Such themes, in my college days, represented the kind of attitude toward which I aspired. Now as I read them over, glancing now and then at the people who came in the door—people whom the tracts had recruited—I knew that the attitudes represented were no longer to be merely aspired toward, but ought indeed to be mine at this moment. *Were* they mine?

"So I said to her, I said, 'Why on earth didn't they put you in a place where . . .'"

"Bill—see you after this meeting for the board conference, O.K.? Right in back of the Sunday-school room."

"Sandy!" This time it was Jenny speaking. "Sandy, you come straight back here. . . . Well, why didn't you say so sooner? The meeting is almost going to start. Oh Margaret, would you hold George while I take Sandy . . ."

The pianist—it was Miss Blake again—struck a few determined chords, executed several runs, and the speaker and song leader took their places on the platform. People hastily found seats and the meeting began, following the same pattern as the prayer meeting on the preceding night —Scripture reading, prayer, and a devotional message from the Reverend Ira J. Perkins, pastor of a large church in Toledo whose Gospel broadcasts had collected a great deal of money for missions in Ecuador. Ecuador was his special project and Mr. Perkins plugged it whenever he had the chance. He was introduced by the chairman of the largest mission board represented at the conference.

"We all know what a blessing Mr. Perkins' broadcasts have been to us—back home in the States and here by short wave—so we're looking forward to a time of real blessing here together this week, with him and with the Lord. Mr. Perkins, we're glad to have you."

Mr. Perkins was a small man with a very powerful voice. He began by telling us what a privilege it was to be a missionary to the missionaries. Then he told one or two humorous stories and proceeded to speak about bearing fruit for Christ, using the fifteenth chapter of John as his text. "The secret, beloved," said Mr. Perkins, "is to abide. Abide in the Vine. Christ is the Vine. Just abide. Now isn't that simple? You and I get so busy running here and there, doing things for Christ, trying to serve the Lord, when all He tells us to do is *abide*." He explained in careful detail how the branches abide in the vine, and left me wondering, as I had wondered all my life, what Jesus had meant by the word *abide*. The secret that Mr. Perkins had set out to divulge was still a secret to me.

"Good message, wasn't it?" I heard afterward. "My, that was a blessing. You get so dried up on your station, it's good to hear something like that. Take in for a change instead of always giving out—you know what I mean."

Then there was a coffee break, called a "Fellowship Hour," during which everyone seemed elated and busy and said the same things over again to one another. I did not find much to say to these people, and spent the time standing with a cup of coffee, trying to overhear others' conversations. "Our work" and "our mission" and "our Indians" and "our tribe" were phrases I heard again and again. They all seemed to belong, they knew the lines, and they wore—I must be imagining it—the same masks. All carried well-worn Bibles, the men large, dog-eared black ones with overlapping Morocco covers, the women smaller ones, some of them with colored bindings, some with names engraved in gold. I noticed in the coffee hour something that had escaped me when I watched the men coming into the church before the meeting. There was a hail-fellow-well-met spirit among them here, but they seemed to see only one another; they acknowledged the presence of women, but without looking any of them straight in the eye. The women on their part—young, pregnant wives, single women with hope in their eyes, overweight older ones, attractive and unattractive—looked as though they had sacrificed much for the cause of Christ, and, stabbed with shame, I thought, Who am I to be their judge? God looks on the heart.

There were certain shades of distinction between members of different mission boards. There were boards which forbade their women to wear make-up, boards whose members were vegetarians, boards which drew their recruits from among midwestern farmers and boards which required attendance at the same Bible college, boards which had a preponderance of single ladies and boards whose members had been born, nourished and cherished by a single denominational group and had survived only by conformity to that regime. I had once heard someone remark that a missionary could be the laziest or the most overworked person in the world. Here I saw both kinds.

Suddenly I felt an overwhelming claustrophobia. It was not only the heat that stifled me. Finding myself inextricably packaged and labeled in the same box with these who bore their labels, it appeared to me, so easily—not to say proudly—put me in a state almost of panic. Someday, God willing (but suppose God willed and I didn't?)—at any rate, someday by the grace or something of God, I would fit into the box. Someday the label would justly apply to me, but not yet. Definitely not yet. I did not meet the qualifications, I could not pass inspection, certainly I was not up to the standards declared on the label. There were still far too many contradictions within me. Perhaps this conference would have some salutary effect.

The next meeting was a series of reports from representatives of the various participating missions. Again it began with a hymn—just two verses, the first and last, of "Send the Light"—and a brief prayer in which the leader asked the Lord's blessing on our gathering together this morning, "that everything might be done to Thine honor and to Thy glory, in Jesus' name, Amen." It was so predictable to me that I hardly had to listen, and caught myself examining the shading of the letters on a motto which had been strung across the front of the room: "All Power Is Given Unto Me." The lettering was neatly done, in gold with red shading, like the motto which arched over the minister's head in my little home church. He had stood, as it were, on exhibit before the words "My tongue shall speak of Thy Word." All that his tongue had spoken had fled from my memory but the claim remained, a convincing label.

Eleven American and two British mission boards participated in the annual conference. A spokesman for each gave a survey of its work and the achievements of the past year. We heard first about evangelism among children of the coastal cities. Four hundred and twenty-three Bible club meetings had been held in churches, homes, stores, and on public plazas. Several thousand Scripture portions had been memorized by the children, four children thus winning a free week at youth camp—they had memorized entire chapters of the Bible. A number of incidents were recounted of the children's having been punished for attending meetings and then of their having won their parents to Christ in the end.

A thin, handsome, well-dressed man told of radio broadcasting in fourteen languages. The Gospel was being given out over the air waves night and day—with cultural programs in between, of course, along with news reports and music—and letters poured in daily to tell of blessings received. "A microphone ministry is not always an easy one—it can be deadening. Pray for us, that the quickening power of the Holy Spirit will anoint each broadcast as it goes out, reaching into homes of people who would never darken the doors of a church."

Then a stocky, red-faced missionary from Nebraska told about importing pure-blooded bulls and a special breed of rooster in order to help the mestizos who live in the lowlands to improve their cattle and poultry. "God can use a thousand methods to get people to listen to the Gospel, and if we can help them physically—they sure need it down our way—then they're more likely to listen to the preaching on Sundays. We have two classes a week for farmers, when we give them instruction on fertilizers and feeds and breeding and things like that, and then at the end we have a little message from the Lord for them." He told of three who had come to Christ through this means, and had found farming more profitable since their conversion.

A missionary from the eastern jungle gave statistics about the numbers of tribes and the probable number of people in each. "Of course, nobody really knows—they haven't made a complete census. We're working in three of the tribes . . ." and he went on to tell of baptisms in jungle rivers ("The crocodiles never seem to come around when we're baptizing somebody. Guess even the devil keeps his distance—for a while anyway!"), schools for Indian boys, prenatal clinics for Indian mothers, snakebite cases successfully treated, portions of Scripture translated into Indian dialects, even a witch doctor who had been converted and insisted on turning over his fetishes to the missionary.

A member of another board reported on their work in a different section of the jungle—schools, clinics, churches, even literacy classes for adult women who until now didn't want to learn to read. "In fact, the men didn't want them to learn for a long time, but now they are loosening up and letting their wives come to classes, so we praise the Lord for this step. One of the younger women has actually been helping my wife in the translation work, an unheard-of thing only a year ago. So pray for the jungle Indians. Scripture says there will be some from every tribe and nation, and we believe God has called us to work with Him toward that end."

"All power is given unto Me." I looked at the words again behind the speaker. He was talking now about the distribution of tracts in market places in the sierra cities. Of the thousands scattered like seed (and here he spoke of the prodigality of nature: "Think of the seeds God wastes!") there were a few examples of fruit, that is, souls saved because of having picked up a tract. "For every thousand thrown away, if we win one soul it's worth it! Amen? *Amen!*" And most of the congregation seconded it.

The chairman closed the meeting with a plea for more concerted prayer for the work which was going on, and for more laborers to be "thrust into the harvest fields."

"Truly," he concluded, "as we look about us in this great field of opportunity here in Ecuador, we see much land yet to be possessed, and the laborers are few. May God give us purer, more dedicated hearts, and a real burden of prayer."

He and the others who had spoken used a language and a distinctive tone that echoed through my mind from a thousand pulpits, pulpits of plain wood, carved wooden pulpits, painted pulpits, but each of them the dais of like men, men who with a notable facility and sameness of phrasing could present what was called the missionary challenge. I had never thought of these phrases as platitudes, and I did not question what they had to say. Like the primitive tribesman who, upon hearing a recording about God, was convinced of its truth because it said the same thing each time it was played, I accepted what they told me as true. It was supported, I believed, by Scripture, and I took it as the voice of God, quite unaware at the time that it little moved me. I deplored, in concord with the preachers, the coldness of my own heart. I capitulated to their arguments that the deficiency of my missionary work now must lie in my own lack of prayer, my failure to surrender to the Lord, and my imperfect apprehension of the power of the Holy Spirit.

"Shall we bow in prayer?" said the chairman. We bowed, and there was a cacophony of coughs and throat clearings.

"Our Father, we thank Thee for what we have heard this morning about Thy work here in Ecuador. We thank Thee for what Thou hast done in this beloved little country, through those who have given themselves to Thee for Thy service here. We ask that Thou wilt bless each work here represented. We pray especially for the believers in each area, that Thou wilt make them strong Christians, faithful to Thee in the midst of temptation and the pull of the old life and its associations. Be with each of the missionaries and guide them in their future service for Thee. Give us a renewed vision of what it means to serve Thee and a deeper burden for souls in Thy great harvest field. May we go forth from this meeting refreshed and strengthened to serve Thee, for we ask it in Jesus' name. Amen."

There were to be separate meetings of the various mission boards during the evening, and I was expected to present my report to the session of Indians for Christ. I spent the afternoon preparing for this. It was quiet in the house while the others were taking their siestas, but concentration was difficult afterward. I went over and over what I had seen and heard in the morning. What could I say to match that kind of success story? What *was* there to say? There was no point in getting panicky about it—after all, there would only be a few people, it would be informal, and obviously they were not going to expect much from a newcomer who had only been working a few weeks on a station. Just tell them about the situation—the ideal location for my house, the thousands of Indians within an hour's walk, the contact with Pedro and Rosa, the beginning on the language. What else would they want to hear? It was very simple, really, and something to praise the Lord for.

It was stifling in the dark little room. The house was long and narrow, and the central rooms had no windows at all, though the ceilings were exceedingly high. I thought of my own little house with its small, cold rooms and its sunshine and red geraniums, the wind whipping around the corners at times, the deep silence at other times. George cried off and on during the afternoon and I could hear Sandy's piping "Mommy!" up and down the hall. I would have given a great deal for some of Indi Urcu's solitude. The general atmosphere of this house was one of confusion, as though the whole family had just arrived from somewhere and had not yet unpacked. It was like that a year ago, too, I recalled.

But for this evening I had been invited to dinner, along with a Dr. Lynn Anderson, to the Rogerses'. Frances had introduced me to Dr. Anderson during the coffee hour and, now that I looked back on it, there was something distinctive about her, something—could I call it reality?—which made me look forward to the evening.

DR. ANDERSON arrived at exactly the hour she had specified, impeccably groomed in a dark cotton dress of simple cut, her ash-blonde hair drawn back carefully in a bun. She wore Ecuadorian earrings of hand-wrought silver with a bracelet to match. I noticed that her car was well polished.

"Well," she said, negotiating smoothly a remarkably rough road, "what sort of day have you had?"

"Oh, it's been very interesting, really. But so hot! I'd forgotten how hot it can get here on the coast."

"Terrific, isn't it?"

"Yes, I suppose I feel it more because the sierra is so cold. Is that where you live, too? Where *is* your work, Dr. Anderson?"

"Please call me Lynn, if you like. I live in Cuenca, in the southern part of the sierra."

"Oh, yes. You have a hospital there, haven't you?"

"Just a clinic. I have four nurses and two national doctors who work with me, but we don't have inpatients."

"What mission are you with?" No one had told me Lynn's connections, and as yet I could not tag her in my mind.

Lynn laughed, tilting back her head. Then she looked at me quickly, her eyes becoming serious again.

"Suppose I didn't tell you? It doesn't really matter much anyway, since my connection with the mission is becoming less and less tangible. Besides, I think it's much more interesting to know people than causes and movements, don't you? As soon as you put somebody in a pigeonhole, you want either to endorse him or cross him off. Did you enjoy the meetings this morning?"

"Why, yes. I enjoyed Mr. Perkins' message."

Lynn said nothing. She waited for me to go on.

"And then, it's certainly encouraging to know that there's so much missionary effort going on. I mean, you see such a need all around and it seems so hopeless to do anything about it, and then when you hear all these reports you're convinced it's not hopeless after all."

"And suppose, after a few years' work, you found that it was?" Lynn watched the traffic and did not give me a chance to learn from her face what she meant.

"Oh, but it couldn't be hopeless," I protested. "You don't mean that that's what you've found?"

"I was asking a question. What would happen to your idea of God, for instance, if you found that your work was useless?"

"To my idea of *God?* Why, nothing, I hope."

We had reached the Rogerses' house and Lynn parked the car with easy skill. She must be a very good doctor, I thought, the picture of confidence and efficiency. I saw that she had a certain dignity in her walk as we went toward the front door.

The house was orderly and cool, with the smell of roast beef coming from the kitchen, the table attractively set at the far end of the living room, fresh flowers in several places. Miss Blake was there, dressed in a very bright crepe dress with pink flowers which cried out for some faint response from her gray face and hair. Frances introduced us to another couple named Ernie and Maxine. Ernie was the one from Nebraska who imported bulls and roosters. Myrtle was there, too, sitting on the edge of a chair beside Maxine.

"Strawberries!" said Maxine. "Where?"

"At the market. And beautiful red ones, too—not those gray squishy ones they usually have. I think Point Four has helped develop them."

"How much were they?"

"Only four sucres a box. I didn't think that was too bad, considering what you'd pay in the States."

Ernie lounged in a corner of the sofa, reading a magazine. I could see the title of the story: "Are Christian Teen-Agers Stuffy?"

"Daddy!" came from the children's bedroom.

"What is it, Linda?" called Woodrow.

"Can I have some ice cream?"

"No, Linda, you go to sleep. You should have been asleep long ago."

"Barry had ice cream."

Woodrow said nothing.

"Barry had ice cream, Daddy. Why can't I have ice cream?"

"Didn't Rosario give you ice cream for your supper?"

"Just some. Not a lot."

"Well, wasn't that enough?"

"Barry got a lot. Can't I have some now?"

"No, Linda, you go to sleep. Daddy means it."

"Why?"

"You'll wake Marilyn. Go to sleep, I said, Linda."

"I want ice cream."

"Linda."

"What, Daddy?"

"You know what. Go to sleep."

"Daddy didn't pray with me."

"Mommie prayed with you a long time ago. Now you be quiet."

"I want Daddy to pray."

Woodrow went into the bedroom. There was a low murmur, then a higher-pitched murmur, and he emerged, closing the door softly. He flopped down on the other end of the sofa and picked up a magazine, leafing through it idly as he turned to Miss Blake.

"Not a bad crowd down for the conference, is it?"

"Daddy! Will I get ice cream tomorrow?"

"Linda, you be quiet this minute."

"O.K., Daddy." There was a pregnant pause. "But Barry won't get any, will he?"

"Linda won't get any if she doesn't go to sleep."

"I'm going to sleep, Daddy. Daddy, I'm going to sleep now."

Woodrow smiled at Ernie with one side of his mouth. Ernie shook his head.

"These kids," said Woodrow.

There was evidence of them in the room, though everything was neat. In one corner stood a low square table with a seat built into an opening in the middle of it. There were toys spread on top of this, and under the coffee table lay a small cement mixer. The floor of the room was of polished brown and white tile and the walls were plastered and painted off-white. Frances' good taste showed in the choice of slip covers and draperies and in the artistic arrangement of flowers on the mantel. She came into the room, wearing a small bright apron, carrying a tray of glasses. Woodrow rose and took the tray and passed it to the guests. Ernie, I noticed, did not get up. He found the magazine story absorbing, and looked up only long enough to take the glass of tomato juice offered him and to say thank you. There was no place for Frances to sit down. Ernie did not notice this and Woodrow had gone to the kitchen for napkins. I had begun to get a chair before Ernie came to and took it from me.

As we sipped the juice Miss Blake described her ride to the meeting that morning in a *colectivo*, a cross between a bus and a station wagon.

"They aren't supposed to stop for you unless they have a seat, but it was rush hour and when I got on there wasn't a seat left so I protested and the driver pointed to the little seat on his *left*—you know the one, don't you, Margaret—that little boxlike affair, hardly big enough for a child, on the *left* of the driver's seat. So of course I told him I couldn't sit on *that*, so a man behind him slid around onto the box and I finally got his seat. But the buses are even worse, and it's worth the difference in price, don't you think so, Frances?"

"Oh, definitely. What's four cents?"

"Well, I used to think it was plenty, but after I got my purse stolen on a bus and lost fifty-five sucres I decided even a missionary had a right to ride the *colectivo*."

Rosario, Frances' maid, was putting the food on the table.

"Ya, señora," she said, and Frances invited us to sit down.

"Frances, this roast is perfect!" exclaimed Maxine, when the food had been passed around.

"Oh, I don't take any credit. Rosario does everything,

[117]

really. I can even leave the meal planning to her if I want to. Of course, she'd like to feed us nothing but rice and *fideo*." Missionaries, I noticed, had an irritating way of throwing in Spanish words as though they were English. "So I have to sorta help her balance the meals for us. She cooks her own rice and stuff, of course, regardless of what we're having. Without rice it's just not a meal in her book."

"Oh, I know," Myrtle put in. "My Filomena is the same way. I never saw such mounds of starch as she can put away. How do they do it, and not get any fatter than they do?"

"They eat in bulk what we eat in variety, you must remember," said Miss Blake.

"Well, with the diet I'm on now there's precious little *variety*," said Maxine, and from there the conversation went on and on about diets. Then it was the heat, the dishonesty of tradesmen and mechanics, poor gasoline which ruined cars, red tape involved in getting things into the country, the conference and the people who attended it, with their poor Spanish, poor health and poor support from home.

"And the way these nationals think we're all *made* of money!" exclaimed Myrtle.

"You can hardly blame them," said Miss Blake, "when you compare our way of life with theirs. We belong to the upper class, by their standards, and we can't get around it."

"Maybe we should learn to identify more," said Woodrow. "Jesus was a poor man."

"Yes, but then how do you reach the upper classes?" said Myrtle. "Besides, if we identified with the lower classes, we'd be spending all our time doing the things they do, and

[118]

we'd never get any missionary work done. How could we take our clothes to the river and wash them by hand? Or cook on a wood stove in a bamboo shack, spending all day making all those complicated soups and things?"

"Well, I guess it's been done. Missionaries have had to do worse than that."

"But this is the twentieth century. We've got to adjust to more modern missionary methods."

I was lost. The arguments disregarded, it seemed to me, the principle of renunciation and sacrifice to follow Christ. What were we here for? And yet I could not answer the questions raised in my mind. Someone noticed my silence, and a few polite inquiries were made about my work in Indi Urcu. I described my house and the village and the great need around me, and they all thought it sounded like a great opportunity and were relieved to know that another missionary had come to work expressly with the Quichuas. Miss Blake talked about her work with the little church in Riobamba, a series of small successes which punctuated her continual giving out of tracts and going from door to door.

"But it's so hard to get people at home to see the need. They think of jungle missionaries as the only ones on the front lines. It's so hard to convince them that we who labor for the Lord in the cities are just as much on the front lines, just as much in need of prayer and support. If only I could get a young couple or a couple of young men to come up there and work with me. My, the opportunities!"

The use of the term "front lines" puzzled me. It was not clear just which were the front ones, now that I was in Ecuador. Once I had thought of all missionaries as on the front lines, but now distinctions were being drawn and I wondered how my work would be classified. Lynn saw the puzzlement in my face, I was sure, though her expression did not perceptibly change.

I did not dream of challenging the truth of Miss Blake's statement. It must be quite legitimate to refer to certain aspects of God's work as strategic, but on what basis did one single them out? I could not argue the thing through, but I knew that it made me uneasy to hear her speak as she did. Perhaps I had an imperfect recognition of the loftiness of my calling, a lack of vision which forbade me to assign to the work its full status in the economy of God. I was an inexperienced, immature worker and it ill befitted me to criticize the terminology used by a veteran of years of service.

Frances passed me a basket of rolls.

"Oh, I couldn't, thank you, Frances. They are delicious, though. Miss Blake, will you have one?"

Miss Blake took one and went on.

"It's a real joy to contact some of those young house-wives there in Rio. They're bored and lonely and it's amazing how receptive they are, for the most part, to the Gospel. They hardly ever refuse the Scripture portions I offer them, and who knows how many are blessed by them? Of course it's another thing for them to come out to the services—their husbands or the priests might find out, and they're afraid, but I do give them the plan of salvation, and then, even if I'm never allowed inside the door again, I know they've had the chance to accept Christ. Of course, some of them are hard all right. Only God could ever break through to them—they slam the door right in my face."

There were small pauses after some of these utterances, as though Miss Blake expected assent from the audience, but I had the odd sensation that we were listening to a recording and consequently need not respond. Finally Woodrow spoke up.

"Well, I've always heard Riobamba is a hard place. Wonder why it is those mountain cities are so hard to crack?"

"I think it's just what I was saying—people don't pray for them, they're just not as interested in that kind of work as they are in more dramatic or romantic work. Then, too, young couples come out, and we try to interest them in working in the cities, but they're always attracted to the Indians and there they go."

"I wonder," Lynn spoke for the first time, "if it is possible that God might have some excellent reasons, quite outside our imaginings, for not doing what we think He ought to do?"

"What do you mean?" asked Miss Blake.

Lynn paused, her water glass halfway to her lips. "We are accustomed to blame the deficiency of missionary work on our own lack of prayer or failure to surrender, or on our inefficient methods or the coldness of the church at home, or even on the hardness of the native heart—the notorious failure of Christian missions among Mohammedans is often accounted for in this way. . . ."

"Would you deny those things?" Miss Blake asked, her eyebrows drawing together.

"I question whether they explain everything."

"Oh well, of course they don't explain everything. But, after all, we have the clear command of God, we know what His will is concerning the evangelization of the world, so if it doesn't get done you wouldn't blame *Him*, would you?"

Lynn took a sip of water. I held my breath. She would surely say no. What other answer could there be if we were not to let the whole structure of our faith collapse? Why were we here if God was not going to keep his part of the bargain? Lynn said nothing, but looked from Miss Blake to me, and then to Frances and Woodrow.

"Oh no," said Frances. "We can't explain the way God works, we know that. Lots of things happen that we can't explain. Look at the beheading of John the Baptist. But then in the end God shows us that it was all for the best, and who knows how much greater glory He got because He allowed John to be killed?"

"That's true, Frances," said Woodrow. "But we're talking about the evangelization of the world and the reasons for its apparent failure so far. I see no other explanation than the indifference of the Church. Christ gave the command, Go ye, and if we don't obey, we're responsible. That's all there is to it. The burden of proof lies with us to show why we didn't go."

"Exactly," said Miss Blake. Her eyes darted from one to the other, missing nothing, as though the moral responsibility for the entire group rested with her. "Why, you'd take the whole motivation out of missions if you put it on any other basis. We know God could have done it some other way, but He chose us to be His ambassadors, and woe unto us if we preach not the Gospel." She looked at me almost accusingly, as though I had taken a position on the other side. Not for the world would I have contradicted her or the others. What they said was to me ineluctable. God keep us, I prayed, from human rationalization which cracks the very foundation of our faith.

"Did God," asked Lynn quietly, "ever destroy anything which He Himself had built?"

"No," said Miss Blake without hesitation, "at least not until men had been so disobedient that He had to. But what are you trying to say? Don't you believe, Dr. Anderson, that we're here to win souls? Don't you believe *that?* What *is* the missionary task, after all?"

"I am no longer as sure as I once was." Lynn smiled, a gentle admission of vulnerability.

"Well, we're here to serve the Lord. I don't know what *you're* here for." Miss Blake attacked the piece of meat on her plate. Frances offered us more mashed potatoes and peas and tried to direct the conversation to a discussion of the hopelessness of the Ecuadorian customs system. Woodrow had spent two entire days trying to retrieve a pair of new glasses which he had had sent down from the States. We all commiserated with him, and other examples were cited which proved the system worse and worse, but conversation was strained for the rest of the meal. A few clear pronouncements on one side and a few honest questions on the other had, in a matter of minutes, shown me that life was not going to be as simple, ever again, as I had thought. It was as though, during a stage performance, someone had peered around from the wings, and though the actors did their best to ignore him and then to make him gracefully retire, the play was ruined. The lines petered out in banality.

There was a little time before the session and I wanted to get away alone. The others went to the church, but I decided to walk. I must determine whether anything I had heard at dinner made it necessary for me to revise what I had planned to say in my report that evening.

I went out to the Malecón and walked by the river, too absorbed this time to notice the things that had bothered me on my first visit to Guayaquil—in fact, my general impression this time was that the city was very modern indeed, a progressive and bustling metropolis.

I was supposed to tell of my work. What was my work? Reaching the mountain Indians, of course. What was my object? Souls. How was I to seek this object? Why, by witnessing, giving out the Gospel. And this, of course, could not be done until I learned the language. That was the obvious first step, and that was what I'd begun to do. There were no texts, no language schools to attend. I must do it on my own. The mission would want to know my specific prayer requests: first of all, my own spiritual needs—a genuine concern for the souls of the Indians, a wholehearted abandon to the task, a willingness to go to any lengths in order to bring others to the Savior. Then I needed prayer for special help in the language, wisdom in knowing how to make contacts with individuals, guidance to those who were prepared by the Spirit of God. That would do it, I thought. That would easily fill my seven or eight minutes; it would be an honest presentation of the work and a good summary of my needs in connection with it.

But the dinner-table conversation kept plaguing me. Lynn's calm questions had shaken me, but Miss Blake's instant answers, which were precisely the answers that had popped into my own head to give to Lynn, shook me even more. It was disquieting to discover now, as I walked by the river and went over the talk in my mind, that what Lynn had said had also been in my thoughts at times and I had not dared to give utterance to it. I had answered myself, at such moments, as Miss Blake had answered Lynn, and had succeeded in silencing the conflicts. They were not so easily silenced now. Then I thought of Woodrow and Frances, kind and generous and anxious to make us all happy; Woodrow, in his position as field director of the mission, obliged to take a certain position while at the same time diplomatically acknowledging the right of another to examine it. I was a member of the same mission. I was committed to the same set of propositions. Just how was I going to blend into this picture? I would have to be careful.

The evening session was as I had expected. There were more reports, detailed this time, sprinkled with "our people," "our work" and "our territory," but the possessive included me this time, since I was a member, so it was my work, my people, my mission. When it was my turn, I said what I had planned to say and sat down, having given no one reason to wonder whether I was qualified to carry the banner, whether I was wholly convinced of the validity of my position or of the mission's. I had said my lines as expected, and I was in.

I lived through the rest of those three days, wishing that they might somehow be shortened, for I wanted to return to my field and begin trying out in earnest the things which were being talked about at such length. The Work was the supreme subject and object of everyone present, it seemed to me, and human relationships went by the board. Except for Lynn, no one seemed to be an individual. They were cogs in wheels, fitting smoothly into their notches, emitting the right kind of squeak—and this, I thought, was as it should be if the task of each was the same. What room was there for questionings, or the exercise of individuality? In answer to an inquiry I had learned to which mission Lynn belonged, and I heard that she had been on the verge of resigning or being asked to resign—my informant was not certain which—but her unimpeachable record as a physician and a missionary kept her superiors from dealing too harshly.

Between the hymn singing and the praying and the

reporting and the devotionals there was time for "fellow-ship," which usually meant food eaten in the company of other missionaries and the sharing of a few jokes and personal anecdotes. I longed to have more conversation with Lynn—or, for that matter, with anyone who would take time seriously to discuss issues—but there was no opportunity. So I settled for faithful attendance at all meetings, where I tried to learn all I could.

CHAPTER

12

ON THE morning after my return home I was making coffee for breakfast, thinking of the victorious testimonies of the many missionary-conquerors at the conference. I, too, must fling out my banner with joy—it is God who will lead me in triumph. When I opened the canister in which I kept the coffee I noticed a slightly moldy smell instead of the rich aroma I had anticipated. I put the can closer to my nose. It was definitely moldy. I had no other coffee in the house. Should I throw this away? Certainly not. No missionary had a right to be fussy about such a trifle. I had left home and kindred to come here in obedience to Christ and would I balk at drinking a cup of ill-tasting coffee? I put the grounds in the pot and proceeded with the meal. It was a victory. A very small victory, to be sure, but nevertheless an indication of singlemindedness. People back in the States with their vacuum-packed Maxwell House—what did they know of doing without? "God, I thank Thee. . . ." The words of the Pharisee, "that I am not as other men" flashed through my mind, not as the words of the Pharisee but as my own, as the prayer of my heart. I was thankful that I was not like others who had ignored the call. Immediately upon the recognition that I had in sincerity said the very words Jesus had condemned the Pharisee for saying, I prayed the prayer of the other in the story, "God, be merciful to me, a sinner."

I put the coffeepot on the table and sat down. A little book of daily readings from the Bible lay on the table, and I opened it to the portion for that day. "If we confess our sins, He is faithful and just to forgive us our sins, and to cleanse us from all unrighteousness." I thanked God for those words. I was a sinful missionary, but then God had entrusted the missionary task to sinners, and if we didn't do it, who would? Too many had left their responsibility unfulfilled. Some had suffered, sacrificed, sailed through bloody seas in order to carry the Light to those in darkness, but not many. "O God, to us may grace be given to follow in their train." As I buttered a roll I thought of the "noble army, men and boys, the matron and the maid," and managed to put myself into the lineup somewhere. I hummed over the other stanzas—the one about meeting the tyrant's brandished steel, the lion's gory mane. How gladly would I do that for the sake of Christ!

I finished the roll, drank the last of the coffee (a deed of courage unlikely ever to be sung about), and began to wash the dishes, thinking over in my mind how to attack the job today. It had all seemed so obvious at the conference. Each missionary had his program—he knew what needed to be done where, and he had a method for doing it. I knew what needed to be done here in the mountains: these poor pagan Quichuas needed to be told about Jesus Christ, and there was one thing above all others that was needed in order to do this—the Bible, translated into their own language.

I decided I would go out again today, try to find Pedro, speak to him about the possibility of working for me as an informant in the language. He was a normally intelligent Indian, I judged—perhaps a little above average, since he had a tile roof on part of his house and enough initiative to work in the market place. I would offer him more than he could earn as a *cargador*, we would have regular sessions on the language, I would teach him the Bible bit by bit as we went along, and I would trust God to open his eyes to his own need of a Savior and then to the need of his own people. He would then be eager to help with the translation of the Scripture. When the Quichuas had the Bible and had been given the opportunity to learn to read it, the responsibility would rest with them to accept or reject the message I had brought.

As I finished the housework, this outline of my plan appeared to me as wholly feasible. Why had I made it all so complicated? I chose a few tracts to carry in my pocket, put on my coat and left the house, walking in the direction of the main plaza. The day was cold, with only thin sunlight filtering through a white sky. There was the feel of rain in the air. This would be a blessing, for the dust lay thick on the road and on the geraniums in my front yard. The rain would make it colder and even more bleak and desolate than it was ordinarily, but it would wash my flowers and clean my lungs. Days of cold, driving wind forced the gritty dust deep into my sinuses and lungs so that each breath seemed to scrape and scratch. How good a rain would be!

When I reached the plaza I was startled to find hordes of Indians converging toward it, far more than the usual market-day crowd, and yet there were fewer stalls set up. There was an atmosphere of jubilance and gaiety I had not seen before. Hats danced in the sunlight and I could hear music coming from somewhere—the birdlike notes of panpipes and the plinking of a guitar. A great throng was pouring from the cathedral on the other side of the market place. It must be a feast day. I went into the little grocery store where I did most of my food buying.

"*Buenos días*, señora," I said. "What is happening today?"

"*Buenos días*, señorita. Do you not know? This is the day of the fiesta."

"A fiesta? Of what?"

"Of the saint."

"Which saint?" I realized I should have known who the patron saint of the town was.

"Of our San Rafael, señorita. It is the biggest fiesta of the year."

How could I have been so ignorant? I could see the woman's incredulity. Ah, these foreigners. I made a few small purchases and went out to watch. Groups of Indians stood here and there, some of them sharing a bottle, some talking, others watching and waiting. The stalls were doing a brisk business selling food and drinks, but there were no clothing stalls open today and I noticed that many of the shops which bordered the plaza were locked and barred. Gradually I became aware of distant shouting and music. There was a movement among those in the plaza, and attention turned to the southwest corner. A crowd of Indians was moving toward the corner, as though preparing for some encounter. I could not make out what was happening. Suddenly a mob of shouting, flailing Indians rushed into the plaza and the crowd swirled and heaved, women and children backed out of the way, policemen swore and swung clubs, and I saw that six or eight free-for-all fights had broken out among the men. In no time it seemed that everyone in the plaza was fighting or cheering for the fighters. The woman from the store had come out of her shop and was standing beside me.

"Why are they fighting, señora?" I asked.

"Oh, it is not permitted any longer, but they used to fight for possession of the plaza."

"For possession of the plaza?"

"Yes, in order to be the leaders of the dance. It is the custom. Perhaps an ancient custom, but that is the way they are, the Indians. They have their customs." She shrugged.

"And now it is against the law?"

"So they say. But who can stop them? And then, the fiestas bring good business."

From another street which gave onto the plaza came a procession of Indians bearing huge candles garlanded with wax flowers and paper streamers. Umbrellas bobbed up and down in the midst of the throng and I heard a weird, melancholy chant. As they spread out into the square I could see that images were being carried under the umbrellas. People jostled for positions nearer to the images, and I caught a glimpse of the face of one old Indian woman, withered as a dried apricot, but with brilliant, intense eyes, joyously following the figure of the Virgin. There was in that look a great hope, the first hope I had seen in an Indian face. Those in the front ranks moved with a springiness in the step, turning their faces back toward the Blessed Mother and surging forward as though drawing the worshipers along with an invisible harness. The music, too, seemed to rise and fall in waves with the surging of the crowd.

In the center of the plaza a band began to play, drowning out the panpipes and guitars with a blast of tubas, trombones and trumpets. They were white men and mestizos who made up the band, and I gathered that they had been hired for the occasion, which was clearly an Indian celebration. White people stood in doorways around the square and watched from balconies and windows, but it was the Indians who today had possession of the town. They began to dance, chanting and stamping in circles, their ponchos swinging, bare feet pounding the earth. There were also men dressed in odd pieces of white men's clothing—sweaters, high-top boots, a policeman's hat or a pair of sunglasses adding a bizarre flourish to the shapeless calf-length trousers and homespun shirts of every day. I found something pitiable and touching about this attempt to assume the white man's status for a day. Inhibitions were forgotten as they gave themselves to the celebration, whirling and throwing back their heads, lifting their elbows and knees with a gay energy, bowing and strutting imperiously. The whole plaza was by now thronged with Indians, some of them fighting, some drinking at the booths, some dancing or playing instruments, some still standing in groups along the edges, some eager and adoring as they followed the processions to the cathedral. The images were being carried into the church to be blessed at the Mass which was soon to be said. Women squatted on the steps selling candles and garlands.

"This must be a very important Mass for them, isn't it?" I asked my friend.

"Yes, señorita. The fiesta Mass is the greatest of the year for this town."

"And they bring the images from their own villages to the Mass?"

"Yes, señorita, to be blessed. They bring them from far away, some of them, and then they take them back again to bless the village."

I wondered why the white people did not participate more in the festival. They were Catholics, the fiesta seemed to be a Catholic one, so why should the participants be only Indians? The custom must have its roots far back in Indian tradition.

The crowd pressed me back toward the walls of the shops and I saw that a new attraction was moving down the street. Several figures dressed in huge, elaborately decorated headdresses with grotesque masks were weaving crazily toward me, flanked by laughing, singing men, men playing tambourines and flutes and panpipes. The shape of the headdresses and the features on the masks reminded me startlingly of the Tibetan devil dancers I had once seen in a missionary film. The decorations were Oriental in character and coupled with the Mongolian features of the faces which surrounded them, reminded me of the mystery of the origin of these people. Where were they when the Apostle Paul wrote, "How shall they hear without a preacher? . . . But I say, Have they not heard? Yes verily, their sound went into all the earth, and their words unto the ends of the world." If Paul meant by "all the earth" all of the known world, where did the American Indian fit into God's design? How was it possible that they had heard the Gospel, and if they had not what provision had God made for the generations which had died before the era of Christian foreign missions? I had heard such questions discussed by people who were considered authorities on missionary work. The answers they gave were facile, and, to me, meaningless.

Here before me was a pageant of paganism, labeled, however, with Christian saints' names, which had its roots probably thousands of years ago, in a past civilization of which almost nothing was known. These Indians had been subjugated by the Incas before the Spanish Conquest, but no one knew to which tribes they had belonged before that. The Incas had perhaps introduced a new significance to the ancient rites of the conquered tribes and in their sun worship had obscured the original meaning. Another religion had more recently supplanted that of the sun, but vestiges of an unknown variety of religions probably remained.

I stood for a long time, watching the dancing, listening to the strange, sad music—when the hired bands stopped their thumping and shrieking, the music the Indians themselves were making came through in thin, plaintive tones. The sour odors of gin and *chicha* became stronger, Indians kept pouring into the plaza until it seemed that there was not room for one more. They danced and sang and drank and went into the church and came out. Finally, some receded into the shops. Others who had bundles of blankets and food with them, and mothers who were carrying their babies, began to set up camp in doorways, under portals, on the sidewalk, wherever they could find a space.

"Will they stay the night?" I asked the señora.

"Oh, yes, señorita! They will stay several nights. You do not understand, señorita. This is a big occasion. Some will go home and come back, but they like to be together. This is their great pleasure, the fiesta. What else have they, the poor things?"

"Their lives are hard, aren't they?" I said.

"Well, yes. It is hard, the life of an Indian. But it does not matter to them. They are used to it."

Like animals. I remembered what the señora had said to me once about the Indians. She called them "poor things," condescendingly, as one might perhaps call a fool or a dumb beast poor. There was no compassion in her tone.

She said they did not mind a hard life. What did they know of any other kind? I yearned to help them. There was, obviously, nothing I could do for them here at the fiesta. I had come to find Pedro but he was nowhere to be seen, and if I did find him how could I intrude my request into his celebration? I was wholly outside the pale for the time being, and must content myself with talking to the shop-keeper.

Perhaps, on second thought, this was why I had come to the plaza today. Perhaps this would be my opportunity to win her. I could not help feeling that a contact with a white woman was second best, but it was clear to me now that this was a day set apart for Indians, and I as a white woman and a foreigner could have no part in it. Ancient loyalties, an irrepressible consciousness of their mystic heritage of a long-forgotten god or system, brought the Indians thronging to the fiesta, eager to give themselves up to the power of the mob, the images, the liquor. Their habitual sullenness and deference to the white man were flung to the winds. I watched them take over the white man's town, crowd out his shops, even elbow him roughly off the sidewalk. Police clumped around through the crowd, half-heartedly seeking to maintain some semblance of order.

The sky overhead had been rapidly darkening although the hour was close to noon, and rain clouds rolled in ominous heaps from the eastern cordillera. Wind blew the dust in tangled veils as the merrymakers scuffed it up with their bare feet. I did not want to be caught in a downpour but was held fascinated by the sights before me. All at once there was a crash from almost directly behind me, several shouts, and the door of a little eating place was flung outward with a bang. A group of Indians erupted, tearing and beating at one another, and I saw in the center of the group a man, half carried and half dragged, whose nose was bleeding profusely.

"Ay, what barbarity!" said the señora, who had been attending a customer in her shop and had come out again when she heard the fracas. "Leave him! Leave him!" The Indians paid no attention, one or two of them still flailing at the others, and the man with the bleeding nose stumbled to his feet and faded into the crowd. The señora went back into her shop.

"Those savages. There is nothing one can do with them when they are drunk. They are savages, animals. They ought to be shut up in prison, but then there is no way to do that. All of them would be in prison. What is there to do? *Caramba!*"

Rain began to fall in huge drops, hitting the dust with little soft explosions, sending up a wet earthy smell, but the dancing went on. Some of the men who had folded the edges of their ponchos up onto their shoulders unfolded them, a few went to push their blankets and bundles closer together against the walls, but most of them seemed oblivious of the weather, of the time of day or the presence of any but their own people. Their stiff felt hats acted as umbrellas and they laughed and chanted and marched and drank and fought and allowed themselves to be what they could never be on an ordinary day. They knew, today, who they were; they accepted themselves and had the courage to reject the rest of us. Today they were able to believe, for a few shining moments, that the white man was not master of all that was good.

The rain was falling now in great gray rods, beating down on the plaza, splashing the water up against us as we stood under the narrow overhang in front of the shops, and I decided it was time to go home.

"When will the fiesta stop, señora?" I asked.

"*Caramba*, señorita, it hasn't started yet!"

"If I come back later this afternoon will they still be dancing?"

"Of course! And tomorrow and the next day." She spread her palms open in front of her shoulders in the Latin gesture of futility. "Drinking and dancing, dancing and drinking—nothing but death will stop them, señorita!"

"Well, then, I think I will go home for a little while. But I do want to see the fiesta. I would like to know all about the life of the Indians."

"When you have seen the fiesta, you will know all. What else is there? What more do they do?" Again she shrugged and lifted her palms.

"Who knows?" I said. "Well, señora, until later. I am going now."

"Until later, señorita."

The rain was pelting down, but I hurried through it toward my house, ruining my shoes but eager for the peace and silence I would find at home.

The dust was washed from the geraniums and from the tiles of my roof, making the reds and oranges clean and bright once more. Water raced between the stones of my front walk, pouring in deltas of mud into the street, streaming in sheets from the eaves. A cold stream ran down my neck as I unlocked the door, but once inside I could not hear the tumult. The rain made a soft murmur which mingled with the ticking of my little Swiss clock. I liked the little clock. It had a pale green enamel case with delicately painted birds, and the hands were lacy. Inside was a charming music box which played the Kaiser waltz. It was really the only thing I had which was personal and permanent in the house, and its gentle sound spoke to me

[137]

like a familiar voice. It was better to be alone, with this small voice and this innocuous face, than to be in a crowd where, because I did not belong, I was even more alone. The faces and the voices in the plaza were directed to something from which I was excluded. Would I ever succeed in being included by the Indians? But the thought of being included in so strange a celebration frightened me, for it was not a thing of which I could or wished to be a part. No, it was not mere inclusion I sought. I wanted them only to open the door a crack so that I could get a foot in. I did not want to be taken into the house. I wanted to take them out of it. And I would have to lure or trick them into coming out.

The impossibilities mounted before me. To try to know the Indians—who had done this before? To be accepted by them—what white man, let alone white woman, had achieved this? To live beside them, as though one of them, but with designs. This idea began to disturb me. The private designs, the double-heartedness which were inescapable made me feel like a conspirator, and although I imagined that some might find excitement in being a part of a plot, I myself could not be set at ease.

As I put the things I had bought into the cupboards in the kitchen, I remembered that I had not seen Pedro, who had been the object of my visit to the plaza. Poor Pedro. He had not the faintest idea that he was a part, too, in a plot—he thought that for once he had met a guileless white person.

The fiesta lasted for three days, and for part of each day I went and stood by the shop and watched. Mercedes, the señora's little daughter, took me around the corner to watch a special dance in a private courtyard. The cacophony of conflicting bands in the plaza would have prevented my hearing the music in the courtyard, and I wondered how many other patios held such groups. About a dozen Indians were reeling and prancing to the boom of a bass drum and the creak of three or four cornets. I stood at the arched entrance with Mercedes, unnoticed by most of the crowd, and listened carefully to the music to see if I could follow any tune. It was very jerky, with sudden plunges and shrieks in addition, it seemed, to the unplanned ones due to the musicians' lack of skill. What was it that made it sound so different from music to which I was accustomed? I did not know very much about music, but had heard that the octave was not the only scale in the world's music, and perhaps this music used a different scale. Was it the pentatonic? I listened some more, and could single out no more than five notes. Yes, that must be what gave it the jerky quality, the wide gaps between notes.

"What is this dance, Mercedes?" I asked the child.

"It is a dance, señorita. They are dancing."

"Yes, I see. But does the dance mean something special?"

"It is a dance of the fiesta."

"But—why would it be that they dance back here in this patio, away from the others in the plaza?"

"Who knows why it will be? They dance for the fiesta of San Rafael, señorita."

I could learn nothing further, though it seemed a very earnest, exclusive group, bent on performing to their utmost whatever it was they were dedicated to doing.

We visited a few of the cafés. Mercedes did not really understand my interest in all of this. Who wanted to watch Indians drink and fight? But she took me. She also guided me through the cathedral, where tawdry jewelry decked hideous plaster images, five-sucre bills covered another, candles flickered and dripped in front of various figures of the Virgin, a priest was intoning something in a little chapel to one side, and black-veiled women knelt to pray. Indians were genuflecting here and there, clasping their hands and moving their lips.

On the last day the plaza was littered with drunken Indians, and little groups dragged one and then another, trying to get them out of the way of the traffic, pleading and cajoling with them to get up and come home. Wives heaved and dragged their besotted husbands, two drunken men wove violently back and forth trying to support each other, heads lolling and eyes rolling. Little children sat and cried in the gutters beside stupefied mothers and fathers. I watched them gradually vacate the plaza, winding up the streets toward their mountainsides. Perhaps if I followed up the street a little way I could help someone. I started in the direction of my own house, seeing several families passing that way. A woman with a baby on her back was stumbling along, clearly on the verge of slumping into the gutter. Her husband, shouting something unintelligible to the skies, grabbed her arm, shoved her, and she fell in a heap, miraculously keeping the baby upright in his sling on her back. He began to wail and she flung her shoulder back as though trying to dislodge him; he screamed louder and she fell forward and lay still. Her husband bent over her in bewilderment as though searching for something and then fell heavily on top of her. I quickened my pace, seeing that this had started a fight. The woman was yelling, thrusting wildly at the man with her fist. He had hold of her hair and was twisting the braid, slapping her face with the other hand. I feared not only for the woman but for the baby on her back.

"Leave her alone!" I cried. "What is going on?"

Both stopped immediately and looked around, their eyes shifting uncertainly into focus. I saw that it was Pedro and Rosa, but they did not recognize me. They gave me a look that said, "Mind your own business," and set at one another again. I tried then to interfere by pulling Pedro's arm. He turned on me with a curse. His lip was swollen with a cut or bruise of some kind, his hair was matted over his forehead and his eyes were bloodshot. At that moment he recognized me, and it was as though blinds were drawn over his face. The intensity of his anger and the freedom of his drunkenness, the real person beneath the humble exterior I had known up until now, receded at once and he looked at me darkly, resentfully.

"Can I help you, Pedro? Rosa?" I hesitated, not knowing what to say.

"*Buenas tardes*, señorita," said Pedro. Even his state of stupor, his anger, and his resentment at my intrusion did not prevent the automatic courtesy.

"*Buenas tardes*, Pedro." Again I had forgotten to greet him. "Can I help you? Are you going home?"

"Home, señorita. *Buenas tardes*, señorita. We are going home."

"May I come with you?" I thought surely they would never reach their destination alone, and I pitied the baby, wriggling and crying on Rosa's back.

"To the house, señorita. Yes. *Buenas tardes*. We are going home, señorita. Until another day, señorita," said Pedro. Probably he was too drunk to have understood my offer, so I tried again. "Can I help you? Can I go home with you?"

"Until another day, señorita. We are going." He was struggling desperately to get to his feet, and I gathered that this was no time to impose help where it was not wanted.

He yanked Rosa to her feet and the pair zigzagged up the road and around the corner of a mud wall, the baby bobbing crazily and watching me from under the brim of his felt hat. It was that look again—the same look I'd seen in Guayaquil. The baby was contented and secure. His parents had him, they had their rare pleasures, they had each other. They were not going to call on me for help of any kind, drunk or sober, and it was I who would have to pursue their help. I stood in the middle of the road and stared at the mud wall behind which they had disappeared.

CHAPTER

13

THERE WAS one drugstore in Indi Urcu, and it was the shop I most liked to visit. It was small, but wonderfully neat, with a very high ceiling and rows and rows of bottles and boxes, many of which had familiar brand names of imported preparations. The smell of the place was antiseptic and fresh, a welcome change from the hot grease and garlic odors of the stuffy shops. The little man who ran the drugstore was as neat as his shop; he wore a white coat with a comb sticking out of the breast pocket and his hair was always impeccably slicked. He treated me with great deference, always searching out the American product when a European or Ecuadorian one would have served. He never called me *madamita*—it was "Ah! La señorita! *Buenos días*, señorita!" whenever I came in, and I had the feeling that he understood my position in the town—he knew it was difficult, he knew I wanted to help people, and he was one with me in the desire, for he wanted very much to help me.

I stopped in one morning on my way to the post office and as I finished making my small purchase an Indian with a deep gash in his head came in asking for a remedy. When he confessed that he had no money the little druggist rolled his eyes toward the ceiling and lifted his palms with a shrug.

"*No hay que hacer*." Nothing can be done.

The Indian pressed a rag to his neck, where blood was staining his collar, looked helplessly from the druggist to me and started toward the door.

"Can I help you?" I asked.

"I have no money," he said.

"That is not important," I told him. "Let me buy you something."

He eyed me dubiously, while the druggist watched me with mild amusement.

"What happened?" I said.

"I was working on a house. A big beam fell on my head."

"Where is the boss?"

"He told me not to work any more."

"Did he say he would pay for your medicine?" As soon as I asked the question I saw from the faces of both men how naïve it was.

"He said Go, señorita. The boss said Go."

"But he paid you for your work?"

"Not today, señorita. He just said Go."

I bought some Mercurochrome and adhesive tape and did the best I could to make a bridge over the wound. It was hard to make the tape stick to the bloodied hair, and it was equally hard to make him believe that he did not owe me any money. The druggist took my payment without a word while the Indian stood, hat in hand, by the door, still wondering what was expected of him. I wanted very much to ask his name, but feared he would think I intended to track him down for payment, so I merely said, "Until another day," and he answered, "May God pay you," and followed me out.

[144]

Oh, this town, this white man's town! Even my little drugstore and my nice little man. But I had met another Indian, as it were by chance. Surely God had ordained the meeting, for He was with me.

The sun shone as it nearly always did in the mornings, and the market place was buzzing. I saw here and there friends I had made, greeted them, happy to find them in their accustomed stalls, and then my steps quickened toward the post office. It was a never-fading delight to go there, past the stamp kiosks, past the little boy who sold magazines on the steps, into the dark little rotunda walled with boxes, each with its tiny window and brass keyhole. "As cold waters to a thirsty soul, so is good news from a far country." That was it. Today there was just one letter. It had an Ecuadorian stamp. Woodrow Rogers in Guayaquil. I tore it open.

"You will be sorry to learn that the Gardners have finally been rejected by the mission on medical grounds. We know how you have looked forward to their coming to work with you, to establish the school. The board feels that if you would prefer to be transferred to a station with another couple on it this might be worked out, although we would be reluctant to see Indi Urcu without a worker. . . .

"God's ways are not our ways. This is of course a great disappointment to all of us, but we must accept it from Him."

Indi Urcu without a worker. No, I could not consider that. I knew that the place in the vineyard to which God had most certainly brought me was His place for me to stay, and although, by worldly standards, it was not an enviable position, it was the object of my most cherished ambitions, a corner of the earth in which to serve my Master, a people to call my people. Would I be willing to labor on alone? The idea of being a solitary missionary was not unthinkable to me—after all, if I had faced the possibility of never marrying (and what calling could more effectively reduce one's chances, if the statistics I had seen were correct? Sixteen women to one man!)—if I was willing to be single, I should be willing to work alone. This kind of hardship fitted in with what I had half expected. But some kind of revision in my outlook was called for. How was I to accept a negative answer to so many people's prayers? The Gardners had been thoroughly prayed for. They had gone so far as to sell their home, they had booked a passage, they had bought their outfit. They had their financial support pledged by several churches, and at the last minute they were stopped by what seemed a very minor physical disability. Could not God have seen to that? It was not mere companionship for a single woman that was at stake. It was not simply the plans of a mission board or a family that had gone awry. The needs of a whole section of Indian population would be unmet. Even if another couple were found to take their place, what of the scores who daily passed into eternity during the delay? I could agree that God's ways are not our ways, all right. But why did we insist on trying to make them so? Was it possible, after all, that the reasons for the shortage of missionaries were sometimes inscrutable, not to be explained so simply as "The church of God is asleep"?

I walked slowly out of the post office, wondering where to turn. The market with its pushing women and their baskets, its jostling men and beasts, its reeking stalls, ordinarily a merely bustling place, seemed to me now in a frenzy of business. If I could just sort them out, shut them up, carry them off to some quiet place, apart, where I could sit them down and say to them, *Listen. God wants to speak to you.* But no. That was of course out of the question, and I could only clench the letter in my hand and send up a desperate prayer, Lord God, *how* will You get through to them?

I worked my way along the sidewalk. My part, the translation of the Scriptures, ought to go hand in hand with other aggressive efforts to help the people. Education was the obvious wedge, and the Gardners were supposed to do that. Now what would happen? Nobody to start a school, no bait to catch the Indians.

There was a sign over a door that I passed, "*Se pone inyecciones,*" and lettered faintly on the door itself was the word "*Clínica.*" I had assumed when I first saw that sign that it meant the presence of a doctor, but had learned that there was no doctor nearer than Wairapamba. A woman who did not even qualify as a nurse had been authorized to give injections, and this was the extent of medical service in the village. Perhaps it was medicine that would provide the wedge if education would not. The idea took hold at once—not that I had had any training, but there might be a lot I could do with common sense and compassion, and was it mere coincidence that I had treated the wounded Indian, received the letter, and noticed again that sign, all within an hour?

I began carrying along a small bag of medicines on my visits to the Indians—aspirin, worm medicine, DDT powder for the ubiquitous head lice, a few first-aid things. Nearly always there were minor needs which I could meet, but often the Indians wanted to know why I did not have a needle to stick them with. "A needle, señorita, is good for anything. Why do you not have a needle?" I explained that I was not a doctor, but this was hardly an explanation to them.

[147]

There was a pregnant girl in the house up beyond Rosa's—I had talked to her several times, a girl not more than seventeen, with an unusually Oriental look about her, smooth, high cheekbones and almond-shaped eyes, and she wore delicate gold earrings in her pierced ears. I would hardly have guessed she was pregnant, for she carried herself beautifully and wore full skirts, but Rosa mentioned it casually one day and I thought how exciting it would be if the girl would let me help in her delivery. It took some nerve on my part to suggest this to her, for I had never done more than watch two births, when a nurse friend of mine, before I came to Ecuador, had secured permission for me to do this in a hospital. I had read one book on midwifery which said that clean hands and common sense were the two basic requirements, and I was confident that I could meet those at least, which was probably more than the old Indian women who were called in to help could have done. Their brand of "common sense," I feared, was often nothing more than superstition. The girl nodded noncommittally at my proposal.

"You send someone to call me when the pain starts," I said.

"*Ari*," she said.

"I would like very much to come and help you," I said.

"*Ari*."

A few weeks later Rosa told me the girl had died in childbirth. Why hadn't they called me? How had she died? Rosa did not know. Was the child living? Oh no, it, too, had died.

"How sad," I said.

"Oh well, señorita, it was a wind child."

"A wind child?"

"That's what it was."

"And what is a wind child?"

"A child born of the wind. It had no other father." And Rosa rubbed her grindstone over the corn.

"But the poor girl. Perhaps if they had called me I could have saved her."

"Perhaps so, perhaps not." Back and forth went the stone. Rosa was right. Perhaps not. And what sort of beginning would that have made?

I kept on the watch for opportunities I might dare to use. I did not want really serious cases if I could avoid them, for I knew how dangerous my little knowledge might be. But I found an item in the newspaper one day about a case of smallpox which had been discovered in a town about twenty miles from Indi Urcu. The government had been vaccinating school children wherever there was a local doctor who could carry out the program. I found from the principal of the Indi Urcu school that he would be only too glad to allow the children to be vaccinated if I could find a doctor who would come. Lynn Anderson had traveled much in the mountains, holding clinics and cooperating with local authorities in medical work, and I wrote to my mission board asking if I might invite her to come and spend a few days with me, vaccinating the children and visiting Indian homes. It might be possible, I added, to announce a clinic to be held in my home during that time, and this could prove an opening wedge in the town as well as in the Indian community.

Lynn's schedule was full, but she arranged to come. I spent hours going from one Indian house to another, inviting them to come to the clinic. I was mystified one afternoon to see a bus stop at my gate—one of those great, swollen wooden things with no aisle down the center into which Indians packed themselves for interminable, airless journeys through the thin atmosphere of the high altitude. What on earth was it doing stopping at my gate? Lynn got off. A small boy swung her sleek blue suitcase off the top of a pile of burlap sacks on the roof of the bus and she came in, looking unrumpled and chic in a gray wool suit with a dark red silk scarf tying her hair back.

"Lynn! Why, I never dreamed you'd have to come in one of those things! Oh dear, the journey must have been awful! I sort of thought maybe Mr. MacDonald . . ."

"Why, it was nothing at all. We had a lovely ride, and the driver was so kind as to bring me up here after he'd let off the other passengers in the plaza."

Dear Lynn! How wonderful of her to come. How exciting it would be to show her around the town, to take her to see my Indians.

There were forty-six children in the school, and seven of these were Indians, the sons of "free Indians," the schoolteacher told me. When I asked what this meant, he explained that many of the Indians in the area were the property of white landowners and did not own their land or their homes. Those who had sent their sons to school had learned through hard experience in the market that white men had a strong advantage over them because they could read and do fast arithmetic. So they had sent their children to school, even though it was very expensive for the children to board in town and it was out of the question for them to walk from their own homes daily.

When the teacher, a young white man in his late twenties, lined up the children for their vaccinations, the seven Indian children were at the end of the line. When they sat down again, I noticed that their seats were at the rear of the room and instead of individual desks like the others' they had a table between them.

The procedure was very simple. I swabbed the arm with alcohol, Lynn scratched it with a needle and applied the vaccine. The teacher maintained the strictest discipline, ordering his pupils around with short, sharp commands. His commands to the Indian children, it seemed to me, were shorter yet, and considerably sharper. One small boy had a hard time rolling his sleeve up high enough to suit Lynn.

"Hurry up! *Caramba!*" said the teacher and cuffed the back of the child's head.

The teacher had given no explanation to the children of the need for vaccine. They submitted willingly to the treatment, though fear showed in some of their faces. Little knowledge did they have of the disease from which they were being protected, much less any desire to be saved from it. If only missionary work were so simple, I reflected. If people could be corralled and injected, like so many cattle branded, without explanation or persuasion or personal sense of need. I had heard missionaries say, "I gave him the Gospel!" as though it had been an injection, and now, as the comparison presented itself, I began to ponder just how important it might be that an individual be prepared for the Gospel. Lynn talked quietly to the children as she vaccinated, and I could feel the tension ease. They even seemed sorry when it was time for us to go, for they saw that she was their friend.

As we left the building, it was gratifying to think of it as a little island of safety, where forty-six human beings were now beyond the reach of a serious disease, simply because Lynn and I had come and spent an hour there.

We walked back up the street toward my house and saw the valley spread out before us, an endless stretch of tiny square fields and little thimble houses sheltering hundreds and thousands of people who were in jeopardy from the same disease, and did not know it. What of them? I spoke of this to Lynn.

She had a way of not responding immediately, of walking on as though she had not heard, and this time, when she was silent, I thought what a bromide my question must have seemed to her. Her reply, however, simple and direct, registered no scorn: "Yes. I suppose anyone who tries to help people in any way soon becomes overwhelmed with the endlessness of the task. So he has two choices. He can give up at the start, or he can accept his limitations and go on doing what he can."

Accept his limitations. This was an idea I had not thought very much about. I was serving the God of the Impossible. Words like "vision" and "challenge" flashed like illuminated captions over my picture of missionary life, and, as I walked along the road with Lynn and my eyes swept the vast bowl of the valley, they still seemed appropriate captions. But when we turned in at my front gate and found the yard filled with people who had heard by the village grapevine of the presence of the *doctora americana* the words blinked out again. Here before us was a definable task, a smaller sacrifice, a commoner duty. The people were mostly of the *mestizo* or *cholo* class—of mixed Indian and white blood, the women with long braids and plaid shawls and shoes and stockings, the men in blue jackets and rope sandals or shoes.

They were silent as we came into the yard, but when we opened the door they pressed around us, trying to get first place.

"I have been here many hours, *doctora*, and I am very sick."

"My daughter here, please, *doctora*, she is very grave."

"Do me the favor, señorita *doctora*, of attending to me, for the love of God!"

Lynn smiled kindly at them and explained that we were not yet ready to see patients, but that she would do her best to see them all in turn. I looked eagerly to see if there were any Indians in the crowd. Their needs were so great, and they had so little means for meeting them. They seldom had money to buy even drugstore medicines, and would not dream of going to Wairapamba to consult a doctor. Why had they not come? The Indians knew the doctor was coming, but there was not a single Indian in the group.

As I set water on the stove to boil and began spreading sheets on the table and laying out bandages and medicines according to Lynn's instructions, I tried to see how it was all to work. I had come to Indi Urcu to minister to Indians, and the means introduced for reaching them succeeded only in bringing to my door white people, those to whom not only did I feel no call, but whose presence inhibited the Indians' coming. It was ironic and I could work up little enthusiasm for the work ahead of us this afternoon. At least it would be good experience, for I could watch Lynn and learn from her and perhaps God would let me use the knowledge gained to help Indians in the future. If I were going to settle for the possible, which I had almost disdained, it was only in the hope that ultimately the impossible would be attained. The *cholos* came at the first invitation (which had not really been meant for them), to offer their aches and pains to the doctor and to take from her whatever she chose to give. The Indians, whose aches and pains were far deeper and less curable, did not come. They had received the invitation, but they did not come. They had not learned to ask anything of the white man. They had learned, instead, to bear their own burdens and this they did, day after day, year in and year out, in the loneliness of the high Andes, in the cold of their fireless huts, on the windswept plains of the grass country where their sheep grazed, and in the hostile white man's village where they knew they were despised. It was their life, and they did not dream that it could be changed.

We took the patients one by one into the living room and Lynn listened to their complaints, many of which seemed to have to do with the liver or kidneys. They were mostly women, and they screwed up their faces with pain and doubled over, a hand kneading the ailing area as they described the attacks. There were one or two cases of advanced tuberculosis, a man with a hernia which had been operated on in a hospital in Riobamba, but they had sewed his insides into knots, Lynn said, and nothing would help him but another operation. There was a young girl, her face gray with pain, who had what she called an earache that hurt her whole head. Mastoid, Lynn said, and nothing could be done for her unless she would go to a hospital. The girl turned in silence to her hovering young husband.

"Is it very serious, *doctora?*" he asked.

"Yes, it is serious. She must go to a hospital."

"Can't you cure her here?"

"No, I can do nothing for her here except give her a pill for the pain. But her ear will only get worse."

"Will they want to operate in the hospital? Will they cut?"

"They will have to operate."

The man stood silent for a moment, fear growing in his eyes. "Is there no other remedy?"

"No. I am very sorry."

The girl shifted the baby in her shawl, her great dark eyes moving from Lynn to her husband and back again.

The man murmured a syllable to her and they went out. Hospital was out of the question for them. Who would pay? The despair in their faces found no answer.

There was no time for lunch. Throughout the afternoon they came, for word spreads rapidly in the sierra in spite of great distances. The foreign doctor was there, and was not charging anything for consultations. She tried to collect a nominal fee for the medicines she dispensed but that was all. A few gave promise of a chicken or a sack of potatoes when they came again.

I learned to give an injection and took notes as fast as I could on the questions Lynn asked and the treatments she gave. A sketchy way to learn medicine but far better than nothing, I told myself, and it was likely that the same maladies would recur in this area.

There were various cases of malnutrition—strange bone formations, goiters, rashes and skin eruptions, anemia. Lynn prescribed vitamins and iron pills, fruits and vegetables, but the people nodded so enthusiastically that we could not help feeling they had no intention of following any consistent course of treatment. They were willing to swallow a pill or two today, but they would see no need for it tomorrow, especially if the pain was lessened at all. As for eating fruits and vegetables, how absurd. They had come to the doctor for medicine, not for food. They themselves knew what to eat.

At the end of the day, as the sun began to drop behind the mountains, I looked out to see how many patients remained. I was astonished to find Pedro just coming in the gate.

"*Buenas tardes*, Pedro," I said.

" '*S tardes*, señorita. Is the *doctora* here?"

"Yes. You have come to see her?"

[155]

"Yes."

He came in silently and began to roll up his trouser leg until we could see a deep, festering wound in the muscle of his calf.

"How did you do that?" asked Lynn.

"It is cut, *doctora*."

"With a knife, no?"

"It hurts me very much."

"How long have you had it?"

"A long time."

Lynn knew there would be no more information forthcoming and set about cleansing and bandaging the wound. Then she administered an injection of penicillin and instructed Pedro to come back for three days in a row so that I could put the needle into him again. She went over again with me the procedure for the injection, and wrote down the dosage.

"*Sí*, señorita," said Pedro.

"Three more days, Pedro. Tomorrow, and the day after that, and the day after that."

"*Sí*, señorita."

"You will not forget?"

He smiled faintly. "Why would I forget?"

"You must be exhausted," I said to Lynn when we finally sat down to supper. "How many did we have?"

"I didn't keep count," she said.

"I should think there were sixty or seventy at least," I said.

"I suppose so. A beginning anyway. If only we could get them to follow up the treatment. That is what is so disheartening about village clinics—some of the cases are beyond help outside a hospital, most of them require a simple but regularly continued treatment—and this, too, is hopeless unless you can follow it up yourself. The people just don't see the need for it."

"You must see some spectacular cures now and then, don't you?—cases which make you feel it's worthwhile?"

"Yes," she said, and the pause this time was longer than usual. "I see some spectacular things all right. But I no longer look for things to make it, as you say, worthwhile."

"What do you mean?"

"I'm not sure I can make you understand what I mean." She stirred her tea and laid the silver spoon carefully in the saucer and then raised her eyes, which were gray and widely spaced. The tiny lines around them, the weariness, did not cloud their kindness.

"You see, when I decided to be a doctor, it was because I wanted to help people. I thought, of course, that I *could* help people by being a doctor. So I went through seven years of study, and I came to Ecuador anticipating the good I was going to do. Gradually I came to see that the results which can be called good are few. And they cannot be the criterion for whether or not what we do is worthwhile. It is hopeless to try to weigh up the good, the bad, the futile, and the merely harmless, and hope that there will be enough of the good—in medical work, enough unequivocal cures—to justify all the rest. Do you follow me?"

"I don't know. I think so. I mean, if the good doesn't justify the rest—is that what you said?" Lynn nodded. "Then what does?"

"Jesus told us to do what is true. I think the truth needs no justification, no defense."

PEDRO RETURNED for his shots as he had promised, and I took this as a happy omen. When the course of treatment was finished as Lynn had prescribed, the leg seemed much improved, but there was still a small opening which drained slightly, and I suggested to Pedro that it would be much better if he did not return to his work in the market place.

"But, señorita, I have to work. There is no money, and my land is very little."

"There are other ways to work, Pedro," I said.

"Not for me. I am a poor man. There is no other work."

"Pedro," I said. "would you like to work for me?"

"For you?" he asked in surprise. "What work? What can I do?"

"I would give you a job at which you could sit down."

"What, señorita? What do you mean, sit down?"

"Not only sit down, Pedro, but sit down in your own house!"

At this he laughed. "You want me to weave. Well, I am a good weaver, but I couldn't earn enough money that way. I earn more money carrying loads."

"No, Pedro. I don't want you to weave for me. I want you to teach me to speak your language."

"You will pay me for that?"

"Yes, Pedro, I will pay you for that. If you will let me come to your house every week—perhaps two or three times each week—and tell me stories in your own language —*your* language, Pedro, not Spanish—I will pay you. We will sit and talk, and then, someday, when I learn to speak, you will help me to translate God's word. I would pay you for that, too."

"You want so much to speak my language that you say, 'I will pay'?" Pedro was still not sure he had correctly understood me.

"Yes, Pedro, I say I will pay."

The idea finally sank in, we agreed on a price, and we began to spend several hours a day three times a week on my lessons. In that time Pedro earned what he would have made in the market in a five- or six-day week, and he seemed pleased with the plan. Rosa was harder to convince, and kept asking Pedro when he was going to town. When he showed her the money she wanted to know what I had given it to him for.

On the days when I was to go to Pedro's I tried to make my route different each time, and visit the huts I passed on the way. I had learned the elementary questions from Pedro and written them down on small cards which I carried in my pocket: "How are you?" "I am fine, and you?" "What is your name?" "Where do you live?" I practiced on a new and unsuspecting audience whenever I found one. Their initial astonishment usually gave place quickly to the urge to talk, and, having said as much as a sentence in Quichua, I found it hard to convince my listener that he had just heard the extent of my Quichua vocabulary. Fortunately this state of affairs did not continue for many days, and I was pleasantly surprised at the ease with which

I learned to give and take in conversation with an Indian who was willing to make even a slight effort to slow down for me.

When I got to Pedro's house we would sit down together by the fire sometimes, or, as I preferred, outdoors where the air was fresher and the light better. I liked the sunshine, in spite of cold wind and dust, but I think Pedro liked better the smell of smoke indoors and the snuffling of the guinea pigs. He loved to smoke as we talked, and very slowly and deliberately would roll his cigarettes, using any scrap of paper he had managed to find. He looked longingly at my small notebooks, the pages of which were exactly the size he needed, and I occasionally gave him a leaf although I knew he could not well afford to buy tobacco and I was not eager to encourage an expensive habit.

When I asked him about his grandparents, his crops or his children, he would sit for a long time, his knees pulled up under his poncho, his eyes fixed on the far mountains. He would blow a long blue curl of smoke, trying to think of the answer.

"My old fathers? The ones-who-lived-in-the-beginning? This whole valley, señorita—you see this valley?—this valley was filled with them, as many as the hair of your head." He gave the lock which hung in front of his ear a shake. "Very, very many they were, and they lived very well. All the land was theirs, the corn and the potatoes and barley, all the towns and all the houses, *all* was theirs, all belonged to the old fathers. Then, after that, the white man coming fooled them. The white man said he was a friend and the old fathers thought, We will live well with these people, but they were deceived. We do not remember that time. My father did not remember that time. It was long ago, señorita, in the beginning time. My grandfather did not remember it, but he had heard about it, and he used to tell me and my brothers about the beginning time. But when I was the size of Romero my grandfather was walking home from the village one afternoon—the sun was just about there"—Pedro stretched his arm toward the western sky, indicating by the angle how near the sun was to setting—"and high in the mountains it began to rain. It was not raining here, but we could see the black clouds and hear the thunder up the ravine. My grandfather was in the *quebrada*—you know the big *quebrada* up by Lame Pedro's house?—he was in there, coming home—he lived up there—and suddenly, suddenly the rain came, the water poured down like an avalanche through the *quebrada* and my grandfather died in the water. We found him the next morning at the bottom of the valley, down where the eucalyptus grows."

I was disappointed in Pedro's ignorance of the history of the Incas. He had no sense of heritage beyond the knowledge that his ancestors had once been free, and the owners of the land. Talk always turned to things he knew first- or second-hand. I asked him about his children, trying to find out if he had any idea of their ages.

"Romero was born the year the corn crop failed. I always sleep in my cornfield when it is ripe, but that year I slept in it for two months. No one had good corn, everyone wanted to steal. They would steal new corn, old corn, unripe corn. I hoped to save my corn, but in the end it was not worth the trouble. Let them steal it all, I said, take it, take it. And I went home from my field before the cock crowed and found that my wife had caused a child to be born, a man. But it was very small and thin and my wife said, 'What will we eat? We will die anyway, this child will die, it is not worth raising, I will throw it away.' So she went outside—still the cock had not crowed—and threw the child away, just outside the wall. But my brother came along and found the child and picked it up and brought it back to my wife and said, 'Here, you must take care of this child, it is your child, is it not?' And she said 'It is my child,' and gave it the breast, and it grew. That is Romero. A good child, after all."

Pedro was intelligent enough to translate word for word when I asked for verb paradigms, and this was a great help in learning conjugations. It often happened, of course, that I asked him for a word which did not exist in Quichua, and he would then explain carefully in Spanish what the Spanish word I asked meant. He did not like to say that there was no Quichua equivalent. I could not resist asking *why* certain things were said in Quichua, why a suffix occurred here or an enclitic there, but soon came to understand that it was a useless question. What did I know of the *whys* of English? Why, for example, when it was correct to say "He went" was it not correct to say "Went he?" instead of "Did he go?" Suppose Pedro had asked me the meaning of *get?* I thought of the possibilities: get your coat, get married, get up, get in, get off, get caught, get out, this language gets me, get him to go, get away, get dinner, get lost. I was thankful I was not teaching English to Pedro.

Many hours were spent listening to stories the "old fathers" used to tell. Now that I had learned to follow the gist of a conversation or story I wanted to concentrate on specific forms of the language, and I taught Pedro to slow down and repeat. It took a great deal of effort to make him understand that by repeating I meant the very words he had spoken, rather than an interpretation or explanation. Finally he learned, and with the great patience characteristic of his people was eventually almost dictating legends and folk tales to me so that I could write every word in my notebooks and then study them at home, filing suffixes, words, syntax and sounds, memorizing phrases and analyzing forms. The content of the tales was just as fascinating to me, many of them dealing with the origins of things, the sun and stars, the seasons and animals, the winds and mountains and rocks. He told me of the legendary twins who, before they were born, guided their mother with instructions from the womb, and after their birth performed marvelous feats of magic and daring. Eventually the twins ascended into the heavens and became the morning and evening stars. There was the story of the condor who, like all other animals, had been a human being. His betrothed was the most beautiful virgin on earth, coveted by every man who saw her. The Sun God, too, saw her and wanted her for himself, so he took her off into the sky and the forsaken young man searched the earth until he became old and white-headed. Walking over the mountains in his black poncho, stooping to search every cranny for the beautiful girl, he finally was transformed into the huge bird which still hangs in the sky, his head bent toward the earth, his poncho outspread. "That is why he seizes our lambs, thinking to himself, 'Here is my woman.'"

The afternoons often found me trekking across the hills again, stopping in the fields to talk with Indians as they rested from plowing or hoeing, calling at huts where I found women weaving or nursing their babies. I was happy in these days, confident that the language work was basic and would one day bear fruit which would remain; gratified, too, to be living simply in a small village, moving about among the farm people as Jesus must have done. The things he talked about—sowing seed and plowing, seasons

[163]

and harvests, sheep and cattle, lilies of the fields, birds of the air—all these things had their place in the lives of my Indians, and it seemed to me that Jesus Himself at times drew near and walked with me. At such moments I was transported by the vision of the great work which had been put into my hands to do. I saw the valley, filled with godless Quichuas, as my parish, and the open Bible, written at last in the language they could understand, as my gift to them.

The little smoky huts with their fleas and stench and darkness, which had at first repelled me and later aroused in me a great pity, I now accepted, as homes, the homes of people I knew. They took on a different aspect entirely, became a part of the furniture of my life, no longer forts of hostility. Inside their blackened walls I learned to respect the people who had built them—how admirably they had adapted themselves to so hostile an environment! Thatch was the only available roofing material, and it belonged to the landscape, to the great stretches of brown grass that glowed and breathed in the wind. The huts had no windows, not because the Indian loved darkness rather than light (though I had once deplored their windowless huts as symbolic of a determination to do evil), but because windows would weaken the mud walls and let in the cold. As for the fleas, I did not learn to love them but was willing to grant after a time that fleas, too, probably had their place in the divine plan. My vehement dislike for them began to seem like a wasted passion alongside the Indians' philosophical tolerance, for like hundreds of generations before them the Indians had cohabited with fleas and were not prepared to panic over them and spend hard-earned sucres on DDT just because the white man did.

I wished for every Indian a metal plow, a pair of good

oxen, better soil and pasture land, and for the Indians who were still held by white *patróns* as serfs, I wished freedom. Someday, I hoped, someone would come who could bring these things—someone trained in agriculture, husbandry, crop rotation, soil conservation. But these were not in my province and I had to accept things as they were. I hardly realized that this acceptance became less and less difficult for me.

My life went on alongside the life of the Quichuas. I do not say *with* theirs, for the two remained separate. All my efforts to make myself one with them ended at the brink of the great abyss—I was not an Indian. The topography of the land associated itself in my mind with this fact. The high sierras of Ecuador are cracked with huge abysses— *quebradas*, they are called, "broken places"—and no one can travel far in any direction without having to descend, bridge or skirt such ravines. My white blood could never become Indian blood, and therein lay the abyss which I could by no means descend, bridge or skirt.

For a time I adopted Indian dress. I bought from Pedro's wife Rosa two hand-woven woolen skirts and a shawl. In the town I found an embroidered blouse and a silver pin for my shawl. The shopkeeper supposed I was buying them for souvenirs—foreigners bought strange things as remembrances. But on the day that I first wore the clothes I met in the street the shopkeeper herself. At first she ignored me, thinking me an Indian, but then my height and gait told her that something was badly amiss. She shot me a look of horror which quickly changed to scorn.

It can't be helped, I said to myself; I didn't expect the whites to like the idea. One must choose the stratum of society with whom one will identify oneself, and run the risk of offending the others. (How had Jesus come to choose the poor working class? I wondered. Might it not have been wiser to be middle class?) I had chosen the Indians and alienated the whites. The sooner I went on up the mountain where my friends were, the better.

The skirts felt very heavy and the blouse was uncomfortably baggy. The shawl scratched my arms. I could not get the pin to stay where I put it. Footwear presented the greatest problem. I had not been able to bring myself to go barefoot in such cold, and over such rough terrain. Impossible, I thought. But then the history of missions told of others who had become all things to all men, sometimes at great personal sacrifice. Hudson Taylor had grown a queue and worn a long Chinese gown. It never occurred to me that he might have minded doing this. When I had looked at the picture of my aunt in her sari I had thought it a very lovely and comfortable costume. But there were costumes which were not so comfortable or so becoming. This did not change the principle. Perhaps it was an unwillingness on my part, despite all I had proclaimed, to pay the price. What were cold feet—even bleeding feet—if they would make me a trifle less alien? But then I would not be able to walk so far, and perhaps even at all after a while. What could be gained? One must not go to extremes. I bought a pair of rope sandals, although women did not wear them. It seemed a sensible compromise. When I tried to walk in them, however, I was not convinced that they were an improvement over bare feet.

Rosa saw me coming and gazed in disbelief. I had told her when I bought the skirts that I was going to wear them, but the sight was a shock to her. A half smile played on her face—was this a kind of joke?

"*Buenos días*, Rosa," I said, but she was too absorbed to

reply. "I am a *runa* today." It was the name the Indians called themselves. It meant "person."

"You are wearing *runa* clothes for-no-particular-purpose?" She used the word *yanga*, a very useful word signifying the absence of a reason. It made a convenient reply to questions one did not wish to answer, and it was a way around explanations one did not wish to make. Rosa expected no better explanation than *yanga*.

"I wear them in order to be like you," I said.

"Like us?"

"Yes."

"You want to be like us?"

"Yes, Rosa. I want to be."

"And . . . your nice clothes? Did you throw them away?"

"No, I have them."

"What will you do with them?"

"Oh, I don't know. Sometimes, when I go to the city, I will wear them."

"Thinking to yourself, 'Today I am a white'?"

Yes. Rosa saw what it would be. A fake Indian one day, a white the next. There was hope notwithstanding that this measure might open some doors. But it did not prove to be so. Indians who did not know me met me with doubled suspicion. This foreign woman was clearly up to no good. Indians who knew me looked at me, I thought, with pity, as though commiserating with me over such a reversal of fortune.

"It's no good," said Pedro to me at last, when I had dressed like a Quichua for only a few days. "You are a señorita, but you look spoiled. You should dress like a señorita. It's no good for a señorita to become a *runa*."

Spoiled. It was the Indians I had thought of as the "unspoiled," but I saw now the unconscious irony of Pedro's words. He and the others of his tribe did not mean to refuse me admittance. They had accepted me from the beginning as a white woman. I must accept myself that way and not ask of them an impossible thing.

Nor should I, I reflected with some contrition, charge God with a botched job. If He had wanted the Quichuas won by a Quichua, He would not have sent them a white woman. It appeared that He *had* sent them a white woman. And God saw that it was good. Pedro's words helped me to see it, too.

"It's no good for a señorita to become a *runa*."

SUNDAY WAS visiting day among the Indians, and while some of them went faithfully to Mass in the church in town everyone spent the better part of the day going from house to house to talk and drink *chicha*, the sweet fermented drink made from corn or rice and occasionally rendered very festive by the addition of a pineapple bought in the market. There were always a few who succeeded in getting drunk and had to be pushed and hauled home, but *chicha* was not powerful enough to do much damage if drunk in ordinary quantities. Rosa made hers on Fridays and set it in clay pots by the door. She often gave me a glassful on Sundays when I would go to visit, and it became almost a habit for the children to beg me for a story as I sat on the little "porch" drinking my glass of *chicha* and listening to the other visitors talk. I had some Bible story books with large colored illustrations and I practiced my Quichua by explaining these pictures to the children and recounting the incidents that went with them. As soon as I arrived Jorge, instead of disappearing as he used to do, would inexplicably appear from nowhere.

"Señorita *shamun!*" he would whisper, "The señorita comes!" and any children present who did not know me would dive for cover while Pava, Romero and Jorge, with any others who had satisfied themselves that I was harmless, crowded around.

"*Huillai, huillai*, señorita!" they begged, using the single Quichua word for "Tell us a story, tell us a story!"

"*Atiu!*" I would hear from the background—this was the expression of astonishment. "You mean she speaks our language?"

"She speaks it!" This was an overstatement, but children are easy to please, and I would begin, showing first a picture, then explaining it and asking questions to find out whether they understood. At times adult conversation ceased and I found everyone listening intently.

"Shut up! She's talking about God."

"About God?"

"Yes. That's the way she talks. Will it be for nothing, or will it be true? Who knows?"

Pava learned all the stories by heart and prompted me when I left out a detail. "No, señorita, not a goatskin—you said his mother put two kidskins on him to deceive his brother!" or, "You forgot to say that David cut off the giant's head—with the giant's own sword. Tell about that, señorita." And she would sit with her chin in her hand, her bright eyes darting from me to the other listeners to see if they were taking it in. Every now and then she would swat Jorge on the side of the head, whispering loudly, "What sort of a child are you, anyway? Shut up! Don't you hear the señorita talking?"

Romero would follow the movements of the story sometimes with pantomimes of his own—picking up five smooth stones and turning them over in his grubby brown hand, wondering, no doubt, if he could kill a man with those. When I tried to translate the Shepherd's Psalm for them, and described how the shepherd anointed the head with oil, I caught Romero rolling his eyes upward and shooting out his lower lip. Oil was a precious commodity, and involuntarily he tried to save it.

Pava persuaded her father several times to come and listen, although he probably felt that he had to listen enough on weekdays to my halting Quichua. Gradually, however, he took more interest in the stories.

"This is what your old fathers used to tell?" he asked.

"Well, yes, Pedro, my grandfather and my father told me these stories, but they learned them from a book, God's book. You know about that. Someday you and I are going to translate it into your language so your people will hear what God says."

"Is it for nothing that God speaks? Or is it true?"

"It is true, Pedro. It is not for nothing."

"It is a nice word. Your old fathers knew some good stories."

Rosa never actually came and sat down. When Pava asked her to listen she only fanned the fire more vigorously and said, "As if I have time to listen to stories!" When I asked her if she would like to hear, she gave me a faint smile and said, "I have to give my visitors *chicha*." I suspected once in a while that she listened with one ear, forgetting herself when the story got absorbing and pausing in her work. She was busy at once when she found me looking.

Months passed, and I continued my weekday work and my Sunday visiting. I had told the story of Calvary several times, but there were some very important words missing— "to save" and "to forsake" were words I had not come across until one day when Rosa told me that while she was at the brook washing her clothes a friend's small child had fallen into the deepest place. By grabbing the child's foot Rosa had "saved" her. I had no sooner written it down than I heard Jorge crying outside and he burst into the house to tell his mother that Romero was going to take him to the lake to sail his reed boat. Between sobs he managed to say, "But Gustavo and Vicente came and Romero ran away with them and forsook me!" Rosa paid very little attention to the recital, and sent Jorge off to bring in some dried grass for the fire. I was overjoyed to learn the word, and the following Sunday I told again the story of the crucifixion of Jesus, quoting the mockers who said, "He saved others; Himself He cannot save," and trying to make clear to the Indians that the death of Jesus was that they might be saved. Pedro's cigarette grew a long ash as I told of Jesus' cry from the cross, "My God! My God! Why hast Thou forsaken me?" The ash fell on his poncho but still he did not move. I did not go on to the end of the story, and the Resurrection. I waited for Pedro to speak. Surely he had something to say this time, for his eyes did not leave my face.

"Señorita . . ."

"What is it, Pedro?"

"My brother is in jail. I was going to visit him today. Will you come with me?"

Pedro had mentioned his brother only once before, and I had not met him. Of course I would go.

The jail was on a tiny narrow street in Indi Urcu which had nothing to distinguish it from other side streets—there were doorways and a few windows on one side, a single double wooden gate set into high mud walls on the other. As we approached this gate a ragged little girl came slithering out from under it. An older girl was waiting nearby.

"Did you see her? What did she say about the money?" she asked the younger one. I could not hear the reply as the two went off down the street. There was a tiny square window in each half of the door, and a hand came through one of them.

"A little charity, señorita. Please, for the love of God a little charity."

Pedro banged on the gate and the face of a guard appeared at the other window.

"What is it?"

"I want to see Juan Chimbu."

"Who are you?"

"I am Pedro Chimbu, brother of Juan."

"Who is with you?"

"The señorita. The foreigner."

The gate opened and the owner of the hand, an old woman, pressed my arm, "A little charity, señorita," while the guard waved us inside. Several women hung around the gate, taking turns at the little window. They too were prisoners, Pedro told me, but they were allowed to beg and to see their children if the children were small enough to squeeze under the gate.

A game of volleyball was in progress in the open courtyard. The players seemed to be mostly of the *cholo* class. Three or four guards stood sleepily by. The one who had let us in led us through the yard into a passageway lined with cells, in each of which were two or three men or women. Most of them got up from their cots to watch us as we went down the passage. At the end of the first passage we came to a cement platform on which were some charred sticks and ashes.

"That is where the prisoners cook their food," Pedro said.

[173]

"They cook their own food?"

"If they have any to cook. When there is food, they cook it there."

"Does the prison not give them food?" I was incredulous.

"Sometimes they give them food. Sometimes the white prisoners get food. Juan doesn't get much. I brought him this." Pedro had a cloth bundle in his hand. The guard turned a corner and gestured toward a cell.

"There he is. What are you bringing him?"

"Some food, captain. Only a little food."

The guard took the bundle, opened it and dug into the cooked corn and beans with his hand, then handed it back to Pedro.

"Half an hour," he said, and left us.

Juan was sitting on a wooden bed with some sort of mattress on it, whittling on what looked like a flute. He looked up without speaking, and Pedro thrust the bundle through the bars.

"Good," said Juan. Pedro turned to me, feeling that something ought to be said, but all he could think of was "This is my brother, Juan." I greeted Juan and told him who I was, that I lived in the town, and I was a friend of Pedro and Rosa. He nodded and whittled. Another man sat behind him, on the other side of the bed, gluing together tiny pieces of wood to make a little toy dresser. He got up and brought one of the finished drawers over to the bars.

"Look, señorita. Would you like to buy this? I am making it to sell."

"He is here for debts," Juan volunteered, and Pedro joined in eagerly, as though he were the man's agent.

"Buy it, señorita Margarita! It is very nice."

The work was indeed skillful and my mind was again

filled with the old turmoils. The bleak prison, the dark cell, the hopelessness of getting out of debt, the numbers who were in similar straits, and here was this charming little piece of furniture, a bauble, a toy to cheer the heart—for a few moments—of some fortunate child. I said nothing. I had learned that an answer was not always required in this country and it spared me from having to think of a truthful and appropriate one. The three men glanced at each other. No one knew just how to pass the allotted half hour. Juan did not ask after Pedro's family or crops, and Pedro offered no information about Juan's. Finally Juan asked, "Have any of my children died?"

"No," said Pedro. "They live. Your wife lives."

Another silence. Then suddenly Pedro turned to me. "Tell a story, señorita." I was taken aback. Tell Juan a story?

"What story, Pedro?"

"The one you told at my house. About killing Jesus."

Juan whittled on his flute without speaking. The other man sat with the toy dresser on his knees, waiting to see what we would do. When I looked back later at that moment I wondered what made me hesitate. Had I failed utterly to grasp the implications of the opportunity? This was the very thing I had prayed and worked and schemed to achieve. But when the request came I saw it very simply —four people who were virtual strangers to one another (indeed, Pedro and Juan seemed hardly to be friends) who needed a way to pass the time. Quichuas loved stories— think of all the stories Pedro had told me. I obliged them by telling as much of the account of the crucifixion as I could with my limited vocabulary and time.

When I finished, Juan looked up from his whittling and said to Pedro, "Do you listen to that?"

"I listen to it," answered Pedro.

"She talks for nothing." Juan kicked away the shavings with his foot. "What is it worth, that talk?"

"Can it be for nothing? It is what God wrote, she says." Pedro spoke gently, not wishing to create an issue with his brother, nor to offend me. Juan's eyes narrowed and he ran the blade of his knife against the palm of his hand.

"That's what the priest says, too. He's always talking about that—about the Virgin and God and Jesus and Our Father and Christ and Our Lady and all those people. Who are they? Who knows them? Why talk so much about them?"

Juan's face was deeply lined, his hair matted, with a few strands of gray showing. He must be a good deal older than Pedro, I thought. I wonder why he is in jail? I had hesitated to ask Pedro, and he had given no hint as to the reason. His crime must be worse than the crimes of those who were playing volleyball in the courtyard.

The guard, a white man with a baggy khaki uniform and a gleaming badge on his cap, appeared and said, "Now." He gave Pedro a small shove and waved me toward the entrance. As we reached the courtyard a great cheer suddenly rose from the players—I thought it was the winning team congratulating themselves, but saw that the gate was opening and a man was leading two sheep into the prison. The game had stopped and the men looked hungrily at the animals. Today they would have meat. Would any of those in the cells share in it?

The guard looked us up and down before drawing back the bolt on the doors. He slammed them hard behind us and I heard the bolt grate in the slot. As we went silently down the sunny street together Juan's face stayed before me—much like Pedro's in its features, but older, more suspicious, more willful and determined. Not that Pedro was anything but strong. He had a ruggedness about him that inspired my honest respect, but there was an openness that Juan did not seem to have, a tenderness with his children that I could not picture Juan displaying. But then, I told myself, I don't know Juan. Certainly I had seen precisely the same expression of suspicion and guardedness in Pedro's face on our first meetings in the market. He was not to be taken in any more than Juan. Perhaps Juan, too, would lay a hand softly on his little daughter's hair as I had seen Pedro do. Both men were members of a once proud race, a people of great intelligence and artistic sensibility. They had worshiped the sun, through which they had received warmth, abundance and life. They were defeated by a people who came to them in the name, they said, of the one true God—and in that name they plundered, betrayed and murdered. I thought of the prince, Atahualpa, shut up in a cell until his ransom—a roomful of gold—should be paid. And over the Andes came hundreds of llama-loads of precious ornaments and vessels of pure gold until the room was filled up to the mark on the wall. The Incas obeyed in good faith, confident that the price would release to them their leader. And then he was hanged, a kindness on the part of his captors, who had intended to burn him at the stake. With a Bible in one hand and a crucifix in the other, they had asked him if he would choose the true God, and he had consented and his punishment was mitigated.

There must be, of course, a just reason for Juan's being in prison. But if the white man had never come, what might he have been? I could not resist glancing sideways at Pedro, who walked a little behind me and to my right. What went on in his mind as he left his brother behind those walls?

What effect had Juan's attitude to my story had on him? Would he tell me what Juan had done against the law?

We did not go through the main plaza on our return. The less Pedro was seen in my company the easier it would be for him, I knew. There was a side street that would take me to my house and when we came to this I said goodbye unceremoniously so that Pedro could slip away without more ado. But it was then, for the first time since we left the jail, that he stopped in the street and spoke.

"Señorita Margarita," he said, "that word that you spoke —it is God's word, isn't it?"

"Yes, it is God's word."

"Juan doesn't believe that. But I, *I* believe it, señorita. It appears to me that the word is true. We ought to put it in my language."

"That is what I want to do, you know. That is why you have been helping me to learn your language."

"Good. I like that word. Juan, too, might like it if he saw it written on paper and knew that God said it."

He stood for a moment, pushing a stone with his toes, as though he had many things on his mind. Then he said, "Well, goodbye. You will be coming to my house soon?"

"Yes, on Tuesday, Pedro, as always. Goodbye."

As I turned up the street toward home I wondered if this was what it meant to be a believer. Pedro had said, "I believe it, señorita." If so, the angels in heaven must be singing. I should be singing, too, in the late Sunday quiet of the village street, but I did not want to make a spectacle of myself, even on the occasion of a soul's salvation, and I silently thanked God that He had not forgotten His promises.

NOT MANY weeks after our visit to the jail I was preparing to go to Pedro's house—this time not just for the usual language study, but to begin in earnest the translation of the Gospel of Mark. Long months of study lay behind me now, hundreds of pages of Quichua text had been analyzed, and the bits of Scripture which Pedro and I had translated had been read many times to the Indians. We needed more, a whole book, with its continuity and completeness, so I decided to begin with the shortest of the Gospels, that of Mark. I was just going out my gate in happy anticipation of the job when Mr. MacDonald's jeep came clattering up the road.

"I've brought a visitor to see you, Margaret," he said, climbing out. "This is Mr. Elmer Harvey of Millions Untold. He is making a mission survey in Latin America and wanted to see the work here in Indi Urcu." A beaming, heavy-set man in a raincoat bounded out of the jeep toward me.

"How do you do, Mr. Harvey." See the work, I repeated to myself. What work? Luckily, today there was something. "I was just going up the mountain to visit my informant. Do you think you'd like to come along?"

"Well, praise the Lord, Miss Sparhawk! Or can I call

you Margaret? No use being too formal. After all, we're all brothers and sisters in the Lord, isn't that right?" He laughed and shifted the camera straps a bit on his shoulder. "Your informant—sounds sort of sinister, doesn't it! You mean the one who helps you with language work?"

"Yes—I'm hoping to do a little translation work today."

"*Bible* translation?"

"Yes."

"Now isn't that wonderful! Guess the Lord brought us here on the right day, Brother MacDonald. Can't think of anything I'd rather do than go visiting with you, Margaret. Not sure I have just the right footgear"—he looked down at his shoes—"but it won't be too rough, will it?"

"It's dusty, and a bit steep," I said, "but I'm sure you can make it."

"Should have brought my old combat boots. They'd have been just the thing, but the airlines only allow you forty-four pounds. These new Florsheims weren't really made for rugged trekking. But then, nothing's too good for the Lord, eh, MacDonald? Ought to be glad to wear out a pair of shoes for Him!"

Mr. MacDonald gave him a thin smile.

"Could I give you a cup of tea before we leave?" I asked. Mr. MacDonald must be thirsty from the dusty drive up to Indi Urcu.

"Oh thank you, Margaret. If you have time, a cup of tea would be lovely," said Mr. MacDonald. This time his smile was warm.

Half an hour later we set out on foot for Pedro's house. The sun struck full on the eastern slope of Chimborazo, the great snowcap, setting it high and exalted above the whole earth, the joy of the valley beneath it. My heart lifted and cheered at the sight of that glory and seemed to run up the shining slopes.

"Cobblestones," said Mr. Harvey, picking his way carefully along the street in his polished shoes. "The genuine article. I suppose they've been here since the Year One."

"Maybe a hundred years," I ventured, not really having any idea how old they were.

We soon came to the end of the cobblestones and took the turn which led up the mountainside. Mr. Harvey, I noticed with some misgiving, was puffing already. The altitude might be too much for him.

"Turn around and look at the view from here, Mr. Harvey," I suggested, in order to give him a chance to rest. "Isn't the sun beautiful on the mountain?"

He paused, his shoulders heaving and making the two cameras rise and fall. He pushed his felt hat back a bit on his forehead, glanced at the mountain, and then looked down toward the village.

"Picturesque little place, isn't it? Wonder if I could get a picture."

Just then a small boy with two pigs came toward us on the road, one of the pigs grunting in time to his trotting, the other zigzagging back and forth across the road as the boy flourished a stick and yelled at him. Mr. Harvey looked apprehensively at the pig, which seemed bent on scurrying between his legs. The boy lunged at the pig, whacked it on the hind quarters, and sent it squealing past us.

"Say—there's a picture now. Could I get a picture of him?" He turned to me. I called to the boy and asked if the gringo might take his picture. The boy smiled shyly and nodded, but kept after his pigs.

"Do you think you could get him to stand over here on the sunny side, Margaret?"

"I'm afraid I can't get him to stand anywhere with those pigs. You'll just have to try to get them on the run."

Mr. Harvey was fussing with a light meter.

"Here. Over here I think the light will be perfect." He peered at the meter, then at the sky, then looked for the boy. He and his pigs were a block away.

"Oh say. That would have been a good one. Guess we'll have to let it go. Maybe I can get one of the town. Let's see. It is picturesque, isn't it, those mountains in the background and all. My. What a view." He looked through the range finder, turned the camera on end and back again, checked the setting, braced himself to snap the shutter, then turned abruptly.

"Oh—here. What's the matter with me? I want you people in this one. Would you mind standing over there by that palm tree—cactus, whatever it is? Both of you, if you don't mind. That's it. Little more to the left. That's good. I can see the whole town in back of you. That will be great." He snapped, grinned broadly. "Thanks a lot."

We walked up the road again. There was a slapping, beating sound, and we came upon a group of women in the meadow by the roadside, kneeling beside a narrow stream of water. Clothes lay all around them on the grass, stiff and humpy, drying in the sunshine. There were several flat rocks at the edge of the stream and over these the women bent, their *fachalinas*, the rectangular cloth worn around their shoulders, flung back, their breasts swinging in the loose blouses. Their hands were red when they lifted their arms out of the water, pounding the clothing into wads which streamed with water as they lifted them and slapped them down hard upon the stones. There was a rhythm in the bowing, slapping, lifting and bowing. It was broken for a moment as they paused to survey the foreigners with a direct, unabashed gaze. Mr. Harvey focused his camera and they bent to the task, their hair falling over their faces again, the water shining and dripping from their arms. One woman was rubbing her hair with a handful of fibrous stuff which made it sudsy. She wore a dark blue cloth tied around under her arms in place of a blouse, and she dipped the glistening black mass of her hair into the icy water, where it waved and swirled in the current.

"How come they don't use any soap?" Mr. Harvey asked.

"It's too expensive for them, I suppose. And they pound the clothes so vigorously they must get most of the dirt out that way."

"How about giving them a tract?" said my visitor. "I have a bunch of Spanish tracts here." He dug into the pocket of his gabardine raincoat.

"I'm afraid they don't read. I doubt if they even *speak* Spanish," I told him.

"They don't read? Oh, I suppose not. But there'll be somebody at home who can read to them. Here, I'll just give them a few. They'll like it, and then it's seed sown. You never know what the results may be."

Seed sown. In Spanish. It would be like planting bananas in Alaska, I thought.

Mr. Harvey started to walk across the grass in the direction of the women. They looked at him apprehensively. All at once he drew up, lifting his feet one after the other and looking at his shoes. He had stepped into a bog, where the water from the stream had spread out into the thick grass. One of the women giggled, quickly covering her mouth with a wet hand. The others smiled furtively and went on washing.

"Guess it's no good going over there. They looked scared anyway, didn't they?" He tiptoed to firmer ground.

The road took us past cornfields and potato fields,

through pastures of grazing sheep and cattle, past a few huts which Mr. Harvey photographed. "Here. I'll have to get some of these thatched roofs. Really primitive, aren't they?" He snapped away, standing with feet apart and raincoat whipping in the wind, then winding his film with a tight-lipped smile of satisfaction. The smile faded as we walked and the powdery dust plastered his wet shoes. He stopped to scrape them on a tuft of grass, then took a clean handkerchief from his pocket and carefully wiped his forehead and the back of his neck. A glance at the color of the handkerchief afterward surprised him, and he quickly folded and stuffed it back into his pocket.

"Dust is terrific up here. How far is it to Pedro's?" he asked.

"Another half hour, perhaps," I told him. "We go by time rather than mileage up here."

"Pretty rugged climb. Do you do this often?"

"Two or three times a week."

"I guess we at home don't know much about what missionaries go through. And that's exactly why I came. I want to see what it's really like, so I can go back and challenge the rest of them." I could hear his breath coming in short gasps behind me for a moment. Then a wave of wind swept the sound away.

We reached Pedro's house and were greeted by the children, who had begun to look forward to my visits. Sometimes I brought them candy or small toys. Rosa was sitting on the porch weaving a *faja*, a narrow woolen belt. Mr. Harvey took a picture of her, after a futile attempt to get her to smile. She watched his movements in bewilderment, for although she knew what the camera was she did not know why he made faces at her. She went on with her weaving, telling us to sit down until Pedro came. He was hoeing potatoes, but was expecting us and would soon be home.

We sat down, Mr. Harvey on a sack of corn, Mr. MacDonald and I on a bench that stood by the wall. A rooster raised a weak cry in the yard, and a couple of skinny hens scraped and picked about where he had been scratching. The valley lay in a veil of dust below us, but the mountain rose clear in the sun. I felt that we were set on a shelf midway between plain and peak. The breadth of this view never failed to gladden me, carrying my eye far down the slope up which we had come, across the wide plain, and up the smooth slopes to the east, beyond which lay the mystery of jungle and Amazon rain forest.

"Nice view up here too," said Mr. Harvey, tearing open a new roll of film. "Think I've about used up that roll, but I want to get Pablo when he comes—and you working with him, of course, Margaret."

Rosa got up from her weaving and went inside. Soon she appeared with bowls of soup for us.

"Do you think it's safe?" asked Mr. Harvey.

"Oh, I think so," said Mr. MacDonald. "I've eaten it many times, and never had any trouble."

"Well, I don't want to take any unnecessary risks. I've got a lot of trips lined up, and then I have to be back for deputation. They're just waiting for my report, you see. I'm not used to foreign foods. Of course, if I lived here like you do—" he broke off. Mr. MacDonald and I were drinking the soup, and Mr. Harvey took a tentative sip. Rosa was watching him closely. She had caught the tone of uncertainty in his voice when she offered it to him. He swallowed, looked at me, sniffed the soup and sipped again. He repressed the grimace he felt coming, and the soup was drunk without social disaster.

Finally Pedro came, his face and neck caked with dust, his clothes powdered to a uniform color. He picked up a rag from the floor near Rosa and wiped his forehead with hard, rough strokes as he greeted us. I knew that he had been working very hard, but he gave no indication that he was tired. He simply sat down on the doorsill, asked Rosa for a drink, and waited for me to start asking questions. I forgot for the moment what I was going to say. There was something in the frank, level gaze of his eyes—an almost innocent manliness—that made me feel a rush of pride and gratitude for him, and I wanted to say, "God bless you, Pedro." Instead, I said, "Today we are going to begin to translate God's word."

"It is so."

I had with me a copy of the New Testament in Spanish and English which I opened to the Gospel of Mark.

"The beginning of the Gospel of Jesus Christ, the Son of God." There was no noun for beginning. The infinitive could sometimes be used in this way, so I gave it a try. "Gospel" presented a problem. I found that it meant simply "good news" but Quichua had no word for news. How about "good word"? Pedro accepted that. There was no preposition "of." The idea had to be expressed as an adjective, as in, for example, "the tree foot" instead of "the foot of the tree," or as a possessive, "the tree's foot." So here it became "Jesus Christ, God's Son—about Him good word begins." Pedro said that was "hearable" all right, so I wrote it down.

"Could you just tilt your face a little bit toward the sun, Margaret?" said Mr. Harvey. "I can't quite get enough light on it. There. That's better. Now get Pablo to take his hand down so I can see the Bible. Oh, that's wonderful. I can even get a corner of the adobe wall and part of the loom in." He clicked, wound, and clicked again. "Better take a couple, just in case."

We went through six verses of the first chapter of Mark in about two hours. There were no Quichua words for messenger, wilderness, baptize, forgiveness, confess, or camel. For each we had to employ a clumsy phrase, a Quichua approximation, or perhaps a Spanish loan word. The result of that first translation session left me feeling utterly deflated. How could I have thought I was prepared to undertake such a task? Two years was too short a time in which to know the Indian idiom sufficiently well to translate the Bible. I had read of missionaries doing it in less time than that—in fact, one missionary had learned a language and translated the whole book of Mark inside two years' time. How did they do it? I had seen pictures of them giving out copies of their translations to eager natives. Who taught the people to read? Were the translations really readable and meaningful? I looked over what I had just written and wondered if it would mean anything to an Ecuadorian Quichua.

"Well, Margaret, this has been a thrill for me!" exclaimed Mr. Harvey. "To think that God brought me here just on the very day you were to begin this great task. Now I can say I have actually seen and heard a missionary translating the Word of God. Wonderful, isn't it, MacDonald?"

The Scotsman did not quite manage to match Mr. Harvey's enthusiasm. He knew how far I was from success, though he did not belittle the attempt.

"It's a beginning, brother. It's a beginning." (And how many more beginnings will there have to be? I wondered gloomily. Surely this would all have to be done over, God knew how many times.) "She's got a long, hard job ahead of her, and of course there's no one, so far, who can teach the people to read Quichua. She'll have to do that, too, before the translation will be of any value."

"Yes." Mr. Harvey looked crestfallen. "I never thought of that. They don't read, do they? How about Pablo? Doesn't he read?"

"Pedro?" I said. "No, he doesn't read."

"Hardly anyone reads even Spanish. No one reads Quichua," said Mr. MacDonald.

"Is that right?" Mr. Harvey was amazed. "So you don't have a mission school here?"

"No. We had hoped to, but the couple who were assigned to establish it could not come."

"How about a church? You have a church here somewhere?"

"No, not yet."

"There must be one someplace among the mountain Quichuas—I mean, I'm sure I heard there was one someplace. Or was that in Peru?"

"There are one or two believers on stations north of here. You couldn't call them churches."

"What about medical work? Do you do any of that?" There was real anxiety in his tone now. Mr. MacDonald looked to me for the answer to this question. I explained as well as I could what I was doing, seeing the bewilderment grow in my visitor's eyes. Desperately he sought proofs, exhibits. What he had found was clearly not up to his expectations of the work of God.

"But in Guatemala we saw a tremendous work—why, there are so many believers among some of those tribes the witch doctors are going out of business! I saw a baptism of eighteen Indians—pure-blooded Indians—all on one Sunday, right there on the station. And schools, clinics, nice little church buildings. But then you're just getting started, aren't you? Well, the Lord will work. Your labor is never in vain in the Lord, you've got to remember that."

The sun had passed its zenith and was sliding around to the west, throwing its rays now on the western slopes of Chimborazo. Pedro's children were peering out at us from the doors of the hut where they had been all during our visit.

"Don't these kids ever play?" asked Mr. Harvey.

"They seem to have little idea of playing as our children do. They work, and they can sit quietly much longer than American children can," Mr. MacDonald said. "I don't know why it is."

Mr. Harvey unsnapped his camera case again, but the children disappeared into the gloom.

"Shucks. Thought I could get a picture of them. They're so cute with their hats and ponchos and things. Won't they come out?"

I asked Pedro if they would mind.

"They are afraid," he said.

I suggested it was time to go, but Mr. Harvey was taking pictures again—of the pigs, the donkey, the view over the valley, Pedro with his rope sandals and dark poncho, the mud hut and the loom.

"I want to get all this stuff. I really want to be able to challenge the folks when I get back." He knelt on one knee to get a backlighted photo of Pedro against the sky, and the shoulder of the hill. I thought of possible captions Mr. Harvey might give it: "A typical Indian of the High Andes, one of millions still without Christ," or, if he chanced to catch Pedro smiling, "The light of the Gospel shines in the face of one of the descendants of the Inca sun worshipers." Challenge the folks back home. What did he mean? I had been "challenged" by men like him, had believed what they told me as though they had been oracles. Today I saw the makings of such a challenge—the swift, superficial glimpse; the intrusion it necessitated into two missionaries' time and an Indian's home; the frame of mind—Harvey had not come to learn but to document what he already assumed; his preconceptions governed his selection of picture subjects. Propaganda, I thought, demands simplification. Choose the pictures which show the poverty and primitiveness of the Indian, the successes of the missionary. Most disturbing of all to me was the realization that neither Mr. Harvey nor I was in a position to assess accurately either the Indians' need (who could say that they were worse off than New Yorkers, for example?) or my own success (who but God knew which were the victories, which the defeats?). For the visitor it was clearcut and simple: "Here is what God is doing." The picture of me with the open Bible and the earnest Indian, "Translating the Scriptures into the mountain Quichua dialect." It was fortunate, I thought with some irony, that Mr. Harvey had succeeded in finding one success of the kind he sought. What would he have done had I not been going to Pedro's that day? Lynn's formula came to my mind: Do the truth. How would Mr. Harvey have photographed that?

We said goodbye and I thanked Pedro and gave him his wages.

"Oh—you pay him for this?" Mr. Harvey was surprised.

"Why, yes."

"Wouldn't he do it without pay?"

"I don't know—but it's hard work for him. Harder than packing sacks of potatoes and firewood in the market."

"But isn't he a believer?"

"I think he is." The *non sequitur* puzzled me.

"A believer and he charges you for helping you translate the word of God?"

"Well—the laborer is worthy of his hire, isn't he? I wouldn't think of asking him to do it for nothing. He has his family to support. You see, Mr. Harvey, if he weren't working for me he would have to be working in the market, and I need him. He is unusually intelligent, I think, he speaks Spanish, and he was willing to do the work. All that means a great deal."

"Too bad, though, isn't it, that they won't do anything without pay. I suppose once you start paying them—well, it would be wonderful if they were willing just to serve the Lord." I thought of the meetings in which Mr. Harvey would show his pictures and of the offerings which would be collected for him just because he was serving the Lord.

We started down the mountainside, the wind flinging dust into our faces so that I could feel grit in my teeth. The cold penetrated our coats as the afternoon progressed. Some beautiful white birds sailed across the valley below us, brilliant against the somber color of the fields beyond them, and came to rest like neat, white boats on the lake.

"Do you see those lovely birds?" said Mr. MacDonald.

"Where?" asked Mr. Harvey.

"There. They've landed on the lake now, away down there."

"Oh. Yes. Pretty, aren't they? Wow, this wind is cold. Funny, you don't think of a country on the equator as being cold. Another one of the things folks back home just don't realize."

He would appear before his audiences as an authority. He had been there, he ought to know. And he could, in all honesty, present what seemed to him facts. Had he not incontestable evidence, there in his pictures, of the need of the Indian, and of the work of the missionary? Who would question the validity of the evidence? Who could gainsay him?

I watched the back of his thick neck, hunched into the raincoat, and heard his hard soles crunching on the stony earth. The cameras bobbed and swung at his side—packed with the evidence, I thought, for cameras "never lie"—material for a thousand illustrated "messages," thrill-packed missionary "challenges."

"Well, praise God!" said Mr. Harvey. *"Praise God!"*

CHAPTER

17

ONE DAY I took a new route home from Pedro's house, going farther up the hill to the north, making a great circle, through the fields, and coming down to the valley again to the east. The sun shone brilliantly and the air was still and warm, even on the highest fields. It was so unusual to breathe dust-free air and to walk without being buffeted by a cold wind that I went slowly, letting my eyes sweep over the beautiful patchwork of the fields, reveling in the world's loveliness as one does in the springtime after a long bleak winter. High above the mountaintop nearest me I saw a condor. I had never seen one before, but I knew him from his likeness on the seal of Ecuador. His great wings seemed to rest on the blueness and his head was bent over the valley below him. A bird of incredible size, he wheeled gently, tipping his wings almost imperceptibly, floating, floating. I stood and watched him sail in the sky, the bereaved lover of the Quichua legend, but I thought of the Spirit of God brooding over the face of the waters at the creation of the world. And as He brooded above that formless, empty darkness, He thought of light and He said, "Let there be light."

Here it was. A glorious brilliance of light all about

me—on the snowcaps glistening in the distance, on the clouds that floated with the condor, on the white sheep that grazed a little way off.

God is light, and in Him is not any darkness at all. In the world He made, though, I thought as I walked along, there is plenty of it still—a great deal of darkness which does not seem to change very much. I had come here as a messenger of light, and for a long time had looked forward to the day when that light would begin to shine in Quichua souls. It occurred to me now that there was really nothing to mark the point at which I became an active missionary. Whatever transition there might have been between being helpless and helpful I had passed over without noticing. All that concern for preparation—what was it for? Perhaps there was, after all, no difference. If I had not noticed it, certainly the Indians hadn't. Had it made any difference to God?

The condor still floated in the sky. I could not see that he had changed his position at all.

I came presently to a hut where a girl was kneeling in the dooryard, grinding corn on a flat stone. Beside her on the ground stood a basket filled with ears of corn, and a great, flat clay plate with toasted kernels. She looked up at me, her black eyes wide with surprise at finding a white woman in her yard. She paused in her grinding, two small brown hands resting on the loaf-shaped grinding stone.

"*Buenos días*," I said. "I am on my way home to the town."

"*Buenos días*," she answered timidly. "To the town?"

"Yes. I live in Indi Urcu."

"You are the señorita that lives there."

"Yes. My name is Margarita."

"Mm."

"Your name? What is your name?"

"I am Manuela." The ease with which she told me, without giggling or hedging as so many of the women did, drew me to her. I wanted to talk some more.

"I come from Pedro Chimbu's house, where we have been translating God's word," I explained.

"God's word?"

"Yes. Did you know that God gave us a word?"

"No, señorita."

"Would you like to hear some of it, Manuela? I will read a little."

"Yes, señorita."

I sat down on the doorstep and she began again with her grinding. I read to her from the fifth chapter of Mark the story of the ruler of the synagogue, Jairus, whose little daughter was dying, and of how Jesus went to the house and found her dead and took her by the hand and said, "Little girl, I say to you, arise." And immediately the girl got up and walked.

"That child got up?" The stone came to an abrupt halt as the young woman asked the question.

"Yes."

"You said she was dead."

"Yes. She was dead. But Jesus, God's Son, came and caused her to get up."

"She got up alive?"

"Yes. Alive. Jesus can raise the dead, He can heal sick ones, He can do anything He wants."

"Where is He?"

"With His Father, God. He lives with God. But He wants to help us, too. He can help us if we trust Him."

"How can He help us? Where is He?"

This was more interest on the part of a woman than I

had met with for a long time, and we talked at some length about Jesus and what He wanted to do for any who would trust Him. I had a hard time explaining what trust meant, for the word I had to use was a Spanish corruption. Quichua had no such expression.

"You can trust Jesus. His word is a true word. You know that He will do what He says."

Manuela sat in silence, as though pondering whether there were such a person—one who would do what he says. I wondered if she understood the kind of faith I was talking about. She said she did. She began to wonder if Jesus could help her too. I did not jump at this as I once might have, aware now that her meaning could be any one of a thousand, and not necessarily indicative of the birth of saving faith. She went on grinding for a long time without speaking. Then she stopped pushing the stone and said, "My children are dead."

My heart sank. Did she want them back? I waited to hear.

"One child died when he was this size." She held her hand about three feet above the ground, fingers extended as though to shake hands, to show his size. "And the other miscarried. Now I am with child. Two months are yet lacking before he will see the light. Who will help me when he is born? He will perhaps die, too."

"I would be glad to come and help you if you wish."

"Can you make him live?"

"I don't know, but I will come and try."

"Can Jesus make him live?"

"Yes, Jesus can make him live if He wants to."

"Will He want to?"

"Perhaps He will want to. I will come if you call me, and

I will do whatever I can to help you. I will ask Jesus, too, to help you and to make your child live."

Leaning her weight on the grinding stone, Manuela searched my face. She had probably tried the witch doctor and the medicines. Whether she thought I could do no worse, or whether something gave her faith in me or even in God I could not tell, but she said, "I will call you, señorita."

Two months later I was awakened from sleep before dawn by a sharp rapping on my door. A child's voice called, "Señorita! Señorita *Gringa!*" I opened it, and found a boy of ten or twelve and a girl perhaps a year younger. "Manuela is giving birth," they announced. "She says come."

I asked them in, got dressed and collected what midwifery equipment I had and we started out.

The street was perfectly quiet at that hour, and the bare feet of the children padded softly on the cobblestones. The sharp night air cut into my lungs. A dog was barking far across the village, answered by others here and there.

As we climbed the hillside the great peaks of the Andes stood like black paper cutouts against the faintly paling sky. Two or three bright planets pierced the deep blue, and the moon, a half disk, floated above Chimborazo. Tufts of grass in the road crackled with frost as we walked.

We reached the hut to find Manuela on her knees facing the wall, her hands pulling on a rope which was strung from the rafters. Her husband, Victor, knelt behind her, lifting her under the arms as she rose and panted with pain. Several women stood about, and her mother, a toothless old Indian with a blue cloth on her head, squatted on the floor beside Victor, instructing him in an urgent whisper to keep lifting, keep lifting. Then she turned to Manuela and said, "Hard now. As hard as you can. Do not stop. *Hard*." The old woman moved over and tightened the woven belt around the girl's waist. This, I learned later, was to keep the child from coming out the mother's mouth.

I asked if everything was all right. Yes, they said, but—someone thought to add, quite casually—perhaps the baby would come feet first. One of the women then insisted that she was sure it would, for Manuela had sheared a ewe that had died during the new moon, and this, all women knew, was taboo during pregnancy.

"I tried to get her to light a candle for our saint, but she would not hear," said the old mother. "Now the child will be born head up and will die."

I went over in my mind all that Lynn had taught me about the procedure for delivering a breech. Only the simplest measures would be possible under these circumstances, but they might be life-saving. I asked that some water be heated and cloths collected. The Indians listened solemnly to my requests but no one hastened to carry them out. They argued among themselves as to who should do it and whether it was worth the trouble.

"What will she do?" they asked one another. "She will not make it live, will she? How can she make it live?"

I found a place on a pile of sheepskins and sat down to wait, since neither Victor nor his mother-in-law seemed willing to relinquish his place to me. Lynn had told me it was useless to insist that a woman in labor lie down unless there was an emergency, since the Indians believed that birth took place by sheer gravity, with a good deal of squeezing and shaking by the husband when the mother's strength ebbed.

It was a long day. I sat through the rest of the morning,

as the sun climbed above the valley and threw its rays into the courtyard between the mud walls, and then as it passed, in the afternoon, toward the Pacific and left the little house in darkness once more. At intervals Victor gave up his task of jerking and jiggling and sat down on another pile of skins to drink his corn soup or chew a mouthful of *máchica*. No one thought of offering Manuela any sustenance until I asked Victor if she might not have some *máchica*, too. He went over and pushed a spoonful of the dry, toasted barley flour under her tongue.

The women sat gossiping, recalling other births they had witnessed wherein mother and baby lived, or the mother died, or the baby died, and they told the details of birth and death with equal relish, while Manuela knelt and sweated by the wall, rising and sinking, crying out in a small voice once or twice, silent the rest of the time. I sat and prayed, listened to the women, tried to talk to Manuela to encourage her, played a little with the two children who had fetched me, and prayed again.

"God save Manuela. O Lord, help her, let her live." But she'll live, I told myself. Nothing wrong, probably. Birth is a normal process.

I looked at Victor, gulping his soup in the corner. He was obviously not worried. Even the old mother, though she urged Manuela intermittently to keep working, was placid enough about it. I had learned a lot from the Indians about accepting life calmly, and the lesson had given me a cooler view of my own hardships and even of my own importance. If my alarm at what had originally seemed the deplorable condition of the Indian had diminished, my sense of being needed by them had diminished correspondingly. Manuela will be all right. No need for any desperate praying yet.

But, Lord, You must have brought me here for some reason. Show me what it is. Show me that I am needed for *something*.

Manuela let go the rope and sank back on her heels, letting her head drop into her hands. "*Aylla*," she said in a whisper, a Quichua expression of woe.

"What's the matter with you?" her mother asked sharply. "Get up there. It's no good sitting down. Get up."

Manuela wiped the sweat from her forehead with a corner of her shawl, rose to her knees again and pulled on the rope. I could not imagine how she had an ounce of strength left. The lack of concern on the part of all present disturbed me. It was all very well to accept life and its conditions without complaining—I had been pleased to find that the crises need not be turned over to the professionals as I had been taught to think. Birth, marriage, accidents, old age, death—all these things were dealt with by the people themselves, in the sanctuary of home as a part of the course of life, not to be interfered with by outsiders, and whatever might be said for the other side, the Indian way seemed laudably humane and in harmony with nature.

But as soon as I heard another cry from Manuela, my philosophizing stopped and I began to think that something must surely be amiss or the baby would have been born by now. Perhaps the women were right—the baby was right side up, and Manuela was in trouble. Something ought to be done. Someone at the very least should be concerned about her.

Lord, give me wisdom. If something ought to be done, show me what it is. Should I do it now? Suppose I delay too long? On the other hand, the Indians are all calm enough. I must not make a fool of myself by declaring an emergency where none exists—I could alienate them.

Manuela sat back once more. "Not yet," she said.

"Not yet?" said the old woman.

"Not yet."

I felt as though everyone drew a slight breath of relief. Perhaps it was only I. How foolish of me to become so agitated by physical suffering when it was the spiritual needs I should have been most deeply concerned about. Had my sense of the Indians' spiritual plight been dulled by familiarity? Probably it had. But whose fault was that? How can the human spirit be held taut for years? Are we not created with resiliency so that we can support the tensions of life? God had given me a task to do in the translation work at least, if not in the area of evangelism. As for the latter, perhaps I had not appropriated the power of God as I ought to have, or perhaps I was never intended for that job, and the sooner my definition of my task was pared down to the size God meant it to be, the better. I hoped with all my soul that I was not to blame, but admitted the possibility that I was, and the burden of guilt became intolerable when I thought that not only was I to be cast aside as unusable, but the millions of Quichuas whom I had taken upon my heart were now without an intercessor. God could do nothing with *me*, and there was no other.

I was not allowed to resolve the hopeless tangle of reasonings. Victor had left the house to get water from the aqueduct half a mile away when Manuela suddenly said, "*Shamun!*" "It is coming!" and reached for the rope.

Things worked better than my highest hopes. The baby was indeed head up as the women had predicted, but I prayed, "Lord help me *now*—let me do this much for them," and then I did what Lynn had taught me, the baby's life was saved, Manuela lay back exhausted and grateful, the women looked at me in wonder. Breech babies never, they said, survived. The pulling and hauling they did would have killed the child, I supposed, if the delay had not first suffocated it, so this to them was a miracle.

Nothing had been prepared for the child, for even if everything had gone smoothly the chances for survival were about equal with the chances of death, so the Indians had hardly thought it worthwhile to take any trouble beforehand. Better to wait and see what the results were. So now they had to rummage through the piles of rags, blankets, and skins to find something to wrap the baby in. Some cloths were finally found, the child was wrapped and then bound round and round with *faja* belting, its little arms pinned firmly to its sides, its legs straightened and pressed together. Then it was laid on the sheepskins like a tiny mummy next to its mother.

CHAPTER

18

———〜———

I HAD been up this mountain many times during the day, but never during a night of pouring rain and roaring wind. By this time the rain was seeping through the coat that was supposed to have been waterproof, and water ran down my neck. "Are they servants of Christ? I am a better one—I am talking like a madman—with far greater labors. . . . Three times I have been beaten with rods; once I was stoned . . . adrift at sea; on frequent journeys, in danger from rivers . . . through many a sleepless night . . . in cold and exposure." The Apostle Paul had listed his hardships, not pretending that he had never made a sacrifice. I might list one or two of my own. I felt exhilarated by the wildness of the night, the streaming, slashing rain, the screaming, lashing wind. But why hadn't the man at least brought a light? My flashlight was feeble, and since I had given it to him to carry I walked mostly in darkness.

The man had come to my house late that night to say that his little daughter was desperately ill with what seemed to be poisoning. Word had run from hut to hut over the mountainside that Manuela had given birth to a feet-first baby, and that the white señorita had made it live, and since that time increasing numbers of Indians found their way to my door in Indi Urcu. Sometimes they came under a pretext of selling me something but often it was with the frank request for medical treatment of one kind or another, or with a plea that I come to visit a sick relative.

Here was another one. The idea of treating such an emergency frightened me—my reputation as a miracle-working midwife did not qualify me for this job, but I did not see how I could refuse at least to attempt assistance. I found an emetic, which I put in the bag with the other standard remedies, and we started off as fast as we could up the mountainside.

The night was perfectly black and the trail soon became a rushing river of water. I could feel the water squelching in my shoes, and apart from the knowledge that they would be ruined I rather enjoyed the memory of childhood puddle splashing that the cool wetness evoked. The trail, however, became more and more slippery as we ascended and I could not see whether I was putting my foot down on a rock or on greasy clay. The effort of trying to keep up with my guide, who was understandably in a hurry, and seeking a foothold at the same time tired me quickly. How far would it be? I knew it was useless to ask—time and again the Indian estimate ("Just over that hill" or "Now we are in my dooryard") had been wide of the mark. I hunched my shoulders up higher to keep the rain from trickling down my neck and hoped most earnestly that this journey would not be in vain.

There was a time when "in vain" to me had meant that there was no visible spiritual result. A study of the public life of Jesus convinced me that he regarded things differently, since comparatively few of his encounters with individuals or groups resulted in manifestations of true faith. I still wanted proof of my effectiveness in some area, and the success with Manuela had been gratifying. Perhaps God had not intended to draw her or her immediate family to Christ through that cure, but at least He had given the physical evidence of His power, and there was reason to hope that spiritual results might ultimately follow. All my life I had been conditioned to regard every chance conversation, every accident by which my path crossed that of another human being (especially if that human being was a stranger—people I knew somehow fell into a different category) as God's way of thrusting in some truth. During the past two years this dream had suffered some revision which, as I hurried along in the dancing fragments of light thrown by my guide's flashlight, I tried to define. What had taken place? Originally I was a missionary with the broad scope of service that the name implied in my thinking: to win souls, to translate the Scriptures, to use medicine and education for the sake of the Kingdom. Then I accepted the role of mere translator—I was prepared for that, I seemed to do better at it than at evangelism, and the task was so demonstrably the work of God. In recent months, however, I had been reluctantly a doctor. The Indians had finally discovered a use they could make of me, and although I dreaded the thought of becoming a quack and studiously avoided advertising my medical skills, there was no escape from duty which presented itself at my door.

We were skirting the edge of a *quebrada*. The wind scooped down into the ravine and rushed upward into our faces, slapping sheets of water against us and tearing at our soaked clothes. It was such a journey as I had never made before, and I thought it would have fit quite nicely into St. Paul's catalogue. His sufferings resulted in triumph. Lord, let this trip, too, at least be worthwhile. I don't mind losing sleep and a pair of shoes if I don't lose the patient or the opportunity to speak of Christ. If Jesus did not always gain a disciple, at least He healed the sufferer who came to Him. Which would it be tonight?

The roar of wind and water made talk impossible, but at last the Indian turned and shouted, "There is my house over there—do you see the light?" I could not see any light, but I thought I could hear another sound above the swish of the wind. The Indian heard it too, for he stopped short, leaning into the wind, and then, the flashlight making a swift arc in the fog, he threw his hands to his head. "Already dead."

It was the death wail that we heard, a wild, hopeless song lament reaching us in waves through the rain.

He resumed his steps, more slowly, and we reached the house to find the mother rocking the child, limp and still in her arms, and a crowd of people shrieking and keening in despair. They stopped long enough to recount the last moments, and I stayed to try to comfort them with the words of Him who said, "I am the Life." But they were in no mood to listen to talk of any kind. It was not talk they wanted. The child was dead; the white woman had not come in time; it was all over. I might have spoken to them, have pronounced a verbal prescription for their need, but I saw that I had no right to presume on their plea for help. They had wanted me to save a life. I had failed to do that; I could go now. No matter what I had to say, what other offers I might make, it was over. The one thing they had wanted from me they had not gotten.

One of the children was sent to guide me home again, and as I walked, still in lashing rain and wind, still in darkness, I told myself that I was not to blame. Clearly I had done what I could. The child could not in all probability have been saved if I had arrived in time—even a doctor loses patients and this child had not been my patient. God knew I had had nothing to do with her death. But if He knew that, He knew ahead of time that she would die. Why this useless frantic race up the mountain in the mud and rain, in the middle of the night?

For nothing. For nothing. For nothing. The rain came in increased force, sending stinging scourges against me. If only this *rain* would stop—now that the job was over, the trip seen to have been fruitless, what was the point in having to keep up the struggle just to get home? I slowed down a little, for there was no reason for urgency now. Still the rain beat down.

A few days after Manuela's delivery I had written a circular letter, asking my friends to pray for her spiritual enlightenment. It was satisfying to be able to recount the medical success, and to tell them of the completion of the translation of the Gospel of Mark—Pedro and I were now working on Genesis, and he had shown real interest in the Scriptures and understanding of the task we were jointly engaged in.

If I were to write of tonight's incident, what would I say? The rain swiped at me, as though a troublesome Providence nagged for my attention when I wanted to focus it even for a moment on my own anxieties. Thoroughly drenched anyway, I resolved to ignore the storm and pursue my thoughts.

Medicine, I had understood, was to be used as the servant of missions, a means for bringing the masses under the "sound of the Gospel." Why didn't it work for me here? Lynn's clinic, the vaccination of the school children, my countless visits, the giving away of hundreds of sucres' worth of drugs, even the resounding success of Manuela's childbirth had produced hardly a single exhibit to prove that medicine was a means to the great missionary end. And if it is an end in itself, I thought wryly, what business have I to be involved in it without proper training? Lynn was legitimately involved—she was a doctor.

But then, of course, if I were to write in my next circular about tonight's journey, I couldn't put it in either category. It was nothing, really, except an adventure—it would seem an adventure to my friends at home, though right now it was sheer misery.

"Are you coming, señorita?" The child was far ahead, and had stopped to call back. I tried to quicken my pace a little but the effort was too great.

"I'm coming," I said.

Why this need to find meaning at every turn? Why do I struggle to sort out the material and the spiritual, to separate the failures from the successes? Well, if you're going to write honest prayer letters . . . That was what tormented me.

I thought of that sunny afternoon when I had traveled down this path with Mr. MacDonald and Mr. Harvey, appalled at the ease with which Mr. Harvey assessed the work of the Lord—these are the victories, these are the defeats. Who was I to label things?

The rain had subsided to a gentle whisper, and I could hear the quick little splashes of the child's feet in the water which still flowed in the trail. By the time we reached my gateway the sky over the eastern cordillera had grayed. The night was past.

"Will you come in and have a cup of coffee?" I asked my little guide.

"*Bueno*, señorita." She followed me inside and I set

about finding something to eat with the coffee. I was suddenly aware of a ravenous hunger.

"Whether therefore ye eat, or drink . . . do all to the glory of God." St. Paul had recognized even the common things. Of course I knew that; I had heard sermons on it. But I saw now that if my task was far smaller in terms of the effect it was to produce, it was far larger in terms of my own life involvement. If there were times when I must be willing to pay any price for what was called the "advancement of the Kingdom" there were also times when I must be willing to let such a price—climbing a mountain, for example, in rain and mud and darkness—be paid in vain. This, too, was a place to glorify God. This must have been what Lynn meant, I thought as I set the table. "Jesus told us to do what is true."

THERE WAS no reason to forge ahead with translation of the Bible, I realized, unless there were readers. And there would be no readers unless I myself taught them. Willy-nilly, I found myself involved in education as well as in medicine and translation. As Pedro and I would sit translating, Jorge and Romero would often hang over my shoulder. In the story of Jacob and Esau I needed a word for "game." I explained to Pedro that it meant meat gotten in the field or forest, not guinea pig or sheep as they were used to. Pedro scratched his head and finally decided that there was no other word for meat. Meat was meat. *Aicha*. I wrote it down, and Jorge said, "She writes *aicha*."

"Where?" said Romero.

"Where, señorita, where is *aicha*? There?" said Jorge.

"Yes," I said. "This part says *ai*, this part says *cha*. *Aicha*." Quichua is a simple language, well-adapted to teaching reading by syllables, and it was not long before the two boys had mastered the three vowels and most of the consonants and could put the syllables together.

My work with Pedro, along with the new reading lessons and my continued medical visits to many homes made it necessary for me to spend a great deal of time walking back and forth from the town. That endless trudge in the rain convinced me that I ought to move closer to the Indians. It would be hard to give up my little house, but how could I stop at the price if such a move would mean closer contact with the Indians? Not that I believed, at this point, that I would ever succeed in identifying myself with them. Nor did I any longer see this as of any great importance. The Indians had become people to me—they were no longer my "field." While I had once declared them to be my equals, I now regarded myself as theirs. Instead of saying, "Oh, you are as good as I—let me help you," I now said, "I am as poor as you. God help us all."

During the first year in Indi Urcu I had coveted the privilege of making noticeable sacrifices—the comfortable village house was one I hoped to make. It was too nice, really, for a pioneer missionary. But at the time there was no way of doing it. Ironically, now that I had learned to be content with lesser self-denials, I saw the opportunity of giving up the house. Pedro told me of an empty house not far from his which could be cleaned up and used if I wanted to put a little money into new tiles for the roof and a new door frame. A young Indian had contracted tuberculosis and been sent to the government hospital, leaving his wife and two small children to run the farm. They had struggled with it but finally given up and gone home to her parents, leaving the house empty and the fields untilled. If I would live in the house Pedro said he would arrange for an Indian to take care of the potato crop. The small rent for the house would cover his wages and the owner would not lose his land. It took some time before the arrangements could be worked out. I looked forward to the move, for funds had been dropping off somewhat of late, and it was expedient for me to look for cheaper quarters. None of my supporters had written directly to explain the decrease in gifts, but one or two had expressed, if not distress, surprise at my sympathy for the Indian outlook. I inferred that they took this as a questioning of the traditional missionary outlook. I searched my form letters for hints that the mission's program was anything but unimpeachable, and found nothing.

Romero, Jorge and Pava had made great strides in reading Quichua. The language had only three vowels, and teaching by syllables was comparatively simple. It was quite another thing to teach them to read with any indication of the sense of the words. The mere idea that the words were supposed to *mean* something was new to them, but Romero finally understood and one day I asked him to read aloud from our translation of Mark so that his mother could hear. Up until this time she had paid little attention to the reading lessons, willing enough to let the children learn whatever it was I wanted to teach them—perhaps because it pacified me as well as them—but ignorant of the purpose. Today I announced to her that the children would read from God's word and she must listen. Obligingly she stopped her work. Romero began to read.

"And they brought him to the place called Golgotha (which means the place of a skull). And they offered him wine mingled with myrrh; but he did not take it." Romero had trouble pronouncing the Spanish words we had introduced for the name of the hill and the myrrh. Here Rosa interrupted.

"This is God's word?"

"Yes," I said, pleased that she had remembered that.

"God speaks Quichua?"

"Yes," I said, "He speaks your language. Men wrote His book in another language and we translate it" (the

Quichua word meant "to take across") "into your language. Pedro and I have been translating it, and now your son can read it."

The boy went on. "And they crucified Him, and divided His garments among them, casting lots for them, to decide what each should take." Again Rosa stopped him.

"Is he reading? Is he reading the paper?"

"Yes," I replied, even more pleased that she had recognized the skill. "Romero is reading the paper. This is what I have been teaching your children all these weeks. It is not easy to read, but Romero has learned, and now he reads God's word for you."

"He is reading Quichua!"

I was delighted. "Yes!" I said. "Quichua."

Rosa's face grew dark and suspicious. "But he *knows* Quichua. Why did you teach him to read Quichua?"

Her anger stunned me. Was she not pleased with Romero's new ability?

"But, Rosa—" I began.

"Why did you not teach him to read Spanish? When people read, they read Spanish. What good is it to read Quichua? Quichua! We are Quichuas! As if he did not know Quichua!" She tore the paper from his hand and flung it toward the fire. Pava snatched it up and clutched it to herself defensively, her eyes snapping like her mother's. "I want my children to *learn*," Rosa went on. "I want them to learn like the white man, to know what the white man knows. Why would I want them to learn Quichua?" She got up from the floor and began violently throwing corn cobs into a basket. Pedro picked at the frayed rope of his sandal. I waited for him to speak, but he said nothing.

"Do *you* understand, Pedro?" I asked.

"Yes, I understand."

"Why did we translate God's word?"

"To take it across from Spanish."

"And why did we take it across from Spanish?" Oh Pedro—if you don't know the answer to this one, after all this time . . .

"To put it into our own language, so that we Quichuas could hear it."

"And you see why I taught your children to read in Quichua, and why I want you to learn?"

"So that we could read what God says, señorita."

"So that you could read what God says. He wants to speak to you."

Pedro picked at his sandal for a while. He pulled out a fiber and began to run it through his teeth. Then he looked at me and said, "Has God not spoken in Spanish?"

"Well, Pedro—you know He has. You know we use the Spanish God's Word—what do you mean?"

"If He has spoken in Spanish, we will hear Him in Spanish. It is enough."

"But, Pedro, we have talked many times of how each man needs to hear it in his mother's tongue."

He considered this for a moment, pensively running the thread through his teeth. Then he spat in the fire and said, "No. It is enough, señorita. The white man hears it in Spanish. We, like the white man, will also hear it in Spanish."

"WHO KNOWS where he will be?" Rosa picked up a huge, flat plate made of clay and set it evenly on the three hearthstones. "Will you wait for him?"

"Yes," I said, disappointed at not finding Pedro at home this afternoon, but unwilling to put off any longer the matter about which I had come to speak.

"Sit down, señorita. Coming he will come. Probably very soon." She began rubbing fat kernels of dried corn off the cobs into the plate. "Pava! The spoon."

The girl climbed onto some sheepskins and pulled a long wooden spoon from the thatch roof. "*Him*." With the nasal grunt which means "Here!" she extended the spoon toward her mother over the plate. Rosa took the spoon and began pushing the corn around and across the plate, turning it over slowly, scraping the clay dish with a soft woody rhythm. A solemn boy of about three—the child who had been on her back when I first met Rosa—sat near her on the mud floor, tapping a corn cob on a piece of broken pottery.

"To translate God's word you come?" Rosa looked at me through the smoke, brushing back a lock of dusty hair with her left hand, never pausing with the stirring.

"No, Rosa, not today. I came today to talk to Pedro."

"*Yanga?* Did you come to talk *yanga?*" She used again the word which means for-no-particular-purpose. It used to infuriate me, and I had at first refused to use it myself. It seemed evasive, senseless, and, for me, a lie. I did not do things *yanga*. God willing, the Indians, too, were going to learn to have some purpose in life. Today, however, I was tempted to agree that I had come for nothing. It no longer seemed like a lie to me, for it was the Indian way of saying all that needed to be said. The Western compulsion to account for everything struck me now as pompous and at times defensive. On the other hand, I may as well tell her my reason for coming, I thought. Not that she will be of any help, but it will make conversation, and this is difficult enough with Rosa.

"I came to talk about the house."

"Oh. The house you want to live in?"

"Yes."

She snatched a kernel of corn from the hot plate and tossed it quickly in her hand, patting it against her mouth for a second, then dropped it back into the plate.

"Your house in the town is no good? You don't like to live there?"

We had been over all this, and I did not know how to make Rosa understand any more than I had already told her.

"It is far away. I have a long way to walk to get to the *runa* houses, and I would like to live near you."

"Oh." She put a corncob between the stones and blew on the fire with a hollow straw. Taking the spoon again, she went on stirring. "You want to live near us, señorita."

"Yes."

"Are you ever going back to your own land?"

"I don't know. I suppose I will, someday, to visit."

"Your mother lives?"

"Yes. And my father."

"And do they not say come?"

"Oh yes, they want me to come home to visit."

"Not to stay?"

"No. My parents want me to do what God wants, and I think God says I should live here."

"Are you going to get married?" She picked up another kernel and tested it as she had before, then crunched it between her yellowed worn teeth, watching me through the smoke.

I laughed. "Oh Rosa, how many times have you asked me that? I don't know, I told you. I don't know if I will ever get married."

"Don't they ask for you? Don't your kind of men ask?"

"No, Rosa. They don't ask."

She scraped some toasted corn from the plate into a basket and rubbed off more kernels to toast. "Pava. Give some *tostados* to the señorita."

Pava came and picked up the basket, brought it over to where I sat. "Do you like these?" she asked timidly.

"Yes. Oh, I think they're very good. We didn't have this kind of corn in my country."

"Is that true?" Rosa looked up in surprise. "What kind of corn did you have?"

I knew very little even in English about varieties of corn and tried to think of a way to describe them in Quichua. When would Pedro come home? Waiting. Always waiting, marking time, wondering when things were going to start.

"Oh, it was a smaller kind than this. We did not have big—" I could not think of the word for kernel—"the big kind that you toast." Would Pedro have been able to get

[217]

me the house by this time? Why didn't he come? He was usually home by this hour.

"What kind do you toast in your country?"

Oh dear. What kind did we toast? Rosa, how am I to explain to you. Why doesn't Pedro come?

"We don't toast corn in my country."

There was a stirring and snuffling in the corner that did not come from the guinea pigs.

"Pava. Bring the baby." Pava rose, went over to the corner where a white cloth was slung between the walls, and stood on tiptoe, her delicate little ankles exposed beneath the cherry-colored wool skirt, the soles of her bare feet showing gray in the smoky light. With some wrestling she extracted the baby from the hammock, draped him over her shoulder, and handed him to his mother.

"You don't toast corn in your country." Rosa sat back with one heel curled under her, one neat small foot stretched out beside the fire, and laid the baby across her lap. He burrowed furiously under her blouse, found what he wanted, and let his feet flop in contentment. His small snortings and smackings mingled with the scraping of the spoon and the rattle of the corn. Firelight, shelter, food to eat, love. You don't know what you've got, Rosa.

"What do you have?" Rosa asked.

I was about to say "Nothing," when I realized that Rosa's question bore no reference to what I was thinking just then. What was it? Corn. We had been talking about not having corn in my country.

"Oh, we have other things. Lots of other kinds of food."

"And if you live near us, you will eat *runa* food?"

"Of course, Rosa! I like *runa* food."

Rosa lifted the plate off the fire and dumped the batch of

tostados into the basket. "You will like it, perhaps. You will not like it, perhaps."

"But I do like it, Rosa. I have eaten all kinds of *runa* food."

"Food! I am talking about the house. Who knows if you will like the house? Who knows if Pedro will get it for you?"

Was there some reason for putting me off from week to week? Each time I had asked him, Pedro had had some reason for not being able to get the house for me. I had offered an increase in the rent I originally proposed and still he put me off. Was it that they did not want me to live near them? I did not really expect them to urge me to come. My presence could hardly have so much importance to them.

There seemed to be nothing to say, and I sat watching the guinea pigs scuffling around the floor. Pava tore bits of leaves from a basket by her side and fed them, careful to give them equal portions. The three-year-old made passes at them with a corncob to hear them squeal.

"Wait for the Lord; be strong, and let your heart take courage; yea, wait for the Lord!" I've been waiting, Lord. Waiting and waiting. Not just for Pedro this afternoon. You know I waited a long time to be a missionary to mountain Indians. Then I waited for the Gardners. They didn't come. Then I waited to see what I was to do next, and You seemed to say translation and medical work. So you gave me Pedro—I don't discount that answer to prayer, Lord, or Manuela's baby. I don't want to belittle Your faithfulness to me. Just being here today, I know, is an answer to prayer. Think what it took. Kindness of friends, help from home, encouragement of people like the

MacDonalds, support that is still coming in (it's probably good for me not to have so much—keeps me looking to You. If I skimp—if I can just get that Indian house—I will be able to live much more simply), prayers of many friends—all these things, good and perfect gifts, coming down from the Father of Lights. I don't complain against You now, Lord—just show me the way. Nothing very startling has happened—maybe it's not supposed to. Let me be content with whatever You want. Just bring Pedro back now, please, for one thing. It gets pretty boring sitting here. Smoke gets in my eyes. My back is tired. There's no school yet, either, Lord. What am I to make of the Indians' attitude toward the translation and learning to read Quichua? There's no visible change *anywhere*. Pedro? What about Pedro? Oh yes, perhaps he is a Christian. I certainly hope so; I trust so. But then, Lord, he is in my pay. No souls to claim, really. No stars in my crown, no figs on the tree.

"Father is coming." Pava jumped up and went to the door. "The señorita is here," she called. "Come quickly. *Atsai!* Mama . . . what is the matter with father?"

"What is it?" said Rosa, looking up sharply.

"Why does he walk that way?"

Rosa lifted the baby in her arms and rose from the floor, peering out into the blinding sunlight of the fields.

"Jesús Santa María, his leg is bad again. It is for that he did not come quickly. *What is the matter with you?*" She shouted at him, not calling his name. I had never heard her address him by name. I got up too, and saw Pedro stumbling across the potato fields toward the gate in the mud wall, his trouser leg rolled up, his hand clutching a rag with which he stooped once to wipe his leg.

"What happened to him, Rosa?" I asked.

"He gets that way *yanga. Yanga* his leg becomes worse."

Pedro came into the house, limping to the bed in the corner.

"*Buenas tardes*, señorita."

"*Buenas tardes*, Pedro."

"Did you bring your needle, señorita?"

I had been earlier that day to visit a child with an infected hand and had with me my penicillin and syringe.

"Yes, I brought it."

"Stick me, please, señorita. It hurts badly."

"What is it, Pedro? What did you do to your leg?"

"It's just that way. It gets well, and it gets bad again. Pus comes out, it hurts badly, I can't walk. Today I was working in my cornfield and it hurt more and more and I worked more and more and then I felt my trousers sticking to my leg when I bent over like this, and I looked at my leg and it had pus coming out, pus running down my leg, and my leg is red and it hurts me so that I could hardly walk home and I thought perhaps I will die, who knows if I will die? Who will cure me? Will God cure me? Will the señorita cure me? Perhaps the señorita will cure me. I will ask her to stick me with her needle. Will you stick me?"

I took out the vial of penicillin. There were still several cc's left, more than enough for an injection. "Yes," I said, "I will inject you. Rosa, would you boil my needle in your pot?"

"Pava! Bring the small pot. Get some water. How much water, señorita?"

"Just a little in the bottom. No, that's too much."

Pava tipped some of the water into the ashes beside the fire. "Like that, señorita?"

"Yes, like that."

"Blow up the fire, Pava! Hurry!" said Rosa. "The señorita says she will boil her needle. There. The needle, señorita? Will you put it in the pot?"

I put the needle, together with the syringe and forceps, into the pot and began to examine the leg which Pedro stretched toward the fire. It was swollen and inflamed, and pus ran in a little trickle between the sparse black hairs of his leg. The wound looked deep and painful. Here I was again, the doctor. There was no escaping it. But how lucky that I was here at this moment with the necessary equipment! No, it isn't luck. It's God. He's the one who leads you, Margaret Sparhawk. He has not left you yet. The work may look unpromising but remember the promises of God. Life isn't easy for anyone. It doesn't fall into neat patterns. It's up and down, trusting in the dark, walking in the light, joy and sorrow, sunshine and shadow, whate'er befall, Jesus my Savior is my All in All. . . . The clichés tumbled emptily in my mind and I realized that the needle was bouncing in the pot. It had boiled long enough, and I picked up a cornhusk to use as a potholder.

"Ay, Señorita Margarita, it hurts." Pedro clasped his hands under the thick calf and rocked back, shutting his eyes and lifting his face. His hat, which he had not taken off, fell behind him and I saw that his forehead was beaded with sweat. Not, surely, from the heat, I thought. He must be in real pain. Poor Pedro. I looked at the strong bones of his face—high cheeks, a solid jaw, and lines that drew his mouth down and converged around his eyes. He had known plenty of pain in his lifetime. He had expected little else, I mused. Not physical pain, perhaps—I did not know how much of that he had had. But if pain could be defined as the absence of pleasure he had certainly known that. He was only one of the million. A million highland Quichuas living in cold and loneliness and poverty and hopelessness.

God help me to help him. At least to help Pedro, Lord. You haven't let me do much for the rest, but You brought me here today. Why was it I came? Oh, the house. I had forgotten to ask him about that. Well, it would have to wait for another time. Now for the injection. This is the right thing to do, isn't it, Lord? What else? Lynn gave him penicillin before, I gave him those three injections on the days following hers. The leg had healed up nicely then.

"Does it hurt here, Pedro?" I prodded the area around the open sore. It felt hot and tight.

"*Ay*, señorita. *Aylla*. It hurts very much. All around there, that whole part. Hurts, señorita, it hurts."

I picked up the forceps, which had cooled a little by now and lifted the syringe from the water. Holding the syringe in my left hand, I lifted the needle and fitted it onto the syringe. Pava watched intently.

"Why do you cook it, señorita?"

"To kill the little things that make sickness."

"What little things make sickness?"

I knew no Quichua equivalent for germ. "They're little things you can't see. Tiny. Much smaller than fleas. They get inside us and make us sick. I cook the needle so that I won't give your father someone else's sickness."

"In the cooking the little things die?"

"Yes." I found a small bottle of alcohol in my bag and a wad of cotton. Pedro moved over to his bed and lay down, familiar with the procedure.

"Gently, señorita, *gently*."

I swabbed the brown flesh and plunged the needle in deeply, drawing the plunger out a little way first to make sure I had not reached a vein, then pressing it slowly until all the white liquid was emptied from the barrel.

"*Aylla!* It hurts very much."

"There. That's all." I rinsed the syringe in the pot and began to put the things away again in my bag.

"Aren't you going to put something on my leg?" asked Pedro.

"Oh. I'm sorry. Of course I will." What should I put on it? The leg was so angry-looking, none of my remedies seemed powerful enough to affect it, but I cleaned up the edges of the wound, fearful to clean the inside lest I introduce further infection. Then I shook in a little surgical powder.

"Will that dust cure me, señorita?"

"I hope it will help, Pedro. The injection is stronger. I think the injection will cure you."

I began to wrap the leg with sterile gauze, holding Pedro's foot in my lap. The toes were thick and club-shaped, coated with earth from his fields. They had walked many, many miles over such earth, and over the roads that led to town, over the cobblestones and over the sidewalks. Strong feet, I thought. The feet of a real man. I wrapped slowly and carefully, holding the leg as lightly as I could. God, heal this leg. What if it doesn't heal? Pedro, a cripple? What would his family do?

"It will heal up all right, will it, señorita?" It was Rosa, who had turned from her place at the fire to watch the bandaging, and now looked into my face searchingly. "He won't die?"

I laughed. "Oh, Rosa. Of course he won't die. It is only his leg, just a bad wound, but the needle medicine will help it."

"*Aylla!* What is it that itches?" Pedro suddenly sat up, pulling his foot from my lap. His lips were stretched in a grimace and he began frantically scratching his hips and thighs.

"It itches, señorita. *Mana pacha*, how it itches! As if there were a thousand fleas biting me. *Aylla!*" His voice rose to a cry and he jumped from the bed and began to dance around the fire, flailing his arms, scratching and digging at his flesh wherever it was exposed, rubbing at the seat of his trousers.

"What is the matter, Pedro?" I asked, suddenly frightened at the violence of his behavior.

"*Taita Dios!* What is the matter with you?" Rosa started from her seat on the ground. "Are you crazy? He's dreaming! He's out of his mind, señorita!"

Pedro threw himself on the bed again, tearing his poncho off and throwing it across the hut. "They are eating me. Father God, they are eating me! Fleas. Lots of fleas. Who will save me? *Aylla*, señorita, who will save me?"

Rosa rubbed his arms and legs vigorously, asking over and over, "What is the matter? What is the matter? Are you dreaming? Are you crazy?"

"Who knows what it is? How it itches! My whole flesh itches. What kind of fleas will they be that can bite like this? *Aylla*, what will become of me?"

"Try bathing him with some hot water, Rosa," I suggested.

"Pava! Hot water! Hurry and heat some water. A lot of water."

Pava jerked a pot out from a corner and dipped water from the huge clay jar that stood in a depression in the earth. She set it on the fire and energetically flapped the reed fan up and down, sticking corncobs and grass into the coals at the same time. "What is the matter with father?" she asked.

"Who knows what has happened to him? *Heat the water!*"

God in heaven, I thought, have I done something to him? What can possibly have caused this? Pedro's arms suddenly stopped flailing and fell along the sides of the bed. His eyes closed and he was mumbling something.

"What are you saying?" Rosa bent over him, beside herself with fear.

"My head spins. Everything goes around."

"Have the fleas stopped biting you?"

"Fleas . . . Around and around my head turns."

"Is this hot enough, Mama?"

Rosa went and dipped a finger in the pot. "I guess it is right. Here. Bring it over here quickly." She sloshed warm water from the pot onto Pedro's face, neck and hands.

"Why do you get me wet? Leave me alone. Leave me . . . My head . . ." His voice trailed off.

"The fleas—the itch. Does it still itch? Does it still itch? Speak!"

Pedro said nothing, but he was not scratching. He lay quiet, his eyes closed, his hands lying limp, with the palms upward, on the sheepskins. Like a flash a word came to my mind from a medical book. Anaphylaxis. Could that be what had happened? O Lord save us and help us—show me what to do, spare Pedro. But it is so rare—reaction to a drug. Fatal unless immediate aggressive treatment is administered. What treatment? What can I do here?

"Pava! Some garlic! Bring some garlic quickly," Rosa shouted.

Pava found a little knot of garlic somewhere in the thatch and gave it to Rosa, who broke it open and rubbed it on Pedro's lips and nostrils. Hardly aggressive, that treatment. What to do? Oh, what, Lord, shall I do? *You* do something. Maybe it's just a temporary setback. Maybe it isn't anaphylaxis at all—one chance in a hundred. Ridiculous of me to get panicky. He's in Your hands, Lord.

I watched the strong, dark face. The boldly chiseled lips, the line of his eyebrows, the straight, large nose. What a beautiful subject for a bronze bust! No . . . a bronze mask. Death mask. Pedro. Oh, Pedro. Open your eyes.

For a second I thought he read my unspoken plea. There was a movement of his eyelids. I leaned forward in an agony of hope. Yes. The eyes rolled under the lids, but did not open. Then I saw that his lips were parted. They moved futilely for a moment, and then he spoke. Rosa put her ear to his mouth.

"*Chunlla!* Shut up, children! Your father is talking."

"What does he say?" said Pava.

"*Chunlla!*" She was listening, her mouth wide open, eyes staring. Pedro spoke, then, clearly enough for me to hear him.

"Señorita. It is dark. All becomes dark. Señorita."

"Dark, Pedro?"

"Yes. Very dark, like night."

"Can you hear me?" I thought his head nodded.

"Can you hear me, Pedro?" Answer me, Pedro, say yes. Oh, please hear me!

"Yes, señorita. I can hear you. Do you hear me? I said it is dark." He spoke clearly, rationally, and my heart gave a lunge of joy. He probably fainted and is coming to, I thought, and now all will be well. Lord, let it be. Let it be well.

There was the sudden thud of bare feet in the dooryard, the guinea pigs went scuttling off into the corners, the sun that lay in a patch on the floor was blotted by a shadow, and Romero and Jorge came tumbling through the door, choking with laughter, and threw themselves on a pile of skins.

"*Caramba! Chunlla!* Your father is dying! Don't you know your father is dying?" The tension in Rosa's voice made her fairly spit the words. "As if anyone had said to you, *Laugh!* Is one to laugh when a man is dying?"

I could see the convulsed faces of the two small boys in the firelight. The light in the flashing black eyes and on the white teeth was extinguished in an instant.

"Dying? Father is dying?" said Romero.

"Dying, I said! Don't you see?"

"What happened?"

"Shut up!"

"No, Rosa. Don't say he is dying," I pleaded. This was an expression I had never been able to accept. The Quichua term for anything other than perfect health was "dying." For them, it was the first possibility. For me, it was the last, and I refused to accept it now. Pedro would not be dying.

"As if he will live!" The scorn in Rosa's voice withered me. "Can't you *see* he is dying, señorita? You put that needle into him; you killed him."

Lord God, Father of us all, if You've never heard me pray before, hear me now. Hear what she says. Lord, for the honor of Your name, show what You can do. Save him, Lord, save him.

A little skinny rooster hopped to the doorsill, crowing thinly. Romero heaved a corncob in his direction and he fluttered off. There was no sound in the house now, except Pedro's faint breathing. The rest of us hardly dared to breathe, waiting.

Pedro began to retch, his chest rising, his belly contracting in great tormented spasms. I could see the tendons in his neck stretch and ripple, a knot rose and fell under the weathered skin, and he gagged uncontrollably.

"He will vomit! Pava! Give me the pot!"

Rosa held Pedro's head over the pot while the retching went on and on, violent, body-racking sounds, until it seemed that his entrails must come forth from his throat, but nothing came. His back arched and writhed and his fingers dug into the sheepskins. Lord, quiet him. Deliver him.

The paroxysms ceased then, and Rosa let his head fall back on the bed. The sleeve of her blouse was wet with his perspiration.

"Señorita! What will become of us? He is going to die! He is dying! Señorita! You said you would make him well! Saying, I will cure him, you gave him the needle. Now he will die."

Jorge began to cry loudly. Romero pushed an elbow into his face. "Shut up!"

"Why should he shut up? His father is dying. He is dying, my husband is dying, what will become of us all?" Rosa put both hands on top of her head and began to rock, her words sliding into the singsong death wail I had heard before.

> "Here you stood alive this morning,
> Beside the fire.
> Here you drank the *mazamorra* that I handed to you,
> Drank it all,
> Not thinking to yourself, Today I will die.
> He is alive, we thought,
> And this is how you die on us.
> My husband, my little husband!
> Who will take care of me?
> Who will work?
> What will become of us, my husband?"

You will find another, Rosa. There are always men ready to take a widow. It will be hard for a time, I know. But he is not going to die! God spare him! O Lord, spare him, for Christ's sake! What will become of Rosa? Of

Rosa? What, Lord God, will become of *Your work?* You started all this, Lord. It wasn't I. You led me here. You answered prayers and gave me Pedro—he is the only one You have given me, Lord, remember that. O Lord, remember that. There is no one else.

No. I must trust Him for healing now. He raised the dead. He healed all kinds of sickness. What is the line from the hymn? . . . "Thy touch hath still its ancient power."

"Rosa, would you like to pray to God that He will help Pedro?"

"To God?" Rosa took her hands from her head and turned her streaming face to me, bewildered.

"Yes, to my God—to the God Pedro believes in."

"Pray, señorita, if you want to. You pray."

"Come here, children, and we will pray," I said. Pava, Jorge and Romero came and squatted in a circle by the fire. The three-year-old had fallen asleep in the shadows. Each child watched me carefully to ascertain the proper procedure. I closed my eyes, and Romero whispered loudly, "Shut your eyes."

"Our Father God, You can do anything You want. We know that You love Pedro, and that if You want to You can make him well. Don't let him die, Lord, please don't let him die. He has believed in You and has served You and You know how he has helped with the translation of Your word. In order that he may go on serving You, Father God, cause him to live. For the glory of Your name, cause him to live. And—because we love him, Lord, cause him to live. In the name of Jesus we pray, Amen."

Pava, who had heard Pedro pray on one or two occasions, said, "Amen."

From the bed behind us we could hear a soft wheeze. Pedro lay very still, breathing shallowly with a sound like a small bellows, his mouth slightly open, the whites of his eyes showing a thin line beneath the lids. Rosa kept feeding corncobs and grass into the fire, as though by sustaining the flame she would prolong the life that flickered on the bed beside her. Carefully, almost stealthily, she chose a bit of straw and put it in place, blowing softly as she did so, watching till the little tongue of fire rose.

What had the medical book said about the symptoms of a drug reaction? I tried to sift my memory for the details. Had it said something about coma or collapse? I could not recall a description of the retching or this wheezing I heard now. Perhaps my diagnosis was mistaken. Lord, let me be mistaken. Perhaps he is delirious from fever, caused by the inflammation. The penicillin has not yet had time to start working. Maybe in a little while . . .

Immediate aggressive treatment. Take him to Indi Urcu? There's no hospital there. The clinic? They wouldn't know anything. Wouldn't admit him, probably, since he's an Indian. Still, we could try. Try? How? There was no one to carry him. There wasn't a man for a mile or so. It's too long a journey anyway. He wouldn't survive the journey. Would he, Lord? Should I try to find someone? No, it's nonsense. Be still and pray. You've done enough damage. I? Was it I who did the damage? My God! I was trying to help him. I was trying to *help* him.

"Pava!" It was Pedro's voice; it was a shout. We jumped with the shock. He was sitting up, blindly fumbling with the sheepskins around him, as though searching for something. "Pava! Get my poncho. My poncho, quickly, Pava. They are coming!"

Pava snatched the poncho from the floor and thrust it toward her father. He opened his eyes, and they moved back and forth wildly, seeing none of us, filled with fear.

He made a movement with his legs, as though to climb off the bed, then turned suddenly and looked behind him. His fingers clutched the skins. "Pava! Señorita! Father God!"

"Pedro." I spoke his name quietly, hoping to arrest his fear. What did he fear? Was he beside himself? Did he know he was dying? Lord, You are our Refuge. Comfort him. Quiet him.

Rosa was staring at him, while at the same time she beat the reed fan up and down with great fervor, causing the fire to flame high for a few moments. Pedro continued to turn and grasp, trying desperately to focus his eyes on something that was not there. Then, with a groan, he collapsed onto the bed again. Rosa's hand let go of the fan, and she gave herself up to weeping, throwing her hands to her head and then clawing at Pedro's arm, rocking and wailing. Once she rubbed the garlic clove on his lips and went back again to renewed hopelessness, seeing that it did not revive him.

It occurred to me to take Pedro's pulse. I reached for his left hand, thrown far on the other side of the bed. It was cold and limp and felt like dry leather in my hand. Oh Pedro, don't die on us. This can't be the time to die.

I pressed my fingertips to the soft side of his wrist. At last I felt a light throb, much too light, much too weak, for a man. I was unsure for a moment whether I had really felt a throb. Yes, there it was again, the tiny signal that the heart still labored.

"What is it, señorita?" Rosa asked, pausing in her wail when she saw me lift the arm.

"His heart, Rosa. I can feel his heart beat."

"There?"

"Yes."

"How is it? Is he alive?"

"Yes." Still alive. God save him. Save him, Lord. Keep the heart beating. Yes, like that. Still going.

The pulse was thready and I thought every minute that I was only imagining that it beat. No, there it was. Tick . . . tick, tick . . . Giver and Sustainer of Life, give him life today, sustain Pedro's life, Lord. You are the doer of all that's been done through him so far. You raised him from eternal death to eternal life, brought him from heathen darkness to Your blazing light. Gave me a soul for the Kingdom, an earnest of the inheritance You would grant me among this tribe, a product of grace. My product, too, Lord, the fruit of all my work here. Spare him. Spare him. Spare him.

I found that I had taken up, in my mind, the rhythm of Rosa's death wail. My prayer was being chanted to the tune of her cry, "He's dying, he's dying, he's dying." Her voice soared again to the narrative, recalling what Pedro did for the family, how he went to work in the morning, how he was unaware of his approaching death. Gradually it sank to the reiteration of her own despair, what would become of her, what would become of the children? And then to the simple declaration of the reality, "He's dying, he's dying, he's dying."

The fire had dwindled to a few embers that waved and blinked. The sun by this time had disappeared and the chickens began to come into the hut to roost for the night. Jorge amused himself by throwing bits of straw and twigs at them, making them cluck and fluff their feathers as they settled themselves on the pole. The baby began to cry, making Rosa halt abruptly in her dirge. She picked him up from his hammock, gave him the breast and settled again on the floor beside Pedro, taking up once more the keening lament.

[233]

Pava and Romero sat hushed in the gathering dark. Their father was dying. The one on whom everything, life itself, depended. Their bulwark against hunger and nakedness and the white man. How much did they comprehend of this?

Now and again Pedro's hands twitched. His head had fallen back at a grotesque angle and I tried to rearrange it. Strange, how heavy it was in my hands. I moved it a little, feeling the weight. Dear Pedro. What will I do? *What will I do?*

Find the pulse again. See if it's working. Tick . . . Is that it? No . . . That? . . . Yes—no . . . Tick. There it is! One tiny throb. I was sure I felt it. Yes, he is alive—his eyes are opening.

Pedro's head fell again into the position from which I had moved it, his eyelids parted a little, his jaw worked back and forth for a few seconds. Then he gave a deep sigh and was still.

"Rosa," I said.

She jerked her head around and looked me full in the eyes, a wild animal look, full of terror and hatred. Then she leaped up from the floor and threw herself shrieking onto her husband's body. The baby was still held in one arm, and he, too, began to shriek. Pava, Jorge and Romero crowded to the mound of skins where their dead father lay, their eyes wide and glittering in the feeble firelight.

CHAPTER

21

———

IT WAS so dark by this time I could hardly see the trail, but I must hurry. I was almost running, putting my feet down recklessly and wrenching my ankles as I tripped on the broken clods of clay. It had never seemed such a long way home. I strained toward the town, pulling it toward me, running and running, trying to push the mountain away behind, pushing the little mud hut back and back.

"Follow the Shepherd, Margaret. He knows the way."

It was too late now. My eyes strained through the dark, trying to light the lamps of the town somewhere there below me. Where was the trail? The turn onto the cobble-stone road? Was it here? Hurry.

Somewhere nearby I heard the bleat of a sheep. I was out of breath and something about the feel of the road beneath my feet was not quite familiar. Every rut and rock was known to me on the usual route. I had better stop. But there isn't time. There's no time to stop. The animal look, the wild shriek, the implacable corpse—were they actually following me? No. They were back in the hut, far up the mountain now. Stop. You've lost your way.

I stood still on the trail and tried to listen, but found that I was panting and my legs were trembling and it took a minute before I could hear the silence around me. The night was still and frigid and the stars, like fearsome watchers, hovered close above me. I should by this time have reached the turn onto my road, but somewhere I had missed it. A sheep cried again—a forsaken, human cry—and I remembered the place where the sheep lived. I was not far from my road. I knew now which way to turn. Hurry. Better start running again.

The light of the stars was not enough to enable me to see anything that I recognized, but to my right, like a jagged orange tear in the fabric of the dark, a fire glowed on the hills. It must be far away, I decided, so it must be to the east. I was going north, then, where I wanted to go. Some Indian must be burning his pasture land. The fire was like a thin dragon, trembling and creeping across the night.

I started to walk again, quickly, and in a few moments I heard a dog bark, then I saw a light, then two lights, and the trail dropped to the cobblestone road. I ran as fast as I could. Perhaps there would still be time.

Time for what? I reached my gate, jerked at the latch and fumbled with it in the dark, wanting to tear it from its screws. It came open, and I ran to the door, but my hands were shaking so that the key would not fit into the lock.

"Fear thou not; for I am with thee: be not dismayed; for I am thy God." Still with me? Still my God? No. It was too late. There. The key turned, the door opened, and I rushed into the house, turned on all the lights, and sank down by the table.

Everything was exactly as I had left it. The rag rug on the floor, the awkward chairs that had long since lost their awkwardness in my eyes, the flowered tablecloth and the teapot, the Swiss clock. But the clock had stopped. Had I forgotten to wind it, or had there actually been, as I seemed to sense, some cosmic change that marked the end of something? I picked up the clock, wound it and shook it, then listened. It was not ticking. Good, I thought, and set it down on the table. That gives me time, then. Time to begin again, slowly, carefully, to sort things out.

Surely there is a way to make it come right. This can't be it. It isn't finished yet. Go back and do it the other way this time. Do it right. For God's sake, *do it right* this time.

Was it the medicine? Would streptomycin have worked? No, no. You have to go back much farther than that. It was something else. There must have been a call that you didn't hear—or was it that you disobeyed? A dozen accusations confronted me. No. I refuse to capitulate. How could I have failed to hear the call that was meant for me? What kind of a shepherd would allow that? No one had ever listened more intently, praying, beseeching, entreating God to guide, to show the way. The call had come, the way had opened, the work had begun. Had I disobeyed? *Had* I? Where could it have been? Is God through with me now, is He saying, "Get out"? The Indians are through with me. Rosa had stabbed me with her hatred.

These four walls—they are still here. My home. My quiet place to come back to after visiting the Indians. The house is still here. They can't reach me here. Nobody can reach me here. But God can. Where is the refuge from Him? I was going to sacrifice this home for You! What of the sacrifices I have already made—did You toy with them? O ineffable, sardonic God who toys with our sacrifices and smashes to earth the humble, hopeful altars we have built for a place to put Your name! Do You mock me? Why did You let him die? Why did You let me kill him? O God! I came to bring him life—*Your* life—and I destroyed him in Your name.

A donkey clopped by on the road outside and I could hear the sound of a whip and an Indian voice. Then there was silence. I looked at the Bible on the table in front of me and started to pick it up. My hand dropped again. I could not find answers there any more. Nothing had worked for me as I had thought it would work. God had nothing to say to me now. Where was He, anyway?

The question, which in my mind was tantamount to declaring myself an atheist, found me sitting there at the table waiting for an answer. Who would answer? Who, if not God Himself? Well, I would wait for Him. Perhaps He would strike me dead. No, that is unlikely. He could hardly bother with me to that extent now. Probably He has forgotten. Or He could answer me out of the whirlwind, vindicate Himself, explain. No, I have probably gone too far astray ever to hear Him again.

What shall I do now? Make some tea. Do something. See if anything works—does water boil as before? This silence! How can things be the same? How can the house stand so smugly as it stood this morning, nothing changed, everything in its place, quiet, neat, oblivious? Only the clock has stopped.

The beginning and the end. I have come to the end of my work. God's work, I thought it was—I came here for Him. I ventured to believe He had given it to me to do, and I staked my life on it. I entered into it in faith and now . . . the end. *And omega.* God! My God!

"Señorita!" I jumped in my chair. It was Pava outside the door. "Señorita Margarita!"

I stumbled to the door and opened it. "Pava!"

"Mama says have you any candles to give us for the wake for Father?"

Candles. A wake for Father. My mind teetered to find its balance again, confronted with two specifics. Did I have any candles?

"Yes, Pava, I think I have. Come in. I will look for them." I found some candles in the kitchen cupboard and brought them out. As though my heart had been hit with a hammer, I realized that had it not been for me they would not have needed candles. Pedro would not have been dead.

"Well, good night, señorita," said Pava. "May God pay you." She turned to go.

"Good night, Pava." I opened the door for her, and saw that Romero was waiting in the dark. She would not have to go home alone. I started to close the door and Romero called, "Señorita."

"What is it, Romero?"

"Señorita—we are having a wake and Mama wanted to . . . Mama said would you come and sit with us?"

Yes, I thought. I can do that. I can go and sit with them.

22

IF I had said no to Romero and Pava, and had not gone to their father's wake, I would probably have forsaken my place among the Indians of the highland, and perhaps my place as a missionary anywhere at all. But then I do not really know. The decision was not one which I weighed carefully. The children came and brought their request, and I went with them. It seems to me now that the decision was right, and that it was indeed the voice of God, still and small, that said, "And omega." Perhaps He would have borne with me even if I had said no, and have brought me by another way. He is indeed of great mercy. Only I know that I was glad to have been at the wake, and I am glad to be here in my house in Indi Urcu.

The sun shines today, as you know that it nearly always does in the mornings, and the great mountain Chimborazo shines with it, lifting its gleaming peak toward heaven, reminding me that the strength of the hills is His also.

The only light at the wake came from the two candles we brought. One was placed at Pedro's head, one at his feet, and Rosa bent over him in the yellow circle, her black hair falling across his face, and wailed the death wail until the cocks began to crow at dawn. People came from all over the mountain, packing themselves into the stuffy little room (the candles flickered for lack of oxygen), crying for a little while, talking, sitting stolidly in the gloom until another mourner arrived, when it was necessary briefly to renew the wailing. Rosa uncovered the face of the corpse when a relative came, and each time she did so the features looked a trifle younger and sharper, the deep tea color of his skin gradually paler. I found myself spellbound by the sight of that face, which had registered nothing when Pedro first met me, then, as time had passed, had shown shy friendliness, trust, interest, eagerness, joy—would it not change now, would not a single tiniest muscle twitch, an eyelash fall? Rosa covered the face again, more tenderly than I had seen her do anything, and then raised her arms to her head once more and rocked and chanted. And then when the cocks had crowed and darkness was driven over the far eastern hills the mourners got up one by one, straightened their ponchos and their skirts, and left the house, filing off over the cracked fields to their work. A few of the men stayed to wait for the coffin which had been sent for from the town. They put the body in it, there was another night of watching, and on the morning of the second day I saw the long file moving toward the village, four men carrying the wooden coffin on their shoulders. I went with them, too, to the Indian section of the little cemetery. The relatives had hired a few professional mourners—poor white people who knew the prayers that had to be said and possessed rosaries which they agreed to use in exchange for some corn and *chicha*.

Pava stood quietly by the open grave, a single ray of sunlight falling across her cheekbones under the wide, upturned brim of her felt hat. As the ropes let the coffin gently into the earth I saw the glitter of tears on her lashes.

When the earth was thrown onto the coffin and stamped down, she wrapped her shawl tightly around her arm, and pushed her nose into the crook of her elbow, her shoulders heaving with sobs. Rosa wept openly, as was expected of her at the grave, and when it was over she took her children home in silence, there to take up what God had left her of life.

I wonder whether I will ever live in an Indian house. Even here in Indi Urcu the people come casually, now and then, to visit me. I go to visit them and they talk as freely or they are as silent as ever. If they talk, they often speak of Pedro's death and my part in it. There is no conspiracy of silence between us on that subject. If they are silent it is not a different silence from before. Some are as hostile and suspicious as they have ever been but not, I think, more so; some are slowly losing their reticence, like Manuela, who asked me if her small relatives could join Pedro's children in the reading classes. I still have the classes. Of course they are not formal. The children come to my house now, when they feel like coming, and we spread out the books on the tiny verandah or, if the group is too large, in the fenced enclosure. Some of them make astonishing strides and then abruptly stop coming. Others, without the slightest flagging of hope and enthusiasm, learn nothing at all, though they come week after week. Perhaps the reading classes will come to an end. God knows about that. As for the translation of the Bible, of course, I cannot go ahead without an informant. God knew about that when Pedro died. I do not write prayer letters any more, for I have nothing to say about my work. It seemed, on the night of Pedro's death, as though *Finis* were written below all I had done. Now, in the clear light of day, I see that I was in part correct. God, if He was merely my accomplice, had betrayed me. If, on the other hand, He was God, He had freed me.

I find that I can no longer arrange my life in an orderly succession of projects with realizable goals and demonstrable effects. I cannot designate this activity as "useful" and that one as "useless," for often the categories are reversed and even more often I am at a loss to apply either label, for the work, in the end, as well as the labeling, is God's.

One day a few weeks ago I went down to the village graveyard again to visit Pedro's grave. The paper flowers that had been put there had faded and were laden with dust. The mound of earth had sunk a little. But at the head of the grave someone had put up a flimsy wooden cross, painted white, and had written in pencil the name PEDRO CHIMBU, and the date of his death.

Nothing else had changed. The sky was vast and blue above me, the mountains calm around me. There was no sound except that of a few sheep beyond the mud wall, and a faint piping as someone—it sounded like a child—went by on the road, playing on his panpipes.

It was as it should be. I found myself alone—Rosa was not here, but carrying out her own work at home; the MacDonalds, Lynn, my colleagues in many places had also their appointed tasks for which they would individually give account; those who prayed for me at home might at this moment be praying, and He to whom the prayers were addressed would know what answer to give. For my part, I was left alone before God—indeed, it seemed to me this morning that for the first time in my life I stood in direct relation to Him as Moses stood when he beheld the burning bush. For me, however, it was no such dramatic vision. There were before me only the dry mound of earth and the pitiful little cross with its penciled legend. What was it about that cross that cleared the way to God? I think it was this: I saw for the first time my own identity in its true perspective. Once I had envisioned Pedro, highland Indian, Christian, translator of the Bible, soldier of the Cross— because I, Margaret Sparhawk, had come. He was my project, he was the star in my crown. But here was another cross, with a name and a date, to mark where a dead man lay—because I, Margaret Sparhawk, had come.

And God? What of Him? "I am with thee," He had said. With me in *this?* He had allowed Pedro to die, or—and I could not then nor can I today deny the possibility—He had perhaps caused me to destroy him. And does He now, I asked myself there at the graveside, ask me to worship Him?

I lay down on the grass and saw that high above me a condor circled, looking down on the tops of the frosted peaks, on the lakes and the serene valley. The child went by the gate once more, piping softly.